Assessment and Instruction of Reading Disability

Assessment and Instruction of Reading Disability

AN INTERACTIVE APPROACH

Marjorie Y. Lipson
The University of Vermont, Burlington

Karen K. Wixson
The University of Michigan, Ann Arbor

HarperCollins*Publishers*

To Michael, Nora, and Theo for their tolerance,
support, and love over many, many months.
M.Y.L.

To my friend and coauthor, with love and gratitude.
K.K.W.

Sponsoring Editor: Christopher Jennison
Development Editor: Anita Portugal
Photo Research: Carol Parden
Editing, Design, and Production: Editorial Services of New England, Inc.
Compositor: Circle Graphics
Printer and Binder: R. R. Donnelley & Sons Company

Chapter Photo Credits

(p. 3)	Ulrike Welsch	PhotoEdit
(p. 44)	Elizabeth Crews	The Image Works
(p. 83)	Elizabeth Crews	The Image Works
(p. 117)	Mark Antman	The Image Works
(p. 165)	Harvey Phillips	Tony Stone Worldwide
(p. 215)	Elizabeth Crews	The Image Works
(p. 277)	Michael Siluk	The Image Works
(p. 329)	Ulrike Welsch	PhotoEdit
(p. 374)	Spencer Grant	Stock, Boston
(p. 427)	David Strickler	Tony Stone Worldwide
(p. 461)	Elizabeth Crews	The Image Works
(p. 502)	James L. Shaffer	PhotoEdit
(p. 537)	Elizabeth Crews	The Image Works
(p. 566)	Harvey Phillips	Tony Stone Worldwide
(p. 617)	Robert Kalman	The Image Works

Assessment and Instruction of Reading Disability: An Interactive Approach
Copyright © 1991 by HarperCollins Publishers Inc.

Library of Congress Cataloging-in-Publication Data

Lipson, Marjorie Y.
    Assessment and instruction of reading disability : an interactive
approach / Marjorie Y. Lipson, Karen K. Wixson.
            p.   cm.
    Includes bibliographical references and index.
    ISBN 0-673-18335-1
    1. Reading disability.   2. Reading—Ability testing.   3. Reading
comprehension.   4. Reading—Remedial teaching.   I. Wixson, Karen K.
II. Title.
    LB1050.5.L54   1991
    428'.42—dc20   90-26777
                                                                                        CIP

ISBN 0-673-18335-1

91 92 93 94   9 8 7 6 5 4 3 2 1

Contents

SECTION II   EVALUATING THE LEARNER

CHAPTER 9   Evaluating Instructional Materials and Tasks   374

SECTION IV   INTERACTIONS

CHAPTER 10 Interactive Decision Making   427

SECTION V INSTRUCTION

SECTION VI   THE READING PROFESSIONAL

Preface

THIS BOOK IS INTENDED as a primary text for pre- and inservice teachers in graduate courses in diagnosis and remediation of children with reading problems. Although a solid foundation in the reading process is expected, no previous coursework targeted specifically at diagnosis and/or remediation is assumed, especially on the interactive view of assessment and instruction presented here. This text presents students with an introduction to the field of diagnosis and remediation while simultaneously extending their knowledge of the reading process so that their skills are sufficient to make decisions about appropriate tools and strategies for assessment and instruction. In addition, it is a goal of this text to enable students to influence school policy in the area of assessment and instruction of disabled readers. To achieve this goal, students are encouraged throughout the text to evaluate current practice and to adapt and modify existing tools and methodologies to achieve a good instructional match for each learner.

This text is based on an interactive view of reading ability and disability. This view suggests that reading is the process of constructing meaning through the interaction among the reader, the text, and the context of the reading situation. From this perspective, disability is no longer seen as an absolute property of the reader, nor is difficulty considered to be an absolute property of a particular reading skill or task. Both a reader's ability and the difficulty of the reading activity will vary as a function of the interaction among specific reader, text, and instructional factors. As a consequence, readers' performance on various reading measures must be considered an indication of what they can and will do under a set of specific reading conditions, rather than a set of fixed abilities and disabilities.

An interactive view of reading disability differs from the deficit models implied by most diagnosis and remediation texts. Deficit models suggest that the cause of the reading problem lies entirely within the reader. Texts based on a deficit model focus primarily on what Sarason and Doris (1979) call the "search for pathology" within the reader. In contrast, an interactive view suggests that reading disability is a relative concept—not a static state—and that the problem often lies in the match between the reader and the conditions of the reading situation.

Consistent with an interactive perspective, this text focuses on the process of evaluating the existing match and identifying an optimal match between the reader and the reading context. The content of this text also reflects our belief that the most important factor in effective assessment and instruction is the knowledge base of the teacher. Features of this text include both understanding and application sections devoted to each topic of discussion, a classroom to clinic section describing applications to different settings, detailed chapter summaries, an extensive bibliography, detailed case studies, and numerous examples of how to implement informal assessment and instructional procedures.

Section I, Perspectives, contains two chapters that provide the knowledge base for using the remainder of the text. In *Chapter 1,* "Reading Ability and Disability," we describe the major ideas and factors influencing remedial reading practices today. We also detail an interactive view of reading and reading disability. *Chapter 2,* "The Assessment-Instruction Process," describes the components of reading and defines the areas to be assessed within the reader and the reading context. This chapter also provides an overview of the assessment-instruction process outlined in this text with a case study example.

The remaining chapters are organized in a manner that parallels the assessment-instruction process described in Chapter 2. *Section II,* Evaluating the Learner, contains five chapters. The first of these is *Chapter 3,* "Getting Started with Assessment," which provides guidelines for gathering initial information about the reader. The next four chapters are designed to provide specific information on how and what to evaluate in reading and writing. *Chapter 4,* "The Foundations of Literacy," is devoted to an understanding of emergent literacy concepts and the assessment of prereaders. *Chapter 5,* "Informal Reading Inventories," provides an in-depth discussion of issues and practices in using IRIs. *Chapter 6,* "Formal Assessment," addresses the understanding of important statistical concepts and provides a detailed description of the characteristics and types of tests commonly associated with reading assessment. *Chapter 7,* "Teacher-Designed Assessment," focuses on more informal, nontraditional methods of reading assessment.

Section III, Evaluating the Reading Context, contains chapters rarely found in textbooks of this type, but integral to an interactive perspective. *Chapter 8,* "Evaluating Setting and Instruction," considers how setting, instructional context, and instructional methods may influence reading and writing performance, and provides tools for evaluating these aspects of the reading context. *Chapter 9,* "Evaluating Instructional Materials and Tasks," describes how reading and writing performance can be affected by these factors and provides additional tools and strategies for assessing the reading context.

Section IV, Interactions, consists of a single chapter, *Chapter 10,* "Interactive Decision Making," which emphasizes the juncture where assessment and instruction come together. This is done through a discussion of the steps in the assessment-instruction process that involve evaluating the match between the reader and the reading context, reflecting and generating hypotheses about the source of interference with learning, and identifying an optimal instructional match.

Section V, Instruction, contains four chapters providing methods for promoting critical reading abilities. *Chapter 11,* "Getting Started in Instruction," describes "high-utility" instructional strategies and provides a rationale for making decisions about the instructional issues and techniques that are described in detail in the other three chapters in this section. *Chapters 12, 13, and 14* provide support to teachers as they plan and refine their instructional program to focus on the specific areas of word recognition (Chapter 12), vocabulary (Chapter 13), and comprehension (Chapter 14).

The final section and chapter of the text, *Section VI* and *Chapter 15,* both entitled "The Reading Professional," place teachers and students in a broader context. This chapter provides techniques and frameworks for reporting information to others, and addresses many of the ethical and legal responsibilities of reading professionals.

In closing, we would like to acknowledge our appreciation to the many people who provided advice, encouragement, and assistance in the development of this text. First, we are greatly indebted to our primary reviewers, Linda Vavrus and Michael McKenna. We also gratefully acknowledge the special assistance provided us by Kathy Hric, Linda Marshall-Mosteiro, Anita Portugal, Melodie Wertelet, Ray Wixson, and by JoAnn Caldwell, who authored the Instructor's Manual. Special thanks are also due Chris Jennison, whose patience provided the ultimate support for completing this project. Finally, we would like to acknowledge the special contribution of the students in our graduate and undergraduate courses who offered us feedback during the development of the manuscript.

We hope that this text will become the basis for a meaningful dialogue on issues surrounding the assessment and instruction of reading disability, and look forward to our readers' response to the challenges presented in this text.

Marjorie Y. Lipson
Karen K. Wixson

SECTION I

Perspectives

IN THE FIRST SECTION of this book we provide a theoretical foundation and rationale for the remainder of the text. The section contains two chapters. In the first, we describe various models of reading. We use available theory and research to advance an interactive perspective on reading, and discuss how reader factors, text factors, and contextual factors influence each other. In the final part of Chapter 1, we describe how an interactive model of reading ability can and should be applied to reading disability. This discussion of the reading process lays the foundation for the remainder of the text.

In the second chapter of this section, we discuss the component skills and strategies required to succeed in reading tasks. This may be a review for some students taking a graduate course in assessment and instruction, but the information is essential for teachers and clinicians to make sound decisions during assessment and to plan appropriate instruction. This chapter also provides an overview of the assessment and instruction process. The overview simultaneously describes the way reading assessment and instruction typically progress, and provides a guided tour of the sequence of this text. The steps of the assessment-instruction process detailed in Chapter 2 are used throughout the remainder of the book. In introductory materials for subsequent sections, we highlight the particular step(s) to be considered in that section.

CHAPTER 1

Reading Ability and Disability

INTRODUCTION

In this chapter, we discuss the need for a theoretical and empirical rationale for reading assessment and instruction. Although many teachers believe that theory can be removed from practice, teacher practices in fact imply various theories or models of reading. This chapter challenges teachers to reflect on their existing knowledge and beliefs, and to consider an interactive view of both reading ability and disability.

Why Theory?

Day in and day out, teachers must be prepared to engage children in some sort of activity. How do teachers decide what to do in the name of reading instruction? Virtually all teachers in the United States have received instruction in planning, and all have been advised to place their statements of instructional objectives at the very beginning of the plan. Despite this training, many teachers start their planning not with desired learning outcomes, but with desirable activities (Clark, 1984). These desirable activities often involve following other people's "good advice," such as the directives contained in teacher's manuals of basal readers.

Even under the best of circumstances, mechanical execution of such directives is not good practice, because good teaching always involves adapting instruction to the needs of specific individuals or groups of students. However, the pitfalls of such practice become painfully evident when we are concerned, as we are in this text, with children who are not learning to read easily and well. These children require thoughtfully planned and executed instruction, fitted to their particular needs. What is needed for one "disabled" reader may be quite different from what is required for another.

How can we make decisions about what to change, how to adapt existing practice, and what to do with these children who have failed to learn when given exposure to the usual and customary instruction? In order to make decisions, teachers need to consider theory. Theory sounds frightening and abstract, but in reality, all teachers have some sort of theory whether they realize it or not. Teachers' theories about reading are extremely important because the particular theory held determines, at least in part, what is done in the name of reading instruction. Theories and models help us to simplify educational decisions in a number of ways. Theories give us explanations for things, but more importantly, they tell us how to behave.

In this chapter, we describe the ways existing models of reading have influenced both assessment and instruction over the years, and provide information that will help readers to refine their own theories or models of reading. In the chapters that follow, we provide information necessary to become an active decision-maker in the process of reading assessment and instruction.

Chapter Overview

This chapter differs somewhat from those that follow because it is entirely devoted to understanding. As Shuy (1981) points out, most teachers have received a great deal more information in their reading methods courses about activities and methods than they have about learning and the reading process.

Specifically, this chapter provides discussions and descriptions of the different models of reading ability, including the interactive view of reading ability that provides the basis for the information in this text. In addition, a brief history of reading disability and the special needs student is provided. It highlights the need for an interactive view of reading disability. Finally, the goals of assessment and instruction are described.

UNDERSTANDING MODELS OF READING

Put most simply, reading entails two related processes: recognizing written words and understanding what has been written. The most obvious feature of reading involves seeing print on a page. It was also the first aspect of reading to be studied. By the turn of the century, several researchers had devised ways to study eye movements to begin answering questions about what readers do when they read (Judd, 1918; Judd & Buswell, 1922).

As a result of this long line of research, we know that readers' eyes move in a series of jumps and stops. Although skilled readers usually feel as though their eyes are moving continuously during reading, the eyes are actually stopped more than they are moving. Readers take in information only when their eyes are stopped. These stops, called *fixations*, generally last for 50 milliseconds. Readers' eyes then jump to the next stopping point. These jumps are called *saccades* and have a duration of 15 milliseconds. Research results indicate that readers are fixated (stopped) about 90–95% of the time and are moving only 5–10% of the time (Just & Carpenter, 1987). Because readers can take in information only when their eyes are fixated, they are effectively blind to the print when their eyes are moving.

All models of reading share this much common ground. However, we have really not gone very far toward describing just what reading is. From this point, the questions get a bit more difficult. Note that a simple mechanical description of the physical activity surrounding reading does not specify, for example, what is being fixated, nor how that information is used by readers. In order to answer the question, What is reading? we need to be able to describe both what is being processed and how that processing occurs. With this much information, you may want to stop a moment and complete the exercise in Figure 1.1 to help clarify your own theoretical orientation to reading.

Many teachers and students describe a model of reading that entails a linear progression, from the recognition of letters, to letter strings, to words and sentences. Despite a lack of empirical support, this model has dominated reading

FIGURE 1.1

What Is Your
Theory of
Reading?

	Yes	No
1. All letter sounds should be taught before the student begins formal reading instruction.	_____	_____
2. Reading should be taught through the sequential development of skills.	_____	_____
3. Young readers should learn to read for literal meaning before they infer or apply meaning.	_____	_____
4. Reading aloud to children enhances their ability to read on their own.	_____	_____
5. Comprehension of words and sentences helps students decode words.	_____	_____
6. Different kinds of text materials demand different kinds of skills.	_____	_____
7. A child's initial encounters with print should focus on meaning, not on exact word recognition.	_____	_____
8. When children do not know a word, they should be instructed first to sound out its parts.	_____	_____
9. It is a good practice to correct a child as soon as an oral reading mistake is made.	_____	_____
10. It is a sign of a poor reader when words and phrases are repeated.	_____	_____

Sources: "What Do You Believe about the Reading Process?" Michigan Department of Education Curriculum Review Committee; "Theoretical Orientation to Reading Profile (TORP)" by Diane DeFord, *Reading Research Quarterly*, Vol. *20*, No. 3, Spring 1985.

instruction in recent years and is evident in almost all current commercial materials. If you tended to answer YES to questions 1–3 and 8–10 and NO to questions 4–7, you have a bottom-up or print-driven theory of reading. If you tended to respond NO to questions 1–3 and 8–10 and YES to questions 4–7, your theory of reading is more top-down or holistic.

Although theories of the reading process existed as early as the turn of the century (e.g., Huey, 1908/1968), the field of reading has tended to operate from atheorectical premises and unexamined assumptions. The emphasis on examining the relationship between underlying theory and instructional practice is relatively recent, emerging strongly since the mid-1960s. To make matters more difficult, theoreticians often differ sharply.

The most serious disputes involve debates regarding the extent to which reading relies on the information on the printed page, as opposed to the information the reader brings to the text. Differences revolve around how much active control the reader exerts, how important reader characteristics are, the control exerted by text characteristics, and whether meaning is in the writer, the text, or the reader.

In the next sections, we consider these differences in greater detail because they are important to instructional decisions. We illustrate these differences by describing three models of reading: bottom-up, top-down, and interactive. The descriptions we provide are actually prototypes of various classes or groups of models and/or theories. None is intended to represent the views of any one theorist or researcher.

Bottom-up Models of Reading

Text-based, or bottom-up, models of reading focus primarily on the recognition of letters, sounds, and words, and are most consistent with existing instructional practice in reading. They are referred to as *bottom-up* because processing begins at the bottom, with the text, and proceeds upward through various levels of analysis to the top, or meaning. The important thing to realize about bottom-up models is that they imply that meaning is on the printed page. They also imply that readers understand the text by analyzing the print as they move through successive levels of analysis.

The levels of processing in bottom-up models are linear and hierarchical. This means that the reader must have the information gained at one level to proceed to the next higher level of processing. The reader works from the smallest units of analysis (e.g., letters) to the largest (e.g., text meaning), making this a part-to-whole model. Each level of analysis triggers the next, with the sum of these analyses adding up to meaning. The emphasis here is on the printed page and what the reader extracts from the page, rather than what the reader brings to the page.

An example of a prototypic bottom-up model is presented in Figure 1.2. The visual input from the text is processed through a series of analyses that proceed in a step-by-step manner. The first level of processing is the *perceptual* analysis of the visual features of the text into distinctive features, letters, letter clusters, and/or words. Many models also include the recoding of visual information into phonological or sound codes that correspond to the visual units. There is some controversy about this, as some believe that skilled readers may be able to go directly from print to meaning without the need for a phonological recoding stage. However, there seems to be common agreement that beginning readers as well as skilled readers who are reading difficult text engage in phonological recoding (Samuels & Kamil, 1984).

At the second level of processing, the visual or sound units that result from the perceptual analysis are analyzed according to word entries in the internal dictionary, or *lexicon*. At the third level, strings of identified words are analyzed according to rules of grammar, or *syntax*. For example, in analyzing a string of words such as *the, cow, barn, the, chased, dog, the,* our knowledge of grammar tells us that something chased something into something. However, there are still a number of syntactically acceptable possibilities for what chased what into what (e.g., "The dog chased the cow into the barn." "The cow chased the dog into the barn." "The barn chased the cow into the dog." "The dog chased the barn into the cow."). It is these types of possibilities that are considered at the final level of analysis when

FIGURE 1.2
A Prototypic Bottom-up Model of the Reading Process

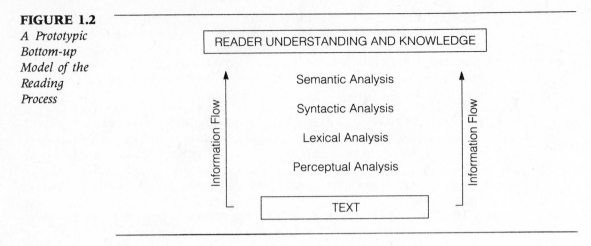

words, phrases, and sentences are analyzed in terms of *semantic* knowledge about events, feelings, and ideas. Therefore, it is our semantic knowledge about cows, dogs, and barns that makes "The dog chased the cow into the barn" the most likely interpretation of this string of words.

Individuals who adhere to a bottom-up model of reading, either implicitly or explicitly, focus a great deal of attention on letter recognition and word analysis, and instructional decisions made from this type of model emphasize these components. Comprehension receives little direct attention, because it is largely accounted for in this model by lower levels of processing. In summary, bottom-up models of reading can be characterized in the following important ways:

- reading is primarily a perceptual process
- meaning resides in the text
- processing proceeds from part to whole (i.e., smallest to largest units of processing)
- model is consistent with skills-based approaches to instruction

Problems with Bottom-up Models: Perception and Thought
One of the problems with bottom-up models of reading is that we do not read letters, words, and sentences in isolation when we read a meaningful passage. Most of us know, for example, that it is possible to "read" without understanding. Think of those times when you read all the words correctly in your attempts to study a foreign language. Although you had satisfied all the criteria noted above, comprehension did not result. Clearly, then, there is more to the reading process than is accounted for by a bottom-up model. In order to clarify what and how people read, researchers and educators have asked two related questions: What do readers perceive? What do they do with their perceptions?

As readers take in information, they are rapidly storing the information in a temporary holding place called *short-term memory*. The information is rapidly analyzed here, and either sent to more permanent storage in *long-term memory* or forgotten. Long-term memory is where all the reader's information about the distinctive shapes and sounds of letters and words, word meanings, syntactic rules, and semantic knowledge are stored.

Studies of perceptual analysis and short-term memory provide some interesting additional information about the reading process. Researchers have discovered what you probably already know, but may not have thought about in some time: it is easier to take in and remember information that is meaningful. For example, look at the following string of what are, for most of you, meaningless symbols:

וְשֹׁ דֹ שֹׁ יַדִקְ תָ בֹ לְ שֹׁ

If you tried to remember this display, each symbol would need to be treated as an individual perceptual item. You would do well to recall seven of those items, even if you had a relatively long time to analyze them. The more meaningful the perceptual display, the more easily you analyze and remember the information. Therefore, *k-l-r-e-w-f-o* is far easier to remember than the first display. Furthermore, *jarmously,* although longer, is easier still, because it is actually treated as one unit, not nine letters.

Consequently, we say that perception is thoughtful, because the knowledge that is stored in the reader's long-term memory (i.e., the top of the model in Figure 1.2) influences what and how information is perceived. The realization that thought influences even this sensory aspect of reading has led other theoreticians to posit a different view of reading. This type of thoughtful processing has been called *top-down* processing, the prototypic model of reading discussed next.

Top-down Models of Reading

Bottom-up models view reading primarily as a perceptual process with meaning located in the text. In contrast, top-down models view reading as a language or psycholinguistic process with meaning located in the reader (see Figure 1.3). According to top-down models, processing begins at the top with the reader's knowledge and predictions about meaning, and continues downward through lower levels of processing, using the text as needed, to confirm predictions and generate new hypotheses. Readers use their knowledge of the perceptual, lexical, syntactic, and semantic systems in language to predict and confirm meaning, and sample only those parts of the text needed to confirm and predict meaning. Therefore, top-down models represent more whole-to-part processing, starting

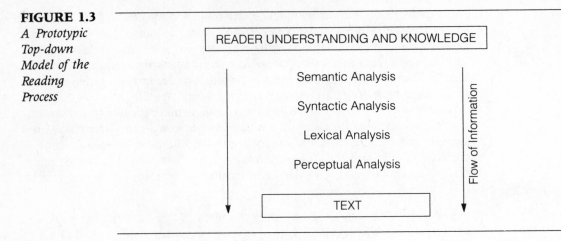

with the largest units (meaning) and working down toward smaller units (e.g., letters and sounds).

Individuals who subscribe to a top-down model of reading, either implicitly or explicitly, focus a great deal of attention on the upper levels of processing such as syntactic and semantic analyses. The reader's knowledge and understanding are viewed as critical, and the unit of processing is the largest possible. Instructional recommendations tend to include a strong focus on "meaning making" and use of context, and little attention is directed toward letter recognition and word analysis. Models that rely most heavily on top-down processes are the basis for whole language and language experience approaches to reading instruction. In summary, the following are important characteristics of top-down models of reading:

- reading is language process
- meaning resides in reader
- processing proceeds from whole to part (i.e., from the largest to the smallest units)
- model is consistent with whole language approaches to instruction

Problems with Top-down Models: Variability and Flexibility

The top-down model of reading has provoked exceptionally fine dialogue and caused researchers and educators alike to examine previous notions of skilled reading, but there are several problems with it. First, it is difficult for this model to accommodate the behaviors of young students just beginning to read. There are many times when their reading is text-driven because they are unfamiliar with both the text and the content of a selection. A skilled adult can remedy this, of course, by reading the material aloud first or by selecting material that provides support from the "top down" (e.g., rhythm and rhyme). However, the fact remains that even with very limited knowledge and skill, beginners can and do read in a print-driven system and, however difficult, can still derive meaning in the process.

Similarly, the top-down model fails to account for times when even skilled readers find the going tough: when the topic is unfamiliar or the material dense. This may not be the preferred mode of reading, but again, the fact is that skilled readers have a text-driven option available to them. Both skilled readers and beginners demonstrate a flexibility and a variability in approach that is not captured by the top-down model of reading.

Interactive Models of Reading

Many researchers have concluded that reading is not strictly either a bottom-up or top-down process. Rather, it is an interactive process in which bottom-up and top-down processes occur simultaneously and *meaning results from the interaction between the reader and the text.* For example, Rumelhart (1977) characterized reading as an "interactive process" in which readers vary their focus along a continuum, from primarily text-based processing to primarily reader-based processing. This view suggests that the processing of text is a flexible interaction of the different information sources available to the reader, and that the information contained in higher stages of processing can influence the analysis that occurs at lower stages of analysis, as well as the other way around.

Evidence of the interaction between levels of processing provided support for Rumelhart's model. Rumelhart summarized this evidence in the following five statements:

1. Perception of letters often depends on the surrounding letters.
2. Perception of words depends on the syntactic environment in which they are encountered.
3. Perception of words depends on the semantic environment in which they are encountered.
4. Perception of syntax depends on the semantic context in which word strings are encountered.
5. Interpretation of what is read depends on the general context in which the text is encountered.

Thus, as readers process print they may rely on any one or more of the following information sources as their primary clues to meaning: the general context, the semantic context, the syntactic environment, and/or the surrounding letters.

Some examples may help clarify these interactions. First, if you were reading along in a text and encountered the word *pgmo,* what would you be most likely to think? Most readers are inclined to say this word is probably a typographical error in the text. Suppose the letters were rearranged, and the unfamiliar word was *gomp.* Would your reaction be the same? Most readers are less inclined to assume that this is a typographical error, because *gomp* is pronounceable according to the rules of English. Many of us will entertain the possibility that this is a real word that we do not know, and adopt a wait-and-see attitude. In short, our knowledge of the spelling rules in our language influences our perception of letters and words.

Second, our perception of words depends on the syntactic and semantic environment in which they are encountered. Note in the following brief example how the reader has altered a subsequent word in the sentence to be syntactically and semantically consistent with a previous error.

Text: The kitten gave a happy meow.
Reader: The kitten *had* a happy *morning*.

After the reader misread *had* for *gave*, the word *meow* was no longer contextually acceptable in this sentence, so the recognition of *meow* as *morning* was influenced by the context in which it occurred.

Third, perception of syntax depends on the semantic context in which word strings are encountered. Rumelhart uses the following examples taken from Schank (1973) to illustrate this:

1a. I saw the Grand Canyon flying to New York.
  b. I saw the Grand Canyon while I was flying to New York.
  c. I saw the Grand Canyon which was flying to New York.
2a. I saw the cattle grazing in the field.
  b. I saw the cattle while I was grazing in the field.
  c. I saw the cattle that were grazing in the field.

Most readers immediately interpret sentence 1a as meaning the same as 1b rather than 1c simply on the grounds that it is semantically anomalous to imagine the Grand Canyon to be flying. In contrast, sentence 2a is ordinarily interpreted to mean the same as 2c rather than 2b. Semantics plays the determining role in which structure is perceived.

Similarly, our interpretation of what we read depends on the general context in which we encounter the text. Bransford and McCarrell (1974) use the following sentences to illustrate:

The haystack was important because the fabric was torn.
The notes were sour because the seam split.

These sentences appear to be anomalous until they are placed in the context of either parachute jumping (sentence 1) or playing the bagpipes (sentence 2). Therefore, the semantic context of a text influences our interpretation of what we read.

The critical features of an interactive model of the reading process are as follows:

- reading is a cognitive process
- meaning results from the interaction between reader and text
- processing proceeds both from whole to part and part to whole
- different emphases in instruction are appropriate at different times

Summarizing Models of Reading

Teachers, like educational researchers, generally hold a view of the reading process that reflects a predominant orientation toward one of three possible models of reading. Both the bottom-up and top-down views have spawned instructional practices that reflect different approaches to the teaching of reading. The interactive model of reading is relatively recent and has engendered fewer instructional responses; although activities drawn from either of the other perspectives might be used at different times.

One of the greatest problems with the prototypic bottom-up and top-down models of reading is that they can account for the reading process under some circumstances, but not others. The interactive model allows for differential use of information sources at different times, under different conditions. Therefore, it also can account for the reader's developmental status so that it can accommodate the possibility that the reading process may differ for novices (beginning and/or less-skilled readers) and experts (mature and/or highly skilled readers). This model and the evidence supporting it are explored in greater detail in the next section.

UNDERSTANDING INTERACTIVE READING

An interactive perspective suggests that readers construct meaning when they comprehend, in much the same way writers construct meaning when they compose. Thus meaning is not in the text to be extracted through a series of analyses. Rather, it is built in the mind of the reader on the basis of information taken from the reader, the text, and the reading context.

Although Rumelhart's work provided the basis for thinking about reading as an interactive process, his work still had bias toward explaining word identification (Samuels & Kamil, 1984). Research in the 10 years following the introduction of Rumelhart's model has led to significant advances in reading theory. Readers' performance on a variety of reading tasks clearly indicates that there are many factors that interact during the processing of print to influence comprehension.

This body of research and our own experiences with students in classrooms and clinics has led us to adopt an interactive view of reading and reading disability. A synthesis of current research suggests that *reading is the process of constructing meaning through the dynamic interaction among the reader, the text, and the context of the reading situation* (Anderson et al., 1985; Wixson & Peters, 1984). Many of the factors that influence this process are represented in the diagram presented in Figure 1.4. These will be described briefly below.

Reader Factors

An interactive model of reading suggests that a variety of reader factors interact with each other and with factors outside the reader to influence reading. Prior knowledge, knowledge about reading, and attitudes and motivation are among

FIGURE 1.4
*Factors That
Interact to
Influence
Reading*

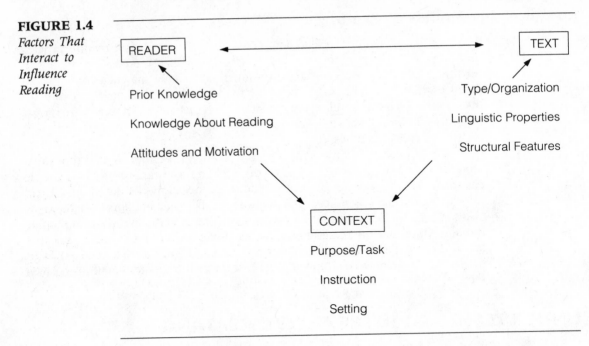

the reader factors that are most important in determining learning and performance in reading.

Prior Knowledge

Put simply, what readers already know about the events, ideas, and objects described in a text influences the meaning they construct from that text (Lipson, 1982, 1983). Current research supports the view that this background, or prior, knowledge is organized in long-term memory as knowledge structures. Each individual structured network is referred to as a *schema*.

Schema theory has had a strong influence on our understanding of how readers understand what they read. A schema-theoretic view of reading suggests that reading comprehension occurs as readers construct relationships between an existing schema and the information suggested by a text. The reader's schema provides a framework of expectations that includes slots for different elements of information.

For example, a restaurant schema contains slots for menus, waitpersons, food prices, and so forth, and these slots are further refined by additional information about the type of restaurant, such as fast food, diner, or gourmet. It is also clear that different people with different experiential backgrounds will have somewhat different restaurant schemas.

Comprehension proceeds so smoothly under ordinary circumstances that most adults are unaware of the process of constructing a model or interpretation of a text that fits with their knowledge of the world. It is instructive to try to understand material for which meaning is not immediately apparent. For example, take a moment to read and try to understand the paragraph in the following exercise, which was used in a classic study by Bransford and Johnson (1972):

> The procedure is actually quite simple. First you arrange things into different groups. Of course, one pile may be sufficient depending on how much there is to do. If you have to go somewhere else due to lack of facilities that is the next step, otherwise you are pretty well set. It is important not to overdo things. That is, it is better to do too few things at once than too many. In the short run this may not seem important, but complications can easily arise. A mistake can be expensive as well. At first the whole procedure will seem complicated. Soon, however, it will become just another facet of life. It is difficult to foresee any end to the necessity for this task in the immediate future, but then one never can tell. After the procedure is completed one arranges the materials into different groups again. Then they can be put into their appropriate places. Eventually they will be used once more and the whole cycle will then have to be repeated. However, that is part of life. (p. 722)

Were there any words you could not pronounce, or for which you do not have some meaning? Is syntax too complex? You probably did not have problems in either of these areas. Yet, for most people, this passage does not make much sense. However, it does become meaningful as soon as we use the title "Washing Clothes." Then the slots for procedures and sorting that are referred to in the passage can be filled with specific knowledge we have about the procedures and sorting that occur as part of washing clothes.

There are many times when a text written for an audience with certain background knowledge is given to an audience with different or limited knowledge of the topic. For example, note the difficulties certain readers will have trying to understand the materials in Figure 1.5 that were taken from newspapers in Vermont and Australia. Now suppose you were asked to identify the main ideas of these texts. If you failed to complete this task successfully, would it mean that you do not know how to "get" a main idea? Obviously not; it simply means that you do not have sufficient background knowledge about the game of cricket, or about dairy cows, to be able to understand the most important points in these texts. Yet we rarely consider our students' prior knowledge in evaluating their performance on comprehension tasks.

A basic fallacy of bottom-up or skills-based views of reading is that skills are static across all reading situations, and that students' skill performance under one set of reading conditions is indicative of their performance under all reading conditions. Clearly, this is not the case for us or for our students. Children do not have the same experiential background as adults, and the meanings they construct for a given piece of text may be different from the meanings constructed by their adult teachers or authors of instructional materials.

FIGURE 1.5

Texts Taken from Newspapers in Vermont and Australia

NIGHT AUCTION
Thursday, Oct. 9th   7:30 PM

Located on the so-called Harry Domina farm on Route #118 between East Berkshire and Montgomery, Vt. Watch for Auction Signs at Route Jct. #105 & #118 in East Berkshire, Vt.

50   Holstein Heifers   50

22 of the heifers are fresh within the last ten days and are milking between 50 to 60 lbs. of weighed milk, balance are all springing, 5 of these heifers are registered with papers that will be handed out the same night. Heifers have good size and condition and are going to be sold for cash regardless of price.
Heifers have all been T.B., blood tested and inoculated from shipping fever and I.B.R. Heilfers are open for inspection anytime on site where auction is to be held. Trucking available.

Auctioneer:	**Ringman:**
Tel.:	**Berkshire, Vt.**
Sales held inside tent	Tel.:
	Owners:
	Berkshire, Vt. Tel.

CRICKET MATCH
AUSTRALIA vs. ENGLAND

A hair-raising century by Australian opener Graeme Wood on Friday set England back on its heels in the third test at the Melbourne Cricket Ground. Unfortunately, living dangerously eventually cost the Australians the match. Wood was caught out of his crease on the first over after lunch. Within ten more overs, the Australians were dismissed. Four were dismissed by dangerous running between creases. Two were dismissed when the English bowlers lifted the bails from the batsmen's wickets. The three remaining batsmen were caught by English fieldsmen. One was caught as he tried for a six. When the innings were complete the Australians had fallen short of the runs scored by the English.

Figure 2 from "Developing Readers' Knowledge Through Analogy" by David A. Hayes and Robert J. Tierney, *Reading Research Quarterly*, Vol. 17, No. 2, 1982.

Knowledge About Reading

Any discussion of the factors that influence reading would be incomplete without reference to terms such as *metacognition*. This term was introduced by developmental psychologists to refer to the knowledge and control children have over their own learning and thinking activities (Flavell & Wellman, 1977; Brown, 1978).

Metacognition in reading refers to one's understanding of the reading process. This understanding is revealed in two ways. First, understanding involves the reader's knowledge of the nature of reading; the purposes and goals of reading; the various factors that influence reading; and the what, how, when, and why of strategy usage in reading. Second, readers' understanding is reflected in the control they have of their actions while reading for different purposes. Active readers monitor their own state of learning, plan strategies, adjust efforts appropriately, and evaluate the success of their ongoing efforts to understand (Brown, Armbruster, & Baker, 1986).

Research suggests that skilled readers know a great deal about the reading process, and that this knowledge influences their ability to select and use appropriate strategies and skills in different reading situations. In the following section, we describe the wide range of reading-related knowledge that skilled readers possess, including knowledge of purposes and goals, knowledge of various text factors, knowledge of task requirements, and knowledge about the skills and strategies used in reading.

Skilled readers know that the purpose of reading is "to get meaning" rather than "to say all of the words right." Skilled readers also realize that reading will be easier if they know a great deal about the topic of the text and if they are interested in it (Myers & Paris, 1978). These examples may seem incredibly obvious, but there are many young and poor readers who do not have even these basic understandings about reading.

Skilled readers also understand how various text factors can influence their reading. Before we ever open a book or read the first words in a text, our knowledge of the type of text we are reading influences the way we will read that text. We know about different types of texts such as encyclopedias, cookbooks, letters from friends, novels, newspapers, and so forth. We have expectations for how these texts will be organized and for the types of information they contain, and this knowledge guides us in the selection of appropriate reading strategies. For example, if someone told you that they had read about a miracle cure for baldness in *Scientific American*, you would be likely to approach the text differently than if they told you they had read about it in the *National Enquirer*.

Knowledge about the tasks that we will be asked to complete following reading also affects strategy selection and usage. When we asked a group of fifth-grade students to tell us why they thought their teachers wanted them to work in their workbooks, one child responded indignantly, "Do you know what she [the teacher] did? She gave us a test on the workbook. You're not supposed to remember that stuff!" His response reflected his awareness that in most class-rooms, students need not remember the material in their workbooks, but simply complete it and put it in the appropriate place.

Skilled readers also have knowledge about different skills and strategies for reading and about how to use them. For example, they are aware of strategies for dealing with words and sentences they do not know (e.g., ask for help, use the dictionary, reread). They are also aware of the purposes for different strategies such as skimming (e.g., to get the general idea), and of strategies such as "look backs" that can be used when comprehension fails (Garner & Reis, 1981; Myers & Paris, 1978). It is not sufficient to know what the strategies are and how to use them; readers must also know when and why to use them

Skilled readers not only have a great deal of knowledge about reading, but they also can apply that knowledge to monitor and regulate their reading. For example, they know when their answers to questions are not satisfactory (Garner & Reis, 1981). There is also evidence that they can adjust their strategies in response to different reading situations (e.g., reading for fun, reading for details or for general impressions, studying), and that they use specific strategies to meet the demands of specific reading situations (e.g., note-taking and underlining in study situations, "looking back" when answering comprehension questions) (Garner & Reis, 1981). In summary, it appears that students' knowledge and control of the reading process plays an important role in their reading performance.

Attitudes and Motivation

Whether children perform or learn in a particular situation depends on whether they can do what must be done and whether they choose to do it (Adelman &

Taylor, 1977). Learning and performance require both skill and will (Paris, Lipson, & Wixson, 1983). Factors such as interest, the amount of time and effort required, willingness to take risks, or perceived competence can influence children's decisions whether to use their skills or not.

The student's attitude toward reading is a central factor affecting reading performance. Good readers generally have more positive attitudes toward reading than do poor readers. Attitudes, beliefs, and expectancies become more negative with failure. This results in less effort, which, in turn, maintains a cycle of failure (Dweck & Bempechat, 1983). A related finding is that high interest in reading material results in greater desire to read and increased comprehension (Asher, 1980). Clearly, students tend to have more knowledge about topics that interest them, so research on interest is somewhat confounded with prior knowledge, which is in itself a powerful factor in comprehension. However, there is also evidence that interest enables students to read beyond their measured ability, and that low-achieving students are more affected by interest than high-achieving students (Shnayer, 1969).

Research indicates that positive self-perceptions promote achievement-oriented behavior, whereas low self-perceptions lead to decreased motivation (Harter, 1981). In addition, positive attitudes and self-perceptions are associated with a sense of control over reading successes and failures. Perceived lack of control can grow out of repeated and prolonged failure experiences. This can have a debilitating effect, sometimes called *learned helplessness*, which in turn causes a general expectation that all events that happen to the person are uncontrollable. The end result can be passive behavior.

This cyclic pattern was demonstrated in a study by Butkowsky and Willows (1980). The poor readers in the study had significantly lower initial expectations for success than did average and good readers, and when confronted with failure, they persisted at the task for shorter periods of time. However, it also appears that children's beliefs about why they succeed or fail in reading vary across reading situations (Hiebert, Winograd, & Danner, 1984). Therefore, it is likely that readers' willingness to exert effort also will vary from situation to situation.

Text Factors

Although an interactive model of reading recognizes the significant contribution of the reader to reading achievement, it also highlights the role of other factors in the process. Research into the ways that text type and text characteristics influence reading is extensive, and consistently demonstrates that the printed material itself influences reading.

In the past, the only text feature that was given much attention was its difficulty, as measured by factors such as the number of syllables in the words and the number of words in the sentences. Current research has demonstrated that there are a number of other factors that have a significant impact on both how much and what readers understand and learn from a text. As a result, texts are often described as either "considerate" or "inconsiderate" (Armbruster, 1984).

Considerate texts are designed to enable the reader to gather appropriate information with minimal effort; inconsiderate texts require the reader to put forth extra effort in order to compensate for the inadequacies of the text. Inconsiderate texts are not necessarily incomprehensible, but they do require more effort, skill, and prior knowledge to comprehend. In the following paragraphs, we briefly describe some categories of text factors that determine if a text will be considerate or not. These include the type and organization of text, the linguistic properties of text, and the structural features of text.

Type and Organization

There is evidence that students' word recognition and comprehension vary as a function of different text types and/or organizations. For example, under certain circumstances, students' oral reading errors have been observed to vary according to the type of text they were reading (e.g., stories versus informational articles; subject area texts versus basal materials). Stories are more easily comprehended than informational texts for many children, and well-constructed stories are more easily comprehended than less well-organized stories (Brennan, Bridge, & Winograd, 1986; Olson, 1985).

Research suggests that major structural differences exist between stories and informational texts. The structure of stories is described by *story grammars* that include elements such as problem, conflict, and resolution (Stein & Glenn, 1979). The structure of informational texts is generally described in terms of its organizational patterns (e.g., cause-effect, temporal sequence). A considerate text marks the type and organization in an appropriate structural manner. We return to these issues in much greater detail in Chapter 9.

Linguistic Properties

Linguistic properties of texts include word usage, sentence structure, and sentence connectives. Each of these surface features influences performance on a variety of reading tasks. For example, texts that include a large proportion of words that occur with high frequency in our language are more easily comprehended than texts with a large proportion of low-frequency words (Ruddell, 1965; Wittrock, Marks, & Doctorow, 1975).

Readability formulas (see Chapter 9) are based on the assumption that shorter sentences are more easily understood than longer sentences. Although this is often true, there is evidence to the contrary (Pearson, 1974–75). Longer sentences often include connective terms that make the relations between ideas explicit. When sentences are shortened, explicit connectives are frequently omitted, requiring the reader to infer a relationship that was previously stated explicitly. For example, in the sentence "The car crashed into the tree, because the wheel fell off the car," the relation between the wheel falling off the car and the car crashing is made explicit by the connective "because." If this sentence were shortened, it would read, "The wheel fell off the car. The car crashed into the tree." Now the reader must infer the relationship between the car crash and the wheel.

This is precisely the way texts are "written down" for younger readers. Other devices that are intended to simplify texts, but may in reality make them less comprehensible, are the overuse of reference, and "round-about" language (Beck et al., 1981). Both of these devices are used to reduce the number of syllables in words, because readability formulas assume that words with more syllables are more difficult to understand. So, multisyllabic words are often replaced with terms of reference, such as "it," or with round-about language. A story about an elephant may refer repeatedly to the elephant as "it," "he," or "she" even when the referent (elephant) may have occurred much earlier in the text, or perhaps only in an illustration.

Structural Features

The structural features of text include all the features of texts that authors and editors use to aid organization and understanding such as headings, boldface type, illustrations, diagrams, and end-of-chapter questions and activities. These, too, influence reading performance. For example, there is evidence that comprehension is enhanced when main idea statements are highlighted through the use of italics or headings (Baumann, 1986). It also appears that students are actually led to attend to unimportant ideas when structural features focus on trivial information. For example, if questions that follow reading focus on insignificant details, children are more likely to learn this information than the more important ideas in the text (Wixson, 1984).

Contextual Factors

The interactive model of reading proposes a triad of factors that influence reading. Of the three elements (reader, text, and context), contextual factors are the least likely to be considered in any discussion of reading. Indeed, the importance of context has only recently been realized.

The subtle, yet powerful, influence of context can be best illustrated by describing two studies. In one of the classic studies demonstrating the importance of prior knowledge in text interpretation, physical education and music majors read a passage that could be interpreted as either a prison escape or a wrestling match. In the original study (Anderson, Reynolds, Schallert, & Goetz, 1977) the physical education majors tended to interpret the passage as a wrestling match, and the music majors tended to interpret it as a prison escape. The researchers concluded that prior knowledge, in the form of expertise, accounted for this behavior.

However, this study was replicated several years later with somewhat different results. It turned out that a basic difference between the two studies was the location of the physical education majors when they participated in the studies. During the first study they were located in a gym, but during the second study they were located in a classroom unrelated to physical education. This demonstrates the significant impact that contextual factors can have on students' reading.

In the following sections, we will briefly describe several aspects of context that have been shown to influence reading: the purpose and the tasks associated with reading, the setting in which the reading event occurs, and the specialized setting apparent in instructional contexts. This brief discussion serves only to introduce ideas that will be discussed at greater length in Chapters 8 and 9.

Purpose and Task

Students' comprehension can vary as a function of the purposes for which they read and/or the *criterion tasks* they must complete in association with their reading. For example, it has been demonstrated that children are better able to identify the main idea of a text when they are asked to choose the best title than when they are asked to write a summary sentence (Williams, Taylor, & deCani, 1984). It has also been shown that children perform better when they are given clear knowledge of the tasks they will be asked to complete following reading (Wong, Wong, & LeMare, 1982).

Questioning is probably the most frequently used task in reading instruction. The evidence suggests that the type of questions children are asked can influence their comprehension. It appears that implicit or inferential questions are more difficult for many children than explicit or literal questions (Pearson, Hansen, & Gordon, 1979). Furthermore, there is evidence that the type of question asked influences the numbers and types of inferences students make. Specifically, questions with answers stated explicitly in the text result in fewer inferences, questions that require the integration of information in the text result in a larger number of text-based inferences, and questions that require students to draw heavily on their prior knowledge result in more knowledge-based inferences (Wixson, 1983a).

Setting

The setting in which reading and/or reading instruction takes place can also affect reading performance. For example, the meaning derived from text may depend on the broader context in which it is being read. For example, imagine the effect that context would have on reading a text on common antidotes to poisoning under the following circumstances: in the evening newspaper; on a test of reading comprehension; when you believe your child has ingested some poisonous substance; and in a first aid course.

Furthermore, researchers have found differences in students' performance on the same task, depending on whether it was administered as part of an informal reading lesson or as part of a formal testing situation (Mosenthal & Na, 1980). Indeed, there are several aspects of classroom settings that have been examined and found to contribute to students' reading achievement. For example, grouping patterns influence both teachers and students. Recent reviews of ability grouping for reading instruction suggest that instructional and social reading experiences differ for students in high- and low-ability reading groups and that these differences influence students learning (Allington, 1983a; Hiebert, 1983).

These different experiences may cause students to generate different views of reading. It has been found that teachers interrupt students proportionally more often following oral reading errors in low-ability than high-ability groups (Allington, 1980). Frequent interruptions to address word recognition are likely to encourage students to view reading as "saying the words right" versus "constructing meaning." Grouping practices may also communicate information to students about their relative ability that eventually influences their learning (Weinstein, 1976).

Instruction

Both the content of instruction (what is taught) and the methods of instruction (how it is taught) can influence students' learning and performance. There is evidence that instructional programs that focus on the process of how to read as well as an understanding of the content of what is being read have a powerful impact on students' performance on a variety of reading measures. Attention to the reading process impacts student awareness of what has been taught, awareness of comprehension strategies, and performance on tasks that require strategic reading (Duffy et al., 1986; Paris, Cross, & Lipson, 1984).

The relative importance of the information contained in instructional activities is another feature of the content of instruction that influences what students understand and remember about their reading (Beck, Omanson, & McKeown, 1982). If the instructional content focuses on important information, students' understanding of important information is increased; if the content focuses on unimportant information, that is what students learn (Wixson, 1984, 1986). Comprehension is also influenced by different types of instructional activities. For example, Hansen (1981a) examined the effects of different types of instruction on students' ability to answer inferential comprehension questions. She found that students who were given a traditional "diet" of literal (80%) and inferential (20%) questions along with "ordinary" story introductions were less able to answer inferential questions correctly than students who were asked to use their own experiences to predict and evaluate story characters' problems and actions prior to reading.

The manner in which the teacher delivers the instruction is also important. Teachers typically provide extraordinarily little "wait time" or "think time" to students after a question has been posed (Rowe, 1974). This limited wait time results in student responses that tend to be low-level and closed. When teachers extend the wait time by even a small amount, however, several things occur. First, student responses tend to be both longer and more thoughtful. Second, the responses tend to be more open-minded. Third, more students respond. Finally, there are fewer occasions in which students fail to respond at all.

Summarizing Interactive Reading

There is ample reason to conclude that reading is accomplished as an interplay among at least three major factors: the reader, the text, and the context. Reader factors that influence process and performance include the reader's prior knowledge, his or her knowledge about reading, and his or her attitude and motivation for reading. In addition, there are text factors that affect the reading process. These include the type and organization of text, the linguistic properties of the text, and the structural features of text including headings, maps, and so on. The context in which the reading event takes place is also a factor in reading. Purpose and task affect the reading process, as do both the general and specific settings in which reading and/or reading instruction occur. Finally, instruction itself, both its content and methodology, influence reading and reading performance.

UNDERSTANDING READING DISABILITY

The foregoing discussion has focused primarily on theories and models of reading ability, without specific attention to reading disability. There is substantial agreement among reading professionals about the interactive nature of reading and reading ability, and this emerging view has been helpful in making decisions about appropriate developmental reading programs for most students. We now turn our attention to a discussion of the area of *dis*ability, including a brief historical perspective, the special needs student, and the politics of disability.

A Historical Perspective

Although the interactive view of reading has become increasingly popular among reading educators, it has not been applied until recently in any significant way to the area of reading disability. Increasingly, we have come to expect that the performance of able readers will vary depending on factors such as those we have just discussed. When a disabled reader fails, however, we presume that the failure reflects some internal disorder or reader deficit, and initiate "the search for pathology" (Sarason & Doris, 1979). This orientation toward seeking pathological explanations for reading problems grows out of the historical roots of the study of reading disability.

The Medical Model
The earliest studies of reading disability assumed neurological impairment and were reported by professionals in the field of medicine. In 1896, P. Morgan published an account of an individual who had failed to learn to read and speculated on the causes of this individual's "congenital word-blindness." About the same time, J. Hinselwood initiated a series of clinical studies that examined the role of the brain in reading failure (dyslexia) and culminated in the 1917 publication of his book *Congenital Word-Blindness*. In 1925, S. Orton introduced a new theory of dyslexia based on the notion of hemispheric imbalance.

Theory and research that assume neurological impairment, including developmental abnormalities, as the basis for reading disability are still popular today (Hynd & Hynd, 1984). The medical model has contributed vast amounts of information about brain functions and the relationship between various types of brain function and certain aspects of cognition. Both early and more recent research have also posed, tested, and refuted a number of hypotheses about the roots of disability.

Although there is little doubt that neurological dysfunction plays a role in certain cases of reading disability, the percentage of cases accounted for by a medical model appears to be extremely small (Chall, 1983; Hynd & Hynd, 1984). The majority of individuals who have difficulties in reading are not likely to be included in the categories of disability described by this model. What is most important for our purposes is the understanding that early medical models influenced later psychoeducational models of reading disability (Guthrie & Seifert, 1978).

The Psychoeducational Model

A major result of the scientific movement in education that occurred around the turn of the century was the development of instruments to be used for educational measurement. Thorndike developed the first norm-referenced group test of reading ability in 1914, and others soon followed. In addition to the development of standardized tests of silent reading, a test of oral reading was published by W. S. Gray in 1915, which led directly to the diagnostic movement and to an emphasis on remediation.

As instruments were developed and used for the measurement of reading, it became evident to educators that many students were either failing to learn to read or were performing far below expected levels. Thus, reading deficiencies became the domain of educators and psychologists as well as medical professionals. This resulted in a different account of reading disability in which various nonmedical factors within the reader were seen as the source of reading difficulties. What distinguished this view from the existing medical models was that neurological impairment was not assumed to be the source of the problem. Neurological factors might be considered as one possible source of difficulty, but the emphasis clearly was on non-neurological factors.

One of the earliest studies conducted from this psychoeducational perspective was Monroe's 1932 study *Children Who Cannot Read*. This study focused on the "atypical child who does not learn to read so well as would be expected from their other intellectual abilities" and posited that such children "may be regarded as having a special defect." Having placed the source of the problem within the reader, Monroe then described the "causative factors in reading defects." These factors will be familiar to professionals in the area of reading disability today. They are visual acuity, visual discrimination, eye-hand coordination, mixed laterality, defects in speech, auditory discrimination, environmental factors, and emotional factors.

Over the next several decades, the vast majority of research related to reading disabilities became focused on finding the cause or causes of reading failure. The notion that reading problems were rooted within the reader became well established, and research based on psychoeducational models of reading disability have dominated the field for the past four decades. This has resulted in extensive tests of single factors believed to cause reading problems.

During this time these models have taken a number of different forms, including those that emphasize developmental factors and those that stress weaknesses in various subskills (e.g., Betts, 1936; deHirsch, Jansky, & Langford, 1966). Most recently, the influence of these psychological models can be seen in information processing models of reading disability (e.g., Perfetti, 1985; Stanovich, 1982a, 1982b). What all of these approaches have in common is the search for causative factors of reading disability within the reader.

Importantly, several key studies demonstrated that reading and reading ability were multiply determined (Robinson, 1946), with an array of factors converging to influence reading performance. During this time, researchers acknowledged the fairly large variability in reading and reading performance among disabled readers. For example, Monroe herself noted that there was great variability among the reading disabled students she studied, and other researchers observed that reading test scores were not comparable when they employed dissimilar materials (see Gray, 1941/1984). Nevertheless, the idea that reading problems might result from one single reader factor that could be "fixed" through remediation has generally prevailed.

The results of these various lines of research have been enlightening. Research driven by earlier models has permitted us to reject some explanations for reading disability. For example, researchers have concluded that perceptual deficits do not account for reading disabilities and that global visual-perceptual training exercises do not remedy the problems (see Vellutino, 1977).

This research has also demonstrated that there are many factors that appear to differentiate good and poor readers. We will discuss the most important correlates of reading ability in the following section. Unfortunately, many of the factors that have been studied do not appear to cause disability. One of the most significant contributions of this long line of research is that it has revealed the complexity of reading performance by demonstrating that these isolated factors do not have sufficient power to explain reading disability (see Stanovich, 1986, and Wixson & Lipson, 1991, for extensive discussion).

Summarizing Early Models of Disability

This brief historical review suggests that there were at least two related models of reading disability that could be identified by 1930: the medical model and the psychoeducational model. The legacy of the two models is the extensive amount of information available on various reader factors that are, or can be, significant in reading achievement. These will be described in some detail in the next section.

The medical model followed a path that led directly to the field of special education, while the psychoeducational model became the domain of psychologists and reading specialists. In both cases, however, the emphasis was placed on pathology. This has caused educators and researchers to focus almost exclusively on the identification of reader deficits, and little attention has been given to the instructional context.

Correlates of Reading Disability

When reading problems are presumed to result always and only from some deficiency on the part of the reader, what emerges as a focus for diagnosis is a listing of the various organic factors that may be abnormal. These factors are frequently referred to as *correlates* of reading disability, because the presence of difficulties in any of these areas is correlated with poor reading performance. When one or more of these correlates is strongly present in a student or a student population, these students are considered *at risk* of school failure (Vacca & Padak, 1990).

It is important to understand, however, that the presence of high correlations does not ensure causality (see Chapter 6), nor has the search for single pathologies yielded, thus far, unequivocal causal relationships between most correlates and reading success. Despite the lack of evidence supporting specific causal relationships, it is still important to be aware of these factors. In individual cases, they may account for reading difficulties, and in others they may contribute to the problem. In still others, they will be ruled out as playing any meaningful role in the reading disability.

In subsequent chapters, we deal with some of the correlates described below in more detail. However, our treatment here is not extensive, because in addition to the problems of causality described previously, it is extremely difficult to evaluate correlates with any precision, and even more difficult to deal with them instructionally, since most are factors internal to the learner (see Figure 1.6). In the following sections, we will briefly describe correlates of reading performance in four major areas: physical development, cognitive development, language development, and social and emotional development.

Physical Development

Within the area of physical development, a student's hearing, vision, general health, and maturation are all important. There are several types of hearing loss. Some make it difficult for students to hear all sounds; others result in loss of hearing for particular sounds. Both types of hearing loss can occur in the same person, and hearing loss can occur in one or both ears. Since reading is based on listening and speaking, children who have difficulty hearing are at a disadvantage in learning to read. An appropriate referral should be made if there is any evidence of impaired hearing, and if at all possible, the loss should be corrected before any further specialized instruction occurs. Hearing loss resulting from more temporary physical conditions (e.g., ear infections) can also interfere with learning and should prompt careful teachers to consider adapting their methods of instruction. For example, intensive oral phonics instruction is unlikely to benefit students with permanent or recurring hearing impairment.

There are several types of visual impairments. People who are farsighted have difficulty in seeing objects up close, as when reading a book. Nearsightedness, on the other hand, results in difficulties seeing distant objects, such as the chalkboard. Astigmatism results in distorted visual images, which could lead to problems such

FIGURE 1.6
Correlates of Reading Performance

Physical Development

Cognitive Development

Intelligence
Information-Processing Abilities

Attention
Perception
Memory

Language Development

Social and Emotional Development

as keeping one's place while reading. Other types of vision problems occur when the eye muscles do not work together in a smooth coordinated fashion. These types of problems can result in fatigue and discomfort that interferes with reading.

Research regarding the impact of these visual problems on reading achievement appears to be equivocal. Harris and Sipay (1985) conclude that there is simply not sufficient evidence to make any real judgment about the relation between problems of visual acuity, poor eye muscle coordination, and reading ability. They also point out that these problems are not likely to be detected by the eye tests commonly used in schools, since the Snellen Chart is designed to detect only problems of nearsightedness. Although adequate visual and auditory acuity are clearly required to learn to read, these are often not assessed during reading diagnostic workups.

Finally, learning and cognitive development depend on acceptable overall development. Poor general health can cause children to fail in any or all areas of learning. Students who are in poor health—who suffer from poor nutrition or chronic illness, for example—may experience frequent absences from school, or fatigue and decreased attention while in school. Insufficient sleep may also contribute to fatigue and lack of concentration. It is important to recognize that these factors can play a role in students' reading, but often do not. It may sometimes be appropriate to request a complete physical for a child who seems to be having difficulty with reading to make sure that diet, sleep patterns, or physical problems are not implicated. A thorough assessment must include consideration of these components of overall development that may impede learning.

Cognitive Development

Reading is a specific example of cognitive activity. Learning how to read requires learning only a handful of skills and strategies that are unique to reading. Many of the things that are required of a reader are required of people engaged in other learning and problem-solving activities as well. For example, students need to be able to listen, attend, and exert effort during learning. Normal reading, like all cognitive abilities, is developmental. This means that beginners know less than experts, but it also means that the quality of their knowledge and skills is different. Therefore, "in relating cognitive factors to reading, both specific prior learning and more general developmental factors influence reading performance at any given time" (Ringler & Weber, 1984, p. 26).

As children grow and mature, they acquire an increasingly sophisticated repertoire of cognitive abilities. Developmental stages or shifts in perspective are often used to capture this changing and increasing knowledge base (e.g., Bruner, 1964; Piaget, 1960; Vygotsky, 1978). Both Piaget and Bruner describe growth during the preschool and school years as a time when children are moving toward the ability to transcend the present and think flexibly about the world. Teachers need to understand how their students think about their world so that they can provide experiences that are appropriate to children's cognitive functioning and that move them to expand and restructure their knowledge.

Cognitive development also includes development in the areas of perception, attention, and memory, as well as encompassing traditional notions of intelligence and verbal ability. Although it is beyond the scope of this text to consider each of these correlates in detail, each will be briefly discussed below to provide an awareness of the scope of the cognitive-developmental factors that may influence reading achievement.

Intelligence. Intelligence generally refers to overall mental ability. Included in the construct of intelligence are such indicators of ability as speed of learning, ability to solve problems, and ability to engage in high-level thinking tasks. Although most people believe intelligence is a broad-based attribute, most textbooks that deal with cognitive development discuss this topic almost exclusively in terms of the results of intelligence tests. In sum, intelligence is viewed as the ability to do well on the tasks presented on IQ tests.

Given the importance of such judgments in school settings, there are several points that need to be made here. First, intelligence is a construct. That is, the components of intelligence are not readily observable. Indeed, there is substantial disagreement about what the components are. Most psychological authorities note that intelligence is actually grounded in culture, and that different societies value different sets of skills and define intelligence accordingly (Kagan & Lang, 1978).

Given this situation, caution needs to be exercised in attributing reading problems to limited overall cognitive ability. In our multicultural society, it is possible for different types of behavior and knowledge to mean different things to different individuals. For example, some cultural groups take aggressive display of information as totally inappropriate behavior—the mark of someone either not very smart or not very polite. Other groups teach children to provide creative, but not necessarily factual, answers to situational questions. To generate conclusions about intelligence in the absence of appropriate cultural context is tricky business.

Reading achievement and intelligence, as measured by IQ tests, are highly correlated, but as we noted earlier, this does not mean they are causally related. It seems possible, perhaps even probable, that higher IQ scores are the *result* of school achievement. In any event, there is little doubt that intelligence tests, as presently construed, probably tap only a small portion of the components that might constitute intelligence.

In the past, intelligence was viewed as a relatively stable characteristic and, as such, was not susceptible to change via instruction. Increasingly, it appears that intelligence, again as measured by existing tests, can be influenced by certain experiences and instruction (Campione, Brown, & Ferrara, 1982). More importantly, there is an increased interest, not in static measures of intelligence as traditionally assessed, but in measures of potential to learn. The evidence to date suggests that measures of potential can contribute important information to the assessment/instruction process and we will return to these in Chapter 10.

Information-processing abilities.   Student learning and comprehension are also associated with aspects of the ability to process information in either written or spoken form. Attention, perception, and memory are all factors that influence learning and comprehension.

The ability and willingness to pay attention to important stimuli is a major factor in school success (Kagan & Lang, 1978). Human beings are surrounded by stimuli, that is, all aspects of the environment that are present to be learned, enjoyed, and noticed. Clearly, if students cannot or do not attend to the parts of the environment that contain essential information, they cannot learn or retain new information and skills. Attention however, is very selective and is influenced by a number of other factors, including motivation, maturity, and instruction. For example, older children are better able to focus their attention and can focus their attention for longer periods of time (Kagan & Lang, 1978).

The ability to impose order on sensory information is called *perception*. It too is central to student learning and performance. Like attention, perception is considered to be selective (Bruner, 1964). As discussed previously in this chapter, the selectivity of perception is influenced by past learning and knowledge. This more active view of how people take in and process information suggests that we organize perceptual information, rather than passively perceive available stimuli. Perception, like attention and memory, is also developmental. That is, important changes occur during childhood and adolescence. Older children have more experience and knowledge, and this allows them to impose order on a greater array of stimuli, thus enhancing perception.

Finally, the development of memory is an important aspect of cognitive information processing ability. *Memory* is the process of storing and retrieving information. For many years, psychologists and educators assumed that all perceived events were registered or stored in memory, and that the inability to remember information was due to a failure in retrieving what one knew. However, recent research suggests that limited memory can result from a variety of factors. As we have seen, children's perceptions of events can differ depending on prior knowledge, affecting what is noticed and stored. Not surprisingly, many of the factors that influence comprehension also influence memory. The less comprehensible the information, the less likely it is to be stored and retrieved effectively.

As with all cognitive abilities, memory changes and develops over time. Older children are better at storing and retrieving information than younger children, and adults tend to be better at this than children. These developmental differences may be due in part to capacity (increased space for coping with information), but most psychologists now believe that memory improves because the ability to organize incoming information improves with age. Older children and adults clearly have better concept formation and a more elaborate network connecting concepts (schemata) that allows for better organization of new information. In addition, older children and adults tend to have better strategies for coping with information, and they are better at understanding what they need to do in order to remember information.

It is easy to see how individual differences in these areas of development can affect students' abilities to cope with school tasks. It is also becoming increasingly clear that these cognitive abilities are not static. Attention, perception, and memory operate in relation to *specific types of information.* It is misleading to talk of children's information-processing abilities without specifying exactly what it is they are trying to perceive and remember (Kagan & Lang, 1978). We see once again how culture, expectations, and experience can influence performance and potentially confound the measurement of these abilities.

Language Development

Language development is a third correlate of reading ability and disability. The acquisition of language competence is a major factor influencing subsequent reading achievement. As children learn language, they develop abilities in understanding and producing speech. This development involves learning how the language is structured, how humans use language to communicate, and the specific words and rules of their own language.

All languages have certain characteristics. The structure (grammar) of a language consists of several major components, including the smallest units of sound *(phonemes)*, the smallest units of meaning *(morphemes)*, the organization of words within sentences *(syntax)*, and the meaning system *(semantics)*. Children must also learn about the communicative functions of language. Humans use language for a variety of purposes, and understanding the functions embedded in language is critical to comprehending the messages sent. The communicative functions include regulating other people's behavior, expressing feelings, pretending and creating, conveying or obtaining information, and establishing and maintaining contact with others.

Children acquire language competence at varying rates and to varying degrees. With few exceptions, children will have mastered the language and communication patterns of their own families prior to entry into first grade. Not all language and communication patterns are equally good matches with the demands of school settings, however. Children with disordered, underdeveloped, or merely "different" language skills are likely to have difficulty with reading.

Indeed, one factor that is likely to place students at risk of school failure is limited English proficiency.

Although it seems obvious to point out that children will not easily learn to read a language they cannot speak, not all schools are equipped to provide the foundation in oral language that may be required for many students. Children's knowledge of the standard structure of language forms the foundation for learning to read. If the child's language differs significantly from the language he or she is encountering in books, the resulting mismatch will make initial learning difficult.

As young children are engaged in experiences with language, thought, and print, they gain an increasing awareness about what is required to accomplish literacy tasks. In addition, they acquire increasing ability to reflect on language as a separate entity. This awareness of and control over cognitive activities is often referred to as *metalinguistic awareness.*

Instruction in reading, like most cognitive tasks, requires some degree of reflective ability, yet not all children have acquired appropriate abilities in this area. Some abilities, though potentially useful, are late in developing in all children. For example, children must understand that sentences are made up of separate words and that words contain separable sounds. This ability to separate words into distinct sounds is called *phonemic segmentation.* Research suggests that most kindergarten and many first grade children cannot segment speech by phoneme (Liberman & Shankweiler, 1979). Because the assessment-instruction process needs to take these factors into account, we will return to the issue of language development in Chapter 4.

Social and Emotional Development

It will be no surprise to teachers that the fourth correlate of students' reading achievement is social and emotional development. Students who have trouble adjusting to various social situations with peers and/or adults may experience academic difficulties. Students with emotional problems may also have difficulty concentrating in school, which often has a negative effect on their learning.

It has been estimated that emotional problems are a contributing cause of the reading problem for about 25% of reading disability cases (Kappelman, Kaplan, & Ganter, 1969). However, it is frequently difficult to determine to what extent emotional and social maladjustment are causes or results of reading problems. "Every poor reader is at risk for psychological disturbance, almost always as a result of, rarely as the cause of, and frequently as a further contribution to, the poor reading" (Eisenberg, 1975, p. 219).

Although Harris and Sipay (1985) note that studies attempting to demonstrate stable relationships between poor readers (as a group) and emotional or social difficulties have been fruitless, individual students may certainly exhibit reading difficulties due largely to social or emotional problems. There are students for whom learning is made more difficult by family upheaval, by neglect, and by interpersonal problems in school. In addition, of course, physiologically-based emotional problems (e.g., from drug-related birth trauma) can lead to students who are easily discouraged or unable to relate to others. Regardless of whether emotional and social problems are the cause or the result of reading problems, if they are interfering with learning and performance, they must be considered in developing an instructional program.

Summarizing Reading Correlates

In this section we discussed four categories of reading correlates. The contributions of students' physical, cognitive, linguistic, and social-emotional development to reading were briefly outlined. We have argued that these correlates are the legacy of psychoeducational models of reading disability. In using terms such as *at risk*, educators acknowledge that relationships between these correlates and reading often exist, although they are rarely causal. In the next section, we describe a different legacy, that of the medical model.

Special Needs Students

Another way to examine the issues and problems of reading disability is to consider the field of special education. Although the psychoeducational model of disability has certainly influenced contemporary special education practice, the field can be considered a direct outgrowth of the medical model of reading disability. Special education has for many years been concerned with organic and/ or medical deficiencies within the learner. However, until recently there were relatively few systematic identification or treatment procedures for students with severe physical, linguistic, cognitive or emotional problems. Judicial and legislative actions over the past 20 years, however, have changed that situation. In this section, we consider the legal and social basis for present-day special education programs and describe the specific provisions for meeting existing legal requirements.

Legal and Social Roots of Special Education

As we have seen, the medical field exhibited the earliest interest in reading-disabled individuals. This interest continued throughout the 1930s and 1940s, resulting in a variety of extraordinary treatments to be used in cases of severe reading disability (e.g., Fernald, 1943). These treatments resided outside the "normal" school environment, however, and children with moderate to severe physical, emotional, or cognitive problems were not typically included in regular classrooms or schools. In areas where placement facilities for these children were scarce, many teachers struggled to address extraordinary problems as best they could. In other areas, in the face of limited facilities, the students were simply excluded from any formal schooling.

During the 1950s and 1960s, a combination of social and political factors combined to create an environment in which unusual and extensive attention was focused on those children who were failing to learn easily and well in the public schools of the United States. National attention was captured by a series of legal battles initiated by a group of advocates who wanted to see that all students received appropriate public education.

Bricker (1986) relates the history of one such legal battle, *PARC v. Commonwealth of Pennsylvania* (1971), in which the court concluded that students had been excluded or excused from attendance in public schools simply because they were retarded. In addition, the court ordered the state to support public education for such students. Thus, "for the first time, any school-age child, no matter how impaired, was eligible to receive a free, appropriate public education" (Bricker, 1986, p. 106).

Access to public education was only one of the problems confronting the field at that time, however. The practices surrounding testing and labeling children were suspect for many reasons. For minority children, the problems of abuses and inadequate protections were particularly apparent. Two other cases were directly related to practices in these areas. The decisions handed down by the court in *Diana v. Board of Education* (1970) and *Larry P. v. Riles* (1972), required that children be tested in their primary language; children from minority groups (e.g., black, Mexican, and Chinese) currently in classes for the mentally retarded be reevaluated; and the state (California) develop and standardize IQ tests appropriate for minority groups.

A final concern among advocates in the area of special education involved the treatment and instruction provided to handicapped individuals once they were placed in specialized settings. Thus, in two cases, *Wyatt v. Stickney* and *New York ARC v. Rockefeller* (Willowbrook), judges ruled that residents of such placements had the right to appropriate treatment, and, in the Wyatt case, the judge specified that this treatment should occur in the least restrictive environment (Bricker, 1986).

The active round of legal rulings prompted both attention and concern and provided the basis for the legislative initiatives to follow. Beginning in the early 1960s, laws were passed that established federal programs related to service, training, and research designed specifically for the handicapped. These legislative actions culminated with the passage of the 1975 Education for All Handicapped Act (PL 94–142), which mandates:

- the right to education—all handicapped children are to be provided with free, appropriate, public education
- the right to nondiscriminatory evaluation
- the right to an IEP (Individual Educational Plan)—a clear statement of objectives for each child along with documentation of the child's current and expected performance
- the right to education in the least restrictive environment
- the right to due process
- the right of parental participation (Gallagher, 1984)

Special Education Identification: Provisions of PL 94–142

The actual procedures for implementing the mandates of PL 94–142 vary somewhat from community to community, but the process must include provisions for meeting each mandate. Practically speaking, a teacher, administrator, or parent may make an initial referral in order to determine whether a student is entitled to special education services. Following this referral, the child's parents must be fully informed abut the prospective assessment process and permission to proceed must be received from them. Only after these stages have been completed are assessment procedures initiated to determine whether the student meets federal and local guidelines for exceptionality. In addition, the assessment is usually designed to determine the category of handicap that will be used for purposes of classification.

PL 94–142 clearly specifies procedures for the assessment phase. The procedures designed to address the mandate that students have "the right to non-discriminatory evaluation" are as follows:

- tests must be selected and administered so as to ensure that results "accurately reflect the child's aptitude and achievement . . . rather than reflecting the child's impaired sensory, manual, or speaking skills"
- no single testing procedure may be used for determining an appropriate educational program for the child
- the evaluation must be conducted by a multidisciplinary team
- the child must be assessed in all areas related to health, vision, hearing, social, and emotional status, academic performance, communicative status, and motor abilities (*Federal Register,* 1977, cited in Morgan, 1981)

In addition, the law provides guidelines for the types of assessment instruments that may be used, stating that tests and other evaluation materials should:

- be provided and administered in the child's native language
- have been validated for the specific purpose for which they are used
- be administered by trained personnel
- include materials tailored to assess specific areas of educational need and not merely those which are designed to provide a single general intelligence quotient (*Federal Register,* 1977, cited in Morgan, 1981)

When the assessment phase is completed, PL 94–142 states clearly that there will be a meeting to develop the child's Individualized Education Program (IEP). As previously noted, the IEP is mandated by the federal government and requires a clear statement of objectives for each child along with documentation of the child's current and expected performance. In addition, the IEP must contain a statement that specifies who will be responsible for each component of the plan and ensures periodic reevaluation of the child's status. The planning group is often referred to as the Committee on the Handicapped and, according to PL 94–142, the following individuals shall be involved in the meeting at which the IEP is developed: a public education representative, who is qualified to provide, or supervise the provision of, special education; the child's teacher; one or both of the child's parents; the child, where applicable; and other individuals at the discretion of the parent or agency (Bricker, 1986).

The parent(s) must agree to the designation of the child under a particular handicapping condition and to the information provided in the IEP. If the parents do not agree with the recommendations of the committee, a series of legal procedures are set in motion to settle the disagreement.

Handicapping Conditions

A student's eligibility for special education services is determined by the type and degree of deficit in a particular area, following the guidelines developed through legal and judicial channels. There are presently nine categories of special needs students:

1. mental impairment
2. hearing impairment
3. visual impairment
4. speech impairment
5. orthopedic impairment
6. other health impairments (limited vitality, strength, or alertness due to chronic or acute health problems)
7. multiply handicapped
8. serious emotional impairment
9. specific learning disability

Eligibility for children in many categories is early and unequivocal because many handicapping conditions are apparent prior to a student's entrance into school. However, learning disability and the less severe cases of mental and emotional impairment are often identified after a student has entered school and failed to meet certain academic expectations.

Reading personnel are often involved with students who have been identified as having special needs in the area of learning disability because the referral is frequently made on the basis of a student's academic performance in the area of reading. Although it is the newest classification, learning disability is presently the largest special education category. By 1982, 41% of all students in special education programs were classified as learning disabled (Plisko, 1984, cited by Sleeter, 1985).

Learning disability is defined by the federal government in the following manner:

> "Specific learning disability" means a disorder in one or more of the basic psychological processes involved in understanding or in using language, spoken or written, which may manifest itself in an imperfect ability to listen, think, speak, read, write, spell, or to do mathematical calculations. The term includes such conditions as perceptual handicaps, brain injury, minimal brain dysfunction, dyslexia, and developmental aphasia. The term does not include children who have learning problems

which are primarily the result of visual, hearing, or motor handicaps, of mental retardation, of emotional disturbance, or of environmental, cultural, or economic disadvantage. (*Federal Register*, Dec. 29, 1977, p. 65083)

It is important to understand how learning disability is related to other volatile issues. For example, the similarity between the definition of learning disability and the definition of dyslexia offered by the World Federation of Neurology has not been lost on most educators:

[Dyslexia] is a disorder manifested by difficulty in learning to read despite conventional instruction, adequate intelligence, and sociocultural opportunity. It is dependent upon fundamental cognitive disabilities which are frequently of constitutional origin. (Critchley, 1975)

These definitions suggest that, for all practical purposes, learning disability and dyslexia are synonymous. What is most important is that both definitions clearly imply an etiology within the reader (either medical or nonspecified).

Although it may appear that special education determinations are straightforward, they are generally far from clear-cut. In addition, schools throughout the country are struggling to decide what programs to offer, who should deliver instruction, and who is eligible for various special programs. For reading professionals and for children who need help in reading, these issues can be troublesome. In the next section, we will describe the extent to which politics may play a part in disability determinations and services.

The Politics of Disability

It appears that the judicial and legislative actions in the area of special education have been most advantageous for individuals with clearly identifiable physical and/or mental impairments. Unfortunately, the situation in the area of reading/learning disability is less clear. Indeed, more than any other classification of handicap, learning disabilities have revived discussion about the source of disability. In the process, troubling sociological issues have been raised as well. With regard to special education services, the question of who gets classified also determines who gets taught.

The political issues arise at least in part from definitions of learning disability. As we have seen, both learning disability and dyslexia definitions are exclusionary. Many researchers have made the point that existing classification schemes work differently for different socioeconomic groups. The requirements of an exclusionary definition effectively "mean that children diagnosed as dyslexic tend to be the bright offspring of 'good' homes attending 'good' schools. There is no reason to suppose that dyslexia is in any real sense a 'middle-class disease,' only that those tend to be the children where psychologists feel most confident they can exclude other obvious causes of reading failure" (Ellis, 1984, p. 106). Indeed, it is the case that minorities are underrepresented in the learning disabilities category (Sleeter, 1985).

Students who are poor readers and who are also less affluent normally receive reading support from a different source, if at all. These students are generally assumed to experience reading difficulties because of one of the other possibilities specified in the government's (exclusionary) definition of learning disability. They are classified into one of the other handicapping conditions (e.g., mental retardation or emotional impairment) or are assumed to need not special education, but compensatory education. Title I of the Elementary and Secondary Education Act of 1965 was passed in order to provide such programs for disadvantaged students:

> In recognition of the special educational needs of children of low-income families and the impact that concentration of low-income families have on the ability of local educational programs, the Congress hereby declares it to be the policy of the United States to provide financial assistance to local educational agencies serving areas with concentrations of children from low-income families in order to expand and improve their educational programs by various means. (NIE, 1977, p. 8, cited in Calfee & Drum, 1979, p. 172)

The practical consequence of these developments is noted by Johnston, Allington, and Franzen (1985): "Two broad notions of reading failure evolved, one linked to environmental deficits and the other to constitutional neurological dysfunction" (p. 8). These authors discuss a number of potential concerns that arise from this situation. First, they note that learning disabled students constitute a protected group under the law, but not "educationally disadvantaged" students. In times of tight fiscal accounting, the special education student will, nevertheless, be "entitled" to appropriate educational provisions. The "educationally disadvantaged" disabled reader is "eligible" for such services, but not entitled to them. Indeed, approximately 60% of economically disadvantaged students do *not* receive compensatory education services (Carter, 1984).

In addition, the existence of two distinct federal systems for handling reading difficulties implies that there really are two distinct and identifiably different groups of reading disabled students, that the source of their reading problems results in different disabilities, and that appropriate instructional programs are also identifiably different (Johnston, Allington, & Franzen, 1985). In many schools today, there are both special education and reading professionals serving students with reading problems. In the vast majority of these situations, there is no qualitative difference between the programs offered.

As Fraatz (1987) has noted, when policy makers and critics became concerned about the performance of middle-class children, they argued and lobbied for school improvement rather than considering what might be wrong with the children. On the other hand, when minority students and students from lower socioeconomic groups do not perform well, schools often look either to the home environment or to the child.

Coles (1978) has argued that the learning disabled label is an example of "biologizing social problems." By positing biological bases for learning problems, the responsibility for failure is put "within the head of the child" rather than placed on the shoulders of schools, communities, and other institutions. "The classification plays its political role, moving the focus away from the general educational process, away from the need to change institutions, away from the need to appropriate more resources for social use toward the remedy of a purely medical problem" (p. 333).

Dyslexia, learning disability, and *reading disability* are clearly imprecise terms. Thoughtful and devoted individuals will still need to teach children, whether labeled or not. Good assessment and instruction will do much to redress some of the problems posed by existing definitions, policies, and political realities.

Summarizing Reading for Special Needs Students

Current research suggests that reading is a dynamic process that is accomplished by the reader in interaction with the text, task, purpose, and setting conditions of the reading situation. Although specific reader factors certainly can affect reading performance, reading efficiency requires active and flexible approaches to the reading context. In addition, the causal link between any one factor and reading achievement has not been demonstrated.

We noted that there is little doubt that neurological dysfunction plays a role in certain cases of reading disability. However, the percentage of cases accounted for by a medical model appears to be extremely small. In addition, a more fruitful approach to instruction awaits a more integrated view of ability and disability that can provide better dialogue between special and regular educators. The majority of difficulties in reading are more likely to result from a complex interaction between the reader and the reading situation. It is this complex interaction to which we turn our attention for the remainder of the text.

UNDERSTANDING AN INTERACTIVE VIEW OF READING DISABILITY

In this text, we use contemporary views of reading ability and the lessons of history to detail a model of reading disability. We are suggesting that an interactive view advanced for reading ability be adopted for reading disability as well. This means that reading disability, like ability, is no longer viewed as an absolute property of the reader, but rather as a relative property of the interaction among specific reader, text, and contextual factors (see Lipson & Wixson, 1986). A refocused orientation to disability offers at least two benefits. First, the model of disability should respond to recent theoretical and empirical evidence; it should account for the reading behaviors of poor readers but should also suggest new areas of investigation. Second, an articulated view of reading disability should enhance instruction. We now turn our attention to these issues.

A Theoretically Sound View of Disability

Current theory and research in reading provide evidence that word recognition and comprehension performance varies for both able and disabled readers, as a function of various interactions with different reading situations. For example, there is evidence that children of all ability levels are better able to recognize words that contain regular phonic patterns, and that they are also more successful when reading high-frequency as opposed to low-frequency words (Juel, 1988). The results of such studies suggest that children's performance on measures of isolated word recognition can be expected to vary as a function of the particular words on a given test.

Oral reading errors are also frequently used as measures of word recognition. Small samples of a reader's errors are often used to characterize performance in all reading contexts. However, studies of oral reading errors suggest that children's word recognition ability is highly variable and is influenced by many factors. These factors include instructional method, type of prose, the reader's prior knowledge of the materials being read, and the difficulty of the text (Wixson, 1979). Thus, it appears that oral reading errors reflect particular strategies a reader employs in interaction with a particular reading activity. As such, they may or may not be representative of the strategies used by a particular reader in other reading situations.

Comprehension performance is also subject to variability in both able and less-able readers. Both groups are similarly affected by differences in prior knowledge, by text organization, and by type of question. In addition, the criterion tasks employed seem to affect readers in a number of ways. For example, Williams and her colleagues have demonstrated in a number of studies that both able and less-able students in Grades 3 through 7 were better able to identify the main idea when they were asked to select the best title than when they were asked to write a summary sentence (Williams, Taylor, & deCani, 1984).

Finally, there is evidence that less-skilled readers perform like skilled readers under certain circumstances. For example, in an examination of the story comprehension patterns of sixth-grade readers, McConaughy (1985) found no differences between good and poor readers in either the quality or the accuracy of their recall summaries. Specifically, McConaughy reports that poor readers' story organization is as good as that of good readers of the same age when the structure of the text is explicit and readers are required to summarize what they think is important, rather than to recall as much as possible.

The foregoing suggests that the strategies students employ as they read should be expected to vary as a function of a number of factors. There is evidence that both the awareness and application of reading strategies varies as a function of the difficulty of the text and task (Olshavsky, 1978). Evaluating strategic behavior in the absence of some consideration of potential sources of variability is problematic. As Jones (1983) has noted, "learning strategies cannot be defined or understood without reference to the text to which they apply because the cognitive processes vary according to the text condition" (p. 6).

When reading disability is viewed from an interactive perspective, it becomes clear how difficult, and probably fruitless, it is to search for a single causative factor within the reader. Yet this is the approach that continues to dominate assessment and instruction in reading disability today. Despite the increased sophistication of our views of reading ability, reading disability is still wedded to the historic "search for pathology" (Sarason & Doris, 1979). An editorial in the *The Learning Disability Quarterly,* a journal that publishes much of today's research on reading disability, summarized this view very well:

> Our entire field is DEFICIT DRIVEN; we spend millions of dollars and hours looking for deficits, defining them, perseverating on them, imagining that we are exorcizing them, and sometimes even inventing them to rationalize our activities. (Poplin, 1984, p. 133)

Research has amply demonstrated that variability in performance is a normal part of the reading process. However, assessment and instruction for most disabled readers still depends on the use of commercial, standardized test instruments that assume the reading process is static, and that reading ability can be measured at some point in time, using one set of materials and tasks to predict performance on other materials in other settings. This is especially problematic given the nature of existing reading tests. We will discuss the problems and advantages of standardized testing in Chapter 6.

A theoretically sound view of disability also draws attention to the need for careful selection of assessment tools. Most existing instruments are based on dated and incomplete notions about reading. When a mismatch exists between the models used to define reading competence and those used to drive assessment and instruction, the assessment information is of little value (Valencia & Pearson, 1987; Wixson, Peters, Weber, & Roeber, 1987).

An Instructionally Significant View of Disability

Earlier views of disability profoundly affected the types of instruction offered to students. Poplin (1988) detailed the types of instruction that grew out of a reductionist model of disability. She noted that instruction has traditionally been delivered within a training model, that it is unidirectional (from teacher to student only), and that school goals but not life goals are promoted.

As a result of research and practice based on earlier models of reading disability, we know a great deal about how people process various isolated words and short, contrived texts. Less is known about the relationship between these measures and performance while reading real texts for real purposes or about learning to read in the classroom. What is needed is a model of reading disability that results in improved assessment and instruction practices.

An interactive view is well suited to the understanding of reading (dis)ability because it predicts variability in performance within individuals across texts, tasks, and settings. This perspective moves discussions of reading disability away from simply specifying deficits and toward the specification of the conditions under which a child can and will learn. In this view, a student's performance on various reading measures is considered an indication of what he or she can and will do under a specific set of conditions, rather than a set of fixed abilities and disabilities (Wixson & Lipson, 1986). Therefore, the necessity for identifying the disability is eliminated, and our attention is refocused on how each child performs under different conditions and which set of conditions is most likely to facilitate learning.

The Goals of Assessment

The problem of learning is the match between the child and the circumstances he or she encounters in the learning environment (Hunt, 1961). The notion of the proper match between child and circumstance is what teachers must grasp if they are to be effective. Therefore, assessment and instruction need to be focused on an evaluation of the existing match and the identification of the optimal match between a reader and the conditions of the instructional context.

The purpose of assessment, then, is to find patterns of interactions that allow us to make relatively good decisions about instruction. Few standardized tests provide this kind of information. Therefore, we suggest a number of assessment strategies that are needed to supplement existing measures. We are not suggesting that current testing instruments be abandoned altogether, but that assessment move forward from a different perspective. Nor are we suggesting that the individual student is not an important factor in the assessment process, but that we must look to the individual in interaction with specified texts, tasks, and methods. In the past, such specification has been incidental to the goal of identifying the reader's problem. This text is designed to help teachers accomplish this in an intentional and thoughtful fashion.

Reader factors clearly contribute to the success of the reading event, and Chapters 3–7 acknowledge this fact by describing procedures for evaluating reader factors. However, an interactive perspective on reading and reading ability dictates that any assessment will remain incomplete if we look only to the ways in which the individual's knowledge and skill contribute to or interfere with reading achievement. Therefore, Chapters 8 and 9 consider the contributions of text and context, and Chapter 10 discusses the interactions of all these components.

FROM CLASSROOM TO CLINIC

A good theory can also help to address the practical issues evident in school settings. An interactive view of reading disability provides a unifying theoretical orientation for teachers and specialized support personnel. The clearest implication of such a reorientation is that the performance of both normal and disabled students is subject to variability. The factors that influence the reading process are the same for both populations of students. At present, there is a tremendous need for coordination of assessment and instruction between classrooms and clinics. If different models of reading underlie the programs in these two settings, problems inevitably arise for students, and the prospects for potential transfer and learning are limited. Both classroom teachers and clinic personnel need to recognize that the reader (student who is experiencing difficulty in reading) is only one component in the reading process.

An interactive view of reading also provides a basis for communication between teachers and support staff. Personnel involved in the education of students with reading problems can begin to talk about the specific contributions of the reader, the text, and the context as determiners of reading performance. All educators need to understand the importance of recognizing this so that we can begin to work together. Since reader performance is likely to be influenced by a wide array of factors, pull-out programs are unlikely to be effective unless there is coordination between the classroom and the clinic. Teachers must provide opportunities for classroom practice and application of the skills and techniques developed in the clinic. Similarly, clinicians can no longer ignore the content and context of classroom instruction, believing that remediation of some specific disability will transfer to other settings.

Finally, an interactive view makes clear the important contribution of context. Both classroom teachers and clinicians must be sensitive to the influences of their distinct environments on reader performance. Thoughtful teachers have always realized that information collected in one situation is not entirely helpful in another. Unfortunately, we have sometimes rejected information from various sources as unreliable because it did not coincide with our own. Such apparently contradictory information can be valuable in planning optimal student instructional settings. For example, it should no longer surprise us when a student performs differently as an individual, in small group settings, and in large group settings. The documentation of these differences can provide the basis for genuinely collaborative professional relationships—relationships that will strengthen the prospects of learning for all children.

CHAPTER SUMMARY

This chapter began with the idea that reading theory is important because it helps us make decisions about assessment and instruction. Prototypic *bottom-up*, *top-down*, and *interactive* models of reading were presented to illustrate differences in reading theories. Bottom-up models of reading focus primarily on the recognition of letters, sounds, and words, and are most consistent with current instructional practice in reading. Bottom-up models view reading primarily as a perceptual process with meaning located in the text. In contrast, top-down models view reading as a language or psycholinguistic process with meaning located in the reader. Top-down models emphasize "meaning making" and are the basis for whole language and language experience approaches to instruction. Interactive models suggest that bottom-up and top-down processes occur simultaneously and that meaning results from the interaction between the reader and the text.

The second section of this chapter presented the *interactive view of reading ability* that serves as the basis for the assessment and instruction process described in this text. This view suggests that reading is the process of constructing meaning through the dynamic interaction among reader, text, and contextual factors. This means that the reading process is not static, but that it varies as a function of *reader factors* such as prior knowledge, knowledge about reading, attitudes and motivation, and *text factors* such as type and organization, linguistic properties, and structural features, and *contextual factors* such as purpose and task, setting, and instructional conditions.

The last half of this chapter was devoted to the subject of reading disability. This portion began with a historical perspective that traces the origins of *medical models* and *psychoeducational models* of reading disability. Medical models originated from the field of medicine and view reading problems as the result of neurological dysfunction. Psychoeducational models were born when educators and psychologists became involved with reading disabilities as a result of the development of reading tests during the scientific movement at the turn of the century. What distinguishes this view from the medical models is that neurological impairment is not assumed to be the source of reading disability.

Both the medical model and psychoeducational models have influenced current programming in special education remedial reading/compensatory education. Although these models have provided important information about the physical, linguistic, cognitive, social, and emotional *correlates* of reading disability, they have resulted in a deficit view of reading disability that places the blame for reading problems entirely within the reader.

In the final sections of the chapter, we described an *interactive view of reading disability* that is consistent with the interactive view of reading *ability* presented previously and that provides the theory that drives this text. An interactive view of disability suggests that students' performance on various reading tasks is an indication of what they can and will do under specified conditions, rather than a set of fixed abilities and disabilities. The necessity for identifying the disability is eliminated, and our attention is focused on how each student performs under different conditions and which conditions are most likely to facilitate learning. Therefore, the problem for assessment and instruction is defined as the *match* between the reader and the reading context, and the goal becomes the evaluation of the existing match and the identification of an optimal match.

CHAPTER 2

The Assessment-Instruction Process

INTRODUCTION

Chapter 1 focused on understanding the reading process and the nature of reading ability and disability. In this chapter and in much of the remainder of the book, we focus on applying this understanding to the assessment and instruction of reading. Decisions about what and how to assess are based on teacher/examiner beliefs about the reading process. They are based, as well, on an understanding of the components of skilled reading and an awareness of the various aspects of context that can be assessed for their contribution to reading performance.

The Assessment-Instruction Process

It is important to understand that the reading process and the assessment-instruction process are not exactly the same thing. The purposes of assessment are to evaluate the existing match and identify the optimal match between the reader and the reading context (see Chapter 1). However, the long-range goal of the entire assessment and instruction process is to produce strategic, motivated readers, and to develop mature readers who can and will apply their skills and strategies independently and in a flexible manner. The process of assessment and instruction requires that we find ways to break down reading into component parts that can be examined within the larger context of the reading process. Our goal is to identify components and procedures for assessment and instruction that are consistent with an interactive view of the reading process. This means that we must identify components that are not so small or specific that they result in assessment and instruction of isolated skills, but that are specific enough to provide direction for assessment and instruction. Traditionally the components of reading have been limited to reader skills or characteristics. However, an interactive view of reading suggests that the components must include factors in the reading context as well. It is essential that both areas be included in assessment and instruction, because reading problems in school arise most frequently from interactions between the reader and the reading context.

Once we have identified the areas within the reader and the reading context that need to be assessed, we must decide what it is we want to know about each of these areas. We will want to gather information that informs us about what the reader knows and how he or she behaves during reading. We will also gather information about the demands of the reading context (e.g., the processing requirements of various methods or materials) that operate across the areas of assessment to influence students' performance and learning.

Before we describe these areas in greater detail, however, we must emphasize that the assessment-instruction process continues to be an art, rather than a science. The best way to become proficient at reading assessment and instruction is to learn as much as possible about readers and reading contexts and how they interact to influence reading.

Chapter Overview

In this chapter, the assessment-instruction process is presented in three major sections. In the first section, we describe the components of skilled reading and the areas to be assessed for *the reader*. The components of skilled reading are each discussed separately, although they are clearly interrelated. They are: word identification, rate and fluency, vocabulary development, comprehension, studying, and writing. The reader's knowledge about reading, prior knowledge, application, and attitudes/motivation are then viewed as areas to be assessed.

Next, we present a process for assessing *the reading context*, including areas to be assessed and issues to be considered. Areas to be assessed include instructional materials, methods, and setting. Each of these is considered in terms of the following considerations: quality, experiences provided, and demands.

In the third section of this chapter, we present a plan for the assessment-instruction process. We explain the reasons for using this plan and describe each of the following steps:

THE STEPS IN THE ASSESSMENT-INSTRUCTION PROCESS

Step 1   Evaluating the Learner: Getting Started
Step 2   Evaluating the Learner: Focusing on Reading and Writing
Step 3   Evaluating the Reading Context
Step 4   Evaluating the Match Between the Reader and the Reading Context
Step 5   Reflection, Decision Making, and Planning
Step 6   Identifying a Better Match: Diagnostic Teaching
Step 7   Focus on Instruction: Continuous Monitoring and Modification
Step 8   Reporting

UNDERSTANDING ASSESSMENT-INSTRUCTION: THE READER

Reading ability develops over time and is a result of a variety of literacy experiences, some formal and some informal. This means that both the reader and the literacy experiences must be assessed. We examine reader knowledge and skill first. There are two things to consider in examining the reader's role in the assessment-instruction process. First, the components of skilled reading must be understood. These skills and abilities, generally acknowledged to comprise reading-writing competence, are described briefly. Then, we turn our attention to identifying the specific reader characteristics to be assessed.

Components of Skilled Reading

The components of skilled reading are described here in fairly traditional terms: word identification, fluency, vocabulary development, comprehension, studying, and writing. These categories are intended to reflect the processes involved in skilled reading, which include recognizing words, inferring the meanings of new words from text, identifying important information in text, integrating existing knowledge with information suggested by text, applying strategies that enable learning and remembering of what was understood from text, and composing thoughts in writing.

We have seen how historical events have led us to assume that these reader factors are stable and static, remaining the same no matter what reading material, method, or task is presented. Although this appears to be inaccurate, it is somewhat useful to discuss each of the reader components separately in order to understand better how they might interact with the components of the reading context and with each other.

Word Identification

Rapid word identification is an essential component of skilled reading. Students must be able to recognize familiar words quickly and to decode unfamiliar words rapidly enough that the process of meaning construction is not unduly interrupted. Skilled readers use a repertoire of word identification strategies, the relative importance of which depends on a variety of circumstances. These strategies can be thought of as a hierarchy, beginning with sight word recognition, which requires the least amount of effort for the reader to use, and ending with the analysis of individual words, which requires the greatest amount of effort on the part of the reader (Crowell, 1980). Skilled readers make use of the least intrusive strategies first and move toward more labor-intensive strategies only when less time-consuming strategies are not successful. The hierarchy of word identification strategies described here consists of sight word recognition and three levels of word analysis strategies: contextual analysis, morphemic analysis, and phonic analysis.

Sight word recognition. The most efficient form of word identification occurs when students recognize words immediately upon sight, without sounding them out or using any other strategy to help identify them. Words that can be recognized instantly are called *sight words* and are considered part of a student's *sight vocabulary.* A large proportion (at least 95%) of the words that children read on a daily basis should consist of sight words. The growth of children's sight vocabularies is necessary for continued progress in reading.

Sight words fall into several categories, especially in early reading. The first words that children can recognize in print are almost always sight words, including such "high potency" words (Hunt, n.d.) as their own and other family members' names, and words with heavy contextual support such as *McDonald's* (Hiebert, 1981). These words are relatively easy to remember because of their visual distinctiveness and/or because of the motivational rewards associated with remembering them (Ashton-Warner, 1963).

A second type of sight words is the high-frequency *function* words (e.g., *the, of, but*) that appear over and over in written texts. These words are difficult to decode or figure out using word analysis strategies, because they are irregular and do not follow basic decoding rules. They are often more difficult to remember than other words because many are similar in appearance (e.g., *where, there, here, when, then*). These words are usually learned as sight words when children are first learning how to read; however, many poor readers have not mastered these words even by seventh or eighth grade. Children need a basic stock of these sight words in order to begin reading fluently and with comprehension.

The last type of sight words includes all of the other words that students have learned to recognize instantly. Many of these words are *content* words (e.g., *meal, bake, animal*) that are already part of a child's speaking or listening vocabularies. These words are often learned initially through the application of various word analysis strategies, and become sight words after repeated exposure through reading. Many poor readers simply do not read enough to acquire a sufficient number of these sight words. Others may rely too heavily on one or another of the word analysis strategies that are discussed in the next section. Either way, children who do not develop an adequate sight vocabulary are likely to have difficulty in all aspects of reading.

Word analysis strategies. These are the strategies that we use to identify printed words that we do not recognize immediately upon sight. Word analysis in the elementary grades has been perceived too often as consisting only of (grapho)phonic analysis, with the result that children are taught primarily "to huff and puff at isolated words in the name of reading" (Spiegel, 1984, p. 2). There are a variety of word analysis strategies that students may employ, and no one strategy is necessarily any better or worse than another.

Although it may seem that skilled readers move through text so quickly that they must be recognizing every word at sight, it is clear that they actually do speed their word recognition by making predictions about words based on the contextual (meaning and sentence structure) and graphophonic (letter/sound correspondence) cue systems within our language. For example, it is the contextual cue system that enables us to predict that the missing word in the sentence "The window in the kitchen of our new _____ is beautiful" could be either *house, home,* or *apartment.* However, it is the graphophonic cue system that assists you in determining that the missing word in the sentence "Our new h r is beautiful" is *horse* instead of *house* or *home.*

The utility of a given strategy depends on its effectiveness in the situation in which it is being applied. Therefore, children need to have a repertoire of word analysis strategies that are available for use in a variety of reading situations. The most commonly recognized word analysis strategies are presented here, in order from most to least efficient. Contextual analysis and morphemic analysis are both meaning-based word identification strategies. Contextual analysis operates at the phrase, sentence, and text levels, and morphemic analysis operates at the level of the individual word. Phonic analysis is a strategy based on sound-symbol correspondence that results in approximate pronunciation of individual words.

1. *Contextual analysis.* Probably the most common method of word analysis is to use the context of the sentence in which the unknown word appears and/or the context that surrounds the sentence to determine what the word is most likely to be. Contextual analysis not only serves as an aid to word identification, but also as an aid to understanding the meaning of an unfamiliar word.

Durkin (1983) makes a helpful distinction between general context and local context. General context is provided by the central topic of a text. Clues provided by the graphic aids in a text such as charts, maps, illustrations, titles, and subtitles are also likely to contribute to the general context of a text. Readers' expectations for what words will be included in a text are guided by general context. For example, one would expect a story about the circus to include words such as *ringmaster, clown, acrobat, elephant,* and *trapeze,* or a chapter on heredity to include words such as *gene, meiosis,* and *chromosome.* These examples emphasize that the use of general context requires prior knowledge about the topic of the text.

Local context is provided by the phrases and sentences that surround the unknown word. The possible choices for a given word are constrained by the syntactic and semantic cues provided by the local context. For example, if you read "Nora wished she had a _____ so _____ could listen to her favorite station," you would expect the first word to be *radio* or possibly *Walkman,* because these are what we use to listen to a station. You would expect the second word to be the pronoun *she,* because of the other references to a girl's name, and *she* and *her* within the sentence. Therefore, use of local context requires knowledge of the structure of our language as well as prior world knowledge.

2. *Morphemic analysis. Morpheme* is a linguistic term for the smallest unit of meaning in our language. Morphemic analysis is a strategy in which the reader breaks down words into smaller meaning-bearing units as an aid to word identification and understanding.

The meaning-bearing units used in morphemic analysis are root words, affixes, and inflections. For example, the word *returnables* can be divided into four meaningful parts, *re-, turn, -able,* and *-s.* The prefix *re-* and the suffix *-able* are affixes that change the function of the root word. The inflectional ending *-s* modulates the meaning of the root word without changing its function. Other common inflections signal possession (*-'s*), verb tense (*-ed, -ing*), or comparison (*-er, -est*). Finally, morphemic analysis can be used as an aid in the identification and understanding of compound words (e.g., *fireman, breadbox*) and contractions (e.g., *don't, he'll*).

Morphemic analysis is often referred to by a different name; *structural analysis.* However, structural analysis categories frequently lump together morphemic analysis, which is a meaning-based strategy, with strategies that are based on the correspondence between letters and sounds (e.g., syllabication and letter clusters). We have chosen to make a distinction between these two types of strategies by listing morphemic analysis separately and placing the letter-sound strategies, normally considered part of structural analysis, in the category of phonic analysis.

3. *Phonic analysis.* Phonic analysis involves using strategies for decoding unfamiliar words by identifying the sounds of each letter or group of letters in an unknown word and then saying the sounds together until the word is recognized. The ability to isolate *phonemes,* the linguistic term for the smallest unit of sound in our language, is central to successful application of phonic analysis. Phonic analysis relies on the graphophonic cues within words as well. Words can be sounded out letter-by-letter or by using spelling patterns, letter clusters, or sylla-

bles that have predictable sounds. However, skilled readers most often use analogy with known words or word parts to pronounce unknown words (Cunningham, 1975–76). Thus, graphophonic analysis proceeds by comparing the new, unknown display with known letter-sound combinations.

The specific graphophonic patterns that are useful in phonic analysis are suggested by a framework for phonics instruction provided by Mason and Au (1990). These are: consonant-sound relations in the initial, medial, and final positions in words; blends of two or three consonants where each consonant retains its own sound (e.g., *spr, fl*); consonant digraphs, or combinations of two consonants that are pronounced as one sound (e.g., *ch, th*); vowel-sound patterns represented by vowels followed by *r* or *l* (e.g., *ar*), and consonant-vowel-consonant (e.g., *sit*), consonant-vowel-consonant-silent *e* (e.g., *lake*), and consonant vowel-vowel (e.g., *meal*); and, we would add, letter clusters or syllables that have consistent sounds (e.g., *-ot, -and*).

Recognition of reliable sound-symbol patterns is useful, particularly when children are first learning to read, because knowledge of a few sounds and generalizations can be used to identify many new words. However, strategies for phonic analysis are also the most time-consuming in our word identification hierarchy, and they render information only about the pronunciation of words. It is important to remember that the successful pronunciation of a word does not ensure understanding of either the word or the text in which it appears.

Although we have talked about these word analysis strategies separately, skilled readers actually use them in combination. One of the more frequently used combinations is context plus the first and/or last letter of an unknown word. In other situations, a combination of morphemic analysis plus analogy with known words would be appropriate.

Poor readers often rely too heavily on one strategy or another. For example, some children pay too much attention to the contextual cues and not enough to the graphophonic cues. These children might substitute *apartment* for *house* in the sentence "The kitchen in our new house is beautiful." Others rely too much on graphophonic cues and not enough on contextual information, and might substitute *horse* for *house* in our sample sentence. It is important to remember that it is not a matter of which strategy to use, but of achieving a balance among these strategies that provides readers with the flexibility they need to be successful in a variety of reading situations.

Rate and Fluency

Fluency and rate are not the same, although they are related, in that fluent readers can enhance rate of reading. *Rate* of reading refers to the speed of oral and/or silent reading as measured in words per minute. Proficient reading requires *automaticity*, or the ability to identify words rapidly enough that sufficient resources are available for attention to comprehension. Research suggests that beginning readers who develop automatic word identification skills are better able to comprehend text (Perfetti & Hogaboam, 1975). How fast is fast enough, and how slow is too slow are questions that are still open for debate, however. Norms for reading rate vary widely, and research designed to improve comprehension by teaching rapid word identification has produced equivocal results. Thus, it appears that reading rate may be a necessary but insufficient condition for proficient reading, and that decisions about the adequacy of a student's reading rate may need to be made on an individual basis.

The important point here is that it is not enough to know the level of accuracy with which a reader identifies words or applies various word analysis strategies. It is also important to know how efficient the reader is in these areas. For example, a student may be able to recognize successfully many words, but may require so much time and effort that few resources remain available for use in comprehending what was read. Reading rate is therefore one of those areas that needs to be examined within the context of other factors, such as general ability, previous experience, and interest in and difficulty of reading materials.

Oral fluency refers to readers' ability to group words into meaningful phrase units as they read. It is regarded by many as a necessary feature of good reading, and a lack of fluency, or word-by-word reading, is often noted as a characteristic of poor readers. Allington (1983b) refers to fluency as "the neglected reading goal," noting that it is often overlooked in assessment and instruction because it is mistakenly viewed as simply symptomatic of poor word identification skills. He states further that unfortunately, this interpretation often leads to further instruction in letters, sounds, or words in isolation, in the mistaken belief that more attention to these areas will result in improved reading.

The exact nature of the relationship between oral fluency and silent reading comprehension is still unclear. However, there is evidence that direct instruction in fluent oral reading produces readers who move from word-by-word reading to a more efficient phrase reading, and in many cases this training has led to improved reading achievement (Allington, 1983b). Fluency, then, appears to be an important area of assessment in helping us to understand how readers process text.

Vocabulary Development

Skilled reading requires knowledge of the meanings of words, and the ability to infer and learn the meanings of new words. Words are the labels for concepts and ideas, making vocabulary knowledge an index of a reader's prior knowledge. Therefore, knowledge of words and their underlying concepts provides the basis for constructing meaning in oral and written communication. If readers do not have adequate knowledge of important words and concepts and/or are unable to determine word meanings, they will have difficulty successfully comprehending their texts.

Vocabulary development is not simply the number of dictionary definitions of words that students have acquired. The primary focus of this area is the depth, breadth, and organization of students' vocabulary knowledge. Guidelines developed by Langer (1981) for evaluating students' prior knowledge of concepts important for text comprehension are helpful in understanding these dimensions of vocabulary knowledge. The highest levels of vocabulary knowledge are represented by knowledge of precise definitions, analogies using the target word, and links among related concepts. Moderate levels of vocabulary knowledge are represented by knowledge of examples, attributes, and defining characteristics, and little awareness of connections or relations among words and concepts. The lowest levels of vocabulary knowledge are characterized by knowledge of sound-alike or look-alike words and associated experiences that provide few, if any, meaning relations. Finally, vocabulary knowledge may actually reflect misconceptions or inaccurate information held by the reader.

In addition to knowledge of specific vocabulary, we must consider the reader's ability to infer and to learn the meanings of new words and concepts. Students are frequently confronted in their reading with new words for which they may or may not already have a concept. Students need to develop strategies, such as different types of contextual and morphemic analysis as described in the previous section, for inferring the meanings of unfamiliar vocabulary and independently increasing their vocabulary learning.

Comprehension

Comprehension is the ability to use previously acquired information to construct meaning for a given text. This area focuses primarily on students' ability to reason their way through a text by integrating existing knowledge with new information, drawing inferences, and forming and testing hypotheses. The goal of comprehension is the construction of an integrated representation of the information suggested by a text that is appropriate for the reading purpose. Other activities that are critical to good comprehension include establishing purposes for reading, identifying important elements of information and their relations within text, monitoring one's comprehension, and dealing with failures to comprehend (Baker & Brown, 1984).

The successful accomplishment of the activities that comprise good comprehension requires the use of a variety of strategies. Given our current knowledge, it is impossible to present an exhaustive list of strategies, or to say for certain exactly which strategies are most appropriate for which activities. We may never be able to do this, because we all use different strategies for different purposes. However, we can identify a range of possible strategies that are appropriate for different activities. For example, the list of possible strategies for dealing with comprehension failures presented by Mason and Au (1990) includes rereading to identify the material not understood, reading ahead and looking for clarifying information, and looking elsewhere for another presentation of the same information. As in the case of word analysis strategies, no one strategy is necessarily more or less important than the others. Rather, the appropriateness of a given strategy is determined by its utility in the interaction between a reader and a specific reading situation. What matters most is how effective and efficient a strategy is for accomplishing a specific purpose.

Rather than focus on the mastery of prerequisite skills, the interactive perspective focuses assessment and instruction on the behaviors or activities that characterize good comprehension. Skills and strategies are the means to achieving the goal of good comprehension, not the end itself. It is important to keep this in mind, lest our old lists of skills be replaced by new lists of strategies, and our assessment and comprehension instruction remains unchanged from past practices.

Studying

Studying is a specialized form of comprehension. Comprehension is reading for understanding, and studying is reading to learn and/or remember what has been comprehended or understood from text. There are three primary activities involved in effective studying. First, students must be able to preview text to familiarize themselves with its form and content and to make plans for reading. Second, students must be able to locate specific information within the text. Third, students must be able to identify the organization of information within the text.

As with word recognition and comprehension, the successful accomplishment of studying activities requires the use of a variety of strategies. These strategies may include outlining, note-taking, summarizing, self-questioning, diagramming or mapping text, and underlining, as well as many of the strategies that are used in comprehending. What is most important is students' ability to select and apply these strategies in a manner that is appropriate to the study task at hand. It is not a question of which study strategies are best, but of how effective a selected strategy is in a given study situation.

Writing

Using language to construct messages in writing enhances readers' ability to understand what others write. Similarly, what children learn about language from reading enhances their ability to express themselves in writing. The strong relation between reading and writing makes writing an important area for assessment and instruction. The writing area consists of students' ability to engage in the writing process and to generate acceptable written products. The writing process refers to the steps that students take to produce a finished piece of writing. These include a planning stage for clarifying purpose and audience, a composing stage which involves writing, reading, and attention to mechanics (e.g., punctuation and sentence structure), and a revision stage which involves rereading and editing.

Students' ability to communicate the intended message in a manner that is appropriate for a particular audience is the primary focus of good writing. Students should be able to produce different types of writing for different purposes and audiences. Each type of writing will have somewhat different features. For example, narrative writing is characterized by the story idea and structure, including its setting and characters, whereas expository writing is characterized more by its central purpose and the organization of the sections and subsections. Mechanics play a role in all writing, but they should be viewed in the same way we view various reading skills—as the means to the end, rather than the goal.

Summarizing the Components of Skilled Reading

The components of skilled reading which we have just discussed are word identification, reading rate and fluency, vocabulary development, comprehension, studying, and writing. These components were discussed in order to help teachers and examiners understand the complex of factors that contribute to reading ability. Competent readers are accomplished in all of these component areas, although they are likely to exhibit varying degrees of expertise, depending on the texts and tasks being read or written.

Areas to Be Assessed: The Reader

Specification of the components of reading assessment and instruction provides a framework for thinking about students' reading. It does not tell us what reader characteristics to assess, nor what information to gather about the components. When a student or group of students is actually in front of us, what exactly do we want to know about each of these component areas? Our goal is not simply to identify how a student performs in each of these areas, independent of the others. It is to understand how a student approaches different reading tasks and how each of these areas contributes to the student's performance in a specific reading situation.

In order to accomplish this goal we need to understand what students know about the process of reading; what prior knowledge they have about the topics of the texts they are reading; how they apply this knowledge; and their attitudes toward and motivation for engaging in a variety of reading activities. We discuss each of these areas below.

Knowledge About Reading

In Chapter 1, we noted that skilled readers have a great deal of knowledge about the reading process, and that this knowledge is correlated highly with performance in measures of reading achievement. Estimates of reading knowledge have not typically been included in evaluations of assessment and instruction, but information of this type is critical to understanding individual readers. Specifically, we need to gather information about readers' understanding of the goals of reading and reading instruction; their awareness of the reader, text, and contextual factors that influence reading; and their knowledge of cognitive control mechanisms that could and should be used in efficient reading.

It is becoming increasingly clear that readers need several types of knowledge in order to become proficient. First, they need to understand that a skill or strategy exists and is available to be used for reading. For example, readers need to be aware that they can use context when they do not instantly recognize a word in print. Many young and less-skilled readers seem unaware of this aspect of skilled reading. When asked what they do when they come across an unknown word, many reply "sound it out," and, when that is unsuccessful, "skip it" (Paris, Cross, & Lipson, 1984). This type of knowledge is called *declarative knowledge* and requires only that the child know that a skill or strategy exists.

Knowing that a particular skill exists is not enough for successful performance. Readers also need to know how to perform the skill or strategy. To continue with our example, it is not sufficient to know that you can use context as an aid to word identification; you must also understand how to go about using context. This type of knowledge is called *procedural knowledge* because it refers to knowledge of the procedures necessary to execute and orchestrate the components of the reading process.

Past practice implies that declarative and procedural knowledge would ensure application. It was assumed that students who knew about the components and how to apply them would surely use this knowledge in the appropriate reading situations. Almost daily, however, teachers encounter students who appear to have mastered a skill or strategy sufficiently to employ it, but who fail to demonstrate any such competence during real reading situations. We would argue that children often fail to apply their existing skills and strategies because they lack a third type of knowledge, *conditional knowledge* (Paris, Lipson, & Wixson, 1983). Simply stated, conditional knowledge is knowledge about when and why to employ a known strategy or skill. For example, skimming is obviously not a universally helpful approach to reading. Readers need to know when and why it is appropriate to use skimming. Conditional knowledge is essential for students to be able to apply the strategies and skills learned during reading instruction in other reading situations.

Prior Knowledge

We have already noted how the quantity and quality of readers' prior knowledge affects reading performance (see Chapter 1). Despite the widespread acceptance of the influence of prior knowledge on reading, until quite recently it was rare for examiners to consider students' pre-existing knowledge. It is still relatively unusual for evaluators to examine prior knowledge in relation to the texts and tasks used in assessment.

Most of us are aware that a well-stocked store of content knowledge is helpful in reading. Readers also need to understand a great deal about social interactions and human relationships in order to connect ideas in texts. This type of prior knowledge seems to be especially important in inferential understanding (Trabasso, 1981). Students who have a rich repertoire of ideas, experiences, and concepts are likely to read a wide range of material with greater ease than students who are not so fortunate.

Both the quantity and quality of prior knowledge will need to be examined, since students' knowledge may include fragmented information and/or misconceptions that can impede comprehension (Hynd & Alvermann, 1986; Lipson, 1982, 1983; Maria, 1986). This is especially troublesome when students attempt to learn from informational texts. Misconceptions and limited information appear to influence comprehension in a number of ways, resulting in poor memory for text, construction of meaning that is anomalous, and even outright rejection of new text information. Because prior knowledge can both help and hinder reading, accurate interpretation of reading performance depends on our ability to gather information about readers' general store of prior knowledge, and to develop ongoing strategies for rapidly and effectively evaluating their knowledge of the specific topics about which they are reading.

Application

Students' prior knowledge, and their knowledge about the process of reading, should always be considered within the context of how it is applied. The information gathered about application traditionally has been limited to the products of the reading effort (e.g., the number correct on some specific measure). However, we are concerned not only with the products of reading, but also with the processes readers use to obtain these products. It is the relation between the products and the processes by which they are created that interests us most.

In order to explore these relationships, we need to observe the quantity and quality of the reader's performance; what skills and/or strategies the reader uses and how they are used; and the effectiveness and efficiency of the strategies in achieving the desired reading outcomes. The most essential component of reading performance is the interaction between the reader and the reading context. We only have half the picture if we do not examine the relations between these two sets of factors. Most reading problems cannot be separated from the context in which they are occurring. When we only examine the reader factors—the traditional practice—we are often misled about the reader's ability to perform under certain reading conditions.

The effectiveness and efficiency of the strategies used in achieving the desired outcome is determined by readers' control over their own cognitive activities. Readers must be able to evaluate different reading situations, plan appropriately, monitor their own success, and regulate their behavior accordingly. These abilities enable readers to employ the most effective and efficient strategies for reading and understanding a given text under particular circumstances (Flavell, 1978; Paris & Lindauer, 1982; Ryan, 1981). For example, if an author has been considerate in writing the text and has made the relations between the major ideas clear, study techniques such as underlining, note-taking, and summarizing should be sufficient for retaining material. On the other hand, if the author has been inconsiderate and the relations are not sufficiently explicit, techniques such as outlining and mapping may be more appropriate, although time-consuming. (Ringler & Weber, 1984, p. 310).

Attitudes and Motivation

Information about students' knowledge and their application of that knowledge must be interpreted within the context of their attitudes toward and motivation for engaging in various reading activities. We must determine, for example, whether they are interested in a particular activity, whether they believe they can succeed at it, and, perhaps most importantly, whether they are willing to become actively involved. A convergence of data from a variety of sources has confirmed what most teachers have always known: positive attitudes and motivation can compensate for relatively weak skills, and negative attitudes can prevent a student from applying existing knowledge or from acquiring new information (Paris, Olson, & Stevenson, 1983). It does no good to determine that a student may be helped by providing knowledge and guidance in a particular area without knowing how willing he or she is to engage in the required activities.

Summarizing Areas to Be Assessed

The reading abilities of individuals can and should be assessed in at least four areas: knowledge about reading, prior knowledge, ability to apply knowledge and skill, and attitude and motivation for reading. In the remaining chapters of this text, we will discuss these factors in greater depth, and provide a wide range of tools and strategies for assessing these reader factors.

UNDERSTANDING ASSESSMENT-INSTRUCTION: THE READING CONTEXT

Because readers' performance is the result of a complex set of interactions between the reader and the reading context, no assessment will be complete until we have assessed the reading context. In Chapter 1, we discussed the text and contextual factors that researchers have found to influence the reading process, so it should be no surprise that these same factors are a matter of concern in the assessment-instruction process. The assessment of the reading context has additional importance, because it is through changing or controlling contextual factors that we are most likely to bring about improved learning and/or performance in the reader.

In this section, we describe the component areas of reading context that can and should be assessed. We also propose some characteristics of these contextual factors that should be considered in evaluating the contribution of the context to reading performance.

Areas to Be Assessed: The Reading Context

There are no traditional categories of assessment within the reading context, because this area typically has been overlooked in the assessment-instruction process. The categories we have chosen to consider are *setting, methods,* and *materials.* These are not intended to represent a comprehensive list of all factors, and there are undoubtedly different ways to examine these factors. However, it is clear that these three areas of assessment represent factors that do play an important role in students' reading, and they are critical for a consideration of reading instruction in a school context.

Setting

Assessment of setting factors can be difficult or even impossible. It is acceptable to acknowledge the difficulties. What is not acceptable is to ignore the influence of many setting variables on students' performance in reading and writing. For example, as we reflect on the setting in which instruction takes place, we must carefully assess the larger sociocultural components of learning for a given group of students. It has become abundantly clear that learning is influenced by factors beyond the classroom walls (Heath, 1983; McDermott, 1985). The community and culture of students exert central, sometimes critical, influence on reading achievement.

Similarly, we are now able to state unequivocally that characteristics of schools, classrooms, and reading groups influence student behavior and achievement. These characteristics can influence students' perceptions about the nature of reading and writing. In addition, these setting factors can have a powerful impact on reading acquisition and performance, and, for this reason, they are an important area of assessment.

Some dimensions of setting are difficult, if not impossible, to alter. However, assessment of setting-related factors can frequently suggest ways in which the instructional match may be improved by adapting other factors that are within our control. Again, the point is not to conclude that any of these components are pathological. Reading problems can certainly result from inattention to the components as they influence each other, however. For example, home environments different from the mainstream are not pathological in themselves. Students can be hopelessly handicapped, however, if the school expects and accepts only one type of entry experience from its students. Although setting factors may seem at first to be the aspects of our assessment-instruction procedure that are the most impervious to change, assessment in this area may actually open up some of the most powerful areas for potential mismatches that could be altered in subtle and not-so-subtle ways.

Methods

In addition to the materials, it is important to evaluate the instructional methods that are being used with a particular student, since the method of instruction can influence both what is learned and how children process information (Roehler, Duffy, & Meloth, 1986). Decisions regarding the effectiveness of instruction and the relative competence of individual readers can only be meaningful to the extent that we know what behaviors to expect and what outcomes are preferred. The outcomes of reading instruction must, of course, be consistent with our views of the reading process. The characteristics of skilled reading, as described in the Report of the Commission on Reading entitled *Becoming a Nation of Readers* (Anderson et al., 1985), provide a coherent summary of important reading abilities:

- *Skilled reading is constructive.* Becoming a skilled reader requires learning to reason about written material, using knowledge from everyday life and from disciplined fields of study.
- *Skilled reading is fluent.* Becoming a skilled reader depends upon mastering basic processes to the point where they are automatic, so that attention is freed for the analysis of meaning.
- *Skilled reading is strategic.* Becoming a skilled reader requires learning to control one's reading in relation to one's purpose, the nature of the material, and whether one is comprehending.
- *Skilled reading is motivated.* Becoming a skilled reader requires learning to sustain attention, and learning that written material can be interesting and informative.

• *Skilled reading is a lifelong pursuit.* Becoming a skilled reader is a matter of continuous practice, development, and refinement.

The success of various instructional methodologies should be evaluated in terms of their success in achieving these major outcomes of reading instruction.

The two major components of instructional methods are the *content* of instruction (what is being taught) and the *delivery system* that is used (how content is being taught). It is frequently assumed that if we know that someone is being taught by a particular approach, such as phonics or language experience, that we know exactly what is being taught and how it is being taught. On closer inspection, we often discover that the actual focus on instruction and the step-by-step procedures to deliver information can vary widely and in important ways among different teachers using the same approach.

The different types of content that need to be considered in evaluating instructional methods are characterized by the three types of instructional outcomes described by Duffy and Roehler (1989). These are *attitude* goals, *content* goals, and *process* goals. First, we must evaluate instructional methods in terms of how well they promote attitudes and beliefs that are likely to produce motivated readers. Second, we must evaluate the informational content of the instructional methods (i.e., what information or ideas are taught). Third, we must determine if the method provides instruction in the process of reading as well as the content of a particular reading selection or skill lesson. Methods used to achieve process goals focus on teaching students the strategies needed to read in various situations (in addition to focusing on understanding the informational content of a particular lesson). Roehler, Duffy, and Meloth (1986) provide excerpts from conversations with children that illustrate differences between process and content-only reading instruction (see Figure 2.1).

There are also different types of delivery systems that need to be considered in evaluating instructional methods. For example, some delivery systems may be characterized as direct instruction, whereas others are considered more indirect. Direct instruction involves explaining or telling students the step-by-step procedures involved in engaging in a particular reading activity. Indirect methods instruct through repeated practice with activities that are examples of the desired reading behavior. These different types of delivery are likely to be effective in meeting different goals and reading objectives.

Much of our current methodology combines a focus on the informational content of a lesson with an emphasis on indirect instruction. However, current research suggests that many disabled readers may benefit from methods that combine attention to process and attitude goals with an emphasis on direct instruction. For example, students who are weak in comprehension are routinely asked to practice reading and answering questions, with the measure of success being improved responses about informational content. As others have noted, such experiences provide little direct instruction about how to go about the process of reading for certain types of information in a text for those who are

FIGURE 2.1
Sample Process and Content-Only Dialogues

Emphasizing the Mental Process

Process-into-content instruction is characterized by an emphasis on the thinking one must do in order to make sense out of text. Consider the following excerpts. In the first, a teacher is teaching how to use context clues to determine the meaning of an unknown word. Note the focus on the mental process involved in using the strategy:

> I don't know what *upbraided* means. I have to figure it out. What do I do first? I look for clues. Are there any clues that might tell me what that means? I look at the words around it and then. . . .

After carefully directing students through this example, the teacher continued to emphasize the mental process when interacting with students:

T: You are reading and you come to that sentence. How are you going to figure out that word? Matt, what would you do first?

S: I would look through the context. I see *rage* (inaudible).

T: Yes. *Did not come* is a clue. When Jerry didn't come, whatever it was he caused, it was caused because he didn't come. Now you are thinking about what you know when people don't come and people getting in rages. What do you suppose that means he was?

S: He was angry or mad at the person.

T: So, do you have a one-word synonym that you could put there?

S: *Mad.*

T: How do you check to see if that makes sense?

S: When he didn't come, Jerry was so mad that he left in a rage.

T: Does that sound reasonable? Yes. Let's try the next one.

In contrast, the mental processing is ignored and answer accuracy is emphasized in the following lesson on main idea taught by a content-only teacher:

T: All right, now here are some possibilities [for a short title]: "A Trip Downtown," "The New Shirt," "The Shirt That Didn't Fit." Let me read them again: "A Trip Downtown," "The New Shirt," "The Shirt That Didn't Fit." Now, of those three possibilities, which one would go best? Annie?

S: "A Trip Downtown."

S: "A Trip Downtown."

T: Okay, Tim, what do you think?

S: "The New Suit."

T: Don, what was your choice?

S: "The New Shirt"

T: I think the girls decided on "The Trip Downtown," and the boys liked "The New Shirt." Mainly, what was the story about?

S: A trip downtown.

S: Getting a new shirt.

T: Getting a new shirt, wasn't it?

"Emphasizing the Mental Process," pp. 89–90, *The Contexts of School-Based Literacy* by Taffy E. Raphael, 1986 Random House. Reproduced by permission of McGraw-Hill, Inc.

unable to do so successfully on their own, and, therefore, may not improve their comprehension ability (Johnston, 1985a). In Chapter 8, we discuss these issues further. We also describe the knowledge gained in recent years that has made it possible to evaluate methods according to general instructional principles that are applicable to a variety of approaches.

Instructional Materials and Tasks

Children read an enormous array of textual materials during their development as readers—comic books, cereal boxes, instructions for constructing models, fiction, nonfiction, notes from friends, letters from relatives, and so on. It is possible, and perhaps even desirable, to consider any or all of these reading materials as having instructional potential. However, the range of materials used for instruction in most classrooms is more constrained than this, and the materials students are exposed to during instruction often differ from the materials they may encounter in other contexts. Therefore, we have limited our examination of this area to four types of instructional material that include the texts and the tasks found in most classrooms.

First, children are asked to read various types of prose, or written texts. Prose selections used for instructional purposes come from a variety of sources, including basal readers, subject area textbooks, children's magazines, reference materials and trade books from the library, weekly readers, and, in some cases, the students' own writing. As noted in Chapter 1, the type and organization, linguistic properties, and structural features of the texts that students encounter in instructional settings can influence their reading, and therefore should be evaluated.

A second type of instructional material emanates from *commercial reading programs and plans.* These materials inevitably become a part of a teacher's instructional set and often determine both what is read and what instructional activity is employed. Recent analyses of the lesson frames provided in most basal reading programs suggest a number of problems (Durkin, 1981). For example, little direct instruction in comprehension appears in teacher's manuals, and not infrequently, the purposes set for reading have little to do with the types of purposes readers set for themselves. In addition, teachers are directed via basal manuals to provide for individual needs among students, and the provisions for less able readers, in particular, need to be evaluated.

Third, students are regularly engaged in *instructional tasks and practice activities* that define reading for them. For example, students often spend more time doing seatwork activities than they do reading prose materials. It should be noted that these materials generally provide practice of separate component areas, not practice in the holistic act of reading. Assessment of this type of instructional material may be particularly important, since these materials appear to have a substantial influence on students' perceptions of the reading process.

The nature of these activities and the cumulative effect of such tasks on reading and writing proficiency must be evaluated. Researchers have also reported that questioning is actually the primary component of reading instruction in many classrooms today (Durkin, 1978–79). Thus, the type, content, and placement of these questions need to be assessed and viewed as instructional material.

Although relatively new in many classrooms, *microcomputer materials and activities* are an important fourth type of materials. Thoughtful assessment of these programs is especially important for teachers who work with disabled readers. There is increasing pressure to operate remedial reading settings through the use of diagnostic-prescriptive management systems that involve microcomputer testing, computer-generated profiles of skill needs, and computer programs for remedial instruction. There are also many other types of computer programs intended for assessment and instruction in reading, and the job of evaluating the usefulness of such materials frequently falls to the reading teacher or reading consultant. If a significant amount of instructional time is being spent with such materials, they too must be evaluated.

Considerations in Assessing the Reading Context

The assessment of the reading context should focus on the characteristics that have been demonstrated to influence students' reading and writing performance. The attributes of the setting can be examined in terms of organization, expectations, and the types of interactions permitted and demanded. Similarly, instruction can be examined for its content and balance, evaluating these in terms of important literacy goals that have been established. Procedures for evaluating the quality of the instructional context are discussed at length in the chapters to follow. Central concerns relate to the degree to which the instructional context reflects our current understanding of the reading process and reading instruction.

An evaluation of the instructional context must include an assessment of the extent to which it provides a meaning-based curriculum that promotes reader independence and self-control. For example, the instructional *setting* should challenge children to become actively engaged in reading and writing, and to take responsibility for their reading. In reviewing the instructional *materials* and *tasks*, we would look for authentic reading experiences. Students should have opportunities to read full-length stories, books, poems, advertisements, and texts. Similarly, when skills and strategies have been isolated for instructional purposes, care should be taken to ensure that the instructional *methods* provide for practice of those skills and strategies for authentic purposes, such as enjoyment, information, and so on.

We must also evaluate the status of the materials, methods, and settings with regard to the demands that are placed on the reader or readers under investigation. Specifically, we need to ask, What does a reader have to do in order to learn and perform successfully in the reading context? Not all material, methods, and classroom or clinic settings place the same requirements on students. Conversely, the interactive nature of reading achievement suggests that students' abilities may not be equally suited to the demands of all materials, methods, and settings.

Finally, we need to determine what experiences are provided by the reading context. Students' learning and performance are influenced by their experiences with certain materials, methods, and settings. Therefore, it is important to understand what the student has learned about reading through previous experience in a particular reading context. Inexperienced clinicians often fail to recognize that students may not have certain skills, knowledge, or abilities because they have not been provided with opportunities to acquire needed expertise. If this is the case, the remedy is clearly quite different than if the student has received instruction but has failed to benefit from it. Reading experiences must also be examined to determine what has been communicated to the student about the nature of reading. It does little good to alter the ways and means by which we evaluate students' performance if we do not also examine the types of instruction and instructional materials provided to them on a daily basis to see what is being communicated.

UNDERSTANDING THE ASSESSMENT-INSTRUCTION PLAN

The goal of the assessment-instruction process is to develop an instructional program that results in improved learning and performance for particular readers, not to identify causes or provide labels. To this end, the information to be gathered about the reader and the reading context must reflect not only the areas within each of these components, but also the interaction between the areas within these two components of the assessment-instruction process. The materials, methods, and settings within the reading context must be assessed not only in terms of their quality, but also in terms of the experiences they provide and demands they place on the reader. Similarly, we must evaluate the reader's knowledge, ability, and motivation to perform various reading skills within the context of specific materials, methods, and settings.

Procedures for the Assessment-Instruction Process

A plan for proceeding with the process of assessment and instruction is described in the next section of this chapter. In keeping with our view of reading as an interactive process, the essence of our plan is the evaluation of the existing match between a reader and the reading context, and the identification of a better match—one that is more likely to promote learning. This is a learning process, so teachers need the same types of knowledge to implement this plan that students need in learning how to read. Teachers must first learn what procedures should be undertaken in each step of the process (i.e., declarative knowledge). In addition, they must learn how to conduct the assessment and instruction activities that will be used as part of the process (i.e., procedural knowledge). Although information about what and how is essential, it is in itself not sufficient for the successful completion of the assessment-instruction process. We need to make decisions at every stage of the process because the complex of factors that interact is never quite the same for any two children. Effective decision making is dependent on knowing when and why we would engage in a particular activity, or use a particular test or instructional technique (i.e., conditional knowledge).

The remainder of this book is designed to provide information about the what, how, when, and why of the assessment-instruction process. The next section of this chapter provides a step-by-step plan for carrying out this process.

The steps in this plan provide the framework for the subsequent sections of this book, and the procedures involved in each step are discussed in detail in at least one or more of the following chapters (see Figure 2.2). Within each chapter, the specific information needed to implement the assessment-instruction process is provided in as much detail as possible, including examples of what procedures to use and how to use them, and explanations of when and why they are appropriate for use.

Steps in the Assessment-Instruction Process

The steps in the assessment-instruction process are guided by three questions that we have adapted from those used by Diane Sawyer (personal communication, 1980). They are:

1. What is the current status of the interaction between the reader and the reading context?
2. What is the primary source of interference with learning or performance?
3. How can learning or performance be established or improved?

The foundation of the steps in the assessment-instruction process is an accurate assessment of the existing match between the reader and the reading context. Based on this information, the next task is to generate hypotheses about the primary source of interference with learning or performance. It is critical that the hypotheses generated in this phase of the process focus on problems of major importance. All readers have minor difficulties with certain aspects of reading, but these problems are rarely a primary source of interference with learning or performance. To ensure that we are focusing on major problems, it is sometimes helpful to ask ourselves, "If I corrected this problem, would the individual in question be likely to demonstrate improved learning or performance?" The steps focus on identifying the means by which learning or performance may be established or improved.

The steps of the assessment-instruction process are summarized below. We follow a case study through all the steps to illustrate how the process was carried out with one student. Detailed information on how to proceed with each step is provided in subsequent chapters.

Step 1: Evaluating the Learner: Getting Started
The assessment-instruction process described here is not a standard set of tests and prescriptions to be used with all students. Rather, it is a dynamic process tailored to the needs of individual students, and continually evolving as each additional piece of information is uncovered. The first step in the process involves identifying the presenting problem, gathering background information, and planning the initial evaluations of the learner and the learning context. Individuals are referred for help in reading, or seek it out, for a wide range of reasons. If there were only one or two sources of reading difficulty, our task would be relatively easy. Since that does

FIGURE 2.2

*Assessment-
Instruction
Process*

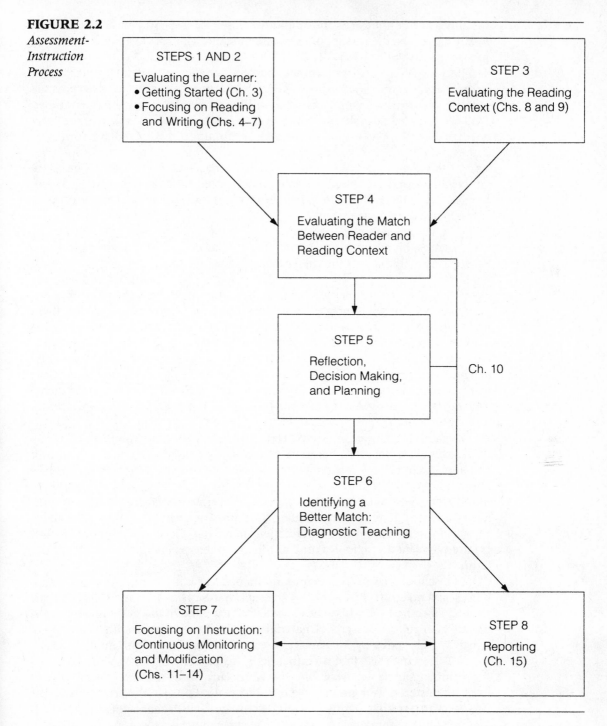

not appear to be the case, and unlimited time rarely is available to explore all possible avenues, the initial phase of assessment must provide a focus for subsequent steps in the process.

Background information provided by the individual reader, parents, school records, interviews, and visitations can yield valuable insights into possible sources of difficulty. Trying to assess an individual reader is rather like reading a good mystery. No clues should be ignored, no information overlooked in the early stages of the story. We cannot be sure at the beginning just what will turn out to be important, even when the evidence seems to lead to an obvious conclusion. The task in this first phase is not to arrive at conclusions, but rather to generate hunches that may be tested. In short, you should try to avoid coming to any conclusions in the early stages, and view your early findings as hypotheses to be tested against reality later on.

Case study. Seth was referred to the reading clinic of one of the authors by Mr. Williams, his Chapter I (formerly Title I) teacher, who had several concerns. First, the available psychological data on Seth were not entirely helpful in planning an instructional program, and Mr. Williams wanted additional diagnostic information to improve Seth's program. In addition, Seth had been referred for evaluation for special education services, but was not presently receiving them because of parental resistance. Therefore, Mr. Williams wanted additional information so that he could make a recommendation about the appropriate placement for Seth. Finally, Seth was failing to make good progress despite receiving remedial reading help in school for the past two years. At the time he was referred, Seth was in the mid-third grade and had repeated first grade once. Seth lived in a state with no compulsory kindergarten and he did not attend school at all prior to entry into the first grade.

In gathering background data on Seth, we spoke to his mother and to his older sister, who was a teacher in his school district. Seth was the youngest of six children and lived on a farm in a rural county. He was small for his age and had limited use of his left hand and arm, which were underdeveloped and deformed. Both parents were busy with farm chores, and Seth was expected to help as well. Because of the family's responsibilities, little time was available for other activities. Family life seemed to revolve around their shared jobs. Seth had little contact with children outside the school setting and had limited experiences with life off the farm.

The school records included annual report cards and a recent report by the school psychologist. The records suggested that Seth had been struggling with reading since he began his school career. At the time of the evaluation, he was placed in regular third-grade material in all areas except reading instruction, which was provided by a Chapter I reading program outside the regular classroom. The records also indicated that Seth was inattentive to assigned tasks, and that he frequently failed to complete his work. On a norm-referenced achievement test administered four months before this evaluation, Seth scored in the first percentile in reading comprehension. The psychologist's report included an estimate of ability within the low-average to average range. In addition, the psychologist suggested that Seth's left-side "paralysis" might be impairing neurological functioning and argued strongly for a "right hemisphere approach" to instruction, involving whole word and language experience activities.

Case discussion. In this first step, we gathered and considered a variety of preexisting information. Briefly, we concluded that Seth was apparently not learning and performing in reading according to expectations based on his age, ability, and educational background. In addition, we had gathered enough background information to form some initial impressions that were used to guide subsequent evaluations of the learner and the learning context. These were summarized as follows.

First, Seth's background and interests suggested he may have had limited experience with and knowledge about reading. This was an area we needed to pursue through interviews with Seth and his parents. Second, his apparent lack of interest in many school-related activities and his failure to complete assignments suggested he may have had little motivation for school in general, and reading in particular. This area needed to be pursued through observations and interviews with Seth, his teacher, and his parents. Third, Seth's history of poor performance, his test scores, and his difficulty completing assigned tasks suggested that his basic reading skills were very poor. This hypothesis needed to be tested, and assessment of sight word recognition, word analysis and comprehension skills were all planned. Fourth, his failure to complete assignments and his dependence on the teacher suggested that the work he was being given may have been too difficult for him. This was an area that needed to be examined through informal measures and an evaluation of the materials and methods being used.

Step 2: Evaluating the Learner: Focusing on Reading and Writing

Each individual reader's abilities, skills, beliefs, interests, and instructional history influence reading achievement. In the initial sections of this chapter, we outlined the components of reading knowledge and skill that must be considered in any assessment, and the type of information about those components that should be gathered. A variety of sources should be used in evaluating the learner because each source of information provides only a small part of the picture. Sources of information will include classroom observations; interviews with the parents, the teacher, and the student; formal assessments; and informal assessments, such as reading from instructional materials used by the student in the classroom.

In the chapters to follow, we describe in some detail the types of procedures that may be employed in evaluating the learner. Generally speaking, these procedures fall into three categories. First, *observational and interview data* are rich sources of information, but are often considered unreliable or subjective (see Chapter 3). We discuss ways of increasing the reliability of data collected in these ways and also describe the unique contributions to assessment that are made by such procedures. Second, more traditional types of information about the learner result from using various *informal assessment* instruments and techniques (Chapters 4, 5, and 7). Both familiar and less-familiar strategies are presented. The third and best-known source of information about learners is *formal assessment,* using standardized, norm-referenced tests (see Chapter 6). Although widely used, most formal tests have significant problems in terms of the value of the diagnostic information they yield. However, a consideration of individual assessment would not be complete without a serious discussion of the role of such instruments in the assessment-instruction process.

Case study. An initial interview with Seth confirmed that his life revolved around family and farm. He reported few other interests, but became animated in his discussions of the animals and his exploits on his "four-wheeler." Seth said that he didn't like television very much, that he didn't like "being cooped up," and that he would rather play outside. Although he said he enjoyed stories, he reported that neither he nor his family read at home. He noted that the classroom teacher was reading *James and the Giant Peach* aloud to the class, and that he enjoyed it very much. However, he was able to tell only fragments from the story.

In response to questions focused on his knowledge about reading, Seth could not give a reason why people read, and said he read because he wanted to be "smart." He appeared to believe that reading involved only accurate word recognition, naming only "sounding out" as a strategy for analyzing unknown words. When asked what his teachers did to help him become a better reader, he said that they helped him sound out the words.

During the interview with Seth's parents, they indicated that he did read a farm journal occasionally and that he received *Humpty-Dumpty* magazine at home. They confirmed that reading aloud to Seth was not a practice in their home. Mrs. C. reported that Seth's health history was normal except that he had a series of ear infections during his first year of first grade. Tubes were inserted to correct this problem and no further difficulty was reported. She also noted that Seth's left-arm "paralysis" resulted from a forceps delivery during which nerves were damaged. Thus, it seemed unlikely that neurological impairment was implicated in his problems.

Seth's classroom teacher reported that Seth seemed much younger than the other children in the class and that he sometimes asked questions or made comments that were "babyish." She indicated that Seth asked for help frequently to get attention. Further, she felt that Seth acted "cute" when he could not do something or wanted help, which was often.

Seth's abilities and behaviors were observed in both the classroom and the clinic. In the clinical setting, Seth appeared highly motivated to work hard in those areas where he felt he was competent and/or where he was succeeding. He enjoyed several of the instructional activities that were used and was always anxious to try reading on his own if appropriate prereading support had been provided. Seth sought help when he perceived work to be too difficult for him, and in those situations he put forth little effort. When pressed, he would attempt difficult tasks, but if success was not immediate, he shrugged and said he could not do it.

Seth was also observed in his classroom for one hour. At the beginning of the observation period, Seth's teacher was phasing children into a painting project. Seth was one of the first students done with his project. While the majority of the class continued to paint, Seth washed his hands and returned to work at his desk. After returning to his desk, Seth looked up from his work only occasionally. Despite the noise level and the proximity of two groups of children chatting, Seth seemed undistracted. However, he was very reliant on his teacher. He asked questions frequently, requiring her help on nearly every individual task on which the examiner observed him working.

Informal assessments of several types were employed with Seth. Information was collected using informal tests of isolated word recognition, informal reading inventories, and tests of word analysis skill. Formal assessments, including norm-referenced tests of reading achievement and vocabulary knowledge, were administered to obtain estimates of Seth's performance as compared to other children his age. The pattern of results indicated that, overall, Seth's reading achievement was at least a year and a half below what we might reasonably expect given his age and school experience. His sight word recognition was inadequate, and his word analysis skills were limited to the ineffective use of phonic analysis. Although his vocabulary knowledge was appropriate for his age, both his listening and reading comprehension were generally poor. In addition, his oral reading errors reflected little attention to meaning or contextual cues. However, in situations where he had adequate background knowledge and sufficient interest, he was able to acceptably answer questions, retell a story, and/or generate a main idea.

Case discussion. At this point in the assessment-instruction process, several specific areas of difficulty had been identified. Seth's responses to interview questions and performance on informal measures suggested that both his knowledge about reading and his reading skill were limited. For example, although Seth believed that he usually understood what he read, he had difficulty retelling stories in a coherent fashion, could not write coherent texts, and could neither identify nor generate a main idea. Seth did not appear to apply what skills and knowledge he had in a consistent way, so the products of his efforts were even less acceptable than might be expected. Although he was not actively resistant to reading, Seth did not appear to be motivated to read or to improve his reading skills; he greatly preferred to do other things. He worked hard when he experienced success, but application during difficult tasks was limited.

Step 3: Evaluating the Reading Context

Despite wide recognition that teachers and teaching methods contribute to academic success, reading assessments rarely include evaluations of these factors. Although this is a matter of some concern, the concern is aggravated by the range of other contextual factors not considered in most assessments. If teachers and methods are rarely considered, the contribution of materials or setting factors are examined even less frequently. Failure to even consider such factors leaves the reader as the sole source of difficulty, and is something akin to blaming the victim (see Coles, 1978).

As in the evaluation of the learner, a variety of procedures should be used to assess the learning context, including classroom observations, interviews, checklists, and visual inspection and analysis. Since most of these procedures are informal, care must be taken to examine this information systematically. Observation guidelines are helpful here, as are checklists. Great strides have also been made in the area of materials assessment. Readability formulas are now only one possible tool, one that can be supplemented with a variety of procedures such as text analysis and comprehensibility checklists (e.g., Irwin & Davis, 1980).

It is not always possible, or even desirable, to evaluate all possible contextual factors. However, it is imperative that the student's performance be examined under several conditions and from several points of view. Not infrequently, students' reading problems are exacerbated, if not actually caused, by contextual factors.

Case study. This step focuses on assessing the instructional context in which Seth was expected to perform. We have already provided a glimpse of the instructional context in the report of Seth's classroom observation. Seth received instruction both in a regular classroom and outside the classroom in a Chapter I reading program. Seth was not part of a regular reading group within the classroom, although workbook tasks were assigned frequently. It appeared that he was rarely expected to read full-length texts in either setting. However, when longer selections were assigned, little was offered in the way of prereading preparation.

Although the teacher read aloud as a daily part of the instructional program, Seth went to his Chapter I reading class during much of this period. Contrary to federal guidelines, Seth did not receive reading instruction in his regular classroom, but only in the Chapter I classroom. His reading instruction was focused largely on word analysis and work was assigned from a program that emphasized visual and auditory perception of letter clusters in words. The method of instruction used by this particular program emphasized the analysis of words into their constituent parts as opposed to beginning with word parts and blending them together to form a word.

The classroom teacher indicated Seth was responsible for the same assigned work required of all other children in the class, and that there was no differentiation of tasks among students. The language arts, spelling, and social studies books used in Seth's classroom were standard third-grade texts with readability estimates ranging from a 2.5 to a 5.0 grade level. Seth was expected to complete all classroom assignments before going to recess. The teacher reported that Seth really liked recess and did not like to miss it, although he frequently did because his work was incomplete.

On the day we observed, Seth still had 12 math problems left to complete when recess time came, despite the fact that he had finished his art project earlier than most of the other children and returned to his seatwork, and despite the fact that he worked industriously and without distraction for the entire period. He repeatedly asked the teacher for help—on every item, in fact. As we observed Seth, we were able to determine that he had little idea about how to approach the math problems assigned. Each time Seth approached the teacher for help, he was given information about how to do the specific problem he was working on, but he never received additional instruction targeted at his lack of understanding about how to do this *type* of problem. More troubling still was our observation that at least some of the assigned work was explained while Seth was involved in reading instruction outside of the classroom. In this particular case, he had little recourse but to continue approaching the teacher for help.

Discussion with Seth provided additional information about his instructional context. After our visit to his classroom, we asked him about his favorite part of the day and he noted again that he really enjoyed the time when his teacher read to the class. It may be recalled that Seth had previously indicated that he enjoyed the period in the day when his teacher was reading *James and the Giant Peach*. During the earlier discussion, he was unable to retell the story in any coherent fashion. This time, Seth explained that he had to go to Chapter I reading class during read-aloud time and was able to hear only the initial portion of each day's reading!

Case discussion. Our evaluation of the learning context revealed the following: instructional materials written at a third grade level and above, little evidence of materials that Seth would be interested in and/or motivated to read, classroom assignments that emphasized task completion, no individualization of classroom assignments, large numbers of classroom assignments, lack of direction and explanation for classroom assignments caused in part by a "pull-out" reading program, no reading instruction in the regular classroom, Chapter I reading instruction focused on word analysis, and little opportunity to read longer texts for meaning.

Step 4: Evaluating the Match Between the Reader and the Reading Context

The fourth step is to evaluate the match between the knowledge, performance, and motivation of the learner and the materials, methods, and settings within the learning context, using the information gathered in the previous steps. This is the culmination of the first phase of the assessment-instruction process. It provides the answer to the first question guiding the assessment-instruction process: What is the current status of the interaction between the learner and the learning context?

Since an interactive view of reading disability predicts variability, it becomes relatively easy to see why some children appear to thrive in the very environments that befuddle others. Thus, our job in this stage of the assessment-instruction process is to pull together all that we know as the result of our professional efforts and experience, and to evaluate how well existing demands, expectations, and supports of the context match the reader's abilities, interests, knowledge, and level of independence.

Case study. As we reached this point in the assessment-instruction process with Seth, we began to see that the match between Seth's abilities, interests, knowledge, and level of independence and the demands, expectations, and supports of his present placement was problematic in several ways. First, it appeared that his daily classroom assignments were mismatched with his abilities and knowledge. The quantity of work was more than he could reasonably complete in the allotted time. In addition, the level of work was too difficult. He could not complete any of this work without additional help. This situation was aggravating his already strong personal tendency toward dependency. Our assessment suggested that he was receiving no in-class support that might help to compensate for limited knowledge and skill.

Second, Seth's interests lay outside the academic setting. He was not internally motivated to complete classwork in order to reap the rewards of school success. The content of the school's instructional materials and tasks was largely devoid of references to lifestyles or interests similar to Seth's. His experiences were limited and little prereading development was done to increase what appeared to be inadequate prior knowledge.

The emphasis on word analysis in Seth's remedial program appeared to represent a closer match to his existing needs and abilities; however, little attention was being given to his problems with comprehension. Finally, he was regularly denied access to the aspects of school life that he did enjoy—recess, book read-aloud time, and so on.

Case discussion. At this stage in the process, there were still many unanswered questions regarding the match between Seth's specific problems and particular instructional approaches. Although our assessment of the learner had revealed a number of problem areas, these needed to be prioritized, and the most effective instructional approaches identified. The issue of instruction was especially critical since it appeared that the existing match was not ideal.

Step 5: Reflection, Decision Making, and Planning

The fifth step is to use the analysis of the existing match to generate hypotheses regarding the second guiding question, What is the primary source of interference with learning or performance? Probably the most critical feature of skilled assessment is the ability to reflect on available data and realize what it means. Collecting information about readers is relatively easy, compared to thinking about it and making sense of it. The assessment-instruction process must include sufficient time to reflect on information gathered. Indeed, the inexperienced clinician may need to spend as much time reflecting on the information as has been spent gathering it. In later chapters, we provide guidelines and formats for summarizing and reflecting on available data.

The answers we have generated in response to the question, What is the primary source of interference with learning or performance? are then used to identify possible solutions to the hypothesized problems. Not all things are equally possible, given the realities of school life and the state of our current knowledge. Thus, decision making is both a thoughtful consideration of instructional priorities (What does the student seem to need most?) and a consideration of the available resources and feasibility of change (How much control do we have over the mismatch?). During decision making, we must specify which components of the problem might be changed in some way, and how this might best be accomplished. These decisions form the basis of the plans for the next steps in the process.

Although many would assume that at this stage, planning means mapping out an instructional program, it is often the case that we are not ready to say with certainty exactly what needs to be done. As we reflect on available information, new questions are often raised that need to be addressed through further evaluation. Therefore, the focus of this step is to identify possible solutions that can be tried out in some systematic way.

Case study. As we reflected on Seth, we had several hunches about his strengths and weaknesses as a reader and the best use of our resources. First, Seth's word identification skills were inadequate. His knowledge of sight words was far from automatic, and he was unable to analyze whole words into their constituent parts. Seth's failure to recognize that the whole was made up of parts was not limited to word analysis. For example, Seth seemed unable to analyze stories at a global level, often failing to see connections between one event in a text and another. His retellings were typically fragmented, and he seemed unable to remedy the problems, even with discussion. Not surprisingly, during oral reading Seth was often content to leave nonsensical miscues uncorrected, suggesting that he was not attending to meaning.

Despite these serious difficulties, Seth's strengths were notable. He had no difficulties in the areas of hearing or discriminating letter sounds. He both knew and regularly applied sound-symbol information for initial and final consonants. Seth's overall reading behavior indicated that he was inattentive to meaning, but he did demonstrate ability in this area during isolated reading events. For example, while reading a selection about a boy's dog being hit by a car, Seth's miscues were consistently meaningful and his responses to subsequent questions indicated a strong ability to bring relevant prior knowledge to bear on the text.

Case discussion. We would identify the primary source of interference with Seth's learning or performance as inadequate word identification skills, coupled with limited background knowledge, interest, and motivation. Secondarily, we were concerned with his ability to read for meaning. Our best guess at this point was that Seth needed an approach that would help him see how the various parts fit into the larger whole of identifying words and understanding what was being read. Therefore, we decided to try a holistic, language-experience approach with Seth, in an effort to address both his problems with word identification and comprehension, and with background knowledge, interest, and motivation. We planned to try out several different methods for enhancing Seth's word identification skills within the context of this approach. The specifics of these diagnostic teaching procedures are described in greater detail in the next section.

Step 6: Identifying a Better Match: Diagnostic Teaching

The sixth step involves continued assessment, based on the hypotheses and possible solutions generated in the previous step. The primary method of assessment used in this step is called diagnostic teaching. The two major purposes of diagnostic teaching are to provide additional diagnostic information about the interaction between the reader and the reading context, and to identify instructional procedures that are likely to be effective in improving learning and performance. Diagnostic teaching is a combination of assessment and instruction that provides information about how students perform under classroom-like conditions and how they might perform if we altered some aspects of the reading instructional set.

Diagnostic teaching usually inovolves systematically manipulating one or more components of the reading act. Teachers are often gratified to know that there is a formal name for what may look like "messing around" or "trying out this and that." All instruction can be viewed as diagnostic teaching, as long as it is thoughtfully planned using our best guesses about what may work for a given student, and as long as we are prepared to monitor our work continually to see how adjustments have affected learning and performance.

Case study. Based on our earlier reflections, we planned a series of diagnostic teaching episodes for Seth. Although we had a great deal of information about him, we also had several questions and concerns that needed to be addressed in order to be able to identify a better match:

1. What approach to instruction should be employed with Seth?
2. By what means does Seth learn most rapidly and retain most consistently?
3. Should the relative focus of instruction be placed on expanding Seth's repertoire of word recognition skills, or could some generic instruction improve both word analysis and passage comprehension abilities?
4. Could reading and writing inform each other in Seth's instructional program?

The first component of instruction we manipulated involved word recognition and retention. Using three different approaches to instruction and three groups of five words, we systematically taught Seth to recognize the words instantly. We timed the instructional sequence so we would know how long it took under each set of instructional circumstances for him to learn the five words in each set, and we also retested him on these words after one and one-half hours to see how many words he had retained from each sequence. Thus, we are able to evaluate both effectiveness and efficiency. Finally, we asked Seth to tell us which method he thought had been most effective for him.

At delayed retesting, Seth knew at sight (2 second flash) all 15 new words. Thus, it appears that all three instructional approaches are equally effective. However, using one approach he learned the 5 new words in 1-1/2 minutes, whereas using a different approach, it took 10 minutes for him to learn the words! In terms of efficiency, Seth was likely to benefit from a phonics program that blends parts into wholes as opposed to a phonics program that breaks the whole into component parts. It should be noted, however, that he learned the words with equal ease when they were presented as sight words. The approach that was least efficient for Seth was the "whole-to-part" phonics approach similar to his current instructional program. Interestingly, Seth's perception conformed to these conclusions. He felt he had learned the words most easily in the "part-to-whole" phonics approach.

These results were a little disconcerting since, as noted earlier, we suspected that Seth could benefit from a "holistic" approach to instruction. In order to clarify issues related to approach and content, we initiated a language experience activity designed to allow Seth to read and write about topics of interest to him. During the first diagnostic teaching segment, we were chagrined to find that while Seth was enthusiastic about discussing a personal encounter with a "coydog" (half dog, half coyote), the story he dictated was sparse and incoherent. Subsequent work with a conference partner did nothing to improve the quality of the product. Two additional trials, yielding similar results, led us to conclude that this was not the most effective method for improving Seth's word recognition or comprehension skills at the present time.

Case discussion. Recall that the questions we wished to address in the diagnostic teaching step of the process included, What should be the focus on instruction for Seth? and What approach to instruction should be employed? After several additional manipulations such as those described above, we concluded that Seth's program would need to contain strong elements of work in both word recognition and comprehension, and these might need to be somewhat separate for the time being. Despite our earlier conclusions, it appeared that Seth needed to develop a strong understanding of the component parts before he would benefit from more holistic instruction. For him, the rather counterintuitive benefits of part-to-whole instruction were obvious. However, he also needed as much exposure as possible to whole texts and read-aloud sessions as a means of increasing his understanding of the purposes for reading and writing.

Step 7: Focus on Instruction: Continuous Monitoring and Modification

The results of diagnostic teaching are used to plan an instructional program that appears to respond to the most important needs of the individual reader. There are times when instruction will proceed before assessment is completed. At other times, the individual responsible for assessment will not deliver instruction. Wherever possible, of course, the preferred arrangement is for both assessment and instruction to be conducted by the same person.

In either case, initial instructional outcomes are established. Although attitude goals, information goals, and process goals may all be included in an individual's program, it is also possible that one or two of these will receive special emphasis. The information gathered in earlier portions of the process is used to inform decisions about what content to include and what delivery system to use. It is understood that these initial decisions may be changed or altered as further information is gathered.

Every instructional encounter with a particular reader is an opportunity for assessing and improving instruction. It is possible, and desirable, to continually monitor the effectiveness of the recommended instructional program and to make fine-tuning adjustments in the program as needed. Continuous monitoring of instructional progress is absolutely essential, and adaptive teaching involving modifications in texts, tasks, and materials is desirable. The full potential of this process can only be realized when it becomes part of daily practice.

Case study. Since there was increasing evidence to suggest that a more parts-to-whole approach would be effective for Seth, we initiated an adapted process writing approach. During the first phase, Seth dictated a story as above. When he believed it to be complete, the tutor then rewrote the story so that it included an introduction, episode, and conclusion. This revised piece was discussed, with the emphasis placed on the components of a strong story. Finally, one component (the introduction, episode, or conclusion) was deleted and Seth was encouraged to write a replacement. This process was continued until Seth had rewritten the entire piece. This practice proved especially helpful to Seth and was later coupled with "story frames" (Fowler, 1982) to encourage Seth to construct whole texts that contained important component pieces.

In addition, contact between school and clinic was maintained to good effect. Although Seth continued to receive remedial reading support outside the classroom during the regularly scheduled reading instruction time, he no longer missed key components of the rest of the day. The support personnel in Seth's school also agreed to incorporate several of the recommended instructional procedures. For example, Seth's program was changed to include daily experiences with whole texts. He was read to daily, and these read-aloud sessions formed the basis for work in comprehension and writing. Similarly, direct instruction in word recognition was planned so that rapid application in text was featured.

Case discussion. It is especially important to recognize that only parts of Seth's instructional program could really be accomplished in the clinic setting. Because some aspects of his progress in reading and writing were governed by the classroom and school setting, it was important to include teachers and specialists very early on in Seth's remedial program. He clearly needed, and could benefit from, some individualized reading instruction. However, he also needed a total instructional program that was more responsive to his needs.

Step 8: Reporting

This step involves the summarization of information obtained in the previous steps in written reports and/or oral conferences. It requires a clear statement of the presenting problem(s); a description of the information collected in the evaluations of the learner, the learning context, and through diagnostic teaching; a synthesis of this information into a clear statement of the primary difficulty; and recommendations for future practice, including descriptions and examples of appropriate materials and methods.

Although procedures for writing and reporting vary, the reporting format should parallel as closely as possible the goals of the assessment-instruction process. For now, it is important only to arrive at a general appreciation of how important clear, concise communication can be for students.

Case study. As a result of the clinic's report (see Appendix A), Seth's parents concluded that he did indeed need the help of special education placement, and requested that he be evaluated for determination of eligibility. The school, in turn, was anxious to use the information gleaned during Seth's assessment in the clinic. Thus, conferences were conducted with the Chapter I teacher and with the special educator, and the school effectively implemented the suggestions detailed in the final report. The special educator was especially interested in the mapping activities that had been done, and incorporated these activities in Seth's program. She also worked with the classroom teacher to find ways to provide prereading support activities for Seth in social studies and science.

You may also recall that there was reason to believe that Seth's daily class work was not entirely appropriate. Thus, the final report had recommended that Seth's program would need to be individualized to accomodate his specific needs and abilities. Therefore, Seth's fourth-grade classroom placement was made with an eye to teacher flexibility. In particular, the teacher's ability to provide consistent and appropriate support, and willingness to adapt and individualize instruction were considered. He was placed with a teacher who had demonstrated these abilities in the past and who was also capable of ensuring that Seth took responsibility for his work.

Case discussion. In later chapters we will discuss these aspects of the assessment-instruction process in some depth. In the meantime, you can find Seth's final report in Appendix A. Continuous assessment is critical, of course. In Seth's case, this will need to be done by the special education team as they conduct their periodic reevaluation of Seth's eligibility for their services. In addition, this will be done to make adjustments to the recommended program. It is likely that Seth will need continued support for some time to come. Only continuous assessment and adjustment will ensure his progress.

FROM CLASSROOM TO CLINIC

Although the components of the assessment-instruction process are the same for both classroom and clinic, the amount of attention devoted to each component and the procedures used to evaluate them are likely to be different. The classroom teacher has the benefit of daily contact with the student or students in question, but limited time to spend with individual students. The specialist or clinician has the benefit of individual time with the student, but limited knowledge about the student's daily interactions with reading in the classroom.

Application to the Classroom

Both formal and informal group-administered assessments of the readers should be a major source of information for the classroom teacher. These assessments would be used to initiate the assessment-instruction process, and as the basis for continuous monitoring and modification of instructional procedures. Therefore, it is important for classroom teachers to develop a repertoire of assessment techniques that can be incorporated easily into their daily instruction (these will be discussed in the chapters that follow). Those students who demonstrate difficulty on these assessments would then be seen individually or in smaller groups for further evaluation. The assessment of the methods and materials that comprise the reading context may be less cumbersome for classroom teachers, because of their daily access and repeated experience with them. Classroom teachers have the added benefit of being able to incorporate trial teaching procedures into the real context of their daily instruction.

Application to the Clinic

The reading specialist or clinician usually only deals with students who have already been identified by some means as having a problem. Whether their problem is primarily a reading problem is one of the questions to be answered through the assessment-instruction process. Specialists usually rely heavily on both formal (Chapter 6) and informal individual assessment (Chapters 3–5 and 7) procedures for an evaluation of the learner. Specialists have the advantage of working closely in small settings with an individual student. This may provide in-depth information unavailable to the classroom teacher. However, specialists are at somewhat of a disadvantage in evaluating the reader in interaction with the reading context, because they do not have daily contact with the student(s) in question in the context in which the problem is occurring. They must rely on limited examinations of the materials, classroom observation, and interviews with the parents, the teacher, and the students for this evaluation. Furthermore, they must be aware of and sensitive to the teacher's style and the organization of the classroom in order to develop trial teaching procedures that would be appropriate for use in the student's classroom. Specialists who are operating in pull-out programs need to be especially aware of the potential difficulties in this situation. Too often, the students who are most in need of consistent, coherent reading instruction are the ones receiving the most fragmented instruction. What is most important, however, is that students may be practicing and acquiring skills and abilities in one setting that are neither valued nor applied in another. Thus, communication between classroom and clinic is of the utmost importance.

CHAPTER SUMMARY

The goals of the assessment-instruction process were described as the development of strategic, motivated readers who are able to apply their skills and strategies independently and in a flexible manner. Learning to read was characterized as a lifelong pursuit in which the knowledge gained from each reading experience affects subsequent reading experiences. The assessment-instruction process was described in terms of reader and reading context factors. For readers, we described the components of skilled reading and the areas to be assessed. For the reading context, we described areas to be assessed and established some criteria for gathering assessment information. Finally, we described the procedures for carrying out the assessment-instruction process.

The components of skilled reading important in assessing the reader were described as follows:

1. *Word identification:* A hierarchy of strategies for identifying words beginning with *sight word recognition,* which requires the least amount of effort, moving to the *word analysis strategies* of *contextual* and *morphemic analysis,* and ending with *phonic analysis,* which requires the greatest amount of effort on the part of the reader.
2. *Rate and fluency:* The speed of oral and/or silent reading as measured in words per minute, and readers' ability to group words into meaningful phrase units as they read.
3. *Vocabulary development:* Knowledge of the meanings of words, and the ability to infer and learn the meanings of new words.
4. *Comprehension:* The ability to use previously acquired information to construct meaning for a given text that is appropriate for the reading purpose.
5. *Studying:* A specialized form of comprehension that emphasizes reading to learn and/or remember what has been comprehended or understood from text.
6. *Writing:* The ability to engage in a process that results in written messages that are appropriate for a given audience and purpose. Areas to be assessed were described as the reader's *knowledge about reading, prior knowledge, application* of knowledge and skills, and *attitudes and motivation.* Information should be gathered about each in relation to a particular reading context, and the *quality* of, *experiences provided,* and *demands* made by the reading context in relation to a particular reader.

The areas to be assessed in the reading context were described as follows:

1. *Materials:* Defined as five types of instructional materials that are representative of the texts and tasks found in most classrooms. These are *written prose, written questions, practice materials, computer-aided instructional software,* and the *teacher's manuals* that are used to guide instruction.
2. *Methods:* The *content* of instruction (what is being taught) and the *delivery system* (how content is being taught). Content is characterized by *attitude, information,* and *process* objectives, and delivery is characterized as *direct* or *indirect* instruction.
3. *Setting:* The various sociocultural conditions that influence learning, including community, schools, classrooms, and reading groups.

In the last section of this chapter we described *procedures* for implementing the assessment-instruction process. The steps in the assessment-instruction process are guided by three questions: What is the current status of the interaction between the reader and the reading context? What is the primary source of interference with learning or performance? How can learning or performance be established or improved? The steps in the assessment-instruction process are as follows:

Step 1   Evaluating the Learner: Getting Started
Step 2   Evaluating the Learner: Focusing on Reading and Writing
Step 3   Evaluating the Reading Context

Step 4   Evaluating the Match Between the Reader and the Reading Context
Step 5   Reflection, Decision Making, and Planning
Step 6   Identifying a Better Match: Diagnostic Teaching
Step 7   Focus on Instruction: Continuous Monitoring and Modification
Step 8   Reporting

Finally, because there are differences between classrooms and clinic, different applications of the assessment instruction process for these two settings were discussed. Classroom teachers have the benefit of daily contact with students, but limited time to spend with individual students. In contrast, the specialist or clinician has the benefit of individual time with the student, but limited access to the student's daily interactions with reading in the classroom. Thus, it was noted that the amount of attention devoted to each component and the procedures used to evaluate them were likely to vary.

SECTION II

Evaluating the Learner

IN THE FIRST TWO CHAPTERS, we provided both a theoretical and a practical framework for thinking about assessment-instruction. The theoretical framework provides the rationale for much of the remainder of the text. Frequent reference is made throughout to the ideas and concepts presented in Section I. In addition, the steps in the assessment-instruction framework, presented in Chapter 2, guide us through the process *and* through this text.

In the figure on the following page, the flowchart of these steps is presented again, this time with one section highlighted. The highlighted section identifies the major focus in this section: Evaluating the Reader. As the flowchart reveals, both Step 1 (Getting Started) and Step 2 (Focusing on Reading and Writing) are addressed in this section.

This section on evaluating the learner is easily the longest section in the book, reflecting the fact that educators know more about how the learner influences reading and reading achievement than they do about other variables in the reading process. Recent attention to other aspects of reading and learning to read has been helpful, but there is not nearly so large a body of knowledge. Similarly, the traditional emphasis on the reader has resulted in the generation of more tools and strategies for assessment than have efforts in other areas. Each of the five chapters in this section contains section(s) on understanding, designed to provide teachers and clinicians with a theoretical or research rationale for the section(s) on tools and strategies for assessment. These include norm-referenced tests and traditional informal measures (e.g., Informal Reading Inventories), as well as innovative, teacher-based tools and strategies.

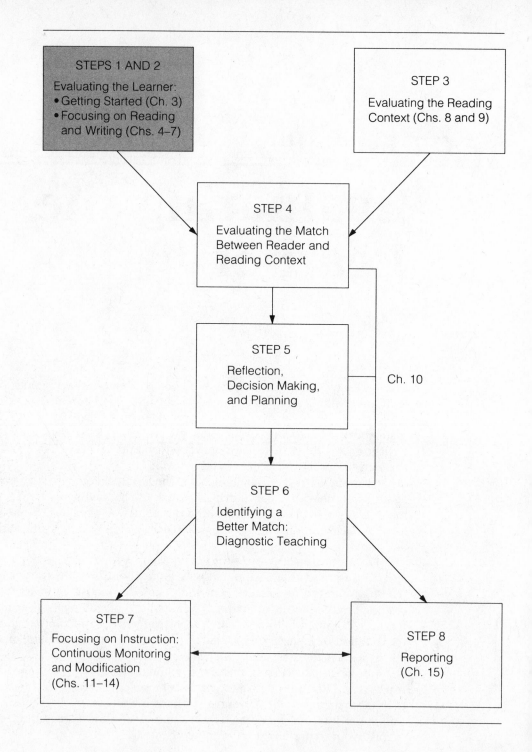

CHAPTER 3

Getting Started
with Assessment

INTRODUCTION

Assessments of student reading ability must begin somewhere. In this chapter, we provide a road map for the initial step of the assessment-instruction process: Getting Started. The interviewing and observational procedures described in this chapter are essential to getting started. However, they should not be viewed as discrete, separable activities that end with this phase of the assessment-instruction process—as in, "That's done, now let's move on to the next step." Talking and observing with an eye toward assessment should be continuous activities in every classroom and clinical setting. Because these are such powerful tools, they are useful in virtually every phase of the assessment-instruction process and are discussed in almost every chapter of this book.

Chapter Overview

This chapter begins with guidelines that are important for the entire assessment-instruction process. Then we provide a rationale and describe procedures for collecting background information and conducting observations and interviews. Specifically, we present examples of these types of procedures, describe how to undertake these forms of assessment, and discuss the types of information that can be derived from these initial assessment devices.

In the Getting Started step of the assessment-instruction process, we are less concerned with gathering information about students' application of reading skills than we are with obtaining a general picture of the factors that may be influencing the performance data we will gather later. More specific details about how to use observation and interview data to assess students' ability to apply reading skill and knowledge are provided in later chapters. In this chapter, observation and interviews are discussed as approaches to the problem of gathering *background information* for the purpose of getting started.

UNDERSTANDING ASSESSMENT
Guidelines

Our current understanding of reading suggests the need to develop assessment procedures for evaluating reading in ways that are more relevant to the holistic, terminal goals of reading instruction (i.e., strategic, motivated reading). In addition, it is essential that we assess directly the factors that are known to influence reading, rather than ignoring them or attempting to create situations where they do not matter. What is needed is a structured approach to determine how an individual handles actual reading materials under conditions that simulate real reading situations both in and out of the classroom. The following guidelines provide the basis for assessment practices that achieve these goals.

Assess Meaningful Activities

To evaluate students' reading and writing abilities, we must assess students as they read and write real texts for real purposes. There are times when it may be reasonable to evaluate some component skill in isolation (e.g., sight word vocabulary). However, we should avoid generating conclusions about the contribution of any single skill to overall reading and writing ability until we have also observed the component in context. In addition, we must consider how relevant the component abilities are for real reading and writing activities. Tests of visual discrimination of shapes or colors, for example, have little to do with reading. Similarly, spelling tests may provide some indirect evidence about reading, but students' performance in spelling and reading is not necessarily directly comparable. On the other hand, asking students to read orally a text containing taught words as a measure of sight vocabulary is directly relevant to the abilities a student needs for skilled reading.

Assessment Should Be Unobtrusive

The most informative assessments are those that occur within the everyday instructional context rather than artificial testing contexts. There is evidence that children are aware of the differences among contexts and alter their performance accordingly (Spiro & Myers, 1984). Anyone who has ever puzzled over the discrepancy between students' performance in the classroom and their test performance is aware of this problem.

In general, children tend to consider formal testing situations to be more important than everyday classroom tasks. However, this perception can have very different effects on different students. Some students perform better in the formal testing situations because of increased motivation to do well, while others perform less well because of the anxiety created by the pressure to do well. Therefore, we do not want to collect information that tells us only how children perform in formal testing situations. We want to be able to make some predictions about students' performance in everyday instructional contexts.

Assessment and Purpose Should Match

No single assessment tool or strategy can do everything. We must think carefully about what we want to know and why we are assessing. If we need comparative data on large numbers of students, then informal, classroom-based assessment probably is not practical. On the other hand, if we want information that will help us plan instruction for individuals or groups of children, then standardized, norm-referenced tests are not likely to be helpful.

Even after the general type of assessment (formal versus informal) has been determined, we need to consider our purpose. For example, if we are interested in making placement decisions, then we do not need procedures that yield a fine-grained analysis of strengths and weaknesses. Alternatively, if we are trying to make decisions about whether to teach or reteach a particular component, then we will need a tool or strategy that provides an evaluation of a specific area.

Assessment Should Be Systematic

Whether we use formal, standardized tests or informal, classroom-based procedures, our assessments must be reliable indices of student performance (see Chapter 6). That is, we need to know that students' performance on a particular assessment would remain constant or stable if the procedure were to be readministered. The results of an assessment would have little meaning if they fluctuated wildly from one administration to the next.

The reliability of formal test instruments typically is addressed through the standardization process and reported in the manual. The reliability of informal assessments depends on the extent to which we are systematic and consistent in our use of these techniques. When making comparisons among individuals, we must attempt to evaluate all of our students under the same conditions, with the same level of support. For example, we should attempt to formalize at least some of the probing questions asked during story retellings. If the student is given additional assistance, then it is important to record the information provided to clarify the conditions under which the assessment occurred.

Assessment Should Be Continuous

Multiple samples of students' performance are always preferable to a single sample. Not only does continuous evaluation improve the reliability of the procedure, it also permits us to observe the *patterns* of behavior that are most informative for assessment and instruction. In addition, it casts assessment and instruction in their proper roles—as interacting elements of teaching. Viewing every instructional interaction with a child as an assessment opportunity enhances our diagnostic powers.

We have found that continuous assessment helps us to view both our own teaching and the student's ability in a different light. For example, a student's failure to perform can be viewed as an opportunity to gather information, rather than a reflection of some static and inherent ability (in either the teacher or the child). It also appears to us as though teachers often distrust their own daily evaluations of children's performance. We are suggesting that these evaluations be taken seriously, and that the majority of assessments in reading and writing be done continuously and in conjunction with the daily instructional program as an aid to planning, adapting, and refining instruction.

Record Keeping

Well-organized record keeping, of necessity, goes hand-in-hand with systematic, continuous assessment. Good records are essential when a variety of standardized and informal procedures are used to plan instruction, evaluate progress, and communicate with parents and administrators. We suggest that records be kept in the form of a portfolio adapted to fit each particular program of assessment-instruction.

According to Valencia, McGinley, and Pearson (1990), the term *portfolio* has both a physical and philosophical sense:

> As a concept, the "idea" of a portfolio forces us to expand the range of "things" we would consider as data to use in instructional decision-making. It is also an attitude suggesting that assessment is a dynamic rather than a static process reflected most accurately in multiple snapshots taken over time. All who have a stake in contributing to the portfolio (students, teachers, and parents) have a right to "visit" it whenever they wish—to reflect on and analyze its contents. But it is also a physical entity, a container in which we can store the artifacts of our literacy—the examples, documents, and observations that serve as evidence of growth and development—so that they are available for visitation and reflection.

Portfolios include materials that exemplify the depth and breadth of a student's expertise. They include a variety of different types of information collected over time as indicators of growth in reading and writing. This type of record keeping makes it easier for teachers, clinicians, and students to understand the development of expertise and to plan the experiences that will encourage additional progress.

It is difficult to say exactly what should be included in any given portfolio, because the contents of the portfolio will vary in relation to the particular program of assessment and instruction in effect. As Valencia (1990a) notes, the range of items to include in a portfolio is almost limitless, but may include written responses to reading, reading logs, selected daily work, pieces of writing at various stages of completion, classroom tests, observational checklists, unit projects, and audio or video tapes. An important addition to these suggestions, for those who follow the assessment-instruction process outlined in this book, is the inclusion of measures designed to evaluate various aspects of the instructional context. "The key is to ensure a variety of types of indicators of learning so that teachers, parents, students, and administrators can build a complete picture of the student's development" (Valencia, 1990a, p. 339).

It is also recommended that the contents of the portfolio be organized into several layers of information: the actual evidence, or raw data, and one or more levels of summary or profile sheets to help synthesize the information. Inclusion of the raw data enables us to examine students' actual work and progress notes, rather than relying simply on a number or grade. Summary or profile sheets assist us in analyzing and synthesizing the information in ways that help us make decisions and communicate with parents and administrators.

HOME AND SCHOOL BACKGROUND
Understanding Information About Home and School

All children, even very young children, come to us with a personal and educational history. One's physical, cognitive, affective, and sociocultural history has a profound influence on what and how the student learns. In some cases, assessments of reading ability can be speeded immeasurably by the careful and thought-ful gathering and analysis of these types of background information.

Many teachers are sensitive to the potential problems of teacher expectations on a student's achievement, or "Pygmalion effects" (Rosenthal & Jacobson, 1968). Therefore, many believe that they should not attempt to gather background information about their students, fearing that such knowledge will color their perceptions and treatment of children. This is a more serious concern when reading disability is viewed as a problem located entirely within the reader (see Chapter 1) than it is when disability is viewed from an interactive perspective. Within an interactive framework of thinking, past history merely reflects the student's performance within a specific context, using particular materials, in-structional approaches, and so on. In short, an interactive perspective implies that patterns observed in the past are not invariable or static, nor are they the only patterns possible. Teachers and clinicians need access to background knowledge so that they can begin to determine what their students have experienced and how they responded to these experiences.

In addition, of course, there are objective aspects of a student's history that are important to know because they can influence instruction directly. For example, if Child A missed a great deal of school because of illness, we know that the student has not had the opportunity to acquire particular knowledge and skill. This background is different than the history for Child B, of the same age and "disabil-ity," who was present during all instructional periods. Although we cannot know immediately why this student has failed to benefit from instruction, we know that the child was exposed to it.

In the Getting Started phase of the assessment-instruction process, it is important to gather as much background information as possible from the home and the school, because we cannot know what information might be significant. There are generally two overall reasons to collect background information. First, it is helpful at the onset of assessment to establish that the primary source of difficulty is *not* a reading correlate (see Chapter 1). Before proceeding with assessment, we need to correct or remedy, if possible, any preexisting condi-tion that may inhibit reading growth (e.g., poor vision). Second, we want to gather as much information as possible in order to inform our decision-making process.

It is important not to leap to conclusions about etiology at this early stage. For example, although the failing marriage of the child's parents may be contributing to the child's reading problems, a great many students whose families are experi-encing stress read well and prosper academically. The purpose of gathering back-ground information is not to attribute cause but to provide insights that allow us to make good decisions about instruction. As we have already noted, we are less concerned in this first step with gathering information about students' abilities to apply knowledge and skill than we are with gathering background that may inform our decisions about what to do next. Therefore, our discussion is focused on the general types of information to be gathered—information about correlates, knowledge about reading, and motivation and attitudes.

Tools and Strategies for Gathering Home and School Information

Background information can be examined from a number of points of view. Like the reading process itself, it resides in a context. The school gathers and reports information on students from a point of view that is different than a parent's. Similarly, the student's view of his or her history is likely to be different from either of these other sources of background information. Each of these points of view can provide important insights during the Getting Started phase.

Home Information

Parents are particularly good sources of information about students' background, because they have enduring contact with them. They have information about their child's overall experiential background and developmental history that includes knowledge about physical, cultural, linguistic, affective, and cognitive factors. Parents are likely to have a somewhat different perspective about students than school personnel. The point of gathering background information from parents is not that all information will be the "truth," but rather that parents have a perspective on their children that cannot be shared by any other individuals. It is often more personal and more graphic, including critical cultural, motivational, and attitudinal data. In addition, parental involvement is often necessary for any lasting change in reading performance, and it is important to enlist parental support as early as possible in the process.

Parents are often confused and intimidated by professionals and their jargon. In addition, many parents of poor readers are frightened and dismayed by their child's apparent inability to read well. For many, this is interpreted to mean that the child is not very bright. Sometimes they are concerned that they have done or not done something that has caused the problem. It is important to be positive and supportive while working with parents, without raising any unrealistic hopes about magic remedies. Recently, one of the authors received a phone call from a frantic parent who was concerned because her child was reading "below grade level," according to school reports; she wanted him to come to our clinic "to get to grade level." We agreed to see him after a clear discussion of the need for further assessment. After the second diagnostic session, the mother approached the tutor and anxiously asked whether her child was getting nearer to grade level. Clearly, this misplaced confidence, although heartening, must be addressed directly so that both the parent and the student can persevere.

Interviewing. During the Getting Started phase of the assessment-instruction process, it is imperative to gather information about family background, parental expectations, health history, and support for reading in the home. We prefer to do this through personal interviews. We try to be informal, using an interview form to remind us of important areas of discussion. McGinnis and Smith (1982) have suggested a set of guidelines for parent interviewing that are helpful:

1. Provide a physical setting that is as comfortable as possible, providing for privacy and confidentiality.

2. Make it clear immediately that the purpose of the interview is solely to help the client.
3. Keep note-taking to a minimum.
4. Use a tape recorder only if the parent agrees to its use, and even then it should be as unobtrusive as possible.
5. Keep the purpose of the interview in mind, and avoid tempting sidetrips.
6. Follow cues provided by the parent.
7. Avoid making judgmental remarks. Attempt to ask open-ended questions such as, "When your child does something you don't want him to, how do you handle it?" versus "Do you punish your child when be misbehaves?"
8. Be tactful.
9. Keep the setting professional but use language appropriate for a lay person, avoiding jargon.
10. Keep control, even with excessive talkers.
11. Encourage less talkative people by avoiding simple "yes or no" questions.
12. Do not be afraid of silences. They often elicit important information.
13. When in doubt, clarify what was said to insure against misunderstandings.
14. Address parental anxiety and try to reassure without painting an overly optimistic picture.
15. Maintain rapport by remaining relaxed and avoiding hostility or impertinence.
16. Assure confidentiality by words, deeds, and implication.

It is usually sufficient to start the interview by asking the parent "Tell me about your child's school experience" or "Tell me about your child's reading problems." This is generally enough to launch parents into a long monologue, because few people ever get enough time to talk specifically about their children. However, we must also be sensitive to cultural differences among parents in our efforts to elicit background information relevant to a child's reading problem. Furthermore, we should keep in mind that an interpreter may be necessary for parents who are willing to be interviewed, but who do not speak English.

Although most parents do not mind sharing family history, some will be concerned. It is important to assure them that this information will be held confidential and not shared without expressed parental consent. In addition, it may be necessary or desirable to explain certain questions, particularly those that refer to family history of academic success and early developmental and health history. Simply telling parents that these can be factors in students' reading achievement is usually enough.

A family information form is presented in Figure 3.1 that can be used either as an interview schedule or, in cases when a personal interview is not possible or practical, as a written form to be completed at home by the student's family. Alternatively, the responses to the written form can be used to guide the development of a personal interview for a specific individual.

It is important to remember that completing a written form can be intimidating to some parents. In particular, we need to be sensitive to the possibility that the parents may not be literate themselves. This may be the case when forms are repeatedly "lost" or "forgotten," suggesting that an extra effort may be needed to make personal contact. It is entirely possible, for example, to have a satisfactory phone interview to gather key background information. Whichever approach is taken, it is essential to gather information from the family about the factors in a student's educational experiences, health history, attitudes toward school and reading, and family background that may be related to problems in reading and learning.

Identifying important information. Parents are often unaware of the potential influence of routine childhood experiences. For example, a history of ear infections can have an inhibiting effect on both language development and phonological awareness (see Chapter 4). These difficulties can, of course, interact with initial instruction to establish an early pattern of school failure. Parents rarely offer this information spontaneously and an interview should elicit it.

Similarly, unreasonable parental expectations, competition with older, successful siblings, or early entrance into academic programs can cause students to avoid reading tasks. Although this information does not necessarily inform us about the specific reading difficulties that the child is experiencing right now, it can help our understanding of the overall context of the reading problem. In addition, parents are very often unaware of the need to provide continuous and supported reading practice in the home. An initial interview can provide information about the amount and type of reading and writing activity that takes place in the home.

School history can, of course, be a critical factor in the child's reading development. Unsatisfactory initial instruction, poor classroom management, or simply lack of readiness for the program offered in the school can result in reading difficulties. Many parents attribute their child's reading difficulties to poor teaching and schooling. Although this is sometimes the source of the problem, it is important to be tactful in responding to parents' concern, frustration, and anger, especially when working in a setting outside the mainstream school environment. The child (and the parents) will probably continue to depend on the school/ teacher in question, and it does little good to create conflict unless it is absolutely necessary.

In the final analysis, even an uneventful personal, family, and educational background provides an important perspective on a student's reading problems. The lack of any unusual or problematic information in these areas helps us begin to rule out certain factors as primary contributors to the student's difficulties in reading.

School Information

As in gathering parent information, we seek information from the school that is uniquely theirs to offer. School records and personnel can suggest how well the child has functioned in an academic setting, what instructional materials have been used, and how far the child has progressed in acquiring age-appropriate reading knowledge and skill. In the best cases, information is obtained about what has worked instructionally and what has not. In addition, school information can help us avoid the duplication of previous assessment efforts. Many children have

FIGURE 3.1
*Family
Information
Form*

General Information

Name _____ Birthdate _____ Age _____
Parent(s)/Guardian _____
Home address _____
Phone (Home) _____ (Work) _____
School _____ Grade _____ Teacher _____
School address _____
Reason for referral _____

Family Members

	Mother	Father
Name	_____	_____
Age	_____	_____
Occupation	_____	_____
Highest grade completed	_____	_____
Learning problems	_____	_____
Marital status	_____	_____

Siblings' names	Age	Health and/or learning problems
_____	_____	_____
_____	_____	_____
_____	_____	_____

Primary language spoken in the home _____
Anything in the home that may be a source of difficulty for your child (e.g., moving, separation, remarriage, illness, financial problems)? _____
_____

Educational History

Did your child attend nursery school? _____ When? _____
Did your child attend kindergarten? _____ At what age? _____
Has your child ever repeated a grade? _____ Skipped a grade? _____
    If Yes, which grade and reason _____

Schools attended by your child:

Name and location	Grade(s)	Dates	Reasons for leaving
_____	_____	____	_____
_____	_____	____	_____

Has your child received special services in or out of school? _____
    If Yes, please explain _____
Has your child had frequent or extended absences from school? _____
    If Yes, please explain _____

Developmental History

Any illness during pregnancy or complications during birth? _____
    If Yes, please describe _____
Is your child adopted? _____ Was your child premature? _____
Age of walking _____ talking in 2–3 word sentences _____
Describe your child's rate of growth. _____
Frequent health problems (e.g., ear infections, colds, allergies?) _____
_____

FIGURE 3.1
(continued)

Speech problems _____
Physical problems _____
Date of last hearing exam _____ Findings _____
Date of last physical exam _____ Findings _____
Date of last vision exam _____ Findings _____
Hours of sleep per night? _____ Problems? _____
What, if any, medication being taken now? _____

Reading Development

Describe your family's reading habits. _____
_____

What newspapers/magazines do you receive? _____
_____

What are your child's attitudes toward reading and school? _____
_____

What do you feel are your child's special learning needs? _____
_____

When were they first noticed? _____
How do you feel your child's special needs have been handled? _____
_____

What are your child's interests? How does your child spend leisure time?
_____

What and how much does your child read at home? _____
_____

What are your child's personal strengths? _____
_____

  Weaknesses? _____
_____

What do you expect for your child's future? _____
_____

COMMENTS: Please write about any other attitudes, behaviors, or information that you
feel are important for us to know.

been evaluated (either informally or formally) by the time they are referred to a
reading specialist. When available, recent test results and observational data may
provide invaluable direction for preparing an assessment plan.

All schools keep records on student progress and achievement. Schools are
sensitive to the permanence of these records, in part because these records are
accessible by parents immediately, and to students at the age of majority (Family
Educational Rights and Privacy Act/Buckley Amendment, PL 93–380, 1974).
Consequently, most schools maintain and retain little except the most standardized information. Schools are not permitted to distribute this information to
any outside professionals without explicit parental consent. Figure 3.2 suggests an
appropriate format for soliciting school records.

Today, school records normally contain only the results of standardized
achievement tests, copies of periodic grading results, and perhaps a list of the

FIGURE 3.2
Parental Release and Request for Records Form

Date:

To:

The following student _____, who lives at _____, is receiving remediation at the Reading Center at _____. In order to facilitate his/her remediation, we would appreciate any test results or records that you might have concerning this child.
Thank you.

_____,
Director
Reading Center

You have my permission to release any records concerning my daughter _____
son _____

_____	_____
Student's name	Parent

curricular materials used by the student (e.g., a listing of basal criterion test results). Some schools have established minimum competencies, and student progress in these areas would be noted. Similarly, some schools give periodic group "intelligence" tests (see Chapter 6) and, if so, these results would be included as well. However, if the child has been tested for eligibility for a special education placement, the school records may contain a great deal more information. This would most likely include an evaluation by a school psychologist, that usually involves administering one or several individual intelligence and aptitude tests. In addition, there would normally be some sort of report from the classroom teacher regarding academic progress and overall functioning. It is also important to note the dates associated with these types of information as an aid to interpretation.

The amount and type of information included in student records varies widely from one school district to another. In some areas, for example, it is necessary to contact support personnel (e.g., Chapter I teachers, speech therapist), directly to collect information about the student, since this information is not included in the overall school records. As a result, school records are not always helpful in providing relevant background information. Certainly it is helpful to know if a child has been retained, and the results of standardized tests may reveal some global information about the student's relative standing compared to age mates. These results can be compared from year to year to determine whether the student's relative standing has changed significantly. Finally, when comprehensive in-school assessment has taken place, the school records can eliminate the

FIGURE 3.3
*School
Information
Form*

Student Background

Name: _____ Birthdate: _____
Age: _____ Grade: _____ Teacher: _____
School district: _____ School: _____
School address: _____ Phone: _____
Principal: _____ Teacher: _____
Parent(s): _____ Phone: _____
Parent address: _____
School attendance: Regular _____ Irregular _____ Reason _____
Ever repeated/skipped a grade? _____ If yes, what grade? _____
   What was result? _____
Is nonpromotion or special class placement now being considered? _____
What, if any, special services is this student now receiving? _____
_____

Describe the student's performance in reading, spelling, writing, math, science, and
   social studies: _____
_____
_____

What concerns, if any, do you have about this student's behavior and/or performance in
   the classroom? _____
_____

Reading Instruction

Instructional personnel   Materials and methods   Progress
Name: _____   _____   _____
Position: _____   _____   _____
Frequency of instruction: _____

Name: _____   _____   _____
Position: _____   _____   _____
Frequency of instruction: _____

Name: _____   _____   _____
Position: _____   _____   _____
Frequency of instruction: _____

Describe any special methods or materials used to help this sudent: _____
_____
What are this student's strengths? _____
   Weaknesses? _____

Test Results

Type of test	Name of test	Date	Results	Examiner
Intelligence				
Achievement				
Vision				
Hearing				
Other				

Other information relevant to this student's performance in school: _____
_____
_____

need for gathering certain types of information. However, these data do not generally permit any specific diagnostic or instructional conclusions.

In addition to formal school records, school personnel can provide important information. Again, most schools and school employees do not discuss specific students without explicit parental consent. If permission is granted, however, present and past teachers can be contacted and student skills, abilities, and performance discussed. Figure 3.3 presents a school information form that can be used either as a guide for interviewing school personnel, or as a written form to be completed independently by school personnel. As with the family information form, the responses to the written form may be used to guide the development of a personal interview for specific school personnel.

Although we might expect specialized school personnel to know a great deal about their students' backgrounds and their daily academic experiences, this is not always the case. Johnston, Allington, and Afflerbach (1985) found that only one-third of the remedial reading teachers interviewed knew what reading instructional materials were used in the regular classroom. Similarly, only 10% of the classroom teachers knew what materials were used in the resource rooms!

Since there appears to be a tremendous lack of coordination between the core curriculum in many schools and the remedial instruction taking place in those same schools, it is important to gather information from both settings when students are involved in pull-out programs. Intake forms, such as those described, and personal conversations with key school personnel can add immeasurably to our understanding of the student and his or her reading history.

We need to know as much as possible about the student's specific knowledge and skill. We also need to know exactly what types of instruction have been offered, how this has been received, and the school's perception of this student. Finally, records of assessment information collected by the school can help us make decisions about the types of assessment information yet to be gathered.

Although these personal histories can provide general information that is extremely helpful, there is also much specific information that can and should be gleaned in the Getting Started step of the assessment-instruction process. In the following section, we discuss student interviews as a source of specific reading information and provide examples of interviews designed to gather information about students' background knowledge, their reading knowledge and skill, and their attitudes and motivations about reading.

STUDENT BACKGROUND

Probably the most neglected source of information regarding a student's reading performance is the student. Poor readers are often surprisingly insightful about their reading difficulties. For this reason, we have devoted a large segment of this chapter to reader interviews and observation. Just as students can provide information related to specific aspects of reading, they can also provide valuable background information.

Understanding Student Interviews

Although interviews are widely used in our society for a variety of purposes, these tools are underused in the area of reading assessment. Reading professionals have recently begun to realize that information elicited from interviews can enhance the diagnostic value of the overall assessment, but they are still not used very often. This may be due, in part, to a perceived lack of time, but it also appears that many teachers and administrators are distrusting of interview information (even though most teachers and administrators were hired on the strength of an interview and the presumed competence it revealed). In part, this distrust results from the fact that interview information is *self-reported*.

In the past, both school personnel and researchers have been troubled by a number of issues surrounding self-reported information (Cavanaugh & Perlmutter, 1982; Nisbett & Wilson, 1977). First, there is a possibility that students might report information that is an inaccurate reflection of their true ideas, beliefs, or inclinations. In particular, it has been argued that students are likely to report what they think the teacher/adult wants to hear.

A second concern revolves around the ability of children to talk about their ideas or abilities. This is a particular concern when students are either very young or have speech/language differences or difficulties. It is clear that we must consider these potentially confounding factors just as we would the factors that can influence performance on other types of assessment instruments, and seek multiple indicators to confirm or validate their findings. However, it is also important to remember that current research suggests that interviews and other types of self-reported strategies can provide both reliable and valid information that is difficult, perhaps impossible, to glean otherwise (Ericsson & Simon, 1980; Lipson, Irwin, & Poth, 1986).

Interviews can also have another advantage. Since they require students to engage in some degree of self-assessment, such discussions can send the message to students that we are genuinely interested in establishing a collaborative working relationship—that we are interested in what *they* think and know. In addition, interviews send a message early in the assessment-instruction process that students are expected to take some responsibility for their own learning. Indrisano (1982) describes an interview used at Boston University that is designed to promote this type of mutually helpful working relationship, which begins with the interviewer saying:

> Today we'll try to discover more about you and the ways you learn. We'll need two kinds of experts, one expert on learning and one expert on you. I've studied about learning and have taught many people, so I could be called an expert on learning. You've been making discoveries about yourself all your life while you've been living there inside you. If we work together we will have the information we need to help you. I'll begin by asking a few questions. (p. 13)

Following this introduction, the examiner asks five general questions:

1. What do you do very well?
2. What is it that you do not do well?
3. How have you learned to do what you can do well?
4. What does not work so well?
5. If you were to give expert advice about you and the ways you learn best, what would you say? (If further prompting is needed, Indrisano suggests asking, "What would you like your teachers to know about you and the ways you like to learn?" Or, "How could they help you more?")

This type of initial interview sets the tone for a mutually supportive working relationship.

Interviewing, like other informal assessment tools, requires a knowledgeable and skilled professional eye. It is important for teachers and specialists to structure interviews and to try to gather information in systematic ways, recording data in a consistent manner. Structured procedures, including tape recording, can increase the reliability of interview information and ensure that teachers interpret thoughtfully the results of such assessments.

Tools and Strategies for Student Interviewing

Student interviews can be best used to gather information about the reader's knowledge about reading, and his or her motivation and attitudes toward reading. The other areas of information to be gathered described in Chapter 1—prior knowledge and application of reading skills—are best evaluated at other times and/or through other means. Prior content-related knowledge is more appropriately evaluated in the context of the ability to comprehend a specific text, whereas the application of reading skills is better evaluated through observation (which is discussed subsequently in this chapter), or through a variety of formal and informal performance measures (Chapters 5–7).

Knowledge About Reading

Current research shows that measures of reading knowledge are strongly related to reading comprehension skill (Paris, Cross, & Lipson, 1984; Paris & Jacobs, 1984; Paris & Myers, 1981). What this means is that interviews offer considerable promise as a method of assessment. As we have noted, interviews can provide us with rich information about students' knowledge of the goals of reading, the processes and skills involved in skilled reading, and their appraisal of their own reading abilities. Consider the following responses to the question, "Do you have trouble with reading?":

> *Jonathon, age 10:* "I have to tell you something. I'm in the fourth grade, but I'm only using a third grade reader. That's not very good."
> *Michael, age 13:* "I must, my Mom's making me come here [the clinic]."
> *Jane, age 11:* "Yes, when I read, the stuff just seems to go out of my head."
> *Sara, age 7:* "Yes, I read too softly."

Embedded in these responses are theories about reading. In their daily interactions with teachers, parents, and print, students construct a vision of reading in general and their ability to perform in particular. When asked to talk about their knowledge of reading and reflect on their abilities, children share with us their view of what it means to be competent. When student theories of reading are inaccurate, or their image of their own competence is askew, learning is difficult. Their theories of reading compete for attention and can make them resistant to learning more efficient and effective reading strategies (see Johnston, 1985b, for several powerful case studies of adults whose concepts of reading have interfered with acquisition of reading skill). In the quotations above, note that both Michael and Jonathon, estimate their ability only in terms of external factors. Sara, on the other hand, estimates reading competence using a criterion appropriate only for public performance. Such definitions can interfere with the ability to learn the important elements of skilled reading, because students often fail to understand the reason for instructional activities. Only Jane has provided a response that suggests she may grasp the nature and demands of real reading and has recognized a serious limitation in her own ability.

Students can reveal what they know about reading in response to several types of questions. It is helpful to examine students' knowledge and beliefs by asking questions about the *functions of reading*, the *goals and purposes of reading, self-appraisal and goal setting,* and the *skills and strategies* necessary for skilled performance.

Functions of reading. Questions designed to elicit students' awareness of the functions of reading might include What is reading? or Why do people read? (see Chapter 4 for additional suggestions). The following samples from two fourth-grade boys are suggestive of the range of responses to questions like these.

Charlie: Charlie could not offer any thoughts about "What is reading?" and he could initially think of no reasons why people read. When pressed, he finally offered that he supposed it was because "they want to be smart."

Jason: Jason offered the following to the question "What is reading?": "You get interested in a book you're reading and you try to imagine the things the book is about." As to why people read, Jason answered, "For enjoyment, something to do. They read books to do a project and they think it's fun."

Not surprisingly, these two boys perform differently during reading. Although both have been classified as "poor readers," their problems are quite different, and these first responses in an interview setting provided important information that was pursued in later sessions.

Goals and purposes of reading. Several researchers report responses from children who possess mistaken notions about the goals of skilled reading (Paris & Jacobs, 1984; Wixson, Bosky, Yochum, & Alvermann, 1984). It appears that many children believe that the goal of reading is flawless word calling or that effective reading is equivalent to verbatim memory of text. Such inappropriate assessments by the reader may lead to a corresponding application of inappropriate strategies (e.g., pay attention only to the graphic cues or read it over and over

FIGURE 3.4

Interview for Assessing Student Perceptions of Classroom Reading Tasks

Reading Comprehension Interview

Name: Date:
Classroom teacher: Reading level:
                                                         Grade:

Directions: Introduce the procedure by explaining that you are interested in finding out what children think about various reading activities. Tell the student that he or she will be asked questions about his/her reading, that there are no right or wrong answers, and that you are only interested in knowing what s/he thinks. Tell the student that if s/he does not know how to answer a question s/he should say so and you will go on to the next one.

General probes such as ''Can you tell me more about that?'' or ''Anything else?'' may be used. Keep in mind that the interview is an informal diagnostic measure and you should feel free to probe to elicit useful information.

1. What hobbies or interests do you have that you like to read about?
2. a. How often do you read in school?
   b. How often do you read at home?
3. What school subjects do you like to read about?

Introduce reading and social studies books.

Directions: For this section use the child's classroom basal reader and a content area textbook (social studies, science, etc.). Place these texts in front of the student. Ask each question twice, once with reference to the basal reader and once with reference to the content area textbook. Randomly vary the order of presentation (basal, content). As each question is asked, open the appropriate text in front of the student to help provide a point of reference for the question.

4. a. What is the most important reason for reading this kind of material?
   b. Why does your teacher want you to read this book?
5. a. Who's the best reader you know in _____?
   b. What does he/she do that makes him/her such a good reader?
6. a. How good are *you* at reading this kind of material?
   b. How do you know?
7. What do you have to do to get a good grade in _____ in your class?
8. a. If the teacher told you to remember the information in this story/chapter, what would be the best way to do this?
   b. Have you ever tried _____?
9. a. If your teacher told you to find the answers to the questions in this book what would be the best way to do this? Why?
   b. Have you ever tried _____?
10. a. What is the hardest part about answering questions like the ones in this book?
    b. Does that make you do anything differently?

Introduce at least two comprehension worksheets.

Directions: Present the worksheets to the child and ask questions 11 and 12. Ask the child to complete portions of each worksheet. Then ask questions 13 and 14. Next, show the child a worksheet designed to simulate the work of another child. Then ask question 15.

11. Why would your teacher want you to do worksheets like these (for what purpose)?
12. What would your teacher say you must do to get a good mark on worksheets like these? (What does your teacher look for?)

FIGURE 3.4
(continued)

Ask the child to complete portions of at least two worksheets.

13. Did you do this one differently from the way you did that one? How or in what way?
14. Did you have to work harder on one of these worksheets than the other? (Does one make you think more?)

Present the simulated worksheet.

15. a. Look over this worksheet. If you were the teacher, what kind of mark would you give the worksheet? Why?
    b. If you were the teacher, what would you ask this person to do differently next time?

Summary Sheet

What does the child perceive as the goal or purpose of classroom reading activities? (see questions 4 and 11)
  Basal reader: Content textbook: Reading worksheets:
What criteria does the child use to evaluate his/her reading performance? (questions 5, 8, 7, 12, and 15)
  Basal reader: Content textbook: Reading worksheets:
What strategies does the child indicate s/he uses when engaging in different comprehension activities? (questions 8, 9, 10, 13, and 14)
  Remembering information
    Basal reader: Content textbook:
  Answering questions
    Basal reader: Content textbook: Reading worksheets:

"Reading Comprehension Interview" from "An Interview for Assessing Students' Perceptions of Classroom Reading Tasks" by Karen K. Wixson, Anita B. Bosky, M. Nina Yochum, and Donna E. Alvermann. Reprinted with permission of Karen Wixson and the International Reading Association.

again). These beliefs may also provide insight into classroom practices that need to be explored more fully.

Wixson et al. (1984) have developed an interview specifically designed to evaluate readers' awareness of the goals and purposes of reading activities, the demands imposed on them by specific reading activities, and the strategies they have available to carry out specific reading activities (see Figure 3.4). This interview assesses students' knowledge of much more than the goals and purposes of reading. Because the interview is designed to be used with actual classroom materials (e.g., a basal reader, a content area text, or workbook pages), the children's descriptions of their own abilities and the strategies they might employ is specific to the reading contexts they encounter daily.

Such systematic probing can lead to a fairly detailed and differentiated profile of the child's understanding of the situations in which reading skills and strategies should be employed. For example, responses to the question "If your teacher told you to remember the information in this story (chapter), what would be the best way to do this?" asked in the context of several types of materials such as a basal reader, a trade book, and a content-area text, can provide information about a reader's level of strategy development and sensitivity to the varying demands that the same task can impose in different reading contexts. Some students provide responses such as "try hard" or "think about it" in both contexts, which may indicate a generalized lack of awareness regarding task demands and strategy usage. One should always remember to probe these types of general responses before assuming that they represent the extent of a student's strategy awareness.

Other students' responses suggest that they have developed context-specific strategies for dealing with a particular task. Within the context of a basal reader, responses such as "memorize the names of the characters," or "think about the exciting action parts" suggest an awareness of the properties of narrative text that may serve as cues for remembering. Similarly, responses in the context of a content text such as "take notes and study," "write out the questions," "have someone quiz you," and "break it up into small parts and memorize it," suggest an awareness that remembering in this context requires a conscious effort on the part of the reader.

Self-appraisal and goal-setting.   As noted previously, it is often helpful to ask students to appraise their own reading abilities and to establish goals for their reading instructional work. The interview just described is, of course, an excellent place to begin. However, a student priority checklist (see Figure 3.5) can also be useful. Some students are unable to complete such checklists reliably and may need some assistance. In our experience, however, students are frequently very accurate in their appraisals of their difficulties and often select appropriate goals. In any event, these early interactions can set the stage for a level of reflection by both the teacher and the student, and for joint effort that can focus the assessment-instruction process.

Self-appraisal is particularly important when working with older students and adults. These individuals are likely to have fairly sophisticated abilities to reflect on their actions and skills. However, they may not have attempted this type of reflection before and self-appraisal may help them to start seeing their reading and study problems more clearly. The self-assessment form presented in Figure 3.6 can be used to help older individuals think about their reading and study needs. It should also help in planning the next steps of the assessment by suggesting which problems may be priorities. Given that the reading demands of this form are fairly heavy, the interviewer should assist adult readers with limited word recognition skills in completing the assessment.

Knowledge about reading skills and strategies.   Although students' knowledge of skills and strategies does not ensure their application, you can gather information about awareness through interviews. The Wixson et al. (1984) interview described previously is appropriate for gathering information about students' awareness of reading strategies and tasks. Lytle (1987) has also developed a scripted interview. This interview is particularly effective with somewhat older students, since it elicits personal reflections on learning experiences as well as more specific reading knowledge, melding the critical components of skill and attitude (see Figure 3.7).

FIGURE 3.5
Student Priorities Checklist

I. 1. I need specific help with   or   2. I need specific help with

A. _____ The letters of the alphabet	A. _____ Short words
B. _____ The sounds for the letters of the alphabet	B. _____ Long words
C. _____ Meanings of words	C. _____ Sounds of each letter
D. _____ Remembering what I hear	D. _____ Sounds of letters together
E. _____ Understanding what I hear	E. _____ Reading faster
F. _____ Writing my name	F. _____ Meanings of words
G. _____ Reading street signs	G. _____ Understanding what I read
H. _____ Using the telephone book	H. _____ Remembering what I read
I. _____ Reading directions	I. _____ Remembering what I hear
J. _____ Reading words on food packages	J. _____ Spelling
K. _____ Reading menus	K. _____ Handwriting
L. _____ Reading the *TV Guide*	L. _____ How to study

II. I want to study material connected with
A. The courses I am taking in _____
B. My job such as a (manual, directories, directions) _____
C. My practical needs such as (forms, maps, schedules) _____
D. My hobby _____

III. I like to read about _____
I like to read

_____ Newspapers	Parts	_____
_____ Magazines	Kinds	_____
_____ Short stories	Types	_____
_____ Fiction	Types	_____
_____ Nonfiction	Topics	_____
_____ Comics	Kinds	_____
_____ Other		

I hope I can be helped to _____

IV. I prefer to work

_____ In a small group with a tutor
_____ With another student
_____ Individually with a tutor

"Student Priorities," pp. 19, 21–22, reprinted with permission of Macmillan Publishing Company from *Bader Reading and Language Inventory* by Lois A. Bader. Copyright © 1983 by Lois A. Bader.

FIGURE 3.6
The Mature Reader: A Self-assessment

Purpose of Self-assessment

Few of us can claim honestly to be mature readers in *all* aspects. It is actually possible to spend an entire lifetime refining our reading/thinking/study skills. Attitude about these matters is an important determinant to successful mature reading. The following activities, then, have two main purposes: (1) to give you the opportunity to assess for yourself your specific areas of strengths and weaknesses; and (2) to introduce you to a sampling of the variety and scope of reading/thinking/study skills to be explored in this text. These exercises should be taken objectively, and any sharing of results in class should be optional.

The following activity is a form of *advance organizer* in that it includes categories of questions representing areas of reading and study skills deemed appropriate for a mature reader. Since *no one* is an ideal reader, you should expect to find some areas that are not as strong as others. Again this survey should be considered private information, with sharing on a voluntary basis.

Quick Survey for Adult Readers: How mature a reader are you?

Directions: Note the organization of this survey. The left-hand side indicates the terminology in the field of reading to which this activity refers; the middle column asks you a question about how you think you function in reading with respect to this category; and a third column is provided for you to write a response to that question. Obviously, this preassessment presupposes no preparation for any given set of answers. Please respond rapidly to the questions. These may be referred to in later class sessions.

Category	Question	Response
1. Motivation	1. List two books you have read lately (*not* work-required or study-related), for the pure pleasure, inspiration, or general expansion of your knowledge of the world.	
2. Interests/ Attitudes	2. If you have the choice between reading a story or watching it on television, which would you choose most often?	
	3. How much time each day do you put aside for recreational or pleasure reading?	
3. Variety of Interests	4. Put a "+" by all those read regularly, a "0" by those read occasionally, and a "−" by those read rarely.	

Fiction
1. Romance _____
2. Adventure _____
3. Mystery _____
4. Historical _____
5. Poetry _____
6. Other _____

Nonfiction
7. Autobiography _____
8. Biography _____
9. Political _____
10. Historical _____
11. Other (specify) _____
_____

Newspapers
12. Sports _____
13. Front page _____
14. Editorial _____
15. Financial _____
16. Other _____

Magazines
17. Women's/Men's _____
18. News _____
19. Literary _____
20. Sports _____
21. Other _____

5. Looking over the above list, would you say that you read widely with a broad range of interests? Circle one:

Very much so　　　　　　Somewhat
Not as much as I should　　Not at all　　I'm not sure

FIGURE 3.6 *(continued)*

Category	Question	Response
4. Vocabulary	6. Describe your system for building up vocabulary. If you have none, leave this blank.	

7. List three new words that you have encountered through reading in the past three months.
   1. _____ 2. _____ 3. _____

8. Circle these strategies you use for identifying unfamiliar words while reading.
   configuration   phonics   context
   dictionary   structural analysis   other

9. List two technical terms you have learned recently and give exact definitions.
   1. _____
   2. _____

5. Syntax

10. Write the meaning of the italicized nonsense words in the following context:
    a. Jerry was *glongering* the data. _____
    b. The man *galurned* the *troper*. _____ _____

6. Rate Adaptability

11. At what rate do you read the following?
    a. very rapid   b. rapid   c. average   d. slow
    1. Novels   _____   4. Magazines   _____
    2. Newspapers   _____   5. Textbooks   _____
    3. Poetry   _____   6. Other   _____

12. Can you skim a text chapter in three minutes and recite the main ideas? (Yes/No/Maybe/Don't Know)
    Do you read everything at the same rate? (Yes/No/Maybe/Don't Know)

7. Getting the Gist of the Topic (literal comprehension)

13. How easy is it for you to:

	Very Easy	Somewhat Easy	Difficult

    a. Spot the topic sentence in a paragraph?
    b. Read to follow directions?
    c. Identify a pattern or a sequence of ideas?
    d. Relate supporting details to main ideas?

8. Thinking About What You Read

14. How easy is it for you to:
    a. Spot cause and effect?
    b. See comparison and contast?
    c. Identify the mood, time, and place?

FIGURE 3.6 (continued)

Category	Question	Response

9. Critical/ Creative Comprehension

15. How easy is it for you to:
    a. Use what you have learned in new situations?
    b. Combine concepts into new and innovative ideas?
    c. Make judgments about your reading while stating your own criteria for judgment?

10. Study Skills

16. List strategies you use for mastering study reading.
    1. _____   2. _____
    3. _____   4. _____

	Very Well	Average	Not Well at All	Don't Know

17. How well do you interpret graphics?
18. How efficient are you in your use of the library to locate "hard to find" materials?
19. How easily do you identify key points in a lecture from your notes after several months?
20. How well do you remember material over a period of time?

11. Self-assessment

Now that you have finished this "survey," look back over your responses and identify those categories that you believe need immediate improvement. Set a few goals for yourself for improving at least two or three of these categories by the end of the term. Write here the areas you have selected (e.g., vocabulary):

1. _____
2. _____
3. _____

At the end of the term look back through this self-assessment to reevaluate yourself in terms of how much change, growth, or enjoyment there has been.

I have changed in the area of _____

I have grown most in _____

I enjoy much more than I did _____

Workshop Activity 1.1, pp. 12–16 from Marian J. Tonjes and Miles V. Zintz, *Teaching Reading, Thinking, and Study Skills in Content Classrooms,* 2nd Ed. Copyright © 1987 Wm. C. Brown Publishers, Dubuque, Iowa. All Rights Reserved. Reprinted by permission.

FIGURE 3.7
Lytle's
Scripted
Metacognitive
Interview

Sample Scripted Interview

1. How would you describe yourself as a reader?
   If you wanted to describe what kind of reader you are to someone, can you think of any words that you might use?
2. How would you describe yourself as a writer?
3. What are some of your earliest memories of learning how to read? Start at home, if you did any reading at home, and continue to when you first began in school, up to the present, what are your memories of reading?
4. Do you remember what people said about you as a reader? How did they describe you when you were young, up to the present?
5. What are your earliest memories of learning how to write?
6. What do you remember that was said about you as a writer, from the time that you first began to write, up to the present?
7. Think of someone who you know, who is a good reader. How do you know that person is a good reader? What would be the best way for a teacher to find out what kind of reader that person is?
8. Now think of someone who is a good writer. How do you know that person is a good writer? What would the best way be for a teacher to find out what kind of writer that person is?
9. Do you read in different ways for different subjects? How do you read differently? How did you learn to read different kinds of texts in different ways?
10. If two people read the same book, would they get the same meaning? How would you explain the difference?
11. When you write a story, how do you put it together? What do you say to yourself?
12. Can you think of a time when you were struggling with something that you were reading? What did you do to try to understand it? How did you learn to do that?
13. Do you talk to anyone about your reading and writing?
14. Have you learned anything about yourself and your reading and writing through our discussion? Have you ever talked about reading and writing in this way with your teachers? What would be important for teachers to know about your reading and writing?

Attitudes and Motivation

Teachers have long recognized that students differ in their attitudes and motivation toward reading. That poor readers are less motivated than good readers is hardly surprising. However, we may not realize the depth of these feelings. Juel (1988) reported on the results of a longitudinal study in which readers were periodically asked to choose preferred activities, with reading listed as one of the choices. One poor reader spontaneously offered the comment, "I'd rather clean scum off the bathtub than read!"

We can learn a great deal by asking students about their reading-related experiences, interests, habits, and attitudes. The following questions suggest some areas where students may provide more focused information.

- Do you read? What? For what reason?
- What are some titles of books that you've enjoyed?
- Have you ever learned anything just because you read about it?
- Have you ever had a teacher who made reading fun and exciting? Tell me about her/him.

FIGURE 3.8
Interest Inventory

Student _____   Grade _____

1. Of all the things you do after school or in the summer, which do you like to do best?
2. Do you have any hobbies? Collections?
3. Do you like to read/do math? Why/why not?
4. What's the easiest thing about reading/math for you?
5. What's the hardest thing about reading/math?
6. What are some titles of books you've enjoyed?/What are some types of math problems you've enjoyed?
7. Who is the best reader/mathematician you know? What does s/he do that makes her/him such a good reader/mathematician?
8. Have you ever had a teacher who made reading/math fun and exciting? Tell me about her/him.
9. What are some of the reasons people read/do math?

- Have you had any experiences that have made you want to read about something?
- Do your parents (or someone else) read to you? How often?
- Do you have a library card? Books? Magazines?
- What kind of help do you think you need with reading?
- How long do you think it will take for you to read as well as you want or need to read?

These initial interviews are most effective when we listen carefully, clarify when needed, and assume a nonjudgmental attitude.

An interest inventory (see Figure 3.8) can also help us examine a student's reading background in the context of his or her overall interests and motivations. In addition, an interest inventory often provides information that can be used later in the selection and design of materials and activities for subsequent assessment and instruction. Finally, it is also an index of the degree to which experiences and personal preference have united to develop a unique and individual view of reading.

Interviews can also provide insights into reader motivations and attributions for success and failure. For example, Joey, age 9 and repeating the third grade, was recently referred to one of the authors' clinics. The results from interest inventories and unfinished sentence forms indicated that Joey did not read and would rather do almost anything else than read. As you read the following excerpt from an initial interview, think about what Joey is saying:

Interviewer: "How do you think you do as a reader?"
Joey: "I'd feel good about reading if I could learn how to read."
Interviewer: "What do you think the problem is?"
Joey: "I don't know. Something inside me stops me when I try to read. I can't spell either."
Interviewer: "What do you enjoy reading?"
Joey: "Nothing. I'm embarrassed 'cause I can't read."

Interviewer: "What do you think might help you to become a better reader?"
Joey: "I don't really know."

Joey is clearly not motivated to read at this point. It would be easy to attribute his reading problem to lack of motivation. During this portion of the interview, however, Joey revealed a much more complex picture of his underlying motivations and attitudes. He appears to be suggesting that his lack of motivation for reading grows from his awareness that he cannot do it. What is especially troubling is the fact that he appears to doubt that he will ever be able to read well.

Over time, feelings such as those expressed by Joey may very well develop into the generalized pattern of learned helplessness (Dweck, 1975) described in Chapter 1. Importantly, the information gleaned through interviews can help teachers to understand the potentially conflicting goals of disabled readers. As Johnston (1985b) so powerfully documents, these readers may want to learn to read, or learn to read better, but other goals may inhibit their progress. Many disabled readers experience high anxiety about the task; many, like Joey, suspect that they cannot succeed in any event; and many may not want to admit to such "failure."

Because discussions of motivation, attributions, and interest can be emotionally charged, we must proceed cautiously. Responses to interview questions such as those posed to Joey can best be interpreted in combination with other sources of information. Remember, it is important to have multiple indicators to confirm and validate the information obtained through interviews. As we are just getting started in the process, the value of these initial interviews lies in their ability to suggest hypotheses. These hypotheses can help to inform the evaluation process and may suggest directions that otherwise might never have been uncovered.

Understanding Observation

Although much information can be obtained through talk and testing, no other single tool can provide such in-depth information about the learner's actual use and application of knowledge and skill as observation. No other tool can demonstrate so clearly whether the reader is both skilled and *motivated.* Observation, in the hands of an experienced evaluator, is one of the most powerful assessment tools a teacher/clinician can possess.

Information about virtually every component of reading can be collected using observation. We have provided in-depth discussions of how to observe specific components in other portions of the book (e.g., observing oral reading miscues in Chapter 5; observing study skills and comprehension ability in Chapter 7; observing written language in Chapter 7; and observation tools for evaluating and assessing classroom interactions in Section III). In this section, we limit our discussion to general observational guidelines and try to capture the power of this tool as a rich source of information about the learner. The observational techniques described in this Getting Started step of assessment-instruction may save many hours of work later on.

As with all informal tools, critics charge that the information gathered is limited because it may not be reliable. Reliability (see Chapter 6) deals with the question of consistency. When we say that a measure is reliable, we mean that students will perform roughly the same on that measure tomorrow as they did today. Reliability ". . . depends, for all practical purposes, on the adequacy of the behavior sample on which the score is based, which, in turn, depends on the stability of the behavior being measured. Our experience indicates that a score based on a single visit to a classroom seldom has adequate reliability . . . Since reliability is primarily a function of the adequacy of the sample of behavior observed, reliabilities can be raised by increasing the number of visits" (Medley, 1985, p. 101).

When reliability is clarified in this way, it can be seen that the observations of classroom teachers may be exceptionally reliable, since teachers have many opportunities to observe student behavior. Their estimates of student strengths and weaknesses can be based on many observations of the same event(s). In truth, most criticisms of the reliability of observation as an assessment tool are really questioning something quite different. Most critics are really questioning the observers' (teachers') objectivity.

> Like everyone else, teachers tend to see things from their own personal perspectives. Some teachers conclude that children are making satisfactory progress when they appear to be busy and attentive. Some teachers are prone to notice certain kinds of behavior and block out other kinds. Some only pay close attention to whatever disrupts classroom routine. Others are more concerned with symptoms of possible unhappiness. . . . (Almy & Genishi, 1979, p. 7)

Teachers must be aware that their observations are subject to personal bias. In order to increase the reliability of observational data, teachers must continuously question the accuracy of their information. This is best accomplished by determining exactly what will be observed. Jaggar (1985) suggests that teachers decide what they will be attending to before observing. In addition, she suggests that they plan how, when, and where to observe. As Medley (1985) notes, the objectivity of observations depends largely on how carefully the observation categories have been defined. If these observation categories are important and well-defined, then observation accuracy will increase.

Perhaps the greatest strength of observation as an assessment tool is that students' performance and behavior can be evaluated in real settings as they are actually performing target tasks. This means that observational data are potentially valid. To ask whether a test is valid is to ask whether students are being evaluated in ways that actually parallel the skill or ability of interest (see Chapter 6). Many teachers question the validity of standardized tests because they feel that students are being evaluated on tasks that are not like real reading tasks. Observation, of course, should normally avoid this problem. However, using observation as an evaluative tool does not ensure validity. Like all assessment instruments, its validity is dependent on how carefully the behaviors to be assessed have been selected. The validity of observation, then, is related to what is worth noticing. In reading, this means looking for behaviors that involve children engaged in a variety of reading activities under a variety of reading conditions—engaged in independent seatwork, sustained silent reading, cooperative work projects, teacher-guided lessons, and so forth.

Teachers can realize the potential value of observation in their assessments by making careful observations of important targeted behaviors over time. Because getting started sometimes includes gathering enough information to decide if there is a problem, observation can be especially useful. The following guidelines may prove helpful:

1. Make clear distinctions between the observations and the interpretations of events (although ultimately both are important).
2. When appropriate, take down exact words and behaviors including the type of body language exhibited by the student(s) involved.
3. Make an attempt to interpret what was observed from the student's point of view (or in other words, ask *Why?*). (Irwin & Bushnell, 1980, p. 64)

Skilled teachers look not only for evidence that is reliable and valid, but they also ask that evidence be *sufficient* (Almy & Genishi, 1979). This means that conclusions should not be drawn from one or even two instances of a particular behavior. Instead, when using observation, we are looking for patterns of performance.

Patterns emerge when the same (or similar) behaviors are observed repeatedly over time. Alternatively, patterns can emerge that reveal the circumstances that influence reading. You can see how the student performs *in interaction* with various texts and contexts (e.g., subject area texts, children's magazines, library research, reading groups, and so on), watching for variability or stability. In this way, it is possible to determine what students can and will do under different conditions.

In planning observations, knowledge of the reading process and learning in general ensures that the information gathered is valid and reliable. Observation can be used as a tool in almost any phase of the assessment-instruction process. For example, observation can be used to get to know individual children, evaluate groups, assess progress, appraise teaching techniques, and identify problems (Almy & Genishi, 1979). Because we are concerned in this chapter only with getting started, this section focuses on techniques for getting to know individual children and identifying problems.

Tools and Strategies for Observing

Observation can provide some information about students' knowledge about reading, but is best used to gather information about their application of reading knowledge and skill, and their attitudes and motivation toward reading. As indicated previously, prior content-related knowledge is more appropriately evaluated in the context of the ability to comprehend a specific text and is discussed in some detail in Chapter 7.

Before presenting various suggestions for observation, we would like to note that some procedures focus on observing the reader while others focus on observing the reader in the context of instruction. Not all observational schemes are equally useful for both purposes. Sometimes we want general information about the reader that is not context specific, and sometimes we want to see how the reader performs in a specific context. As we have already noted, we return to each of these topics repeatedly throughout the text.

The forms and ideas presented here are examples of the ways in which observations can be structured so that the information gathering is fairly objective. We share the perspective of Jaggar (1985): "With increased skill and confidence, teachers can devise their own strategies and techniques. The important thing is that teachers think of observation as a form of problem solving; it is a selective search for knowledge to guide instruction" (Jaggar, p. 6). The observer's knowledge base is extraordinarily important in the identification of the behaviors to be observed. Observing in a busy classroom may require fairly structured observations. Checksheets and anecdotal records of various types can be extremely helpful—but only if the behaviors being observed are important.

Knowledge About Reading

As we have already noted, observation is simply not the best way to gather information about *knowledge*. We can make inferences about students' knowledge from watching them, but we cannot be sure that students' actions reflect all the knowledge they possess. They may know what and how to do many things, but choose not to use this knowledge. It is really only when we compare knowledge information with application information that a more complete picture emerges.

Making educated guesses or inferences about students' knowledge from their observed behavior is not all bad, however. By watching young children, we can make some hypotheses about what they know about reading and about their world in general. For example, children who regularly subvocalize during silent reading time may not know that reading is creating meaning in the head. Indeed, they may be entertaining a view of reading such as: "Reading is saying all the words." Another example might be that some children, no matter what the reading task, start reading at the beginning of the text and read to the end. If they have been asked to read for total memory, this may be an appropriate strategy. However, if they have been asked to scan for specific information, this behavior suggests that they may lack the knowledge required to execute the task. Samples of the types of behavior we might want to look for to inform us about our students' knowledge of reading are presented in Figure 3.9.

Unstructured observation may also be very helpful. This type of observation involves procedures such as making anecdotal records of what students say during different reading activities or during conversation, or keeping running records (see Chapter 7) of students' behavior during various portions of the day. When observations are conducted in this manner, it is difficult to know what will be important, and the insights often grow out of the observations. This is a particularly useful approach for students who are getting lost in the hustle and bustle of daily schedules. This is also a useful approach for those who are not the regular classroom teacher. Observations of the child functioning in the regular classroom can provide information that is not available in a one-to-one clinical setting.

FIGURE 3.9
An
Observation
Guide for
Reading
Knowledge

Observing Reading Knowledge

_____ Demonstrates flexibility in approach to reading tasks
_____ Handles different genre with ease
_____ Always seeks the same type of literature
_____ Reads about a range of topics
_____ Reads at different pace for different material
_____ Adapts reading strategies to task demands

_____ Subvocalizes during silent reading
_____ Can use books for recreation
_____ Can use books to find information
_____ Checks books out of the library
_____ Talks about books
_____ Uses literary references in informal ways (e.g., "When I'm six, I'll fix Matthew.")

FIGURE 3.10
Reading Activity Observations

Date:		Setting:					
		Sara	Kelly	Jon	Marc	Shawn	Laura

1. Sustained interest in silent reading
2. Self-selection of books
3. Appropriate journal entry
4. Completed homework
5. Participation in book discussions
6. Sustained activity, independent work period
7. Read when directed to
8. Completed book-related activities
9. Completed library projects

Skill Application

As we get started, it is unlikely that we will make detailed observations of students' application of reading knowledge and skill. These are done as we get further into the assessment-instruction process. However, there are a number of general guidelines that might be used for observing students' application of reading skills and knowledge at this point in the process. Indeed, some of these are useful as a periodic check-up to make certain that we are not overlooking something that needs attention. Questions such as the following are worth asking about all students:

1. For what purposes does the student read—to accomplish classroom tasks, or for pleasure?
2. How does the student respond to different types of comprehension questions?
3. How would you characterize the student's ability to do the following: retell or summarize; make predictions; identify relations among important ideas; monitor and repair comprehension failures?
4. How does the student adjust his/her rate and strategy usages to meet the demands of different purposes, texts, and tasks?

The important thing to remember is that there must be a convenient and accurate way to record information. One of the authors used to wear a carpenter's apron with markers and pens in the pockets. Whenever she observed something of interest, she pulled out a card and jotted down the time, date, and student information. It should be easy to remember important events, but by the end of a busy day, we frequently have forgotten what we meant to remember. Alternatively, a checklist such as the one in Figure 3.10 may be generated to systematize observations of important classroom activities. Remember, we are trying to locate possible sources of difficulty for students and to establish patterns of behavior that can help generate instructional ideas. This can best be done using multiple sources of information.

Attitudes and Motivation

One of the simplest and most effective ways of finding out children's interests is to watch their daily behavior and listen to their conversations. The alert teacher can find many leads concerning possible reading interests by observing the children (Harris & Sipay, 1985, p. 576).

As we have already discussed, children's attitudes can have a significant and cumulative effect on their reading achievement. Often children do not like to read because they are not skilled in reading. However, it is also the case that skilled reading requires practice. Teachers and clinicians are obliged to help children find reading material that responds to their individual interests and that helps children to see the functional value of reading. Observation can assist in determining students' attitudes and motivation toward reading. The following are examples of the types of questions that can be used to guide these observations:

1. How does the student approach reading activities (e.g., active involvement or passive resistance)?
2. What types of reading activities does the student engage in during his/her spare time at school and at home?
3. Does the student persist at reading activities or give up easily?
4. What types of positive or negative comments does the student make about his/her reading? When?

Gathering information in response to these questions will not provide a solution to the reading problems. It can, however, indicate whether the student understands and appreciates the value of reading and is willing or able to use this knowledge to support the hard work of becoming a skilled reader.

FROM CLASSROOM TO CLINIC

There are a number of ways that the information in this chapter is likely to be used differently by classroom teachers than by clinical or resource personnel. Because classroom teachers have greater opportunity for ongoing data collection than do specialists, they will probably use the procedures described here for gathering background information, interviewing, and observing more informally. For example, classroom teachers are more likely to have access to the type of background information sought by the family and school information forms through personal contact with a student's family and through personal knowledge of their own classroom practices than are clinical personnel. Clinical personnel, on the other hand, are more likely to need to gather background information through the use of these types of forms in order to begin planning for further assessment.

Differences in ease of access to students on a daily basis also have implications for the reliability of the information that is gathered through the types of informal interview and observational procedures described in this chapter. Because classroom teachers have easier access to ongoing data collection, they are in an excellent position to collect enough samples of a behavior to allow greater reliability of the information gathered than are clinical or resource personnel who must rely on more limited samples of behavior.

Classroom teachers, however, are busy people with a multitude of responsibilities. It is often difficult, and sometimes impossible, to find the time to engage in the type of information gathering we have suggested here. Clinicians or specialists are no less busy, but may have greater opportunity to focus on an individual or a small number of students. This ability to focus on individual students permits in-depth assessments that may not be possible for classroom teachers. Resource personnel are also in a better position than classroom teachers to evaluate the relations between students' knowledge, skills, and attitudes, and the various settings they encounter. The resource professional has the potential for stepping back to obtain a bigger picture of the situation in ways that can produce exceptionally helpful insights.

The obvious solution to the problem of achieving both in-depth and ongoing evaluation is a strong collaborative working arrangement among classroom teachers and specialists or resource personnel. Classroom teachers can benefit from the assistance of specialists in obtaining more detailed information about students and how they perform in a variety of settings. Resource personnel can benefit from the assistance of classroom teachers in obtaining continuous assessments of students' knowledge, skills, and attitudes in various classroom contexts. This type of collaboration also allows teachers and specialists to coordinate their instructional efforts and to evaluate the extent to which students are able to transfer their knowledge and skills from one setting to another.

Despite the differences between classroom and clinical practices, there is no tool described in this chapter that is necessarily more appropriate for use in one type of setting than any other. All can be used profitably by all types of professionals, although some may need to be adapted for use with groups rather than individuals. Both classroom professionals and clinical resource personnel can make excellent use of background information, interview data, and observational records. Indeed, they will probably be missing some important information if they do not.

CHAPTER SUMMARY

The purpose of this chapter was to assist the reader by providing the knowledge and techniques necessary for getting started in the assessment-instruction process. We began with a set of guidelines that are important for the entire assessment-instruction process. These guidelines are designed to promote assessment that examines how individuals handle actual reading materials under conditions that simulate real reading and writing situations both in and out of the classroom. They are as follows:

- assess meaningful activities
- assessment should be unobtrusive
- assessment and purpose should match
- assessment should be systematic
- assessment should be continuous

In addition to these guidelines, it was suggested that records be kept in the form of a portfolio of relevant reading and writing materials (e.g., written responses to reading, reading logs, or work samples) to be used in planning instruction, evaluating progress, and communicating with parents and administrators.

The second major section of this chapter dealt with information about students' home and school background that it is important to obtain as we are getting started with assessment. The importance of knowing about a student's physical, cognitive, affective, and sociocultural background as a means of understanding difficulties with reading and writing was discussed. In addition, tools and strategies such as interviews and informational forms that can be used to gather information about a student's home and school background were described.

The third major section of this chapter focused on the student as a source of information about his or her own reading problems. Specific interviewing and observational techniques were described for the purpose of evaluating various aspects of students' knowledge about reading, and their attitudes and motivation toward reading and writing activities.

The chapter concluded with a discussion of the differences between the classroom and clinic in the application of the knowledge and techniques provided in the previous sections. This section ends with a call for increased cooperation between classroom teachers and specialists or resource personnel in the implementation of the assessment-instruction process.

CHAPTER 4

The Foundations
of Literacy

INTRODUCTION

Now that we have gotten started in the assessment-instruction process, we need to consider how to evaluate the reader in greater depth. To do this, it is important to understand the competencies that underlie learning to read and write. An understanding of the foundations of literacy is essential to the development of an appropriate program of assessment and instruction. Research by Clay, Ferreiro, Sulzby, Mason, and others is used to illustrate the emergent competence of young children in the areas of reading/language arts and the critical importance of these competencies to initial reading success. Research in the area of emergent literacy provides teachers and clinicians with information that can be used to develop more effective assessments and instructional programs than have been possible with previous conceptualizations of reading readiness. A clarification of these issues and their implications for assessment are the focus of this chapter.

Chapter Overview

This chapter is divided into three major sections. The first section traces the history of traditional definitions of readiness that underlie both readiness assessment and instruction in today's schools, and introduces a more current conceptualization of readiness known as emergent literacy. The second section elaborates on two major areas of competence necessary for literacy learning derived from an emergent literacy perspective: language development, and literacy experiences, which include developing print awareness, understanding the forms and functions of print, analyzing print, and controlling reading and writing processes. The last major section of this chapter describes strategies and tools for assessing the previously identified elements of emergent literacy.

UNDERSTANDING READINESS

Educators continue to be divided about what causes children to be ready to learn how to read and write. Some argue that children simply grow into readiness, much the way a tree or plant develops. Others argue that readiness is either caused or facilitated by the environment. Most recently, current research has led to a reconceptualization of readiness as *emergent literacy*, or the gradual emergence of written literacy skills in the context of oral language development. Each of these views is described briefly, followed by a short discussion of reading readiness instruction in today's schools.

A Developmental View of Readiness

Reading readiness is most frequently discussed from a developmental perspective. Teachers have often been taught that readiness is an objectively measurable state of being that reflects *the* point when an individual is sufficiently mature in cognitive, affective, and psychomotor areas to be *able* to learn to read. Most educators attribute the developmental view of reading readiness to Gesell's writing during the 1920s (Teale & Sulzby, 1986). Indeed, Gesell described reading readiness as "neural ripening," and argued that "behaviors unfold automatically." At the center of a developmental view of readiness are two related ideas: children's learning is biologically determined; and there is an orderly and predetermined development of abilities.

Developmental views of readiness received additional momentum in 1931, when Morphett and Washburne published a study concluding that children were unlikely to succeed in reading before they had attained a mental age of 6.6 years. Many educators believed that this finding validated the concept of readiness as an organically determined phenomenon. The combination of neural ripening theories of development and the assertion of a set mental age for reading readiness was taken as an instructional mandate for inaction by educators. The implications for educational practice were straightforward—instruction should be withheld until the child is "ready" (Teale & Sulzby, 1986).

Developmental views of reading readiness continue to exert strong influence today, which is evident in both assessment and instruction practices for preschool- and kindergarten-age children. For example, in many parts of the United States, Gesell's developmental screening tests are still used to make decisions about students' readiness for entry into kindergarten. In addition, debates about the appropriate age for entry into kindergarten programs continue. Mental age, perceptual-motor development, social maturity, and general physical development are all considered critical aspects of reading readiness.

Certainly, there is both intuitive and empirical evidence to indicate that children must arrive at some developmental milestones before they are able to cope with print. For example, infants clearly do not have sufficiently well-developed cognitive systems to learn to read in any normal sense of the word. It is equally obvious that language competence is closely related to the ability to learn to read. However, neither the available empirical evidence nor the anecdotal accounts of teachers and parents support an account of beginning reading development that is orderly and unchanging. In addition, it is not clear which, if any, of these traditional abilities are prerequisite to others. Finally, the available evidence suggests that development, and therefore readiness for school tasks, is influenced by both experience and instruction.

An Experiential View of Readiness

Over the past fifty years, there have always been those who questioned the rigid, linear notion of readiness as requiring certain prerequisite and maturationally controlled abilities. However, during the 1950s and 1960s, more and more educators began to move toward a notion of readiness as a product of experience. For example, Dechant (1970) wrote:

> There are both biological and environmental determinants of readiness for and achievement in reading. Among the more important factors are the child's intellectual,

physical, social, and emotional development, his general proficiency in language, and his sensory equipment. Success in reading also depends on the child's proficiency in auditory and visual discrimination. It is assured by a wide background of personal experience, by a genuine interest in reading, and by an adequate instructional program. (Dechant, 1970, p. 40)

Dechant, like others of this era (e.g., Tinker & McCullough, 1968), believed that instruction should be offered to develop readiness where there was none. This increased focus on teaching as a remedy for lack of readiness led to a wide array of training programs. With few exceptions, these programs were designed to train students in one or more subskill areas, these subskill weaknesses having been identified using one of the available readiness tests. Indeed, many of the subskills were related to abilities that had been tested on earlier developmental tests (e.g., perceptual motor ability, visual discrimination, and so on).

The development of training programs moved educators beyond the notion of simply waiting for children to become ready, excepting screening programs that restrict students' entrance into school. Training programs in readiness were, and remain, common features of beginning reading programs. The content of both the assessment instruments and the instructional procedures has been dictated by the notions of reading readiness we have just described. Two points are especially important to understand: tests of reading readiness typically result in profiles of subskill abilities; and the appropriate response to lack of readiness has been a curriculum designed to train children in these subskills, and to delay reading instruction until these subskills have been mastered.

It is equally important to understand that few of the early attempts at readiness training have resulted in better reading achievement. One of the reasons that so few of these earlier readiness programs affected reading achievement is that we now know that many of the readiness skills described in older reading textbooks and embedded in most commercial readiness programs are not necessary for learning to read. Knowledge of shapes and colors, for example, may indicate overall cognitive development, but this knowledge is not required for students to begin to learn to read (see Durkin, 1987; Shepard, 1986).

Similarly, many gross motor skills, once believed prerequisite for readiness, have proven unnecessary for learning to read. It is unwarranted, for example, to withhold reading instruction for a child who cannot skip (Spache & Spache, 1986). Indeed, instructional programs aimed at developing prerequisite skills listed in older textbooks, such as visual-motor integration, have not enhanced reading achievement. As a general rule, the only perceptual-motor training programs that have demonstrated any level of success in promoting reading achievement are those that move rapidly to involve children with letters and words, preferably in a meaningful context (see Klesius, 1972; H. Robinson, 1972).

Older notions of readiness have been challenged further by the findings of current research discussed in the next sections. Given these findings, it is probably more sensible to view reading readiness as a continuum, rather than a specific point in development. Such a view is consistent with the perspective on readiness known as emergent literacy.

Readiness as Emergent Literacy

From an emergent literacy perspective, children are acquiring abilities, skills, and knowledge at home during their early years that are themselves literate behaviors. As Teale and Sulzby (1986) assert, "the first years of the child's life represent a period when legitimate reading and writing development are taking place. These behaviors and knowledges are not *pre-* anything, as the term *pre-reading* suggests" (p. xix). In addition, we know that children seem to acquire some of the readiness skills *in the process of learning to read* (Ehri, 1979). That is, they develop knowledge and skill as they receive reading instruction or engage in reading and writing tasks. From an emergent perspective, reading readiness is reconceptualized as the process of becoming literate as opposed to a series of discrete, specifiable skills that must be developed before learning how to read.

An emergent perspective also focuses our attention on all aspects of literacy, not just reading. Children cannot become ready to read in the absence of competence in a wide array of language related and cognitive areas. The most recent research findings suggest that children are developing competence simultaneously in all aspects of literate behavior: reading, writing, listening, and speaking. Current research also indicates that there are many abilities that provide the underpinnings for literacy learning that have been ignored in the past (Lomax & McGee, 1987). Among these are: competence as a language user, knowledge about story structure, books, print, and facility with the language of instruction.

Finally, an emergent perspective does not deny the developmental nature of literacy learning, but places it in a framework that identifies children's early years as a period of high activity rather than passive waiting for readiness to unfold. Children, even very young children, are viewed increasingly as intentional learners—as strategic problem solvers. Such a view of the learner results in a conceptualization of reading as a special case of more generalized processes, and the acquisition of reading skills and strategies as a continuation of socio- and psycho-linguistic development.

> Learning to read involves the acquisition of a few skills specific to reading and the use of many other abilities that are common to a variety of cognitive processes. Previously acquired linguistic and conceptual knowledge relevant for understanding oral language and interpreting visual experience is also necessary for reading. (Juola, Schadler, Chabot, McCaughey, & Wait, 1979, p. 91)

We will turn our attention shortly to a discussion of the knowledge and skills that provide the foundation for literacy and to a description of the behaviors and abilities that are emerging as young children become literate. But first, it is important to consider the state of readiness instruction in today's classrooms.

Readiness Instruction Today

Most educators persist in talking about readiness as though they were describing a developmental phenomenon. However, the reality in most schools is that teachers and administrators are actually using the term in quite a different way. When teachers say that a particular student is not ready to learn to read, they do not usually mean that the student is incapable of learning to read by some means that we might devise. Rather, they usually mean that the student is not ready to take advantage of the reading instruction that will be offered.

Searfoss and Readence (1985) make a useful distinction between "basic readiness" skills and "specific readiness" skills. They argue that all students need some prerequisites before they can learn to read effectively. For example, it is difficult to conceive of a child learning to read who had not yet mastered the rudiments of language or acquired some understanding of the structure of stories. Similarly, children who have no sense of the functions of print are unlikely to learn to read, although they may acquire certain taught skills. These *basic prerequisites* are discussed in depth in the next section of the chapter.

Specific prerequisites, on the other hand, are those skills and abilities that are necessary for learning to read *in particular programs.* For example, the ability to discriminate individual sounds or phonemes within words and name the corresponding letters or graphemes is a specific prerequisite. Reading programs that place a heavy emphasis on phonic analysis require students to be able to do this. Students who cannot name letters and isolate phonemes will not be ready for the instruction in these programs. In contrast, beginning reading programs with an emphasis on language experiences, reading dictated stories, and acquiring a store of sight vocabulary do not require this ability. Students may learn to do these things as they begin to learn to read. Students with limited language competence/experiential background and/or poor visual memory, however, might be judged not ready for these types of programs.

Kindergarten and first-grade programs typically offer only one type of reading instruction. It is possible, then, for students to be judged ready for reading in one school system and not ready in another. Thus, as Durkin notes (1978; 1987), children have to adapt to the program rather than the other way around.

> The question of a child's readiness for reading has a *two*-fold focus: (a) his capacity in relation to (b) the instruction that will be available. . . . Ideally, of course, the educator's question would be: Given this child's particular abilities, what type of instruction can we offer that will make use of them and thus allow the child to experience success? (Durkin, 1978, pp. 162–163)

Although there is increasing variability in the types of beginning reading programs used today, the traditional skills-based programs are still the predominant form of beginning reading instruction in the United States. Teale and Sulzby (1986) indicate that most of the reading readiness programs in use today assume the following:

1. Instruction in reading can only begin efficiently when children have mastered a set of basic skills prerequisite to reading. The most important skills predict subsequent achievement most strongly.
2. The area of instructional concern is reading. It is implied that composing and other aspects of writing (except for letter formation—or handwriting) should be delayed until children learn to read.

3. Sequenced mastery of skills forms the basis of reading as a subject to be taught; instruction focuses almost exclusively on the formal aspects of reading and generally ignores the functional uses of reading.
4. What went on before formal instruction is irrelevant, so long as sufficient teaching and practice presented in a logical sequence are provided when instruction begins.
5. Children all pass through a scope and sequence of readiness and reading skills, and their progress up this hierarchy should be carefully monitored by periodic formal testing. (p. xiii)

In summary, it is probably misguided to think of reading readiness in terms of the prerequisites for reading. The gradual emergence of reading makes it difficult, if not impossible, to identify specific prereading as opposed to emerging reading skills, and to determine which skills and abilities are best acquired prior to rather than during reading instruction. It is more reasonable to think in terms of facilitating abilities, since it is evident that students who can name letters, segment print, and discriminate visual symbols are apt to be able to take advantage of a wide range of learning programs. We prefer the term *emergent literacy* to reading readiness because it reflects more accurately the current state of our knowledge in this area (see Clay, 1966; Teale & Sulzby, 1986).

UNDERSTANDING EMERGENT LITERACY

In the sections that follow, we consider two important aspects of emergent literacy. First, we consider the nature of oral language development and how the acquisition of oral language competence prepares children for reading tasks. Second, we discuss the types of literacy experiences necessary for effective emergence into reading. Four interrelated experiences are identified and discussed: developing print awareness; understanding the forms and functions of print; analyzing print; and controlling reading and writing processes.

The issue of whether the various aspects of emergent literacy discussed here are "prerequisite" or "facilitating" is still unresolved. It appears that these abilities emerge more or less simultaneously and that none is mastered before children enter school. Even at age 7, children continue to refine their understanding and control of literacy tasks (Lomax & McGee, 1987). However, it is increasingly clear that each of these abilities affects the process of learning to read. Children with significant difficulties in any or all of these areas are much more likely to experience reading problems in school than those without problems in these areas (Juel, 1988).

Learning to Talk

In this section we describe why and how oral language acquisition is so important to subsequent success in reading. Learning to talk (Wells, 1986) is one of the first productive cognitive tasks confronting young humans.

There is much for children to learn: not just the words, but their pronunciation and the ways of combining them to express the relationships between the objects, attributes, and actions to which they refer. They also have to learn how the more subtle distinctions of intention are expressed—indirect and direct requests, questions of various kinds, and expression of different attitudes, such as sympathy, anger, apology, and so on—through different selections and orderings of words and structures and the use of different patterns of intonation and facial and bodily gestures. (Wells, 1986, p. 39)

The ways in which children accomplish this task can tell us a great deal about how humans learn to acquire cognitive competence in general. Studying language acquisition is particularly productive for reading, because success in learning to read is highly correlated with oral language competence. This relationship probably exists for a number of reasons. First, reading is a language-based, cognitive task. Second, both written language and spoken language are communicative processes. That is, both reading and talk are used to exchange ideas, request information, demand and elicit help, share feelings, and so forth. Finally, both oral language communication and reading are interactive, taking place in a context that influences the active search for meaning. By studying how children learn language, we can gain tremendous insight into the cognitive structures and strategies they will employ in learning to read and write.

Obviously, we cannot provide a comprehensive discussion of the issues surrounding oral language acquisition in this book. However, several issues should be considered. First, a discussion of what children must learn about oral language can provide a great deal of information about what children must know in order to learn to read. Second, a discussion of how children learn language can inform us about how children acquire general cognitive competence. Finally, it is important to consider what language acquisition can tell us about how children learn and, therefore, how we might teach.

What Children Must Learn About Language

What does it mean to know or to learn a language? According to Lindfors (1980):

When you know a language, you know unconsciously, intuitively, the set of possible sounds in that language, the set of possible meanings in that language, and a finite set of abstract principles for relating these meanings and sounds. (p. 40)

These are the common features of all that are essential components of language learning.

One of the first tasks that confronts babies is to figure out that the auditory sounds of humans are meaningful. Although infants are typically surrounded by human talk, there is no reason to assume that they would automatically know that these sounds, in distinct combinations, had specific and special meanings.

The sounds of a language only provide the starting point, however. Children must learn how to express their intentions by using language. In order to accomplish this, they must figure out how to name the objects and ideas in their language. In addition, they must figure out the grammar of their language. This grammar is composed of the rules for mapping meaning onto words. The grammar typically dictates that various meaning relationships are described by particular word orders or syntactic structures (see Chapter 2).

It is important to understand that not all languages have the same rules for mapping meaning on strings of words. In most romance languages (e.g., Spanish), adjectives follow the noun they are describing, whereas in English these modifiers are placed before the noun. Children must learn what word order is dictated by their particular grammar, and the rules that tell them how to combine words.

Although knowledge of the grammar of a language enables children to produce words and to put those words together in ways that conform to the demands of the language, there are other important skills and abilities that are required of the competent oral language user. For example, at very early ages children come to recognize a range of *language functions*. Halliday (1975) has studied and categorized the functions of language. In Figure 4.1, these functions are coupled with examples from a young boy from the ages of 18 to 20 months.

Language is learned in order to express certain intentions and to perform certain functions. In addition, these intentions and purposes are executed in the context of social interaction. It is our knowledge of the language that allows us to translate the sounds speakers produce into a representation of the messages that they are trying to communicate. The end result of language learning is not simply mastering the language structures. Children master the forms of language in order to communicate. Mastery of vocabulary and word order results in nothing if the learner cannot use those forms for the purpose of producing and understanding thoughts, ideas, and feelings.

Thus, word and sentence level understanding must be derived from the context of the language event. Single words and sentences are hardly ever fully comprehensible without considering the contexts in which they are used. For example, the sentence "That's an ugly dress" could be: agreement, argument, simple comment, disagreement, criticism, complaint, or apology.

Researchers who study language have increasingly concluded that language acquisition is an interactive process (Genishi & Dyson, 1984). This has led to increased interest in and study of the rules for communication, or social conventions, of language that determine how we should speak to different individuals in different contexts. These conventions are part of what must be learned to become a competent language user. As will be seen in Chapter 9, the social conventions of language are an important determinant of school achievement. Mismatches between school conventions and the conventions that children have learned at home can lead to poor performance and wrong judgments about children's ability to learn in school.

How Language Is Learned

Most humans appear to move toward oral language competence through a series of more or less similar stages (see Figure 4.2). The presence of these developmental stages across cultural and linguistic boundaries provides strong evidence that

FIGURE 4.1
Functions of
Language

Language Function	Example
Instrumental language 　the "I want" function; language used 　to satisfy needs	"I wanna the cookie too." Or, reaching 　for toy another child has "Mine!"
Regulatory language 　the "do as I tell you" function; 　language for controlling others	"I do it myself."
Interactional language 　the "me and you" function; language 　for interacting with others	"What you doing?" [Said over and over 　to elicit response from adult]
Personal language 　the "here I come" function; 　language for expressing feelings and 　personality	"I scared."
Imaginative language* 　the "let's pretend" function; 　language used to create own 　environment.	(Putting a construction worker's hardhat 　on his head): "Going to work. 　Bye-bye."
Heuristic language 　the "tell me why" function; language 　for exploring the environment	"Emma crying. What happened?"
Informative/representational language 　the "I've got something to tell you" 　function; language for communicating	"It's darking" (at the end of the day).

(*) As children get older, their use of language for imaginative play is very evident: "You pretend that you're sick and that's the hospital and I'll pretend I'm the mommy." (T's older sister, age 5).

Functions as described by Halliday (1975). *Learning How to Mean* (pp. 18–21). New York: Elsevier North Holland, Inc.

humans have some biological basis for language production. It appears that human babies have a biological predisposition toward learning language. However, it should also be noted that this predisposition is played out in environments where loving adults attribute meaning to their child's early language attempts (Wells, 1986). For this and other reasons, it is important to interpret so-called stage theories of development as general guidelines rather than rigid, unalterable stages.

Attention to meaning is a striking feature of early language development. From the beginning, young children's utterances reflect semantic intent. Their productions reflect an awareness that the functional purpose of language is to create and communicate meaning. This is most evident at the two-word utterance stage, when children seem capable of producing only two-word constructions. During this stage, researchers have observed what is termed *telegraphic* speech, so called because children leave out the words that are left out in telegrams and retain

FIGURE 4.2
Language
Acquisition
and
Development
Table

Age	General Language Characteristics
3 months	• The young child starts with all possible language sounds and gradually eliminates those sounds that are not used around him.
1 year	• Many children are speaking single words (e.g., "mama"). Infants use single words to express entire sentences. Complex meanings may underlie single words.
18 months	• Many children are using two or three word phrases (e.g., "see baby"). Children are developing their own language rule systems. Children may have a vocabulary of about 300 words.
2–3 years	• Children use such grammatical morphemes as plural suffix /s/, auxiliary verb "is," and past irregular. Simple and compound sentences are used. Understands tense and numerical concepts such as "many" and "few." A vocabulary of about 900 words is used.
3–4 years	• The verb past tense appears, but children may overgeneralize the "ed" and "s" markers. Negative transformation appears. Children understand numerical concepts such as "one," "two," and "three." Speech is becoming more complex, with more adjectives, adverbs, pronouns, and prepositions. Vocabulary is about 1500 words.
4–5 years	• Language is more abstract and most basic rules of language are mastered. Children produce grammatically correct sentences. Vocabularies include approximately 2500 words.
5–6 years	• Most children use complex sentences quite frequently. They use correct pronouns and verbs in the present and past tense. The average number of words per oral sentence is 6.8. It has been estimated that the child understands approximately 6,000 words.
6–7 years	• Children are speaking complex sentences that use adjectival clauses, and conditional clauses beginning with "if" are beginning to appear. Language is becoming more symbolic. Children begin to read and write and understand concepts of time and seasons. The average sentence length is 7.5 words.
7–8 years	• Children use relative pronouns as objects in subordinate adjectival clauses ("I have a cat which I feed every day"). Subordinate clauses beginning with "when," "if," and "because" appear frequently. The average number of words per oral sentence is 7.6.
8–10 years	• Children begin to relate concepts to general ideas through use of such connectors as "meanwhile" and "unless." The subordinating connector "although" is used correctly by 50 percent of the children. Present participle active and perfect participle appear. The average number of words in an oral sentence is 9.0
10–12 years	• Children use complex sentences with subordinate clauses of concession introduced by "nevertheless" and "in spite of." The auxiliary verbs "might," "could," and "should" appear frequently. Children have difficulties distinguishing among past, past perfect, and present perfect tenses of the verb. The average number of words in an oral sentence is now 9.5.

Reprinted with permission of Merrill, an imprint of Macmillan Publishing Company, from *The Effective Teaching of Language Arts* by Donna E. Norton, Copyright © 1980.

only those most essential to conveying meaning, for example, "baby ride," and "Mommy cookie."

Most parents would assert that they "taught their children to talk" and that children learn language largely through imitation. However, the available research evidence suggests otherwise. Children are not deliberately taught the language, and they don't learn to talk through imitation. Instead, it appears that children construct the grammar of their language through the internalization and genera- tion of rules. What the child learns is not a set of utterances, but a set of rules for processing utterances.

For example, young children frequently produce utterances such as these: "He *goed* to the store"; "It's *darking* outside"; or "I'm going to school today, *amn't I?*" These examples demonstrate how children produce speech that could not have been imitated, as no competent speaker of English produces them. The child creates order by generating hypotheses, testing them out, and then modifying them in the face of new evidence. Children create mistakes because they know something, not because they don't.

As children generate rules for the language they are learning, their speech reflects this growing knowledge. For example, when children come to know that nouns can be converted to verb forms (as in "That room is a mess" and "You're messing up my things"), they may create errors that are consistent with this knowledge. Examples of these types of errors can be seen in sentences such as "We'll airplane to Florida," and "You're germing it all up." These types of examples provide insight into how children search for regularities, create rules, simplify the task, and overgeneralize and extend the information they have to new situations. They are creating rules for producing and understanding speech. In short, they are engaged in the development of strategies.

Although it is clear that children are not taught language, they do not learn it without help. Children need to have language available to them so that they can work out the regularities. In addition, they need responsive conversational part- ners who will help them to see how the language works and provide feedback on their efforts.

> Learning to talk should thus be thought of as the result of a partnership: a partnership in which parents and other members of the community provide the evidence and then encourage children to work it out for themselves. Andrew Lock sums it all up in a single phrase when he describes the process as "the guided reinvention of language." (Wells, 1986, p. 51)

Language Acquisition and Reading

It is probably not the case that learning to read is entirely dependent on oral language knowledge (Menyuk, 1984). Preschool children have not acquired all the knowledge and skill they will need and use as they proceed through school. Children continue to acquire new vocabulary, more complex structures, and encounter new contexts for meaning as they grow and learn in school. In particu- lar, children are exposed to new types of communicative encounters with different people, especially those out of their own linguistic community. In addition, the language of books is not exactly the same as the oral language children have learned.

However, it certainly is true that the development of oral language abilities lays the foundation for successful acquisition of reading competence. Taking all the evidence together, oral language competence is important to reading for these reasons:

1. In learning to talk, children develop (or demonstrate) a number of general cognitive strategies for learning.
2. In learning to talk (and listen), children acquire much that they will use to aid them in bringing meaning to print: vocabulary, understanding of syntax, the ways in which meaning is carried in language structures, and alternative structures for communicating similar and dissimilar ideas.
3. Children's oral language abilities permit them to use prediction and hypothesis testing to support their initial reading attempts.

As we will see shortly, learning to read requires that an understanding of certain linguistic properties be brought to conscious awareness. Menyuk (1984) concluded that oral language development is important for learning to read because beginning readers who have not yet acquired certain features of oral language competence will not be able to bring them to conscious awareness for the task of reading.

Literacy Experiences

The foundations of literacy begin with language acquisition, but also include learning that: print and speech are related, print encodes a message, pictures are guides to the message, some language units are more likely to occur than others, certain words in certain orders reflect particular messages, and memory may be used as a guide to understanding (Clay, 1979). For those youngsters fortunate enough to have been introduced to reading on the laps of their parents, these lessons are well-learned long before the onset of schooling.

The foundations of literacy are laid in homes, parks, preschools, and stores— anywhere that children encounter print. Children are most likely to acquire useful and refined ideas about print, however, as they interact with, observe, and are guided by literate adults. Researchers have repeatedly identified the following types of literacy experiences as central to the development of early and/or successful reading:

1. Parents read aloud to their children.
2. Parents take their children to the library.
3. Parents report an early interest in writing.
4. Parents report the prevalence of "playing school."
5. Parents put their children to bed with books.

6. Parents support and respond to their children's efforts to learn to read. (Kastler, Roser, & Hoffman, 1987, p. 91)

Although there is much that we have yet to learn about how these experiences set the stage for learning to read, there is also much that we now know about what is learned through these experiences. There are many possible ways to describe literacy experiences. We have chosen the following abilities as organizers for the discussions to follow: developing print awareness; understanding the forms and functions of print; analyzing the task of reading; and gaining control of literacy behaviors/activities.

Developing Print Awareness

Children in our society are surrounded by print—on doors, cereal boxes, signs, etc. It appears that they acquire, at an early age, a fairly sophisticated understanding that these symbols convey meaning. Although some researchers question the utility of this generalized awareness (e.g., Ehri, 1987), it does appear that situational print awareness is part of a larger progression of acquired skill and knowledge. It is likely that most children understand something about the functions of print in environmental settings and use this information to arrive at key conclusions about the links between print and speech; however, it is also important to remember that some do not.

Just as children must come to understand the functional, meaningful nature of spoken language, they must come to appreciate that print is communicative, functional, and meaningful. Recent evidence suggests that most children in our society have a fairly well-developed "sense of print awareness in situational contexts" by the time they reach school age (Y. Goodman, 1980, 1986; Heath, 1983; Hiebert, 1981; Mason, 1980). For example, Hiebert (1981) found that 3-, 4-, and 5-year-old children were all sensitive to differences between print and drawing stimuli. In addition, when presented with words and letters in meaningful contexts, even very young children have demonstrated competence in understanding concepts such as word and letter, provided they are not asked to use or understand specific terminology.

Y. Goodman (1986) argues that children must learn that print is meaningful prior to formal schooling since, at present, beginning reading programs most often focus on the relationships between sound and symbol. Although this appraisal may be a bit harsh, it is clear that initial instruction must take into account the students' level of print awareness. Children who do not have a strong sense of the meaningfulness and functional value of print are unlikely to benefit from most beginning reading instruction. Such a situation may result in long-term reading difficulties.

Understanding the Forms and Functions of Print

Although environmental print awareness is necessary for emergent literacy, it clearly is not sufficient for success in beginning reading. Children need to acquire much more specific ideas about how print is organized and why we read. Knowledge of the forms and functions of print is typically acquired in rich literacy environments prior to schooling, and includes understanding the language of books and the structure of stories.

Understanding the language of books. Long before children begin to read they have already acquired substantial competence in oral language and clearly understand that the purpose of speech is communicative—to carry meaning (Bowerman, 1978; Slobin, 1979). Despite many commonalities, oral and written language are not identical, and young children need to learn the language of books. Read-aloud transactions provide a pleasurable and supportive environment for this type of literacy learning.

The Commission on Reading concluded in its 1985 report that "the single most important activity for building the knowledge required for eventual success in reading is reading aloud to children" (Anderson et al., 1985). One of the specific benefits of reading aloud to children in the preschool years is that children learn to "talk like a book" (Fox, 1987). The following excerpt, for example, is hardly the stuff of daily conversations: ". . . and he sailed off through night and day and in and out of weeks and almost over a year to where the wild things are . . . " (Sendak, 1963). During read-aloud transactions, children learn to deal with a different type of communicative style (book language) and with a communicator who is not present (the author).

In the process of being read to on a regular basis, children also become familiar with the look of print, the direction of it, the fact that it has been written by someone, the ways in which pages are turned to move through text, and so forth (Clay, 1979). Indeed, children who are read to learn a great deal about the language and functions of books. For example, one of the most important differences between spoken and written language is that written language is "decontextualized." This means that written language is produced so that it does not require the writer and the reader to share a physical context. In order to accomplish this, authors use a variety of cohesive devices to link information together in a meaningful whole. Children must learn to attend to the cues and referents that authors use so that they can sort out events and motives.

Increasingly, researchers are studying not only the specific knowledge gleaned during reading aloud, but also the lessons learned from the exchanges themselves. Indeed, the concept of "read-aloud transactions" carries with it the sense that something is being negotiated. This negotiation has strong parallels with the types of exchanges commonly documented as crucial for oral language development. Just as children learn that they must be actively involved in creating oral language, the conversations surrounding reading aloud encourage children to be active participants in creating meaning from text. This active interaction with text is necessary, of course, if children are to become competent readers (see Chapter 1). In addition, these read-aloud transactions teach children to question the meaning of text and encourage children to begin to think and use language in ways that will later be critical for school success (Altwerger, Diehl-Faxon, & Dockstader-Anderson, 1985; Wells, 1982).

Understanding story structure. Read-aloud transactions provide children with much information about the ways stories are organized. Children begin to internalize different structures for different types of text. For example, they begin to understand that "Humpty Dumpty" will have a certain structure and pattern and that this will be different than the structure and pattern for "The Little Red Hen." Many experiences with different types of texts encourage children to see that stories have certain predictable features and these can be relied upon to aid comprehension and memory.

Stories are a particular kind of narrative discourse identified by their structure, content, and language. The three basic elements of structure—setting, character, and plot—are so interrelated that the development of one affects the development of the other. A concept of story involves knowledge of these story elements and their interrelations. It can be thought of as a mental representation of story structure, essentially an outline of the basic story elements and their organization (Golden, 1984). Well-read-to youngsters generate a mental map for stories during the many interactions they have with this type of text (Mandler & Johnson, 1977; Stein & Glenn, 1979). These mental maps, or "story schema," are generalized structures that people use to comprehend (McConaughy, 1982).

Several types of story structures have been proposed. It is, however, important to understand that these story grammars are descriptions of specific texts. The components of stories suggested by Stein and Glenn (1979) are generally used to describe the types of stories very young children encounter:

- Setting—generally, the physical setting and characters
- Initiating event—"it all started when . . . "
- Internal response—how the main character reacts to the initiating event
- Attempt—an action or series of actions by the character(s) to try to reach a goal or solve a problem
- Consequence—what happens as a result of the attempt
- Reaction—a final reaction or event that ties the rest of the story together (also called a resolution)

These elements actually describe the elements present in stories that come out of an oral tradition (e.g., fairy and folk tales). Other stories may have different types of arrangements (see Chapter 9).

Research suggests that young children need a well-developed sense of story to comprehend text fully. In addition, story sense appears helpful in generating predictions about upcoming text and also in remembering (or reconstructing) stories. Thus, children who have not yet formed a solid mental map of stories are likely to have more difficulty reading and remembering textual information.

General literacy experiences such as read-aloud transactions provide children with the information they need to generate good hypotheses about book orientation, importance of print, directionality, and, typically, some level of word identification (Clay, 1982; Y. Goodman, 1980, 1986). Most importantly, they teach children that print is meaningful and useful and that it requires active participation. In order to become successful readers, however, children also must acquire the ability to analyze and to control their interactions with print (Bialystok & Ryan, 1983).

Analyzing Print

Oral language skills and general literacy experiences facilitate children's understanding of reading and writing, but the special requirements of decoding print are not obvious to the novice. G. Mason (1967) suggests: "One of the first steps in learning to read seems to be the realization that one doesn't already know how" (p. 132). It is not uncommon for young children at age three to assert that they can, indeed, read and/or write. They often proceed to demonstrate this ability by providing an oral or scribbled rendition of a favorite and familiar text. Clay (1979) provides a particularly delightful example of this phenomenon. She describes how one young child closed his eyes, recited a story, and proudly proclaimed, "Look, I can read with my eyes shut!"

Children must begin to analyze print in the early stages of learning to read and write. If children are to make progress in becoming literate, they need to come to understand the discrete parts that comprise the "whole" of reading and writing. At the very least, they must come to understand the rule-governed nature and critical features of reading and writing (Downing, 1970; Ehri, 1979; Leong 1976–77). They need to understand which aspects of speech are selected for representation in print. They must also learn how the meaning is carried in the specific features of print.

More specifically, children must come to realize that speech is segmented into sounds or *phonemes*, that letters represent phonemes and not some other unit of speech (a syllable, for example), that words have specific boundaries, and that speech and print match word-for-word. Whether such concepts are prerequisite to beginning reading/writing or whether they are the result of instruction is debatable. It seems entirely possible that children achieve something of the awareness that is necessary to become literate in the process of receiving instruction. It is as though the children had never thought to analyze speech, but in learning to read and/or write had been forced to recognize units and subdivisions (Francis, 1973).

Young children typically demonstrate limited awareness of the specific features of oral and written language. This *metalinguistic awareness,* or conscious knowledge of the linguistic elements of language, appears to be critical for the beginning reader/writer. Although metalinguistic awareness clearly continues to develop throughout the school years, there are several areas of knowledge and skill that seem critical to learning to read and write: understanding the concept of word, the ability to segment speech into phonemes, and the ability to match speech to print.

The concept of word. Because the strategy "pay attention to meaning" works so well for speech, young children seem not to be aware of the component pieces of language. For example, speech provides few cues to tell children about the word as a unit of analysis. Words that name objects are easily isolated, but in the flow of normal speech, individual words are not clearly marked. Thus, children must come to answer the question What is a word?

The following example demonstrates how children who appear competent may have incorporated unanalyzed items into their language. A 3-year-old girl sings: "Baa-baa black sheep, *have you any* wool . . . " (a favorite song which she has sung for months). Then she asks: "Mom, what's *'pabuany'*?" What has been understood by the informed listener (Mom) as "have you any" has actually been perceived and produced by the child as a single unit, "pabuany." However, the child's question does indicate her growing demand for clarity in language.

Not only must children begin to reliably identify the word as a distinct unit, but as Downing (1978) points out, beginners must also understand the technical concepts involved in reading and writing. Even if children have come to recognize that print is related to speech in some systematic way, they must also possess some additional awareness of the ways in which print is organized in order to learn to read and write. For example, children must learn that words are bound configurations that are separated by white space in print and that the term *word* is used to refer to a specific aspect of language.

The available evidence suggests that 4- and 5-year-old children have a difficult time selecting a word from among letters, numbers, phrases, and sentences (Ferriero & Teberosky, 1979/1982; Hare, 1984). J. Reid (1966) interviewed 5-year-old English children, asking them whether a variety of stimuli were "words." Some identified whole sentences as words, some made only random guesses, and some said that words, phrases, and sentences were all words. Similarly, when American kindergarten and first-grade children were given sentence strips and asked to "cut off" a word with a scissors, they sometimes cut off a word. Just as often, however, they cut off a portion of the word or cut off two words together (Meltzer & Herse, 1969). Even when children are asked about reading and words with a book in front of them, many 4- and 5-year-olds demonstrate substantial confusion about what constitutes a word and what people look at when they read (Downing, 1970).

Children obviously do not acquire the concept of word in one flash of insight. As with all such knowledge and skill, the concept develops over time. In addition, it is probably not the case that a well-defined concept of word is prerequisite to reading and writing, although it clearly facilitates initial instruction. For example, Hall (1976) reported a significant correlation between children's ability to segment printed text into words and their progress in a basal reader series. However, the correlation between ability to segment and reading was significantly less than the correlation between segmentation ability and length of time in school. These findings have led many researchers to conclude that children learn about the concept of word during the process of learning to read and write (Ehri, 1979; Hall, 1976; Sulzby, 1986a).

Phonemic segmentation. The ability to separate words into constituent sounds, or phonemic segmentation, is one ability that increasingly appears to distinguish children who have difficulty learning to read and write from those who make good progress (Juel, 1988; Stanovich, 1986; Yopp, 1988). For example,

Juel's longitudinal study of a large group of "at risk" children suggests that children who are poor readers in first grade remain poor readers in fourth grade. In addition, one hallmark of the poor readers in first grade was very limited phonemic awareness. Indeed, Juel's findings suggest that, although poor readers' phonemic awareness grew steadily in first grade, they left first grade with a little less phonemic awareness than the children who became average or good readers possessed upon entering first grade.

Clearly, children must be able to distinguish separate sound units in words before they will be able to identify letters in words that relate to these sounds. It is important to note that phonemic segmentation ability does not require that children know what letter stands for each sound they hear in a word. Phonemic segmentation is not the same as auditory discrimination, which refers to the ability to distinguish between two different sounds. Indeed, it appears that auditory discrimination tests are poor predictors of ability to segment speech (Yopp, 1988).

Research suggests that young children may take quite a long time to understand print concepts. Liberman and Shankweiler (1979), for example, report the results of a study investigating the ability of 4-, 5-, or 6-year-old children to segment speech into constituent phonemes and syllables. None of the children at age 4 was able to segment by phoneme, although half of these children could segment by syllable. Only 20% of the 5-year-old children were able to segment by phoneme and, even at age 6, only 70% were able to do so. Other authors have reported similar findings based on a variety of criteria (Calfee, Lindamood, & Lindamood, 1973; Fox & Routh, 1976; Hall, 1976).

Most existing readiness programs do not include instruction designed to help children segment words into phonemes. Since ability to segment speech into phonemic units appears to have strong predictive power, most researchers suggest that early instruction in this area is needed (Tunmer, Herriman, & Nesdale, 1988). Indeed, recent research suggests that direct instruction in phonemic segmentation is related to reading achievement at the beginning stages of reading development (A. Cunningham, 1989).

However, caution is needed in this area. Although the ability to segment sounds is clearly important, most researchers have also concluded that phonological sensitivity is necessary, but not sufficient, for reading achievement (Tunmer, Herriman, & Nesdale, 1988). For most children, good instruction in reading and writing leads to greater linguistic awareness: "Being taught to read helps to develop awareness of phonological segments" (Menyuk, 1984, p. 109). Thus, early successful experiences with print can develop student's abilities in this critical area.

Speech-to-print match. As we have seen, children typically do not have the capacity to analyze speech into all its constituent parts until after instruction and/or practice in reading and writing have begun. Emergent readers must begin to recognize that phonemes are represented in print with letters and letter combinations, and some direct information about this relationship is probably necessary before children can take control of their reading and writing.

In a longitudinal study of 30 children between the ages of three and six,

Ferreiro (1980) examined the development of children's hypotheses and strategies for reading. Her findings demonstrate that children's early "guesses" about the nature of reading and writing are quite different from those of older children. Although unconventional in nature, there was considerable agreement among children as they moved through several stages. For example, at some point, all the children she studied believed that the label for a single object was represented by using one letter. In a somewhat later stage, all the children began to require several letters to represent a single name.

At this later point, the children clearly realized that words are written with strings of graphemes. However, their analysis of the relationship between speech and print was still unconventional since, during this phase, similarities and differences between words were determined by the characteristics of the referent items, not by any similarities in sound. Thus, more letters were needed to write the name of a large item than were needed to write the name of a small one. Ferreiro (1980) provides the following marvelous example from a child in this stage:

> Maria (aged 4) was asked how many letters it would take to write her name. She said 4 (as many years as she was old). When asked how many letters it would take to write her mother's name, she responded, "6." But, for her father (a large man), she responded: "As many as a thousand."

Eventually, the children in Ferreiro's study all evolved a "syllabic hypothesis." During this period, the children believed that each letter represented one syllable. Clearly, when children arrive at the syllabic hypothesis, they have begun to see the formal relationships between speech and print.

Controlling Reading and Writing Processes

As children increase their understanding of the requirements of reading and writing, they begin to acquire more cognitive control over their own literacy skills. Clay (1979) suggests that children must develop an understanding of how print functions that includes the knowledge and abilities we have just described. In addition, she notes that children must learn letter identification, directionality, linearity (that letters in a word and words in a sentence are ordered from left to right, and that by changing the order you alter the meaning), word identification, and capitalization and punctuation. It is in school that children typically come to control and expand their knowledge to include these aspects of literacy learning.

However, we cannot "give" students the knowledge they need; we must help them to acquire it. The nature of emergent literacy suggests that it is the children's own struggle to make sense of available data that moves them toward analysis and control.

> At certain levels, the children do not even see the conflicts in their own thinking. Conflicting notions are simply compartmentalized, and no need is felt to reconcile them. *Only if children recognized and were bothered by a conflict did they sometimes manage to construct a more adequate notion to coordinate the two conflicting ones.* (Duckworth, 1979, p. 303, emphasis added)

Thus, a 3-year-old named Dana can write her name "ADNA" and be quite content with the production, since all the requisite letters are present. Indeed, efforts to correct the display are completely ignored. Just two weeks later, however, she is confused by her display. Although she is now sure that the production "ADNA" does not say "Dana," she cannot correct it, since she has not yet learned that *linearity* is essential.

For many years, educators assumed that the ability to read preceded the ability to write. In addition, reading was typically considered to be a decoding activity, requiring reception of data, and writing an encoding activity, requiring the production of data. Increasingly, research in the area of emergent literacy has brought these assumptions into question. Although the exact relationship between reading and writing has not been determined, it is clear that reading and writing behaviors emerge simultaneously. In addition, it appears that early writing experiences produce growth in many of the areas we have just discussed (e.g., concept of word, phonemic segmentation, etc.).

> Given encouragement, children will begin to write before they begin to read . . . Writing entails spelling, and spelling entails both working judiciously with letters of the alphabet and analyzing spoken words into their component sounds. Analyzing sounds in words requires an ability to make words hold still in the mind while the analysis is carried out, which in turn depends on having a stable concept of what a word is. (Gillet & Temple, 1982, p. 163)

Because of these relationships, examining children's early writing can provide a rich source of insight into their development of competencies important for learning to read.

The form and function of writing. The parallels between writing development and oral language development are substantial. It seems clear that young children acquire writing competence by writing—in much the same way that they become competent in speech by talking. This does not, of course, happen without a supportive environment. The following stages are evident in the writing development of most children (DeFord, 1980, p. 162):

1. scribbling;
2. differentiation between drawing and writing;
3. concepts of linearity, uniformity, linear complexity, symmetry, placement, left-to-right motion, and top to bottom directionality;
4. development of letters and letter-like shapes;
5. combination of letters, possibly with spaces, indicating understanding of units (letters, words, sentences), but may not show letter/sound correspondence;
6. writing known isolated words—developing sound/letter correspondence;
7. writing simple sentences with use of intensive spellings;
8. combining two or more sentences to express complete thoughts;
9. control of punctuation—periods, capitalization, use of upper- and lowercase letters;
10. form of discourse—stories, information material, letters, and so on.

Caution should be exercised in interpreting this information, because many of these characteristics will be evident simultaneously as children gain control over written forms. However, recent research does not support the notion that writing is developmental. That is, younger/less-skilled children perform differently than older/skilled children and, more importantly, there are identifiable stages of ability. Nowhere is this finding more helpful to reading professionals than in the work related to invented spelling.

Invented spelling. The term *invented spelling* is a considered one. It is used to refer to a consistent phenomenon observed in young emergent readers/writers: the ability to invent spellings on their own. The underlying assumptions in the term are captured in the following quotation from Ferreiro (1978):

> In order to understand the writing system which society has forged for them children must reinvent writing and thereby make it their own. (p. 39)

It is increasingly clear that children, do, in fact, "reinvent" the writing system as they gain control of their linguistic knowledge. Several findings provide evidence that children are engaged in this process. First, children have not been taught to spell words the way they often do (see Figure 4.3). Second, spelling errors are not random, as can be seen from the sample in Figure 4.3. As discussed previously with regard to oral language, this child has made errors because she knows something, not because she doesn't. A third piece of evidence is the substantial similarity in invented spellings from child to child. Finally, children appear to move through distinctive developmental stages—moving from very immature spellings to those that approximate standard spellings.

Studies of emergent readers/writers suggest several distinct stages of spelling development (e.g., Beers & Henderson, 1977; Forester, 1980; Chomsky, 1981). These stages represent an expansion of DeFord's (1980) writing stages (especially 6 and 7), which were presented previously. Although there are some disputes about the content of each stage, the following distinctions are generally made:

> *Pre-phonemic Spelling:* Children use alphabetic symbols to "write" words, but these are generally unrelated to the target word. There is no sound-symbol relationship present and these are likely to reflect earlier notions about how the writing system works (see Ferreiro above).
>
> *Early Phonemic Spelling:* Children exhibit a clear awareness that there is a relationship between phonemes and print. However, children represent very little of the phonemic information in print—sometimes the initial, sometimes the final, graphemes. "What defines early phonemic spelling is that the letters represent phonemes but only an incomplete number of phonemes for each word" (Gillet & Temple, 1982, p. 169). Example: DR GML = Dear Grandma.
>
> *Phonetic (and Letter Name) Spelling:* Children hear and produce sequences of sounds in words. At this stage, children may produce spellings that are quite readable (e.g., *wns* for *once* and *bik* for *bike*). However, children at this stage are also often using a strategy that results in rather strange productions. As they try to represent more and more sounds in words, they begin to use a *letter-name strategy* (Beers & Henderson, 1977). That is, they analyze the word they want to spell into its component sounds and

FIGURE 4.3
*Writing
Sample
(Age 6)*

MᵒBᵣUᵗᵣAᴰᵗ
MˢˢE5ᵗᵣ
ᵗAᵣSᴀᴰEₕBᵒMᵒ
HWS

My brother and my sister are
standing by my house

then find a letter name to represent each sound. They then spell each sound by
choosing the letter name that most closely resembles the sound they want to represent
(Gillet & Temple, 1982). Thus, children in this stage also produce such words as *lavatr*
for *elevator* (Morris, 1981). This approach causes problems in correct production of
vowels, and certain consonant combinations, in particular.

    Transitional Spelling: Children's spellings bear a much closer resemblance to stan-
dard spellings. In this stage, children make use of visual as well as phonemic information (Gentry, 1982). Thus, children generally represent short vowels appropriately in
this stage and also mark long vowels, even though these often represent overgeneral-
izations of learned rules. Thus, spellings such as the following are typical of this stage:
dres for *dress* and *rane* for *rain*. As Morris (1981) notes, "These transitional spellings,
which begin to appear in late first-grade or early-second grade, are to be welcomed by
the teacher, for they signal advancement in the child's understanding of English
spelling. No longer does the child believe that spelling is a fixed, simple code in which
letters map to sounds in a left-to-right, one-to-one fashion." (p. 664)

Children's inventive spellings can provide a great deal of information about
their literacy skills. We return to invented spelling for diagnostic purposes shortly.
For the moment, it is enough to understand that students who are not progressing
along these dimensions are unlikely to be able take advantage of most beginning
reading programs. It is also important to understand that "when children reach
the transitional stage, reading and spelling diverge from each other; that is, they
may continue to make progress as readers at the same time that they continue to
make many spelling errors . . . Once the transitional stage is reached, it is not

particularly productive to analyze spelling to learn about children's reading" (Gillet & Temple, 1982, p. 187).

Summary: Understanding the Foundations of Literacy

A large body of research suggests that older views of readiness provide an inadequate description of the abilities needed to learn to read and write. Teale and Sulzby (1986, p. xviii) summarize these findings and suggest that the following conclusions must be drawn:

1. Literacy development begins long before children start formal instruction.
2. *Literacy* development is the appropriate way to describe what was called *reading* readiness: The child develops as a writer/reader. It is no longer viable to think of reading as preceding writing or of oral and written language as distinct domains.
3. Literacy develops in real-life settings for real-life activities in order to "get things done."
4. Children are doing critical cognitive work in literacy development during the years from birth to six.
5. Children learn written language through active engagement with their world.
6. Although children's learning about literacy can be described in terms of generalized stages, children can pass through these stages in a variety of ways and at different ages.

STRATEGIES AND TOOLS FOR ASSESSING EMERGENT LITERACY

Readiness Assessment

Gathering dependable and useful information about the literacy abilities of young children can be a very tricky business. In the following section, we briefly discuss the theoretical problems involved in using most existing formal assessment instruments, saving a discussion of specific standardized tools for later in the text (see Chapter 6). In this chapter, we describe a number of informal assessment strategies for observation, structured informal assessment, and diagnostic teaching. Before we turn our attention to these specific practices, it is important to consider the problems associated with readiness assessment in general.

Reading readiness tests can only be judged useful if they predict students' subsequent success in reading or place students appropriately in beginning instructional programs. However, the problems associated with existing readiness tests prevent them from meeting these criteria successfully. For example, almost all of the readiness tests used today are variations of earlier tests that evolved from older, developmental views of reading readiness. Between 1930 and 1943, 12 reading readiness tests were published (Betts, 1946), including the Metropolitan

Readiness Test which is still used widely today, in a revised version. Thus, the primary result of these tests is some type of global score for use in evaluating students' mental readiness for reading.

It is hardly surprising to find that, until recently, most measures of reading readiness were really tests of general verbal aptitude and/or general overall development. As we have seen, early models of readiness suggested that a specific mental age was necessary before children could learn to read. Thus, the first item on a readiness checklist from the late 1940s asked, "Is the child 6.5 mentally?" (see Robinson & Good, 1987). The next item on that checklist was, "Does the child score well on a reading readiness test?" Indeed, most early readiness tests demonstrated their validity by providing evidence that test scores were highly correlated with tests of intelligence.

The match between readiness assessment and beginning reading instruction has become increasingly poor as our knowledge and understanding of emergent literacy has continued to expand. As Teale, Hiebert, and Chittenden (1987) note, "Young children's reading and writing are being measured in ways that do not reflect an adequate conceptualization of early literacy development or sensitivity to the fact that children of 4 or 5 have special social and developmental characteristics" (p. 773). Few readiness tests, for example, evaluate children's awareness of the purposes for reading; nor, for that matter, do they ask children to glean meaning from print. Similarly, few permit teachers to assess whether children know how to handle a book, understand the conventions of print, or understand the language that will be used in beginning reading instruction (Day & Day, 1986).

In addition, most reading readiness tests include some tasks not directly related to the act of reading (e.g., identifying and/or matching geometric shapes). Finally, few of the available readiness instruments permit observations of readiness linked to the question: Readiness for what? The demands of specific programs of beginning instruction have been ignored almost completely. As Nurss (1979) states, "Because most (readiness tests) attempt to be nationally standardized tests equally applicable to a variety of situations, none fully accounts for the questions 'what methods' or 'what materials' will be used for instruction" (p. 43).

Now, however, the climate seems much more hospitable for examining students, their knowledge and abilities, and acknowledging some of the contributions of methods and materials. For example, Teale, Hiebert, and Chittenden (1987) recently asserted that assessment of emergent literacy must include the following characteristics:

1. Assessment is a part of instruction.
2. Assessment methods and instruments are varied.
3. Assessment focuses on a broad range of skills and knowledge reflecting the various dimensions of literacy.
4. Assessment occurs continuously.
5. Literacy is assessed in a variety of contexts.
6. Measures are appropriate for children's developmental levels and cultural background.

Because so few standardized instruments have been developed to respond to these concerns, educators have begun to devise ways to gather this information informally. Advances in the *informal* assessment of emergent literacy have been substantial. We turn our attention to some of these advances in the next section, devoting the remainder of this chapter to descriptions of assessment strategies that can be conducted during everyday instructional exchanges.

Informal Assessment of Emergent Literacy

Initial assessments of emergent literacy should yield suggestions for appropriate instruction, hinting at an answer to the question: Ready for what? (Nurss, 1979). This requires generating more and better information than is provided by standardized tests of reading readiness. This need, coupled with our growing body of knowledge about how and what children learn as they develop proficiency in written literacy, forces us toward new ways of assessment. Searforss and Readence (1985) suggest two principles that should drive assessment efforts in the area of emergent literacy:

- *Principle 1*—Assessment of basic competencies such as print awareness, concepts about book print, story sense, and oral language will be functional, relying on the observation and recording of children's behaviors during reading, writing, and related tasks.
- *Principle 2*—Assessment and instruction of basic competencies must be merged, because good teaching requires that both processes work together in a constant interplay.

These two principles suggest that assessment of emergent literacy should be embedded in daily instructional exchanges and rely heavily on continuous observations of children in actual literacy settings. In this way, teachers are gathering information that is relevant in terms of the task they actually expect children to perform. In the following sections, we describe several informal strategies that can provide information about children's emergent competencies and discuss their usefulness in evaluating the emergent reading process. These classroom-based strategies involve both careful observation of children engaged in normal instructional events and observations of children in situations that have been structured by the teacher to assess specific components of literacy.

As can be seen from Figure 4.4, most informal assessment strategies permit us to gather information about a number of component areas. Thus, for each technique described here, we indicate the types of information that can be gathered. In general, the techniques we describe are designed to gather information about the following component areas of emergent literacy: oral language; concepts about the functions and conventions of print; understanding of stories and story structure; and knowledge of words and the writing system.

FIGURE 4.4

Components of Emergent Literacy Assessment

Components of Emergent Literacy Assessed by Various Informal Techniques

Assessment Strategy	Oral Language Competence				Print Awareness			Concepts of Book Print				Story Sense			Phonemic Awareness				Speech-Print Match			Control of Reading-Writing			
	Developmentally appropriate articulation and syntax	Adequate vocabulary	Elaborated use of language	Wide range of language functions	Recognizes environmental print	Recognizes various functions of print	Print carries a message	Parts of book	Directionality/orientation	Language of book print (word/letter)	Punctuation	Recognizes/recalls story elements	Produces well-structured stories	Retains structure during recall	Segmentation of words (oral)	Segmentation of syllables (oral)	Segmentation of phonemes (oral)	Rhyming	Matches spoken words to print	Some sight vocabulary	Sound-symbol correspondence (initial)	Attempts reading/writing	Knows letter names	Knows some sound-symbols	Uses some invented spelling
Informal Observation	x	x	x	x	x	x	x																		
Structured Interviews	x	x	x	x	x	x	x	x	x	x	x				x		x								
Structured Observation					x	x	x	x	x	x	x														
Retelling Guides	x	x	x	x								x	x	x											
Dictated Stories	x	x	x	x			x					x	x						x	x	x				
Writing Samples	x	x					x							x	x	x	x		x	x	x	x	x	x	x
DLTA						x	x	x	x	x		x	x	x											

FIGURE 4.5

Summary/
Planning
Form for
Emergent
Literacy
Assessment

Student: _____   Age: _____   Date: _____
Examiner: _____

I. Oral language
II. Literacy knowledge/experience
    A. Print awareness (environmental)
    B. Language of books (directionality, linearity, etc.)
    C. Story sense
    D. Concept of word
    E. Phonemic segmentation
    F. Speech-to-print match
III. Knowledge of words and the writing system
    A. Word recognition
    B. Phoneme-grapheme correspondence (invented spelling)
IV. Observations and comments

Planning the Assessment

A summary form such as the one shown in Figure 4.5 should be used to organize information as it is gathered. This form can also be used to help determine what information is already available from sources such as those described in Chapter 3. In general, it should be used to help systematize the information about to be gathered. As assessment is planned, it is helpful to reflect on the following questions:

- What do I already know about this child?
- How do I know that?
- What do I still need to know to plan instruction?
- How can I find this out?

As we evaluate and monitor the results of our assessments, it is very important to provide specific examples of the behavior, language, or products that enabled us to make specific inferences. Informal assessments can provide rich data about children, but it is important to guard against hasty judgments and assumptions. Conclusions *must* be documented. The strategies and forms provided below can help with this task.

Observing Spontaneous Use of Knowledge and Skill

The procedures described in this section expand the focus of the observational techniques on knowledge and attitudes about reading, described in Chapter 3, to include observation of emergent literacy in the areas of oral language development and concepts about print.

Oral language checklists. Researchers and educators have come to realize that language is difficult to evaluate through short, controlled samples. Therefore, people who study language acquisition now frequently recommend evaluating language in naturalistic settings (see Lund & Duchan, 1988). This means talking and listening to children engaged in everyday school activities.

Teachers need to assess oral language competence to ensure that children can accomplish the tasks required in school settings (see Chapter 9). School tasks demand language use that is quite different from the language used in homes and among peers. Thus, even if children have language development appropriate to their home environment, they may not have acquired language appropriate for functioning in a school setting.

Previously in this chapter, we described Halliday's taxonomy of language functions. Halliday's categories are drawn from actual observations of children, and can be used fairly easily as the basis for the type of evaluative checklist shown in Figure 4.6. The checklist in Figure 4.6 clearly is designed to gather information about a number of children. Alternatively, it is possible to evaluate one child more carefully by using a checklist that provides for more detail. In this case, it is important to note the time and the setting (Pinnell, 1985b). In addition, examples of the language used should be noted next to each function.

Checklists for concepts about print. Although there are several contrived ways to assess students' knowledge about the functions of literacy, evaluation in this area can be accomplished largely through observation. Many kindergarten and first-grade classrooms are rich print environments. Print appears on labels, charts, schedules, and so on. In this type of environment, it is possible to observe how often and how well children employ print in their daily activities.

As children use print to label, describe, and follow directions, teachers can document the growing competence of each child. For example, the teacher might watch children as they reread familiar books, charts, and papers. The following examples are suggestive of the types of events that are noteworthy:

> Example A: 4½-year-old Kelly picks up a newspaper and opens it appropriately, remarking: "Oh, here's some news."

> Example B: 5-year-old Joel works intently to make a label to describe his show-and-tell object, so that people who see it on the science table "will know what it is."

These children clearly are acquiring a sense of the functional nature of print. These types of observations should focus on behaviors that demonstrate that children understand the various functions and conventions of literate behavior, not on accuracy (do they read/write correctly?).

As teachers watch for specific behaviors that will inform them about their students' emergent literacy, they should keep the following questions in mind:

- How well does the child distinguish print from pictures?
- How well does the child recognize the functions of print in the environment (e.g., signs, posted information, and so on)?
- How does the child reread familiar books (i.e., does she "talk like a book," using the structure and vocabulary of book language)?

FIGURE 4.6
Observation Form: Functions of Language

	Functions							Activity							
	Instrumental	Regulatory	Interactional	Personal	Imaginative	Heuristic	Informative	Sharing time	Group lessons	Book discussions	Free play	Structured play	Small group lessons	Projects	Cooperative work groups
Names															
1. _____															
2. _____															
3. _____															
4. _____															
5. _____															
6. _____															
7. _____															
8. _____															
9. _____															
10. _____															

- What distinctions does the child make among pictures, scribbling, and print?
- In what ways does the child attempt to read familiar books, labels, charts, and so on?
- What distinctions can the child make among different forms of print (e.g., labels vs. stories)?

Continuous observations of these types of behaviors yield a much richer picture of literacy knowledge than is permitted by formal measures alone.

Despite the usefulness of observation, relying on spontaneous use of knowledge and skill cannot ensure that we have gathered information about all that students can do. Thus, systematic task structuring can be helpful. Morgan and Argiro (1987) developed a useful (and validated) battery of tasks to assess written language awareness (see Figure 4.7). This battery is based on the research of several authors and it pulls together many of the techniques we have described above. Much of this information can be gathered in daily encounters with students. However, some of this information requires simple structuring of either the task or the context, so that a complete picture can be obtained of the child's abilities in these areas. This measure provides specific information about students' general print awareness and about their emerging abilities to analyze the task.

FIGURE 4.7
Checklist:
Functions and
Conventions of
Literacy

SUMMARY FORM: PRINT AWARENESS

Development of an Understanding That Print Conveys Meaning and Serves a Useful Function

Spontaneous use: Does child exhibit competence in using/reading:
1. Labels
2. Cubbies
3. Signs
4. Name recognition
5. Book print

Structured observation: Present children with stimuli and evaluate ability to recognize by name or function.
1. Cartons or containers for common household foods
2. Advertisements/logos for local fast food chains (e.g., pizza or McDonald's)
3. Common directional signs (e.g., EXIT)
4. Newspaper, magazines, storybooks, adult novels

Development of an Awareness of Writing Conventions

Using the stimuli above:
1. Can child show "where you read"?
2. Name any words or letters?
3. Show you how to read the print (directionality)?

Structured Interviews

Ferreiro (Ferreiro & Teberosky, 1979/1982) has devised a number of ingenious tasks that are quite easy to administer and that yield a number of insights into children's understanding of the conventions of print. The tasks are administered in a structured interview format that includes probing and discussing of children's responses to elicit more information about their print concepts. These interviews are designed specifically to explore children's ideas about what is readable. We have used these techniques with very young children and found that they are manageable, and also that they do discriminate among children who are more or less aware of the demands of beginning reading. Two of these tasks are described briefly below.

"Word" reading. This task involves sorting word cards. The stimulus cards should include letter strings, real words, "possible" words, repeated strings, and numbers. Some sample items include:

> two   5   zzzz   me   n   iiio   PIE   jot

To administer this task, simply ask the child:

- Which are something to read?
- Which are not something to read?
- Can you read the cards that are "good for reading?" What do they say?

The examiner should also probe to determine what criteria the child is using to classify the cards.

In evaluating the child's responses, the following questions should be considered:

- What distinctions does the child make between words and numerals, and words and letters?
- What distinctions does the child make based on the length of the display?
- How sensitive is the child to repeated elements?
- How do upper- and lowercase letters influence the child's decisions?

Patterns of response can indicate how aware the child is of the forms and conventions of written words.

Working with kindergarten children, we found that some children argue that all the cards are "good for reading." As we noted above, an interview of this type allows us to explore responses. In defending this response, two explanations are common. Some children assert that although they could not read the cards, other "older" or "bigger" people could. Other children demonstrate that all the cards are "good for reading" by reading the letter names. Thus, the card *iiio* is read "i-i-i-o," and the card *jot* is read "j-o-t." In neither case do these children appear to have satisfactory ideas about the forms and functions of reading and writing.

Reading with pictures. Using cards like the ones displayed in Figure 4.8, the examiner/teacher engages in an open-ended dialogue with the child by asking the following questions:

- Is there something to read on this card? (Have children point to it.)
- What does it say? or What do you think it says?
- (Using a portion of the child's response) Where does it say _____?
- Do you think it might say _____?

The exchange that is documented in Figure 4.8 demonstrates how one 6-year-old proceeded with this task, suggesting how such exchanges can reveal a great deal about children's concepts of print. This one reveals that Nicole knows that the print is what is read. She also has a well-established sense of directionality. However, she clearly lacks a sense of speech-print match. She also lacks clarity about the terminology associated with reading instruction.

It is helpful to consider the following questions in evaluating a child's performance on this task.

- How well does the child understand the speech-print match?
- How well does the child appear to understand word boundaries?
- How well does the child appear to understand directionality?

The purpose of these types of structured interviews is to delve into children's understanding and to gather instructionally useful information. Some of these same components are explored in the *Concepts About Print* test, discussed in the following section.

FIGURE 4.8
*An Interview
with a
6-year-old
"At Risk"
Kindergartner*

THE DOG RUNS

Examiner: Where is there something to read on this card?
Nicole: Points to the words and runs her hands along the print.
Examiner: What does it say?
Nicole: I don't know.
Examiner: What do you think it says?
Nicole: The dog is chasing the cat.
Examiner: Where does it say, "The"?
Nicole: Points to "THE"
Examiner: Where does it say, "cat"?
Nicole: Points to "DOG"
Examiner: Where does it say "dog"?
Nicole: Points to "RUNS"
Examiner: Where does it say "chasing"?
Nicole: Laughs . . . There aren't any more of those . . . things.
Examiner: That's right. What do we call those "things"?
Nicole: Letters. Or, numbers.

Structured Observation of Print Concepts

Some years ago, Clay (1985) created an informal test designed to assess young
children's knowledge and use of print concepts. In its most recent form, the
Concepts About Print (CAP) test is part of a diagnostic survey designed to detect
reading difficulties among young children (Clay, 1985). Two books, *Sand* and
Stones, are used to assess children's knowledge of print conventions. During an

exchange that is much like the interview techniques just described, the examiner asks 24 questions as the book (*Sand* or *Stones*) is read. The child is told to help the examiner read the book by pointing to features in the book. The examiner makes observations related to the following concepts: how to hold a book for reading; print orientation; print, not pictures, carries the message; upper- and lowercase letters; punctuation marks; and directionality.

A recent review of the available research suggests that the *Concepts About Print* test is a valid measure of emergent literacy independent from intelligence (Day & Day, 1986). For the classroom teacher, the CAP has the advantage of structuring observations. It can provide teachers with a place to start, and it also increases reliability, since the same tasks and materials are used for each child. In general, it can provide you with a quick assessment of children's experiences with books.

It is also possible for teachers to obtain similar information in more natural settings from regular picture books. Genishi and Dyson (1984) provide an adaptation that is quick and easy to use. This procedure permits teachers to select their own materials, and perhaps to use several different types of materials for purposes of comparison. This may prove more valuable than using the predetermined materials provided in other assessments, such as the CAP.

To implement this basic book-reading procedure, simply select a book and ask the child to do the following:

- Show me the front of this book.
- I'll read you this story. You help me. Show me where to start reading; where do I begin to read?
- Show me where to start. Which way do I go? Where do I go after that?
- Point to what I am reading. (Read slowly and fluently.)
- Show me the first part of the story. Show me the last.
- (On a page with print on both the left and right sides) Where do I start reading?

Figure 4.9 provides a list of the concepts (e.g., distinctions between print and pictures, directionality, speech-to-print match) that can be used as a guide in evaluating the child's responses to these requests.

It is fairly easy to get a sense of the child's experience with books and print from the types of assessments described in this section. However, for a comprehensive view of students' emergent reading abilities, the results of these types of assessment will need to be supplemented with information from other assessment activities, such as dictating stories and/or listening comprehension (see Clay, 1985).

Story Retelling Guides

Story retelling can provide a wide range of assessment information. Since young children read or listen to many stories, it is relatively easy to embed this assessment into the regular instructional program. Because this assessment strategy is discussed at length elsewhere (see Chapters 5 and 7), the discussion in this chapter is

FIGURE 4.9

Print Concepts Form

Name: _____ Date: _____

Directions: Using a book the child has never seen before, test the following concepts:

1. Identifies front of book/back of book
2. Can indicate title
3. Identifies print as "what is read"
4. Can indicate picture
5. Knows where to start reading
6. Shows correct direction of print display
7. Indicates beginning of story on a page
8. Can indicate return sweep for a line of print
9. Indicates end of story
10. Identifies bottom of page
11. Identifies top of page
12. Can locate a word (by circling, cupping, etc.)
13. Can locate two words that appear together
14. Can locate the space between words
15. Can locate a letter
16. Can locate two consecutive letters
17. Can indicate a period (full stop)
18. Can indicate a comma, question mark

limited to two aspects of emergent literacy that can be assessed using retelling procedures: sense of story and oral language development.

The ability to recognize and use story structure clearly aids comprehension. As we assess children's retellings, we are looking for evidence that children have made use of the major components of stories to understand the text and to aid their recall. For young children, it is important to determine if they have noted characters, events, and resolutions. In addition, the children should make the sequential and causal connections between events and resolutions explicit and clear.

To conduct a story retelling, simply ask the child to retell a story that he or she has just heard or read. Ask the child specifically to retell the entire story just the way the author did. When the retelling has stopped, ask the child if there is anything else he or she can remember about the story. Record the child's retelling in writing and/or by audiotaping.

The form presented in Figure 4.10 can be used as a guide for evaluating the retelling with regard to the child's language and sense of story structure. In addition, it may be helpful to collect retelling data from children on both familiar and unfamiliar stories. In this way, it is possible to evaluate whether the child generates more complex relationships from text through repeated exposure. Repeated exposure to the same material should also permit the child to capture the language of the text.

If the quality and quantity of the retelling does not improve with repeated exposures, it is likely that the children need more guidance in making use of story structures or that their oral language development (and experience) is not well-matched to the text. Over time, regular and frequent use of retelling procedures can permit us to evaluate and document a child's growth in a number of areas, including language fluency, complexity, vocabulary, usage, and specific aspects of knowledge about story structures.

FIGURE 4.10
Story Retelling Form

Child _____   Date _____   Story Title _____

Language
Fluent
    Word count
    Absence of verbal fillers
Complete sentences
A variety of sentence patterns to express ideas
Precise, descriptive words

Story Structure
All major events
Accurate sequence
Linked events

Key: + — always or completely   √ — usually or most   − — seldom or few

From *Language Assessment in the Early Years* by Celia Genishi and Anne Haas Dyson. Reprinted with permission of Ablex Publishing Corporation.

Dictated Stories

Reading and writing experiences in the instructional programs of young children are increasingly linked through the use of dictated stories. This type of instructional approach, often referred to as *language experience* or *whole language*, grows out of the belief that reading and writing are natural extensions of linguistic development, and that these abilities are acquired naturally if instructional practices are in keeping with their linguistic competencies and abilities (Harris & Sipay, 1990). Dictated stories are also a rich source of diagnostic information about children's print awareness, sense of story, and control of reading and writing.

Generally, dictated writing samples are collected in one of two ways. In some classrooms, children produce journal entries several times a week. For very young children, this usually involves drawing a picture and "writing" any portion of the accompanying story that is possible. Then, the child dictates the intended story to the teacher, who writes it down exactly as produced (see Figure 4.11). Alternatively, the teacher may set a topic for a child (or group of children) and then proceed as above. Some children provide only a label (Figure 4.11), while others generate text-length stories, sometimes continuing their story for several days (see Figure 4.12).

Dictated stories are a rich source of information about oral language, print awareness, knowledge of the conventions of print, and story structure (Agnew, 1982; Dixon, 1977; Ringler & Weber, 1984). As children dictate and reread their stories, information about each component of emergent literacy can be gathered, using the type of form shown in Figure 4.13. In addition to the items on this form, it may be helpful to reflect on the following:

- What does the child do as the story is transcribed?
- Does the dictation have clarity and organization?

**FIGURE
4.11**
*Dictated Story
(School Bus)*

This is a school bus.

- Does the child provide a title that shows a grasp of main idea?
- How does the child (attempt) to read back his or her dictation?
- How easily and fluently does the child dictate?
- Does the child use appropriate grammatical structures?
- How does the child use language appropriate to the task?

After a dictation is completed, it is possible to gather information about other aspects of emergent literacy (Agnew, 1982). For example, the child's ability to match speech to print can be observed, using the following voice-pointing procedure (see also Genishi & Dyson, 1984). Using the dictated story, simply ask the child:

- To find a word (by circling or framing it)
- To match a story word on a card to the story itself
- To find a letter and/or a sentence
- To find a word that begins the same as another
- To point "to the letters you can name"
- To point "to the words you can read"
- To "reread" the story

At the conclusion of a dictated story activity, it is helpful to reflect on the following:

- What evidence is there that the child understands the concepts of word, sentence, paragraph, and story?

**FIGURE
4.12**
*Lengthy
Dictated Story*

This is a house and it lives near a forest. There were two girls who lived together.

The girls names were Nava and Shoshana. One day they dis-Obeyed the rules and went out in the forest. They were'nt watching and they stepped in a hole.

Well, they were in the hole. A person was standing in the hole, up on earth. And the person had a rope.
Nava and Shoshana called, "Help, send down the rope". But,

the person was a nasty person. And very nasty creatures came flying out. A hawk came flying out And a nasty bird came flying out.

**FIGURE
4.13**
*LEA
Summary
Form*

Dictated Experience Story Inventory

Name: _____   Date: _____

Directions: Present stimulus for student to discuss or experience directly. Ask them to tell
you something about it.
  Dictated Story:

  Assessment:
  1. Does the child speak in sentences, in single words, or word clusters?
  2. Does the child use descriptive names for objects and events or many ambiguous
     terms like ''it,'' ''that,'' ''this thing''?
  3. Does the child speak clearly and pace the dictation to allow the teacher to record?
  4. Does the child provide adequate information to reconstruct the experience?
  Comments:

- What aspects of the speech-to-print relationship does the child understand?
- In what ways does the child use memory for text as an aid to reading?
- What sight vocabulary does the child appear to have mastered?
- How does the child use graphophonic information to read?

Observations of the child's use of directionality, graphic clues, and so forth can be
enriched by collecting samples of children's independent writing, as described in
the following section.

Writing Samples

Current research suggests that reading and writing are mutually supportive activities. Information from one source is used to inform the other. However, not all
young children come from homes where reading and writing are modeled. More
importantly, not all children enter school settings that support the relations
between reading and writing. The writing of 5- and 6-year-old children:

> . . . is often not acceptable in schools, where conventional, adult-like writing may be
> the only writing of interest. As Freddy remarked, 'I used to write, but not any-
> more . . . I come to school now.' Freddy reported that he stopped writing when he
> started kindergarten. . . . In an environment supportive of writing, children do write,
> and teachers can gain information about children's knowledge of our alphabetic
> writing system, the writing process, and the functions that writing can serve. (Genishi
> & Dyson, 1984, p. 173)

If the child's classroom does include many opportunities for writing, spontaneous samples of children's work can be gathered. This is desirable because it
permits an evaluation of not only what the child *can* do, but what he or she does.
Genishi and Dyson (1984) suggest a number of questions that can be considered as
various aspects of children's written work are observed (see Figure 4.14).

**FIGURE
4.14**
*Guidelines for
Observing
Kinder-
gartners'
Writing*

When observing (watching, listening to, talking to children about) their writing, you might consider the following questions:

The Message

1. Does the child believe that he's written a message? If so,
2. Does the child know what the message is? That is, can he read it? If so,
3. Did the child freely formulate his own message? Or, did the child simply copy something? Or, was the message confined to a small set of words which the child could easily spell?
4. How long was the message?
   one word or a list of unrelated words
   a phrase
   a sentence
5. How does the child's written message relate to other graphics on the page?

The Encoding System

1. Can you read the child's message? If not,
2. Does there seem to be any system to how the child went from the formulated message to the print? For example, the child may have:
   put down a certain number of letters per object
   rearranged the letters in his name
   written a certain number of letters per syllable
3. If you can read the child's message, can you tell how the child encoded it?* For example, the child may have:
   recalled the visual pattern (e.g., *COOW*, child intended to write *moo*)
   based spelling on letter names (e.g., *PT*, which is read *Petie*)
   requested spellings from peer or adult
   based spelling on phonological analysis (e.g., *APL*, which is read *apple*)

The Written Product

1. How conventional are the child's written symbols? (Do they look like letters?)
2. Did the child follow the left-to-right directionality convention?
3. Is there any order to the way the letters or words are arranged on the page? Or, does it appear that the child simply put letters where there was empty space?

Message Decoding

1. Does the child appear to have written without any particular intended message? If so,
2. Did the child attempt to decode the written message?
3. If so, how did the child go from text to talk? The child may have:
   engaged in apparent fantasy behavior
   requested that an adult read the unknown message (e.g., "What does this say?")
   based the decoding on the perceived text segments (i.e., matched a number of oral syllables to the perceived number of segments in text)
   used a letter-name strategy (i.e., "read" a word containing the name of a written letter, as reading "Debbie" for *PARA NB*)
   based decoding on visual recall of a word similar in appearance

Writing Purpose

1. Why did the child write? Possible reasons include:
   simply to write: no clearly identifiable purpose exists beyond this (e.g., "I'm gonna' do it how my Mama does it.")
   to create a message: the meaning of the message is unknown to the child (e.g., "Read this for me.")
   to produce or to practice conventional symbols (e.g., the *ABC*'s, displayed written language) without concern for a referent

FIGURE 4.14
(continued)

to detail or accurately represent a drawn object (e.g., the *S* on Superman's shirt)

to label objects or people

to make a particular type of written object (e.g., a book, a list, a letter) without concern for a particular referent

to organize and record information (e.g., to write a list of friends)

to investigate the relationship between oral and written language without concern for a particular referent (e.g., "If I do [add] this letter, what does it say?")

to express directly feelings or experiences of oneself or others (i.e., direct quotations, as in writing the talk of a drawn character), and

to communicate a particular message to a particular audience

* It may be that the child *is* using one of these methods, but you simply cannot read it. After asking the child to read the paper, you may be able to detect patterns in the child's encoding system.

From *Language Assessment in the Early Years* by Celia Genishi and Anne Haas Dyson. Reprinted with permission of Ablex Publishing Corporation.

If spontaneous writing samples are not available, assessment information can be gathered by simply asking the child to write anything she or he knows how to write. It may be necessary to provide additional structure, because many young students balk at this. Two tasks that can be used to help generate writing samples are All the Words I Know and Supported Writing.

All the words I know. We have found that children often know how to write some words, even if they believe they are not yet writers. Thus, a paper headed "All the Words I Know" can sometimes produce results when the more generalized request to write has failed. Most children, for example, can write their own names, the names of some other people, and a few other high-potency words (Clay, 1985). When the child has completed this task, it may help to probe further by asking the child to attempt to write specific words such as his or her mother's name, color names, the name of the month, the words on street signs or logos, and so forth. Such samples provide information about the child's word knowledge and attention to recurring environmental print.

Supported writing. Children will often be able to write some connected discourse if they are provided with a little support. There are many ways to do this. For example, the child can be asked to draw a picture, then write about it. Alternatively, it is possible to brainstorm with the child, generating several possible topics.

Eliciting writing samples of connected text is important. The word-writing task just described cannot provide evidence of the child's awareness of text organization, directionality, or concept of word boundaries. These areas can only be assessed when children write several words or sentences. In addition, when the connected writing sample generates the need to use some words that are unknown, the child's strategy for spelling can be assessed.

An analysis of children's writing strategies can provide much information about the status of emergent literacy. Students' development can be traced from

**FIGURE
4.15**
*Kindergarten
Writing
Sample*

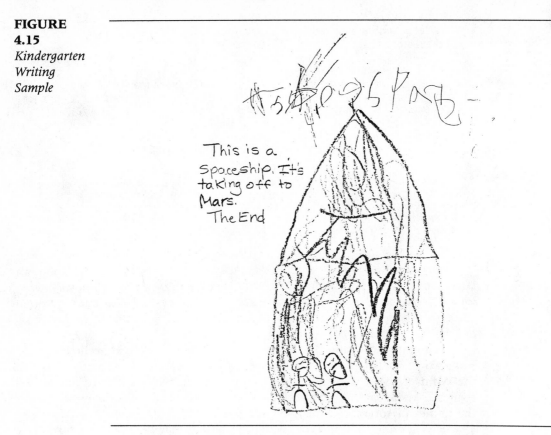

scribbling through invented spelling to conventional orthography (Sulzby & Teale, 1985) by reflecting on questions such as:

- What forms is the child using—drawing, scribbling, or making letter-like squiggles?
- How does the child use letters or strings of letters?
- How does the child copy?
- What types of invented spellings does the child produce?
- In what ways does the child use the visual display to recall high-frequency sight words?

Figures 4.15 to 4.17 provide samples of work from the same kindergarten class in which journal-writing is a daily experience. These samples suggest how this activity can provide continuous assessment information about the emergent abilities of young children. They also reveal a broad range of development in the class, from scribbling (Figure 4.15) to emergent (Figure 4.16) into formal conventions (Figure 4.17).

**FIGURE
4.16**
*Kindergarten
Writing
Sample*

Directed Listening Thinking Activity

It is helpful to observe children engaged in the actual school tasks they are expected to perform. Throughout this section, we have encouraged a type of assessment that can be embedded in daily classroom exchanges. Indeed, most of these assessments can and should be done as a part of regular classroom routines.

The Directed Listening Thinking Activity (DLTA) was developed by Stauffer (1980) as an instructional strategy. It is easy to use on a continuous basis for assessment because it fits naturally in the classroom routine. The strategy simply involves the teacher reading a well-crafted story aloud to children and stopping periodically to solicit predictions. The children are also directed to monitor their predictions to see if they were correct. Retellings can also be incorporated into the DLTA. Throughout the activity, the teacher asks the children questions such as:

**FIGURE
4.17**
*Kindergarten
Writing
Sample*

This is a gingerbread cookie, and it has a pink foot and a blue one.

ThiSiSaJiNJerBredCuKey
andIfHaSapicFutanda
Blue
TheEnd

- What do you think this story will be about?
- What clues did you use to help you?
- Were your predictions right?
- What do you think will happen next?

Gillet and Temple (1986) suggest guidelines for assessing a child's participation in a DLTA. These have been adapted into the record-keeping form shown in Figure 4.18. When used regularly, this form can help evaluate change in students' knowledge and ability to perform various types of school tasks.

The *Primary Language Record*
The *Primary Language Record* (1988), or PLR, was developed by teachers and other groups of educators in London for use by teachers of young children in recording progress in language learning. The PLR is based on the belief that the primary purposes for record keeping are: to inform and guide other teachers who do not yet

FIGURE 4.18
DLTA Summary Chart

Name: _____   Date: _____

Story used: _____

Directions: Read a story aloud pausing before important events and ask for predictions. Use a story with a strong story structure.

    Reaction when activity is announced:

    Examples of predictions:

    Oral retelling:

Analysis of predictions:

___ Can/does child predict from title, cover, pictures?

___ Are these predictions plausible?

___ Are these predictions based on real life?

___ Are they based on story structure expectations?

Ability to monitor predictions? (Is text used to revise/monitor?)

Are the following included in the retelling?

___ Setting   ___ Initiating event   ___ Goal   ___ Attempt(s)   ___ Resolution

---

know the child; to inform administrators about a child's work; to provide parents with information and an assessment of a child's progress; and to support and inform day-to-day classroom instruction. Consequently, the seven principles that underlie the development of the PLR are as follows:

1. the involvement of parents;
2. the involvement of children;
3. the involvement of all teachers who teach the child;
4. the involvement of children with special educational needs;
5. the importance of recording children's progress in the other community languages they know, as well as in English;
6. the importance of recording developments across the curriculum, in all major language modes;
7. the importance of a clear framework for evaluating progress in language.

The PLR has two major components: the main record and supplementary observation and sample sheets. The main record is designed to be completed at several points in the school year in order to inform the teaching that goes on during the year. It is expected that the completed records will be passed on throughout a child's school career to form a cumulative language profile.

The main record is divided into three parts. The first provides space to record the discussion with parents and the first language/literacy conference with the child. The second part has sections on talking and listening, reading, and writing. Each section provides space for comment on various aspects of the child's language development, as well as space to record what experiences and teaching have helped or would help development in this area, and the outcomes of any discussion with administrators or parents about the child's development. The instructions for recording comments about the child's progress in each of the three areas provide a sense of the types of information the PLR elicits. They are:

> *Talking and listening:* "Please comment on the child's development and use of spoken language in different social and curriculum contexts, in English and/or other community languages: evidence of talk for learning and thinking; range and variety of talk for particular purposes; and experience and confidence in talking and listening with different people in different settings."
>
> *Reading:* "Please comment on the child's progress and development as a reader in English and/or other community languages: the stage at which the child is operating . . . ; the range, quantity, and variety of reading in all areas of the curriculum; the child's pleasure and involvement in story and reading, alone or with others; the range of strategies used when reading and the child's ability to reflect critically on what is read."
>
> *Writing:* "Please comment on the child's progress and development as a writer in English and/or other community languages: the degree of confidence and independence as a writer; the range, quantity, and variety of writing in all areas of the curriculum; the child's pleasure and involvement in writing both narrative and non-narrative, alone and in collaboration with others; the influence of reading on the child's writing; growing understanding of written language, its conventions and spelling." (PLR, 1988, pp. 16–17)

The third part of the main record allows for the addition of information to the second part, so that the information on the child's language progress is as current as possible. There is also space for parents to comment on the record, and for a report of a second language/literacy conference with the child.

The second major component of the PLR consists of sheets for commenting on supplementary observations and samples of reading and writing. These sheets are organized into four parts: Talking and listening—diary of observations; reading and writing—diary of observations; reading samples; and writing samples. Space is provided to record significant developments in language and literacy in a diary format, and to analyze in depth particular examples of a child's reading and writing.

Finally, it should be noted that the *PLR Handbook for Teachers* provides a great deal of information about language and literacy that is invaluable for anyone interested in understanding and evaluating a child's progress in this area. The PLR is an impressive addition to the tools and strategies we have available for the continuous assessment of emergent literacy, and it should be given careful consideration by all who are engaged in this effort.

FROM CLASSROOM TO CLINIC

The primary difference between classroom and clinic in the application of the knowledge and procedures described in this chapter lies in the age and the progress of the individuals for whom these matters apply. Classroom personnel are most likely to need and use this information in their dealings with young children who are progressing normally in prekindergarten, kindergarten, and the first grade. In contrast, specialists and resource personnel are most likely to need and use this information in relation to individuals who are experiencing difficulty in learning to read and write in the second or third grade and up.

As the age of the individuals being evaluated increases, there is a decrease in the applicability of the specific techniques described here. However, the general areas of concern remain the same. Although the evaluation of older individuals may require different assessment techniques, it is still important to examine the areas of oral language competence, print awareness, knowledge of the forms and functions of print, and the ability to analyze print and control the reading and writing process.

There are differences between how and which procedures are used in classroom and clinic, as with the techniques for gathering background information described in Chapter 3. Classroom teachers are more likely to use the procedures that can be incorporated into their daily instruction for the purposes of ongoing planning and assessment. Resource personnel are more likely to use the procedures that can be administered most efficiently for the purposes of understanding the problems and/or evaluating the progress of specific individuals. For example, classroom teachers are likely to find the *Primary Language Record* more appropriate for their setting and purposes than will clinical personnel. Conversely, clinical personnel are likely to find that the *Concepts About Print* test is more appropriate for their setting and purposes than do classroom teachers. The ideal situation involves collaboration between classroom teachers and resource specialists. In this manner, the most complete picture of an individual's ongoing literacy development can be obtained, greatly increasing the likelihood of improving instruction and learning.

CHAPTER SUMMARY

The first section of this chapter described two traditional views of reading readiness that underlie both readiness assessment and instruction in today's schools. The developmental view suggests that children simply grow into readiness, much the way a tree grows and develops. The experiential view emphasizes the role of the environment in developing readiness. This section also describes the more current conceptualization of readiness as emergent literacy. The gradual emergence of written literacy skills in the context of oral language development provides a better perspective for understanding this stage of children's literacy development.

The second section of the chapter detailed two major areas of competence necessary for literacy learning derived from an emergent literacy perspective: oral language development and literacy experiences. Oral language development was described in terms of what children must learn about language, how language is learned, and the importance of language development in literacy learning. Essential literacy experiences were defined as *developing print awareness; understanding the forms and functions of print,* including the language of books and story structure; *analyzing print,* including the concept of a word, phonemic segmentation and the speech-to-print match; and *controlling reading and writing processes,* including the form and functions of writing and invented spelling. We noted that most children acquire important literacy abilities long before they enter school.

The third section of this chapter described a variety of informal assessment procedures. These informal strategies can be used to gather information about a variety of different emergent literacy abilities. For example, *dictated stories* can be used to gather information about children's language development, sense of story, awareness of the speech-to-print match, and memory for print. Other strategies include guidelines for using *structured observations and interviews, checklists, retellings,* and *writing samples.*

Consistent with the guidelines for assessment provided in Chapter 3, the techniques described in this chapter allow for meaningful, unobtrusive, systematic, and continuous assessment of emergent literacy. Recognizing that readiness must be viewed within the context of the instructional program and tasks that children are going to encounter in school, many of the techniques described here are designed to be used with children *during instruction* and/or as they engage in tasks like those they will be expected to accomplish.

CHAPTER 5

Informal Reading Inventories

INTRODUCTION

The information obtained through interviews and observations provides the background for further evaluation of the learner, using formal and informal assessment instruments. We pursue the evaluation of the learner in this chapter with a discussion of informal reading inventories (IRIs). In the hands of a skilled examiner, an IRI can yield exceptionally useful information about a student's knowledge and application of reading skills and strategies.

Although informal reading inventories have generated considerable controversy over the past 40 years, they are potentially the most powerful assessment instruments available to both the classroom teacher and the clinician. Informal reading inventories reflect the demands of classroom reading better than most available assessment instruments. When adapted in the ways we suggest in this chapter, they can also provide useful information about the ways in which the factors that influence reading affect achievement in individual readers, thus capturing the interactive nature of reading in ways that more formal tests cannot.

Chapter Overview

This chapter presents an overview of various IRI procedures, rather than a single set of guidelines that might give the mistaken impression that there is only one way to construct or use an IRI. The specific topics addressed in this chapter are: traditional IRI usage, including construction, administration, scoring, and interpretation; issues and problems with traditional IRI construction, administration, scoring, and interpretation; guidelines for constructing and selecting IRIs; and alternatives to traditional IRI procedures, such as miscue analysis, retellings, and multiple administrations.

UNDERSTANDING TRADITIONAL USAGE OF IRIs

Definition

The Informal Reading Inventory (IRI) is probably the most widely known form of systematic informal reading assessment. An IRI is an individually administered reading test composed of a series of graded word lists and graded passages that the student reads aloud to the examiner. The examiner notes oral reading errors as the student reads, and asks comprehension questions when the student has finished reading each passage. Many informal reading inventories also include silent reading passages and passages that are read to the student to determine a listening comprehension level, along with comprehension questions for each. When the student has finished reading, errors are analyzed and percentage scores are calculated for word recognition performance on the graded word lists and the oral reading passages. In addition, the examiner tallies performance on the comprehension questions for the various reading passages.

The two primary purposes for administering an IRI are to place students in materials at the appropriate levels by establishing their *independent, instructional,* and *frustration* reading levels; and to identify strengths and weaknesses in the areas of word recognition and comprehension by analyzing the amount and type of word recognition and comprehension errors. The first half of this chapter focuses primarily on the traditional usage of IRIs for placement purposes, and the second half focuses on the evaluative functions of an IRI.

Placement Levels

Four different levels of reading can be identified by applying established criteria to a student's word recognition and comprehension performance.

1. *Independent level:* This is the level at which students read fluently and make very few word recognition or comprehension errors. The reader can handle material at this level easily, without the assistance of the teacher. Free or recreational reading materials should be at this level, as well as reading assignments such as homework, tests, and seatwork that the student is expected to complete independently.

2. *Instructional level:* At this level, the reader makes some errors; however, word recognition errors are not excessive, and comprehension is adequate. This is the level at which the student will benefit most from direct instruction. For each child, the materials used for direct instruction—such as basal readers, subject area textbooks, and skill activities—should be at this level.

3. *Frustration level:* This is the level at which reading is often slow and halting, and the reader makes an excessive number of errors. Materials at this level are too difficult for the reader, even with assistance. Students should not be placed in materials at this level, because effective learning is unlikely to occur.

4. *Listening comprehension level:* This is the level at which the student can satisfactorily comprehend material that has been read aloud. This level provides a rough estimate of the student's receptive language comprehension and is often used as a measure of the student's potential reading level.

Background

Betts (1946) and Kilgallon (1942) are frequently credited with the development of the IRI, although similar techniques were suggested by others even earlier (e.g., Gray, 1920). Betts (1946) originally designed the IRI to be constructed by the teacher, using reading materials in which the students might actually be placed and procedures for administration that were similar to those used in classroom reading instruction, such as silent reading followed by oral rereading. The intent was to evaluate students' reading performance under circumstances that were as similar to classroom reading conditions as possible. Today there are many types of IRIs and a variety of administration procedures. Some teachers still construct their own IRIs, but many prefer to use IRIs that have been prepared by a publisher to accompany a particular basal reading series. Others use IRIs that have been prepared commercially, independent of any particular reading series (see annotated list of commercially prepared IRIs on p. 214).

A key feature of an IRI is that the activities it involves closely approximate the activities found in daily classroom reading instruction. For this reason, the results obtained from an IRI are more likely to be generalizable to classroom performance than results obtained from formal tests using activities that are further removed from classroom practice. A second important feature of IRIs is that they are informal measures, and can be used more flexibly than formal tests.

Formal tests are designed to compare a student's score to that of other students (see Chapter 6). Standardized procedures are used to administer these tests to large numbers of students in order to establish the standards for comparison. Teachers or test examiners must administer formal tests in exactly the same way as they were administered in the standardization process in order for the scores to be valid. In contrast, IRIs are designed to compare a student's scores against some criteria for mastery (e.g., 99% word recognition and 90% comprehension) that have been established independent of how any particular group of students might perform on the same test.

Few, if any, published IRIs provide scoring criteria based on the performance of other students. Since the scores are not based on a standardized administration of the IRI, the teacher or examiner can make many decisions about the procedures used for constructing, administering, scoring, and interpreting IRIs. This is one reason why so many different procedures have developed since the IRI was first introduced. This is also the reason that we present an overview of various IRI procedures in the next section, rather than a single set of guidelines which might give the mistaken impression that there is only one way to construct and/or use an IRI.

Components of an IRI

The basic components of an informal reading inventory are graded word lists, graded reading passages, comprehension questions, and a summary/analysis sheet. To help illustrate some of these components, examples of an examiner's copy of graded word lists, a graded passage, and a summary sheet are presented in Figure 5.1(a—c).

Graded Word Lists

Most IRIs begin with lists of words that have been graded to correspond with the grade levels in basal reading series. Although not originally included in the IRI, graded word lists have become a standard part of today's IRIs, particularly those that are published rather than teacher-constructed. Graded word lists are used primarily to determine accuracy of word recognition in isolation, and to assist the examiner in determining the level at which the student should begin reading the graded passages.

**FIGURE
5.1(a)**
*Sample IRI
Components*

Form B • Graded Word Lists • Performance Booklet

List B-B (Pre-Primer)	Timed	Untimed	List B (Primer)	Timed	Untimed
1. we			1. they		
2. and			2. she		
3. house			3. will		
4. the			4. of		
5. duck			5. blue		
6. one			6. it		
7. street			7. are		
8. happy			8. his		
9. lost			9. now		
10. know			10. dress		
11. do			11. if		
12. at			12. from		
13. very			13. morning		
14. party			14. father		
15. out			15. ask		
16. find			16. back		
17. goat			17. green		
18. wish			18. time		
19. first			19. who		
20. sing			20. cookie		
Number Correct			Number Correct		
Total Score			Total Score		

Scoring Guide for Graded Word Lists

Independent	Instructional	Frustration
20 19	18 17 16 15 14	13 or less

**FIGURE
5.1(b)**
*Sample IRI
Components*

BASIC READING INVENTORY PERFORMANCE BOOKLET

Jerry L. Johns
Northern Illinois University

Student _____ Grade _____ Sex ☐ M ☐ F Date of Test _____

School _____ Examiner _____ Date of Birth _____

	Word Recognition		Comprehension		Listening	Estimate of Levels
SUMMARY OF STUDENT'S PERFORMANCE						
Grade	Isolation (Word Lists)	Context (Passages)	Oral Reading Form ___	Silent Reading Form ___	Form ___	
	Total Score / Level	Percent Correct / Level	Percent Correct / Level	Percent Correct / Level	Percent Correct	
PP						
P						
1						Independent _____
2						
3						Instructional _____
4						
5						Frustration _____
6						Listening _____
7						
8						

SCORING GUIDE FOR READING LEVELS

Percent of Word Recognition in Context	100 99	98 97 96	95	94 93 92 91	90 or less
	Independent Level	Independent or Instructional	Instructional Level	Instructional or Frustration	Frustration Level
Percent of Comprehension	100 95 90	85 80	75	70 65 60 55	50 or less

INFORMAL MISCUE ANALYSIS SUMMARY

Type of Miscues	Frequency of Occurrence			General Impact of Miscues on Meaning		
	Seldom	Sometimes	Frequently	No Change	Little Change	Much Change
Substitutions						
Insertions						
Omissions						
Reversals						

Consistent Strengths (+) and Weaknesses (−)

Check (✓) Consistent Difficulties

Comprehension

☐ main idea
☐ fact
☐ inference
☐ evaluation
☐ vocabulary
☐ lower level
☐ higher level

Word Recognition

☐ use of context
☐ single consonants
☐ consonant clusters
☐ short vowels
☐ long vowels
☐ syllabication
☐ flexible word attack

Oral Reading

☐ fluency
☐ word by word
☐ ignores punctuation
☐ lacks expression
☐ loses place
☐ repeats from habit
☐ requests assistance

Observations

**FIGURE
5.1(c)**

*Sample IRI
Components*

B-B (Pre-Primer)

F   1. ___   What happened to Pete?
(he lost his ball)

F   2. ___   What did the ball Jill found look like?
(blue and small)

E   3. ___   How do you think Pete lost his ball?
(any logical response)

I   4. ___   How did Pete know that the ball Jill found wasn't his?
(any logical response; it was small and blue; it wasn't red)

V   5. ___   What does "find" mean?
(to locate; to look for something and then see it)

"I cannot find my ball," said Pete. "It is a big ball. My ball is red."

"Here is a ball," Jill said. "The ball is blue. It is small. It is not red."

"I see a ball," said Pete. "It is red. It is big. It is my ball."

Percent of Word Recognition ____

$\overline{)3000}$ WPM

Percent of Comprehension ____

Scoring Guide: Pre-Primer

Percent of Word Recognition in Context

100 99	98 97 96	95	94 93 92 91	90 or less
Independent Level	Independent or Instructional	Instructional Level	Instructional or Frustration	Frustration Level
100 95 90	85 80	75	70 65 60 55	50 or less

Percent of Comprehension

Reprinted from "Basic Reading Inventory Performance Booklet" from *Basic Reading Inventory: Pre-Primer–Grade Eight, Third Edition*, by Jerry L. Johns. Copyright © 1985 by Kendall/Hunt Publishing Company. Used with permission.

Each graded word list typically contains between 10 and 20 words, and includes different types of words ranging from a large number of function words, such as *the* or *want* at the lower grade levels, to multisyllabic content words that may or may not be easily decoded at the upper grade levels. If the IRI has been constructed by a publisher or a teacher for a particular series, the words are usually selected from the word lists that appear frequently in the teacher's manual or in the back of the pupil edition for each level in the reading series. It is often unclear how the word lists have been generated for commercially prepared IRIs (Jongsma & Jongsma, 1981). Some are created from previously published lists of graded words or word frequency lists such as *Dolch* (Dolch, 1942), *San Diego Quick*

Assessment (LaPray & Ross, 1969), *New Instant Word List* (Fry, 1980), and *Slosson Oral Reading Test* (Slosson, 1983). However the lists are created, there is generally an effort to represent high-frequency features in the language, providing a sampling of words that students who read a great deal would not find difficult to recognize.

Graded Reading Passages

The graded word lists are followed by a series of graded reading passages. Most IRIs have two or three passages at each grade level, so comparisons can be made among oral, silent, and listening comprehension. Alternatively, the various forms for each level may be used as pre- and post-tests (before and after instruction). The purpose of the graded reading passages is to provide a basis for evaluating comprehension and for examining oral reading accuracy in context.

Graded reading passages range in length from 25 to 350 words. Typically, the length of the passages increases gradually, from the lowest to the highest grade levels, along the following lines: preprimer and primer, 25–60 words; Grade 1, 75–100 words; Grades 2 and 3, 75–150; Grades 4, 5, and 6, 150–200 words; Grades 7 through 10, 200–350 words. When an IRI is constructed by a publisher or a teacher from a particular series, the passages are excerpts from the readers in the series. The authors of commercially prepared IRIs often construct their own passages or select excerpts from children's materials found in the library.

Passage difficulty is determined by the level of the material from which it is taken and/or through the use of readability formulas (see Chapter 9 for detailed explanation). Beyond this, little attention is given to the text characteristics described in Chapter 1, such as type of text, organization, coherence, or familiarity.

Comprehension Questions

The graded passages are accompanied by a series of open-ended comprehension questions. The number of questions may vary by grade level and among different IRIs. Most commercially prepared IRIs have between 5 and 10 questions per passage, although a few have more.

Most IRIs categorize the comprehension questions according to types such as main idea, detail, literal, inferential, vocabulary, sequence, and cause-effect. Guidelines for constructing IRIs also recommend that different types of questions be used (e.g., Johnson & Kress, 1965; Silvaroli, Kear, & McKenna, 1982). Valmont (1972) provides the following general guidelines for constructing questions, which may also be used to evaluate existing sets of questions:

- Avoid yes/no questions, and questions stated in the negative.
- Make certain questions do not overlap (that the content in one question does not answer another).
- Keep questions short and simple.
- Begin questions with who, what, when, where, how, and why.
- Avoid writing questions with multiple answers that cannot be specified.

Student and Examiner Materials

The student materials include the word lists and passages that are to be read. The teacher materials include the record sheets that are used for recording and summarizing the student's responses. The student materials for graded word lists usually are either separate lists of words or individual words presented on index cards.

The materials designed for student reading vary greatly. In IRIs developed for a particular reading series, the students may read from the printed textbook itself or from a reproduction of the text (with or without illustrations). Commercially prepared IRIs will contain a booklet of printed passages. A review of commercially prepared IRIs indicated that 2 of the 11 inventories reviewed included illustrations along with their passages (Jongsma & Jongsma, 1981). It is also accepted practice to vary the size of the print type, in a manner that is consistent with the grade level of the passage.

The examiner or teacher materials for the graded word lists are copies of the lists with spaces for recording the student's responses. Commercially prepared IRIs often include a scoring guide that indicates the number of errors corresponding to the different placement levels. This assists the examiner in making decisions about the next step in administering the IRI.

Copies of the passages (triple-spaced to make room for recording oral reading errors) and scoring guides are also included in the teacher's materials for the graded reading passages. Scoring guides for calculating the student's rate of reading may also be provided. In addition, the examiner's materials include the comprehension questions and suggested answers, with room for recording student responses. Some IRIs also provide motivational statements that are to be read to the student before the presentation of the passage, to provide background and stimulate interest. Scoring guides are often included on the examiner's copy of the reading passages as well.

Finally, most published IRIs provide some type of summary sheet for recording student performance on word lists, oral reading, and oral, silent, and listening comprehension at each grade level. These scores are used to determine a student's independent, instructional, and frustration reading levels, which are recorded on the summary sheet. Many summary sheets also provide for recording the numbers and types of oral reading and comprehension errors made by the student.

Issues and Problems

The first major area of concern regarding the construction of IRIs focuses on the representativeness of the reading selections. When a passage is selected from a basal reader for use in an IRI, it is assumed to represent the materials the student will find in that reader. This may have been an accurate assumption when IRIs were first suggested and the vocabulary and content of basal readers were more highly controlled than they are today. However, in today's basal readers, passages taken from a single level can vary from first to twelfth grade readability (Bradley & Ames, 1977).

If a book designated as being at the fourth reader level contains selections that range from first to eighth grade readability, then a student's performance on a fourth reader selection may vary considerably depending on the passage selected for use in the IRI. In fact, Bradley and Ames (1976) used several passages from the same reader and found that approximately 40% of the students tested had scores that ranged from the independent to the frustration level. Given that there appears to be no systematic variation of intrabook readability, it is difficult, if not impossible, to determine which portion of a book is related to IRI results (Bradley & Ames, 1977). Harris and Sipay (1990) have suggested that the problem of intrabook variation in readability can be addressed by sampling a large number of selections from each level, averaging their readability estimates, and then selecting the passages that come closest to the average for each level.

A second problem related to the reading selections involves the comparability of alternate passages at each grade level. Although there is a clear advantage to having several alternate passages at each grade level, it is difficult to be certain that these passages are comparable. Some authors suggest creating different passages by using different portions of the same selection. However, there is also variability in readability within selections, although perhaps not as great as within a book. When passages from the same selection are used, there is also the problem of accumulated prior knowledge affecting performance from one passage to the next.

Most IRIs do not account for the fact that there are *many* text factors that are likely to influence student's performance. For example, it has been found that the effects of interest are sufficiently strong to cause comprehension scores to vary between the frustration and instructional levels (Estes & Vaughan, 1973). Another finding is that the type and length of the passage influences the number and types of oral reading errors (see Wixson, 1979). Other factors, discussed in Chapter 1, include text organization and topic familiarity.

A third major area of concern in the construction of IRIs focuses on the nature of the comprehension questions. Peterson, Greenlaw, and Tierney (1978) constructed three sets of questions for a single IRI according to a popular set of guidelines that called for one vocabulary, two literal, and two inferential questions. When these three sets of questions were used in testing, approximately 65% of students examined were assigned two different instructional levels, and 10% were assigned three instructional levels. This suggests that different questions for the same passages can produce different results.

Finally, we must also be concerned with the degree to which comprehension questions are *passage dependent*. Questions that are passage dependent have answers that depend on information provided in the passage, rather than on the reader's prior knowledge about the topic. To illustrate this problem, read and answer the following questions taken from Johns (1988):

1. Skyscrapers are different from other buildings because they are: a. bigger; b. higher; c. cleaner; d. prettier.
2. A person who "operates with a frying pan" uses the pan for: a. cutting fish; b. cooking fish; c. hitting fish; d. cleaning fish.

How did you do? Johns found that 134 of 160 fourth- and fifth-grade students answered the first item correctly, and 131 answered the second one right *without* reading the passages. These questions were part of a study in which students scored significantly better than chance when they answered the reading comprehension questions from a test *before* they read the passages.

Studies of IRI-type tests suggest that results may be influenced by questions that are passage independent. For example, an analysis of the comprehension questions on four IRI-type tests indicated that 23–31% of the questions were passage independent (Allington, Chodos, Domaracki, & Truex, 1977). In addition, the analysis demonstrated that there was a large degree of variability in the number of passage independent items from one passage to the next within each test. In other words, the results of these studies suggest that in some cases, the variability in scores observed between passages may be attributable to differences in the comprehension questions, not to real differences in ability.

Administering an IRI

IRIs are administered individually, and require 30–40 minutes for administration. They can be administered in more than one session. IRIs typically are administered in a quiet place, with the examiner and the student sitting at different sides of a table. It is usually a good idea to audiotape the administration for later reference. As with all aspects of the IRI, there is no one right way to administer it. Decisions about how to administer the IRI must be based on the purpose for administration and the types of information desired.

Graded Word Lists

The word lists are introduced by saying something like, "I have some words I would like you to read for me today. Please read carefully, and if you come to a word you don't know, just try your best." The word lists are then presented, either as a whole or one word at a time, through a window cut in a manila folder or on individual index cards. Administration of the word lists begins with the list that is at least two years below the student's grade placement. If the student misses any words in the first list that is administered, the examiner drops to lower lists until the student achieves 100% accuracy. As the student reads, the examiner makes a specified mark to indicate when the words are read correctly, and writes down exactly what the student says when a word is miscalled. The student is encouraged to read words that are unfamiliar, and the administration of the word lists continues until the student makes some specified number of errors (e.g., five errors in a list, or three consecutive errors).

Some published IRIs only have a timed administration of the word lists, in which the student is given anywhere from 2 to 10 seconds to respond. Some only have untimed presentations, where the student is given unlimited time to respond. Still others have some combination of the two; for example, a timed administration followed by an untimed administration of the words that were missed the first time. The combined administration provides the greatest amount of information; however, the final decision about the manner in which the word lists should be administered depends on the purpose for administering the IRI.

Oral Reading Passages

Administration of the oral reading passages begins with the passage that is at the same level as the word list on which the student achieved some specified criterion (e.g., 100%). If the student does poorly on the first passage, the examiner drops down one level at a time until performance is satisfactory. The examiner begins the administration by saying something like, "Now I have some passages I would like you to read out loud to me. Please read carefully, because I will ask you some questions when you are finished. If you come to a word you don't know, just try your best." Then the examiner reads the motivation statement, if there is one, and asks the student to begin reading. The examiner may also wish to begin timing the student's reading in order to calculate the oral reading rate.

The examiner follows along as the student reads, and uses a code to mark every deviation from the printed text on the teacher's response sheet. If the student stops reading at a difficult word, the examiner waits some specified amount of time (e.g., 5 seconds) and then either pronounces the word or directs the student to skip it and continue. The administration of the oral reading passages is stopped when the student is visibly frustrated or is making excessive word recognition and comprehension errors. Since it is not always possible to score the test immediately, the decision to suspend testing is frequently based on the examiner's judgment.

The oral reading errors that are commonly coded include *omissions, insertions, substitutions, repetitions, hesitations, ignoring punctuation, prompts, reversals,* and *self-corrections.* The sample coding system presented in Figure 5.2 is just one of many that can be used. Which particular system is used is not as important as becoming familiar enough with one system so that it can be used quickly and consistently. It is important to code all deviations from the text, so the student's performance can be reconstructed at a later time. Audiotaping the administration can also help with this.

Silent Reading and Listening Passages

In addition to oral reading passages, the examiner can administer silent and/or listening comprehension passages. The examiner may also want to time the silent reading to determine the student's silent reading rate. There are a number of variations in the order of administration for oral, silent, and listening passages. Several of these variations are listed below:

1. oral reading only;
2. an oral reading passage followed by a silent reading, and possibly a listening comprehension passage, all at the same grade level before going on to higher levels;
3. oral reading passages until frustration level is achieved, followed by silent

FIGURE 5.2
*Sample
Coding System*

Error	Sample Notation
SUBSTITUTIONS — mispronunciations or real word replacements	I saw ~~cats~~ *cars* and ~~dogs~~ *dojes*.
INSERTIONS — letters, syllables, or words added to the text	I saw *the*ʌcats and dogs.
OMISSIONS — letters, syllables, or words deleted from the text	I saw cat(s and dogs.
REVERSALS — reversed order of words	I saw cats and dogs.
PROMPTS — words pronounced by the examiner	**P** I saw cats and dogs.
PUNCTUATION — obvious omission of punctuation	I saw cats and dogs₀
HESITATIONS — obvious pause	I saw **H** cats and dogs.
REPETITIONS — part of a word, a word, or words repeated	I saw cats and dogs.
SELF-CORRECTIONS — spontaneous corrections by the reader	*cars* ✓ I saw cats and dogs.

reading passages starting at that level or one level below until frustration level is achieved, which is then followed by listening comprehension passages;

4. silent reading followed by oral rereading of all or parts of the same passage.

A review of commercially prepared IRIs indicates that 6 of the 11 inventories examined either disregard silent reading or make it optional (Jongsma & Jongsma, 1981). The reviewers speculate that the most likely reason for this practice is to shorten administration time. As before, decisions about how to administer the reading passages should be based on the purposes for which the IRI is being administered and the information that one wishes to obtain.

Comprehension Questions

After the student finishes reading, the passage is removed and the examiner says something like, "Now I am going to ask you some questions about the passage you just read." The examiner reads each question and provides ample time for the student to make a response. If the student does not respond, or appears to have misunderstood a question, the question may be asked again or rephrased. Additional information may be elicited by neutral questions, such as "Can you tell me more?" However, leading questions that provide information related to the answer should be avoided.

Issues and Problems

The major issue in the administration of an IRI is the effect that different procedures might have on students' scores. For example, Brecht (1977) reports a study in which children were administered IRIs both with oral reading at sight and with silent reading followed by oral rereading. Only 20% of the students obtained the same instructional level under both types of administration. When the rereading format was used, 70% scored at least one grade level higher, and 10% scored at least one grade level lower.

Another factor in administration that may influence students' scores is the directions provided to both students and teachers. According to Jongsma and Jongsma (1981), some inventories clearly emphasize the importance of reading accurately and not making mistakes. Although this may seem trivial, they point to evidence that directions can influence the number and type of oral reading errors, the degree of comprehension, and the rate of reading. One inventory actually directs the students to decrease their speed for subject area material and to reread sections or words on which they made "careless mistakes." Two inventories direct the teacher to start all students, regardless of age or reading ability, at the lowest levels on both the word lists and passages. This practice could result in boredom and fatigue for both the student and the teacher.

A final issue to be considered in the administration of an IRI is the effect of different procedures for administering oral, silent, and listening passages. If passages are only administered orally, is it safe to assume that performance can be generalized to silent reading? Research has yet to provide a definitive answer to this question. However, an interactive view of reading suggests that there will be differences in performance under different reading conditions. This means that performance may vary when students are asked to read a passage orally, as opposed to silent reading followed by oral rereading. Therefore, caution is urged in generalizing from one reading situation to another. It may also be necessary to administer an IRI under various conditions that are representative of those the student encounters frequently in the classroom to obtain a complete understanding of a student's reading abilities (see Multiple Samples, p. 200).

Scoring an IRI

Preliminary scoring occurs while the IRI is being taken, because scores are needed to make decisions about subsequent steps in administration. The final scoring is completed when the student has finished the IRI, and the scores are entered on a summary sheet.

Graded Word Lists

The examiner determines the percentage correct on each word list and enters the number and the placement level, when one is provided, in a scoring guide on the examiner's response sheets. Unfortunately, this is not quite as easy as it may appear at first glance. As soon as we attempt to score an IRI, we are confronted with the question, What is an error? or, conversely, What is an acceptable response? Once again, there is no one correct way; it depends on the situation.

The biggest decisions that have to be made in scoring the word lists are how to handle self-corrections and the time factor. In other words, does a student know a word if it takes 10 seconds to identify it, or if it is misread and then self-corrected?

Some commercially prepared IRIs provide no guidelines for time limits or how to score self-corrections. Those that do recommend time limits for acceptable responses suggest time limits ranging from 10 to 15 seconds. Some IRIs suggest that all deviations, self-corrected or not, count as errors, while others do not count self-corrections as errors.

Clearly, when there are only 10 to 20 words in a list, decisions about what constitutes an error are not trivial. Each error translates into a 5–10% difference in the scores, which can have a significant impact on decisions about placement levels and the entry level into the reading passages.

Oral Reading Passages

The examiner counts the oral reading errors and determines the percentage of word recognition accuracy. The percentage of word recognition accuracy can either be determined from a scoring guide of some type, or calculated by hand using the following procedure:

1. Subtract the number of errors from the total number of words in the passage to obtain the total number of words correct.
2. Divide the total number of words correct by the total number of words in the passage.
3. Multiply the result by 100 to convert to a percentage.

The percentage of word recognition accuracy and the placement level, if provided by a scoring guide, are entered on the summary sheet. In addition, the number of errors of each type is calculated and recorded on the summary sheet.

The question of what constitutes an error becomes even more complex in scoring the oral reading passages. Guidelines for scoring oral reading range from counting every deviation from the text as an error, to the other extreme, counting only those deviations that alter the meaning of the text. Most scoring guidelines lie somewhere between these two extremes.

A review of the scoring guidelines of 11 commercially prepared IRIs indicates that the majority consider omissions, insertions, substitutions, reversals, prompts, and repetitions to be scorable errors, and self-corrections, hesitations, and punctuation to be scorable but not reportable errors (Jongsma & Jongsma, 1981). In an attempt to recognize that some errors may be more serious than others, some authors have recommended weighting the errors by deducting one point for each error that deviates from the text and disrupts meaning, and one-half point for each error that deviates from the text but does not disrupt meaning (Harris & Sipay, 1990). Whatever decisions are made regarding the scoring of oral reading errors, it is clear that they will have an impact on the percentage scores and must be taken into consideration when establishing or applying the criteria for placement.

Comprehension Questions

The examiner determines if the answers to each comprehension question are correct, incorrect, or partially correct, based on the suggested answers and on an awareness of acceptable alternatives. It is important to consider any oral reading errors that may have interfered with comprehension. The percentage comprehension score is calculated using a scoring guide, or by dividing the number of questions that were answered correctly by the total number of questions and then multiplying by 100. The percentage comprehension score and the placement level, when provided by a scoring guide, are then recorded on the summary sheet. In addition, the number of each type of questions missed is calculated and entered on the summary sheet. Because there are often as few as five comprehension questions per passage, scoring decisions have a major impact on the final results of the IRI.

Rate

The examiner determines the number of words read per minute for silent and/or oral reading, using the following procedure:

1. Convert the amount of time it took to read the passage to seconds.
2. Divide the number of seconds by the number of words in the passage.
3. Multiply the resulting number by 60 to reconvert it into words per minute.

When the rate in words per minute has been calculated, it is entered on the examiner's response sheets and the summary sheet, when appropriate.

Issues and Problems

A major area of concern regarding the scoring of an IRI is that decisions about what gets counted as an error are going to make a difference in the scores used for determining placement levels. Betts (1946) was not entirely clear about what constituted an error; however, an examination of the summary sheets he used suggests that all deviations from the text were counted as errors. Much of the controversy about scoring oral reading errors centers around so-called good errors; that is, errors that do not disrupt the meaning of the text and appear to arise from the reader's meaningful processing of the text, rather than some faulty skill or strategy.

The particular error type that has received the most attention is the repetition error. Some argue that repetitions should not be counted as errors, because they represent the reader's attempt to preserve the meaning of the text (K. Goodman, 1973). Others argue that repetitions should be counted as errors, because failure to do so will result in readers becoming physiologically frustrated before they reach the percentage of errors normally recognized as the student's frustration level. Ekwall and Shanker (1983) sum up the situation as follows: "Although it may not seem 'fair' to a student to count repetitions because the student ends up with more errors, it is in reality less fair not to count these errors. If the student appears to be a better reader than is actually the case, the student will be given reading material that is too difficult" (p. 374).

For our part, it is difficult to make a single rule that accommodates all situations satisfactorily. In general, we do not consider repetitions, especially those that are accompanied by self-corrections, to be scorable errors. However, there are instances when repetitions are so disruptive that they are clearly interfering with effective reading. In these cases, repetitions should be counted as errors.

A second area of concern focuses on the practice of aggregating different types of oral reading errors across passages and looking for patterns. Research has shown that the type of errors that readers make is directly related to the difficulty of the material. In fact, Kibby (1979) found that including frustration-level errors in an analysis can give a distorted view of the reader's skills and strategies. Our position on this is that, when possible, oral reading errors should not be aggregated across passages. However, if some aggregation is necessary, then they should only be aggregated for passages on which the student's performance was relatively comparable.

A related problem is that many commercially prepared IRIs analyze oral reading errors in isolation (Jongsma & Jongsma, 1981). The focus of this type of analysis is on letter-sound differences, without any attention to context, the effects of previous errors, and/or the reader's background knowledge. We believe that oral reading errors should be analyzed both in terms of letter-sound differences and in relation to the contexts in which they occurred (see Miscue Analysis, p. 188).

Finally, traditional IRI scoring procedures do not provide any mechanism for evaluating the interaction between oral reading and comprehension errors. Oral reading accuracy has a differential effect on various types of comprehension. Nicholsen, Pearson, and Dykstra (1979) report the results of research that revealed the following:

1. Accurate word recognition is important for comprehension of specific information, but relatively unimportant for global interpretation.
2. Errors that make sense in a sentence (e.g., *giant* for *gorilla*) are more likely to disrupt comprehension of specific information than errors that clearly do not make sense (e.g., *wall* for *gorilla*), because students are more likely to maintain a faulty interpretation that makes sense than one that is unreasonable.
3. Comprehension questions that require students to relate the ideas in two sentences are affected more by the word recognition error rate than questions that require responses based primarily on prior knowledge.

Thus, it is important that oral reading and comprehension errors be examined in tandem to determine the interaction between word recognition and comprehension abilities for a particular reader.

Interpreting an IRI

The examiner evaluates the information on the summary sheet regarding the percentage of word recognition accuracy and comprehension at each level, and determines the student's independent, instructional, and frustration reading levels. In addition, the examiner evaluates the information on the summary sheet regarding different types of oral reading and comprehension errors to determine specific strengths and weaknesses.

FIGURE 5.3

Betts'
Placement
Criteria

	Word Recognition		Comprehension
Independent	99%+	AND	90%+
Instructional	95%+	AND	75%+
Frustration	90% or less	OR	50% or less
Listening Comprehension			75%+

Placement Levels

Some IRIs provide placement-level criteria for the graded word lists, while others do not. There is no general agreement among those that do provide placement levels as to what the criteria should be. A review conducted by the authors of a limited sample of commercially prepared IRIs provided the following range of placement criteria for lists of 10–20 words: independent level, 90–100% (0–2 errors); instructional level, 80–90% (2–4 errors); and frustration level, 80% and below (2–4+ errors).

Determining the criteria for a student's general independent, instructional, and frustration levels on the reading passages is a complex issue. The original criteria, established by Betts (1946) and still the most widely accepted today, are presented in Figure 5.3.

Reviews of commercially prepared IRIs indicate that the majority continue to use Betts' criteria. There are several problems associated with the use of these criteria. First, they leave a scoring gap between the frustration and instructional levels that can make interpretation fairly difficult (e.g., What happens to the student who scores 65% in comprehension?). Second, the Betts' criteria were developed on the basis of a study with fourth-grade students, and subsequent research suggests the need for criteria that account for the differential effects of age, grade, and/or the difficulty of the materials (Cooper, 1952; Powell & Dunkeld, 1971). Finally, the procedures for administering IRIs have changed somewhat from those under which the Betts' criteria were first developed. Most guidelines for administering either published or teacher-constructed IRIs call for oral reading at sight, rather than Betts' procedure of silent reading followed by oral rereading.

As a result of the problems with the Betts' criteria, some believe that different placement criteria should be used. Powell (1980) has suggested the criteria presented in Figure 5.4 to account for both the grade level of the materials and two methods of administration—oral reading at sight and silent reading followed by oral rereading. Given the disparity between the Betts' and Powell criteria, Figure 5.5 presents the ranges based on the actual criteria used in the majority of commercially prepared IRIs as a guide for establishing reasonable placement criteria.

FIGURE 5.4
Powell's Placement Criteria

Reading Levels by Grade	Reading at Sight		Oral Rereading	
	Word Recognition	Comprehension	Word Recognition	Comprehension
Independent				
1–2	94%+	80%+	94%+	80%+
3–5	96%+	85%+	96%+	85%+
6+	97%+	90%+	97%+	90%+
Instructional				
1–2	88–94%	55–80%	92–94%	70–80%
3–5	92–96%	60–86%	95–96%	75–85%
6+	94–97%	65–90%	97–97%	80–90%
Frustration				
1–2	86% or less	55% or less	91% or less	70% or less
3–5	92% or less	60% or less	91% or less	75% or less
6+	94% or less	65% or less	96% or less	80% or less

FIGURE 5.5
Ranges of Criteria Used by Published IRIs

	Word Recognition	Comprehension
Independent	96–99%+	75–90%+
Instructional	92–95%+	60–75%+
Frustration	90–92% or less	50–70% or less
Listening Comprehension		60–75%+

Oral Reading

The traditional interpretation of oral reading errors is based on a preponderance of errors of a particular type. The following interpretations of error types are adapted from Ekwall and Shanker (1983).

Omissions. Students who do not read carefully may skip over some words; these are not serious errors if meaning is kept intact. Some students who have trouble with longer words may simply pronounce the first syllable, indicating a need for instruction in word analysis. Some omissions, particularly those of word endings, may be due to language differences.

Insertions. When the insertions are correct within the context of the sentence, it can usually be assumed that the student is comprehending the passage.

These errors may be a sign of carelessness or an indication that the student's oral language ability may surpass his or her reading ability. If the insertions do not make sense within the context of the sentence, the student may be having difficulty with comprehension.

Substitutions. Substitutions or partial mispronunciations may suggest a careless reader, lack of word recognition skills, or reflect the language of a dialect speaker. Students who constantly make gross mispronunciation errors usually require help in any or all of the word-analysis skills, but especially in phonics and structural analysis.

Prompts. Students who ask for aid or wait for assistance usually lack sight vocabulary and/or word analysis skills. They may also lack self-confidence in their ability to identify strange words.

Reversals. Students make reversals for a number of reasons. Most beginning readers tend to make reversals because they have not yet learned certain important perceptual distinctions. Reversals may also accompany more serious problems in severely disabled readers. The common assumption that students who make persistent reversal errors will have serious reading problems has not been supported by research.

Repetitions. Repetitions may indicate that the student is attempting to figure out a word or phrase. Sometimes repetitions are due to nervousness. Some believe that repetitions are a sign of normal, effective processing. Others believe they indicate some type of reading difficulty.

Punctuation. Disregard of punctuation and expressionless reading may simply indicate a need to work on the meaning of various punctuation marks. In some cases, ignoring punctuation is symptomatic of more serious word recognition or comprehension problems.

Hesitations. A student who pauses longer than is normal before words is usually either lacking in sight vocabulary or word analysis skills, has formed a habit of word-by-word reading, or has determined that there is a problem of some kind.

Comprehension

The interpretation of a student's comprehension skills is based on an analysis of errors on different types of comprehension questions. Students with a preponderance of errors on a particular type of comprehension question are believed to have difficulty with certain types of comprehension subskills. Depending on the types of comprehension questions included on the IRI, these problems might include understanding literal ideas or factual information, drawing inferences, identifying main idea or supporting ideas, and understanding cause and effect or sequential relations.

Rate

The interpretation of a student's reading rate is based on the number of words read per minute during oral and/or silent reading. A slow reading rate may indicate a reading problem, but an acceptable rate does not guarantee that the material is

FIGURE 5.6
Reading Rate in Words per Minute

Instructional Reading Level	Oral Reading Rate at Sight	Silent Reading
Grade 1	45–65	45–65
Grade 2	70–100	70–100
Grade 3	105–125	120–140
Grade 4	125–145	130–180
Grade 5	135–155	165–205
Grade 6	140–160	190–220

being comprehended at a satisfactory level. Desired silent reading rates are similar to oral reading rates at first- and second-grade instructional levels, but begin to increase sharply at the third-grade instructional level, when word identification becomes more automatic. It is also important to remember that reading rates will vary according to the conditions of the reading situation, and that norms or standards are good only for the conditions under which they were obtained.

Guidelines provided by Powell (n.d.) for evaluating the oral and silent reading rates obtained on IRIs for students at different instructional levels are presented in Figure 5.6. When using these guidelines, it is important to remember that students' instructional levels may be different than their grade levels.

Issues and Problems

The biggest problem confronting those who use IRIs for placement purposes is that there is no evidence that reading levels established through IRI testing actually correspond to classroom performance. The validity of IRI placement levels hinges entirely on readability estimates of the IRI passages. The results of an IRI must be interpreted cautiously when placing a student in appropriate instructional materials, given the variability among different basal programs and the levels within each program, and among commercially prepared IRIs (Jongsma & Jongsma, 1981).

For those who assume that IRI levels are indeed indicative of classroom performance, the next problem is to decide on the criteria for placement. The decision about which placement criteria to use seems not so much a question of which are best, but rather which are most appropriate, given the administration procedures, criteria for scoring, and purposes for administering the IRI. Decisions about the appropriateness of placement criteria should not be made independent of decisions about administration and scoring.

For example, a decision to administer an IRI using oral reading at sight, to count all deviations from the text as errors, and to use the Betts criteria for placement would be the strictest test and is the most commonly used set of procedures in commercially prepared IRIs. A decision to administer an IRI with silent reading preceding oral reading, to count only those errors that alter meaning, and to use the Powell criteria would provide very different results, and a much less strict test of reading proficiency. Although the majority of published IRIs use the Betts' criteria, there is still enough variability to make this an important concern. Variability in placement criteria *can* result in different placement levels. This is one reason why we are much less enthusiastic about using IRIs for placement, as opposed to the evaluative purposes discussed in the second half of this chapter.

A second area of concern is how well traditional error analysis reveals students' strengths and weaknesses in word recognition and comprehension. The major problem with these types of analyses is that they treat each error type as a separate entity, as though they occurred independent of each other. Research has demonstrated again and again that this is not the case; rather, error types are all interrelated and cannot be separated in this manner.

Several authors have summarized the problems with using a variety of question types of each passage in the hope of finding a student's relative strengths among an array of subskills (McKenna, 1983; Schell & Hanna, 1981). These include reliability problems due to the small number of questions per subskill, lack of objective standards for classifying questions by subskill, and lack of a comparable scale for examining subskill scores. Perhaps the most damaging of all is evidence of the high interrelationships among categories of questions, which suggests that they are all measuring the same skill (Drahozal & Hanna, 1978). Therefore, traditional analyses of oral reading and/or comprehension errors should not be relied on to produce a complete picture of a student's strengths and weaknesses in these areas.

Guidelines for Traditional Usage of IRIs

The significant concerns that have been raised about the construction, administration, scoring, and interpretation of IRIs indicate that caution needs to be exercised in developing or selecting IRIs for use in placing students in appropriate grade-level materials. The following guidelines, based on the information in this chapter and the recommendations of Jongsma and Jongsma (1981), McKenna (1983), and Pikulski and Shanahan (1982), are provided to assist those who choose and/or need to use IRIs for placement purposes. However, "keep in mind that when using an IRI, as with any test, you're just sampling behavior. On another set of passages, given on another day, you might get different results" (Jongsma & Jongsma, 1981, p. 704).

1. Look for selections that correspond to regularly used instructional materials with regard to content, difficulty, style, and length. Be alert to differences in the interest level of passages for different groups of students.
2. Stay alert to readability problems. Don't assume that texts are representative of classroom materials, or that texts on alternate forms are comparable.
3. Ensure the passage dependency of questions by "field testing" them. Do not assume that questions on published instruments are passage dependent, and do not hesitate to replace some of them with your own.
4. In writing questions, limit the number of types. In using commercial tests, be

wary of summary sheets that break down student responses into a large number of comprehension subskills.

5. Determine procedures for administering and scoring, and placement criteria within the context of the purpose(s) for using the IRI.

6. Consider carefully how the oral, silent, and listening passages will be presented.

7. Be sure that instructions for administering, scoring, and interpreting are clear and complete. Consider carefully what student directions communicate to the students.

8. Carefully consider what constitutes an error on the word lists and oral reading passages.

9. Consider which factors should be weighed most heavily in establishing placement levels, that is, word recognition, comprehension, or rate.

10. Do not aggregate oral reading and comprehension errors across passages. Differentiate errors that occur at students' independent, instructional, and frustration levels.

In summary, we do not believe that the primary strength of IRIs and IRI-like measures lies in their use as placement procedures. Furthermore, we object most strenuously to the use of a single (usually commercially prepared) IRI as the sole criterion for placement. Having said this, we also believe that various informal procedures modeled after the basic structure of IRIs can provide valuable information in the placement process. The following section addresses the use of IRIs and IRI-like procedures for the evaluative purposes for which they are best suited.

TOOLS FOR USING IRIs TO EVALUATE

A Basic Strategy

The previous section highlighted the many problems associated with using IRIs for placement purposes. In this section, we turn our attention to another, more valuable, use of IRIs. We believe that IRIs are most useful for the purpose of evaluating the way readers interact with different types of texts and tasks. We share the view of Estes and Vaughan (1973) that teachers should approach IRIs not as tests, but as a strategy for studying the behavior of the reader in depth.

The following sections describe various adaptations that can be made to traditional IRI usage for evaluative purposes. We have combined these variations into an assessment strategy with the following components:

1. analyzing oral reading miscues;
2. analyzing fluency;
3. analyzing comprehension;
4. analyzing performance on different IRI materials.

We describe each component of this strategy, using examples from a case study to illustrate the utility of these various techniques. These techniques can be used to evaluate the word recognition (miscue analysis), fluency (Aulls' fluency scale), and comprehension components (retelling and questions) of the assessment-instruction process in a more interactive way. This interactive focus is most apparent in the final discussion of multiple administrations of IRIs, a technique that can be used to assess word recognition, fluency, and comprehension. Finally, we present an alternative to this strategy, in the form of a recently published, innovative IRI known as the *Qualitative Reading Inventory* (Leslie & Caldwell, 1990).

Miscue Analysis

Miscue analysis describes procedures that attempt to identify how readers process print by analyzing their oral reading errors. Interest in the ideas underlying miscue analysis dates back to Huey (1908/1968), but is most often associated with Kenneth and Yetta Goodman (K. Goodman, 1969; K. Goodman & Y. Goodman, 1977) and their colleagues. The fundamental assumption underlying miscue analysis is that reading is a psycholinguistic guessing game. Readers use their knowledge of language to sample, predict, and confirm the meaning of a text (the top-down view of reading described in Chapter 1). Therefore, oral reading provides a means for examining readers' use of the language systems that cue meaning—graphophonic, syntactic, and semantic.

Miscue analysis procedures provide a structure for the analysis of oral reading errors. Oral reading errors have been renamed miscues, because it is believed that they are not random errors, but rather are mis-"cued" by the graphophonic, syntactic, and semantic systems the reader uses to process written material. It is assumed that both expected and unexpected oral reading responses are produced by the same process. Therefore, miscues are viewed as a "window on the reading process" (K. Goodman, 1973). The concept of miscues has become so popular that the term is commonly used when referring to oral reading errors, even when they are analyzed in a traditional manner.

Reading Miscue Inventory (RMI). The miscue analysis procedures developed by the Goodmans and their colleagues were simplified for research purposes and published as the *Reading Miscue Inventory* (Y. Goodman & Burke, 1972). A further revision and a set of alternative procedures for administration, depending on the purposes for which the inventory is to be used, were published more recently (Y. Goodman, Watson, & Burke, 1987). The RMI is designed specifically to identify and evaluate the strategies used by a particular reader to process written material. The following is a summary of the basic procedure:

1. A reading passage providing a continuity of meaning is selected for the reader. The selection must be somewhat difficult and long enough to elicit a minimum of 25 miscues.
2. The selection is retyped, and each line is numbered to correspond with the appropriate page and line from the original text, to be used as a code sheet for recording miscues.
3. The reader is asked to read aloud and informed that the reading will be

unaided. The code sheet is marked as the selection is read. The reading is tape-recorded for future reference.

4. The substitution miscues are coded.
5. Miscue patterns are studied, interpreted, and translated into instruction.

The reader is encouraged to guess after a 30-second hesitation. If hesitations are continuous, the reader is told to continue reading even if it means skipping a word or phrase. The RMI procedures also include a retelling of the selection, which is scored subjectively by the examiner. More will be said about retellings in the next section.

Although all types of miscues are marked, only substitution (including mispronunciation) miscues are coded, according to RMI procedures. Each substitution miscue is coded on the basis of the answers to a specific set of nine questions.

1. *Dialect.* Is a dialect variation involved in the miscue?
2. *Graphic similarity.* How much does the miscue look like what was expected?
3. *Sound similarity.* How much does the miscue sound like what was expected?
4. *Intonation.* Is a shift in intonation involved?
5. *Grammatical function.* Is the grammatical function of the miscue the same as the grammatical function of the word in the text?
6. *Correction.* Is the miscue corrected?
7. *Grammatical acceptability.* Does the miscue occur in a structure that is grammatically acceptable?
8. *Semantic acceptability.* Does the miscue occur in a structure that is semantically acceptable?
9. *Meaning change.* Does the miscue result in a change of meaning?
(Y. Goodman & Burke, 1972, pp. 49–50)

In the most recent version of the RMI (Y. Goodman, Watson, & Burke, 1987), the Dialect question is subsumed by the Meaning Change question, the Intonation question is subsumed by the Syntactic and Semantic Acceptability questions, and the Grammatical Function question is listed as optional. Thus, the 1987 version recommends six, rather than nine, basic questions. There is also some variation in how these questions are used within each of the alternative procedures presented in the revised RMI.

The major advantage of miscue analysis over traditional analyses of oral reading errors is that it recognizes that some errors are better than others. Miscue analysis emphasizes the quality of errors as a reflection of the quality of strategies students are using to process text. Quality exists along a continuum, from not-so-good to good.

Differences in the quality of miscues can be illustrated best by the following examples, taken from Hood (1978). Suppose a reader encounters an unknown word during reading. Reader A may try to sound it out and pronounce either a real word that does not fit the context, or a nonsense word; or Reader A may just wait for the teacher to pronounce the word. Reader A's responses are poor ones because there is little attempt to focus on meaning. Reader B might pay more attention to the context and guess a word that makes sense, though it may or may not look much like the text word. This error is better than Reader A's because it shows more focus on meaning, but it still may represent a poor response. For example, suppose the error fits the preceding context but does not make sense when the rest of the sentence is read. In this instance, the error is not acceptable, and the reader should self-correct.

Reader C might take a quick look at the subsequent as well as preceding context before guessing an unknown word. If it fits the whole sentence context, Reader C's substitution is considered better than the errors made by Readers A and B. But what if the meaning of Reader C's sentence is different from what the author had in mind? Reader D uses context cues to predict several meanings that may be contained in the next bit of print, and uses print cues to decide which meaning may be the right one. When reading aloud, Reader D may substitute words that mean the same as the text, such as reading "frightened" for "afraid." In addition, Reader D may omit unessential words, for example, by reading "told what he heard" instead of "told what he had heard." Words may be inserted, such as reading "the little old lady" for "the old lady." The writer's exact words may be read correctly but in different order, such as reading "put the tent up" for "put up the tent." Unlike other errors which do not sound sensible, these specific examples are all good errors because they represent the same meaning as the words in the text. More importantly, they reflect the use of effective strategies to process the text.

There are no normative data to guide the interpretation of readers' miscue patterns. However, miscue analysis research does suggest the existence of several trends. A summary of these trends provided by Wixson (1979) includes the following:

1. Most readers, regardless of age or proficiency, produce a greater number of contextually acceptable miscues than graphophonically similar miscues.
2. As readers become more proficient the proportion of graphophonically similar miscues stabilizes and the proportion of contextually acceptable miscues increases.
3. Less proficient readers make fewer attempts to correct their miscues than more proficient readers.
4. Less proficient readers tend to correct acceptable and unacceptable miscues at almost an equal rate; whereas more proficient readers tend to correct unacceptable miscues at a higher rate than acceptable miscues.

Problems with the RMI. Miscues should be interpreted with caution, however, because there is evidence that patterns vary as a result of the complex interaction among factors such as the instructional method; the reader's background, skills, and purpose for reading; and the specific nature of the written material. As with any test, miscue analysis provides a sample of behavior that may or may not be representative of the way a student interacts with different types of texts under different reading conditions. Miscue patterns are best regarded as a reflection of the particular strategies employed by a particular reader to satisfy his or her purpose for reading a particular passage.

The best way to address the problem of variability in miscue patterns is to obtain repeated samples of a particular reader's miscues under a variety of predetermined conditions. The nature and content of the reading selections should be varied with regard to each individual reader's skills and background, in an attempt to present the reader with a range of reading tasks and materials. An analysis of the miscues generated by a particular reader under a variety of conditions may reveal any pervasive problems the reader may have, as well as the particular conditions that present the reader with the greatest difficulty. An example of this is given later in this chapter under the topic of multiple administrations.

In addition to the problem of variability, the two biggest problems with the RMI are that it is designed to be used with materials that are at least one grade level above the student's reading placement level, and the administration and scoring are too complex and time-consuming to make them practical for either classroom or clinical use. Procedures we advocate to simplify miscue analysis are provided in the next section.

Modified miscue analysis procedures. The first step is to select text materials at what is believed to be the student's instructional level of difficulty, so that information is being collected about the way the student is likely to perform during real classroom reading situations. Next, the substitution miscues are analyzed within the context of the following four questions:

1. Does the miscue change the meaning of the sentence?
2. Is the miscue contextually acceptable within the context of the whole passage?
3. Was the miscue self-corrected?
4. Is the miscue graphophonically similar to the intended word?

In reflecting on the answers to these questions, we can begin to discover patterns of performance. In particular, we can begin to determine whether the student is attending to the meaningfulness of text (Are most of the miscues acceptable? Does the student self-correct most of those miscues that are not acceptable?). The chart in Figure 5.7 illustrates Marvin's miscues on several sentences from a level-three selection on the Burns and Roe *Informal Reading Inventory* (1985).

One or two errors of a particular type do not make a pattern, but a predominance of a particular type of error may suggest a pattern that can provide information about how the student is approaching a particular text. One of the most important findings of miscue research focuses on the self-correction patterns of skilled and less-skilled readers. Skilled readers tend to self-correct errors that are contextually unacceptable and to leave uncorrected errors that are contextually acceptable. Less-skilled readers are just as likely to correct acceptable as unacceptable errors.

If we examine Marvin's self-correction behavior, we see that there are six contextually unacceptable errors (2, 4, 5, 7, 9, and 10) that we would expect a

FIGURE 5.7
Modified
Miscue
Analysis

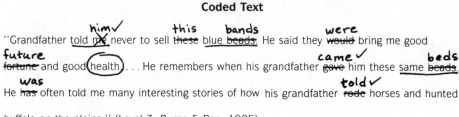

Coded Text

"Grandfather told me never to sell these blue beads. He said they would bring me good fortune and good health. . . . He remembers when his grandfather gave him these same beads. He has often told me many interesting stories of how his grandfather rode horses and hunted

buffalo on the plains." (Level 3, Burns & Roe, 1985)

Miscue Analysis

Text	Marvin	Meaning Change	Contextually Acceptable	Self-Corrected	Graphophonic Similarity
1. me	him	no	yes	yes	no
2. these	this	no	no	no	yes
3. beads	bands	yes	yes	no	yes
4. would	were	no	no	no	no
5. me	my	no	no	no	yes
6. fortune	future	no	yes	no	yes
7. gave	came	yes	no	yes	some
8. beads	beds	yes	yes	no	yes
9. has	was	no	no	no	yes
10. rode	told	yes	no	yes	some

skilled reader to correct. Marvin corrected two of these (7 and 10) and left four uncorrected (2, 4, 5, and 9). There were also four contextually acceptable errors (1, 3, 6, and 8) we would expect a skilled reader to leave uncorrected. Marvin corrected one of these (1) and left the other three uncorrected (3, 6, and 8). Although not entirely random, Marvin's pattern of self-correction for this text is more like that of a less-skilled than a skilled reader.

Additional information can be obtained by examining the graphophonic similarity of the errors to the intended word. Eight of Marvin's ten errors have at least some graphophonic similarity to the word in the text (2, 3, and 5–10). Even the two errors that are not graphophonically similar (1 and 4) are common sight word confusions. This pattern, coupled with the fact that only 4 of his 10 errors were contextually acceptable, suggests that Marvin is relying heavily on the graphophonic cues in this text.

Finally, it is important to consider the effect of the errors on the meaning of the passage. In most cases, when an error is contextually acceptable, it will not change the meaning of the text; and vice versa, if an error is contextually unacceptable, it will change the meaning of the text. However, occasionally unacceptable errors do not change the meaning of the text, and acceptable errors do. There are several examples of this among Marvin's errors. Errors 2, 4, 5, and 9 are contextually unacceptable, yet they do not change the meaning of the text. In Marvin's case, these errors are all examples of common sight word substitutions, adding to the evidence that Marvin still has not mastered the graphophonic cue system. However, these types of errors can also result from language differences, such as those of a dialect speaker. It is important to consider the source of these errors before automatically classifying them as either good or bad.

Marvin also has two errors (3 and 8) that are contextually acceptable, but *do* change the meaning of the text. The first time he encounters the word *beads,* he calls it *bands,* and the second time he calls it *beds.* This is a good error in that it suggests that Marvin is using both contextual and graphophonic cues and he does not correct it, because it makes sense in the passage. However, it is clear that this error is also likely to have a profound effect on his comprehension of this passage. Therefore, the meaning change column can provide further insight into readers' miscue patterns.

Before going on, it is important to remember that this is a very small sample of miscues taken from a single text. In order to make generalizations or predictions about Marvin's reading, we must examine a large number of miscues taken from a variety of texts under a variety of conditions. This issue will be considered further in the section on multiple administrations.

Aulls' Fluency Scale

Fluency can be defined as the extent to which readers organize the words in sentences in a manner that preserves the syntax of the author and signals the relations among word meanings. An assessment procedure developed by Aulls (1982) evaluates fluency by providing an estimate of whether or not a student consistently reads sentences predominantly word-by-word; in two-word groups with occasional word-by-word reading; in phrase groups with some two- or three-word groups; or in phrase groups.

Selecting materials. Research with good and poor readers in Grades 1 through 6, using a procedure similar to the one described here, suggests that word grouping strategies change as a function of the difficulty of the material, reading ability, and years of exposure to reading and reading instruction (see Aulls, 1982). Most good readers in Grades 5 and 6 read consistently in phrase groups when reading instructional level and even frustration level material. However, good readers in Grades 1 through 4 typically read material at the independent level with better word grouping strategies than they do material at the instructional or frustration level. What appears to be unique about poor readers at any grade level is that they group words in material at the independent and at the instructional level in the same fashion.

Aulls recommends using material at the student's independent level in order to confidently estimate the reader's optimum ability to organize words into phrase groups. However, since most instruction is carried out at the instructional level, and since poor readers perform similarly at all levels, instructional level materials seem acceptable. In any event, it would be helpful to gather information about a reader's ability to read fluently at the instructional level.

The materials should be no less than 250 words in length. The longer the text, the better the estimate. Texts of 500 to 1,000 words are equally appropriate, and have the advantage of offering a highly confident estimate of the student's ability to consistently organize words into groups when reading texts of similar readability and text organization or type.

Scoring.   The teacher scores an oral reading sample by putting a slash mark between each word or word group that characterizes the reader's intonation. These patterns result from pitch sequences and pauses during oral reading. For the examiner, pauses provide the primary signal of the division of words into groups. Pitch provides a secondary signal of the meaning assigned to each group. If a student rereads a phrase or sentence, the word grouping used in the first reading is scored. This provides the best estimate of how the student typically and spontaneously performs. Students can and do self-correct word groupings, but the intent is to characterize their spontaneous patterns for organizing text information fluently, not their self-corrections of disfluent reading. The sample markings below characterize different students' ability to organize words into groups:

1. Word-by-word: *The/brown/pony/galloped/toward/the/fence./ It/was/* . . .
2. Beyond word-by-word reading, but not consistently in phrases: *The brown pony/galloped/toward/the fence./ It was/* . . .
3. Consistently in phrases: *The brown pony/galloped toward the fence./ It was/* . . .

In the first example, all words except two were read word by word. The words *the fence* were organized into a two-word group. Since the majority of words were read word by word, the student must be considered to be a word-by-word reader. In example two, only two of seven words in the first sentence were read word by word, and other words were grouped in two-word groups. In the third example, the entire text was read in phrase groups. Even if *galloped* has been read as part of the first word group (*The brown pony galloped/toward the fence*), it would still be an acceptable phrase group. The exact phrase grouping is not as important as the preservation of sensible word groupings.

After all sentences have been marked, the teacher assigns a value of 1, 2, 3, or 4 to each sentence. Each weighted value represents a category for characterizing how each sentence was read. The values and associated categories are:

1. A value of 1 is assigned to a sentence if the majority of words in the sentence were read word by word.
2. A value of 2 is assigned to a sentence if the majority of words were read in two-word groups with a few read word by word.
3. A value of 3 is assigned to a sentence if the majority of words were read in phrase groups with some two- or three-word groups.
4. A value of 4 is assigned to a sentence if all the words are grouped in phrases.

To obtain an overall estimate of a student's word grouping during reading, the teacher adds all the values and divides the total by the total number of sentences read. A sample of Marvin's fluency rating using this scoring procedure is provided

FIGURE 5.8

Sample Fluency Rating: Marvin

Introductory Statement

"Joe wanted more than anything in the world to buy the electric train set in the trading post window. But should he do this? Please read the following story."

Joe sat down/ on the sidewalk/ in front of/ the/ trading post with his/ buckskin jacket/ thrown over his shoulder.　　Value: ___2___

He/ felt worried/ because/ it was difficulty/ to know/ what to do.　　Value: ___2___

"Grandfather told me/ never to/ sell/ these blue/ beads.　　Value: ___2___

He/ said they would/ bring me/ good fortune and/ good health.　　Value: ___2___

Grandfather is/ a wise/ and understanding man.　　Value: ___3___

He is proud/ to be an American Indian.　　Value: ___4___

He remembers/ when his grandfather/ gave/ him these/ same beads.　　Value: ___2___

He/ has often told/ me/ many interesting stories/ of/ how his grandfather rode/ horses/ and hunted buffalo/ on the plains."　　Value: ___3___

Joe/ held the/ string of/ beads/ high into the aid/ toward the/ sunlight.　　Value: ___2___

"These/ are perfectly beautiful/ beads,"/ he said/ out loud.　　Value: ___2___

"I can't sell them/ because/ I too am proud/ of/ my great past.　　Value: ___4___

Yes,/ I will keep the beads."　　Value: ___4___

Summed Value: ___31___

Mean Value: ___2.6___

Source: *Analytic Reading Inventory,* Woods & Moe, 1985, Grade 3 Selection.

in Figure 5.8. This passage was made up of 12 sentences. The sum of the values assigned to these sentences is 31. This is divided by the total number of sentences (12), with the result of a mean fluency rating of 2.60. If the frequency of sentences assigned a value of 2 is counted, it can be seen that this was Marvin's most consistent pattern of grouping words. He is beyond word-by-word reading the majority of the time, is able to read some sentences in complete phrases, but is not consistent in doing so.

Interpreting the score. Figure 5.9 provides a scale for interpreting the total word grouping score obtained. From studying this table, it is clear that scores of 1.0 and 4.0 represent the two extremes: either not being able to group words at all, or having learned to consistently group words. Scores from 1.1 to 3.9 represent students who are acquiring word grouping strategies. The major distinctions within this score range are between 1.7 to 2.6 and 2.7 and 3.9. Those poor readers in the category between 1.7 and 2.6 are different from those in the 2.7 to 3.9 category in their ability to get beyond two-word groups to reading in phrase groups with relatively high frequency. This is an important shift, because it seems to allow those in the 2.7 to 3.9 score range to give much more attention to the development of the more advanced strategies for processing sentence meaning (Aulls, 1982).

FIGURE 5.9

Aulls' Scale for Interpreting Total Word Grouping Score

Total Score	Judgment of Word Grouping Ability
Category one 1.0 1.1 1.2 1.3 1.4 1.5 1.6	If 1.0, reads word by word consistently without exception. If 1.1 to 1.6, reads predominantly word by word.
Category two 1.7 1.8 1.9	*If 1.7 to 1.9, reads about as often in two-word groups as word by word. This is a clear shift toward beginning to group words. Therefore, category two may best represent the reader's word-grouping ability.
2.0 2.1 2.2 2.3 2.4 2.5 2.6	If 2.0 to 2.6, reads predominantly in two-word groups with some word-by-word reading.
Category three 2.7 2.8 2.9	*If 2.7 to 2.9, reads predominantly in two-word groups, with some phrase or three-word groups, but virtually no word-by-word reading. Therefore, category three may best represent the reader's word-grouping ability.
3.0 3.1 3.2 3.3 3.4 3.5 3.6 3.7 3.8 3.9	If 3.0 to 3.9, reads predominantly in phrase groups but not consistently.
Category four 4.0	If 4.0, reads consistently in phrase groups without exception, even though intonation or interpretative expression may be lacking and at times the flow of processing is disrupted.

* Because every scale has a margin of error, the recommendation to assign these score ranges to the next highest categories seems useful because of their instructional implications.

From Mark W. Aulls, *Developing Readers in Today's Elementary School.* Copyright © 1982 by Allyn and Bacon. Reprinted by permission.

Students in the 1.0 to 1.6 range need to become more fluent before moving on. They may need to be provided with easier materials until they have learned to group words better. Those students in the score range between 1.7 and 2.6 will be much more likely to be ready to refine the less complex sentence processing strategies involved in confirming word identification cues or integrating them. Once the student has attained a score between 2.7 and 3.9, the teacher should begin stressing the development of more sophisticated sentence processing strategies.

It appears that Marvin is just on the verge of becoming a fluent reader. His ratings here are encouraging, given the large numbers of miscues present in his readings. This score sheds light on his performance because it suggests greater fluency (and potential comprehension) than a simple miscue analysis would suggest. However, Marvin is in fifth grade, and the passage described is a third-level selection from an IRI. His plight highlights the caution noted by Aulls (1982):

> When a poor reader is an older, intermediate grade pupil who cannot read material beyond third-grade difficulty at the independent level, it is very likely that all or part of the reading problem is inability to read words in phrase groups and/or inadequately developed strategies, or the lack of use of them, for processing sentence meaning. A teacher who cannot or does not assess the sentence processing strategies of poor readers may incorrectly conclude that teaching word identification cues will be sufficient to enable a poor reader to become a fluent reader. (pp. 622–623)

Retellings

Readers' understanding of textual materials has traditionally been evaluated using question response scores. Indeed, the practice of answering questions is so pervasive that it is sometimes difficult for teachers to recognize that the ability to answer questions is not the same thing as understanding. It is possible that a reader could construct meaning from a passage that was not captured by question responses. Retellings can add immeasurably to our understanding of readers' comprehension because they allow us to get a view of the quantity, quality, and organization of information gleaned during reading.

Student's initial responses to the material should involve free recall of the text, without the interference of the examiner. Text recall is natural for children and does not necessarily bias them to process text in a particular way, as questions do. It provides the examiner with information about how the student is constructing meaning from the text without external influence.

Because it is important to influence student response as little as possible, initial requests for retelling should be intentionally open-ended. The examiner can initiate the retelling of text with questions such as these:

- Tell me what you have read, using your own words.
- What is the text about?
- Tell me as much information as you can about what you have just read. (Ringler & Weber, 1984)

Students should be allowed ample time to recall and relate information, and it is important that the examiner not interrupt the student until the retelling is completed. In this way, readers express what they have reconstructed during reading without any external cueing. This free recall can provide valuable insight into how the student processes text.

Following the uninterrupted retelling, probing statements or questions can be used to elicit further information and to probe readers' understanding of the text. Probes constructed by the examiner/teacher should be based directly on the retelling. The following are examples of probes to be used immediately following the retelling:

- Tell me more about what you have read.
- Tell me more about what happened.
- Tell me more about the people whom you just read about.
- Tell me more about where this happened.

A caution is in order before definitive conclusions are made regarding students' ability to understand based on retellings. Some young or less-skilled readers have had little experience in retelling. In fact, they may be surprised that you are not asking them questions. For them, the novelty of the task may influence results, and you may want to attempt another retelling shortly after an initial attempt.

In addition to free and probed retelling, teachers and clinicians may also want to consider using structured questions. The examiner should avoid their use until students have provided all possible information during free and probed retelling, since structured questions impose someone else's view of what is important on an evaluation of text understanding. In this way, the examiner is able to distinguish among information generated freely, information elicited with minimal cueing, and information generated through direct cueing. More will be said about structured questions in Chapter 7.

Selecting and analyzing short passages. Although the addition of retellings can enhance the diagnostic value of an IRI tremendously, some cautions are in order. As we have already suggested, a number of factors can influence the comprehensibility of textual material. This, of course, affects students' ability to recall text information as well. Both the quantity and quality of student recalls can be affected by the type and quality of the text. For example, when students recall stories, we would expect to see appropriate recall of sequence and story line. In contrast, recalls of informational text may not rely so heavily on sequence, but should reflect an understanding of the relationships among key facts and ideas.

The coherence of a text can also affect recall. Many IRI passages read more like fragments of text than intact stories or informational selections. This can hamper student recall, because it may be difficult for students to organize and retrieve the content presented. Finally, remember that reader interest in or familiarity with passage content can affect understanding, memory, and recall. Familiarity appears to influence the content of recall, and both interest and familiarity seem to have an effect on the amount of inferential comprehension achieved during reading.

Before making final judgments about a student's ability to retell passages, it is important to be sure that samples of the student's best efforts have been gathered. To do this, the selections that are used should provide a good match for the student's interests, prior knowledge, and development ability. It may also be desirable to gather information regarding performance on materials that are routinely assigned to the reader in class. The point is that we are simply sampling the reader's abilities, not measuring them in some definitive way. The selections we make should reflect our assessment purposes.

Scoring and interpreting short passages. A number of systems for scoring and interpreting passage recall have been proposed in the past several years. One of the most useful and straightforward systems was designed by Clark (1982) specifically for use with IRIs. The steps in this procedure are as follows:

1. Break the passages to be used for retelling into pausal units by placing a slash wherever a good reader would normally pause during oral reading. The boundaries for these units typically fall at punctuation marks and at connectives such as *and, but,* and *because.*
2. Make a numbered list of the separate pausal units in the order in which they occur.
3. Rate the level of importance for each pausal unit by assigning 1 to the most important units, 2 to the next most important units, and 3 to the least important units. To simplify this process, read through the units and assign 1 to the major units, read through the units again and assign 3 to the least important information, and then assign 2 to all remaining units.
4. Record the order in which the pausal units are recalled by numbering them in the order in which they are retold. Give the student credit for responses that capture the gist of the unit.

Three types of information result from this technique: the amount recalled, the sequence of recall, and the level of recalled information. The amount recalled is determined by dividing the number of units recalled by the total number of units in the passage. The score is then converted to a percentage by multiplying by 100. There are no available guidelines to evaluate the amount recalled. Clark reports that generally acceptable levels will be below the 75–90% criterion level of the IRI, and numerous research studies have reported average recall levels ranging between 33% and 50% depending on the level of the students and the nature of the materials.

The assessment of sequence is purely subjective. A judgment should be made about whether the order of the retelling was reasonable. Finally, to get an indication of the level of information that was recalled, add the importance value of each recalled unit and divide by the total number of recalled units. The resulting average score shows if the most significant information (as judged by the examiner) has been remembered. The closer the average value is to 1, the higher the level of recall. Clark cautions that it is important to remember that there is a normal developmental tendency; older, better readers recall more information at higher levels of importance and in better sequence, so comparisons among individuals of different ages and abilities is inappropriate.

A sample of Marvin's recall has been scored using this system and is provided in Figure 5.10. As can be seen, Marvin has recalled a reasonable amount of the text, in good sequence. In addition, the mean importance level of units recalled is good. However, it is also important to note that he has failed to recall any of the last portion of the text. This failure to report crucial information about the resolution of the problem presented in the early part of the passage is serious, and warrants further investigation with additional samples, using this and other procedures.

Multiple Samples

To accomplish our goal of discovering patterns of interactions that allow us to make relatively good decisions about instruction, we have found it helpful to administer several IRIs or IRI-like procedures to the same student, in order to examine the learner's performance under several different sets of reading conditions. The goal of this type of assessment is not the specification of deficits, but rather a description of the circumstances under which children perform well and less well. This information can then be used to alter reading contexts (see Chapter 10) to yield educationally significant suggestions for instruction.

We continue with the case of Marvin in illustrating the potential benefit of using multiple samples. Although three published IRIs are used with Marvin, it should be emphasized that there are a variety of ways in which multiple samples can be used. Notably, the time factor involved in using multiple samples make this procedure best suited for use within the context of regular classroom reading instruction.

The three IRIs used in Marvin's case are the *Analytic Reading Inventory* or ARI (Woods & Moe, 1985), the *Classroom Reading Inventory* or CRI (Silvaroli, 1982), and the Burns and Roe (1985) *Informal Reading Inventory.* These three IRIs vary considerably in several important ways, and it is important to consider each briefly before we examine Marvin's performance.

ARI. The ARI passages are narrative selections from levels primer through Grade 4. Most are excerpts from longer texts. All selections are preceded by an introductory statement that allows the reader to cope with the text as though it were a complete work. The one notable exception appears on Form B, Level 4. This selection from *Justin Morgan Had a Horse* reads like a fragment, and the initiating event occurs before the excerpt begins. Thus, the conflict described is difficult to understand. In addition, the selection ends with no resolution. From Level 5 on, the passages are expository selections of a much more technical nature. The introductory remarks are quite focused and often provide useful purpose-setting information. The selections gradually increase in length, from approximately 50 words per passage to 250 words at Level 7. Eight questions follow each selection. These questions vary in quality from passage to passage. Most are reasonable and require a range of text processing, but some passages are weighted fairly heavily toward recall of details.

CRI. The Silvaroli CRI has been revised in its latest edition. Marvin read selections from the 1982 edition; therefore, the remarks below refer to the selec-

FIGURE 5.10

Sample
Retelling
Evaluation

Importance Number	Pausal Unit	Recall Sequence
3	1. Joe sat down	2
3	2. on the sidewalk	
2	3. in front of the trading post	3
3	4. with his bucksin jacket thrown over his shoulder.	
1	5. He felt worried	1
1	6. because it was difficult to know what to do.	
1	7. "Grandfather told me	4
1	8. to sell these blue beads.	5
2	9. He said they would bring	
2	10. me good fortune and good health.	
2	11. Grandfather is a wise	12
2	12. and understanding man.	13
1	13. He is proud	
1	14. to be an American Indian.	
2	15. He remembers	6
2	16. when his grandfather	7
2	17. gave him these same beads.	8
2	18. He has often told me	9
2	19. many interesting stories	10
2	20. of how his grandfather	
3	21. rode horses and hunted buffalo	11
3	22. on the plains."	
3	23. Joe held the string of beads	
3	24. high into the air toward the sunlight.	
3	25. "These are	
2	26. perfectly beautiful beads,"	
3	27. he said out loud.	
1	28. "I can't sell them	
1	29. because I too am proud of my great past.	
1	30. Yes, I will keep the beads."	

Total number of units = 30
Number of units recalled = 13
Percentage recalled = 43%
Sequence evaluation = Good
Mean importance level recalled = 1.85 (Fair to good)

tions from that earlier test. All the CRI passages except the primer selections are short expository selections. The longest passage is only 118 words in length. Each is prefaced by a motivational statement and accompanied by a picture. The selections are generally very straightforward presentations of factual information, followed by five questions of varying quality. Most questions require recall of stated details, but many questions can be answered without reference to the text. For example, the following two questions appear in the Level 3, Form C selection of this IRI: "What does the word 'sip' mean?" and "Where do baby birds grow up?" Again, these questions represent two of the five available questions.

   Burns and Roe IRI.   This IRI uses narrative text throughout. All selections are excerpts, and many continue from one form to the next. For example, at Level 2, the story is introduced in Form A and continued in Form B. The selections tend to have a rather weak story line and an almost lyrical quality about the events presented. For example, one Level 4 passage describes how a little girl comes to understand death by watching a snowflake melt. All passages are introduced with a sentence or two (e.g., "Read this story to find out about an animal named Whiskers."). In some cases, the selection can only be understood with reference to the introductory remarks, and in a few cases, questions are posed about information presented only in the introductory remarks. The selections at the lowest levels are relatively long (65–100 words), but they increase in length only slightly over the reading levels (e.g., Level 7 has 171 words).

   Figures 5.11a, b, and c compare Marvin's performance on the three IRIs in the areas of silent reading comprehension, oral reading comprehension, and word recognition. The substantial variability in the results demonstrates the precarious position we are in if we assume reading ability/disability to be a stable construct. For Marvin there is obvious variability across texts and tasks. There are occasions when he performs like an average or even above-average reader, given his grade placement. Similarly, there are occasions when he looks more profoundly disabled then the overall data would warrant. Note, for example, the summary of Marvin's silent reading comprehension scores (Figure 5.11a). At both grade Levels 4 and 5, the estimates of his ability to deal with text of this difficulty range from frustration to independent, depending on the instrument used.

   If any one of these instruments had been used alone and viewed as a reliable indicator of his ability, the range in Marvin's abilities or disabilities would have been seriously miscalculated. Examination of the patterns of Marvin's performance provides some interesting information. His word recognition scores are consistently poor, and he reaches frustration level on word recognition at Level 3 on all three IRIs (see Figure 5.11c). On the other hand, his comprehension scores are consistently higher than his word recognition scores, and on two IRIs, he does not reach frustration level in comprehension until Grade 6 or 7. The disparity between his word recognition and his comprehension performance is substantial. However, he also demonstrates differential ability across texts and tasks. Note both his peak (silent reading at Level 5 on the CRI) and his valley (frustration comprehension at Level 3 on the oral reading Burns and Roe).

FIGURE 5.11

Marvin's Results (Multiple Administration of IRIs)

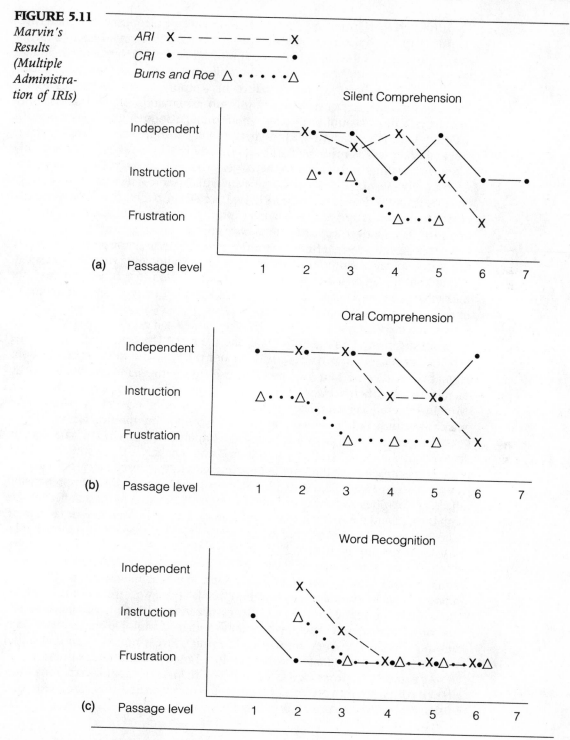

Although Marvin's comprehension abilities are quite robust, it is obvious that the Burns and Roe passages are more difficult for him than any others. In fact, if only the Burns and Roe IRI had been administered, it would appear that limited power and automaticity in decoding skills inhibit his comprehension. This conclusion would have been warranted, since his comprehension decreases as his decoding accuracy decreases. This bottom-up explanation of reading disability obviously cannot account for Marvin's performance at other times, however. His performance on the other two IRIs suggests exactly the opposite: that comprehension ability drives his reading efforts, and that he is likely to perform poorly only when the reading process cannot be driven from the top, or comprehension.

Marvin's weakest performances occur while reading several rather ambiguous texts in the Burns and Roe IRI. Two are set in a foreign country and are guided almost entirely by a type of lyrical, internal response structure. All three are fragments from longer texts, and none have very strong story grammar structures (see McConaughy, 1985). Note, for example, the Burns and Roe passage in Figure 5.12. This passage is interpreted by Marvin to be about a dog that acts like a cat. While Marvin understands all the relevant information in this text, he does not make the one critical inference necessary to answer the questions, although his inference certainly is permissible.

When the final question, "Was Whiskers a well-fed cat?" was posed, Marvin asked in surprise, "You mean this was about a *cat*?" Thus, although neither the type of text (narrative versus exposition), nor the type and number of questions significantly affected Marvin's performance, his performance was affected by factors such as coherence and conformity to expected story structure. In particular, Marvin's overall performance appears to have been affected by the degree to which he can generate a meaningful framework for interpreting a text.

In Figure 5.13, we provide a comparative analysis of Marvin's miscues for one level across the three IRIs. We selected the Level 5 passages to illustrate Marvin's miscues because this is the level of difficulty where the discrepancies among IRI results are most marked. As can be seen, not only is Marvin's comprehension affected by various text features, but the quality of his miscues is also affected. On both the CRI and the ARI, Marvin's oral reading comprehension is estimated to be instructional at this level. On the Burns and Roe IRI, however, his results suggest a frustration reading level.

Recall that the miscue analysis presented previously indicated that Marvin's self-correction behavior tends to be random, and that his overall performance indicates that he attends to the graphophonic display to the detriment of his attention to comprehension; or, at the very least, that his ability to monitor and self-correct are suspect. The power and advantage of multiple administrations is that the student's miscues are sampled in much larger numbers, so that initial hypotheses can be evaluated within a wider range of reading situations.

As can be seen from Figure 5.13, during the multiple administrations Marvin's performance in word recognition is almost as varied as his comprehension results. Marvin's self-correction rate (29–30%) is roughly the same on all three

FIGURE 5.12
*Burns and
Roe IRI
Passage*

Motivational Statement

Read this story to find out what happened to Whiskers the cat.

Soon after Whiskers sharpened his claws, he saw some blades of grass move to and fro. A human being might have said to himself, ''That grass is moving against the breeze. There must be a mouse on the ground!'' But Whiskers could not talk, to himself or anyone else, and he did not take time to think things out. Instead, he crouched down and began to creep forward and pounced upon it.

   Dogs and wolves bite their prey and hold it, but Whiskers did not bite. He struck the mouse with one paw and then backed away. When the mouse got up and tried to escape, Whiskers struck it again. He did this several times until the mouse was dead. Then the cat picked it up and carried it to the house. When his mistress opened the door to let him in, he laid the dead mouse at her feet.

Adapted from Carroll Lane Fenton and Herminie B. Kitchen, *Animals That Help Us: The Story of Domestic Animals*. Rev. Ed. (New York: John Day, 1973). Copyright © 1973 by Mildred Adams Fenton and the Estate of Herminie B. Kitchen. Copyright © 1959 by Carroll Land Fenton and Herminie B. Kitchen. Used with the permission of the HarperCollins Publishers.

IRIs. However, as noted previously, students are unlikely to correct miscues that are contextually acceptable. When Marvin's self-corrections and contextually acceptable miscues are viewed together, Marvin's performance on these three IRIs looks quite different.

   On the CRI, Marvin's combined rate of self-corrected miscues and contextually acceptable miscues is 70%. On the ARI, this rate is 55%. On the Burns and Roe IRI, his combined rate of self-corrected miscues and contextually acceptable miscues is only 29%. Indeed, Marvin corrected only two miscues on the Burns and Roe IRI and both of those miscues were contextually acceptable! Thus, the miscue analysis parallels previous conclusions. Marvin's overall performance is tightly linked to his ability to comprehend reading materials.

   Other information is also apparent, of course. For example, Marvin's miscues are overwhelmingly similar in graphic appearance to the text. He is clearly attending to the print, but appears to have somewhat limited word recognition abilities. Marvin needs additional decoding skills, and a great deal of attention should be directed toward increasing his automaticity.

   Marvin's strength is comprehension. However, his performance in comprehension is not universally strong, and he might be expected to perform poorly on tasks that require identification of complex main ideas. In addition, material that is symbolic and/or lyrical will most likely cause him difficulty. This is especially problematic because Marvin is less attentive to correcting nonsensical miscues when he cannot grasp the meaning of a text selection. As a result, both his word recognition and comprehension suffer. However, since we rarely ask young students to read texts as ambiguous as those presented in some of these IRIs, it would appear that Marvin is capable of handling most material at his grade level, especially if he receives prereading preparation.

FIGURE 5.13

Marvin's Miscue Analysis on Three Level 5 Selections

Text	Marvin	Meaning Change	Contextually Acceptable	Self-Corrected	Graphohonic Similarity
ARI, GRADE 5					
determined	demanded	yes	no	no	some
talking	taking	yes	no	no	yes
trainer	trail	yes	no	no	yes
dripping	dipping	yes	no	no	yes
doubts	doubting	yes	no	no	yes
decided	deceased	yes	no	no	yes
accepted	competeble	yes	no	no	some
career	carrious	yes	no	no	some
famous	farther	yes	no	no	little
her	the	no	yes	no	no
riding	racing	no	yes	no	no
placing	racing	no	yes	no	no
fast	faster	no	yes	no	no
this	the	no	yes	no	no
she	so	yes	no	yes	no
ability	advility	yes	no	yes	no
had	and	yes	no	yes	no
being	behind	yes	no	yes	no
onion	union	no	yes	yes	no
CRI, GRADE 5					
trained	trimmed	yes	no	no	yes
experts	expect	yes	no	no	yes
also	always	yes	no	no	yes
tap	top	yes	no	no	yes
scientists	students	yes	yes	no	no
meant	means	no	yes	no	no
made	make	no	yes	no	no
learned	learn	no	yes	no	no
expect	explect	yes	no	yes	no
difference	different	yes	no	yes	no
when	then	yes	no	yes	no
were	give	yes	no	yes	no
they	to	yes	no	yes	no

FIGURE 5.13

(Continued)

Text	Marvin	Meaning Change	Contextually Acceptable	Self-Corrected	Graphohonic Similarity
BURNS and ROE IRI, GRADE 5					
threshold	darnhold	yes	no	no	yes
terrible	trouble	yes	no	no	yes
experience	expressing	yes	no	no	yes
cured	curled	yes	no	no	yes
daze	drazed	yes	no	no	yes
chuckled	looked	yes	yes	yes	no
the	a	no	yes	yes	no

Summarizing IRI Usage

This section has described various adaptations that can be made to traditional IRI usage, which focuses primarily on placement, to a more interactive assessment, focused on an evaluation of reader strengths and weaknesses. Furthermore, it was suggested at the beginning of this section that the techniques described can be combined into an assessment strategy, with the following components:

1. analyzing oral reading miscues;
2. analyzing fluency;
3. analyzing comprehension;
4. analyzing performance on different IRI materials.

When used in conjunction with each other, the procedures described here form an assessment strategy that provides a great deal of information about the reader in a fairly parsimonious fashion. Miscue analysis of a student's oral reading is used to evaluate word recognition strategies in relation to text comprehension. The Aulls' procedure is then applied to the same oral reading samples to evaluate the student's oral reading fluency. Retellings are then used to evaluate various aspects of a student's oral, silent, and/or listening comprehension. Finally, multiple samples are used to evaluate word recognition, fluency, and comprehension under a variety of different reading conditions (e.g., text type and coherence, topic familiarity, and task demands).

In many cases, the assessment strategy proposed here may be all that is needed in following up initial observations and interviews to provide a sufficient evaluation of the reader. For this reason, it is well worth the investment of time necessary to become proficient in these techniques.

Qualitative Reading Inventory

An alternative to the basic assessment strategy presented in the previous section is the recently published *Qualitative Reading Inventory* or QRI (Leslie & Caldwell, 1990). The QRI is an IRI "designed to provide diagnostic information about (1) conditions under which subjects can decode and comprehend successfully, and (2) conditions that appear to result in unsuccessful decoding and/or comprehension" (Leslie & Caldwell, 1990, p. 1).

The QRI has undergone extensive pilot testing to develop the procedures used to answer the following diagnostic questions:

- Can the student identify words automatically? more words in context than in isolation?
- When reading orally, does the student correct oral reading errors that do not make sense? use meaning clues? use graphic or letter clues?
- Can a student successfully comprehend narrative but not informational material? goal-based but not non-goal-based narratives? familiar but not unfamiliar text?
- What is the quality of the student's comprehension? Does the student organize recall in stories according to elements of story structure? Does the student organize recall in informational texts according to main idea and supporting details? Can the student answer questions that require inferences as well as those whose answers are explicitly stated in the text? Does the student have a low knowledge base overall?

Innovations

Although a complete description of the QRI is not possible here, there are important differences between the QRI and other IRIs that should be highlighted. First, the QRI provides both narrative and informational texts at each level. At the primer through second-grade levels, there are two types of narrative passages: goal-based and non-goal-based. Goal-based narratives reflect the structure of simple stories where the major character has a goal or a problem, attempts to achieve the goal or solve the problem, and achieves a resolution, usually by accomplishing or changing the goal, or by solving the problem. Non-goal-based narratives either have no goal-directed action, or the goal is not stated directly. The narratives at third-grade level and above are all goal-based. Both narrative and informational selections are intact texts, not excerpts, and are highly representative of the structure and topics of selections found in basal readers and subject area texts.

The QRI also provides a means for assessing the student's familiarity with passage content. Each reading selection includes a word association task as a means of determining the level of a student's familiarity with the topic of the selection. These tasks allow the examiner to identify each passage as either familiar or unfamiliar to each individual student. The use of passages that vary in familiarity enables the examiner to arrive at a more complete description of a student's reading ability.

In addition to evaluating prior knowledge, the QRI assesses comprehension using both questions and unaided recall. Each selection has an accompanying text map for recording and evaluating the student's unaided retelling. The comprehension questions are of two kinds: explicit and implicit. Answers to explicit questions are directly stated in the text, and answers to implicit questions require the reader to make inferences from textual clues.

Another innovative feature of the QRI is that the word lists contain words taken from the reading selections. As a result, the examiner can assess students' use of context by comparing their word recognition during passage reading to their performance on the word lists.

Scoring and Interpreting

Although the QRI does provide quantitative scores, they will vary for many students as a function of the type of text read, the familiarity of the passage content, and the manner in which comprehension is assessed. The interpretation of the scores must therefore be qualified by the above factors. This is what sets the QRI apart from other IRIs and the reason it has been called *qualitative*. As the authors of the QRI suggest:

> While it was once common, it is now simplistic to talk about a single independent, instructional, or frustration level for an individual. The act of reading is highly complex and contextual. (Leslie & Caldwell, 1990, p. 14)

The authors go on to explain that students who possess extensive background knowledge about a topic can read and comprehend at a higher level than in unfamiliar material. In addition to prior knowledge, the structure of the text can affect a student's reading performance, as can the mode of reading and the nature of the comprehension task. The variety of passages on the QRI allows the examiner to evaluate the effects of topic familiarity, text structure, and reading mode on the independent, instructional, and frustration levels of the student. "It is not inconceivable that a single reader may have different levels for familiar and unfamiliar text, for narrative and expository material, and for oral and silent reading modes" (Leslie & Caldwell, 1990, p. 14).

The authors further note that the major strength of the QRI is that it provides a profile of an individual reader's strengths and weaknesses across different types of text and in relation to the familiarity of the reading selections. These comparisons are facilitated by the inclusion of two summary sheets—the Subject Profile Sheet and the Levels Comparison Sheet (see Figure 5.14). The Subject Profile Sheet is designed to provide the examiner with maximum flexibility in the amount of

FIGURE 5.14
Qualitative Reading Inventory

SUBJECT PROFILE SHEET

Name _Jamie_ .... Birthdate _11/12/75_ Grade _5 (retained)_

Sex _M_ Date of Test _11/8/86_ Examiner _JC_

WORD RECOGNITION	Grade	3	4	5						
	% Automatic	70	55	25						
	Level Automatic	INS	Ques	Fr						
	% Total	85	65	40						
	Level Total	INS	Ques	Fr						
ORAL READING	Name	Zoo	Amelia	Columbus		Beavers				
	Readability Level	3	4	5		4				
	Passage Type	GN F	GN F	GN F		E F				
	% Total Accuracy	95	95	88		95				
	Accuracy Level	INS	INS	Fr		INS				
	% Total Acceptability	96	98	91		97				
	Acceptability Level	INS	IND	Fr		INS				
	% Free Association	66	78	67		66				
	# Explicit Correct	4	3	3		2				
	# Implicit Correct	3	3	2		0				
	% Comprehension	88	75	63		25				
	Comprehension Level	INS	INS	Ques		Fr				
	Total Passage Level	INS	INS	Fr		Fr				
	Rate									
SILENT READING	Name	JOHN A								
	Readability Level	4								
	Passage Type	GN F								
	% Free Association	92								
	# Explicit Correct	3								
	# Implicit Correct	2								
	% Comprehension	63								
	Total Passage Level	Ques								
	Rate									

FIGURE 5.14
(Continued)

LEVELS COMPARISON SHEET

Subject

WORD IDENTIFICATION

Comparison

Instructional level: sight vocabulary
  (Total of Automatic column on word list) — *questionable 4*

Instructional level: word identification
  (Total of Automatic and Decoded columns on word list) — *questionable 4*

Comparison

Instructional level: words identified in isolation
  (Word list) — *questionable 4*

Instructional level: words identified in context
  (Oral reading of passages: total accuracy or total acceptability) — *4*

COMPREHENSION *(Total Passage Levels)*

Comparison

Instructional level: oral reading comprehension — *4*

Instructional level: silent reading comprehension — *questionable 4*

Comparison

Instructional level: goal-based narrative text — *4*

Instructional level: expository text — *below 4*

Comparison

Instructional level: familiar text — _____

Instructional level: unfamiliar text — _____

Comparison (primer through grade 2)
Instructional level: goal-based narrative text — _____

Instructional level: nongoal-based narrative text — _____

IDENTIFICATION OF READING DISABILITY

Comparison

Instructional reading level (familiar text) — *4*

Chronological grade placement — *5 (retained)*

Discrepancy — *2*

From *Qualitative Reading Inventory* by Lauren Leslie and JoAnne Caldwell. Copyright © 1990 Scott, Foresman and Company.

information to be recorded for a given student. The Levels Comparison Sheet is designed to facilitate comparison of a subjects' reading ability across different contexts.

In summary, the QRI provides a set of procedures that is both conceptually and psychometrically sound and that represents a major step forward in the development of interactive assessment devices. We believe that this tool will make a valuable contribution to teachers' and clinicians' understanding of the variability and complexity of reading and reading problems and in so doing will have a positive effect on the instructional programs that result from its use.

FROM CLASSROOM TO CLINIC

IRIs and IRI-like procedures are potentially high-utility techniques for both classroom teachers and clinical personnel. For placement purposes, it is important that anyone using IRIs understands the issues associated with the representativeness of the reading selections to the materials in which a student is being placed. Although some might argue that IRIs should not be used for placement purposes, in reality there is no one measure that can serve this purpose adequately. The key to successful placement, both in the classroom and in the clinic, is the use of multiple indicators of performance on materials comparable to those in which the student is to be placed.

For the purpose of evaluating reader strengths and weaknesses, the issues of IRI usage differ somewhat between the classroom and the clinic. Classroom teachers obviously do not have the time to administer a traditional IRI individually to each student in their class. Even if they did, it is not clear that this would be entirely appropriate or necessary. However, by virture of their daily contact with students in a variety of reading situations, classroom teachers are in a position to incorporate the adaptations that form the basic assessment strategy described in this chapter directly into their regular reading instruction.

Retellings, for example, are an easy addition to the normal question-answer format that follows reading in most classrooms. Using a scoring form prepared ahead of time, teachers can collect information on each child over time (see also Chapter 7). In addition, teachers can easily collect samples of student miscues during regularly planned oral reading activities (either individual or group) and examine these samples for patterns that may suggest instructional needs. In effect, teachers gather information from multiple samples on a daily basis as a function of the different types of texts, tasks, and methods that are employed as a part of their regular reading activities. It is more a matter of knowing what to attend to than a matter of having indefinite amounts of time to work one-on-one with students.

If the information collected as part of regular reading instruction suggests the need for more structured or focused assessment, then the teacher can consider the individual administration of an IRI and/or some other instrument (see Chapters 6 and 7). It is also important to recognize that the types of information that can be gathered about word identification, fluency, and comprehension, using the procedures described in this chapter, should be collected on a continuous basis throughout the year for each student in a classroom. These types of information can and should be incorporated into some form of ongoing student record or portfolio that documents student progress and provides the basis for instructional decision making (see Chapter 3).

In contrast to classroom teachers, specialists and clinical personnel typically do not have the amount of regular contact with individual students necessary to successfully implement the adaptations to traditional IRI procedures that comprise the basic assessment strategy described in this chapter. However, the interactive nature of the QRI makes it an excellent alternative for clinicians and resource personnel. The QRI also fits well with the purposes for which resource personnel are likely to find IRI-like procedures most useful. Whereas classroom teachers are likely to find these procedures most useful for ongoing assessment and instructional decision making, clinical personnel and specialists are most likely to find these procedures useful for making programmatic curricular and instructional decisions for a given student.

Resource personnel must be particularly sensitive to the potential abuses of IRIs, given the limited amount of time that they are likely to come in contact with individual students. In particular, it may be difficult to predict a student's performance in the classroom from a small sample derived from administering just one IRI. However, in the hands of a skilled specialist, IRIs can provide a great deal of valuable information about the reader within a relatively short time period.

CHAPTER SUMMARY

An *Informal Reading Inventory* (IRI) was described as an individually administered, informal reading test designed to place students in materials at the appropriate levels and to identify their strengths and weaknesses in the areas of word identification and comprehension. Traditionally, IRIs are used to identify students' *independent, instructional,* and *frustration* reading levels.

The *components* of an IRI include graded word lists, graded passages, comprehension questions, and separate materials for the student and the examiner. There are a variety of procedures that can be used for *administering* and *scoring* an IRI, and different procedures produce different test results. Similarly, the criteria used for *interpreting* students' placement levels can have a significant effect on the results of the IRI.

The first half of the chapter concludes with some *guidelines* for the traditional use of IRIs for placement purposes. These include looking for selections that correspond to regularly used instructional materials; evaluating the passage dependency of the comprehension questions; and determining administration and scoring procedures, and placement criteria, together and within the context of the purpose for using the IRI.

The second half of the chapter describes interactive *adaptations* of the IRI that can be used to evaluate reader strengths and weaknesses. When combined, these adaptations form an assessment strategy that includes analyzing oral reading miscues, fluency, comprehension, and students' performance under different reading conditions. The techniques described as part of this assessment strategy include:

1. procedures for analyzing readers' oral reading *miscues* to determine the language cue systems (i.e., graphophonic, syntactic, and semantic) they are using as they process a particular text;

2. *Aulls' fluency scale* as a method for identifying the extent to which a reader organizes the words in sentences in a manner that preserves the author's syntax and signals the relations among word meanings;
3. procedures for evaluating a reader's comprehension using *retellings;*
4. a technique involving *multiple samples* of different IRIs or IRI-like procedures as a means of evaluating students' word identification and comprehension skills under a variety of reading conditions.

Finally, a recently published IRI known as the *Qualitative Reading Inventory* is described as an alternative to the adaptations that form the recommended basic assessment strategy.

ANNOTATED BIBLIOGRAPHY OF IRIs

Burns, P. C. & Roe, B. D. (1989). *Informal reading inventory* (3rd ed.). Boston: Houghton Mifflin. Grades 1–12. Two graded word lists and 4 sets of graded passages per grade level (preprimer–Grade 12). Eight questions at preprimer to Grade 2 levels, and 10 at the other grade levels.

Ekwall, E. E. (1986). *Ekwall reading inventory* (2nd ed.). Boston: Allyn & Bacon. Grades 1–9. Each of 4 forms consists of 11 graded word lists (preprimer–Grade 9). Five comprehension questions at the preprimer level and 10 at the other grade levels. Also contains Quick Survey Word List and the El Paso Phonics Survey.

Johns, J. J. (1988). *Basic reading inventory* (4th ed.). Dubuque, IA: Kendall/Hunt. Grades 1–8. Each of 3 forms consists of 10 graded 20-word lists (preprimer–Grade 8). Four comprehension questions at preprimer level; ten at other grade levels.

Silvaroli, N. J. (1986). *Classroom reading inventory* (5th ed.). Dubuque, IA: Wm. C. Brown. Grade 1–adult. Each form has 8 graded 20-word lists and 8–10 graded passages followed by 5 comprehension questions. Forms A and B for Grades 1–6; C for junior high; and D for senior high and adults.

Spache, G. D. (1981). *Diagnostic reading scales.* Monterey, CA: CTB/McGraw-Hill. Criterion- and norm-referenced battery for Grades 1–7. Three word lists (40–50 words each), two sets of 11 graded passages (preprimer–Grade 7) with 7–8 comprehension questions each. Twelve supplementary decoding tests yielding grade equivalent scores.

Woods, M. L., & Moe, A. J. (1989). *Analytical reading inventory* (4th ed.). Columbus, OH: Merrill. Grades 1–9. Each of 3 forms consists of 17 graded 20–word lists (primer–Grade 6) and 10 graded passages (primer–Grade 9). Six comprehension questions at primer and first grade; eight at the other grade levels. Two expository subtests consist of graded social studies and science passages (Grades 1–9).

CHAPTER 6

Formal Assessment

INTRODUCTION

Formal assessment devices typically are published tests that provide standardized methods of administration, scoring, and interpretation, and are often at the heart of the procedures used in traditional reading diagnosis. That these types of measures have not been considered until almost halfway through this text is intentional. The reason is simply that most formal tests do not reflect current definitions of reading. Despite this fact, most professional educators are required to evaluate, use, and interpret both formal and informal assessment instruments. This chapter is intended to provide teachers and clinicians with information about the properties of formal instruments that are important for intelligently evaluating the usefulness of available tests, in light of their purposes for assessment.

Chapter Overview

The first half of this chapter describes the aspects of standardized testing that are essential for evaluating formal tests, including issues of type and purpose, important statistical concepts, validity, reliability, the characteristics of norming populations, test fairness, and the interpretation of test scores. The second half of this chapter provides detailed examples of formal reading tests of different types, including survey, diagnostic, emergent literacy, and other language arts and related areas.

UNDERSTANDING FORMAL TESTS

As indicated previously, much of what we know to be important in the reading process is not reflected in formal assessment devices. We know that reading is a holistic, constructive process that varies as a function of the interaction among reader, text, and contextual factors (see Chapter 1). However, most existing formal instruments treat reading as an aggregate of isolated skills. As noted in *Becoming a Nation of Readers* (Anderson et al., 1985):

> If schools are to be held accountable for performance for reading test scores, the tests must be broad-gauged measures that reflect the ultimate goals of instruction as closely as possible. Otherwise, the energies of teachers and students may be misdirected. They may concentrate on peripheral skills that are easily tested and readily learned. Holding a reading teacher accountable for scores on a test of, say, dividing words into syllables is like holding a basketball coach accountable for the percentage of shots players make during the pre-game warm up. (p. 100)

Most existing formal reading assessments also imply that reading is a static process—that students can be evaluated under one set of conditions and that this performance will be representative of their performance under all conditions. For example, formal tests evaluate students on passages that are much shorter than those students are expected to read in their classroom texts, and assume that the results will generalize to classroom reading. These tests do not take into account differences in genre or the coherence of reading selections. Neither do they consider how students' reading performance is affected by their background knowledge of the reading topics; their knowledge about the purposes, goals, and strategies of reading; or their attitudes and motivation toward reading.

The widespread use of formal reading tests makes it important to understand a number of different aspects of standardized testing in order to become a critical consumer of these types of assessment devices. We begin with a description of the general information needed about each test, and proceed to more specific information about the various psychometric properties of tests.

General Information

Test selection and evaluation begin with understanding that the title, author, publisher, and date of publication reveal information about a test's quality and the appropriateness of its purpose and content for different students or testing situations. For example, a test with the word *survey* in the title suggests that the test will provide general information about a student's achievement, rather than specific information about strengths and weaknesses. Similarly, the reputation of the test author and/or publisher in reading or testing may suggest something about both the content and quality of the test. A recent date of publication or revision increases the likelihood that the test reflects the most recent theory and research, and that any norms used for scoring are current.

Other general characteristics of a formal test that are important for determining its appropriateness for specific students or testing situations include the level of difficulty and type of administration. Some tests are appropriate for a wide range of age, grade, and ability levels, while others are appropriate only for restricted levels. Still others have different forms for different levels. Therefore, it is important to determine that a test is appropriate for the age, grade, and ability of the student with whom it will be used.

The appropriateness of the test administration for specific students and purposes depends on factors such as whether the test is group or individually administered, and whether it is timed or untimed. Group tests are efficient to administer, but tend to provide more general information than individual tests and do not allow for the variety of response formats (e.g., oral reading) that are allowed by individual tests. Individual tests require significantly more time to administer than group tests, but tend to provide more specific information about the student. Timed or speed tests determine what a student can do under specified time constraints, whereas untimed or power tests evaluate a student's performance without any time constraints.

Norm- and Criterion-Referenced Tests

The two basic types of tests we discuss in this chapter are norm-referenced and criterion-referenced measures. Criterion-referenced tests are procedures that assess an individual's skill in relation to absolute mastery of a body of knowledge.

Norm-referenced measurements examine a given student's performance in relation to the performance of a representative group. The emphasis in norm-referenced testing is on the individual's relative standing, rather than on absolute mastery of content (Salvia & Ysseldyke, 1988). Although the term *standardized* is often used synonymously with norm-referenced tests, criterion-referenced tests can be, and often are, standardized. *Standardized* means only that all students answer the same questions under uniform directions (Swanson & Watson, 1982).

Another distinction between the two types of procedures is that criterion-referenced measurement is designed primarily to provide information that relates easily and meaningfully to specific objectives and specific standards of performance that have been determined independently of the measurement process. The emphasis is on describing the level of performance of individuals and groups on the behavior a test is measuring. In contrast, norm-referenced instruments are designed primarily to rank individuals on the characteristic being measured. The emphasis is on discriminating among the performances of a number of individuals and comparing one person's performance to that of others with similar characteristics (Salvia & Ysseldyke, 1988).

The difficulty of test items and the manner in which they are selected also differs between norm- and criterion-referenced tests in ways that are consistent with the different intents of these two types of tests. The basic intent of norm-referenced tests is to determine an individual's relative position in comparison to a group of his or her peers. This is done by using test items that produce a wide range of scores and discriminate well between high-scoring and low-scoring individuals. Therefore, the best norm-referenced items are those which 40 to 60% of the students answer correctly, because they produce the greatest variance in test scores. In well-constructed norm-referenced tests, half of the population will score above the average, and half will always fall below the average.

Criterion-referenced tests are designed to describe performance accurately in relation to some external goal, so there is no reason to restrict the range of item difficulty. Criterion-referenced items can range in difficulty from 0 to 100% accuracy, depending on the nature of the specific learning tasks to be measured. If the learning tasks are easy, the test items should be easy. No attempt is made to modify item difficulty, or to eliminate easy items from the test, in order to obtain a range of test scores. On a criterion-referenced test we would expect all or nearly all students to obtain high scores, when the instruction has been effective (Gronlund, 1985).

Developers of criterion-referenced tests must give first priority to content validity, or the relationship of items to specific objectives. Developers of norm-referenced tests must give first priority to item discrimination. According to Swanson and Watson (1982), there is a shift in emphasis between criterion- and norm-referenced tests from items that best measure performance in a domain of knowledge to items that provide the greatest diversity in scores. They further note Popham's (1978) conclusion that the procedures used to construct norm-referenced tests are likely to result in the exclusion of items that measure the major instructional emphases of the schools.

Reading tests can be categorized in a variety of ways in addition to the distinction between criterion- and norm-referenced devices. Specifically, they can be grouped according to the purposes of the assessment. For example, survey tests are used to evaluate general achievement, whereas diagnostic tests are used to determine individual strengths and weaknesses. These and other types of tests are described in the second half of this chapter.

Important Statistical Concepts

There are several statistical concepts that must be understood in order to evaluate formal tests accurately. One of the major purposes of statistics in test use is to allow us to describe and summarize data. In this section we briefly summarize several major concepts in descriptive statistics: normal distribution, measures of variation and centrality known as the standard deviation and the mean, and a measure of relatedness known as correlation.

Normal Distribution

One way of summarizing test data is to describe the distribution of test scores. The two characteristics of a distribution that are most important for the interpretation of educational tests are the mean and the standard deviation. The mean is the arithmetic average of the scores, and provides a central value or representative score to characterize the performance of the entire group. The standard deviation is a unit of measurement based on the degree to which the scores deviate from the mean. A large standard deviation indicates greater spread around the mean than a smaller one. Test scores can be referred to in terms of the number of standard deviations they are above (+) or below (−) the mean, depending on whether the score is greater than or less than the mean.

A very useful property of the distributions of many of the behaviors and psychological characteristics we are interested in measuring is that they are normally distributed; in other words, the scores are distributed symmetrically around the mean. The normal curve is a symmetrical, bell-shaped line that has many useful mathematical properties. One of the most useful for test interpretation is that when it is divided into standard deviation units, each unit under the curve contains a fixed percentage of cases (see Figure 6.1). This means that in any normal distribution:

1. approximately 68% of the population will be between + 1 and − 1 standard deviations from the mean;
2. approximately 95% of the population will fall between + 2 and − 2 standard deviations from the mean;
3. approximately 99.7% of the population will fall between + 3 and − 3 standard deviations from the mean.

Raw scores from two different tests have been placed beneath the row marking the standard deviations in Figure 6.1 to illustrate how knowing the standard deviation and the mean contribute to the understanding of relative

FIGURE 6.1
*Normal
Distribution
and Sample
Test Scores*

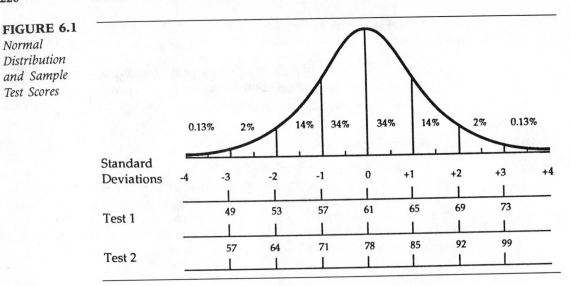

position within a group. Test 1 has a mean of 61 and a standard deviation of 4. Test 2 has a mean of 78 and a standard deviation of 7. Therefore, a score of 65 is equivalent to +1 standard deviation on Test 1 and a score of 85 is equivalent to +1 standard deviation on Test 2. If we convert all of the raw scores on the two tests to standard deviation units, it is possible to directly compare performance on the two tests. Knowing the mean and standard deviation permits us to convert raw scores to a common scale that has equal units and that can be interpreted readily in terms of the normal curve.

Salvia and Ysseldyke (1988) use the example of intelligence tests to present another illustration of why it is important to understand the means and standard deviations of the tests we use. The Stanford-Binet Intelligence Scale, a well-known intelligence test, has a mean of 100 and a standard deviation of 16. Assuming the scores on this test are normally distributed, approximately 68% of the school population would be expected to have IQs between 84 and 116. Another well-known intelligence test, the Slosson Intelligence Test, has a mean of 100 and a standard deviation of approximately 24. Again, if scores on the Slosson are normally distributed, approximately 68% of the school population would be expected to have IQs between 76 and 124.

The fact that the meaning of a score depends on the mean and the standard deviation of the distribution is often overlooked, according to Salvia and Ysseldyke (1988). Specifically, they cite the example of states that use an absolute score in the school code for the placement and retention of mentally retarded children in special educational programs; for example, a score of 75 (+ or −5) for determining eligibility for placement. On the Stanford-Binet, a score of 80 is more than one standard deviation below the mean; on the Slosson, a score of 80 is within 1 standard deviation of the mean. If a single absolute score is specified, different levels of eligibility for special education classes could be unintentionally built into the school code.

Correlation

Another statistical concept that is important in the interpretation of test data is correlation. While the mean and standard deviation describe a single distribution of scores, correlations describe the degree of association between two or more sets of scores. This measure is important in describing the relationship of test scores to other variables of interest and is critical to the evaluation of reliability and validity.

The strength of the correlation is expressed using a *correlation coefficient.* The values of correlation coefficients range from + 1.00 to .00 to − 1.00. A positive correlation (+) indicates that high scores on one variable are associated with high scores on the other variable. A negative correlation (−) indicates that high scores on one variable are associated with low scores on the other variable. A correlation coefficient of .00 between two variables means that there is no relationship between the variables; the variables are independent, changes in one variable are not related to changes in the other variable. A correlation coefficient of either + 1.00 or − 1.00 indicates a perfect relationship between two variables (Salvia & Ysseldyke, 1988).

Measures of correlation provide useful information about the various components of tests and can also be used as an index of test validity and reliability (see below). However, educators must use correlational information sensibly, which means, in part, understanding that correlation is not the same as causation. Correlation is a necessary but insufficient condition for determining causality. The mere presence of a correlation between two variables does not imply that one causes the other.

Salvia and Ysseldyke (1988) point out that "for any correlation between two variables (A and B), three causal interpretations are possible: A causes B; B causes A; or a third variable, C, causes both A and B" (p. 80). Correlational data do not tell us which of these three possible interpretations are true; therefore, we must never draw causal conclusions from such data. So, for example, the simple fact that there is a positive correlation between reading achievement and factors such as balance-beam walking or alphabet knowledge does not, by itself, mean that these factors cause skilled reading.

Validity

Validity is a second primary concern in evaluating formal tests. A test is valid to the extent that it measures what it claims to measure. To determine a test's validity, test users must understand what is to be measured. Although it is fairly common to start test development by simply generating test items, experts agree that test validity requires careful definition of the skill or content to be measured.

In addition to the question of whether a test measures what it is intended to measure, the concept of validity is concerned with the theoretical and applied usefulness of a test (Walsh & Betz, 1990). The usefulness of a test depends on our ability to make inferences about people or situations from the test scores. Different tests have different purposes. These purposes dictate the types of inferences we may want to make. For example, survey tests of reading are designed to tell us, generally, how proficient students are in reading. From the test results, teachers want to be able to make inferences about the level of materials students can read.

The *Standards for Educational and Psychological Testing* (AERA, 1985) published jointly by the American Educational Research Association, the American Psychological Association, and the National Council on Measurement in Education, indicate that tests should include evidence of validity that specifies what inferences can be made reasonably. In addition, this document argues that test consumers should be warned against making specific kinds of inferences if the evidence that these inferences are warranted is not available. Again, it is the range and accuracy of possible inferences to other real-world phenomena (other tests, classroom performance, future success, etc.) that constitute evidence for a test's validity.

Finally, Salvia and Ysseldyke (1988) point out that test validity is also related to the claims made by users of the test information. The valid use of tests is the responsibility of both the test author and the test user. A major factor in the valid use of tests is the extent to which there is a match between the test's and the test user's conceptualization of the domain being measured. We agree with Salvia and Ysseldyke (1988):

> Validity is the only technical characteristic of a test in which we are interested. All other technical considerations, such as reliability, are subsumed under the issue of validity and are separated to simplify the issue of validity. We must know if a test measures what it purports to measure and if scores derived from the test are accurate. Adequate norms, reliability, and lack of bias are all necessary conditions for validity. None—separately or in total—is sufficient to guarantee validity. (p. 142)

The following sections discuss two major types of validity: content and criterion-related.

Content Validity

Content validity refers to how well the particular items used to sample the behaviors of interest reflect performance in the entire domain of behaviors that constitutes the characteristic being measured (Walsh & Betz, 1990). Content validation involves judging the extent to which the test's content is representative of the universe of content being sampled by the test. Content validation requires first that we have a precise definition of the domain the test items are intended to reflect, including a delineation of both what is and what is not included in the domain. The more precise the definition, the better able we are to establish content validity; the greater the content validity, the better able we are to make generalizations about the domain of interest from the sampling of that domain represented by the test.

Content validation involves a careful examination of the content of a test, in which judgments are made on the basis of the definition of what the content should be. Specifically, Salvia and Ysseldyke (1988) indicate that content validity is established by examining three factors. The first factor considers the appropriateness of the types of items included. To examine this factor we must ask, Is this an appropriate test question? and Does this test item really measure the domain? So, for example, one should question the validity of the items on a reading test that require the use of skills that are not used outside the testing situation in real reading contexts, or the use of skills that are not age appropriate.

The second factor to be examined is the completeness of the item sample. For example, one would reasonably expect a test of reading achievement to include a far broader sample than a short word list to be read aloud. The third factor concerns the task demands imposed by the format of the items. For example, reading skills can be evaluated in a variety of ways, including multiple-choice items, open-ended questions, retellings, oral reading samples, and so forth. This is especially important because different formats require the use of different skills.

Walsh and Betz (1990) indicate that the most common type of evidence presented in support of content validity is the judgment of those who construct the test, or of other experts familiar with the domain of interest. Given that this type of evidence is usually somewhat subjective, they assert that it should be accompanied by a detailed definition of the domain being measured and a clear specification of the methods used to select items. "In a sense, content validity is best ensured by a detailed, thoughtful plan used to guide the initial construction of the test" (p. 60).

Content validity of reading tests. As models of literacy have changed, the match between the definitions of reading and writing and the content and methodology of standardized tests has become weaker (Wixson, Peters, Weber, & Roeber, 1987). Indeed, the degree of mismatch between theory, instruction, and assessment has become quite alarming. Valencia and Pearson (1987) provide a summary of some of the ways in which information about the reading process is poorly aligned with testing (see Figure 6.2).

There is a clear threat to validity when test content is a poor reflection of the reading process as we understand it. Reading professionals must understand these issues and carefully evaluate the content validity of their instruments. Too many of the existing standardized tests of reading distort the process by testing nothing more than subskills, or by requiring students to read only a series of short passages while answering multiple choice questions. Instructional interventions aimed at improving the reading and writing abilities of poor readers must be evaluated using tests that do not trivialize the process.

Criterion-Related Validity

Criterion-related validity refers to the extent to which a person's performance on a criterion measure can be estimated from that person's test score (Salvia & Ysseldyke, 1988). The criterion often represents the actual behavior of interest for which test scores are intended to be used as a predictor. The relationship between test scores and the criterion measure is usually expressed as a correlation known as a validity coefficient. Consider the example of the Graduate Record Examination, which is used to predict success in graduate degree programs. Success in a graduate program is the behavior of interest, and the magnitude of the correlation

FIGURE 6.2

Issues in Reading Assessment

A Set of Contrasts Between New Views of Reading and Current Practices in Assessing Reading

New views of the reading process tell us that . . .	Yet when we assess reading comprehension, we . . .
Prior knowledge is an important determinant of reading comprehension.	Mask any relationship between prior knowledge and reading comprehension by using lots of short passages on lots of topics.
A complete story or text has structural and topical integrity.	Use short texts that seldom approximate the structural and topical integrity of an authentic text.
Inference is an essential part of the process of comprehending units as small as sentences.	Rely on literal comprehension test items.
The diversity in prior knowledge across individuals as well as the varied causal relations in human experiences invite many possible inferences to fit a text or question.	Use multiple choice items with only one correct answer, even when many of the responses might, under certain conditions, be plausible.
The ability to vary reading strategies to fit the text and the situation is one hallmark of an expert reader.	Seldom assess how and when students vary the strategies they use during normal reading, studying, or when the going gets tough.
The ability to synthesize information from various parts of the text and different texts is a hallmark of an expert reader.	Rarely go beyond finding the main idea of a paragraph or passage.
The ability to ask good questions of text, as well as to answer them, is a hallmark of an expert reader.	Seldom ask students to create or select questions about a selection they may have just read.
All aspects of a reader's experience, including habits that arise from school and home, influence reading comprehension.	Rarely view information on reading habits and attitudes as being as important as information about performance.
Reading involves the orchestration of many skills that complement one another in a variety of ways.	Use tests that fragment reading into isolated skills and report performance on each.
Skilled readers are fluent; their word identification is sufficiently automatic to allow most cognitive resources to be used for comprehension.	Rarely consider fluency as an index of skilled reading.
Learning from text involves the restructuring, application, and flexible use of knowledge in new situations.	Often ask readers to respond to the text's declarative knowledge rather than to apply it to near and far transfer tasks.

From "Reading Assessment: Time for a Change" by Sheila Valencia and P. David Pearson, *The Reading Teacher*, April 1987, p. 731. Reprinted with permission of Sheila Valencia and the International Reading Association.

between scores on the GRE and success in graduate school is an important index of the validity of the test.

There are two types of criterion-related validity—concurrent and predictive validity. Concurrent validity refers to the relation between a person's score and an immediate criterion. Salvia and Ysseldyke (1988) suggest, for example, that if we were developing a test of achievement, the basic question would be: How does knowledge of a person's score on our achievement test allow the estimation of that person's score on a criterion measure? In other words, how do we know that our new test really measures achievement?

To establish the concurrent validity of this new achievement test, we would first have to find a valid criterion measure of achievement. Since there are no perfect measures of achievement, we can use other achievement tests that are presumed to be valid, and/or teacher judgments of achievement. "If our new test presents evidence of content validity and elicits test scores corresponding closely (correlating significantly) to teacher judgments and scores from other achievement tests presumed to be valid, we can conclude that our new test is a valid measure of achievement" (Salvia & Ysseldyke, 1988, p. 138).

The second type of criterion-related validity is predictive validity. Predictive validity refers to the relation between a person's score and performance on some measure at a later time. It is used when there is interest in how present status on the test predicts future status on the criterion measure. Our previous discussion of the GRE provides an example of predictive validity. According to Salvia and Ysseldyke (1988), the basic predictive validity question is: Does knowledge of a person's test score allow an accurate estimation of that person's score on a criterion measure administered some time in the future?

If we were developing a test to determine reading placement, for example, we would ask, Does knowledge of a student's score on our reading placement test allow an accurate estimation of the student's ability to perform successfully in certain materials? Successful placement in reading materials can be evaluated by another assessment (presumed valid) or by teacher judgments. If our placement test has content validity and corresponds closely with either later teacher judgments of appropriateness of placement or validly assessed ability to read certain materials, we can conclude that ours is a valid test of reading placement.

The nature of the criterion is extremely important in both concurrent and predictive validity. In effect, the value of the test is being established by comparing it to another measure. To do this, the other measure must be appropriately effective or representative of the behavior under investigation. Therefore, the criterion measure clearly must be valid itself (Salvia & Ysseldyke, 1988). In addition, in the document *Standards for Educational and Psychological Testing* (AERA, 1985), test developers are urged to provide thorough, accurate descriptions of the criterion measures and a rationale for using them. Finally, test authors are expected to provide complete, accurate statistical information regarding the degree of relationship between the target test and the criterion measure(s). The utility and value of tests rely on their validity. No matter what else is true, if the behavior or performance is not characteristic of the student in other related settings/tasks, then the information is misleading.

Reliability

Reliability is another major consideration in evaluating a test. Reliability refers to the consistency or stability of a test and involves the extent to which some attribute has been measured in a systematic and therefore repeatable way. If a test is reliable, a person will receive the same score on repeated testings. When we administer a test, we would like to assume that those taking the test would earn the same scores if tested again with the same instrument. Test results would have little meaning if they fluctuated wildly from one occasion to the next. We would not administer a test if we knew that the student's score might be 15 or 20 points higher or lower if retested. For a test to be useful, it must be reliable.

An easy way to think of reliability is to think of an obtained score on a test as consisting of two parts: true score and error. A *true score* represents the obtained score uncontaminated by chance, while the *error* represents the extent to which scores are attributable to chance. Error is unrelated to the true score and is random; it can either inflate or decrease a score. The reliability of a test is usually expressed as a correlation coefficient (reliability coefficient) which provides an estimate of how much error there is in the test.

Reliability Measures

There are several methods of estimating a reliability coefficient, depending on the particular test and the preferences of the test authors. The two we describe here are test-retest and alternate form reliability. Test publishers should report reliability estimates and the methods used to obtain them. Test users should look for reliability information in test manuals in order to evaluate the adequacy of the test.

Test-retest. Test-retest reliability measures the stability of tests scores over time. It assesses the degree to which test scores are similar after a time delay versus the degree to which they change or fluctuate with repeated testing (Walsh & Betz, 1990). If test scores are relatively stable across repeated testings, we have some basis for believing that the test is measuring something in a consistent manner. The procedures for establishing test-retest reliability usually involve two administrations of the same test to the same individuals, with a time interval of at least one week between the administrations. The test-retest reliability coefficient is the correlation between the sets of scores obtained at the two administrations of the test.

Alternate form. Alternate form reliability assesses the degree to which two different forms of the same test yield similar or consistent results. If an individual's score on one form of a test is similar to his or her score on an alternate form of the same test, we have increased confidence that the test items are measuring some common domain in a relatively consistent manner (Walsh & Betz, 1990). The procedures for establishing alternate form reliability involve developing two equivalent forms of the same test, and then administering both forms to a single sample of students. The reliability coefficient is the correlation between the scores obtained on the two forms of the test.

It is important to keep in mind that equivalent or parallel forms of a test are never perfectly correlated or reliable. Errors of measurements occur because the two tests differ somewhat in item sampling. This can be an important factor in interpreting pre- and post-test scores using alternate forms of the same test.

Standard Error of Measurement

One of the primary reasons for obtaining a reliability coefficient is to be able to estimate the amount of error associated with an individual's obtained score (Salvia & Ysseldyke, 1988). The standard error of measurement (SEM) permits the test user to do this. In other words, we can use the SEM to suggest the distance between the true score and the actual score. The SEM provides information about the certainty or confidence with which a test score can be interpreted. When the SEM is relatively large, the uncertainty is great. When the SEM is relatively small, the uncertainty is minimized.

An individual's true score actually may be either above or below the obtained score. Using the SEM, we can define a range, or confidence interval, within which we can be relatively certain the individual's true score lies. Several options are available, depending on how "confident" we wish to be. Since the SEM is based on a normal distribution of scores, we can say that 68% of the time the individual's true score will fall within + or − 1 SEM of his or her obtained score. Therefore, if an individual's obtained score is 60 and the SEM is 4, the person's true score is somewhere between 60 + or − 4, or between 56 and 64. This means that an individual's score fluctuates within 4 points on either side of the true score 68 times out of 100. This also means that the obtained score is likely either to underestimate or overestimate the student's true score about 30 percent of the time. If we want a higher degree of confidence, we can expand the size of the interval. A 95% confidence band is represented by + or − 2 SEM and provides the interval within which an individual's true score will lie 95 out of 100 times.

It is important to realize what the SEM means for the interpretation of test results. When we say that someone's raw score corresponds to a grade equivalent of 4.5, it sounds very precise. But consider the SEM and the confidence intervals. If the SEM is .3, we are only 68% certain that the true score falls between 4.2 and 4.8 and 95% certain that it falls somewhere between 4.0 and 5.1—a range of over one year. A larger SEM would mean even larger intervals.

Swanson and Watson (1982) offer a related example of a child who has scored 75 on an IQ test with an SEM of 5. A 68% confidence level represents an interval of 70 to 80 and a 95% confidence level represents an interval from 65 to 85. Thus, even though the student's score was in a range typically labeled as mentally retarded, it is possible that the true score was in fact in the low-normal category.

Desired Standards

As Salvia and Ysseldyke (1988) indicate, no test can be valid unless it is reliable, and no score is interpretable unless it is reliable. Therefore, it is important for test authors and publishers to present sufficient information about test reliability for the test user to interpret test results accurately. Reliability information for each type of score should be reported for each age and grade. In addition, Salvia and Ysseldyke (1988) "recommend that the estimated true score and a 68 percent confidence interval for that true score also be reported" (p. 128).

In terms of the absolute level of reliability that is acceptable, Salvia and Ysseldyke (1988) recommend three standards or cutoff points for reliability coefficients. If test scores are to be reported for groups rather than individuals and are to be used for general administrative purposes, a reliability coefficient above .60 is acceptable. If test scores are to be used to make decisions about individual students, the standard should be much higher. For important educational decisions, such as placing a student in a Chapter I class, a reliability of .90 should be considered minimum. For more general purposes such as initial screening, a reliability of .80 is acceptable.

Criterion-Referenced Interpretation

The raw score, or the number of points received on a test, is the basic score in both norm- and criterion-referenced tests. These raw scores alone tell us very little, since we neither know how other individuals performed, nor how many total points might be reasonable or possible on the test. As Gronlund (1985) notes, "we can provide meaning to a raw score either by converting it into a description of the specific tasks that the pupil can perform (criterion-referenced interpretation) or by converting it into some type of derived score that indicates the pupil's relative position in a clearly defined reference group (norm-referenced interpretation)" (p. 347). Each of these modes of interpreting test performance can be useful under some circumstances and occasionally both are reasonable.

Criterion-referenced test interpretation permits us to describe an individual's test performance on some preestablished standard, or criterion. In this way, it is not necessary or even desirable to refer to the performance of others. Thus, students' performance might be described in terms of the speed with which a task is performed, the precision with which a task is performed, or the percentage of items correct on some clearly defined set of learning tasks.

Although percentage correct scores are often used as the standard for judging whether a student has mastered each of the instructional objectives measured by a criterion-referenced test, there are many ways to report these scores. Swanson and Watson (1982) present five measures, or *metrics*, commonly accepted as appropriate for criterion-referenced interpretation, several of which are basically raw scores.

1. A rate metric simply refers to the time it takes to complete the specified task.
2. A sign metric indicates the mastery or nonmastery of the task.
3. An accuracy metric gives the proportion of times the examinee is successful.
4. A proportion metric specifies the portion or percent of the population of items in a domain on which the student performs.

5. A scaling metric describes the point along a continuum at which the student's performance occurs (pp. 55–56).

Gronlund (1985) points out that criterion-referenced interpretation of test results is most meaningful when the test has been designed specifically to measure a specific set of clearly stated learning tasks. In addition, enough items are used to make it possible to describe test performance in terms of a student's mastery or nonmastery of each task. The value of criterion test results is enhanced when the domain being measured is delimited and clearly specified and the test items are selected on the basis of their relevance to the domain being measured. Finally, there should be a sufficient number of test items to make dependable judgments concerning the types of tasks a student can and cannot perform.

Although standardized tests typically have been designed for norm-referenced interpretations, it is possible to apply criterion-referenced interpretations to the test results. This simply involves analyzing each student's test responses item by item and summarizing the results with descriptive statements. Some test publishers aid this type of interpretation by providing a list of objectives measured by the test, with each item keyed to the appropriate objective, and by arranging the items into homogeneous groups for easy analysis.

However, as Gronlund (1981) notes, "just because it is possible to make criterion-referenced interpretations of standardized survey tests does not mean that it is sensible to do so. Since these tests were designed for norm-referenced interpretation, they have built-in characteristics that are likely to make criterion-referenced interpretations inadequate" (p. 369). Although norm-referenced survey tests may serve their intended function well, they typically do not provide a satisfactory basis for describing the specific learning tasks that students can and cannot perform. However, if such criterion-referenced interpretations are attempted, the following factors should be taken into account:

1. Norm-referenced tests often contain a conglomerate of learning tasks with relatively few items representing each specific type of task. This makes it difficult to obtain dependable descriptions of the tasks a student can and cannot perform.
2. The easier items are often omitted from the test during construction to obtain maximum discrimination among individuals taking the test. This can severely limit the description of what low achievers can do.
3. Many norm-referenced tests use only recognition-type items that may or may not be a relevant measure of the objectives. This may distort any criterion-referenced interpretation of the results (Gronlund, 1985; 1981).

Norm-Referenced Interpretation

Norm-referenced interpretation indicates how an individual's performance compares to that of others who have taken the same test. According to Gronlund (1985), the simplest type of comparison is to rank-order the raw scores from highest to lowest and to note where an individual's score falls. Noting whether a particular score is second from the top, about in the middle, or one of the lowest scores provides a meaningful report to both teachers and students. If a student's score is second from the top in a group of 10 or more, it is a high score whether it represents 95 or 60% of the items correct. The fact that a test is relatively easy or difficult for the students does not alter the interpretation of test scores in terms of relative performance.

Although the simple ranking of raw scores may be useful for reporting the results of a classroom test, it is of limited value beyond the immediate situation. To obtain a more general framework for norm-referenced interpretation, raw scores are typically converted into some type of derived score. The most common types of derived scores are grade and age equivalents, percentile ranks, and standard scores. The conversion of raw scores to derived scores depends on the scores of a *normative sample*—a representative group of the individuals for whom the test is designed.

Norms

The concept of comparing one person's test score to those of other people is the basis for test norms, i.e., the test scores of a representative sample of people. Test norms usually are obtained using a standardization sample—a sample designed to be representative of the people for whom the test is designed to be taken. Based on the responses of this standardization, or normative sample, raw scores obtained from any subsequent examinee can be converted into a measure of relative standing in comparison to the normative group.

There are two important points related to the fact that test scores are based on the performance of individuals in the normative sample. First, even the slightest variation of the administration procedures for norm-referenced tests from those used with the standardization sample will render the norms, and therefore the test scores, invalid. Second, the fact that norms are only applicable to individuals of the same age and/or grade as the students in the normative sample can be a major problem when testing students with serious academic difficulties. If a test at the appropriate age/grade level is administered, the norms are of questionable value because the student is at the extreme end of the distribution (not to mention the student's frustration at taking a test that is far too difficult). However, if a test designed for younger or lower-grade students is administered, the norms are inappropriate because older students were not included in the normative sample. To get around this problem, some tests provide norms for out-of-level testing that make it possible to obtain valid scores for students on tests that approximate their skill level more closely than their age/grade level.

According to Salvia and Ysseldyke (1988), norms are important for two reasons: the normative sample is used to obtain the various statistics on which the final selection of test items is based; and an individual's performance is evaluated in terms of the performance of the individuals in the normative sample.

Even if a test is reliable and otherwise valid, test scores may be misleading if the norms are inadequate. The adequacy of a test's norms depends on three factors: the representativeness of the norm sample, the number of cases in the norm sample, and the relevance of the norms in terms of the purpose of testing. (Salvia & Ysseldyke, 1988, p. 114)

An evaluation of representativeness requires particular attention to demographic variables because of their theoretical and/or empirical relationship to what the test is intended to measure. According to Salvia and Ysseldyke (1988), representativeness hinges on two questions: Does the norm sample contain individuals with the same characteristics as the population that the norms are intended to represent? and Are the various kinds of people present in the sample in the same proportion as they are in the population represented by the norms? Among the factors that must be considered in answering these two questions are the age, grade, sex, acculturation of parents (SES and education), geographic factors, race, and intelligence of the individuals in the norm sample in relation to the characteristics of the population for whom the test is designed.

Another, often overlooked, consideration in assuring representativeness is the date the norms were collected (Salvia & Ysseldyke, 1988). Ours is an age of rapidly expanding knowledge and rapidly expanding communication of knowledge. Children of today know more than the children of the 1930s or the 1940s, and probably less than the children of tomorrow. "For a norm sample to be representative it must be *current*" (Salvia & Ysseldyke, 1988, p. 102). Finally, tests used to identify children with particular problems should include children with such problems in their standardization sample.

According to Salvia and Ysseldyke (1988), the second factor related to the adequacy of norms—the number of subjects in a norm sample—is important for several reasons. First, the sample should be large enough to guarantee stability. If the size of the sample is small, the norms will be undependable because another group might produce significantly different results. The larger the sample, the more stable the norms. Second, the sample should be large enough so that infrequent elements in the population can be represented. Third, the sample should be large enough to produce a full range of scores. As a rule of thumb, the norm sample should contain a minimum of 100 subjects per age or grade, although in practice the sample should have more than 100 cases.

The major question regarding the third factor related to the adequacy of norms is the extent to which individuals in the norm sample can provide relevant comparisons in terms of the purpose for which the test was administered (Salvia & Ysseldyke, 1988). For some purposes national norms are the most appropriate, whereas in other circumstances norms developed on a particular portion of the population may be more meaningful.

A final note concerns the ethical issues associated with reporting and using tests with inadequate norms. If the test publisher or author recognizes that the test norms are inadequate, the test user should be explicitly cautioned (AERA, 1985). "The inadequacies do not, however, disappear on the including of a cautionary note; the test is still inadequate" (Salvia & Ysseldyke, 1988, p. 107). Inadequate norms can lead to serious misinterpretation of test results.

Grade and Age Equivalent Scores

Grade norms are widely used with standardized achievement tests, especially at the elementary school level. They are based on the average scores earned by students in each of a series of grades and are interpreted in terms of grade equivalents expressed in years and months (i.e., a grade equivalent of 4.7 indicates the fourth grade, seventh month). For example, if students in the norming groups who are beginning the fifth grade earn an average raw score of 24, this score is assigned a grade equivalent of 5.0. Tables of grade norms are made up of such pairs of raw scores and their corresponding grade equivalents.

The popularity of grade norms is due largely to the fact that test performance is expressed in common units with which we are all familiar. Unfortunately, this familiarity often leads to interpretations that are misleading or inaccurate. The most serious limitation of grade equivalents is that the units are not equal on different parts of the scale or from one test to another. For example, a year of growth in reading achievement from grade 3.0 to 4.0 might represent a much greater improvement than an increase from grade 1.0 to 2.0 or 7.0 to 8.0.

A related problem is the uncertain meaning of high and low grade equivalent scores. Raw scores, corresponding to grade equivalents at the extremes of the distribution of test scores, are usually estimated rather than determined by direct measurement of a norming sample. More precisely, they are *extrapolated* by "projecting the average performance of students at grade levels that were tested to performance of students at grade levels that were not tested" (Baumann, 1988, p. 37). In interpreting grade equivalents at the extremes, therefore, it is well to remember that they do not represent the actual performance of students at these levels. Indeed, because of the widespread misinterpretation of grade equivalents, the International Reading Association has recommended that their use be discontinued in reading assessment (IRA, April 1981) and several major diagnostic tests have excluded these scores in their most recent revisions.

A common misinterpretation is that grade norms are equivalent to performance standards. It is especially important to remember that grade equivalents indicate the *average* score obtained by the students in the standardization sample at a particular grade level. This means that half the students in the norming group at this grade level scored above and half the students scored below this norm. Therefore, we should not interpret a particular grade norm as something all of our students should achieve. It is important to remember that the norm represents the typical performance of average students in average schools and should not be considered a standard of excellence to be achieved by others (Gronlund, 1985).

A related misconception is that students who earn a certain grade equivalent score in a subject are ready to do work at that level. For example, we might conclude that a fourth-grade student should be doing sixth-grade work if she earns a grade equivalent of 6.0. However, students at different grade levels who earn the same grade equivalent score are apt to be ready for quite different types of instruction. It certainly could not be assumed that she has the prerequisities for sixth-grade reading. This would be especially true at the outer reaches of scores where no individuals from the grade group were included in the norming sample.

Age norms operate on the same principles as grade norms. Therefore, they have essentially the same characteristics and limitations as grade equivalents. Specifically, they are based on the average scores earned by students in the norming group at different ages and are interperted in terms of age equivalents. Thus, if students who are 10 years and 2 months of age earn an average raw score of 25, their score is assigned an age equivalent of 10−2. Conversely, a student with a reading age of 11−6 has earned a score on the reading test equal to that of the average 11½-year-old in the norming sample (assuming that age group was represented).

The major differences between age and grade equivalent scores are that test performance is expressed in terms of age levels instead of grade levels, and the expression of months in age equivalents runs from 0 to 11 months to reflect the calendar year as opposed to a range of 0 to 9 months that reflects the school year in grade equivalents. As with grade equivalents, age equivalents present test performance in units that are apparently easy to understand, but can be misleading. Literal interpretations of either should be avoided.

Percentile Ranks

A percentile score or rank indicates a student's relative position in a group in terms of the percentage of students scoring below a given raw score. For example, if we consult a table of norms and find that a student's raw score of 31 equals a percentile rank of 70, we know that 70% of the students in the reference group obtained a raw score lower than 31, and that this student's performance surpasses that of 70% of the reference group.

Percentiles should not be confused with the familiar percentage scores. The latter are raw scores, expressed in terms of the percentage of correct items. Percentiles are derived scores, expressed in terms of percentage of persons scoring below a given raw score. A raw score of 90% could have either a low or high percentile rank depending on the performance of the other individuals in the group. We must always refer to the norm group used for comparison when interpreting a percentile rank.

A student does not have a percentile rank of 75. It is a percentile rank of 75 in some particular group. For example, a raw score on an achievement test may be equivalent to a percentile rank of 88 in a general group of high school seniors, 66 in a group of college-bound seniors, and 27 in a group of freshmen in a highly selective college. Relative standing varies with the reference group used for comparison. Therefore, a test must have separate norms for each group to which students are to be compared.

The major limitation of percentile ranks is that they are not equal units on all parts of the scale. A percentile difference of 10 near the middle of the scale (e.g., 45th to 55th percentile) represents a much smaller difference in test performance than the same percentile difference at either end of the scale (e.g., 5th to 15th or 85th to 95th percentiles). This is because the largest number of scores fall in the middle of the scale and relatively few scores fall at the extreme upper or lower ends of the scale. The difference between the 45th and the 55th percentiles represents fewer raw score points than the difference between the 5th and 15th or 85th and 95th percentiles. Thus, percentiles show each individual's relative position in the normative sample but not the amount of difference between scores.

Standard Scores

Standard scores express individuals' scores in terms of standard deviation units from the mean. There are a number of different types of standard scores used in testing; however, only the most common ones are discussed here. These are deviation IQs, stanines, and normal curve equivalents.

Deviation IQ. One widely used standard score is the deviation IQ where the mean is set at 100 and the standard deviation at 15 or 16, depending on the particular intelligence test. Thus, a score of 100 has been taken to indicate the average IQ, an individual with an IQ score of 84 or 85 falls one standard deviation below the mean, and an individual with an IQ score of 115 or 116 falls one standard deviation above the mean.

Stanines. Stanines are standard-score bands that divide a distribution into nine parts with a mean of 5 and a standard deviation of approximately 2. The fifth stanine is located precisely in the center of the distribution and includes all scores within one-fourth of a standard deviation on either side of the mean. The remaining stanines are evenly distributed above and below stanine 5. Each stanine, with the exception of 1 and 9, which cover the tails of the distribution, includes a band of raw scores the width of one-half of a standard deviation unit.

Normal curve equivalents (NCEs). NCEs are like percentile ranks with equal units. The NCE scale has been set with a mean of 50 and a standard deviation at 21.06. NCEs of 1, 50, and 99 correspond to percentiles of the same values. However, unlike percentiles, NCEs are equal units of measure whether they are at the low, middle or high range of the distribution. A gain of five NCEs represents the same amount of improvement in performance for students at the extremes of the distribution as it does in the middle of the distribution. Federal education programs such as Chapter I often use NCEs for evaluation.

Comparison of Scores

A comparison of different types of scores to the normal curve is presented in Figure 6.3. This figure illustrates the interrelated nature of various types of scores for reporting relative position in a normally distributed group. For example, a raw score that is 1 standard deviation above the mean can be expressed as a percentile rank of 84, a deviation IQ of 115, or a stanine of 7. Thus, various scoring systems provide different ways of presenting the same information, and if we assume a normal distribution and comparable norm groups, we can convert back and forth from one scale to another.

The selection of which particular type of score to use depends on the purpose of testing and the sophistication of the consumer. In the opinion of many, grade and age equivalents should never be used because they are so easily misinterpreted (Salvia & Ysseldyke, 1988). Standard scores are convenient because they allow test authors to give equal weight to various test components, can be converted

FIGURE 6.3
*Score
Comparison*

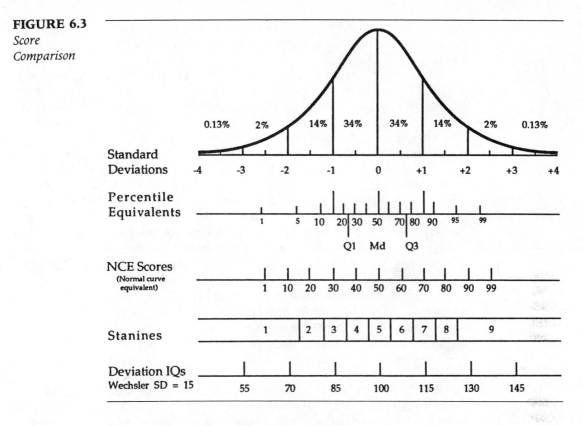

easily to percentile ranks if the distribution is normal, and are useful in developing individual profiles. Percentile ranks require the fewest assumptions for accurate interpretation and present test results in terms that are easily understood (Salvia & Ysseldyke, 1988).

Test Fairness

Gronlund (1985) describes well the increasing attention in recent years to the issue of test fairness to racial and cultural minorities. Concern with the fairness of tests parallels the general public concern with providing equal rights and opportunities to all citizens. Critics have charged that tests are biased and discriminatory and provide barriers to educational and occupational opportunities for minorities. The charge of test bias, or lack of fairness, can be examined from two perspectives: the possible presence of bias in the test content and the possible unfair use of test results.

Much of the concern with bias in test content focuses on the fact that minority group members frequently earn lower test scores than their more advantaged peers. At the most fundamental level is the fact that tests are, almost by definition, culture-bound. It is impossible to construct a test that is independent of a cultural content, and to assume that tests can be made culture-free is as erroneous as the assumption that behavior and attitudes can be made culture-free (Walsh & Betz, 1990).

According to Gronlund (1985), standardized tests of the past typically emphasized content and values that were more familiar to white, middle-class students than to racial or cultural minorities and students of lower socioeconomic status. As a result, the content of some tests contained vocabulary, pictures, and objects that minorities had less opportunity to learn. Some reading tests contained stories and situations that were unfamiliar. In addition, minorities were seldom represented in pictures, stories, and other test content, and when they were, it was sometimes in a manner that was offensive. It is impossible to say how much these types of bias might have lowered the scores of individual students, but most persons familiar with testing would acknowledge some adverse effect.

Special efforts are now being made to correct preexisting problems. Major test publishers employ staff members representing various racial and cultural minorities, and new tests being developed are routinely reviewed for content that might be biased or offensive to minorities. Statistical analyses are also being used to detect and remove biased test items. Gardner (1978) cautions, however, that low test scores do not necessarily indicate test bias. It is important to distinguish between the performance the test is intended to measure and factors that may distort the scores in a biased manner.

Gronlund (1985) indicates that the most controversial problems concerning the fair use of tests with minority groups are encountered when tests are used as a basis for educational and vocational selection or placement. Much of the difficulty lies in the definition of fair test use. One view is that a test is fair, or unbiased, if it predicts as accurately for minority groups as it does for the majority group. This traditional view, which favors a common standard for selection, has been challenged as unfair to minority groups because they often earn lower test scores; thus, a smaller proportion of qualified individuals tends to be selected. Alternative definitions of test fairness favor some type of adjustment for minorities such as separate cutoff scores or bonus points.

Walsh and Betz (1990) remind us of the importance of understanding that the quality of a test and the uses of test scores are two separate issues. The existence of bias in tests is a psychometric issue involving the concern about how tests are constructed and evaluated, while questions concerning how and when tests should be used are social issues. A test can be valid and relatively free of bias, yet still produce scores that have negative effects for minorities. In short, answers to validity and test bias questions do not provide answers to social policy issues.

Taylor, Harris, and Pearson (1988) note a fairness issue related specifically to reading assessments that is often overlooked. Because most poor readers are also poor test takers, formal tests may not fully reveal the competence and knowledge of these students, since they may be penalized by the way in which they are asked to display their knowledge. Similarly, the total test score for a poor reader may have little to do with what he or she actually knows or can do. As Taylor et al. (1988) point out, the majority of the items on norm-referenced tests are geared to the level being tested. Although a few easy and a few hard items are included, not enough of either are included to provide a reliable spread among students at the extreme ends of the distribution. As a result, the tests are likely to fail to measure what low-achieving students do know.

Some teachers feel that it is best to give students who have reading problems a standardized test that matches their achievement level rather than their age/grade level. However, there are also certain problems inherent in this procedure. First, there may not be a content or format match with the reader. Second, great care must be taken in interpreting the results. The scores have been determined on age/grade peers and are not appropriate for use unless the publisher has also developed out-of-level norms. Even when out-of-level norms are available, teachers should study the population on which these norms were developed to determine whether there is a match with their students.

Summarizing the Guidelines for Evaluating Standardized Tests

In the sections to follow, we consider a variety of formal assessment tools. The quality and usefulness of these tools should be considered in terms of the information we have just presented. Informed educators and reading professionals need to be critical consumers of assessment information. To do so, they must consider the validity and reliability of the assessment tools they employ. In addition, they must consider the methods for reporting and interpreting test scores. Finally, concerned educators need to evaluate tests for potential sources of bias, and exercise care in administering and interpreting results with special populations. The format in Figure 6.4 can be used to guide the evaluation of formal assessment tools.

FORMAL ASSESSMENT TOOLS

Reading professionals do not need to be experts on the technical or psychometric properties of formal tests, but they can and should be careful consumers of test information. Reading professionals should be able to evaluate critically the information provided by the tests themselves and know where to find critical reviews if necessary. Reading teachers and reading curriculum specialists are often the only professionals in school buildings who have sufficient expertise to raise critical questions about the use of tests and the quality of test information.

In this portion of the chapter, we describe several types of reading and reading-related formal assessment tools and provide detailed descriptions and evaluations of exemplars of each test type. The tests described in this section are grouped according to their primary purposes: survey (including the reading portion of achievement batteries), diagnostic (including oral reading and criterion-referenced tests), readiness/emergent literacy, and tests of other language arts and related areas. Each type of test is described briefly before we begin the description of specific tests. No effort has been made to evaluate all published tests.

FIGURE 6.4
Guidelines for Test Evaluation

General Information

Name:
Publication date:
Author(s):
Contents:
Age:
Administration:
Scores:
Interpretation of results:
(Criterion-referenced, norm-referenced, or both?)

Type and Purpose

Type: Note whether this is a Survey, Diagnostic, Readiness/emergent literacy, or other language arts/related tests.
Purpose: What purposes are stated by the author(s)?

Validity

Evidence of validity: What definition or domain is defined for assessment? (Face validity)
Evidence of content validity:
Evidence of criterion-related: (concurrent and predictive)

Reliability

Measurement: Test-retest, alternate form, or other?
Standard error of measurement: Is this acceptable?
Desired standard: Is this acceptable for this type of test?
Other factors: Sufficient number of items to test specific components, to determine a year's growth, etc.?

Norms and Scores

Norming: Consider whether the norms and norming procedures are acceptable and the norming sample comparable to your students.
Scores: Note the types of scores generated and the types of interpretation provided.

Special Considerations

Test fairness: Consider both content and use.
Provisions for testing students with reading or other problems: Consider administration flexibility, content, and interpretation (e.g., provision of out-of-level).

General Evaluation

Special features or problems of this test: Consider length, novel formats, etc.
Appropriateness for purposes and students: Consider ease of administration, time to score/interpret, difficulty, etc.
What do others say about this test? If possible, consult specialized colleagues, written reviews, etc.

Recommendations

Would you use this test?
For what?   With whom?
What cautions should be exercised?

Instead, the most commonly used tests are used as prototypes, and the guidelines for test evaluation (see Figure 6.4) are used to focus the discussion. At the end of this chapter, there is a special test resources section that lists sources of information on tests and test reviews.

Survey Tests

Survey reading tests are norm-referenced tests of global reading achievement. Generally speaking, the purpose of survey tests is to compare the performance of students or groups of students. They are most commonly used to screen large numbers of students for approximate reading levels and to identify those who may have serious or severe problems. Survey tests are also often used to make general judgments about program success. For example, many Chapter I programs use a global test of reading achievement for program evaluation purposes. Under these circumstances, reading professionals should be especially concerned that they are using valid tests of reading. Average scores on these tests should parallel acceptable performance on the reading tasks assigned or expected in that age bracket.

Although survey tests are generally designed for group administration, this is not always the case. The *Peabody Individual Achievement Battery–Revised* (Markwardt, 1989), for example, is individually administered. Often survey reading tests are embedded in a larger achievement battery such as the *Iowa Test of Basic Skills* (Hieronymus, Hoover, & Lindquist, 1986). These tests generally yield quite general scores of reading. For example, reading performance on the *Gates-MacGinitie Reading Test* (W. MacGinitie, Kamons, Kowalski, R. MacGinitie, & MacKay, 1978) is reported only in terms of comprehension and vocabulary. The results are meant to indicate general ability, and subscores designed to identify strengths and weaknesses are not provided.

Survey reading tests are easy to administer and score, and are useful screening devices. However, because of their general nature, they often lack content depth. The general scores do little to indicate specifically what a student knows or has trouble with. Also, because survey tests are intended for large general populations, they tend to estimate more accurately the ability of average students than those who are either very good or very poor readers. Furthermore, a low score indicates only that a reading difficulty exists, but does not reveal the nature or degree of difficulty. Finally, these tests often evaluate reading in a most cursory fashion, using limited samples of reading behaviors.

A Group Survey Test: *Gates-MacGinitie Reading Tests*

One of the most commonly used group survey tests of reading is the *Gates-MacGinitie Reading Tests* (MacGinitie & MacGinitie, 1989). The third edition of this test, like its predecessors, has two subtests at Grades 1 through 12: Vocabulary and Comprehension. There are two parallel forms for Grades 1, 2, 3, 4, 5/6, 7/9, and 10/12. The administration of this test is timed, with the vocabulary tests taking 20 minutes and the comprehension tests taking 35 minutes. Raw scores are converted into percentile ranks, stanines, grade equivalents, NCEs, and extended scale scores. As with earlier versions, there is also a level *R* test designed for use in first grade. This is primarily a test of initial and final consonants and other sound-symbol information. There is also a new, PRE-level test for use in kindergarten. This untimed test includes items related to Literacy Concepts, Reading Relationship Concepts (e.g., word meanings), Oral Language Concepts (including phonemic segmentation), and Letter and Letter-Sound Correspondences.

Consistent with its purpose as a survey test, the authors state:

> The basic premise of the Gates-MacGinitie Reading Tests is that it is useful for teachers and schools to know the general level of reading achievement of individual students, throughout their entire school careers. This objective information obtained from tests, complemented by teachers' evaluations and other sources of information, is an important basis for selecting students for further individual diagnosis and special instruction, planning instructional emphases, locating students who are ready to work with more advanced materials, making decisions about grouping, evaluating the effectiveness of instructional programs, counseling students, and for reporting to parents and the community. (Directions for Administration, 1989, p. 29)

The authors describe specific efforts to ensure the validity of the Gates-MacGinitie, including careful selection of vocabulary and balancing passage content across several disciplines. However, they do not directly demonstrate either the construct or criterion-related validity of the test. Instead, the authors are careful to state that users should evaluate the test for validity in terms of their specific school and students.

Both the content and the format of the Gates-MacGinitie will be familiar to most educators. The comprehension subtest requires students to read short paragraphs/selections and to answer several multiple choice questions about the text. On the Vocabulary subtest, students select a synonym for a word that is presented in a phrase or sentence. Most revisions result in an improved test. However, like earlier editions, "the materials and the format cover only a small subset of the reading curriculum. Students are expected to do much more in reading than to select a single distinctive alternative from a set of four" (R. Calfee, in Mitchell, 1985, p. 593).

The reliability of the Gates-MacGinitie is acceptable for its stated purposes. Measures of internal consistency were determined for each level and generated reliability coefficients from .88 to .94. Alternate form reliabilities are also acceptable for the total score, but less so for subtests. Similarly, the norming procedures for this test are good, but becoming dated (the 1970 census was used for the stratified sampling). Approximately 5,000 students per grade were assessed and the norming sample includes a representative proportion of black and Hispanic students. The test also provides norms for out-of-level testing. In addition, the authors have made extensive efforts to remove bias from the test items and from the scoring.

To summarize, the Gates-MacGinitie is a survey reading test with acceptable reliability. Its validity is acceptable using traditional standards, but users must decide whether the test measures reading competencies important to them and their program. Teachers and administrators must be clearly informed that vocabulary is measured in terms of students' ability to identify synonyms in a multiple choice format and comprehension is defined as the ability to answer multiple-choice questions after reading brief paragraphs in a timed forum.

Individually Administered Survey Reading Tests

Reading achievement is commonly surveyed in batteries of general academic achievement. Both the *Peabody Individual Achievement Test–Revised* or PIAT-R (Markwardt, 1989) and the *Wide Range Achievement Test–Revised* or WRAT-R (Jastak Assoc., 1984) have been used extensively by the special education community, since most states require a demonstrated disparity between ability (IQ) and achievement in order to place students in special education programs.

The PIAT-R is a general achievement battery containing six subtests in the following areas: general information, reading recognition, reading comprehension, math, spelling, and written expression. For the reading subtests, the following scores are available: percentile ranks, stanines, grade and age equivalents, standard scores, and normal curve equivalents (NCEs).

The PIAT-R is designed for use with students from kindergarten through Grade 12 and is considered a screening tool, although the author also suggests that it can be used for individual evaluation and program planning. It is an untimed test that is estimated to take one hour to administer. Only the reading subtests are reviewed here, and it should be noted that the response mode is not the same for all subtests.

Both the content and the criterion-related validity of the PIAT-R are somewhat suspect. The Reading Recognition subtest involves pronouncing words presented in a list of 100 increasingly complex words (from *you* to *oligochaete*). On the Reading Comprehension subtest, students read isolated sentences, then turn the page and match the sentence from memory, to one of four picture choices. No contextualized story comprehension is involved, nor are students expected to answer questions or summarize information. Instead, students read a brief statement from one page then turn to the next page and select the picture that corresponds to that statement. For example, students read, "The puppy is in the pan," and select from one of the four pictures displayed as in Figure 6.5. The only criterion-related validity that is offered is a correlation with the *Peabody Picture Vocabulary Test–Revised* (Dunn & Dunn, 1981), a test of verbal ability that seems an inappropriate benchmark for comparison.

The reliability of the PIAT-R is substantially improved from the PIAT. Both the test-retest and the internal consistency coefficients are generally well within the acceptable boundaries for such an instrument. Test-retest reliability composite scores range from the low to the upper .90s. Most subtest correlations fall in the mid-.80s to high .90s, with low values at Grade 6 in reading comprehension (.78). Although there are generally at least seven items per year's growth on the test, Reading Comprehension is a notable exception. This is especially problematic at the upper grades where the limited item pool restricts its utility. With a SEM of 3.8 for Reading Comprehension and 2.6 for Reading Recognition, there is reason to exercise caution.

FIGURE 6.5
PIAT-R Item

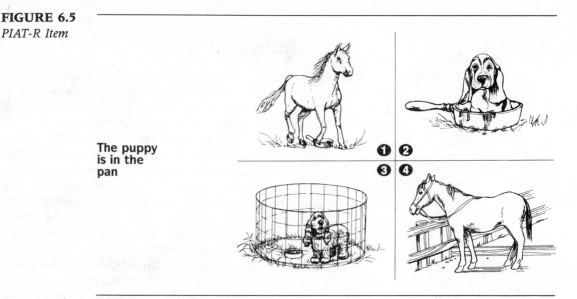

**The puppy
is in the
pan**

"The puppy is in the pan," *Peabody Individual Achievement Test–Revised PIAT-R* Manual by Frederick G. Markwardt, Jr. Copyright © 1989 American Guidance Service, Inc. Reprinted by permission.

Finally, although the norming procedure is adequate, the roughly 120 students per grade level is just acceptable. This test is often used to determine eligibility for special education programs, yet there were no special education students included in the norms.

In summary, the PIAT-R is a generally reliable screening instrument that can provide some information to teachers who know very little about the student they are testing. Because of serious concerns about the content validity of the Reading Comprehension subtest, however, it seems likely that teachers might find more useful survey data upon which to rely.

The PIAT-R is most often compared to another individual achievement battery, the *Wide Range Achievement Test–Revised* or WRAT-R (Jastak, 1984). Although there are some difficulties with the reliability and norming procedures of the WRAT-R, its most serious problem is its lack of content validity, especially in reading. The reading subtest consists of letter recognition, letter naming, and isolated reading of words on a page. The entire reading subtest is displayed on one single sheet. No information is gathered regarding students' oral reading accuracy or comprehension of even sentence length discourse. As Salvia and Ysseldyke (1988) note:

> A teacher who adjusted a student's reading curriculum on the basis of scores obtained on the Reading subtest of the WRAT-R would be on shaky ground indeed. The subtest assesses only skill in decoding isolated words and is not designed to measure the derivation of meaning from those words. (p. 343)

Diagnostic Tests

Diagnostic reading tests are designed to provide a profile of a student's relative strengths and weaknesses. According to Gronlund (1985), diagnostic tests differ from survey tests in three major ways: they have a large number of subtest scores and a larger number of items; the items are devised to measure specific skills; and difficulty tends to be lower in order to provide adequate discrimination among students with reading problems. Rather than providing one or two general scores that represent a student's overall reading performance, diagnostic tests break reading into various components such as knowledge of phonics, structural analysis, literal comprehension, inferential comprehension, and reading rate, and provide scores for each of these areas. The rationale underlying diagnostic tests is that instruction can be planned to help a student improve in areas where performance is low.

To have confidence in a diagnostic reading test, test users must satisfy their concerns for content validity. It is entirely possible that a subtest is measuring nothing of consequence or that it measures something that does not lend itself to instruction. Although the issue of content validity is always important to consider, the utility of diagnostic tests relies entirely on the relationship between the subtests and the prevailing conceptions of what is important in learning to read—both the users' views and those of the school curriculum.

Diagnostic reading tests can be individually or group administered, and either norm- or criterion-referenced tests. For example, the 1984 *Stanford Diagnostic Reading Test* (Karlsen & Gardner, 1986) is designed for group administration, while the *Woodcock Reading Mastery Test–Revised* (Woodcock, 1987) is an individually administered diagnostic reading test. Others include IRI-type oral reading tests such as the *Gray Oral Reading Test–Revised* (Wiederholt & Bryant, 1986). Finally, some diagnostic tests are embedded in criterion-referenced skills management systems. The *BRIGANCE® Diagnostic Inventories* (Brigance, 1976) provide an example of this type of testing.

Group Administered Diagnostic Tests:
The *Stanford Diagnostic Reading Test*

The third edition of the *Stanford Diagnostic Reading Test,* or SDRT (test copyright, 1984, manual copyright Karlsen & Gardner, 1986) is the latest version of a widely used group diagnostic test. There are four test levels that provide testing from first grade through junior college: Red, Grades 1 to 3; Green, Grades 2 to 5; Brown, Grades 4 to 9; and Blue, Grades 9 to 13. There are two forms at each level. Like most traditional comprehensive diagnostic tests of reading, there are a number of subtests (see Figure 6.6). All subtests use a multiple choice format.

The SDRT is a timed test, requiring from one and a half to two hours, depending on the level. Raw scores, for both subtests and total tests, are routinely converted to percentile ranks and stanine scores. Schools may also choose scoring options that include scaled scores, grade equivalents, and normal curve equivalents (NCEs). In addition, criterion-referenced interpretation is offered.

FIGURE 6.6
SDRT Content Chart

	RED LEVEL — Grades 1.5–3.5	No. of Items	GREEN LEVEL — Grades 3.0–5.5	No. of Items	BROWN LEVEL — Grades 5.0–9.5	No. of Items	BLUE LEVEL — Grades 8.5–13	No. of Items
Decoding	**Auditory Discrimination**	**30**	**Auditory Discrimination**	**30**				
	Consonants	15	Consonants	15				
	Single Consonants	5	Single Consonants	5				
	Consonant Clusters	5	Consonant Clusters	5				
	Consonant Digraphs	5	Consonant Digraphs	5				
	Vowels	15	Vowels	15				
	Short Vowels	5	Short Vowels	5				
	Long Vowels	5	Long Vowels	5				
			Other Vowels	5				
	Phonetic Analysis	**40**	**Phonetic Analysis**	**30**	**Phonetic Analysis**	**30**	**Phonetic Analysis**	**30**
	Consonants	24	Consonants	15	Consonants	15	Consonants	15
	Single Consonants	8	Single Consonants	5	Single Consonants	5	Single Consonants	10
	Consonant Clusters	8	Consonant Clusters	5	Consonant Clusters	5	Consonant Digraphs	5
	Consonant Digraphs	8	Consonant Digraphs	5	Consonant Digraphs	5	Vowels	15
	Vowels	16	Vowels	15	Vowels	15	Short Vowels	5
	Short Vowels	8	Short Vowels	5	Short Vowels	5	Long Vowels	5
	Long Vowels	8	Long Vowels	5	Long Vowels	5	Other Vowels	5
			Other Vowels	5	Other Vowels	5		
			Structural Analysis	**48**	**Structural Analysis**	**78**	**Structural Analysis**	**30**
			Word Division	24	Word Division	48	Affixes	15
			Compound Words	6	Compound Words	6	Syllables	15
			Affixes	9	Affixes	18		
			Syllables	9	Syllables	24	**Decoding Total**	**60**
			Blending	24	Blending	30		
			Compound Words	6	Affixes	10		
			Affixes	9	Syllables	20		
			Syllables	9				

Vocabulary	**Auditory Vocabulary** 36	**Auditory Vocabulary** 40	**Auditory Vocabulary** 40	**Vocabulary** 30
	Reading & Literature 14	Reading & Literature 18	Reading & Literature 16	Reading & Literature 10
	Math & Science 10	Math & Science 12	Math & Science 12	Math & Science 10
	Social Studies & the Arts 12	Social Studies & the Arts 10	Social Studies & the Arts 12	Social Studies & the Arts 10
				Word Parts 30
				Affixes 15
				Roots 15
				Vocabulary Total 60
Comprehension	**Word Reading** 30			
	Reading Comprehension 48	**Reading Comprehension** 48	**Reading Comprehension** 60	**Reading Comprehension** 60
	Sentence Reading 28	Literal 24	Literal 30	Literal 30
	Kernel Sentences 12	Inferential 24	Inferential 30	Inferential 30
	Sentence Transforms 12			
	Riddles 4	and	and	and
	Paragraph Comprehension 20	Textual	Textual 20	Textual 20
		Functional	Functional 20	Functional 20
		Recreational	Recreational 20	Recreational 20
Rate		**Reading Rate**	**Scanning & Skimming** 33	**Scanning & Skimming** 32
				Scanning 16
				Skimming 16
				Fast Reading 30
				Rate Total 62
Total	**SDRT Total** 184	**SDRT Total** 196	**SDRT Total** 241	**SDRT Total** 242

The stated purpose of the SDRT is to "diagnose pupils' strengths and weaknesses in reading. The SDRT results can be used to help teachers group pupils according to their specific instructional needs, thus facilitating the development of appropriate teaching strategies and materials" (Karlsen & Gardner, 1986, p. 3). Although the manual suggests that this test is appropriate for evaluating program effectiveness, for measuring student gains, and for reporting to the community, we believe that most people prefer a more global test of reading behavior for these purposes.

The internal consistency data for the SDRT suggest that all subtests have acceptable levels of reliability (greater than .80), except the Auditory Vocabulary subtest at Grades 2 and 3 (.79 and .76 respectively). The alternate form reliabilities are lower (.66 to .78). This is somewhat troubling because no information is offered at all about the test-retest reliability of any forms or subtests.

The authors press hard to establish the validity of the SDRT, arguing that the subtests and subskills represent instructional objectives common to most reading programs. Despite an effort to link the test content to more recent models, inspection of the tasks on the test suggests that it still reflects a heavy reliance on curricular validity from two decades ago, rendering the validity of this test suspect. As Salvia and Ysseldyke (1988) note, "data on validity are not convincing" (p. 376).

The content of some of the tasks is also questionable. The decoding subtests pose particular problems. For example, the phonetic analysis subtest of the Blue level (Grades 8–13) asks students to read a word and match the underlined sound with a word containing the same sound, for example: size: nurse, six, knows. As several critics have pointed out, this involves identifying variant spellings of phonic elements but does not necessarily have much to do with the type of sound-symbol analysis required during actual reading (Mitchell, 1985). Similarly, the structural analysis subtests of the Green and Brown levels require students to create a word using random word parts (e.g., *important* from *port er im ant*).

A notable feature of the SDRT is its intended audience. The authors intended that the SDRT be used with below-average readers and used an item development procedure that ensured that the test would not be too difficult for poor readers. This feature enhances the confidence we can have in the accuracy of students' scores. Although this test can provide some information about relative strengths and weaknesses, the utility of it is diminished by the questionable validity of the many subtests that reflect a dated view of the reading process.

Individually Administered Diagnostic Tests:
The *Woodcock Reading Mastery Test–Revised*

The *Woodcock Reading Mastery Test–Revised* or WRMT-R (Woodcock, 1987) is a battery of individually administered tests designed to diagnose students' readiness for reading and their mastery of various components of the reading process. The six distinct subtests are grouped and reported as the readiness cluster, a basic skills cluster, and a comprehension cluster. There are two parallel forms of the

WRMT-R. Form G contains all three clusters while Form H is used to measure basic skills and comprehension only (see Figure 6.7).

The WRMT-R is a norm-referenced test that is untimed, requiring between 45 and 90 minutes to administer. It is designed for use with students from kindergarten through college. This test provides several options for scoring and interpretation. Included among these are percentile ranks for total reading score and relative performance indices (RPIs) for subtests. RPIs indicate the individual student's percentage of mastery for tasks that the norming group performed with ease (90% mastery). With somewhat more effort, it is also possible to generate grade and age equivalents, a variety of standard scores, and confidence bands for the RPIs.

The test manual provides little documentation of validity, and it will be left to users to decide if reading has been appropriately tested by the subtests. The Readiness Cluster contains two subtests: Visual-Auditory Learning and Letter Identification, and Word Identification. The Visual-Auditory Learning subtest, taken from the *Woodcock-Johnson Psychoeducational Battery* (Woodcock & Johnson, 1977), is designed to measure students' ability to learn to read. Familiar words are represented by novel graphic displays (rebus-like graphics). Students must learn these novel graphics and use them to read sentences. Twenty-six "words" and two inflectional endings (-ing, -s) are used in this subtest.

On the Letter Identification subtest, students are asked to name letters written in several different type faces. The 51 items include a variety of types that are rarely used in the school setting (e.g., serif, sans serif). A supplementary checklist is available for testing letter names and sound associations. There are 27 capital letters and 36 lowercase letters on this list, which constitutes the only criterion-referenced portion of the WRMT-R.

The Basic Skills Cluster also contains two subtests: Word Identification and Word Attack. The Word Identification subtest requires students to read real words in isolation. The 106 items on this subtest increase in difficulty so that high-frequency words appear earlier and words with lower frequency appear later. On the Word Attack subtest, students encounter 45 nonsense words used to measure phonic and structural analysis skills. Beginning with simple syllables like "tat" and "op," the test proceeds to multisyllabic nonsense words and unusual vowel combinations like "quox" (item 30) and "untroikest" (item 40). This subtest is among the most controversial since many critics feel that reading nonsense words in isolation does not parallel normal reading. Clearly, the reader can neither check the approximation against known vocabulary words nor use the syntactic and semantic clues available in connected text. The WRMT-R authors defend its use, however, arguing that this does approximate real-life decoding (p. 6).

The Comprehension Center is comprised of Word Comprehension and Passage Comprehension. The Word Comprehension test has been expanded in this latest edition, and students are now required to display word knowledge by generating antonyms, synonyms, and analogies on three separate sections on the test. The word analogies task remains from the previous test edition. The subtest

FIGURE 6.7

Table of the WRMT-R Subtests and the Clusters

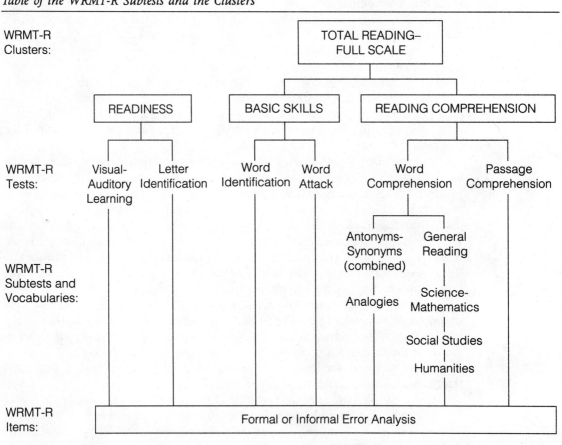

Test or Subtest

Readiness Cluster (Form G only)
  Test 1: Visual-Auditory Learning
  Test 2: Letter Identification

Supplementary Letter Checklist
  Capital Letters
  Lowercase Letters

Basic Skills Cluster
  Test 3: Word Identification
  Test 4: Word Attack

Reading Comprehension Cluster
  Test 5: Word Comprehension

  Subtests
    Antonyms-Synonyms (combined)
    Analogies

  Vocabularies
    General Reading
    Science-Mathematics
    Social Studies
    Humanities

  Test 6: Passage Comprehension

From *Woodcock Reading Mastery—Revised,* Examiner's Manual, pp. 2 and 4. Copyright © 1987 American College Guidance Service, Inc. Reprinted by permission.

requires students to complete a word analogy (physics is to science as algebra is to
_____). On the other two parts, students are asked to provide either a word
opposite or similar word as stimulus words are presented. These two additional
tasks were added in response to critics of the previous edition, who complained
that this subtest was a difficult, inadequate test of vocabulary (Laffey & Kelly,
1979).

The Passage Comprehension subtest consists of 68 sentences or short paragraphs containing a missing word (a modified cloze activity). Approximately one-
third of the items are one-sentence stimuli coupled with a picture. Students are
required to read each segment and supply the missing word.

The manual reports somewhat dated information asserting acceptable concurrent validity with unspecified editions of the *Iowa Test of Basic Skills*, PIAT
reading subtest, and the WRAT reading subtest (see WRMT-R manual, 1987,
p. 100). Norming procedures for the WRMT-R were reasonable, although the
sample size for adults (ages 20 to 80) was quite small. However, most users who
want to use this test in K–12 school settings will find adequate representation for
their purposes.

The authors report internal consistency reliability coefficients for all subtests.
These range from .34 on letter recognition to .98 on word identification. However,
the reliabilities for all clusters are above .80 and most are above .90. No test-retest
reliability data are provided.

The results of the WRMT-R will be most helpful to teachers with a skills
approach to teaching reading. In addition, general areas of difficulty can be
highlighted using the clusters making it useful in identifying students for special
and remedial services. We believe, however, that this test should be used cautiously, recognizing that it provides little new information to those who have
extensive diagnostic information from other sources.

Individually Administered Diagnostic Tests:
The *Gray Oral Reading Test–Revised*

First published in 1915 as the *Gray Oral Reading Standardized Paragraphs*, this test
has been revised recently and is enjoying a revival as the *Gray Oral Reading Test–
Revised* or GORT-R (Wiederholt & Bryant, 1986). The GORT-R has two alternate
equivalent forms, each containing 13 passages of increasing difficulty. Five comprehension questions follow each passage, and each passage is timed. The authors
suggest four purposes for using the GORT-R that involve identifying students with
oral reading problems, evaluating the strengths and weaknesses of individual
students, documenting progress in remedial programs, and measuring reading
ability in research investigations.

Targeted for first through twelfth grade, the test is similar to an informal
reading inventory in format and construction. However, norm-referenced scores
are available for reading rate, accuracy, and comprehension. Standard scores and
percentile ranks are both reported. In addition, an oral reading quotient is generated which is a combination of the oral passage reading score and the comprehen-

sion score. Finally, guidelines and scoring aids are provided to conduct a miscue analysis of oral reading behaviors.

The face validity of the GORT-R is quite good, since oral reading of passages followed by responses to questions is a common school task. In addition, evidence of construct validity is reasonable, since the authors attempted to use recent theory and research to guide their selection of passages rather than relying solely on readability formulas (see Chapter 9). The unprepared oral reading required throughout the test is a source of some concern, however, especially since there are no opportunities for silent reading at all. In addition, the criterion-related validity of the GORT-R is relatively weak, and it appears that extensive validity studies have not been conducted.

Norming procedures for the GORT-R appear nationally representative; however, no information is presented about the numbers of students at each level. The reliability of the tool appears acceptable. A limited sampling of students was used to conduct internal consistency estimates of reliability and the resulting coefficients were greater than .80. Alternate form reliabilities for a larger sample ranged from .80 to .83 for the various scores. No test-retest reliabilities were determined.

The GORT-R is relatively easy to administer and can provide guidance to a novice diagnostician, since the record form is quite comprehensive and helps to organize information (see Figure 6.8). Although most of the information provided can also be obtained by using an IRI (see Chapter 5), the availability of normative data may be desirable when reporting of standardized scores is necessary.

Diagnostic Tests of Specific Areas:
The Test of Reading Comprehension

There are times when test users are interested in exploring a particular component area of reading (e.g., word analysis or comprehension) in greater detail than is possible with more generalized test batteries. The *Test of Reading Comprehension* or TORC (Brown, Hammill, & Wiederholt, 1986) is an example of a norm-referenced test that focuses in depth on one area of reading: comprehension.

The TORC is a silent reading test designed for use with students aged 7 to 17. The test should be administered individually, although group administration is possible. The authors assert that the test can be used as a general measure of reading ability because the various components are combined to determine a basic Comprehension Core, expressed as a Reading Comprehension Quotient, or RCQ. Raw scores can also be converted to standard scores and percentile ranks. Diagnostic information of a sort can also be generated by comparing results generated from the various subtests. The four subtests of the TORC are: General Vocabulary, Syntactic Similarity, Paragraph Reading, and Sentence Sequencing. Optional subtests (e.g., content vocabulary) are available as well.

The reported reliability of the TORC is above .90 for all age groups. On the various subtests, coefficients of internal consistency are equally strong. Test-retest reliability for the RCQ is good (.91), but unacceptably low for several subtest scores.

The authors make a strong case for the content validity of the TORC, discussing newer theoretical perspectives at some length. However, an examination of the face validity of the test suggests they have not always succeeded in operationalizing these ideas. For example, Paragraph Reading is a fairly typical test of comprehension, requiring students to read only six short passages and answer multiple choice questions. This appears to be a very limited sampling of comprehension ability. The weak evidence for content validity is especially troubling given that the test also fails to demonstrate reasonable levels of criterion-related validity.

Other than Paragraph Reading, the subtests represent fairly unusual assessment formats and techniques. General Vocabulary, for example, requires students to read and consider three words that are related in some way by meaning. Then, the students read four other words, selecting two of the four that are most closely related to the original three. However, this subtest has been criticized as requiring high degrees of classification ability and as not representative of the type of vocabulary knowledge required for reading and understanding connected text (Hood, 1985).

The tests of Syntactic Similarity and Sentence Sequencing are equally controversial. The first of these requires students to select two sentences that have the same meaning expressed with different syntactic structure. Sentence Sequencing involves 10 items, each containing 5 randomly presented sentences that require reordering to create a meaningful short paragraph.

The TORC is a reliable test that may provide valid information about the overall reading comprehension of individual students using the Reading Comprehension Quotient score. However, diagnostic information derived from subtest analysis is likely to be both less reliable and less valid. The information generated from the TORC is not likely to be informative, and users are likely to find it most functional as a numerical measure when meeting federal or state guidelines for screening purposes.

Criterion-Referenced Diagnostic Tests:
The *BRIGANCE® Diagnostic Inventories*

As we have already noted, criterion referenced tests (CRTs) are designed to assess students' abilities and describe their strengths and weaknesses without making comparisons to other students. CRTs have proliferated since their initial appearance in the 1960s. The success and utility of a CRT depend extensively on the degree to which the tasks and behaviors sampled on the test are closely related to a reasonable view of skilled reading and are like the tasks and behaviors teachers intend to address.

The *BRIGANCE® Diagnostic Inventories* (Brigance, 1976) provide an example of this type of testing. There are five different BRIGANCE® batteries aimed at evaluating a wide range of ages and skills, from preschool early development through the basic skills of the elementary years to a test of essential skills designed for use with secondary students. There is also a test designed to screen students for

FIGURE 6.8
GORT-R Summary Form

PRETEST: Form _____

	Year	Month	Day
Date tested	___	___	___
Date of birth	___	___	___
Chronological age	___	___	___

School _____ Grade ____

Examiner's name _____

Examiner's title _____

POSTTEST: Form _____

	Year	Month	Day
Date tested	___	___	___
Date of birth	___	___	___
Chronological age	___	___	___

School _____ Grade ____

Examiner's name _____

Examiner's title _____

Section I. Record of GORT-R Scores

	PRETEST: Form ___		POSTTEST: Form ___	
Story	Comp. Score	Passage Score	Comp. Score	Passage Score
1	___	___	___	___
2	___	___	___	___
3	___	___	___	___
4	___	___	___	___
5	___	___	___	___
6	___	___	___	___
7	___	___	___	___
8	___	___	___	___
9	___	___	___	___
10	___	___	___	___
11	___	___	___	___
12	___	___	___	___
13	___	___	___	___
Raw Score	___	___	___	___
%ile	___	___	___	___
Std. Score	___	___	___	___
Sum of Std. Scores	___		___	
%ile	___		___	
Oral Reading Quotient	___		___	
Quotient Difference		___		

Section II. Record of Other Test Scores

Test Name	Test Date	GORT-R Equiv.
1. _____		
2. _____		
3. _____		
4. _____		
5. _____		

Section III. Profile of Scores

Std. Score	GORT-R Scores		Other Scores						
	Comp. Score	Passage Score	ORQ	1	2	3	4	5	Quotient
20	•	•	•	•	•	•	•	•	150
19	•	•	•	•	•	•	•	•	145
18	•	•	•	•	•	•	•	•	140
17	•	•	•	•	•	•	•	•	135
16	•	•	•	•	•	•	•	•	130
15	•	•	•	•	•	•	•	•	125
14	•	•	•	•	•	•	•	•	120
13	•	•	•	•	•	•	•	•	115
12	•	•	•	•	•	•	•	•	110
11	•	•	•	•	•	•	•	•	105
10	—	—	—	—	—	—	—	—	100
9	•	•	•	•	•	•	•	•	95
8	•	•	•	•	•	•	•	•	90
7	•	•	•	•	•	•	•	•	85
6	•	•	•	•	•	•	•	•	80
5	•	•	•	•	•	•	•	•	75
4	•	•	•	•	•	•	•	•	70
3	•	•	•	•	•	•	•	•	65
2	•	•	•	•	•	•	•	•	60
1	•	•	•	•	•	•	•	•	55

FIGURE 6.8
(Continued)

Section IV. Record of Miscues

PRETEST: Form _____	POSTTEST: Form _____

A. Summary of Categorized Miscues (left) / **A. Summary of Categorized Miscues** (right)

	Number	Percentage		Number	Percentage
Meaning Similarity	_____	_____	Meaning Similarity	_____	_____
Function Similarity	_____	_____	Function Similarity	_____	_____
Graphic/Phonemic Similarity	_____	_____	Graphic/Phonemic Similarity	_____	_____
Multiple Sources	_____	_____	Multiple Sources	_____	_____
Self-correction	_____	_____	Self-correction	_____	_____

B. Summary of Other Miscues

	Number		Number
Omissions	_____	Omissions	_____
Additions	_____	Additions	_____
Dialect	_____	Dialect	_____
Reversals	_____	Reversals	_____

C. Summary of Other Observations
(check statement and circle each part)

Posture	_____	Posture	_____
Word-by-word reading	_____	Word-by-word reading	_____
Poor phrasing	_____	Poor phrasing	_____
Lack of expression	_____	Lack of expression	_____
Pitch too high or low	_____	Pitch too high or low	_____
Voice too soft or strained	_____	Voice too soft or strained	_____
Poor enunciation	_____	Poor enunciation	_____
Disregard of punctuation	_____	Disregard of punctuation	_____
Head movement	_____	Head movement	_____
Finger pointing	_____	Finger pointing	_____
Loss of place	_____	Loss of place	_____
Nervousness	_____	Nervousness	_____
Poor attitude	_____	Poor attitude	_____
Other _____	_____	Other _____	_____

Section V. Comments/Recommendations

_____

_____

_____

_____

_____

_____

_____

From *GORT-R Profile/Examiner Record Form* by Wiederholt and Bryant, 1986. Reprinted by permission of PRO-ED.

kindergarten and first grade. The batteries including reading, language arts, spelling, math and a variety of life skills.

Each of the inventories contain a sizeable listing of skills to be tested. The *Inventory of Early Development*, for example, tests 98 skills, and the *Diagnostic Inventory of Basic Skills* contains 141 skills. There are 33 distinct skills listed for reading alone on this battery (see Figure 6.9). The tests produce grade level scores for each of the skills, and teachers are encouraged to plan their instructional programs based on the specific items missed.

Unfortunately, the tests provide no information regarding the validity of these skills. "The assumption is made that if children master each of the subskills in the hierarchy, they will be able to read" (Witt in Mitchell, 1985, p. 218). This absence of validity information is especially troubling. The BRIGANCE® Inventories have enjoyed wide use, in part because the results are so easily translated into instructional objectives of the sort used by many special educators to write IEPs. Indeed, any item that is not mastered on this test is likely to be listed as a desirable outcome on an IEP.

The BRIGANCE® also provides no information about either the reliability or developmental appropriateness of the test(s). Thus, it is not reasonable to use the BRIGANCE® as a placement tool, a purpose suggested by the author (Smith in Mitchell, 1985, p. 216). The most defensible use of the BRIGANCE® is to reveal fairly quickly to the uninformed or busy teacher some of the areas that may require further testing or evaluation. However, Brigance himself notes that the test should be used together with other information, such as classroom observational data and work samples.

Tests of Other Language Arts and Related Areas

Reading professionals often require information about student performance in areas other than reading. This may include information related to the correlates of reading performance (see Chapter 1), such as general cognitive ability or emotional/physical development. Assessments in these areas may be necessary in order to eliminate or identify these correlates as factors in reading performance.

The role of general cognitive development in influencing reading achievement is well documented. As measured by standardized tests, the relationship between verbal ability and reading achievement is very strong. It is important for educators to examine the issues surrounding intelligence testing and for reading professionals to use this information cautiously, since test scores are obviously influenced by what is measured and by students' opportunity to learn what is expected (see Chapters 1 and 8). However, limited verbal ability *can* contribute to reading problems, and in the case of students who have significant limitations in verbal ability, special placements and provisions should be considered.

In addition to the usual cautions about test use and misuse, one major caveat regarding intelligence test information is in order. Many schools continue the practice of routinely collecting IQ data using group tests of intelligence. Sometimes the tests are piggybacked on the group achievement tests used by the district

FIGURE 6.9
BRIGANCE®
Diagnostic
Inventory of
Basic Skills—
Reading
Sections

A. Word Recognition

Test	Title
A-1	Word Recognition Grade Level
A-2	Basic Sight Vocabulary
A-3	Direction Words
A-4	Abbreviations
A-5	Contractions
A-6	Common Signs

B. Reading

Test	Title
B-1	Oral Reading Level
B-2	Reading Comprehension Level
B-3	Oral Reading Rate

C. Word Analysis

Test	Title
C-1	Auditory Discrimination

C. Word Analysis (cont.)

Test	Title
C-2	Initial Consonant Sounds Auditorily
C-3	Initial Consonant Sounds Visually
C-4	Substitution of Initial Consonant Sounds
C-5	Ending Sounds Auditorily
C-6	Vowels
C-7	Short Vowel Sounds
C-8	Long Vowel Sounds
C-9	Initial Clusters Auditorily
C-10	Initial Clusters Visually
C-11	Substitution of Initial Cluster Sounds
C-12	Digraphs and Diphthongs

C. Word Analysis (cont.)

Test	Title
C-13	Phonetic Irregularities
C-14	Common Endings of Rhyming Words
C-15	Suffixes
C-16	Prefixes
C-17	Meaning of Prefixes
C-18	Number of Syllables Auditorily
C-19	Syllabication Concepts

D. Vocabulary

Test	Title
D-1	Context Clues
D-2	Classification
D-3	Analogies
D-4	Antonyms
D-5	Homonyms

From BRIGANCE® *Diagnostic Inventory of Basic Skills*, Copyright © 1976, 1977 Curriculum Associates, Inc. Reprinted by permission.

or school, and at other times schools use the available independent group intelligence tests. There are a wide range of problems associated with the use of these tests (see Salvia & Ysseldyke, 1988). Most are not adequately normed and have limited validity as measures of intelligence. In addition, the reliability for individual test scores is often low. For these reasons, group intelligence data are permissible as data when making major placement and eligibility decisions (e.g., special education determinations). Given the limited utility of this information and the volatile nature of the data, it is hard to understand why schools persist in this practice.

Reading professionals are also increasingly aware of the relationship between reading development and ability in other areas of language arts. In particular, the links between oral language development and reading and between writing and reading appear critical. When serious problems of speech or language development are suspected, reading professionals will obviously want to refer children to a specialist in these areas. However, there are several tests that can be used to guide the prereferral process.

Although we cannot possibly review all of these types of instruments in this text, some are administered or encountered so frequently by reading professionals that they need to be addressed here. For example, the *Test of Written Language* (Hammill & Larsen, 1988) is often used to determine whether students are experiencing difficulty in written expression similar to their problems in reading. Similarly, the *Peabody Picture Vocabulary Test—Revised* (Dunn & Dunn, 1981) is widely used to evaluate students' receptive vocabulary.

Tests of Oral and Written Language

Test of Oral Language Development–2 Primary (Newcomer & Hammill, 1988). The revised TOLD-2 Primary is an individually administered, norm-referenced test designed for use with children ages 4.0 to 8.11. The seven subtests provide information about a student's skills in specific language areas. The phonological aspects of language are evaluated in the Word Articulation and Word Discrimination subtests. The semantic aspects of language are tested in the Picture Vocabulary and the Oral Vocabulary subtests, and the syntactic aspects of language are represented in the Grammatic Understanding, Sentence Imitation, and Grammatic Completion subtests.

The TOLD-2 Primary is intended for use in identifying children whose language development is atypical, providing information about the strengths and weaknesses of individual children, and documenting progress in specialized programs. Administration time ranges from 30 minutes to an hour. Raw scores can be converted to percentile ranks and standard scores for both subtests and composites.

Fairly extensive evidence of the criterion-related validity of the TOLD-2 is offered in the manual. The authors compared the subtests of the TOLD-2 to nine criterion tests, with the correlation coefficients for all students ranging from .69 to .84. The correlation coefficients for subtest scores for various age groups were smaller, however. The authors use expert judgment to establish the content validity of the TOLD-2 Primary. While the tasks are similar to those used on many formal tests of language, the question of face validity must be raised here. Westby (1988) asks, "Do the test tasks represent anything that the child actually does with language in the real world?" She concludes that the test has serious flaws in this area and suggests using it for screening only, supplementing it with language samples gathered in more natural language contexts.

The authors provide a good discussion of reliability and provide coefficients that consistently exceed .80. Using a measure of internal consistency, the composites range from .91 to .95, with subtests somewhat lower. These results suggest that the test has adequate reliability at both the subtest and composite level for screening purposes. For diagnostic conclusions at the subtest level, only some ages and subskills attain a .90 coefficient. Test-retest reliability information is limited to a small sample and reference to previous editions.

The norming procedures appear entirely acceptable, with representative stratified sampling of acceptable numbers of students. However, the norms are based on speakers of mainstream English only and there is some evidence that dialect or bilingual speakers may perform poorly on this test (Westby, 1988).

The TOLD-2 is most likely to be useful in providing normative screening data to reading professionals, especially when they are considering a referral to a language specialist. However, test users should be especially careful about possible dialect usage and should also be alert to evidence of acceptable language use in normal daily discourse.

Test of Written Language–2 (Hammil & Larsen, 1988). The TOWL-2 is a test of both receptive and expressive language designed for use with students ages 7 to 17. Students are asked to read, listen, and write in response to several stimuli. Both contrived and spontaneous writing formats are employed. With the exception of the 15 minutes allocated to story writing, the TOWL-2 has no set time limits. The test takes approximately two to two and a half hours to administer, and inexperienced examiners should allow considerable additional time to score the test. Unlike previous editions of this test, the TOWL-2 provides two alternate forms.

The 10 subtests of the TOWL-2 can be reported as raw scores, percentiles, subtest and composite standard scores, and written language quotients (see Figure 6.10). Five of the subtest scores are generated by analyzing a spontaneous writing sample, a story that is written in response to a picture stimulus: Thematic Maturity, Contextual Vocabulary, Syntactic Maturity, Contextual Spelling, and Contextual Style. Extensive checklists are provided for this purpose.

The other five subtests involve contrived writing tasks. For example, subtest 4, Logical Sentences, requires students to rewrite sentences that have something wrong with them so "that it makes perfect sense" (p. 21). Some of these sentences are corrected using general semantic knowledge. Item 1 is an example of this type: "John blinked his nose." Others, however, require much more subtle distinctions, such as those in item 13: "While farmers work long days, most of them are satisfied with their lives." The authors note that *while* should be replaced by a connective that shows opposition, such as *although* or *whereas* in this item. Spelling and Style are both evaluated using the same dictation task, and the Vocabulary subtest requires students to write 30 stimulus words in sentences.

The norming procedures for the TOWL-2 are carefully described and appear acceptable. The stratified standardization sample included over 2,000 students, distributed in a representative fashion across geographic areas. Other demographic factors were also considered. The authors provide reasonable evidence regarding the reliability of the TOWL-2. The overall reliability of the test, using interscorer reliability, content sampling, and time sampling, ranged from .87 to .96. The TOWL-2 can be considered a reliable test of students' written language.

The TOWL-2 provides reasonably strong evidence of its validity. The content validity is derived from the theoretical orientation of the test and from examination of the types of tasks generally required of students in school settings. Item development and selection seem adequate. Criterion-related validity was examined in two studies. The first study compared students' performance on the TOWL-2 to their language arts composite score on the SRA Achievement Series. The second compared the performance of students on the TOWL-2 with student-generated essays that had been rated by experts. The coefficients presented are large enough to lend support to the contention that the TOWL-2 has adequate criterion-related validity. Test-retest coefficients range from .59 to .99, with most in the high .80s. Interscorer reliabilities are reported ranging from .93 to .99.

**FIGURE
6.10**
*Summary
Sheet from
TOWL-2*

TOWL-2

Test of Written Language

A B
Form ☐ ☐

PROFILE/STORY SCORING FORM

Donald D. Hammill & Stephen C. Larsen

IDENTIFYING INFORMATION

Name _____ Male _____ Female _____

	Year	Month	Day
Date Tested	_____	_____	_____
Date of Birth	_____	_____	_____
Age	_____	_____	_____

School _____ Grade _____

Examiner's name _____

Examiner's title _____

SECTION I RECORD OF SUBTEST SCORES

Subtests	Raw Scores	%iles	Std. Scores
I Vocabulary	_____	_____	_____
II Spelling	_____	_____	_____
III Style	_____	_____	_____
IV Logical Sentences	_____	_____	_____
V Sentence Combining	_____	_____	_____
VI Thematic Maturity	_____	_____	_____
VII Contextual Vocabulary	_____	_____	_____
VIII Syntactic Maturity	_____	_____	_____
IX Contextual Spelling	_____	_____	_____
X Contextual Style	_____	_____	_____

SECTION II RECORD OF OTHER TEST SCORES

Name	Date	Std. Score	TOWL-2 Equiv.
1			
2			
3			
4			
5			
6			
7			
8			
9			
10			

SECTION III COMPUTATION OF COMPOSITE SCORES

TOWL-2 COMPOSITES	STANDARD SCORES										SUM OF STD. SCORES	QUOTIENTS
	VO	SP	ST	LS	SC	TM	CV	SM	CSp	CSt		
Contrived Writing	☐	☐	☐	☐	☐						= ☐	( )
Spontaneous Writing						☐	☐	☐	☐	☐	= ☐	( )
Overall Written Language	☐	☐	☐	☐	☐	☐	☐	☐	☐	☐	= ☐	( )

In general, the TOWL-2 is a reasonable standardized measure of writing. The spontaneous writing sample, from which five scores are generated, should be considered carefully, however. Students are given one and only one opportunity to write a story. There is no prewriting or editing permitted and students are not given time or opportunity to reflect on either the content or the mechanics.

Teachers and students who are accustomed to a process-writing approach will find this a somewhat limited view of writing competence.

Although the TOWL-2 does not really generate any information that could not be collected by a clever and knowledgeable teacher during classroom instruction and observation, the standardized information can be used to document and substantiate students' weaknesses in written language for placement in special education programs. Polloway's conclusions (in Mitchell, 1985) regarding the TOWL are even more true of the improved TOWL-2: "It does offer the most structurally sound and instructionally relevant instrument currently available in the area of written language" (p. 1602).

Tests of General Cognitive and Verbal Abilities

In this section, we describe three tests that are commonly used to make decisions about students' cognitive abilities: the *Bender Visual Motor Gestalt Test* (Koppitz, 1963; 1975), the *Peabody Picture Vocabulary Test* (Dunn & Dunn, 1981), and the *Slosson Intelligence Test* (Slosson, 1983). These tests were selected because they are so widely used and because they are often administered by teachers who have no specialized training in psychological testing. Each has serious limitations that are also described to help school personnel evaluate these and other similar tools used to make judgments about students.

***Bender Visual Motor Gestalt Test* (BVMGT).** Although this test is not, strictly speaking, a test of general cognitive ability, it is used to draw conclusions about minimal brain dysfunction and emotional disturbance. According to Salvia and Ysseldyke (1988), "the test has become one of the most frequently administered psychometric devices" (p. 280).

The BVMGT requires only that students copy nine geometric designs, which are then scored according to a system described by Koppitz (1963, 1975). Shape distortion, perseveration, integration, and rotation errors are scored, generating a raw score that can be converted to age equivalents and percentile ranks. It is administered individually and norms are available for use with children ages 5 to 11.

Inter-rater reliability scores suggest that it is possible to reliably score the BVMGT. Test-retest reliability, however, is much lower. The mean reliability coefficient for studies reported in the 1975 manual was .71 (Salvia & Ysseldyke, 1988). This does not meet the criteria of stability we would demand of a test used to make the types of serious judgments described above. However, the most serious problem with the BVMGT is its validity.

Neither the original test as described by Bender (1938) nor the descriptions and guidelines offered by Koppitz adequately support copying of geometric figures as a measure of visual perceptual functions. In addition, there is inadequate evidence offered as to the validity of Koppitz's (1963) suggestions that the test can be used as a measure of intelligence, brain dysfunction, and emotional disturbance. Despite admonitions to use this test cautiously, the suggestion that perceptual-motor skills such as copying can predict reading or other academic success is difficult to justify. Indeed, the available evidence now suggests that there is no causal relationship between perceptual motor abilities and reading success (see Chapter 1). Certainly, the suggestion that tests of copying could provide adequate evidence of general cognitive ability is even less reasonable.

Peabody Picture Vocabulary Test–Revised (Dunn & Dunn, 1981). The PPVT-R is a norm-referenced, individually administered test of receptive vocabulary. It is designed for use with people from the ages of 2$\frac{1}{2}$ through 40 years and contains two parallel forms. Each form consists of an easel-booklet of stimuli plates. Each plate page contains four pictures, one of which illustrates the meaning of the stimulus word that is read by the examiner. Students need only point or gesture to the correct picture. Administration time is approximately 20 minutes.

Raw scores can be converted to standard scores (mean of 100, SD of 15), percentile ranks, stanines, and age equivalent scores. In addition, the scores are displayed so that confidence bands appear around each of the derived scores. The norming procedures for the PPVT-R are good, both in terms of representativeness and stratified sampling methods. The norms for the group 2$\frac{1}{2}$ to 18 are more reliable than those for adults, since there are 200 individuals per age group in this range, but many fewer to cover the ranges above age 19.

The authors offer no evidence of criterion-related validity, nor is there much information regarding content validity. In general, the authors simply assert the general utility of vocabulary measures in measuring cognitive ability. Although procedures for item development appear to be adequate, Jongsma (1982) notes that there is no evidence offered for the curricular relevance of these words.

The manual reports reliability coefficients for internal consistency, test-retest, and alternate forms. These range from .61 to .91 and are generally acceptable for screening purposes. As the authors advise using this test for those purposes only, the reliabilities seem reasonable.

The PPVT is a reasonably reliable test that is quick and easy to administer and score. Although the test offers little evidence of validity, the authors suggest that it serves as a measure of achievement when viewed as a test of receptive vocabulary. It can also be considered to be a quick global measure of one aspect of verbal ability. Previous versions of this test resulted in so-called intelligence quotients and the test was frequently, but wrongly, viewed as an IQ test. In this latest version, the authors are careful to characterize the test as a receptive vocabulary test only and to caution against using it as a comprehensive test of intelligence. Like the TOLD-2, however, it can help reading professionals decide whether they wish to recommend further testing.

Slosson Intelligence Test (Slosson, 1983). The SIT is a short, easy-to-administer, individual screening tool. It yields an estimate of intelligence as measured by a subset of items taken from the *Stanford-Binet Intelligence Test* (1972). The test requires only about 15 minutes to administer, and scoring is also quite simple.

Although the test manual implies that it is appropriate for individuals as diverse as infants and adults with significant handicaps, the 1981 norms used to interpret the data from this test were developed on a sample of people from 27 months to 17 years, 2 months. This standardization group, although apparently representing diverse demographics, consisted of a narrow sample drawn solely from the New England states. In addition, the numbers of individuals per age group was inadequate at ages 2–6 and 13–18, rendering age equivalent (mental age) scores suspect. Scores can also be converted to deviation IQs (mean = 100, SD = 16), percentile ranks, NCEs, and stanines.

Items at the earliest levels (age range two weeks to two years) and derived from the *Gesell Developmental Tests of School Readiness* (Ilg & Ames, 1965) (described in a subsequent section of this chapter). The remainder of the test is comprised of a subtest of items from the Stanford-Binet test. All items are administered orally, and testees are not expected to read or write, except for several items requiring that they draw a circle, square, etc. Not surprisingly, the SIT scores are highly correlated with scores derived from the Stanford-Binet, which serves as the basis for its validity. Most troubling, however, is the author's assertion that the SIT is reliable, although the data presented are actually generated from the Stanford-Binet test-retest coefficients.

The SIT may be used as a global screening measure, since its correlation to the Stanford-Binet Intelligence Test is understandably strong. However, the absence of evidence of reliability renders this relationship suspect for any individual child. At the upper age ranges of the test, the number of items per age equivalent is quite thin (there is only one item for age 27, for example). Extreme caution in using and reporting the information from the SIT is suggested.

Readiness/Emergent Literacy Assessment

Traditional tests of reading readiness are intended to determine whether students are ready to learn to read (see Chapter 4). Thus, they can only be judged useful if they predict students' subsequent success in reading or appropriately place students in beginning instructional programs. Indeed, many school systems continue to use readiness tests for both screening and placement purposes, often as the basis for recommending special classes or delayed entry into school.

Most existing readiness tests share several significant problems. First, few readiness tests are sufficiently reliable to make educational decisions. The test results of very young children are often unstable, and existing readiness tests are no exception. Second, few have sufficient predictive validity to warrant making judgments about students' future performance. As Shepard and Smith (1986) note:

> The lack of high correlations with later school success is caused by the instability of the very traits we are seeking to measure. Four- and five-year-olds experience developmental bursts and inconsistencies that defy normative charts. In addition, the cognitive domains that can be sampled at younger ages are only moderately related to the cognitive skills demanded later by reading and other academic tasks. (p. 83)

A third problem relates to the degree to which readiness tests reflect recent advances in our knowledge of literacy development. Most commercially available readiness tests were developed 50 years ago and are either developmental tests of readiness or subskills tests of component parts. These generally do not provide useful information regarding the foundations of literacy, and therefore may not differentiate among students in instructionally useful ways.

More recently, tests developed in response to an emergent literacy view of reading/writing development have begun to appear. Although these are not without flaw, they can offer different types of information to a careful and thoughtful evaluator. Tests such as the *Test of Early Reading Ability–2* (Reid, Hresko, & Hammill, 1989) attempt a global assessment of emergent literacy, while tests like the *Test of Awareness of Language Segments* (Sawyer, 1987) examine some single component assumed to be critical to literacy development.

Gathering dependable and useful information about the literacy abilities of young children can be a very tricky business. We have addressed many of the salient issues in previous portions of this text (see Chapter 4). Before we examine some of the widely used standardized tools, it is helpful to consider the recommendations made by Nurss (1979) over a decade ago for the improvement of commercial, standardized tests in this area:

1. Readiness tests should include information about Language Concepts (understanding of the reading task, words, sounds, and letters).
2. Prereading assessment in the future should be based on reading-like tasks using actual letters, sounds, and words.
3. Readiness tests should assess instructional skills that can be related to specific methods and materials.
4. Prereading measures should focus upon content validity related to instruction rather than upon predictive validity.
5. The focus of prereading assessment should shift from readiness to beginning reading skills . . . The skill scores should be related to beginning reading so that they can be used to suggest which beginning instructional steps should be tried for each child (vs. which kids aren't ready). (Nurss, 1979, pp. 55–56)

The following sections provide some prototypic examples of both developmental and subskill tests of readiness that are still widely employed, followed by examples of several more recent tests of emergent literacy.

Developmental Readiness Tests

Many school systems continue to use developmental tests, most often to make judgments about whether children are ready to enter school programs (Durkin, 1987). They are also commonly used to make decisions about placement into special programs (i.e., transitional kindergarten/first grades) or to limit entrance into kindergarten (who should stay home for a year). These tests often evaluate readiness using global data regarding physical and cognitive development. The *Gesell Developmental Tests of School Readiness* (Ilg & Ames, 1965) is such a test. Alternatively, developmental readiness is often evaluated using measures of conceptual achievement. The *Boehm Tests of Basic Concepts–Revised* (Boehm, 1986) and the *Test of Basic Experiences–2* (Moss, 1979) are examples of this type.

Gesell developmental tests of school readiness. The *Gesell* (Ilg & Ames, 1965), as it is often called, consists of a small battery of interview and manipulative tasks to be used with children ages 5 to 9. Students are required to build with blocks, complete a picture of a man, copy forms and letters, name animals, and so forth. A subset of these tasks comprise the *Gesell School Readiness and Kindergarten Screening Test* (1978), which is to be used for children entering kindergarten.

Normative responses and age trends are provided in a separate document, *Scoring Notes: The Developmental Examination* (Ilg, 1982). However, there is inadequate information about both the norming procedures and the validity of these tools. There is reasonable face validity for some tasks, but others are very questionable. For example, during the interview portions of the test, children are asked to respond to a number of inquiries, for example, to tell how old they are, to show their right and left hands, to identify body parts, and to name their interests. During other portions of the test, children are asked to copy figures from memory and to manipulate number concepts. These tasks might very well elicit some reasonable information about language and cognitive development important to school performance. However, in other portions of the screening, the examiner is asked to consider such factors as the time and development of tooth eruption activity.

Still widely used, the Gesell tests have recently been singled out as being questionable instruments for making decisions regarding children's readiness for reading (Shepard, 1986; Shepard & Smith, 1986). Shepard and her colleagues note that these tests do not meet the standards of the American Psychological Association for validity, reliability, or normative information. In particular, they note that although the reliability is so questionable that distinctions between 4-year-old and 5-year-old performance are not possible, this is precisely the difference that is used to decide who should start kindergarten and who should not. Accordingly, teachers and administrators should exercise exceptional caution when making important decisions based on these tests.

Tests of Basic Concepts. Estimates of verbal and conceptual readiness are less controversial than estimates of physical and emotional development, but no less difficult to evaluate in young children. One advantage to tests of basic concepts is that they are often simple to give and score. For example, the *Boehm Test of Basic Concepts—Revised,* or BTBC-R (Boehm, 1986), is a group-administered, norm-referenced test that takes only 15 to 20 minutes to administer.

The BTBC-R is designed to measure students' knowledge of concepts thought to be important for school achievement. According to the author, it can be used to identify children who are at risk for learning problems and children who have not mastered basic concepts, so that remedial instruction can be planned. The test evaluates students' understanding of 50 concepts representing various relationships (e.g., *next to, inside,* or *several*) by having them mark pictures that reflect concepts read by the teacher. The author provides documentation that these concepts are generally important to school settings.

Alternate test forms are available for pre- and post-testing. Pass-fail scores are generated for each item and percentile ranks are available for total scores. The normative sample does not appear to include any children in special programs,

FIGURE 6.11
Summary Chart: Subskill Tests of Readiness

Skill category	Skill	CIRCUS, 1974	Clymer-Barrett, 1968	Gates-MacGinitie, 1968	Harrison-Stroud, 1956	Lee-Clark, 1962	Metropolitan Readiness, Level 1, 1976	Metropolitan Readiness, Level II, 1976	Murphy-Durrell, 1965
Quantitative Skills	Observation scale	×××	×				×	×	
	Quantitative operations							×	×
	Quantitative concepts	×					×	×	×
Language Comprehension Skills	Divergent thinking	×							
	Problem solving	×							
	Information	×							
	Productive language	×××							
	Following directions			×					
	Language structure	×					×	×	
	Listening	×		×	×		×	×	
	Word meaning	×				×			
Auditory Skills	Sound-letter correspondence						×		
	Auditory blending			×					
	Rhyming		×				×		
	Auditory memory						×		
	Auditory discrimination			×					
	Auditory matching	××		×		××	×		××
Visual Skills	Visual-motor coordination	×	××	×			×	×	
	Word recognition (reading)			×	×				×
	Figure-ground perception						×	×	
	Visual memory	×							
	Letter recognition	×	×	×	×		×		
	Visual discrimination	×		×		××	×		
	Visual matching		×		×	××	×	×	
	Practice test	×					×	×	

X indicates that the test includes one, two, or three subtests measuring the skills indicated.
Source: Nurss, J. R. (1979). Assessment of readiness. In T. G. Waller & G. E. MacKinnon (Eds.) *Reading Research: Advances in theory and practice.* Vol. 1, 31–62.

and the data regarding socio-economic status are questionable. Similarly, re-liability coefficients are weak for test-retest estimates. Salvia & Ysseldyke (1988) conclude that "the device has inadequate reliability and norms for purposes other than screening" (p. 442).

The *Test of Basic Experiences–2* or TOBE-2 (Moss, 1979) also relies on students' concept achievement to judge readiness for school learning. Most of the test assesses vocabulary knowledge; however, there are also items related to letter recognition and letter-sound associations. There are additional sections on vocab-ulary knowledge for mathematics, social studies, and science.

Like the BTBC, the TOBE-2 is group-administered and takes approximately 45 minutes to give (there is also a 20-minute practice test). There are two forms of the TOBE-2: one for kindergarten and one for first grade. The norming procedures seem entirely acceptable, and the reliability of this test is acceptable.

Unfortunately, there is little information regarding validity. Indeed, the au-thor relies on its similarity to other accepted tests to demonstrate face validity. Without a well-conceived description of the readiness framework used to con-struct the test, there is reason to question the rationale and the predictive validity of this instrument.

Subskill Tests of Readiness

Subskills tests of reading readiness are by far the most prevalent type of instrument used in schools today. These tests are composed of a battery of subtests, each assessing some readiness skill. The listing in Figure 6.11 summarizes the most commonly used of these readiness tests and the types of skills they evaluate. Because of its widespread popularity, the *Metropolitan Readiness Test* or MRT (Nurss & McGauvran, 1976/1986) has been chosen as a prototype for discussion of these types of tests.

The 1986 edition of the MRT is the most recent update of one of the oldest tests of readiness. It is a group-administered test with two levels. Level 1 is designed to assess a "range of prereading skills," while Level 2 is designed to assess "more advanced skills that are important in beginning reading and mathematics" (Nurss & McGauvran, 1986, p. 7). The subtests included in these two levels are summarized in Figure 6.12.

The MRT is generally considered to be very strong technically (Ravitch, 1985). However, as with other tests of this type, it has only marginal predictive validity. Given that the MRT is not meant to predict future school performance, this should not be a particular problem. Unfortunately, that is not the case, because the MRT is often misused for predictive purposes. Furthermore, the MRT lacks the predictive validity for specific instructional programs necessary for its intended purposes of helping teachers plan and organize activities to meet individ-ual needs. As Salvia and Ysseldyke (1988) note, "educators want to know how students will fare in their various curricula. . . . The information presented is inadequate to establish either content or construct validity" (p. 450).

Raw scores on the MRT can be converted to "content-referenced" scores. However, because no rationale is provided for the criterion levels established for

FIGURE 6.12
MRT Subtests

Level 1 Subtests

Auditory Memory assesses immediate recall of words read by the tester.

Beginning Consonants assesses the discrimination of initial sounds.

Letter Recognition assesses both upper and lowercase letters.

Visual Matching assesses a child's ability to match a series of letters, words, numbers, or other symbols.

School Language and Listening assesses "basic cognitive concepts, as well as complex grammatical structures"; "the questions require children to integrate and reorganize information, to draw inferences, and to analyze and evaluate" oral material.

Level 2 Subtests

Quantitative Language assesses various mathematical concepts (for example, one-to-one correspondence).

Beginning Consonants assesses discrimination of beginning consonants.

Sound-Letter Correspondence requires a child "to identify letters that correspond to specific sounds in words."

Visual Matching requires the matching of various arithmetic, English, and nonsense symbols.

Finding Patterns requires the child to find various arithmetic, English, and nonsense symbols embedded in larger groupings of symbols.

School Language is essentially the same as the School Language subtest in Level 1.

Listening is about the same as the Listening subtest in Level 1.

Quantitative Concepts assesses various mathematical concepts (for example, conservation and part-whole relationships).

Quantitative Operations assesses "counting and simple mathematical operations."

Copying is an optional subtest that requires the copying of a printed sentence.

content scores, its value as a criterion-referenced measure is limited. A variety of norm-referenced scores are also provided, including percentile ranks, stanines, scaled scores, and normal curve equivalents—none of which are likely to be very helpful for instructional planning.

Given the questionable validity of the contents of subskills test such as the MRT and the general lack of reliability in tests for young children, we would suggest that they be used only to verify the observations and judgments made by teachers in daily contact with students. The face validity of the MRT and most other measures of early literacy is weak, because these tests are not based on a validated model of readiness. Several recent attempts at constructing theory-based readiness instruments are described below.

Tests of Emergent Literacy

Although most schools administer one or another of the types of readiness tests just described, there are other options. Instruments such as those described in the following sections have been developed recently to evaluate individual skill and knowledge of the foundations of reading.

Test of Early Reading Ability–2. The TERA-2 (Reid, Hresko, & Hammill, 1989) is designed to identify students who are below the average in reading development and to monitor progress in intervention programs. It is individually administered and takes 15 to 30 minutes to complete. The TERA-2 test items relate to three component areas of early reading behavior: constructing meaning, alphabet knowledge, and conventions of print.

The original TERA, published in 1981, was "a significant departure from current readiness tests in that it provides a norm reference for the direct measurement of reading behaviors of preschool children" (S. Wixson, 1985, p. 544). The revised edition (TERA-2) has maintained the strong features of the previous edition test while remedying some of the problems. For example, the stimulus materials are now bound in a spiral book, and some items include advance preparation in order to avoid cultural or geographic bias. The authors note the serious problems associated with age-equivalent scores, and these are not provided in this second edition. In addition, standard scores, percentile ranks, stanine scores, and instructional target zones are available (see Figure 6.13)—the set of items that lies between the child's chronological age (the solid line) and his or her mental age (the dotted line).

Normative data from a large sample are provided in the manual, and generally seem adequate. Although the manual suggests that the TERA-2 is designed for use with children from 3.0 to 9 years 11 months of age, the standardization group is best for ages 5, 6, and 7. The reliability of this test is supported using internal consistency coefficients, which exceed .90 for both forms. The reliability coefficients for ages 8 and 9 are weaker.

The item selection and test construction of the TERA-2 appear reasonable, but its validity really rests on its theoretical orientation. The TERA-2 is notable for its attempt to assess areas of emergent literacy that have been identified by recent research. The Constructing Meaning portion of the test contains items designed to assess environmental print awareness, knowledge of relationships among vocabulary words, print awareness in connected discourse, the ability to anticipate written language (a cloze test). Examiners must prepare cards with logos of local stores, common grocery items, and so forth, prior to testing. On the Alphabet Knowledge portion, students are required to name letters, recite the alphabet, and read orally. Conventions of Print measures students' knowledge of left-right orientation, punctuation, spatial presentation of the story on a page and general book-handling ability.

Students respond to retelling a story, choosing correct answers, comparing answers, filling in a missing word, or finding a mistake in printed material. The test manual suggests basal levels of various ages of children. Unfortunately, the score sheet does not permit notation regarding specific components of each item passed or failed. This limits the amount of diagnostic information that is targeted, and even a sophisticated examiner has no place to organize the data.

The TERA-2 has acceptable levels of reliability for testing concepts related to emergent reading. Of the available readiness tests reviewed in this chapter, the TERA-2 is the best match with current models of readiness. Several traditional aspects of readiness (e.g., letter knowledge) are assessed, as well as several aspects of metalinguistic awareness. The test is reliable, and young children seem to enjoy it and find the format nonthreatening.

FIGURE 6.13

Summary Form from TERA-2

Section V. Instructional Target Zone

Age	Meaning	Alphabet	Convention	Age
	TERA-2 Constructs			
10-0	46		44, 45	10-0
9-9				9-9
9-6	43			9-6
9-3				9-3
9-0			42	9-0
8-9				8-9
8-6			41	8-6
8-3	40			8-3
8-0	38	39		8-0
7-9		37		7-9
7-6	34, 35		36	7-6
7-3	32, 33			7-3
7-0	30, 31			7-0
6-9		28, 29		6-9
6-6	— 26 —	— 27 —	—	6-6
6-3		23, 24, 25		6-3
6-0		22	20, 21	6-0
5-9	18	18		5-9
5-6			16, 17	5-6
5-3		15		5-3
5-0	12	13	14	5-0
4-9			11	4-9
4-6			10	4-6
4-3			8, 9	4-3
4-0				4-0
3-9		6, 7		3-9
3-6				3-6
3-3	3, 4	5		3-3
3-0	2		1	3-0

Section VI. Interpretations & Recommendations John's score on the TERA-2 indicates that his early reading ability is above average. His DTLA-P aptitude score is also above average. Comparing the results of these two tests indicate that John is achieving at a level that is to be expected. Thus, his instruction should continue at its current pace, with emphasis on the content covered by items on his Instructional Target Zone (see above.)

From *Test of Early Reading Ability—2* by D. Kim Reid, Wayne P. Hresko, and Donald D. Hammill. Copyright © 1989, 1981 by PRO-ED, Inc. Reprinted by permission of PRO-ED.

Linguistic Awareness in Reading Readiness (LARR). The LARR test is based on the assumption that "to benefit from instruction in reading and writing the pupil must understand the functions of literacy skills and must comprehend such concepts as 'word,' 'letter,' 'top line,' 'print,' and so on" (Downing, Ayers, &

Schaefer, 1983, p. 1). The LARR is designed for use by kindergarten and first-grade classroom teachers. It can be group administered, has two parallel forms, and consists of three parts: Recognizing Literacy Behavior, a measure of the child's recognition of the kinds of activities involved in reading or writing; Understanding Literacy Functions, an assessment of the child's understanding of the purposes of reading and writing; and Technical Language of Literacy, a measure of the child's understanding of such terms as *letter, word, number,* and *sentence.*

Each subtest takes 15 to 20 minutes to administer and should pose little difficulty for the average 5-year-old. A separate booklet is provided for each subtest and for each child. The children are required to draw a circle around pictures or portions of a picture. If the test is administered to a group, the teacher will need to monitor carefully while testing children so young.

Downing et al. (1983) suggest that classroom teachers can make judgments about which children are likely to profit from formal instruction in reading. There are no normative data available on this test, but the authors do suggest that a beginning kindergarten child should normally achieve 50% or better on subtests 1 and 2, and 30% or better on subtest 3. In addition, the manual provides fairly specific guidelines for generating local norms. The data that are provided suggest reasonable reliability for this instrument. However, both the reliability and the predictive validity (reported in the manual) are based on a very small sample of children in one small area of Canada.

The strengths of the test clearly lie in the face validity of the tasks themselves. The subtest, Recognizing Literacy Behavior, has 22 items requiring students to circle their response to picture stimuli. For example, children are asked to circle the portions of a picture "that someone can read," to circle "each person who is reading," and "each person who is writing" (see Figure 6.14). Similarly, the 23 items on the Understanding Literacy Functions subtest require children to circle pictures showing different purposes for reading. For example, children are asked to indicate "each person who is enjoying a story," "each person who is leaving a message," and "each person who knew how to remember what groceries to buy." On the Technical Language of Literacy subtest, children identify and circle letters, numbers, printing, writing, words, punctuation marks, first and last letters and words, etc. Few other tests provide evaluative information about these aspects of emergent literacy.

Test of Awareness of Language Segments (TALS). The TALS (Sawyer, 1987) is based on a body of research that suggests phonological segmentation ability is necessary for successful early reading achievement. It is designed for use with children ages 4½ to 7 to "assess a child's ability to segment the stream of spoken language into words, syllables, and phonemes (sounds)" (Sawyer, 1987, p. 1).

There are three subtests in the TALS, each focusing on a different element of speech analysis. Part A tests children's ability to segment sentences into constituent words, Part B asks children to segment words into syllables, and Part C requires children to segment one-syllable words into phonemes. Part A is administered to all students, while Parts B and C are offered depending on age and performance on the other parts.

FIGURE 6.14

Items from the LARR

From *Linguistic Awareness in Reading Readiness (LARR) Test,* Administrative Manual, by John Downing, Douglas Ayers, and Brian Schaefer. © Downing, Ayers, and Schaefer 1983. Reprinted by permission of NFER-NELSON Publishing Company Ltd.

The results of the TALS are interpreted in terms of "readiness for basal instruction," and three cutoff points are provided. Students are classified as "Ready for Instruction in Basal Reading Series," "Approaching Readiness for Basal Reader Instruction," and "Not Ready for Basal Reader Instruction." In addition, however, there is an exceptionally good chapter in the manual that describes how to plan instruction based on TALS results. Not only is the kindergarten-Grade 1 teacher informed of procedures for adapting instruction, research data are provided to demonstrate the advantages of these adaptations. In general, these adaptations involve teaching phonemic segmentation and blending with a language experience or reading-writing program.

The content validity of the tests is good. In addition, predictive validity data are provided that suggest the test adds considerable information about students' future success in reading. Although the reliability is acceptable (Part B is low), the norming population is somewhat limited and caution should be exercised when interpreting scores since all subjects (about 250) were from a single geographic area.

FROM CLASSROOM TO CLINIC

Important information can be obtained from formal tests of reading and related areas. Many of the most serious problems with formal testing involve test abuse, that is, people using test information inappropriately. The primary differences between the classroom and clinic lie in the types of tests used most frequently and the ways in which tests are most commonly used. It is absolutely essential that both teachers and resource personnel be critical consumers of formal tests to ensure that they are used properly.

Classroom teachers are likely to have the most direct contact with survey tests. In many districts, classroom teachers annually administer achievement batteries that survey several subject areas as a measure of student progress. When these tests are administered at the beginning of the year, they are often used to assist in placing students into groups or materials, and to screen for referral to special programs. When they are administered at the end of the school year, they may be used for decisions about promotion and retention and about placing students in summer programs or fall classes.

Many districts also involve kindergarten and first-grade teachers in the administration of tests of readiness and emergent literacy for screening and program placement. Given all that has been said about the problems with many formal tests, it is clear that great caution should be exercised in using these instruments for these purposes.

Teachers are also likely to encounter formal diagnostic and psychological tests when dealing with students who are participating in special programs, such as Chapter I, or receiving special education services. Classroom teachers are unlikely to actually administer these tests, but they are likely to receive reports describing the results of the administration of these types of tests by the reading specialist, special education personnel, or school psychologist. Because the classroom teacher often spends considerably more time with these students than the specialists, they shoulder a major portion of the responsibility for understanding the nature of these students' special needs and addressing them through their classroom activities. Therefore, it is extremely important that classroom teachers are knowledgeable about the tests being administered to their students, so they can follow up the results with informal measures in the classroom that will lead to appropriate classroom practice.

Specialists and clinic personnel are more likely to have direct contact with diagnostic reading tests and those focusing on other language arts and related areas than are classroom teachers. Resource personnel are most likely to use these tests to demonstrate program effectiveness with individual students, to identify specific strengths and weaknesses as an aid to program planning, and as an aid in the identification of students with special needs. Even when the limitations of formal tests in these areas are recognized, there is still a need for their administration, because of legislative mandates and the need to have common measures that cut across schools, districts, and states. This makes it that much more important that the individuals administering and interpreting these tests have a clear understanding of what they can and cannot tell us.

It is our belief that instructional decisions should never be made solely on the basis of formal assessment instruments. It is absolutely essential that formal tests be followed up with informal measures that are more reflective of classroom demands before decisions are made about placement or about instructional programs.

The public appetite for numerical answers to literacy questions has been fed by the educational community. Classroom teachers and clinic personnel are often caught in the middle, forced to teach content they do not believe is useful so that students can perform well on standardized tests. We need to help the public understand both the uses and limitations of test information. In particular, educators need to be especially alert to the types of information *not* available from traditional standardized tests, especially information about students' abilities to read and write the different types of complex tests that are important in today's society.

CHAPTER SUMMARY

The chapter began by emphasizing that much of what we know to be important in the reading process is not reflected in formal assessment devices. However, the widespread use of formal reading tests makes it important to understand a number of different aspects of standardized testing. The information necessary to become a critical consumer of formal assessment devices was the focus of the first half of the chapter, beginning with the understanding that the title, author/s, publisher, and date of publication reveal information about the quality of a test and the appropriateness of its purpose and content for different students or testing situations. The importance of determining the appropriateness of the level of difficulty and type of administration for the students with whom the test will be used and the purposes for which it is intended was also discussed.

The two basic types of tests discussed in this chapter were *norm-referenced* and *criterion-referenced*. Criterion-referenced tests were defined as procedures that assess an individual's skill in relation to mastery of a specific set of objectives. Norm-referenced tests examine a given student's performance in relation to the performance of others with similar characteristics. Several statistical concepts were described as important to evaluating formal assessment devices. These were *mean, standard deviation, normal distribution,* and *correlation.*

Content validity was discussed as a primary criterion for test evaluation. A test is valid to the extent that it measures what it claims to measure. Adequate norms, reliability, and lack of bias are all necessary conditions for validity; however, none is sufficient to guarantee validity. Content validity refers to the extent to which the test's content is representative of the universe of content being sampled by the test, and requires that we have a precise definition of the domain the test items are intended to reflect. The more precise the definition, the better able we are to establish content validity; the greater the content validity, the better able we are to make generalizations about the domain of interest from the sampling of that domain represented by the test. *Criterion-related validity* was also described.

Reliability was also described as a major criterion of test acceptability. Reliability refers to the consistency or stability of a test and involves the extent to which some attribute has been measured in a systematic and therefore repeatable way. The two types of reliability discussed here were *test-retest* and *alternate form.* The *standard error of measurement* (SEM) was also described as an estimate of the distance between the true score and the actual score, based on the amount of error in the test (i.e., its reliability). The SEM helps the test consumer determine the confidence with which a test score can be interpreted.

The interpretation of norm-referenced tests was described in terms of the adequacy of the test norms. Norms are the test scores of a sample of people representative of those for whom a test is designed. They are important because an examinee's performance is evaluated in terms of the performance of the individuals in the normative sample. The adequacy of a test's norms depends on factors such as the size and representativeness of the norm sample.

Based on the responses of the standardization or normative sample, raw scores obtained from any subsequent examinee can be converted into a variety of *derived scores* designed to measure relative standing. For example, *grade* and *age equivalents* are derived from the average scores earned by students in the normative sample at a particular grade or age level. Other types of derived scores discussed include *percentile ranks* and *standard scores.*

Guidelines for criterion-referenced interpretation were also provided. The issue of *test fairness* to racial and cultural minorities was discussed in terms of the possible presence of bias in the test content and the possible unfair use of test results. The first half of the chapter concluded with summary guidelines for evaluating formal assessment instruments.

The second half of the chapter described several types of formal assessment tools and provided detailed descriptions and evaluations of exemplars of each type of test. *Survey* tests were described as norm-referenced tests of global reading achievement used to screen large numbers of students for approximate reading levels and to identify those who may have serious reading problems. Described in detail were a group-administered survey test—the *Gates-MacGinitie Reading Test* (MacGinitie & MacGinitie, 1989)—and two individually administered tests, the *Peabody Individual Achievement Battery–Revised* and the *Wide Range Achievement Test–Revised* (Jastak Assoc., 1984).

Diagnostic reading tests were described as designed to provide a profile of an individual's relative strengths and weaknesses. Described in detail were a group-administered diagnostic test, the *Stanford Diagnostic Reading Test* (Karlsen & Gardner, 1986); an individually administered diagnostic test, the *Woodcock Reading Mastery Test–Revised* (Woodcock, 1987); a diagnostic test of oral reading, the *Gray Oral Reading Test–Revised* (Wiederholt & Bryant, 1986); a diagnostic test of reading comprehension, the *Test of Reading Comprehension* (Brown et al., 1986); and a criterion-referenced diagnostic test, the *BRIGANCE® Diagnostic Inventories* (Brigance, 1976).

Tests of other language arts and related areas described in some detail were: *Test of Written Language–2* (Hammill & Larsen, 1988), *Test of Oral Language Development–2 Primary* (Newcomer & Hammill, 1988), *Bender Visual Motor Gestalt Test* (Koppitz, 1963), *Peabody Picture Vocabulary Test* (Dunn & Dunn, 1981), and *Slosson Intelligence Test* (Slosson, 1983). Finally, traditional tests of reading readiness—the *Gesell Tests of School Readiness* (Ilg & Ames, 1965), the *Metropolitan Readiness Test* (Nurss & McGauvran, 1976/1986), the *Test of Basic Experiences–2* (Moss, 1979), and the *Boehm Tests of Basic Concepts–Revised* (Boehm, 1986)—were described, as were more recent tests of factors associated with emergent literacy, including the *Test of Early Reading–2* (Reid et al., 1989), the *Linguistic Awareness in Reading Readiness* (LARR) *Test* (Downing et al., 1983), and the *Test of Awareness of Language Segments* (Sawyer, 1987).

In conclusion, this chapter suggested that formal tests should be used with a great deal of caution; and that they should be used primarily as general estimates of various aspects of reading, to be followed up by more in-depth, instructionally valid, informal measures, such as those described in the next chapter.

ASSESSMENT SOURCES AND RESOURCES

Professionals in the fields of reading, special education, and psychology often find it helpful to refer to test reviews and critical analyses completed by experts in these fields. Perhaps the most commonly used referenced is a series of books called the *Mental Measurements Yearbooks*. Started and edited for almost 50 years by Oscar Buros, these references are often called simply "Buros," although they are presently edited by Mitchell. These volumes are unique because they provide independent, critical analyses of the tests by knowledgeable professionals. In addition to the *Mental Measurements Yearbooks,* Buros published a descriptive volume of reading test reviews that is now somewhat dated (Buros, 1975). These, and a very few other volumes of critical review or description, can be helpful to teachers and testers who wish to make assessment choices.

Blanton, W. E., Farr, R., & Tuinman, J. J. (Eds.). (1972). *Reading tests for secondary grades: A review and evaluation.* Newark, DE: International Reading Association.
Buros, O. K. (Ed.). (1975). *Reading tests and reviews II.* Highland Park, NJ: Gryphon Press.

Buros, O. K. (Ed.). (1978). *The eighth mental measurements yearbook,* Vols. I & II. Highland Park, NJ: Gryphon Press.

Mauser, A. J. (1981). *Assessing the learning disabled: Selected instruments* (3rd ed.). Novato, CA: Academic Therapy Publications.

Tests Cited

Bender, L. (1938). *A visual motor Gestalt test and its clinical use* (Research Monograph No. 3). New York: American Orthopsychiatric Association.

Boehm, A. E. (1986). *Boehm Test of Basic Concepts–Revised.* San Antonio, TX: The Psychological Corporation.

Brigance, A. H. (1976). *BRIGANCE® Diagnostic Inventories.* North Billerica, MA: Curriculum Associates.

Brown, V. L., Hammill, D. D., & Wiederholt, J. L. (1986). *Test of Reading Comprehension.* Austin, TX: PRO-ED.

Downing, J., Ayers, D., & Schaefer, B. (1983). *Linguistic Awareness in Reading Readiness (LARR) Test.* Slough, England: The NFER–Nelson Publishing Company.

Dunn, L. M., & Dunn, L. M. (1981). *Peabody Picture Vocabulary Test–Revised.* Circle Pines, MN: American Guidance Service.

Gesell School Readiness and Kindergarten Screening Test (1978). Gesell Institute of Child Development. Rosemont, NJ: Programs for Education.

Hammill, D. D., & Larsen, S. C. (1988). *Test of Written Language–2.* Austin, TX: PRO-ED.

Hieronymus, A. N., Hoover, H. D., & Lindquist, E. F. (1986). *Iowa Test of Basic Skills.* Chicago, IL: Riverside Publishing.

Ilg, F. L., & Ames, L. B. (1965). *Gesell Developmental Tests of School Readiness.* Lumberville, PA: Programs for Education.

Jastak Associates (1984). *Wide Range Achievement Test–Revised.* East Aurora, NY: Slosson Educational Publications.

Karlsen, B., & Gardner, E. (1986). *Stanford Diagnostic Reading Test,* 3rd ed. San Antonio, TX: The Psychological Corporation.

Koppitz, E. M. (1963). *The Bender Gestalt Test for Young Children.* New York: Grune & Stratton.

Koppitz, E. M. (1975). *The Bender Gestalt Test for Young Children: Volume II: Research and Application, 1963–1973.* New York: Grune & Stratton.

MacGinitie, W. H., & MacGinitie, R. K. (1989). *Gates-MacGinitie Reading Test* (Third Edition). Chicago: Riverside Publishing.

MacGinitie, W. H., Kamons, J., Kowalski, R. L., MacGinitie, R., & McKay, T. (1978). *Gates-MacGinitie Reading Test—Readiness Skills.* New York: Columbia University, Teachers College Press.

Markwardt, F. C. (1989). *Peabody Individual Achievement Battery—Revised.* Circle Pines, MN: American Guidance Service.

Moss, M. (1979). *Test of Basic Experiences, (TOBE).* Monterey, CA: CTB/McGraw-Hill.

Newcomer, P. & Hammill, D. D. (1988). *Test of Oral Language Development–2 Primary.* Austin, TX: Pro-Ed.

Nurss, J. R., & McGauvran, M. E. (1976/1986). *Metropolitan Readiness Test (MRT).* San Antonio, TX: The Psychological Corporation.

Reid, D. K., Hresko, W. P., & Hammill, D. D. (1989). *The Test of Early Reading Ability–2 (TERA-2).* Austin, TX: PRO-ED.

Sawyer, D. J. (1987). *Test of Awareness of Language Segments (TALS).* Rockville, MD: Aspen Publications.

Slosson, R. L. (1983). *Slosson Intelligence Test* (2nd Edition). East Aurora, NY: Slosson Educational Publications.

Spache, G. (1981). *Diagnostic Reading Scales.* Monterey, CA: CTB/McGraw-Hill.

Thorndike, R. L. (1972). *Stanford-Binet Intelligence Scale,* (Third Revision, Form L-M). Boston: Houghton Mifflin.

Wiederholt, J. L., & Bryant, B. R. (1986). *Gray Oral Reading Test–Revised.* Austin, TX: PRO-ED.

Woodcock, R. W. (1987). *Woodcock Reading Mastery Test–Revised.* Circle Pines, MN: American Guidance Service.

Woodcock, R. W., & Johnson, M. B. (1977). *Woodcock-Johnson Psychoeducational Battery* (1977). Allen, TX: DLM Teaching Resources.

CHAPTER 7

Teacher-Designed Assessment

INTRODUCTION

In this chapter, we complete our discussion of Step 2: Evaluating the Learner. If the flow of assessment activity has been followed, much information has been gathered about the students being evaluated. They have been interviewed and observed. They have responded to one or more informal reading inventories, and have probably taken at least one standardized norm-referenced test. It is time to refine the assessment and to decide which aspects of each student's reading and writing require a closer examination.

In the preceding chapters, we described tools and strategies for assessing the reader. These assessment strategies have provided information about the student's prior knowledge of reading and his or her motivations and attitudes about reading. In addition, the performance data collected from informal reading inventories or norm-referenced tests provides some general insights into the student's ability to comprehend short selections. Finally, if oral reading data from the IRI was analyzed using a miscue analysis and a fluency scale (Chapter 5), there is specific information about the student's word identification skills and the degree to which these skills are automated. All of this information helps in forming some hunches about sources of difficulty and strength for the student.

This information will be used to make decisions and to shape the assessment in order to look more closely at selected aspects of reading. In particular, teachers need more specific information about students' application of reading knowledge and skill. This requires careful collection and interpretation of performance data; and information about student's skills and strategies as they read and respond to various school tasks. The primary goal, as always, is to glean information that will help us make relatively good decisions about what and how to teach.

Chapter Overview

This chapter focuses on assessment strategies that are selected and/or created by teachers and examiners interested in gathering additional information about each component of reading. These differ from the norm-referenced standardized tests introduced in the previous chapter because they tend to be more informal and because the content and tasks can be closely fitted to the type of knowledge and skill promoted by an individual teacher or school. In addition to traditional types of teacher evaluation (e.g., skills mastery tests and comprehension questioning), we describe assessment strategies and instruments that can be used for ongoing assessment of the student in interaction with reading instruction. Many of these can (and should) be done as a routine part of the instructional program.

After a brief discussion of the role of the teacher in assessing students' reading, we identify some critical issues in the development and use of informal assessment strategies. Finally, a wide range of strategies and tools are described for assessing component areas of reading: word recognition, vocabulary, comprehension, studying, and writing. The assessment strategies described are almost exclusively *performance* measures. These are techniques for evaluating students' ability to *apply* the knowledge and skill that you evaluated earlier.

UNDERSTANDING TEACHER-DESIGNED ASSESSMENT

The assessment-instruction process described in this text relies very heavily on the knowledge and skill of the teacher/examiner. Extensive description of formal tests, the traditional heart of reading "diagnosis," is not the centerpiece of the process. Instead, we acknowledge the complexity of reading and learning to read, recognizing that more informal assessment can often provide powerful and flexible evaluation strategies. In this regard, we agree with Easley and Zwoyer (1975):

> If you can both listen to children and accept their answers not as things to just be judged right or wrong but as pieces of information which may reveal what the child is thinking you will have taken a giant step toward becoming a master teacher rather than merely a disseminator of information. (p. 25)

The Role of the Teacher/Evaluator

One of the most serious problems with existing assessment practices is that they often lead teachers to believe that assessment and evaluation are someone else's job. When teachers rely too heavily on standardized test results, they may stop using their own good judgment (Valencia & Pearson, 1987). It may also cause teachers to discount or become inattentive to the high-quality information they themselves have. It tends to be high in quality because it provides evidence about students' ability to perform the actual tasks required in their instructional settings. This information is, by definition, valid (see Chapter 6). Of course, the quality and nature of these in-school tasks needs to be examined closely as well, and we address this issue in Chapters 8 and 9.

Another important advantage of teacher-designed assessment is that evaluations can be based on knowledge of the specific cultural and/or linguistic characteristics of individual students. This is critical, since standardized tests can distort information for some students, as they tend "to reflect the language, culture, or learning style of middle- to upper-middle-class" students (Neill & Median, 1989).

In order to make good instructional decisions, teachers must come to trust that assessment is a continuous process that takes place within the instructional program. It should be designed to increase the "goodness" of the fit between each child and the materials and methods of instruction. According to Johnston (1987), teachers can—indeed they must—become expert evaluators. We have already noted one of the most important attributes of an expert evaluator: the ability to listen. Another important characteristic of an expert evaluator is the ability to recognize patterns. Expert evaluators are not concerned about an isolated event or behavior, but are able to connect pieces of information to create an integrated vision of the student's knowledge and skill.

Informal, teacher-designed assessment can provide exceptionally powerful and helpful information. However, Valencia (1990b) reminds us that:

> The concept behind a "good" reading assessment, whether it is a standardized test or alternative classroom assessment, is the same. First it should be authentic; it should assess what we have defined and value as real reading. Second, it should be trustworthy; it should have clearly established procedures for gathering information and for evaluating the quality of that information. (p. 60)

Teacher-designed assessment requires reflection and planning. As Johnston (1987) points out, effective assessment requires procedural knowledge. Teachers must be able to create a context that elicits the types of reading/writing behaviors that they have decided to examine, and they must be skilled in managing all aspects of the assessment-instruction process. As teacher/evaluators reflect on the assessment information they have gathered about individual students, it is important to think about what is already known. Next, consideration should be given to the specific evidence that revealed this knowledge. It is especially important to avoid untested assumptions. Finally, teacher/evaluators must ask what remains to be discovered about *this* learner. Then, teachers can design the types of additional assessments that will provide them with the information needed.

Effective evaluation also requires an informed teacher who is capable of articulating a rationale for alternative assessment procedures. Informed teacher/evaluators are obviously knowledgeable about reading and writing. They are well-versed in child development and can recognize developmentally appropriate responses. Further, they can translate this knowledge into teacher-designed assessment strategies that focus on areas of identified interest.

This does not mean that teachers must generate all of their own tools and techniques. It does mean that from a variety of tools and approaches, they can choose the ones that will yield high-quality information about specific students. These choices may include commercially available informal instruments, teacher-designed tools, and student self-assessment procedures. The variety of assessment strategies presented in this chapter are designed so that teachers can select from among a repertoire to examine some particular component area more closely. Before turning our attention to some less familiar tools and strategies, we examine the types of teacher assessments that are already used widely.

Traditional Informal Assessment

In Chapter 6 we described the problems associated with many formal tests. As teachers turn to more informal assessment options, they should proceed cautiously. Informal tests offer no guarantee of excellence. We have already noted the problems associated with many informal placement tests (see Chapter 5). Many other common informal assessment tools also need to be carefully considered. Two pervasive assessment methods are mastery criterion-referenced tests and comprehension questions.

Skills Mastery Tests

Skills mastery tests are a common feature in many classrooms. All basal reading programs provide for periodic end-of-level or end-of-unit testing to assess students' mastery of skills that have been taught, and many school systems employ some form of skills management system to assess student learning. These instruments are "criterion-referenced" tests that have been designed to compare students' performance to some pre-established "criterion" or standard. As such, they are meant to determine whether, and how well, a student has learned what has been taught. They are not designed to compare a student's performance to the achievement of other students, although they are frequently used as accountability measures, somewhat like standardized achievement tests.

The periodic administration of skills mastery tests can provide for continuous assessment of individual and/or class performance throughout the year. However, a major problem with these measures is that they frequently assess skills in isolation on a series of discrete subtests. For example, they often evaluate a skill such as main idea recognition under highly restricted conditions (e.g., short, unfamiliar, informational passages with initial topic sentences) that do not reflect the complexity and variety of factors that are likely to influence students' ability to grasp a main idea under real reading conditions. In addition, mastery tests presume that the order of skill acquisition is invariable; that students must master a specific skill before proceeding to other skills and/or materials. Neither the assumption that reading skills are hierarchical nor the assumption that reading skill can be evaluated in discrete parts is warranted, given current knowledge about the reading process (Mason, Osborn, & Rosenshine, 1977).

Questioning

Perhaps the most common form of informal reading assessment is questioning. Teachers use questions to evaluate all aspects of students' reading ability, although they are most often employed to assess comprehension. The use of question responses to evaluate student ability needs to be examined quite carefully, since it appears that the questions students are asked influence both the products they produce and the manner in which they process information. The comprehension that is revealed through questioning is, at least in part, a function of the questions that have been asked. Children's ability to answer questions is influenced by both the type and content of the questions they are asked (Pearson et al., 1979; Raphael, Winograd, & Pearson, 1980). In addition, both the type and content of questions influence what children recall and the types of inferences they make (Wixson, 1983a, 1984). (See Chapter 9.)

Because the demands of questions affect student performance, information gathered in this way requires careful consideration. Both basal reading programs and popular classroom management programs use a classification scheme to label comprehension questions. These classification schemes are typically based on one of several well-known taxonomies (e.g., Barrett, 1976; Bloom, 1956). However, there is little evidence that these taxonomies represent real differences in comprehension skills or in the level of difficulty of different questions. In addition, the questions in many commercial programs require memory rather than under-standing, or divert students' attention from important to unimportant information.

To summarize, although informal tests can be a potent form of assessment, the techniques employed must be carefully examined for evidence that these capture what we know about skilled reading. A serious problem in many existing tests, both formal and informal, is the lack of relationship between how reading is measured and what we expect children to do during reading. The truth is that we do *not* want children to know how to complete workbook-like pages. Rather, we want children to be able to employ their skills during the reading of real texts.

Reading professionals must continue to press for better commercial assessments and, in the meantime, supplement these with good information about important reading/writing behaviors. This means that we need to develop assessment procedures that assess more clearly the holistic terminal goals of reading instruction and the factors that are known to influence reading. As Wood (1988) notes, what is needed is a structured approach to determine how an individual handles the reading of actual textbook material under conditions that simulate the classroom situation.

The guidelines for assessment offered in Chapter 3 should be reconsidered as guiding principles in teacher-designed assessment. These guidelines are important for *both* standardized and teacher-designed assessment. However, teacher-designed assessment is too often discounted as sloppy, haphazard, or unreliable. Consequently, teachers need to be especially careful to attend to important principles of assessment. Well-crafted informal assessment can assess meaningful reading activities in a nonintrusive way, and teachers can ensure that it is systematic, continuous, and well-organized.

STRATEGIES AND TOOLS FOR TEACHER-INITIATED ASSESSMENT

In the remainder of this chapter, we describe specific techniques for evaluating the various components of reading ability. These techniques—some old, some newer—can provide the initial repertoire for both classroom teachers and clinicians who want to expand their assessment practices. They are only suggestions, however. There are many other ways to evaluate performance informally. As teachers develop more refined skills for assessing students' knowledge and application of reading-related abilities, their confidence in making good assessment decisions will also develop. Each of the strategies is designed to provide for ongoing student assessment during instruction. Throughout, we also provide forms that can be used to summarize and display this information. If an assessment portfolio is being used, these forms can facilitate analysis and interpretation. If this documentation is providing support or confirmation within a more traditional case evaluation, the summary forms are equally helpful in making sense of the documents.

Word Recognition

Rapid and automatic word recognition, using a combination of strategies, is a hallmark of skilled reading (see Chapter 2). Not surprisingly, many poor readers have a limited repertoire of word recognition and word analysis strategies. If the results from informal reading inventories or standardized tests suggest difficulty in these areas, it may be useful to collect additional information to refine the assessment. However, the strategies suggested can also be used *before* administering an IRI. The classroom teacher, in particular, is likely to start with these informal techniques first, because they are less time-consuming than administering an IRI. In general, information is needed regarding two areas of word-level performance: sight word recognition and word analysis. In addition, it will be important to assess students' word recognition during reading.

Word Lists

As we have already noted, it is generally wise to evaluate component skills in use, rather than in isolation. Clearly, using a word list to test word recognition skills is a very constrained procedure. However, one attribute of skilled reading is *automaticity* in word recognition. Good readers are able to recognize large numbers of words rapidly. Allington and McGill-Franzen (1980) found that the scores generated by isolated word recognition tests were markedly different from those generated by in-context word recognition tests. The scores were especially divergent for less-able readers. It appears that context does facilitate word recognition, but it is used more heavily by poor readers than able ones. Thus, students' ability to recognize high-frequency sight words (see Chapter 2) should be evaluated both in isolation and in context.

There are many lists of high-frequency sight words. One of the most widely used is the *Dolch Basic Sight Word Test* (Dolch, 1942). This test consists of 220 high-frequency sight words, grouped into lists deemed appropriate from pre-primer to third grade. The list has generated controversy and many prefer to use one of the more recently created lists (e.g., Fry, 1980; Johnson, 1971). The *Fry Instant Word List* (1980) appears in Figure 7.1. Fry's analysis suggests that one-half of all written material is comprised of the first 100 of these instant words. The complete list of 300 instant words makes up 65% of all written material, and studies by a variety of researchers have confirmed the utility of various high-frequency core words (Durr, 1973). Assessment of sight word skill is essential, since students will find fluent reading difficult if they do not master these words. Students can be expected, as a general rule, to have instant recognition of the entire list by the end of Grade 3.

Administration of sight word lists requires some preparation. It is necessary to have a prepared record form (a copy of Figure 7.1) and a set of flash cards of the list words. The cards are used to control the rate of presentation, so that students' instant recognition can be evaluated. Most specialists suggest presenting cards or words at a rate of one second per word. When the lists have been completed (or stopped due to frustration), the words that were missed can be presented again to see whether the student can recognize the word(s) using further analysis. Most people suggest a criterion level of 90% or better for each list; however, Botel (1982)

FIGURE 7.1
The Fry Instant Word List

The Instant Words: First Hundred

First 25 Group 1a	Second 25 Group 1b	Third 25 Group 1c	Fourth 25 Group 1d
the	or	will	number
of	one	up	no
and	had	other	way
a	by	about	could
to	word	out	people
in	but	many	my
is	not	then	than
you	what	them	first
that	all	these	water
it	were	so	been
he	we	some	call
was	when	her	who
for	your	would	oil
on	can	make	now
are	said	like	find
as	there	him	long
with	use	into	down
his	an	time	day
they	each	has	did
I	which	look	get
at	she	two	come
be	do	more	made
this	how	write	may
have	their	go	part
from	if	see	over

Common suffixes: *s, ing, ed*

The Instant Words: Second Hundred

First 25 Group 2a	Second 25 Group 2b	Third 25 Group 2c	Fourth 25 Group 2d
new	great	put	kind
sound	where	end	hand
take	help	does	picture
only	through	another	again
little	much	well	change
work	before	large	off
know	line	must	play
place	right	big	spell
year	too	even	air
live	mean	such	away
me	old	because	animal
back	any	turn	house
give	same	here	point
most	tell	why	page
very	boy	ask	letter
after	follow	went	mother
thing	came	men	answer
our	want	read	found
just	show	need	study
name	also	land	still
good	around	different	learn
sentence	form	home	should
man	three	us	America
think	small	move	world
say	set	try	high

Common suffixes: *s, ing ed, er, ly, est*

The Instant Words: Third Hundred

First 25 Group 3a	Second 25 Group 3b	Third 25 Group 3c	Fourth 25 Group 3d
every	left	until	idea
near	don't	children	enough
add	few	side	eat
food	while	feet	face
between	along	car	watch
own	might	mile	far
below	close	night	Indian
country	something	walk	real
plant	seem	white	almost
last	next	sea	let
school	hard	began	above
father	open	grow	girl
keep	example	took	sometimes
tree	begin	river	mountain
never	life	four	cut
start	always	carry	young
city	those	state	talk
earth	both	once	soon
eye	paper	book	list
light	together	hear	song
thought	got	stop	leave
head	group	without	family
under	often	second	body
story	run	late	music
saw	important	miss	color

Common suffixes: *s, ing, ed, er, ly, est*

The instant word list, pp. 286–87 from ''The New Instant Word List'' by Edward Fry, *The Reading Teacher*, December 1980. Reprinted with permission of Edward Fry and the International Reading Association.

suggests a mastery level of 70%, arguing that since reading words in isolation is more difficult than reading words in context, the scoring procedure should be adjusted accordingly.

In evaluating the student's responses to the word list task, the following questions should be considered:

Does there appear to be any consistent pattern to the errors?

Is the pattern of these errors comparable at each level, or does it change with increasing difficulty?

Does the student substitute initial consonants? final consonants?

Does the student attend to the medial portions of words?

Does the student confuse vowel patterns?

Does the student reverse letters or words?

What is the student's overall level of mastery of high frequency sight words in isolation?

Although some authors recommend equating the results from a sight word list with reading level ability, we caution against this practice. All that can reasonably be accomplished by administering a word list is an appraisal of the reader's instant recognition of words, without benefit of context. This can provide a quick, efficient clue as to the student's in-text reading, and perhaps an idea of what may be impeding progress. Of course, it does not yield direct information about the student's word recognition during reading. Remember, children often misread different words in context and in isolation (Allington & McGill-Franzen, 1980).

An important next step, then, is to compare students' word recognition during reading to word recognition in isolation. Different patterns of response can be suggestive. For example, some children perform much better during reading than on isolated lists. This suggests good use of context and is frequently accompanied by better comprehension than word recognition. When there is a large discrepancy, it can be expected that students are actually over-relying on context. The student may not have achieved automaticity in word recognition and reading may proceed very slowly.

Other children demonstrate exactly the opposite pattern. That is, they perform better on isolated word lists than they do in context. There may be several reasons for this, but often these students have too little experience with real reading. This limited reading experience often occurs in classrooms where students learn words in isolation (by completing workbook tasks, using flash cards, or playing games). Thus, these students have competence in recognizing words (or analyzing them, see below), but have not learned to transfer this skill to reading continuous text.

Of course, students' sight recognition of other words can be assessed as well. For example, Glazer and Searfoss (1988) suggest assessing students' word recognition using "personal word lists." These lists are compiled by the teacher (and perhaps the student) using words from the students' own experiences or current topics of study. Since these lists will be idiosyncratic, it may not be possible to compare children. However, it is possible to evaluate a student's performance over time by recording the initial performance (baseline) and tracking improvement as more words are recognized. Charts or graphs are always useful for both student and teacher. Raw scores of total words read instantly can be displayed, along with the date. Alternatively, with increased availability of databases on microcomputer, teachers could create a file for all students, adding new words as they become part of the students' word recognition repertoire.

Similarly, word lists can be prepared from the instructional materials used in classroom or clinic. Lists created from basal readers or required trade books can be helpful in evaluating readiness to read specific materials and/or in assessing progress. If students are participating in a literature-based reading program, it may be advisable to examine high-frequency words derived from the literature commonly used in such programs. (See Chapter 12 for a list of "bookwords.")

Informal Tests of Phonics and Structural Analysis

Although we favor analyzing knowledge and application of phonics during reading of actual text (see Chapter 5 and running records below), most diagnostic batteries include some form of isolated assessment of phonics skill. Teachers sometimes find it helpful to use these commercial materials as they build their own knowledge base and increase their ability to reliably identify important phonic elements that may be influencing students' reading. Once information has been gathered about the student's knowledge and skill in phonics, it will be important to generate record-keeping forms that summarize the patterns of strength and weakness that were observed (see Figure 7.2). These may also be used to aid analysis of writing samples, which can provide powerful information about phonics skill (see below).

Both informal and formal tests of phonic and structural analysis typically contain lists of nonsense words that embody one or more of the sound-symbol patterns. A sample test might look something like the following:

1. fload _____	6. mait _____
2. zam _____	7. glavorful _____
3. drowt _____	8. kneef _____
4. dispount _____	9. jarf _____
5. strabble _____	10. bluther _____

The *El Paso Phonics Survey* (Ekwall, 1979), the *Sipay Word Analysis Tests* (SWAT) (Sipay, 1974), and the *Gates-McKillop-Horowitz Diagnostic Tests* (Gates, McKillop, & Horowitz, 1981) are among the commercially available informal tests of this type.

The advantage of nonsense words is that it is possible to evaluate students' knowledge and application of word analysis strategies as they are used with totally unfamiliar "words." The disadvantage of this practice is that reading nonsense words is a more difficult task than reading real words in context (Harris & Sipay, 1990). Baumann (1988) devised a phonics survey that compensates for this difficulty to some extent.

The *Baumann Informal Phonics Test* requires children to read both real and nonsense words involving the same phonic element. For example, *walk, chalk,*

FIGURE 7.2
Summary Chart of Phonic and Structural Analysis

Directions: As the child reads, note how frequently she or he:

	Always	Sometimes	Never
Demontrates knowledge of sounds-symbol relationships			
Recognizes major sounds of consonants			
Uses major CVC vowel patterns			
Recognizes consonant influenced patterns			
Uses major CVVC clusters			
Uses other patterns (clusters/phonograms)			
Uses structural analysis			
Uses morphemic analysis			
Uses a combination of context/decoding			

falk, and *jalk* all appear on this test. In this way, students' recognition of phonic elements in familiar words can be compared to their performance on nonsense words. However, these words still appear in isolation, and it will be necessary to contrast performance on this type of test with performance during reading. This is especially important since some children consistently attempt to make real words from nonsense words. Their attempts to make meaning override the visual display. Consequently, they may appear to have limited sound-symbol knowledge when, in fact, they regularly employ word analysis strategies during reading, in combination with their meaning-seeking strategies.

Running Records During Oral Reading

Of course, the most effective way to assess children's word recognition and word analysis skills is to do so as children read aloud. It is possible to achieve a very detailed picture of students' word recognition and monitoring abilities by using the Reading Miscue Analysis (RMI) procedure (see Chapter 5). Because that assessment strategy is very time-consuming, many teachers find it difficult to do with any frequency.

The *Running Record,* on the other hand, is a method of assessment that is ideally suited to continuous assessment. An adaptation of the RMI, "this task requires the teacher to observe and record the strategies the child uses 'on the run' while attempting to read a whole text" (Pinnell, 1985a, p. 74). The technique was originally described by Clay (1979, 1985) and is based on the work of the Goodmans and their associates (K. Goodman, 1969, 1973; K. Goodman & Y. Goodman, 1977; Y. Goodman & Burke, 1983). Although the running record may seem complex at first, it is especially useful for the classroom teacher because no special preparation is required. A running record can be created as long as the text being read by a child is visible as he or she reads. Therefore, it is possible to collect data any time you are listening to a child read aloud. Of course, it could also be used to adapt the administration of an IRI. In Figure 7.3, you will find a sample running record, along with a key to the various markings.

FIGURE 7.3
*Sample
Running
Record*

Text	Child's Reading

Text

Isabel saw a kitten.

It was on the side of the street.

It was sitting under a blue car.

"Come here, little kitten," Isabel said.

The kitten looked up at Isabel.

It had big yellow eyes.

Isabel took her from under the car.

She saw that her leg was hurt.

"I will take care of you," Isabel said.

She put her hand on the kitten's soft, black fur.

"You can come home with me."

The kitten gave a happy meow.

Child's Reading

✓ was/saw ✓ ✓

✓ ✓ ✓ ✓ ✓ ✓ stairs/street

✓ ✓ sutting/sitting ✓ ✓ ✓

✓ ✓ ✓ ✓ ✓

✓ ✓ ✓ uṗ ✓ ✓

✓ ✓ a/ȯ ✓ ✓

Sa-bel/Isabel ✓ ✓ ✓ ✓ ✓

✓ was/saw ✓ ✓ eyes/leg were/was ✓

✓ ✓ ✓ ✓ ✓ ✓ ✓

✓ ✓ ✓ ✓ her/the ✓ ✓ ✓

✓ ✓ ✓ ✓ ✓ ✓

✓ ✓ had/gave ✓ ✓ morning/meow

Key for running record:

Accurate Reading   ✓ ✓ ✓

Substitution   substitute/text word

Appeal   A̲

Told   T̅

Self-Correction   ı sc

Omission   text wȯrd

Insertion   inserted worḍ

Repetition   ✓R

Return & Repetition   ↶✓✓✓ R

After the record has been taken, the teacher uses it to analyze miscues. Although a full miscue analysis can be done, classroom teachers usually generate more global, less specific inferences about what the child is doing to construct meaning from text and which strategies seem to be used most often to accomplish this (Pinnell, 1987). A teacher's summary of the small sample you have examined in Figure 7.3 might read something like this:

> David's most consistent miscues are word substitutions. These substitutions are made using both language structure (syntax) and meaning (semantics). ("Isabel was a kitten" is both structurally and semantically acceptable, as is "The kitten had a happy morning.") In fact, David uses this combination of cueing systems so well that he actually makes one miscue in order to accommodate an earlier miscue (" . . . her *eyes were* hurt"). What David does *not* do is monitor effectively for miscues. He makes virtually no use of rereading or self-correction. He appears to prefer moving forward, even if text must be altered to conform to earlier miscues. In addition, David does not make full and effective use of the graphophonic information available, nor does he appear to have mastered all high-frequency sight words. Miscues in this area ("was," "sutting") are tolerated even when they result in syntactically and/or semantically unacceptable productions. Although he generally seems to "read for meaning," his comprehension is affected by word recognition.

As with any "test," running records provide a *sample* of behavior that may or may not be representative of the way a student interacts with different types of texts under different reading conditions. Students' miscue patterns vary depending on a number of factors (Wixson, 1979). The best way to address the problem of variability in miscue patterns is to obtain repeated samples of a particular reader's miscues under a variety of predetermined conditions (see Chapters 5 and 10).

Vocabulary

Knowledge of word meanings clearly influences reading performance. This fact has been unchallenged for decades, yet surprisingly few assessment techniques have been suggested for validating individual differences in this area. Most diagnosticians employ one of the available standardized tests to estimate relative vocabulary strength, and we have described several of these in Chapter 6. Most of these involve word level assessments (finding definitions, picture associations, etc.).

A word is a label for a concept or idea. Of course, readers with more word meanings at their disposal read more types of texts with greater comprehension. It has recently been suggested that vocabulary words are important, not because they are directly helpful in understanding text, but because the individual words reflect generalized knowledge about a topic. When a reader knows a word, he or she probably knows many other, related words. The generalized knowledge (concepts) facilitates comprehension, not just the words (Anderson & Freebody, 1981). For example, a knowledgeable sailor generated in a few seconds the following words when asked what she thought of when she heard *spinnaker:*

spinnaker: jib; fore; aft; mainsail; port; bow; sheets; heel; winch; cleat; starboard; heading; gaff; sloop; schooner; 12-meter; galley; tack

It should be apparent that simply learning a definition for the word *spinnaker* would not be as helpful as the knowledge base that results in knowing *spinnaker*, but also knowing all those other words.

Word meanings are related in such a way that they form concepts that are organized in a network of relationships. When asked to think about one word related to a concept, people generate many associated words. These concept relationships may be organized in a number of ways.

Class relations are hierarchical networks. Words are related to each other by superordinate and subordinate concepts. For example, *spinnaker* is part of a larger class, *sails*.

Examples are exactly what they appear to be. Every concept has associated examples and nonexamples. Thus, *spinnaker, jib*, and *mainsail* are all examples of sails, while sheeting is a nonexample of a sail.

Attribute relations provide us with organizational networks that focus on the characteristics of concepts. Thus, *mainsail, spinnakers*, and *jib* all have certain common features that connect them to the class of sails.

Although these organizations capture how sets of words may be related to concepts, there are other ways that words are related to each other. They may be organized according to aspects of language. For example, words are changed and interrelated by adding morphemes (affixes, inflectional endings). The richness and flexibility of students' vocabulary must consider these aspects of language as well as the conceptual density of the words and word networks. Vocabulary assessment must consider both aspects. In addition, the relationship between vocabulary and comprehension for each reader must be examined.

Word Sorts

The *word sort* (Gillet & Temple, 1990) is a flexible assessment strategy that can be used to assess a variety of word level abilities. Although Gillet and Temple suggest using the word sort as a way to assess word recognition and/or word analysis, we have found it useful for evaluating vocabulary as well. This technique capitalizes on the fact that words are organized in human memory by a series of connecting relations. Two types of word sorts are described: *open* and *closed*. In an open sort, no criteria for sorting the words are provided. Since students must impose their own organization on the words, it is possible to observe the types of relationships available to students. In a closed sort, the teacher establishes the criteria for sorting in advance. Using word cards prepared in advance (or selected by students from their own word bank), the examiner/teacher asks the student:

Put the words that go together in the same pile (open sort).

Put all the words together that are examples of something else. Then, name the group (closed sort).

Put all the words together that have something the same and label the characteristic.

Put all the words together that have the same semantic feature (e.g., "have a prefix that changes meaning").

As the student's performance is evaluated, it is helpful to consider the following questions:

Does the child attend to meaning features or graphic features?
Can the child generate relational categories?
Does the child recognize multiple meanings for words?
Does the child recognize and use affixes?
Does the child recognize and use root words?
Can the child generate superordinate categories?

It is possible to get a general idea of the range and flexibility of students' vocabulary knowledge using word sorts. However, it is so intimately linked to instructional issues that it can be used repeatedly. This type of assessment strategy can be especially helpful if you are selecting content area texts, are examining students' ability to understand basal texts, or you want to compare your students' knowledge of some new theme or topic.

Vocabulary Knowledge and Reading

No matter how sophisticated the general measures of vocabulary knowledge, teachers also need to know how vocabulary is interacting with specific reading demands. Fortunately, vocabulary measures are relatively easy to incorporate into regular assessment-instruction efforts. Since prior knowledge can and does produce variation in reading performance, we suggest evaluating students' prior knowledge (vocabulary) throughout the assessment process.

There are a variety of ways to assess vocabulary knowledge. Holmes and Roser (1987) identify and compare five techniques for evaluating prior knowledge that can be used during instruction and assessment: free recall, word association, structured questions, recognition, and unstructured discussion. The special value of the work of Holmes and Roser (1987) is that they have actually collected data to determine the utility and efficiency of these assessment strategies. The five strategies are easily adaptable to any assessment or instructional setting. Each approach requires only an observant teacher who understands his or her purpose in gathering such information.

Free recall: The teacher asks students: "Tell me everything you know about _____," and records the responses. Free recall provides the most information in the least time, but can pose problems for young and/or disabled readers who have retrieval problems and/or disorganized information.

Word association is much like PReP (see below). Teachers select several key words and ask children what comes to mind when they hear each one. These are fast to prepare and administer and generally yield more information than free recall.

Structured questions are posed to determine what students know *prior* to reading. This technique is both the most effective and efficient, yielding by far the most information. However, it is time-consuming to prepare.

Recognition requires that the teacher prepare several statements or key terms beforehand. Then, students select the words, phrases, or sentences they believe are related to the key terms or would be present in a particular selection. Recognition is second only to structured questions for efficiency and to free recall in effectiveness, and is helpful for children who have trouble retrieving for production tasks.

Unstructured discussion is most like what is traditionally done in reading instruction, since students freely generate their own ideas about a topic, with no focusing from the teacher. However, this approach may not be worth the effort since it is the least effective and efficient procedure of the five.

These procedures are designed to gather information that can be used to inform instruction. They can provide rather quick, on-the-spot assessments of students' conceptual base regarding specific text information.

In Chapter 5, we described The *Qualitative Reading Inventory* (Leslie & Caldwell, 1990), which contains provisions for assessing readers' prior knowledge for each selection. If this tool is used, it may be less important to obtain other measures, since the influence of prior knowledge on the reader's performance will already have been examined somewhat. Using these strategies, educators can be more confident of the quality of their assessment information and can also be more focused in their instruction.

PReP

One procedure that has been well researched and is easily incorporated into instruction is a word association procedure developed by Langer (1982; 1984). This procedure is called Prereading Plan, or PReP, and is designed to assess both the quality and quantity of students' prior knowledge. PReP is a particularly effective strategy because it can be used for assessment purposes at the time of instruction.

To implement this procedure, preview the materials to be used and list two to four key concepts. The following questions are then used as the basis for a discussion:

What comes to mind when you hear/read . . . ? Write the students' responses on the board.

What made you think of . . . ?

Given our discussion, can you add any new ideas about . . . ?

Following the discussion, student responses are evaluated using the following classification scheme:

Much prior knowledge: precise definitions, analogies, relational links among concepts.

Some prior knowledge: examples and characteristics, but no connections or relations.

Little prior knowledge: sound-alikes or look-alikes, associated experiences, little or no meaning relations.

The technique can be used to generate diagnostic conclusions about how students' vocabulary (conceptual) knowledge is contributing to their reading difficulties, to make decisions about grouping and pacing, or to make decisions about appropriate instructional adaptations. If this information is needed for a group of students, Langer advocates creating a matrix. Students' names appear down one side and the three categories (*Much, Some, Little*) appear across the top.

To summarize, vocabulary assessment can, and probably should, be done in association with the demands of reading selections. Teachers will obviously need to make decisions about which of these vocabulary assessment strategies is most effective for their purposes. However, it is also important to note that different procedures may actually provide different types of information. Valencia et al. (1987) found that different measures may assess different aspects of vocabulary (prior) knowledge. Here again, it is important to recognize the value of multiple measures of prior knowledge. This is obviously most easily accomplished by a skilled teacher during actual instruction. Again, each of the documented events (employed over time or over tasks) can contribute to the utility of any assessment portfolio.

Evaluating Comprehension

There are really two issues to be examined carefully in the assessment of comprehension. First, we are concerned with students' comprehension of a specific selection. Second, and more important, we need to assess students' growing comprehension *ability* (Johnston, 1985a). In this section, the descriptions of tools and strategies for assessing comprehension have a dual focus: to evaluate whether students have understood what they have just read, and also to reveal whether they are developing the tools needed to understand other texts.

As we have already seen, a number of factors can influence the reading performance. For example, students' ability to recall information and answer questions can be affected by the type and quality of the text. Similarly, the coherence of the text will affect recall and recognition (see Chapter 9). Although Informal Reading Inventories can provide a great deal of valuable information, most IRI passages are extremely short, and many read more like fragments of text than like intact stories or informational selections. This can hamper student recall, since it may be difficult for students to organize and retrieve the content presented.

Because we are interested in evaluating students in meaningful reading settings, it is important to assess students' comprehension of materials that are similar to those they are expected to read every day. These are likely to be much longer, more complex selections than any that appear on most commercially available tests.

Selecting and Analyzing Long Passages

The quality of teacher-designed assessments will obviously depend significantly on the knowledge and skill of the teachers doing the designing. Because the text can exert such a strong influence on comprehension performance, we suggest becoming somewhat adept at analyzing the selections to be used for assessment purposes. The issue of evaluating text will be examined at length in Chapter 9. For now, we limit the discussion to the types of procedures that are needed to develop effective reader assessments.

An important first step in developing comprehension measures is constructing maps for the reading selections. The purpose of these maps is to identify important elements within each of the reading selections to ensure that test questions (or recall evaluations) are focused on important information. Stories and informational texts will, of course, differ. We expect students to recall the sequence of events from narrative texts, for example. On the other hand, recalls of informational text may not rely so heavily on sequence. Students' recalls should reflect an understanding of the relationships between and among key facts and ideas.

Story maps: Analyzing narrative text. Story maps reveal the underlying relationships between characters, events, and settings in a given story. They create a visual representation of the elements of setting, problem, goal, events, and resolution (Beck & McKeown, 1981; Pearson, 1982; Reutzel, 1985). The display in Figure 7.4 demonstrates a general map for narrative stories that has been used to represent the familiar story "Jack and the Beanstalk."

Story mapping generally begins with the identification of the problem, the attempt (or plan), and the resolution. The characters, events, and setting revolve around these elements. Sometimes, of course, these other elements are more important. For example, in many books by Ezra Jack Keats, the setting plays a central role (e.g., *Snowy Day, Evan's Corner*). Once completed, the maps are used to generate assessment questions (see below) and/or to generate alternative assessment tasks.

For assessment purposes, it is important to remember that the map should reveal the central ideas and should also capture the underlying relationships among events. To do this, teachers may need to use somewhat more elaborate maps than the generic one displayed in Figure 7.4. The more complex maps reveal how events are organized and how they are related to each other. In Figure 7.5, the map of a fourth-grade basal story reveals its problem-solution framework.

Although text mapping may seem time-consuming, we have found that teachers (even preservice teachers) can learn to do this with just a little practice. Careful analysis of texts is likely to increase both the reliability and validity of informal assessments. Structuring our assessment tasks around carefully analyzed reading material is likely to increase the degree they provide us with *trustworthy* (Valencia, 1990a) information. In addition, most teachers report that they begin to view comprehension differently when they analyze selections carefully. They are much less likely to ask trivial, detail questions, and much more likely to pose thought-provoking, theme-related questions. Once the basic frameworks are

FIGURE 7.4
Story Map for "Jack and the Beanstalk"

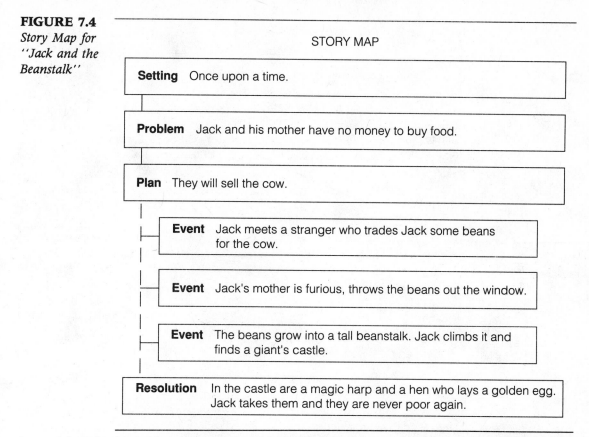

STORY MAP

Setting   Once upon a time.

Problem   Jack and his mother have no money to buy food.

Plan   They will sell the cow.

Event   Jack meets a stranger who trades Jack some beans for the cow.

Event   Jack's mother is furious, throws the beans out the window.

Event   The beans grow into a tall beanstalk. Jack climbs it and finds a giant's castle.

Resolution   In the castle are a magic harp and a hen who lays a golden egg. Jack takes them and they are never poor again.

Adapted from *Asking Questions about Stories* by P. David Pearson, Number 15 of the GINN OCCASIONAL PAPERS, © Copyright 1982, by Ginn and Company. Used by permission of Silver, Burdett & Ginn, Inc.

learned, mapping takes relatively little time. Certainly, a battery of such selection maps could be developed by a small group of teachers working together.

Conceptual maps: Analyzing expository text. Few assessment instruments provide sufficient information about students' abilities to read nonfiction materials. Yet older students and adults read disproportionately more informational text than they do fictional material. There are simply no available commercial materials that provide good diagnostic information about this critical area of reading ability. For the purposes of evaluating comprehension in general, and studying in particular, it will be necessary to examine actual textbook passages closely (see Chapter 9).

A conceptual map is used to analyze informational selections, identifying relationships in the same way that story maps do for narrative selections. Conceptual maps visually display important elements such as central purpose, main and

FIGURE 7.5

Story Map for "The Sociable Seal"

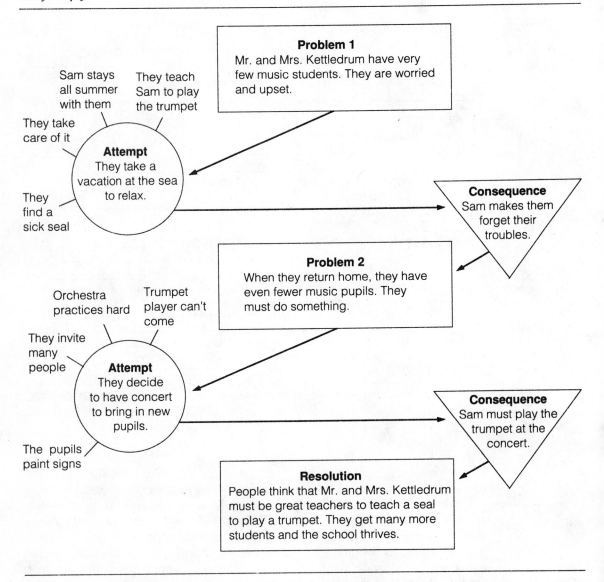

From *Instructor's Resource Book to Accompany Reading Instruction for Today* by Jana M. Mason and Kathryn H. Au. Copyright © 1986 Scott, Foresman and Company.

FIGURE 7.6

Concept Map for "The Sea Otter"

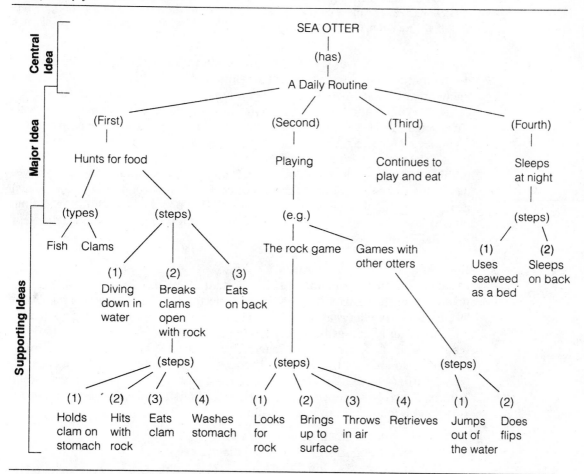

Reprinted by permission of the publisher from Wixson, Karen K., & Peters, Charles W., "Teaching the Basal Selection" in Winograd, Peter N., Wixson, Karen K., & Lipson, Marjorie Y., eds., *Improving Basal Reading Instruction* (New York: Teachers College Press, © 1989 by Teachers College, Columbia University. All rights reserved.), p. 30.

supporting ideas, and text organization. In Figure 7.6 you will see a conceptual map of a nonfiction selection from a second-grade basal reader. Wixson and Peters (1989) provide a functional description of the steps involved in creating a conceptual map:

> Concept mapping begins with the identification of major concepts within the text, through reading and an examination of important text features such as headings and photographs. These concepts are then arranged hierarchically to form the first two levels of the concept map—central purpose(s) and major ideas. Then the map is

expanded to include a third level of information—supporting ideas. Relations between concepts are highlighted by adding relational links specifying how the concepts are connected. The more clearly organized the text, the more coherent the concept map. If the relation between two concepts is not clear, a link cannot be established. (pp. 29–30)

In Chapter 9, we will provide more information about how to evaluate informational texts. For the moment, it is important only that you can identify any major organizational patterns and use these to guide your comprehension assessment. As Wixson and Peters (1989) note, the conceptual map in Figure 7.6 reveals a well-organized text. The ideas are linked together very clearly and each concept is connected by a linking concept which appears in parentheses (e.g., first, types, steps). The map also shows that the relationships among the levels of information in this selection are clearly hierarchical. The first level (central purpose) involves describing the daily routine of the sea otter. Then the second level (major ideas) describes the sequence of sea otter activity during one day (e.g., hunting, eating, playing, and sleeping). Finally, the third level (supporting ideas) details the steps involved in these activities.

Retellings of Long Selections

Armed with a representation of the important elements of a particular text, it is possible to elicit recalls and assess lengthy selections with high levels of reliability. We discussed retellings at some length in Chapter 5. The overarching guidelines for evaluating retellings of full-length selections are no different from those already described, so we will not reiterate them here. However, it is important to remember to start with open-ended requests to recall as much as possible.

Eliciting recalls. For fictional selections, it is often desirable to ask probe questions, using elements of story grammar (Marshall, 1983). Thus, questions such as the following are appropriate:

"Where did _____ happen?" (setting)
"What is _____'s problem?" (initiating event)
"What did _____ do about _____?" (attempt)
"How did _____ solve the problem?" (resolution)

Using these or similar probes, teachers can gather information about a child's ability to recall and infer important story information. Marshall suggests using a checklist to organize the assessment information (see Figure 7.7).

It is possible to structure the retellings even more at this point by asking probe questions, using elements of text structure appropriate to the type of reading selection. The following are examples of probe questions students might be asked for thematic stories and informational selections (Lipson & Wixson, 1989):

Story Selections
What is the main problem the characters face? (problem)
What makes it difficult for the characters to solve their problem? (conflict)
How is the problem solved? (resolution)
What lesson(s) are there in the story? (theme)

FIGURE 7.7
*Checklist of
Retelling
Behaviors*

Student Names	Retelling Contains						
	Theme	Setting	Character	Goal/ Problem	Attempts	Resolution	Reactions

From "Using Story Grammar to Assess Reading Comprehension" by Nancy Marshall, *The Reading Teacher*, March 1983, p. 619. Reprinted with permission of Nancy Marshall and the International Reading Association.

What is the main thing that happens in the story? (theme)
What do you learn about the main characters? (characterization)
How is the setting of the story important? (setting)
Which event is a "turning point" in the story? (events)

Informational Selections
What is the central idea of this selection? (central purpose)
Using the headings to divide the text into sections, tell the main ideas in each smaller section. (major ideas)
What information does the text provide to tell more (support) about the important main ideas? (supporting details)
How does the author organize the information to tell you about the central and major ideas? (structure)

Analyzing recall information. Gathering retelling data is the easy part of this assessment strategy, resulting in a wealth of rich information about students' ability to comprehend and about what students choose to share. The problem is less in the gathering than in the interpretation. How to make sense of, and evaluate, this wealth of information is an altogether different (and more difficult) job. It may be helpful to reflect on the following:

What does the child recall about this selection?
How does this recall compare with the map of the text (quantity and quality)?
How does the student organize the recall?
How does the recall rate as a whole?

FIGURE 7.8
*Retelling
Analysis*

Identify the Following Elements

STORY MATERIAL

Character Analysis:

  Recall: Student names characters in the story.

  Development: Student provides relevant information about the characters: appearance, feelings, behavior, etc.

Events: The things that happen in the story (these can be divided into episodes first).

Plot: The plan that defines how events will evolve given the major problem in the story.

Theme: The idea that unites the story events; often the theme is the major point, or ''truth'' the author wishes to reveal about the world.

INFORMATIONAL MATERIAL

Specifics: The informational content of the text; events, examples, etc.

Generalizations: General information related to the main topic of the material that can inferred by examining relationships between and among the specifics.

Major Concepts: Information beyond the text; the large, or universal, ideas that can be generated from generalizations.

Point Distribution for Retellings

STORY MATERIAL Maximum Points		INFORMATIONAL TEXTS Maximum Points	
Character Analysis		Specifics	50
Recall	15	Generalizations	25
Development	15	Major Concepts	25
Events	30		100
Plot	20		
Theme	20		
	100		

Adapted from C. L. Burke and Y. M. Goodman (1972). *Reading Miscue Inventory: Alternative Procedures.* New York: Richard C. Owen.

Of course, some system for analyzing and interpreting recall data is needed in order to answer questions like these. Both quantitative and qualitative systems are available, some easier to use than others (Kalmbach, 1986a; Morrow, 1988).

The retelling guidelines suggested by Y. Goodman and Burke (1972) involve a point system. The student's retelling is compared to an analysis of the original selection. Classification systems are provided for both narrative and informational text, each yielding a retelling score totaling 100 points. The procedures are summarized in Figure 7.8. It should be noted that more recent versions of the RMI have simplified the distribution of points for scoring stories, because some distinctions were difficult to make. Less sophisticated users may wish to use a simplified point system suggested by Y. Goodman, Watson, and Burke (1987). This revised system assigns 20 points each to character recall and character development, and 60 points to events.

FIGURE 7.9
Sample
Retelling

Marvin's Retelling of "The Sociable Seal"

They were at their house. They went to the beach and saw a seal on the shore. When they first found it they took it, a boat, and went out to the sea. They left him and he came back and went to the shore as fast as he could. They couldn't believe it so they said they'd keep him 'til the end of the summer and they did. He wanted to stay. He took baths at night and they took baths at daytime in the morning. They had a music store and she needed people to play and one kid didn't show up so they went to get the seal to play the trumpet and he played it better than ever and they decided to keep him for as long as they wanted. They had a musical seal and he played good and everyone else did and they had sign-ups so you can play with him and all the people who wanted to sign up for practice with the seal and everybody signed up so they had enough people to play so they were happy and . . . um . . . that's the end.

Probe Questions and Marvin's Responses

1. Who found the seal?
   The people, Mr. and Mrs. Kettledrum.
2. What did they do for a living?
   They had a school music store.
3. What problem did the Kettledrums have?
   They couldn't find a . . . . A boy was sick and he couldn't play so they had to get somebody else so they picked the seal.
4. What was Sam like?
   Funny.
5. Where did the story take place?
   At the ocean and the music store.
6. What problem was the story trying to solve?
   That they couldn't keep the seal and they did because he didn't want to leave.
7. What do you think the story was telling you?
   That seals play just as good as people, if not better.
8. Why do you think they took Sam out to sea?
   So they could have him find his family, but he didn't want to. He swam back to shore and they saw him and decided to keep him.
9. Why did the Kettledrums go to the beach?
   Because they wanted to get away from all their problems.
10. What kind of problems were they having?
    They had problems with their orchestra and their school. Ummm. I don't know.
11. Why do you think they had the musical?
    To get money.
12. Why were they happy at the end?
    Because the seal could play the instrument and they liked the seal so they kept him.

To use this retelling procedure, point values are assigned to various aspects of the maps created earlier. Then, the student's recall is evaluated according to how well it reflected these major components. In Chapter 5, we analyzed a short retelling from Marvin. Figure 7.9 shows the transcript of Marvin's retelling of the much longer story, "The Sociable Seal" (mapped in Figure 7.5). Using the Y. Goodman and Burke (1972) system, we would evaluate Marvin's retelling in the following way:

Character Analysis:		Marvin's Score
Recall	= Adequate	10
Development	= Limited	5
Events	= Unimportant events	20
Plot	= Very weak	10
Theme	= Very weak	5
		50/100

Although Marvin did note the main characters, he did not refer to them by name (and, in fact, seems uncertain that "Sam" is the seal during probed questioning). In addition, his grasp of character development was very weak. More seriously, Marvin focused on events that were not central to the story. This significantly weakened his recognition of the plot and the theme. Note that when asked what the story was telling, Marvin concluded, "That seals can play just as good as people, if not better," a theme that is not supported by the text analysis (see Figure 7.5).

The advantage to this type of system is that it is relatively easy to use and it reduces large amounts of data into manageable and reportable pieces. The disadvantage to any quantitative system is that it is possible to miss the qualitative aspects of the retellings, a point we made in Chapter 5 with regard to Clark's retelling system.

Irwin and Mitchell (1983) have proposed a more holistic scoring system, borrowing from approaches used to assess writing. This system attends to the "richness of retellings," assessing not only such features as the inclusion of major points and details, but also the degree to which students have gone beyond the text to generate cohesive generalizations and create a comprehensible whole. The system employs a 5-point scale designed to assess the retelling as a whole. The criteria for assigning retellings to one of these levels are displayed in Figure 7.10. When Irwin and Mitchell's holistic scoring system is applied to Marvin's retelling, we would rate the richness of his retelling somewhere between 2 and 3. Marvin did include some major ideas and included appropriate supporting details. There is a cohesiveness and coherence to his recall. However, he did not include the major thesis (problem) of the selection in his retelling and, even with probing, failed to make appropriate connections between episodes, events, and problems.

To extend the diagnostic value of a qualitative assessment even further, specific aspects of the retelling can be summarized and evaluated (see Figure 7.11). The qualitative analysis in Figure 7.11 clearly demonstrates that Marvin had difficulty generating inferences from text, especially with regard to major ideas and themes. His abilities to summarize, generalize, and organize the text information were all weak. On the other hand, Marvin did recall detailed information from text and clearly responded affectively to what he read.

Both of the systems just described are typically employed to analyze *oral* retellings. With older students, written recalls may be employed. In either case, however, the task must be absolutely clear to students. As with all assessment procedures, task demands will most likely influence results (see Chapters 8 and 9). When written retellings are to be used, it is especially important that you differen-

FIGURE 7.10
Guidelines for Evaluating the Richness of Retellings

Judging Richness of Retellings

Level	Criteria for establishing level
5	Student generalizes beyond text; includes thesis (summarizing statement), all major points, and appropriate supporting details; includes relevant supplementations; show high degree of coherence, completeness, comprehensibility.
4	Student includes thesis (summarizing statement), all major points, and appropriate supporting details; includes relevant supplementations; shows high degree of coherence, completeness, comprehensibility.
3	Student relates major ideas; includes appropriate supporting details and relevant supplementations; shows adequate coherence, completeness, comprehensibility.
2	Student relates a few major ideas and some supporting details; includes irrelevant supplementations; shows some degree of coherence; some completeness; the whole is somewhat comprehensible.
1	Student relates details only; irrelevant supplementations or none; low degree of coherence; incomplete; incomprehensible.

5 = highest level   1 = lowest level

Checklist for Judging Richness of Retellings

	5	4	3	2	1
Generalizes beyond text	X				
Thesis (summarizing) statement	X	X			
Major points	X	X	X	?	?
Supporting ideas	X	X	X	X	?
Supplementations	Relevant	Relevant	Relevant	Irrelevant	Irrelevant
Coherence	High	Good	Adequate	Some	Poor
Completeness	High	Good	Adequate	Some	Poor
Comprehensibility	High	Good	Adequate	Some	Poor

The above matrix describes the evaluation of retellings in a holistic fashion on the basis of criteria similar to a procedure used to grade written compositions. This technique is an alternative to questioning for assessment of student comprehension of both narrative and expository text.

From "A Procedure for Assessing the Richness of Retellings" by Pi Irwin and Judy Nichols Mitchell, *Journal of Reading*, February 1983, pp. 391–396. Reprinted with permission of Pi A. Irwin and the International Reading Association.

tiate a retelling from a summary. Although the evidence is slim, it does appear that written retellings are likely to generate more limited productions than oral ones. On the other hand, written retellings are frequently more coherent and organized. Ringler and Weber (1984) report good success using brief written recalls that focus attention on important story components. Using very holistic ranking procedures, we also have arrived at high degrees of reliability between teachers on such written protocols. When used over time, students' progress can be assessed and the effects of instruction can be demonstrated.

These techniques can be used to gather information about the child's ability to recall and infer important text information. In addition, affective responses to readings can be checked regularly with questions such as: Did you learn anything from reading this? Did you find this selection interesting? Did you enjoy reading

FIGURE 7.11
Diagnostic Summary of Marvin's Retelling

Directions: Indicate with a checkmark the degree to which the reader's retelling includes the reader's comprehension in terms of the following criteria:

	None	Low Degree	Moderate Degree	High Degree
1. Retelling includes information directly stated in text.				✓
2. Retelling includes information inferred directly or indirectly from text.		✓		
3. Retelling includes what is important to remember from the text.		✓		
4. Retelling provides relevant content and concepts.			✓	
5. Retelling indicates reader's attempt to connect backgrond knowledge to text information.			✓	
6. Retelling indicates reader's attempt to make summary statements or generalizations based on the text which can be applied to the real word.		✓		
7. Retelling indicates highly individualistic and creative impressions of or reactions to the text.			✓	
8. Retelling indicates the reader's affective involvement with the text.				✓
9. Retelling demonstrates appropriate reader's language fluency (vocabulary, sentence structure, language conventions, etc.).			✓	
10. Retelling indicates reader's ability to organize or compose the retelling.		✓		
11. Retelling demonstrates the reader's sense of audience or purpose.			✓	
12. Retelling indicates the reader's control of the mechanics of speaking or writing.			✓	

Interpretation: Items 1–4 indicates the reader's comprehension of textual information; items 5–8 indicate reader's response, and involvement with text; items 9–12 indicate facility with language.

Source: Mitchell, J. N., & Irwin, P. A. *The Reader Retelling Profile: Using Retellings to Make Instructional Decisions.* Submitted for publication.

this? Kalmbach (1986b) suggests that careful analysis of the retellings themselves can provide important information about students' responses to the text. "The way students structure a retelling will often tell you more about what they thought of the story than they can themselves" (p. 331). Although Kalmbach offers no specific suggestions, the following might prove helpful:

Is the child's personal interpretation evident from the retelling?
Does the child make evaluative statements about the characters or events?
Does the child attend to the language of the text, using it to support his or her interpretation?

Before making final judgments about students' ability to retell passages, be sure that the samples gathered represent the students' best efforts. The selections used for assessment should provide a good match for the students' interests, prior knowledge, and developmental ability. Of course, examiners can decide to gather information regarding performance on materials that are routinely assigned to the reader, regardless of appropriateness. The point to remember is that these procedures are sampling the reader's abilities, not measuring them in some definitive way. The goal is to learn more about the reader, and the selections teachers make should reflect their assessment purpose(s).

Questioning

In addition to free and probed retelling, teachers may also use structured questions. For classroom teachers, questioning will continue to be a mainstay in comprehension assessment. Although we believe that retellings enrich the picture, careful questioning can reveal much about students' understanding of a particular selection and about their ability to comprehend in general. Since structured questions impose someone else's view of what is important, they should be avoided until students have provided all possible information during free and probed retelling. In this way, distinctions can be made between the information generated freely, information elicited with minimal cueing, and information generated through direct cueing.

We noted earlier that there are problems associated with most of the taxonomies used to classify questions. As Pearson and Johnson (1978) point out, questions must be considered in relation to the probable source of the answer if we are to know what is required to respond correctly. Pearson and Johnson originally devised a three-level taxonomy that captured the relationship between a question and its answer source: text-explicit questions, text-implicit questions, and scriptally-implicit questions. This taxonomy has been extended and used widely as an instructional tool by Raphael (1982; 1986). Her latest refinement of these *question-answer relationships* (QARs) includes the following categories:

1. *Right There QARs.* The answer is explicitly stated in the text, usually easy to find. The words used to make up the question and words used to answer the question are right there in the same sentence.
2. *Think and Search QARs.* The answer can be inferred from text information. The answer is in the story, but you need to put together different story parts to find it. Words for the question and words for the answer are not found in the same sentence.
3. *In My Head QARs.* These scriptally implicit questions (the question must be answered by referring to prior knowledge) have been divided into two types:
   a. *Author and You.* The answer is not in the story. You need to think about what you already know, what the author tells you in the text, and how it fits together.
   b. *On My Own.* The answer is not in the story. You can even answer the question without the story. You need to use your own experience.

Distinguishing between questions on the basis of the source of the answer is extremely important in assessment. We need to be able to characterize children's comprehension strengths and weaknesses as accurately as possible. If we are not sure what is required to answer the questions we ask, then it will be difficult to make instructional decisions about comprehension. For example, if we think the answer is right there, when in fact the answer requires connecting text information through inference, then we may incorrectly assume that students cannot locate detail information in text while the problem is actually related to inferential ability. Therefore, the first task in assessing students' comprehension with questions is to determine the task demands of the questions themselves (see Chapter 9).

Consideration should also be given to the effects of question placement. A far more comprehensive picture of students' comprehension abilities emerges when examiners systematically vary the position of the questions. Most teachers regularly ask questions after the selection has been read. Questions in this position place a premium on student recognition of important information. However, if students come to expect that they will always be asked detail, text-explicit questions, they will attempt to remember small details at the expense of more global, inferential understanding. Another aspect of comprehension, however, is students' ability to locate and recognize information depending on their purpose. Thus, teachers may want to ask questions before reading. This permits evaluation of students' ability to read for differing purposes and/or to locate key information.

Finally, questions can be posed during reading. Questions asked during reading can help determine whether students are making connections and integrating relevant information. Imagine, for example, that a student was progressing through the text, making necessary inferences, and apparently understanding it (as determined by interspersed comprehension questions). Imagine, further, that this student was unable to answer questions posed at the end. At least two possible explanations come to mind. First, it is possible that the comprehension questions were not good ones. That is, perhaps they required the student to recall information that was not essential to understanding the text. Second, it is possible that the problem is not student comprehension, but student memory for text information (either ability to store information or retrieve it). By refining the questioning strategies, important instructional information can be gathered.

Issues surrounding the quality and placement of questions in general are important, but so are concerns about the content and focus of questions. It is important to devise some means for mapping or outlining text. Maps or outlines like those we described earlier can serve as the basis for constructing comprehension questions. For example, the charts in Figures 7.12 and 7.13 were used in combination with story or conceptual maps when generating assessment questions for a new state test (Wixson, Peters, Weber, & Roeber, 1987). These matrices can provide helpful structure to a novice teacher/evaluator. When the matrix is completed, an array of possible questions has been generated about important aspects of text. In addition, the various types of questions are well represented (the three types correspond directly to the three types of QARs described above).

Although these strategies may seem time-consuming, the instructional value of assessment information is enhanced. Students do not have to be characterized simply as "good comprehenders" and "poor comprehenders." Instead, teachers can describe quite precisely what and how they understand.

FIGURE 7.12
Narrative Grid

Story Components	Intersentence Level	Text Level	Beyond Text Level

Themes
  Main Idea Level
  Abstract Level			

Plot
  Setting (Location and
  Relation to Theme)			

Characters (Traits and Functions)			
Problem Conflict Resolution			
Major Events			

FIGURE 7.13
Informational Text Grid

Text Components	Intersentence Level	Text Level	Beyond Text Level
Central Purposes			
Major Ideas			
Supporting Ideas			
Adjunct Aids			

Evaluating Comprehension Processes

We have described a variety of ways to gather information about the products of comprehension. Analyzing students' recall and question responses can provide good information about how students comprehend, but this information is indirect; it must be inferred. Recently, educators have tried a number of novel assessment strategies designed to uncover the activity that goes on "inside the head."

Think-alouds. Verbal report procedures simply involve asking readers to stop at various points during their reading and "think aloud" about the processes and strategies they are using as they read. Wixson and Lipson (1986) suggest that think-alouds can produce insights into readers' approaches to text processing. They provide the following example of a student's verbal report:

Stacy: (reads title) Space Ship Earth.
Tutor: What were you thinking about when you read that title?
Stacy: A space trip to earth. (reads first portion of text, haltingly and with many repetitions) Boy! I had a lot of trouble with that one.
Tutor: What makes you think you had trouble with it?
Stacy: I kept messing up.
Tutor: What do you mean by "messing up"?
Stacy: I kept reading sentences twice.
Tutor: What do you think caused you to read sentences twice like that?
Stacy: Not understanding it.
Tutor: Okay, did any of the words give you trouble?
Stacy: No. (pp. 139–140)

Stacy's verbal report reveals a view of reading that is governed by attempts to understand. "Although miscues were obvious during this segment, Stacy's 'fix-up' strategy was driven by a desire not to sound good but to construct a sensible text representation" (Wixson & Lipson, 1986, p. 140).

Procedures for eliciting students' reports of mental activity generally include the following (Alvermann, 1984; Lipson, Bigler, Poth, & Wickizer, 1987; Wade, 1990):

1. Teacher/evaluator selects a text (generally about 200 words, but longer selections have been used).
2. The text is segmented and marked so that students will stop at predetermined spots.
3. The teacher/evaluator reminds students to think aloud about the text and/or their thoughts as they read the text.

Sometimes students are asked to provide text-based think-alouds. Wade (1990), for example, has designed a think-aloud procedure that requires students to generate hypotheses about the text as they read. Students are told to "tell what is happening," and they are then asked to detail the portions of text that led to their hypotheses. Student reports are analyzed in terms of the information they yield about the reader's ability to make hypotheses and integrate and revise information during reading.

On the other hand, Lipson et al. (1987) focused on readers' use of mental processes. Consequently, they asked students "to tell what you were *doing* and *thinking* as you read that part." Using this approach, students' verbal reports are analyzed for evidence that they employed various strategies known to enhance comprehension (see Chapter 14). It is important to understand that verbal reports reflect what readers are doing as they read a specific text with specific task directions. There is good evidence that students' reading behaviors may vary as texts and tasks change (Olshavsky, 1978). The somewhat contrived and ambiguous short selections used by Wade (1990), coupled with the student directive to think about "what is happening" no doubt produce different student behaviors than the intact exposition and request to talk about mental activity used by others.

As Maria (1990) has pointed out, think-aloud assessment procedures are very intrusive and require considerable teacher time. In addition, single think-aloud excerpts will not capture the variability we noted above. Both concerns can be addressed if teachers turn to careful observations of strategy use during normal instruction.

Continuous comprehension assessment. As Wixson and Lipson note (1986), "specifying the factors related to text and varying them systematically will greatly enhance the contributions of verbal report data to the total assessment" (p. 140). This generally requires regular, ongoing assessment of students as they read and interact with a variety of texts and tasks. Good assessment should capture the full range of students' comprehension ability; not just their best or worst efforts.

A versatile assessment procedure, designed by Wood (1988), is the Individual Comprehension Profile. As described by Wood, a profile, or matrix, is created

FIGURE 7.14

Individual Reading Record

Name: _____   Teacher: _____

Grade: _____   School: _____

	Date	Text Description	Topic Familiarity	Attitudes and Interest	Reading Task(s)	Process Knowledge/ Strategy Use	Reading Performance	Level of Support
Text 1								
Text 2								
Text 3								

using the results from information that has been gathered by the teacher/evalua-tor. The information is recorded as students read from their basal, under conditions that parallel the daily expectations in the classroom. Although Wood provides a sample profile, the matrix is meant to be teacher-made, allowing teachers to enter columns for whatever conditions appear most important for their program and student(s).

We have used a variation on this procedure to create an Individual Reading Record (see Figure 7.14). As students read, information relevant to their perform-ance can be recorded. If students are thinking aloud (see above), for example, the information generated would probably be used to fill the "Process Knowledge/ Strategy Use" column. The data recorded, coupled with specific information about the texts and tasks (see Chapters 8 and 9), will be valuable in summarizing and reflecting on the reading/writing abilities of individual students (see Chapter 10).

Studying

Studying is a specialized type of comprehension (Anderson & Armbruster, 1984b). Studying involves intensive reading for specific purposes, typically to organize, retain, and retrieve information. Often the purposes for reading have been imposed by others. However, many of the skills required for studying in the school context are also required in work settings. Even students who have a good foundation in the skills and strategies of reading through the elementary years may find the special demands of study and work reading difficult. We recommend assessing the study skills and habits of all students who have reached the sixth grade or beyond, since weaknesses in this area often cause serious academic problems.

Although it is helpful and important to assess all components of reading ability in natural contexts, it is absolutely critical to do so when assessing study skills. If they are to provide any useful information, assessments of studying ability must be specific to the content to be learned and related to the materials to be studied (Rakes & Smith, 1986). In planning an assessment of study skills, Estes and Vaughan (1978) suggest the following steps:

1. Identify the study skills that students will need for success in their studying activities.
2. Construct a diagnostic checklist to record your assessments of students' studying abilities.
3. Prepare a student self-appraisal survey based on the study skills you consider important [see Chapter 3].
4. Construct informal activities to assess the study skills you have identified as critical.
5. Informally observe students' ability to use their study skills as they perform tasks during daily classroom activities (paraphrased, p. 114).

Developing a Checklist of Critical Studying Skills and Strategies

The specification of skills and strategies as reading-studying abilities is somewhat problematic, since many of these might arguably be considered generic comprehension skills. Rogers (1984) has made a distinction between casual and study reading that is helpful: "Deliberate procedures for retaining or applying what is read are called study-reading skills. They permit people to complete tasks which they would not do as successfully if they read only casually" (p. 346). Long lists of study skills generally include specialized abilities, such as: alphabetizing, skimming, note-taking, outlining, scanning, and reading maps, graphs, tables, and diagrams.

Such lists are not entirely helpful, however, because the use of these studying skills does not ensure good comprehension, nor do all good readers use all of these skills (Armbruster & Anderson, 1981). Assessment of students' studying abilities should move forward cautiously. Clearly students may be aware of these skills and strategies but not use them during studying. In addition, many of these skills can be executed passively (e.g., outlining by copying headings and subheadings). In this context, it is apparent how important it is to determine what is really required to understand a particular text or accomplish a specific task. In addition, observation of skills in use is absolutely essential.

There are many checklists available to guide observations of students as they engage in studying activities. Rogers (1984) has collapsed the long lists of reading-study skills into three large categories: (1) special study-reading comprehension skills, (2) information location skills, and (3) study and retention strategies, and has designed a comprehensive checklist of discrete abilities (see Figure 7.15). As always, this checklist should be adapted to specific settings. As students are observed, engaged in study activity, the examiner should consider the following questions:

Does the student have an organized approach to the task?
Does the student seem to know what to do and how to use the text to accomplish the task?

FIGURE 7.15

Study-Reading Skills Checklist

	Degree of Skill		
	Absent	Low	High

I. Specific study-reading comprehension skills
  A. Ability to interpret graphic aids
    Can the student interpret these graphic aids?
      1. maps
      2. globes
      3. graphs
      4. charts
      5. tables
      6. cartoons
      7. pictures
      8. diagrams
      9. other organizing or iconic aids
  B. Ability to follow directions
    Can the student follow . . .
      1. simple directions?
      2. a more complex set of directions?

II. Information location skills
  A. Ability to vary rate of reading
    Can the student do the following?
      1. scan
      2. skim
      3. read at slow rate for difficult materials
      4. read at average rate for reading level
  B. Ability to locate information by use of book parts
    Can the student use book parts to identify the
    following information?
      1. title
      2. author or editor
      3. publisher
      4. city of publication
      5. name of series
      6. edition
      7. copyright date
      8. date of publication
    Can the student quickly locate and understand the
    function of the following parts of a book?
      1. preface
      2. foreword
      3. introduction
      4. table of contents
      5. list of figures
      6. chapter headings
      7. subtitles
      8. footnotes
      9. bibliography
     10. glossary
     11. index
     12. appendix

FIGURE 7.15
(continued)

	Degree of Skill		
	Absent	Low	High
C. Ability to locate information in reference works			
Can the student do the following?			
1. locate information in a dictionary _____			
a. using the guide words _____			
b. using a thumb index _____			
c. locating root word _____			
d. locating derivations of root word _____			
e. using the pronunciation key _____			
f. selecting word meaning appropriate to passage			
under study _____			
g. noting word origin _____			
2. locate information in an encyclopedia			
a. using information on spine to locate volume ____			
b. using guide words to locate section _____			
c. using index volume _____			
3. use other reference works such as:			
a. telephone directory _____			
b. newspapers _____			
c. magazines _____			
d. atlases _____			
e. television listings _____			
f. schedules _____			
g. various periodical literature indices _____			
h. others ( ) _____			
D. Ability to locate information in the library			
Can the student do the following?			
1. locate material by using the card catalog			
a. by subject _____			
b. by author _____			
c. by title _____			
2. find the materials organized in the library			
a. fiction section _____			
b. reference section _____			
c. periodical section _____			
d. vertical file _____			
e. others ( ) _____			
III. Study and retention strategies			
A. Ability to study information and remember it			
Can the student do the following?			
1. highlight important information _____			
2. underline important information _____			
3. use oral repetition to increase retention _____			
4. ask and answer questions to increase retention ____			
5. employ a systematic study procedure (such as SQ3R) ___			
6. demonstrate effective study habits			
a. set a regular study time _____			
b. leave adequate time for test or project preparation			
c. recognize importance of self-motivation in learning			

FIGURE 7.15
(continued)

	Degree of Skill		
	Absent	Low	High

B. Ability to organize information
Can the student do the following?
1. take notes _____
2. note source of information _____
3. write a summary for a paragraph _____
4. write a summary for a short selection _____
5. write a summary integrating information from more than one source _____
6. write a summary for a longer selection _____
7. make graphic aids to summarize information _____
8. write an outline of a paragraph _____
9. write an outline of a short selection _____
10. write an outline for longer selections _____
11. write an outline integrating information from more than one source _____
12. use an outline to write a report or make an oral report

From "Assessing Study Skills" by Douglas B. Rogers, *Journal of Reading*, January 1984, pp. 353–354. Reprinted with permission of Douglas B. Rogers and the International Reading Association.

Does the student exhibit enthusiasm and/or interest?
Does the student appear to be using appropriate study skills and strategies?
Does the student appear to read with a flexible rate?

Ideally, checklists like this one would become a part of the continuous and on-going assessment (portfolio) for each student, an idea implied by Rogers: "It (the checklist) can be completed as opportunities arise for observing each student and it can be kept in the student's records" (p. 347). As a matter of practicality, however, it may be necessary to create planned opportunities or informal tests to make these observations efficient.

Constructing or Using Informal Study Skills Assessments

There are many commercially available informal tools that assess study skills and habits. For example, the *Shipman Assessment of Work-Study Skills* (SAWS) (Warncke & Shipman, 1984) contains a number of subtests for evaluating alphabetizing, dictionary usage, ability to use reference sources, use of graphic materials, and organizing skills. The *Content Inventories: English, Social Studies, Science* (McWilliams & Rakes, 1979) contains a similar battery of informal tests. These commercial materials permit teachers to gather a wide variety of information about groups of children quickly. Therefore, they are quite useful if screening data are needed. However, these tests are not generally linked to the books or curriculum used in the classroom. Thus, the amount of information generated about students' ability to actually perform in that setting is somewhat limited.

To collect information about students' application of knowledge and skill, teachers will need to construct their own inventories. A *Group Reading Inventory* (GRI) is designed for use in the classroom and is helpful for gathering information about how well students can read their textbooks (Rakes & Smith, 1986). A GRI typically has two components; a book-handling component and a comprehension section. Both parts of the GRI are constructed using the actual textbook employed in the classroom. Resource room teachers, of course, will need to construct an inventory that samples several types of texts.

Part I of the GRI is constructed by generating 10 to 12 questions about the various parts of the text (see Figure 7.16 for sample items). Part II of the GRI is akin to an IRI. A relatively short selection (e.g., 500 words) is drawn from a chapter in the text. Ten or fifteen questions are generated to test comprehension. Whereas students are directed to complete Part I of the GRI while using their textbook, the questions in Part II are to be answered without referring to the book. The information gleaned from this type of assessment can be used to complete an observation checklist like the one proposed by Rogers (see Figure 7.15).

A similar procedure is the Open Book Reading Assessment (OBRA) (Bader, 1980). As its name suggests, students have access to the text throughout this assessment. The OBRA is based on the following assumptions: "To determine the skills to be evaluated, one must give consideration to (a) the nature of the tasks to be performed with the material and the levels of comprehension required and (b) the enabling skills required to perform the tasks or comprehend the information." Bader suggests creating items about such things as technical vocabulary, use of context clues, using charts, and using book parts. In addition, she suggests testing students' ability to answer questions that require making inferences and interpreting text information.

To create an OBRA tailored for specific settings, examine the textbook carefully and consider the types of tasks generally expected of students (see Chapters 8 and 9). The OBRA is a very flexible assessment strategy since, it can accommodate almost any type of text-task context. The example in Figure 7.17 was developed by a vocational education teacher who was concerned about his students' failure to do well on tests. He constructed the OBRA to accompany an assigned chapter entitled "Electronic Fuel Injection Systems." The chapter contained the following notable features:

- Chapter Preview
- List of Objectives
- Clearly labeled section headings (e.g., 53.3, Fuel Flow System)
- Fourteen (14) complex figures with detailed labeling
- A New Terms section, with new vocabulary in boldface, and brief definitions
- Chapter Review
- Discussion Topics and Activities section

After the students have completed the OBRA, the following questions should be considered in evaluating students' performance:

Using Book Parts

Introduction: These questions are designed to help you understand the organization of your text and to enable you to use it more effectively. You may use your text in answering the questions.

1. Where would you look to locate a short story in the text if you could not recall the title or the author?
   a. Glossary
   b. Table of Contents
   c. Literary Terms and Techniques
   d. Index of Authors and Titles

2. If you came across the word "demagoguery" in your reading in the text, where would you look *first* for a definition?
   a. Table of Contents
   b. Literary Terms and Techniques
   c. Glossary
   d. The Composition and Language Program

Excerpted from "Assessing Reading Skills in the Content Areas" by Thomas A. Rakes and Lana Smith in *Reading in the Content Areas: Improving Classroom Instruction, Second Edition,* edited by Dishner et al. Copyright © 1986 by Kendall/Hunt Publishing Company. Used with permission.

Do the students recognize the parts of the text?
Are students able to make use of graphic materials?
When the text is available, can students locate specific information?
Can students use the text to figure out unfamiliar, specialized vocabulary?
Does the problem appear to be ability to use the text or ability to retain information?

This information is summarized and used to plan and adapt instruction. Bader (1980) suggests using a chart to display the information for the class. The chart in Figure 7.18 displays a portion of the one generated by the vocational teacher who constructed and administered the informal assessment described earlier. He learned, to his surprise, that most of his students were unable to make effective use of the diagrams and charts in their textbook. Similarly, few of them were adept at using the helpful features of the book to derive information. Whereas he had previously attributed the students' poor performance to lack of effort and/or motivation, he now realized that at least some students were unable to learn the information using the text. Instruction in textbook use and/or additional support for reading and studying would be needed.

Again, teachers may be concerned about the time-consuming nature of these assessment strategies. Although short-cuts are possible, the information gathered will not be as useful. As Rogers (1984) has noted, "Students' use of study-reading can best be assessed by observing them while they are engaging in studying-reading for some personal interest or need. Contrived situations such as often occur when students are asked to complete worksheet pages from published materials are not as effective for assessing and teaching study-reading" (p. 352).

**FIGURE
7.17**
*Sample
Open Book
Reading
Assessment*

Auto Mechanics

Name _____(KEY)_____

1. Circle the components of an airflow system (pages 536, 539)
   a. air flow meter
   b. main jet
   c. throttle chamber
   d. throttle valve
   e. injector
   f. choke plate
   g. air regulator
   h. electronic control unit
   i. back pressure relief valve
   j. throttle body
   k. fuel distributor
   l. turbocharger

2. Using the diagram on page 540, indicate the order that fuel flows through the following components, starting with the fuel tank

1	Fuel Tank
5	Fuel Distributor
3	Fuel Damper
6	Injector
4	Fuel Filter
2	Fuel Pump

3. Using the following chart, circle the cars that should have an idle speed of 800 RPM if equipped with automatic transmission.
   a. 84 AMC Alliance
   b. 82 Renault
   c. 83 Toyota 4 cyl
   d. 82 Ford Bronco
   e. 80 Toyota Cressida
   f. 83 Toyota 6 cyl
   g. 83 Renault Fuego
   h. 79 Toyota Supra

Idle Speed and Mixture Adjustments

Application		Idle Speed			Idle Mixture		Voltmeter Leads	
Year	Model	M/T	A/T	Adjustment Location	Voltage	Fluctuation	Positive	Negative
AMC								
83	Alliance	650	650	Thrott. Hsg. Screw	6.0–7.0	0.5	D2-2	D2-7
84	Alliance, Encore	700	700	Thrott. Hsg. Screw	6.0–7.0	0.5	D2-2	D2-7
Renault								
82–83	Fuego Turbo	750	...	Thrott. Hsg. Screw	6.5–7.5	0.5	8	2
82–83	All Others	800	650	Thrott. Hsg. Screw	6.5	0	8	2
Toyota								
79–80	Supra	800	800	Thrott. Hsg. Screw	*	0.5	VF	B+
80	Cressida	800	800	Thrott. Hsg. Screw	*	0.5	VF	B+
81–82	All AFC	800	800	Thrott. Hsg. Screw	3.0–9.0	*	VF	E1
1983	4-Cyl.	800	800	Thrott. Hsg. Screw	5.9–9.0	2.0	VF	E1
1983	6-Cyl.	650	650	Thrott. Hsg. Screw	0.1–0.2	0.1	10 or 20	B+

In my textbook, to find quickly:

4. __e__ definition of technical word
5. __d__ A statement of the book's purpose and features
6. __b__ Name of the book's publisher
7. __c__ Outline of what is in the book
8. __a__ Location in the text of a key term

I would turn to:

a) Index
b) Title Page
c) Table of Contents
d) Preface
e) Glossary

On page:

9. 563
10. beginning
11. beginning
12. beginning
13. 566

Note: If a section does not have a page number, indicate if it is in the beginning, middle, or end of the book.

FIGURE 7.18

Open Book Reading Assessment Summary Form

	Literal Details Content												Using Diagrams and Charts														Using Book Parts									
	1												2 (Diagrams)						3 (Charts)																	
	a	b	c	d	e	f	g	h	i	j	k	l	a	b	c	d	e	f	a	b	c	d	e	f	g	h	4	5	6	7	8	9	10	11	12	13
Lorie				✓			✓													✓	✓																
Jack				✓			✓																					✓	✓	✓							✓
Mark				✓			✓	✓																✓												
Judy				✓			✓															✓	✓													
Shane				✓			✓	✓																✓												
Mike				✓			✓	✓																					✓	✓	✓	✓				
Greg			✓										✓								✓															
Jack R.						✓	✓																							✓	✓	✓		✓		
Keith				✓		✓	✓																							✓	✓					

Adapted by permission of Macmillan Publishing Company from *Reading Diagnosis and Remediation in Classroom and Clinic* by Lois A. Bader. Copyright © 1980 by Lois A. Bader.

Writing

In Chapter 2, we noted that there is a strong relationship between reading and writing, and argued that learning to generate messages in print enhances readers' ability to understand what others write. In Chapter 4, we discussed at length the role of writing in learning to read. In particular, we described the ways in which the assessment of early writing efforts can provide information about student's knowledge of print conventions and their word analysis abilities.

An analysis of writing ability can provide useful information at later stages of reading development as well. It has become increasingly common to include writing assessments in an evaluation of reading competence, as educators recognize how similar the cognitive and language demands of writing are to those involved in understanding written materials (Tierney & Pearson, 1983; Stotsky, 1984). The evidence about reading-writing relationships is not unequivocal, but it does appear that examination of students' written productions can reveal a good deal about students' intentions (meaning generation), strategies, and language development. In the discussion to follow, we will focus less on analyzing writing competence and more on analyzing writing as it can provide insights into literacy development.

Process-Product Measures

Traditionally, writing has been evaluated by examining written *products*, just as reading has traditionally been evaluated by examining the products of reading (e.g., question responses). Product assessments have generally consisted of evaluating two aspects of written work: composition and mechanics (Cramer, 1982). These aspects of written work can be evaluated holistically or analytically. Many norm-referenced tests of writing involve analytic evaluations of written products (see Chapter 6). Holistic scoring of written products is quite common both in classroom assessment and in large-scale assessment (even statewide assessment of writing) and can be especially useful for screening purposes.

Using a holistic scoring system, you arrive at a rating that represents a global judgment about the overall quality of a written product. Criteria are established before scoring begins, and then general evaluations are made about the written work, typically using a three-level scale (High-Middle-Low). An example of standards for holistically evaluating narrative and expository writing are reproduced in Figure 7.19. As you can see, the composition is judged separately for narrative and exposition, whereas mechanical skills are judged together.

An analytic scoring system, on the other hand, involves assessment of various elements of the writing process: syntax, vocabulary, and so on. It is, of course, possible to use an analytic framework after a more holistic score has been derived. Stoodt (1988) has proposed an Analytic Scale for Holistic Scoring. This scale involves holistically scoring each of the following more discrete aspects of written work: wording, ideas, organization, syntax, usage, spelling, punctuation. When students control these features of print sufficiently to use them in their own writing, it is reasonable to assume that they can make use of them during reading as well.

Increasingly, educators and linguists are concerned with students' grasp of the writing *process*. Clearly, it is possible to make inferences about students' growing knowledge and control of the process by examining written products. However, students' behavior as they engage in writing is also of concern. Most experts suggest that the writing process involves several stages: a planning stage, for clarifying purpose and audience; a composing stage, which involves writing, reading, and attention to mechanics; and a revision stage, during which rereading and editing occur.

Folders of ongoing and completed work are a normal part of classrooms where a process writing approach is used. Samples of written work should be gathered and provide exceptionally good evidence regarding student growth. Graves (1983) recommends that evaluation start with what he calls Folder Observation. This entails evaluating the written work in preparation for other types of observation. "Trends in children's writing will be important observation points, along with the specifics that make up the trends" (Graves, 1983, p. 287). In completing a folder observation, it may be helpful to reflect on the following:

What types of writing is the student producing?
What topics seem to fuel his/her writing?
What new ideas are being generated?
Is there evidence of topic or theme change/growth?
What skills can and does this child employ?

FIGURE 7.19

Standards for Evaluating Narrative and Expository Writing

	Standards for Evaluating Composing Skills for Narrative Writing		
	Low	Middle	High
Story structure	No identifiable beginning, middle, or end. Story problem unclear. Action and characters not developed or related. Essential details missing or confusing. Story problem not solved, or resolution unrelated to events.	Beginning, middle, and end present, but not always identifiable. Story problem presented, but not completely developed. Some conversational or descriptive details included. End may not show logical resolution of problem.	Identifiable beginning, middle, and end. Characters introduced and problem presented. Characters and problem well-developed with appropriate conversational or descriptive detail. Story ends with believable resolution of problem.
Story setting	Setting of the story not identifiable. Details inappropriate and confusing.	Time and place of story are hinted at. But uncertain. Further references to setting may be inconsistent with original time or place.	Time and place of story clearly set. Specific details related to setting given in appropriate context. Setting consistent throughout.
Story characters	Characters not believable. Details related to character development are inconsistent, inappropriate, or missing. Difficult to distinguish one character from another. Action of characters unrelated to problem.	Characters somewhat believable. Some descriptive or conversational details given. Details may not develop character personality. Action of characters not always related to problem. Major and minor characters not clearly discernable.	Characters believable. Descriptive or conversational detail develops character personality. Action of characters relates to problem. Major characters more fully developed than minor ones.
Story conversation	Conversation among characters haphazard, incomplete, or muddled. Much of the conversation inappropriate to circumstances and to personality of story characters. Conversation seems unrelated to story being told.	Conversation sometimes appropriate to circumstances and to characters. Conversation may reveal character personality or relationships among characters. Conversation sometimes not clearly related to story.	Conversation appropriate to story circumstances and to personality of each character. Conversation used to reveal character and develop interrelationships among characters. Conversation clearly relates to story.
Story idea	Story idea is trite or otherwise uninteresting. Story lacks plot or plot is vague. Story ends abruptly or reaches no definite conclusion.	Story idea is interesting. Idea may lack freshness or imaginativeness. Story has a plot. Plot may not be well-developed or entirely consistent. Story ending may not be satisfying or interesting.	Story idea is fresh or imaginative. Story plot is well-developed, is consistent, and comes to a satisfying, surprising, or otherwise highly effective ending.

	Standards for Evaluating Composing Skills for Expository Writing		
	Low	Middle	High
Quality of ideas	Most ideas vague, incoherent, inaccurate, underdeveloped, or incomplete. Details often unrelated to topic. Nothing imaginative or thoughtful about the ideas.	Unevenness in completeness and development of ideas. Most ideas related to the topic; a few unrelated. Sound, but unimaginative ideas.	Ideas relevant to the topic, fully developed, rich in thought and imagination, and clearly presented.

FIGURE 7.19

(Continued)

	Standards for Evaluating Composing Skills for Expository Writing		
	Low	**Middle**	**High**
Quality of organization	Introduction, development, and conclusion unclear. Emphasis of major and minor points indistinguishable. Sentences and paragraphs seldom related by transitions. Overall lack of coherence and forward movement.	Introduction, development, or conclusion not easily identified. Emphasis on major or minor points sometimes not well-balanced. Transitions between sentences and paragraphs used, but without consistency. Forward movement variable.	Introduction, development, and conclusion well-structured, complete, and easily identified. Emphasis of major and minor points well-balanced. Sentences and paragraphs clearly related by transitions. Logical forward movement.
Selection of words	Word selection inexact, immature, and limited. Figurative language seldom used.	Word selection usually suitable and accurate. Over-used words and clichés somewhat common. Figurative language may lack freshness, when used.	Facility and flair in word selection. Writer experiments with words in unusual and pleasing ways. Figurative language used, often in interesting and imaginative ways.
Structure of sentences	No variety in sentence structure; often only simple sentences are used. Transitions limited to such words as **then**; conjunctions to **and**. Awkward and puzzling sentences common. Run-on sentences and fragments often appear.	Some variety in sentence length and structure. Transitions used when necessary. Few sentence constructions awkward and puzzling. Run-on sentences and sentence fragments appear, but do not predominate.	Sentence length and structure varied. Sentences consistently well-formed. Smooth flow from sentence to sentence. Run-on sentences and sentence fragments rarely appear.
Structure of paragraph	Topic sentences seldom used. Irrelevancies common. Order of details haphazard. Little or no command of the four common paragraph types.	Topic sentences usually stated. Irrelevancies uncommon. Order of details usually suitable. Limited ability to use the four common types of paragraphs.	Topic sentences stated and supported with relevant details. Appropriate variety used in ordering details (chronological, logical, spatial, climactic). Four types of paragraphs used when appropriate (narrative, explanatory, descriptive, persuasive).

Evaluations of this type are richer than examining one, or even several, final products. However, it is extremely difficult (perhaps impossible) to evaluate students' control of the writing process by considering only final products. Evaluation of student control over the process of writing requires that students be observed, over time, in a classroom that values process writing and encourages author development.

Observation Checklists

An effective observation framework should include examination of written work, but it should also provide for examining the writer at work. Kemp (1987) has proposed an observational checklist of behaviors to watch for as children

FIGURE 7.19
(Continued)

Standards for Evaluating Mechanical Skills for Narrative or Expository Writing		
Low	**Middle**	**High**
Grammar and usage Frequent errors in the use of nouns, pronouns, modifiers, and verbs.	Grammatical conventions of inflections, functions, modifiers, nouns, pronouns, and verbs usually observed. Grammatical errors sometimes occur.	Grammatical conventions of inflections, functions modifiers, nouns, pronouns, and verbs observed. Grammatical errors infrequent.
Punctuation End punctuation often used incorrectly. Internal punctuation seldom used. Uncommon punctuation is almost never used correctly.	Sentences usually end with appropriate punctuation. Internal punctuation used, with occasional errors. Uncommon punctuation sometimes used, but often inaccurately.	Sentences consistently end with appropriate punctuation. Internal punctuation and other less common punctuation usually correctly used.
Capitalization First word of sentence often not capitalized. Pronoun/often a small letter. Proper nouns seldom capitalized. Other capitalization rules usually ignored.	First word of sentences nearly always capitalized. I always capitalized. Well-known proper nouns usually capitalized. Other capitalization rules used, but not consistently.	First word of a sentence and the pronoun/always capitalized. Well-known proper nouns nearly always capitalized. Good command of other capitalization rules regarding titles, languages, religions, and so on.
Spelling Frequent spelling errors. Shows a frustration spelling level (less than 70%). Unable to improve spelling accuracy in edited work without help. Misspellings often difficult to recognize as English words.	Majority of words spelled correctly. Shows an instructional spelling level (70 to 80%). Approaches 90% accuracy in edited work. Misspellings approximate correct spellings.	Nearly all words spelled correctly. Shows an independent spelling level (90%). Approaches 100% accuracy in edited work. Misspellings close to correct spellings.
Handwriting/ neatness Handwriting difficult or impossible to read. Letters and words crowded. Formation of letters inconsistent. Writing often illegible.	Handwriting usually readable, but some words and letters difficult to recognize. Some crowding of letters and words.	Handwriting clear, neat, and consistent. Forms all letters legibly with consistent spacing between letters and words.

From *Language: Structure and Use, Teacher's Edition* 8 by Ronald L. Cramer et al. Copyright © 1981 Scott, Foresman and Company.

write. The results of these observations can be used to evaluate children's developmental progress and also to identify areas that might require instructional attention. The form, which appears in Figure 7.20, parallels the major stages of writing, focusing on the student during planning, composing ("drafting"), and revision phases. In addition, this checklist addresses the critical affective outcomes addressed by creating good written products, and provides for evaluation of student attitudes.

A similar system of writing analysis is proposed by Temple and Gillet (1989). They suggest that in addition to the assessments of the writer in the writing process, students' written work should be evaluated in terms of the functions of the writing, writing style, writing fluency, and mechanics. The checklist devised by Temple and Gillet (1989) delineates the kinds of questions to ask during the evaluation of students' writing. These include:

Functions of Writing
　　What types of writing have been produced? (e.g. stories, expressive writing, descriptive writing, etc.)
　　What topics have been selected by the writer?
　　Who is the audience for this child's writing? (e.g., teacher, classmates, etc.)
　　How sophisticated is the writer's awareness of audience?
Qualities of Writing Style
　　Does the writing reflect good choices in language use?
　　Does the writer make good use of descriptive language?
　　Does the writer maintain a focus throughout the work?
　　Are papers well-organized, given the purpose of the work?
　　Are the written products defined by effective openings and endings?
Mechanics of Writing
　　How much control of standard English usage/grammar is reflected in the written works of this writer?
　　Are complete idea units (sentences) used throughout?
　　Are punctuation and capitalization used appropriately?

These examples demonstrate how teachers can focus on and gather evidence of the writer's reading interests, knowledge, and skill. It is possible to conduct much more extensive analyses of student's writing abilities. For our purposes, however, we are interested in collecting information that will inform us fairly directly about students' reading abilities. If other academic abilities, such as writing, spelling or ability to attend, appear to be primary sources of difficulty, then these should be examined more closely. Not all good readers are good writers, but it is very difficult to be a fine writer and not be a good reader as well.

Student Self-Evaluation

According to Valencia, McGinley, and Pearson (1990), one of the characteristics of newer perspectives on assessment is the realization that it should be *collaborative*. "The essence of collaborative criterion lies in collaboration with students. When we work *with* students in developing assessments, we communicate our support of their learning process" (Valencia, McGinley, & Pearson, 1990). This means that students should share some responsibility for monitoring their own progress, but this also means that they must have access to information. They need to be clearly informed of the purposes for various work assignments, and important evaluative criteria will need to be shared with them as well.

　　Collaboration necessarily involves at least some student self-evaluation. Indeed, the ability to evaluate one's own work should be viewed as an important goal in most literacy programs, since it is a necessary requirement of independence (Johnston, 1987). Writing is one arena in which self-evaluation has been

FIGURE 7.20
Writing Analysis

Name of Child: _____   Name of Teacher: _____

Date of Assessment: _____   Levels: 1, 2, 3: _____

Title of Sample: _____
(attached, if to be used in discussion with parent or teacher)

A. Orientation to Writing

1. Is able on most occasions to engage in discussion of a theme or topic.
2. Is positive on most occasions when given writing opportunities.
3. Responds well to 'conferencing' or seeks out others for trying out ideas or words.
4. Engages in writing without need of persuasion or direction.

B. Drafting

5. Manages, when motivation is high, to produce a draft.
6. Contributes drafts to a personal journal or writing folder.
7. 'Rehearses' with drawing, talking, verbal composing.
8. Takes risks in using words when their spelling or precise meaning are not known.
9. Aims to write.
10. Responds to conferencing whilst composing drafts.
11. Reflects on efforts so far.
12. Avoidance strategies are rare.
13. Appears on most occasions to have purpose, that is, to write for an audience and/or a publication or self.

C. Revising, Rewriting, Editing

14. Makes judgements about own writing.
15. Submits drafts for others' comments.
16. Can 'see the words as temporary' (and) 'the information as manipulable.'
17. Is prepared to work over drafts.
18. Is careful in final stages about mechanics, such as spelling.
19. Revisits 'risk' areas to work over them.
20. Understands that own writing can be manipulated for better effects and to match changing intentions.
21. Seeks information, facts, opinions to strengthen writing.

Comments

What signs are there of the child's self-direction, self-monitoring and incentive to write?

What kinds of freedom does the child show in engaging in the first writing stages?

Is he/she an 'explorer' with words, styles, structures, ideas?

What successful changes have taken place between drafting and final writing?

What are some of your perceptions of the writer's recent development?

FIGURE 7.20
(Continued)

D. Production	**Comments**
22. Produces sustained writing effort from time to time.	*What does the writer do with the final products?*
23. Takes pride in a completed work.	
24. Is sensitive towards the writing efforts of others.	
25. Achieves a 'voice' in some writing.	
26. Achieves completeness of some writing.	
27. Final presentation is accurate in mechanics, such as spelling and handwriting.	
28. Reads own and others' writing.	*Are the final products valued/re-read? With whom?*

E. Additional Observations

29. _____

30. _____

31. _____   *Would transformations assist the growth of self-editing skills?*

32. _____

33. _____   *What were the most successful strategies used this time to sustain the writing?*

used productively for some time. Generally, teachers use teacher-student and peer conferences to establish criteria for evaluating success and/or progress (see previous section). Then, students are invited to contribute by evaluating their own efforts (see Figure 7.21). These self-evaluations must be taken seriously and must become part of the total assessment process.

For our purposes, it is especially important to note the extent to which students' self-evaluations reflect their development and progress as writers. Comments such as the following reflect differences that are important to recognize: "I liked this story because it's long"; "I tried to make a good beginning to this story and I think I did"; "I was trying to make people understand how the boy in this story felt." We want to attend as well to changing self-evaluations. Students can help us understand their purposes in this way, but they also show us whether they have begun to take risks in writing or have internalized new standards for their work.

FIGURE 7.21
Self-Evaluation Guide for Writing

Self-Evaluation

Name _____ Date _____

Title _____

Why I wrote this paper (no more than two sentences) _____

The best thing about my composition is _____

The hardest thing about writing this paper was _____

I can make my paper better if I _____

I think my grade should be _____

Figure from *Teaching Language Arts* by Barbara D. Stoodt. Copyright © 1988 by Harper & Row, Publishers, Inc. Reprinted by permission of HarperCollins Publishers.

FROM CLASSROOM TO CLINIC

Educators must continue to press for assessment instruments and methodologies that provide instructionally useful and contextually valid information. The assessment efforts described in this chapter can and should provide much more specific information about how and what to teach, but they are suggestive only. Ingenious teachers will find many other ways to evaluate their students' performance for the purpose of making placement and curricular decisions. In this chapter we argued that assessment is continuous, lasting as long as the working relationship with the child. Assessment is viewed as an ongoing process. Each encounter with a child must be seen as an opportunity for interactive assessment. In this manner, teaching and testing become integral events. By adopting this stance, we have taken a positive step toward providing instructional programs that are responsive to the needs of all children.

Most of the assessment strategies we have suggested can be easily incorporated in daily instructional programs. Indeed, the strategies described may be difficult for a teacher in a pull-out program to implement without the cooperation of the classroom teacher. It does little good to evaluate component skills and abilities without observing them in action. Students can, and often do, perform differently on tests of isolated skill, or on tasks in constrained and artificial environments, than they do in real classrooms accomplishing real assignments. In Chapters 8 and 9 we will describe ways to evaluate the contributions of materials and programs to reading performance. In the meantime, clinicians must make every effort to assess students in situations that mimic real reading.

On the other hand, support personnel may have more time to analyze task demands or observe students in action. Collaborative assessment efforts can and should be undertaken if we want to understand how and why young children are struggling in the area of reading.

CHAPTER SUMMARY

In this chapter, we described the role of the teacher in an effective program of assessment, arguing that high quality information about students requires knowledgeable teacher/evaluators. We described a number of informal assessment strategies for evaluating specific components of reading competence. Several traditional assessment tools were presented (e.g., word lists, criterion tests, and questions). In addition, we suggested ways to gather information as students engage in actual reading and writing activities. For example, we described methods for gathering information about students' vocabulary knowledge using strategies such as free recall and PReP. In the area of comprehension assessment, we suggested techniques for enhancing the information that can be gathered using traditional techniques like questioning and retelling. In addition, we have described a verbal report, or think-aloud, procedure for assessing students comprehension abilities. Strategies for gathering information about students' studying abilities were also discussed, stressing the need to assess this area in naturalistic contexts. Finally, several informal techniques for assessing writing were described, and a section of student self-assessment was provided as well.

In each case, the assumption has been made that the information will become a part of a systematic, continuous, and well-organized assessment designed by well-informed teacher/evaluators. We will return to the issue of continuous assessment in Chapter 10, where we introduce the principles of diagnostic teaching and decision making.

SECTION III

Evaluating the Reading Context

THE DISCUSSIONS IN these two chapters provide the basis for the execution of Step 3 of the assessment-instruction process: evaluating contextual factors. In this section, we describe more fully the contextual factors of setting, methods, materials, and tasks. We discuss the contributions of these factors to reading performance and describe ways in which these factors can be evaluated for individual students. The measures we suggest are designed to help summarize information about the setting, the specific instruction, the reading materials, and the tasks students face in their current reading contexts. Each of these areas is considered in light of the most current research, and also in terms of the desirable outcomes for reading instruction.

In the preceding chapters, we focused on strategies, tools, and techniques for gathering information about the reader's knowledge, skill, and ability. Now we turn our attention directly to the two other components of the reading process: setting/method and materials/tasks. In Chapter 8, we describe the ways that setting factors contribute to reading and reading achievement. In particular, we describe how the instructional context and methods can enhance learning or lead to difficulty. In Chapter 9, we take a close look at reading materials and tasks, providing a more lengthy discussion of these than was possible in the earliest sections of this book.

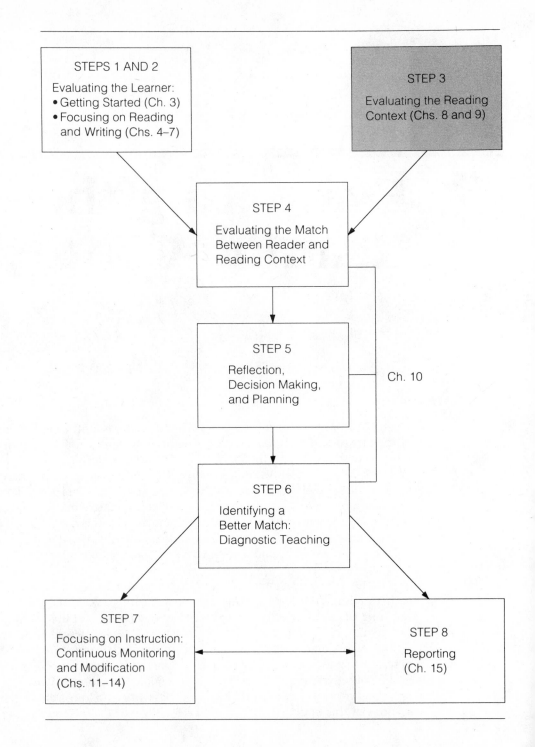

STEPS 1 AND 2

Evaluating the Learner:
• Getting Started (Ch. 3)
• Focusing on Reading
  and Writing (Chs. 4–7)

STEP 3

Evaluating the Reading
Context (Chs. 8 and 9)

STEP 4

Evaluating the Match
Between Reader and
Reading Context

STEP 5

Reflection,
Decision Making,
and Planning

Ch. 10

STEP 6

Identifying a
Better Match:
Diagnostic Teaching

STEP 7

Focusing on Instruction:
Continuous Monitoring
and Modification
(Chs. 11–14)

STEP 8

Reporting
(Ch. 15)

CHAPTER 8

Evaluating Setting
and Instruction

INTRODUCTION

In this chapter, we discuss how different aspects of setting and methods influence reading performance and describe methods of evaluating these factors. In our discussion of setting, we return to the issue of special needs and at-risk students, describing the ways in which specific cultural and home factors may influence reading achievement. This chapter also addresses the relationship between contextual factors and student motivation and describes an instructional framework for assessing instruction.

Why Assess Setting and Methods?

Traditional assessment looks only to the student as the source of reading difficulties. Clearly, students' knowledge, skill, and motivation are crucial factors in reading achievement. However, a growing body of research demonstrates that instructional context and methods can support learning or contribute to disability. One of the most important reasons for engaging in assessment is to inform instruction. This requires careful descriptions of how different setting and task conditions influence learning in general and how they match the needs of a particular student being considered.

Gaskins (1988) notes that one of the strongest impediments to change in schools is the belief, even among very good teachers, that the need for change must reflect poor or incompetent teaching. An interactive view of reading ability and disability suggests otherwise. School success and/or failure result from a complex interaction among many factors (Coles, 1987). Some factors that seem to influence a particular student negatively do not affect a second student at all. Similarly, the program that has been successful in the past may not work for the student who is struggling now. Thus, the focus should be on assessing the context and method in terms of their likely impact on specific students' performance in reading.

Chapter Overview

After a discussion of literacy and the role of cultural context in defining the goals of literacy, we describe the subtle interactions that can and do influence school achievement. Next, we turn our attention to understanding and assessing instructional settings, discussing four aspects of setting that merit attention: teacher expectations and classroom environment; classroom activity and organization; patterns of verbal interaction; and congruency across instructional settings. The third major section contains a discussion of instruction. A model of instructional goals and methods is provided and used to guide the assessment of instruction.

UNDERSTANDING THE ROLE OF CONTEXT IN READING PERFORMANCE

Children learn to read in a variety of settings. American children are often exposed to books in the home prior to formal schooling, and many children participate in social groups devoted to story time or reading in their homes, nursery schools, or kindergartens. One aspect of the reading context relates to the settings in which the student encounters reading activities. This includes settings both in and out of school. In school they usually learn to read in small groups with their classmates. In all of these settings children are exposed to print, and the actions of reading as a functional social activity are guided by knowledgeable adults.

The complexity of factors related to setting and method makes assessment very difficult. We have attempted to keep a focus on gathering and integrating information about factors known to influence learning (see Figure 8.1). Most often, educators examine only those aspects that involve instructional method. Before turning our attention to these factors, however, we will briefly consider settings external to the school.

Informal reading activities removed from school often reflect the same characteristics wherever they occur—at home, in the marketplace, or in religious training. Becoming literate occurs in social situations that shape purposes, conditions, constraints, audiences, standards, and motivation to engage in reading and writing activities (Paris & Wixson, 1987).

FIGURE 8.1

Some Attributes to Consider in Assessing Reading Context

Attributes of the Classroom Setting	Attributes of Instruction	Attributes of Instructional Materials and Tasks (Chapter 9)

Organization
  Types of activity
  Management efficiency
  Grouping patterns
	Focus of Instruction
	  Content
	  Materials
	  Balance
	    Attitude outcomes
	    Content outcomes
	    Process outcomes
	  Similarity to instruction for
	    average/above average
	    students
		Texts
		  General nature of materials
		    (e.g., basal, trade book,
		    workbook, etc.)
		  Genre and variety
		  Salient features (length,
		    vocabulary, organization,
		    etc.)

Expectations
  Teacher/student beliefs
  Literacy environment		

Classroom Interactions	*Method/Approach Being Used*
	  Salient features
	  Similarity to approach for
	    average/above average
	    students
	  Congruence from one
	    instructional setting to
	    another
		Tasks
		  Purpose
		  Salient features (content and
		    form)
		  Relationships to program goals
		    and outcomes
		  Variety and duration of tasks

Literacy and Home/School/Community Settings

Every educator knows that literacy is not accomplished in schools alone. The children themselves contribute to learning and achievement, but so do parents, siblings, and the general community. Attributes that are important to consider regarding the larger literacy setting include: the nature of the linguistic community (language(s) spoken in the home/community), the literacy status of the home/community, the relationships between home/community and school, and the socioeconomic status of home/community. All of these factors in turn affect individual and community literacy goals.

The discussion of setting features external to schools must be conducted with great care, to guard against a tendency to lay blame. If the public blames teachers and schools for poor achievement, it is also true that schools and teachers tend to blame families and communities. These discussions do little to promote better school experiences for students who need our best effort. It is true that teachers often can do little to influence the external, or larger, settings that affect students' achievement. The enormity of these external setting features can paralyze schools and teachers, causing them to feel powerless to do anything at all. On the other hand, a tendency on the part of schools to expect the same things from all students and families renders many parents powerless and angry.

Identifying attributes that contribute to school achievement should not be a process of laying blame. Rather, careful examination and description of the settings children encounter can promote both understanding and adaptation. Poor instruction is a less prevalent problem than instruction that is unresponsive to the needs of individual students. The ways in which various setting features interact can be both extremely subtle and profoundly important, affecting student learning and motivation. Teachers and clinicians must consider the results of recent research which offers insights into the ways that home experiences can produce a mismatch between student and teacher expectations. One of the most illuminating of these is a study by Heath (1983).

Heath studied the patterns of language use in three communities in the southeastern United States and concluded that patterns of language use and social interaction differed strikingly for children in homes from these communities. In "Maintown," a middle-class, school-oriented community, the focus of literacy-related activities was on labeling, explaining, and learning appropriate interactional patterns of displaying knowledge. Children learned how to use language in literacy events and were socialized into the interactional sequences that are central features of classroom lessons.

Families in "Roadville," a white working-class community, also focused on labeling and explanations; however, they did not link these ways of taking meaning from books to other aspects of their environment. Consequently, children from these homes were well prepared for the literal tasks of early reading instruction, but not for reading assignments that call for reasoning and affective responses.

The third group of homes under investigation were located in "Trackton," a black working-class community. The children in these homes were not taught labels or asked for explanations; rather, they were asked to provide reasons and express personal responses to events in their lives. As a consequence, these children were unprepared for the types of questions often used in beginning reading instruction and unfamiliar with the interaction patterns used in reading lessons.

These differences resulted in mismatches in the patterning of teacher-pupil interactions during reading instruction (Heath, 1981). For example, a predominant characteristic of teachers' questions was (and still is) to ask students to name the attributes of objects or events in isolated contexts. Trackton parents did not ask the children these kinds of questions, and Trackton children had different techniques for responding to questions. Teachers reported that it was difficult to get responses from Trackton students, Trackton parents reported that teachers did not listen or that "we don't talk to our children the way you do," and Trackton children reported that teachers asked "dumb" questions they already knew about.

Heath then shared with the teachers examples of how Trackton children interacted at home and teachers incorporated questions similar to those the children were familiar with in their instruction. As a result, the children participated much more frequently, and in time the teachers were able to involve them in more traditional question-answering as well. This research illustrates the point that the children from these homes were initially disabled by virtue of the fact that they had not engaged in the type of interaction that is characteristic of classroom instruction, but that their disabilities were remediated by the social interaction they subsequently experienced with their teachers (Gavelek & Palincsar, 1988).

Goals for Learning Literacy

Teachers and schools are often frustrated by the apparent lack of motivation and achievement among students. Recent research and reflection has lead to a more complex conclusion: all children are motivated to achieve, but they may direct their actions toward different goals, under different conditions and for different reasons. It must be recognized that at least some children are motivated toward different goals than those emphasized by educators.

It is also important to realize the existence of different definitions of achievement and motivation. Students' achievement and motivation can only be understood in relation to the cultural contexts in which they live. Different cultures and different contexts dictate norms of behavior that vary. Individual behavior reflects, and is constrained by, these different norms. To the extent that subcultures define achievement goals differently, differences in observed motivation to achieve those goals would be expected.

Experts cannot agree on a single definition of literacy because the attributes and standards are relative to the context in which reading and writing are observed. An African boy chanting the Koran in a language he cannot understand, a teenager striving to read the driver's test manual, and a student in a classroom stumbling to pronounce words in a primer are all participating in literate activities.

Literacy is a social and cultural phenomenon that encompasses much more than school-oriented values and practices. Furthermore, as cultures change, so do definitions of literacy. New technological advances require new knowledge and skills, and societies expect both more and different abilities from literate individuals.

Because literacy definitions vary, many scholars describe literacy activities in terms of how print is used and how reading and writing fit into the total fabric of a cultural group (Scribner & Cole, 1981). These uses and purposes partly determine the value that is placed on literacy by the community. They may also determine who has access to literacy within a particular culture. It is well known that literacy is given different levels of priority in various societies, and that many cultures restrict access to literacy to certain portions of the population (Downing & Leong, 1982).

Although it is relatively rare today for cultures to restrict access to literacy by law or stricture, there are other, less direct ways to control access to literacy. Cultures define the social functions of literacy, methods of instruction, and standards of competence. For example, Western societies historically restricted females' access to scientific and mathematical literacy by denying women entry into certain types of employment and by establishing certain norms of behavior.

Similarly, the culture of the school informs students of acceptable forms of achievement behavior and motivation (Dreeben, 1968). Schools do vary in the way they operate, and these differences may result in differing expectations for students to achieve. For example, a school may routinely provide excused absences from class and even classwork for certain students (e.g., athletes, student government representatives, job training participants). System features of the school, such as its size, neighborhood, formal structure, and informal climate, may also influence students' motivation and achievement by affecting their expectations for success, self-esteem, and time on task (Schmuck, 1980).

Different cultural groups can have similar or dissimilar frames of reference for the functions and activities of literacy (Green & Bloome, 1983). When students do not share with teachers the same expectations or rules for communication and participation in the classroom, they often devalue literacy or exempt themselves from instruction, thereby diminishing their opportunities to become literate. Although cultural setting is a vague and global term, it is important to recognize at the outset that the functions, values, and frames of reference in particular contexts influence who has access to literate activities and the opportunity to learn to read (see Fraatz, 1987).

INSTRUCTIONAL SETTING

In this section, we discuss how various aspects of instructional context interact with cultural and home environments to influence student learning and motivation. In addition, we describe ways to assess these features, providing tools and strategies for examining and describing the instructional setting. The complexity of factors related to setting and method makes assessment very difficult. There are, however, four aspects of setting that merit attention: teacher expectations and classroom environment; classroom organization, including grouping patterns; patterns of verbal interaction; and the role of multiple instructional settings.

Understanding the Role of Instructional Setting in Reading Performance

Setting factors do not operate in isolation from curriculum and instructional methods of course. The evidence suggests that instead, setting factors interact with each other and with curriculum and instructional methods. We have separated them somewhat for purposes of discussion and as a guide to the factors that must be considered in evaluating the instructional setting. Wherever possible, however, we have tried to suggest the interrelationships between and among the elements.

Teacher Beliefs, Context, and Curriculum

Perhaps no single factor influences the instructional setting more than a teacher's knowledge and beliefs about teaching and learning. As we noted in Chapter 1, teachers are often unaware of the extent that their views about learning and reading influence and shape classroom instruction and the learning experiences offered to students.

> Beliefs will serve as a frame of reference for a teacher in selecting materials for instruction and for presenting and guiding the use of these instructional materials. These values will be communicated to the students, both verbally and nonverbally. Students will adhere to and improvise upon the contextual demands, or will find ways to change the nature of those demands through active, or passive, negotiation. (DeFord, 1986, p. 166)

Thus, children's behavior and the degree to which they participate in academic tasks is often determined by what others expect of them.

Teacher expectations are shaped by their beliefs about reading, learning, and literacy in general. In turn, these beliefs influence the type of classroom environment that is established. Children attend to these subtle and not-so-subtle clues as they determine how to behave and what to learn. Evidence of how these beliefs and actions influence each other is provided by DeFord (1986), who studied three separate classroom literacy environments—traditional, literature-based, and mastery learning. The three teachers, who had all been identified as "exemplary," created dramatically different classroom settings, described below.

The context in the *traditional* classroom was formed by the teacher. Within this curriculum model, the teacher set up a series of general rules for classroom participation, some explicitly stated, others implied. Lessons were thoroughly planned, allowing for a limited number of child-initiated decisions, and usually structured so that they could be completed in one work period. Reading groups were generally organized according to the basal program, with seatwork consisting of workbook pages and phonics worksheets. If the seatwork was a writing activity, the topic was assigned by the teacher; very little writing was student-initiated. The overriding teacher concerns were for a productive, smooth-flowing, moderately quiet day, and to provide assignments that allowed students to work at levels that minimized confusion.

The children in the traditional classroom were responsible and cooperative. They participated actively in discussions led by the teacher and worked diligently to complete their assignments. Verbal interactions were most commonly teacher-child or teacher-group conversations, although quiet child-child conversations were allowed during seatwork time to discuss assigned work.

The teacher and children formed the context in the *literature-based* classroom together as they wrote, read, and explored the environment both in and out of their classroom. Teacher goals and student goals were negotiated to produce the curriculum and context. The rules, set by the teacher and children together, revolved around issues of productive work and social/child development. Reading and writing instruction were handled individually or in small-group situations, with the teacher assessing and teaching on a daily basis from information gathered during the work period. Instruction involved a variety of topics, materials, and methods, including numerous field trips that provided the content for reading and writing. Teacher planning for student projects usually extended from several days to several weeks, during which time progress was evaluated continuously until the projects were completed.

The teacher structured open-ended activities and helped students make decisions about personal outcomes. The children in the literature-based classroom were active, independent, and generally responsible for the social climate of the room. They helped each other and collaborated on projects. Child-child conversations and teacher-child conversations were most common, with fewer teacher-group interactions.

In the *mastery learning* classroom, "the literacy context was directed by the curriculum, the teacher serving as mediator and manager of the reading and writing program" (DeFord, 1986, p. 174). Since the content of the curriculum was delivered within a highly structured management system, students worked independently at their seats a significant amount of the time. The teacher created an orderly and quiet work environment for the execution of these tasks. Reading groups met to receive teacher-directed instruction within the programmed materials. This instruction involved introducing, practicing, reviewing, and testing word lists and vocabulary. Assigned workbook and basal reader pages were executed independently, and tests were administered periodically.

Writing activities and oral exchanges occurred almost exclusively at the initiation of the teacher. Writing tasks were assigned each day, and discussions generally occurred only in teacher-led forums. Planning occurred only within the prescribed program materials, and work was assigned so that it could be completed in a half-day block of time.

This observational research (DeFord, 1986) highlights the extent to which classroom organization, activities, and discourse may vary as a function of teacher beliefs about reading and reading instruction. The unique attributes of classroom settings influence the nature of students' literacy learning.

Classroom Interaction

Teachers are generally unaware of the extent to which they rely on verbal interactions to make educational decisions and judgments. According to Cazden (1986), "spoken language is the medium by which . . . students demonstrate to teachers much of what they have learned. Spoken language is also an important part of the identities of all participants" (p. 432).

Variation in ways of speaking is a universal fact. When the variation is significant, it can lead to painful mismatches for individual students or groups, and these mismatches can affect achievement (Cazden, 1986; Flanders, 1975). Differences in how and when something is said may only require a temporary adjustment, or they can seriously impair effective teaching and accurate evaluation.

Teachers, like other groups of specialists, have unique ways of talking. Some of the more obvious features of teacher talk include asking known-answer questions and evaluating students' answers to questions. Teacher talk is also characterized by its preoccupation with control of behavior and of talk itself. Students must "learn how to participate in reading, what effective reading means, and the definitions of reading held by the teacher and school" (Green & Bloome, 1983, p. 23) to be regarded as skilled in literacy activities in school.

However, studies of cultural differences also suggest that students would be better served if teachers took differences in prior experiences in the home community into account more than they now do; and that "teachers now differentiate among their students in ways that may continue, even increase, the inequalities of information and skills that are present when students start school" (Cazden, 1986, p. 445). Research evidence suggests that some children come to school with an oral style of discourse that is inconsistent with teachers' literate style. These children often do not gain access to the kind of instruction and practice required to develop a more literate discourse style, resulting in less-skilled performance in school-based literacy activities.

Linguistic and interactional patterns are important considerations because teachers base judgments about students' abilities and behavior on them. For example, Michaels (1981) studied first-grade "sharing-time" experiences and found that when children's narrative styles were very different from the teacher's expectations, the event was generally unsuccessful. In addition, the teacher frequently made negative assessments of the students' ability and sanctioned the students' performance.

Because interaction styles are so subtle and interwoven with individual identity, they can be difficult to assess. However, there is evidence that when instruction is shaped to respond to these differences, achievement and interaction improve. Research with native Hawaiians provides another example of the importance of cultural compatibility in the patterns of interaction between teachers and students in reading lessons.

Boggs (1985) learned that native Hawaiian adults rarely ask children questions for information, as is common with white middle-class parents. They use direct questions primarily when reprimanding their children. When telling a story, Hawaiians cooperate in taking turns to construct the story with voices overlapping, an activity called "talk story." In addition, Hawaiians delegate household chores to an older child, who, in turn, is responsible for making certain that the work is done. Apprenticeship and observation, rather than explanation or discussion, are used to teach children new skills.

Consistent with this knowledge about the interaction patterns of native Hawaiians, Au (1980) observed that Hawaiian children were more successful in reading lessons using the participation structures of the talk story than with the conventional recitation pattern commonly used in reading lessons with children from the mainstream culture (Au & Mason, 1981). The results of this comparison indicated that the lessons of the teachers using these two participation structures were clearly different kinds of social events, and that Hawaiian students demonstrated much higher levels of achievement-related behavior in the lessons incorporating the culturally compatible talk story pattern.

Classroom Activity

Over the past several years, research descriptions of classrooms have demonstrated what most classroom teachers know only too well: classrooms are busy places, and teachers are very active participants in classroom events. These features of classroom life are critical to understanding what is expected of students, and also whether teachers do think about individual students, instructional purposes, or content.

Because the environment is busy and demanding, organization is a major factor in classroom teaching. According to Doyle (1986), the activity is the basic unit of classroom organization. Activities are relatively short blocks of classroom time during which students are arranged in a particular way. Labels for activities reflect either their organizational focus (e.g., seatwork, discussion) or their focal content (e.g., reading, journal writing). More than 30 separate activities occur each day in the average elementary school class.

Teachers must also divide their attention among competing demands. For example, in a study of third-grade classrooms, approximately half of the teachers' acts involved instructional activities such as questions, feedback, and imparting knowledge (Gump, 1969). The rest of the time, the teachers were involved in organizing students for instruction and orienting them to tasks (23%), dealing with deviant behavior (14%), and handling individual problems and social arrangements (12%).

Consequently, management of activity can take precedence over instructional content. Indeed, there is evidence to suggest that subject matter is often reduced by teachers and students to a set of procedures to be followed in completing assignments in order to satisfy management demands (Doyle, 1986). "Neither teachers nor students talk much about the meaning, purposes, or underlying operations of the content. The work is often . . . done without understanding" (Doyle, 1986, p. 417). This disturbing conclusion is consistent with the finding that while in class, students often focus a significant part of their attention on information about how to do the work they are assigned as well as what behavior they are to display (King, 1983). Clearly, the degree to which students have an opportunity to learn content or to practice significant literacy behaviors will depend, at least in part, on the types and quantity of classroom activity provided. In addition, teachers who can increase the amount of academically engaged time produce students who achieve at higher levels (Rosenshine, 1979).

Examination of the types of activities can also provide an indication of how productive the classroom environment is likely to be. For example, the amount of time teachers spend organizing and directing students, interacting with individual students, and dealing with inappropriate and disruptive behavior is likely to be lower in teacher-directed activity. Student involvement is highest in teacher-led small groups (90%), slightly lower for whole-class recitations (80–85%), and lowest for seatwork (65%) (Kounin, 1970; Rosenshine, 1979). Open-ended, small-group activities result in higher levels of academic and intellectual engagement (Blumenfeld et al., 1983; Bossert, 1979).

Differences among classrooms can and do account for differences in student performance and achievement. Although classroom organization and management may vary within and among schools, the predominant pattern appears to be the teacher-directed classroom, in which students are expected to work independently and to interact primarily with the teacher and the instructional materials. For some students, the traditional patterns of organization pose especially serious problems.

Researchers contend that families and cultures vary considerably in the extent to which they prepare children for such settings (Fillion & Brause, 1987). Children who are accustomed to assisting others in accomplishing tasks, collaborating on projects, and generally working together, are at ease in the cooperative classrooms in which these activities are rewarded, but uncomfortable in more traditional classrooms. Hispanic homes have been characterized as fitting into the cooperative format (Tikunoff & Ward, 1983). Similarly, Philips (1982) found that Native American children were accustomed to independent activities and were unaccustomed to the noise and competition characteristic of many classrooms. Differences between cultural values and classroom values were so extreme as to alienate the children from their teachers and their classmates. Thus, it is important to examine the match between classroom organization and cultural or individual patterns of achievement.

Ability Grouping

Grouping patterns in classrooms constitute a special type of organizational response. Teachers need to exercise caution if they group students for instruction, because such arrangements have implications for student motivation and achievement. Key components of the grouping structure in the classroom include size and number of groups, basis for grouping, consistency of groups across content areas, stability of groups over time, labeling of groups, mobility of individuals between groups, number of groups functioning as groups at one time, and amount of time spent in individual, group, or whole-class structure (Marshall & Weinstein, 1984).

Reviews of research on ability grouping for reading instruction suggest that instructional and social reading experiences differ for students in high- and low-ranked reading groups, and that these differences influence student learning (e.g., Allington, 1983b; Hiebert, 1983). The social properties of ability groups are derived, at least in part, from the fact that students are grouped with those defined to be similar and separated from those defined to be different. Group placement is based on socially valued criteria, so that group membership immediately identifies some individuals as better than others. Therefore, high- and low-ranked reading groups are likely to form unique instructional-social contexts that influence the learning outcomes of the individuals within those groups.

As a consequence, students make judgments about their own and others' competence. Reading assessment can be enriched by a clear understanding of the types of social distinctions that accompany grouping patterns in the classroom. For example, when researchers ask students about how they learn how smart they are, students commonly refer to group membership (Marshall & Weinstein, 1984). We see this repeatedly when we interview students in our clinics. This type of awareness was displayed by 10-year-old Jonathon, who was asked to talk about what kind of reader he was: "I have to tell you something. I'm in the fourth grade, but I'm only using a third-grade reader. That's not very good."

Student feelings of efficacy and motivation are affected by grouping decisions, but research suggests that students in different groups also receive distinctly different instruction. Students in low-ranked groups spend considerably less time in actual reading tasks than students in high-ranked groups (McDermott, 1977). High-ability groups read silently more often than they read orally, while low-ability groups read orally much more frequently than silently (Allington, 1983b). In addition, teachers interrupt students following oral reading errors proportionally more often in low-ability than high-ability groups, and are more likely to emphasize word identification with low groups and comprehension with high groups (Allington, 1980).

The nature and extent of such differential treatment varies from teacher to teacher, and at least some of the variation can be seen as appropriate differential instruction (Brophy, 1983b; Haskins et al., 1983). Too often, however, low groups receive less exciting instruction, less emphasis on meaning and conceptualization, and more rote drill and practice activities (Good & Marshall, 1984).

The differential treatment, coupled with the simple fact of group membership, provides students with more messages about their potential for success in reading (R. Weinstein, 1986). Average- and low-ability students who are in ability groups give lower self-evaluations than those who are not in ability groups (Rosenbaum, 1980). Research suggests that most groups based on homogeneous ability levels are relatively stable over time with infrequent mobility of students from one group to another (Rosenbaum, 1980), and that membership in reading groups of different ability levels contributes significantly to the prediction of reading achievement beyond initial individual differences (R. Weinstein, 1976).

In sum, the evidence suggests that a low-group psychology develops wherever ability grouping is practiced, even in schools whose low-group students would be high-group students somewhere else (Good & Brophy, 1987). Such students may be prime candidates to become underachievers because it may be easier for them to remain passive and to pretend indifference rather than risk failure by trying their best.

Before leaving this topic, it is important to note that some groups are formed for reasons other than ability, such as grouping for student interests or specific skill needs; promoting interaction among students of varying backgrounds; and promoting learning in all students (Marshall & Weinstein, 1984). Research on cooperative learning groups has demonstrated a positive effect on achievement, race relations, and student self-esteem (Slavin, 1983). In contrast to stable and homogeneous groups, students have greater opportunity to work with more of their peers and to observe their own and others' strengths in a variety of areas when a flexible grouping strategy is used. Where external rewards are distributed, more children have the opportunity to receive recognition than where stable hierarchical grouping strategies result in the high group consistently receiving more rewards and privileges.

In light of the foregoing, Good and Brophy (1987) offer the following guidelines for within-class ability grouping:

1. The number, size, and composition of groups should be determined by teacher goals.
2. Groups should not be formed for the sole purpose of altering the pace of instruction. Instead, they should promote differentiated instruction for individual students.
3. Assignments to groups should be flexible, not permanent, and the scheduling and instruction of these should be subject to change as well.
4. Students should be assigned to a group for a specific purpose and should be managed in such a way as to limit the impact on their other activities, both academic and social. For example, members of the same reading group should not be seated together, nor should membership in a reading (or other group) dictate the students' grouping for other subjects.
5. The organization and instruction of groups should result in extra instruction for low achievers.

Grouping patterns often affect poor readers more profoundly than other students, but grouping is common across a wide range of settings. In the next section, we examine instructional contexts that are unique to the disabled reader.

Congruence of Context and Curriculum

The school life of many poor readers involves not one, but several, instructional contexts. Until recently, most poor readers received special instruction outside of the classroom (called pull-out programs), a configuration that is still quite common. However, many less-skilled readers now receive their instruction via *push-in* delivery systems, receiving special reading instruction within the regular classroom. This instruction is still planned and delivered by a special teacher. In either arrangement, it is likely that students are experiencing two settings, two teachers, and, frequently, two sets of program materials.

Researchers such as Allington and Johnston have examined the relationships between supplemental reading programs and regular classroom instruction (Johnston, Allington, & Afflerbach, 1985; Allington & Johnston, 1989). Their results revealed that an astonishing 80% of classroom teachers did not know what instructional materials were being used with the remedial students in their room. The data also indicated that only 50% of the reading teachers could specify the reading book used by classroom teachers. If classroom and supplemental teachers do not know this general information it is, of course, extremely unlikely that they have coordinated any other aspects of the students' reading instruction.

Examinations of the instruction remedial students receive in the classroom and in the remedial setting suggests that there is little congruence. On a typical day, remedial students are receiving instruction on different skills, using different materials, and with a different focus in two different environments (Allington, Stuetzel, Shake, & Lamarche, 1986). As Johnston and his colleagues (1985) point out, this means that the students who have the most difficulty integrating information and transferring learned skills to new situations are presently receiving the most fragmented, least unified instruction of all.

The coordination of efforts between the classroom and the special teachers is at the heart of most definitions of what Walp and Walmsley (1989) call "procedural congruence." These authors note that organized mechanical coordination does little to ensure that students will encounter a coherent and well-conceived instructional environment. Simple push-in programs will not assure congruent instruction either. "It is quite possible to have classroom and remedial teachers occupying the same space yet delivering unrelated programs" (Walp & Walmsley, 1989, p. 365). It seems likely that congruence between instructional settings for remedial readers will depend on teachers having serious discussion about the nature of reading and the rationale for delivering "more of the same" or "different" instruction.

Strategies and Tools for Assessing Setting

Recognizing the contribution of the instructional setting to student achievement, educators and researchers have periodically developed, and occasionally validated, instruments for evaluating some aspect of instruction. Until recently, however, assessments of the instructional context have been rare. Fortunately, there is now a spare but growing number of strategies and tools for assessing the instructional context.

In the following section, we describe some techniques for examining and describing instructional factors and school settings in order to determine how they may be contributing to a particular student's struggles or successes. The point is not to pass judgment, but to collect information—information that can be used to make sound decisions aimed at improving instruction for children who need our help. The techniques described focus on the following components: teacher beliefs and classroom environment, classroom organization, grouping patterns, classroom interactions, and congruence across settings.

Teacher Beliefs and the Literate Environment

As painful as it can be, from time to time we all need to carefully examine our beliefs and practices in light of new information and new innovations. When preparing an assessment of a student who is working with other professionals, information should be gathered that can be used in assessing the type of instructional environment experienced by the student. These reflections should include a consideration of implicit beliefs and an analysis of the types of literary environment provided in the classroom.

Teacher beliefs. Several instruments have been developed to help identify teachers' beliefs and theories about reading and learning. We provided a self-assessment questionnaire in Chapter 1 (see Figure 1.1, p. 6). Interviews can also provide insights into teachers' theoretical orientations. Recognizing how much classroom practice is influenced by teacher beliefs, Gove (1983) designed an instrument for helping teachers see the relationship between their theories and methods.

After the questionnaire or interview has been completed, the salient features of the teacher's conceptual framework should be described and then analyzed. Focus on questions such as these:

What does the teacher (or, do I) believe:
1. is the purpose of reading and reading instruction? of writing and writing instruction?
2. are the goals of reading/writing instruction?
3. is necessary for children to know and do before they will become skilled readers and/or writers?
4. are appropriate activities to promote reading/writing competence?
5. are most important priorities in teaching literacy?

Teachers' knowledge and beliefs can be considered in relation to accepted theories and concepts (see Figure 8.2).

Another type of evaluation links beliefs to practice, examining the extent to which classroom practice is consistent with the theories teachers hold. Teachers are occasionally surprised to find that although they believe that something is important, they do not provide for it in their own program. For example, most teachers believe that prior knowledge influences reading and that building background is important, but relatively few teachers actually include these features in their instruction. Recognizing mismatches between belief and practice can begin with an assessment of the classroom environment.

The classroom environment. The types of learning that are valued should be reflected in the classroom. Duffy and Roehler (1989) note that the literate envi-

FIGURE 8.2

Conceptual Framework and Rating Scale of Reading Interview

Concept Areas	Summary of Beliefs	
	Bottom-up conceptual framework of reading	Top-down conceptual framework of reading
Relationship of word recognition to comprehension	Believe students must recognize each word in a selection to be able to comprehend the selection	Believe students can comprehend a selection even when they are not able to recognize each word
Use of information cues	Believe students should use word and sound-letter cues exclusively to determine unrecognized words	Believe students should use meaning and grammatical cues in addition to graphic cues to determine unrecognized words
View of reading acquisition	Believe reading acquisition requires mastering and integrating a series of word recognition skills	Believe students learn to read through meaningful activities in which they read, write, speak, and listen
Units of language emphasized instructionally	Letters, letter/sound relationships, and words	Sentences, paragraphs, and text selections
Where importance is placed instructionally	View accuracy in recognizing words as important	View reading for meaning as important
Student evaluation	Think students need to be tested on discrete subskills	Think students need to be tested on the amount and kind of information gained through reading

ronment in classrooms really contains several environments: physical, intellectual, and social-emotional environments.

There are many formats for examining the *physical environment* in classrooms. Most focus on assessing the general attractiveness and orderliness of the environment (e.g., Glazer & Searfoss, 1988). Observation and assessment can, however, focus more specifically on aspects of the environment that directly influence the acquisition of reading and writing skill. Assessment questions about physical setting might include:

1. Does the environment reflect the many types, functions, and uses of print?
2. Are the children's own written works prominently featured in the classroom? (Are they displayed? Is there an "author's chair"? and so on?)
3. Is there a writing center where children can store writing folders, get materials, display and share work, and so on?
4. Is there a reading corner where children have access to a wide array of print materials and opportunity to share books read?

The physical environment can communicate to students both what is valued and

FIGURE 8.2

(Continued)

Interview Probe	Rating Scale			
	Bottom-up model	Top-down model	Nonreading rationale	Not enough information

Ask about:

1. Instructional goals
2. Response to oral reading when reader makes an error
3. Response to oral reading when a student does not know a word
4. Most important instructional activity
5. Instructional activities reader should be engaged in most of the time
6. Information from testing
7. How a reader should respond to unfamiliar words during silent reading
8. Rationale for best reader

Overall Rating: Use the conceptual framework to complete the rating scale.

Strong bottom-up: gave 0 or 1 top-down response; all others are bottom-up, not-enough-information, or non-reading-rationale.

Moderate bottom-up: gave 2 to 4 top-down responses.
Moderate top-down: gave 2 to 4 bottom-up responses.
Strong top-down: gave 0 to 1 bottom-up response.

Adapted from "Clarifying Teachers' Beliefs About Reading" by Mary K. Gove, *The Reading Teacher*, Vol. 37, 1983, pp. 266–268. Reprinted with permission of Mary K. Gove and the International Reading Association.

what is acceptable. Inaccessible reading/writing centers and uninviting activities and spaces affect students' understanding of the value and purpose for reading and writing. They also influence children's voluntary reading and writing. Similarly, rigid seating arrangements do little to advance the cooperative or verbal interaction patterns that are necessary for many students' literacy development. Consequently, these factors are related to the intellectual environment as well.

The *intellectual environment* is established and affected by teacher expectations, student motivation, and literacy goals. Elements related to the development of an appropriate intellectual environment are discussed at length in the section on instruction (see p. 352).

The amount and type of reading and writing that children do is also influenced by the *social-emotional environment*. According to Duffy and Roehler (1989), the social-emotional environment is strongly determined by social interactions, grouping practices, and a general sense of purposefulness. These are discussed in the next section.

Classroom Organization

The teacher's ability to organize the classroom and manage the daily routine influences the amount of time available for teaching and learning. A sound knowledge base and a commitment to literacy are extremely important, but teachers must also know how to maintain a functional learning environment for fairly large groups of children.

Some key focus questions for assessing the organizational factors in classrooms are suggested in Figure 8.3. These highlight various aspects of effective organization, such as the degree to which the teacher has organized classroom routines so that activity focuses on instruction versus management. Any continuing factors or conditions that make it difficult to deliver instruction smoothly should also be identified. Although we have adopted a teacher decision-making stance throughout this text, we are aware that a number of factors can influence teachers' ability to make and execute good decisions. There are a variety of constraints that may be imposed on an individual teacher that influence the organization of the classroom (Mason, Roehler, & Duffy, 1984). For example, teachers in some schools have difficulty arranging their schedules so that they have large blocks of instructional time within which to organize their literacy activities. Such factors obviously contribute to the conditions of instruction and should be identified.

Finally, it is important to consider how effectively the instructional context is managed. Assessment should involve examination of the instructional setting to determine how much time is spent locating materials, identifying students for instruction, and/or transitions. These are obviously worth noting, since they influence students' ability to take advantage of new instruction or gain access to it.

Grouping

As we have seen, grouping practices seem to exert a strong influence on student achievement and motivation. Consequently, effective assessment must include a consideration of school and classroom grouping practices (see Figure 8.4). Teachers often use a variety of organizational patterns in their classrooms. It will be particularly important to identify the variety of patterns and their associated purposes.

Both observation and interviews may be necessary to get a clear picture of the complex ways in which students are organized. For example, it is important to determine what information teachers use to make their placement decisions. Although most teachers make careful and intentional grouping decisions using some systematic procedure, others generate groupings on the basis of "untested assumptions" (Good & Brophy, 1987). An example of an untested assumption might be something like: "Her brother had trouble in reading, so she will too." Placement decisions based on this type of reasoning are obviously problematic, especially because "teacher judgment" is often used to make other educational decisions as well.

FIGURE 8.3

Assessing Classroom Organization

Focus Questions	Yes	No

1. Are classroom rules displayed? If not displayed, are they clearly understood by all?
2. Are there clearly understood classroom routines?
3. Are procedures for seeking help and getting supplies well established and nonintrusive?
4. Do students share the responsibility for routine tasks?
5. Are routine scheduling problems handled smoothly (e.g., movement by some students to special services or activities)?
6. Are transitions between activities handled smoothly and quickly?
7. Describe any notable disrupting factors or significant constraints on optimal organization.
8. Does the teacher make effective use of the available instructional time?

Comments:

FIGURE 8.4

Assessing Classroom Grouping Practices

Focus Questions

1. Is the classroom organized into groups of different sizes?
   _____ Whole   _____ Small
   _____ Pairs   _____ Individual
2. Are these groups permanent or temporary?
3. How are these groups formed?
   _____ Achievement/ability
   _____ Interest
   _____ Specific instructional need
   _____ Other (describe)
4. What criteria are used?
5. For what purpose are these groups used?
   _____ Direct instruction
   _____ Practice
   _____ Support/aid
   _____ Other (describe)
6. How much time is spent in each type of grouping arangement?
7. What labels are used to describe these groups?
8. Is cooperative grouping a present organization? Is paired reading, buddy reading, or peer tutoring used for instruction?
9. What judgments have students made about membership in one or another of these groups?
10. If ability grouping is used:
    a. How much time does each spend in teacher-directed instruction?
       _____ High   _____ Mid
       _____ Low
    b. How much time does each spend in silent reading of connected text?
       _____ High   _____ Mid
       _____ Low
    c. In oral reading of connected text?
       _____ High   _____ Mid
       _____ Low
    d. In paper-pencil seatwork?
       _____ High   _____ Mid
       _____ Low

The assessment of grouping practices should also examine the extent to which membership in a group for one purpose (e.g., a reading group) defines access to other tasks, activities, and levels of achievement. This is a problem especially in middle and junior high schools where scheduling is complicated and the need to receive specialized instruction in reading, for example, may dictate the classes and sections for all other subjects. To gather this information, it may be necessary to observe, or inquire about, the grouping arrangements and grouping characteristics for subjects other than reading/language arts.

As we have already seen, one of the reasons this information about grouping is so important is that it influences the patterns of interaction that occur among peers and between teachers and students. The quantity and quality of these interactions may profoundly affect both achievement and motivation. In the next section, we consider these issues directly.

Classroom Interaction

The nature of classroom interaction can have a substantial effect on student achievement and motivation, but this influence is often very subtle. It is important to recognize how difficult it may be to describe the features of classroom interaction, much less assess its impact. In this section, we will suggest two types of assessment tools that can be used to evaluate the quantity and quality of classroom interaction. The first is a global checklist that can provide a general sense of the linguistic environment in the classroom. The second is much more labor-intensive and would be used sparingly by teachers only when they wanted/needed the most detailed of information about a particular student.

It is possible, and probably useful, to characterize the general pattern of interaction in a classroom. Several short observations can provide answers to general questions displayed in Figure 8.5. The answers to these global questions can give a sense of the amount and type of verbal interaction that occurs in the classroom and the demands and opportunities likely to be present for individual students. In particular, unusual linguistic, cultural, or classroom characteristics can be revealed with this general observation. Occasionally, a much closer examination is desirable or necessary to gather quite in-depth information about the interactions between the teacher and a particular child or group of children. In this case, careful and systematic classroom observation will be necessary. A procedure described by Page and Pinnell (1979) is useful in both classrooms and clinics. This procedure involves tape-recording a "conversation" with the student and then analyzing the verbal interaction using the checklist displayed in Figure 8.6. The authors report that teachers are often chagrined at the analyses that result, since the patterns were not always what they intended: "Teachers only asked questions and students only gave answers. As a result, the language of both was limited" (p. 62). When teachers use these initial results to shape subsequent interactions, there is often dramatically more verbal *interaction*, versus question-response.

If very detailed information is needed, consideration should be given to the Brophy-Good Dyadic Interaction System (Good & Brophy, 1987). This detailed and reliable observation system is quite complex, so we have not duplicated it

FIGURE 8.5
Observing
Classroom
Interactions

Focus Questions

1. How is language/literacy used in the community?
2. Are there any notable characteristics to the linguistic community of the student you are assessing?
3. What judgments does the teacher make about students' linguistic background or the community's use of literacy?
4. In the classroom, who typically initiates language exchanges, decides on the form and content of written work, or controls discussions?

5. Is student-student interaction permitted? encouraged? for what purposes?
6. How often does oral/written interaction serve the purpose of eliciting "set" or "known" responses, versus open discussion or divergent responses?
7. How much nonverbal interaction occurs? What types (e.g. smiling, signaling, physical contact)?

FIGURE 8.6
Checklist for
Analyzing
Teacher-
Student
Conversations

Verbal Behavior	Adult	Child
Asks a question		
Answers a question		
Gives personal information about self		
Gives information about something other than self		
Refers to past events		
Makes a prediction		
Draws a conclusion		
Makes an evaluative statement		
Gives an order		
Makes a request		
Other		

From *Teaching Reading Comprehension: Theory and Practice* by William D. Page and Gay Su Pinnell. Reprinted by permission of the National Council of Teachers of English.

here. However, it can provide important guidance when a close, systematic observation of individual students is needed. Educators should be aware of this instrument, whose purpose is "to determine if individual students receive more or less of certain behaviors than do other students (e.g., Are high achieving female students treated differently than low-achieving male students?)" (p. 84). As we have seen, differential treatment of students within the classroom has serious implications for student learning and motivation. This is especially true to the extent that it influences the quantity and quality of *instruction*.

Congruence Across Settings
Among the most critical aspects of an assessment of the instructional context will be the degree of congruence from one setting to another. In essence, it will be

FIGURE 8.7
Comparing
Instruction
Across Settings

Student Record Sheet
Student Name _____   Homeroom Teacher _____
Week of _____   Grade _____

	Classroom Program	**Remedial Program**
Monday		
Tuesday		
Wednesday		
Thursday		
Friday		

Homeroom Teacher Comments:

Remedial Teacher Comments:

Reprinted by permission of the publisher from Shake, Mary C., "Grouping and Pacing with Basal Materials" in Winograd, Peter N., Wixson, Karen K., & Lipson, Marjorie Y., eds., *Improving Basal Reading Instruction* (New York: Teachers College Press, © 1989 by Teachers College, Columbia University. All rights reserved.), p. 75.

necessary to observe in, and collect information about, multiple settings. A first step involves collecting information about the relationship between classroom instruction and any supplemental or replacement instruction. Shake (1989) has developed a simple form that can be used to summarize this information and that could be completed with relative ease by both the classroom and the remedial teachers (see Figure 8.7). If a communication system such as this already exists, it will obviously be easy to assess the degree of congruence between instructional settings for students receiving special services.

Once the instructional context for a particular student has been described, the information needs to be analyzed and evaluated. In particular, teachers need to examine the degree of similarity between instruction for average/above average students and that received by poor readers. Similarly, consideration should be given to the similarity of approaches used for these groups of students. Guidelines that may help answer these questions are provided in Figure 8.8. If there are substantial and significant variations in the two programs (of the sort described previously in this chapter), teachers and assessment personnel should examine the assumptions and rationale for these programs and procedures very carefully. It is possible that some students may require unusual programs or that remedial programming will be needed in some cases to compensate for unbalanced classroom instruction. However, such conclusions should be based on careful consideration, not unsupported assumptions.

FIGURE 8.8
*Self-
Evaluation of
Instructional
Practices*

Observe your practices with your reading groups for five consecutive days, then answer the following questions.

Content Coverage

1. What is the average number of words read daily in connected text during reading instuction by your
   above-average readers? _____
   average readers? _____
   below-average readers? _____
2. What is the average number of pages read daily during reading instruction by your
   above-average readers? _____
   average readers? _____
   below-average readers? _____
3. What is the average number of stories read each week during reading group by your
   above-average readers? _____
   average readers? _____
   below-average readers? _____
4. What is the average number of new words introduced per story to your
   above-average readers? _____
   average readers? _____
   below-average readers? _____
5. What is the average number of read-ing workbook/worksheet pages com-pleted daily by your
   above-average readers? _____
   average readers? _____
   below-average readers? _____

Are the foregoing numbers for each reader group comparable? If not, which of the following suggestions would be most appropriate in your particular teaching situation?

1. Meet for a longer period of time with the group that has been moving at the slowest pace.
2. Allow the more slowly paced group to engage in repeated readings.
3. Have each student in the more slowly paced group read to an aide or parent volunteer several times weekly.
4. Other _____

Success Rate

1. Can your readers read orally with approximately 95-percent word recognition accuracy
   above-average readers? _____
   average readers? _____
   below-average readers? _____
2. Can your readers answer comprehension questions about what they have read with approximately 75-percent accuracy
   above-average readers? _____
   average readers? _____
   below-average readers? _____
3. Do your readers exhibit mastery of the reading skills and strategies previously taught
   above-average readers? _____
   average readers? _____
   below-average readers? _____
4. Are your readers able to compre-hend successfully when reading independently
   above-average readers? _____
   average readers? _____
   below-average readers? _____

Are any of your students exhibiting reading performance (word recognition and/or comprehension) that falls in the frustrational range?

Reprinted by permission of the publisher from Shake, Mary C., "Grouping and Pacing with Basal Materials" in Winograd, Peter N., Wixson, Karen K., & Lipson, Marjorie Y., eds., *Improving Basal Reading Instruction* (New York: Teachers College Press, © 1989 by Teachers College, Columbia University. All rights reserved.), pp. 78, 80–81.

INSTRUCTIONAL METHOD

In this portion of the chapter, we summarize recent research on effective instructional practices and then suggest several strategies and tools for evaluating how instructional method may be affecting reading performance for individual students.

Understanding the Role of Instruction in Reading Performance

There are two ways in which this research can help in the assessment-instruction process. First, descriptions of good teaching provide a framework for specifying the important attributes of the instructional context. Second, it is important to understand what characterizes good instruction in order to evaluate its contribution to the reading process for individual students.

The question of what constitutes effective instruction has been of consuming interest to educators and researchers for decades. However, during the past 30 years there has been a great increase in efforts to specify the attributes of successful schools, classrooms, and teachers. The important lessons from recent research are that students need to be actively engaged in order to learn, and that initial learning requires teacher modeling and explanation. There is also support for the general conclusion that students need multiple opportunities to learn (Cooley & Leinhardt, 1980). These findings suggest that the effects of instructional method are intimately connected to the classroom management practices and teacher expectations described previously in this chapter. Unfortunately, the evidence also suggests that teachers are spending too much time managing and assessing children through materials by assigning them activities and asking questions, and too little time teaching (e.g., Durkin, 1978–79). It appears that existing methods encourage teachers to view instruction as placement in a program rather than a series of decisions to be made about what content should be taught or what methods might work best.

Research has also identified factors that result in improved performance. Among the most critical is the teacher. Two decades ago, Flanders (1971) found that the teachers in his studies who were least knowledgeable in their content discipline produced the least learning in their students. He concluded: "There is no substitute for knowledge of what is being taught" (p. 66). This has been reiterated more recently as well. Roehler and Duffy (1991), for example, concluded that the key to instructional effectiveness is not the development of newer commercial programs. Rather, it is helping teachers flexibly adapt their instructional actions to fit particular situations. Effective reading programs are created by informed, thoughtful teachers.

In the following sections, we describe the goals, content, and methods of effective instruction as a guide to the evaluation of instructional contexts. However, it is important to emphasize that research on effective instruction in reading is far from definitive. Indeed, the research in this area is so diverse that it is possible to find evidence supporting contradictory practices. Effective teaching can occur within the context of many programs and many materials, but no one set of materials nor any single program is likely to address the needs of every student. Our instructional guidelines are derived from two sources of information: our conclusions about the best theoretical perspectives on the reading process, and our understanding of the best available research evidence regarding effective reading practices.

Considering What to Teach

Reading instruction should be as consistent as possible with our understanding of the reading process. Both instructional activities and student outcomes should emanate from a definition of skilled reading (see Chapter 1). Reading programs should hold as their goal the development of *strategic, motivated readers:*

> The goal of reading instruction should be to develop students' understanding of and control over the reading process. If it does not—if instruction causes students to view reading as a series of tasks rather than a sense-making process—students will probably never experience the full potential of reading. (Duffy & Roehler, 1989, p. 5)

If instruction is to be effective, especially for children who are struggling with reading, then it must be linked to personal "sense-making" for the students. In addition, of course, children must acquire sufficient skill and control to use reading to meet this sense-making goal. In order to accomplish these ambitious—but critical—goals, students need opportunities to learn about *all* aspects of the reading process, in situations that provide for as much authentic application and practice as possible.

Effective teachers establish goals, objectives and specific outcomes for students (Rupley, 1976). In addition, students who are made aware of objectives prior to reading are more successful than those who do not have this benefit. Despite these findings, many teachers are not clear about their goals, and many schools do not have well-considered program outcomes.

Evaluating the instructional context requires consideration of both *overall curricular goals* and *specific lesson objectives*. The fundamental questions to be asked regarding instructional goals and objectives are: What is being taught? and Is the student likely to be a better reader because she or he has achieved this goal or objective? The answers to these questions are explored for general curricular goals in the next section and for lesson objectives in the following section.

Curricular goals. Reading instruction in the United States has too often focused on easily measured subskills. Little attention has been directed toward the acquisition of important overall ability (Brown, Collins, & Duguid, 1989).

> In a well designed reading program, mastering the parts does not become an end in itself, but a means to an end, and there is a proper balance between practice of the parts and practice of the whole. (R. C. Anderson et al., 1985)

The rationale for teaching certain content should be extremely clear, and the ultimate goal of creating strategic, motivated readers must be highlighted. Strategic readers are able to recruit an extensive knowledge and a wide range of skills for reading. In addition, they can use this knowledge and skill flexibly, adapting their approach for different purposes, tasks, and reading materials. For example, strategic readers recognize that recreational reading of light fiction does not require the same intentions or skills as assigned reading of a physics text. Not only do they recognize this, they act accordingly, making adjustments before, during, and after reading.

Motivated readers are those who not only *can* read, but *choose* to do so for a variety of recreational and functional purposes. They generally understand the various purposes for reading and are reasonably skilled at using reading to meet their needs. Not all motivated readers do enjoy and select the same types of reading material, but they do have one thing in common—they read voluntarily.

In addressing these goals, much of the traditional content of reading instruction will continue to be important, but students and teachers must not focus on the acquisition of knowledge and skill as an end in itself. Instead, the goal is for students to use their knowledge and skill as they read widely.

The total reading curriculum across ages and grades must attend to the interplay among these outcomes. A program that does not balance these primary aspects of reading may produce students who can, but will not, read; or students who enjoy books but cannot read them independently. Both breadth and depth are desirable in the developmental reading program, but the relative attention to different aspects of the curriculum may vary across the developmental continuum.

Just as the emphasis on different outcomes may vary across the developmental continuum, it will also vary for individuals who are experiencing reading difficulty. Some children will need to acquire knowledge about reading; others will need ample opportunity to apply and adapt their reading skills; still others will need to develop an increased appreciation for the functional value of reading and reading practice. The issue here is a critical one: *both the content and the delivery system of reading instruction are factors in student achievement.*

Lesson objectives. At the outset, it is important to understand that lesson objectives are not synonymous with activities (e.g., journal writing, dictating stories). When objectives are equated with activity completion, both teachers and students are likely to misconstrue the purpose of instruction. In addition, successful instruction is likely to be measured in terms of the number or levels of activities completed, rather than the extent to which knowledge and/or competence have increased. This is an extremely important distinction that must be understood, both to evaluate and plan effective instructional programs.

The goal of developing strategic, motivated readers can be translated into three types of lesson objectives that relate to the outcomes required for students to become expert readers (Duffy & Roehler, 1989). Sound instruction must contain provisions for each of the following types of outcomes:

1. *Attitude outcomes:* Students need to develop the motivation and desire to read for a variety of personal purposes.

2. *Content outcomes:* Students need to be able to comprehend and learn the content of texts.
3. *Process outcomes:* Students need to understand how the reading process works and acquire skill in using this knowledge.

We begin our discussion of specific types of lesson objectives with the most neglected area in reading instruction: attitude objectives. Although most teachers assert that they want students to be motivated to read, few instructional programs provide directly for the development of attitude outcomes and fewer still include assessments of attitude when they evaluate the effectiveness of their programs. Just as students vary in their knowledge and skill, they may differ in their attitudes and motivation toward reading. Some students find reading gratifying, and therefore read widely outside of school. Others do very little reading and may come to view skilled reading as tedious word calling, required to complete a number of discrete tasks.

Attitude outcomes are important, legitimate concerns for all teachers. It is possible to argue that "love of reading" must be accepted as a desirable goal without further explanation. However, such declarations are abstract, and unfortunately, many teachers feel guilty when they spend time engaged in activities that might encourage positive reading attitudes. When this happens, teachers too often abandon good practice so that they can spend more time "teaching." However, personal belief in the value of reading is not the only reason for concern about attitudes.

In order to become effective readers, students must demonstrate both *skill and will* (Paris, Lipson, & Wixson, 1983). If they are not willing to engage in independent reading, students will not have sufficient opportunity to practice acquired skills, nor will they develop the facility to read flexibly for their own purposes. The relations between positive attitudes and achievement are becoming increasingly clear. Students' expectations and values have a significant effect on both their effort and achievement (Covington & Omelich, 1979; see Wigfield & Asher, 1984 for a complete review).

If attitude outcomes have been neglected, the same cannot be said about content outcomes. The directed reading portion of lessons has traditionally focused almost exclusively on methods and techniques for helping students to understand the content of specific texts. Teachers should not abandon their efforts to help students comprehend during reading. Obviously students who are struggling to understand the content of texts should be helped in this effort. However, all reading does not entail studying and detailed understanding of the content of text, and children should not be led to believe that it does. Nor should instruction aimed at an understanding of specific content be divorced from instruction in the processes and values associated with a particular type of reading.

Instruction designed only to help students understand specific stories or textbooks aids comprehension, but does little to develop comprehension ability (Johnston, 1985a; Paris, Wixson, & Palincsar, 1986). Effective reading instruction must achieve the delicate balance between focusing on content and developing the ability to process different types of materials for different purposes. Students must acquire the skills and strategies required to comprehend and learn *on their own*, and teachers need to think carefully about how they address these important process objectives.

The absence of instructional focus on process objectives that promote control and independence is especially troubling because research suggests that students learn best what is emphasized in instruction. For example, in an informal study conducted by one of the authors, students in two different classes of fifth-grade students in the same building appeared to be learning very different things about how to understand and remember the information presented in the social studies textbooks. When asked how they would go about remembering the information in their texts, students in the first class consistently responded with "I don't know" or "try hard." Students in the second class consistently responded with strategies such as "well, you have to take notes. Then you have to find a partner and go over your notes."

When speaking with the teachers of these two classes, the teacher of the first class indicated that the students could not read their texts, so he did not ask them to read it independently nor did he give tests in this subject area. The teacher of the second class indicated that he expected students to learn the information in their texts, that he assigned independent reading as homework, and that he gave frequent tests. Although we cannot be certain that the students in the second class actually used the strategies they described, at least they have some knowledge about which strategies are appropriate.

What to teach vs. how to teach. One of the problems with much of the research on effective instruction is the failure to make judgments about what is worth learning and learning to do. The first step in improving reading instruction is to start with important goals and objectives. Once these have been determined, attention can be directed to the best ways to help students meet these goals—the focus in the following sections, in which we move now from *what* is being taught to the methods of instruction or *how* it is taught. The following section is organized according to the categories of goals and objectives described in the previous section. First, there is a discussion of practices associated with achieving the general curricular goals of developing motivated, strategic readers. This is followed by a discussion of specific lesson practices that address attitude, content, and process goals simultaneously.

Creating Motivated Readers—Effective Practices

Students should seek to gain the intended knowledge and skill benefits from instructional activities. They should also be motivated to set goals and use cognitive strategies that are appropriate for doing so. Students' motives, goals, and strategies developed in response to classroom activities will depend both on the nature of the activities themselves and on how the teacher presents these activities to the students.

Reading and reading achievement are powerfully influenced by motivation and attitudes (see Chapter 1). Good and Brophy (1987) concluded that most current research supports an *expectancy × value theory* of motivation. According to this theory, the effort that people will be willing to expend on an activity is a product of the degree to which they expect to be able to perform the task successfully if they apply themselves, and the degree to which they value the rewards that successful performance will bring. This theory of motivation implies that teachers need both to help their students appreciate the value of school activities and to make certain that their students can achieve success in their school activities if they apply reasonable effort.

It is important that teachers use strategies designed to motivate their students to learn from academic activities. But Good and Brophy (1987) argue that certain preconditions must be in place in order for motivational strategies to be effective: (1) the teacher must have created a classroom atmosphere that is supportive of students' learning efforts; (2) students have been given tasks of an appropriate difficulty level; (3) activities have been selected with worthwhile academic objectives in mind; and (4) the teacher shows moderation and variation in using motivational strategies.

Once these preconditions are established, there are several different types of motivational strategies that teachers use to promote students' expectations for success and value of learning.

Motivational strategies. In order to meet challenging goals, students must possess confidence and be willing to take risks; they must *expect* to be successful. Good and Brophy (1987) describe strategies that teachers might use to promote students' expectations for success. Not surprisingly, the most basic strategy here involves assigning tasks on which students can succeed, if they apply reasonable effort, and instructing them thoroughly so that they know what to do and how to do it. Other strategies include helping students to: set appropriate goals; commit themselves to these goals; use appropriate standards for appraising their levels of success; recognize the linkages between effort and outcome through modeling, socialization, and feedback; and view effort as an investment rather than a risk.

Although all teachers are aware of these strategies, they take considerable thought and often additional effort. Good and Brophy (1987) point out that the class as a whole may respond to one level of motivational support, but students who have become discouraged to the point that they give up at the first sign of difficulty or frustration need more intensive and individualized encouragement. Some students will require arranging instruction that virtually guarantees success.

Such strategies are essential because students' expectations for success are often patterned by their judgments about why they succeed or fail, which affect their willingness to try difficult tasks. These judgments are called *attributions*.

Attributing success to ability and failure to lack of effort means the person generally will expect to succeed and will be willing to try more challenging tasks. In contrast, attributing success to a variable factor (like task ease) and failure to lack of ability means that the person will not expect to succeed. When the person fails, he or she will

> give up quickly since extra effort will not overcome the person's perceived lack of ability. (Wigfield & Asher, 1984, p. 425)

Thus, many less-able students may also benefit from "attribution retraining" (e.g., Fowler & Peterson, 1981).

In this case, instruction is aimed at teaching students to: concentrate on the task at hand rather than worry about failure; cope by retracing their steps to find their mistakes or analyzing the problem to find an alternative approach; and attribute their failures to insufficient effort, lack of information, or reliance on ineffective strategies rather than lack of ability. It is important to understand that expectancy affects motivation. In addition, the degree of objective success that students achieve is less central than how they view their performance: what they see as possible for them to achieve with reasonable effort, whether they define this achievement as successful or not, and whether they attribute their performance to controllable factors such as effective strategy usage or to uncontrollable factors such as ability.

Expectancy is not the only factor that influences student motivation. Remember that students must also value the activity. Good and Brophy (1987) suggest different strategies to address the *value* aspects of student motivation. These strategies emphasize motivation for *learning,* not merely performing. Much traditional instruction attempts to motivate students to read and learn in order to meet some performance standard (e.g., to take a test).

> If students are motivated solely by grades or other extrinsic reward and punishment considerations, they are likely to adopt goals and associated strategies that concentrate on meeting minimum requirements that will entitle them to what they see as acceptable reward levels. They will do what they must in order to prepare for tests and then forget most of what they have learned. (Good & Brophy, 1987, p. 308)

Strategies focused on learning, on the other hand, should motivate students to study and learn because they find the information or skill interesting, meaningful, or worthwhile. Although the affective, emotional aspects of this approach to motivation are important, Good and Brophy (1987) argue that these will be insufficient for students in academic settings. Students should be focused on sense-making and importance, not just enjoyment. This, they argue, will result in effective and motivated student effort. Teachers, especially teachers of older students, should attend to these distinctions.

The three general features of classroom learning environments that support the development of student motivation to learn are modeling of the thinking and actions associated with motivation to learn, communicating expectations and attributions implying motivation to learn in students, and creating a supportive environment for learning by minimizing the role of factors that produce performance anxiety. In addition, there are a number of other strategies for inducing student motivation to learn that are more situation-specific. For readers who are struggling in school settings, the issue of motivation and the importance of communicating the value of becoming literate cannot be overemphasized. Effective teaching requires the acquisition of a sophisticated repertoire of ways to focus students on learning.

Voluntary reading. The cost of failing to address motivational issues is high. Too often, repeated experiences with failure or school experiences that do not make the value of reading evident result in students with poor attitudes and limited willingness to attempt reading and writing tasks. The relationship between motivation and reading is painfully illustrated in the following fourth-grade student's response to a question about voluntary reading: "I'd rather clean scum off the bathtub than read" (Juel, 1988). Students with such strong negative feelings about reading are not likely to read voluntarily. These attitudes, in turn, influence ability.

There is a strong association between voluntary reading and general reading achievement (Greaney, 1980; Morrow, 1983). For example, children who demonstrate voluntary interest in books are rated significantly higher by teachers on school performance than are children with low interest in books (Morrow, 1986). They also score significantly higher on standardized tests and in work habits, social and emotional maturity, and language arts skills. Other evidence suggests that time spent in voluntary reading of books is the best predictor of reading achievement gains between second and fifth grade (Anderson, Wilson, & Fielding, 1988). Finally, research suggests that independent reading is one of the major determinants of vocabulary growth, especially during and after third grade (Nagy & Anderson, 1984).

It is clear that most reluctant readers will need experiences that go beyond the instruction provided in commercial programs if they are to become independent, voluntary readers. Morrow (1983; 1986) has conducted a series of studies that have examined instructional practice and its influence on students' motivation to read and their involvement in voluntary reading. Specifically, she has examined the influence of classroom environment (e.g., library corners) and literary activities like book talks on students' selection of reading as a voluntary activity. The following practices appear to influence students' voluntary reading (Morrow, 1989):

1. *Print rich environment.* It appears that children need attractive and accessible library corners that provide a range of materials (books of all types, magazines, and so on).
2. *Active student involvement with reading.* Morrow suggests various teacher-initiated activities and projects related to books. However, she also acknowledges the importance of ample practice time through recreational reading periods.
3. *Adult-child interactions focused on literature.* Teachers must invite children to interact with these materials by reading aloud and telling stories.

These practices are not new, but their importance has been reaffirmed. Teachers need to model their love of reading, but they also need to consider the nature of their planned instructional activities. "If through a teacher's presentations, children learn to associate reading only with repetitious skill drills and testing, they will probably not be encouraged to reach for books on their own'' (Morrow, 1989, p. 220). Reading educators need to recognize how self-regard and motivation are influenced by instructional practices in order to avoid the negative consequences of repeated failure.

Creating Strategic Readers—Effective Practices

Good teaching must include instruction in how to read, remember, and think about text independently. This means both that students acquire reading skill and that they are able to transfer this knowledge to a variety of reading situations and tasks. The problem of how to maintain and transfer skilled and strategic behavior has become a major issue facing educators today. The traditional practice of teaching isolated component parts of reading has proven less effective in improving reading ability on transfer tests and on subsequent achievement tests than instruction that is embedded in more meaningful events.

Current research suggests that it is possible to teach students how to be strategic readers. This research suggests a need for instruction based on the principle of gradually releasing responsibility for learning from the teacher to the student (Pearson & Gallagher, 1983). In the initial stages of acquisition, the teacher has primary responsibility for students' learning. In the final stages of learning, the student has the primary responsibility for practicing and applying what has been learned. What comes between is a form of guided instruction that represents joint responsibility between the teacher and the student. These features are discussed at some length below.

During the acquisition phase of the instructional process, the teacher has the primary responsibility for learning. The attributes of teacher-based instruction that have demonstrably improved reading performance include: clear teacher presentations (Roehler & Duffy, 1984); good direct explanation (Paris, Cross, & Lipson, 1984); modeling and guided practice (Palincsar & Brown, 1984); high levels of active student involvement (Palincsar & Brown, 1984); and providing for review and feedback (Adams, Carnine, & Gersten, 1982). Using these techniques, researchers have demonstrated improvement in students' decoding abilities (e.g., Cunningham, 1990), vocabulary knowledge (e.g., Pany & Jenkins, 1978), and comprehension ability (e.g., Paris, Cross, & Lipson, 1984).

Although the relative contributions of these separate teaching practices have yet to be determined, it appears that clear, specific, teacher explanation is particularly important to students' improvement. Clear explanations provide students with knowledge about how to accomplish various reading tasks. However, knowledge about *how* to perform a skill or strategy does not ensure that students will use it.

To increase the likelihood that students will use their skills, teachers must provide students with information about when and why to use the skills they are learning. Research suggests that this is a critical factor in students' ability to transfer the skills they have learned to other reading contexts (Cunningham,

1990; Paris, Lipson, & Wixson, 1983). Although it may seem obvious to teachers, students frequently do not understand how skills acquisition is related to real-life reading. Thus, effective reading instruction must also involve feedback on the utility of the action (Lipson & Wickizer, 1989) and instruction in why, when, and where such activities should be applied (Paris, Cross, & Lipson, 1984).

As the student becomes more skilled, the responsibility for continued learning becomes shared between teacher and student. A study by Gordon and Pearson (1983) can be used to illustrate how this gradual release of responsibility might actually be accomplished. In this study, learning to make inferences was conceived as involving four tasks: (a) posing a question, (b) answering it, (c) finding evidence, and (d) giving the reasoning for how to get from the evidence to the answer. Release was accomplished through four stages of instruction. In stage 1, the teacher modeled all four tasks; in stage 2, the teacher did (a) and (b) while the students did (c) and (d); in stage 3, the teacher took responsibility for (a) and (c) and the students did (b) and (d); and in stage 4, the students did all but (a).

Once students have acquired sufficient knowledge and skill to work independently, the primary responsibility for learning is transferred to the student. Effective instruction provides students with many opportunities to advance their learning by using their literacy skills in productive and authentic ways. The effects of practicing reading and writing in holistic settings have become increasingly evident in recent years. Beginners can enjoy intensified gains when provided with increased opportunities to read and write large numbers of texts (Pinnell, 1985a); 7- and 8-year-olds enjoy significant increases in meaning vocabulary when they listen to good books (Elley, 1989); individuals at many ages recognize more words after reading them in continuous text (Herman, Anderson, Pearson, & Nagy, 1987; Nagy, Herman, & Anderson, 1985); and both comprehension and vocabulary have been improved when students' recreational reading is increased (Anderson, Wilson, & Fielding, 1988).

We will return to these issues in later chapters, but the point should be made, since the evidence is quite impressive: students need to read to become good readers, and write to become good readers and writers. Simple workbook completion activities do not provide enough substantial practice and may actually contribute to students' lack of motivation for reading authentic texts outside of school.

The following sections discuss three notable characteristics of the gradual release model of learning and instruction: scaffolding; social interaction; and level of instruction.

Scaffolding. The hallmark of instruction involving the gradual release of responsibility is *scaffolding*. Scaffolding has been described as instructional assistance that enables someone to solve a problem, carry out a task, or achieve a goal that he or she could not accomplish without support (Wood, Bruner, & Ross, 1976). The metaphor of a scaffold calls attention to a support system that is both temporary and adjustable. Teachers should expect students to need their support in moving from one level of competence to the next so that, in time, they will be able to apply problem-solving strategies independently and wisely (Paris, Wixson, & Palincsar, 1986).

Scaffolded instruction begins with selecting a learning task for the purpose of teaching a skill that is emerging in the learner's repertoire but is not yet fully developed. The task is evaluated to determine the difficulty it is likely to pose for the learner. This is done to facilitate decision making about how to make the task simpler and the learner more successful. Modeling, questioning, and explanation are used during instruction to make the task explicit and to represent appropriate approaches to the task (Palincsar, 1986).

There is considerable emphasis on student participation in the learning activity for the purposes of providing opportunities to use the skills being instructed and evaluating student performance. This evaluation is conducted to determine the level of difficulty of the task, make appropriate adjustments in the level of instructional support, and provide the learner with information regarding their performance. Finally, the aim of scaffolded instruction is generalization to less-structured contexts. Such generalization is facilitated by the gradual withdrawal of the scaffold as the learner demonstrates increased competence (Palincsar, 1986).

Dialogue. Instruction in the gradual release model is also characterized by the ongoing interplay between teacher and learner in the joint completion of a task. These dialogues are the means by which support is provided and adjusted. When children engage in subsequent problem solving, they display the types of behaviors that are characteristic of dialogues they had when they were collaborating with a more expert individual. Palincsar (1986) suggests the following characteristics of dialogue:

1. The teacher supports students' contributions to the dialogue, eliciting and supporting responses at the idea level (versus asking for one-word, discrete responses).
2. The teacher uses student ideas and links those ideas to new information.
3. The dialogue has a focus and direction.
4. The teacher makes use of explicit instruction.
5. The teacher uses feedback constructively to help students improve their responses.

The relationship between teacher and learner in this supportive dialogue is to be contrasted with that observed when students are left to discover or invent strategies independently, or when students are passive observers who receive demonstration and are "talked at" regarding strategy use. When this type of dialogue occurs with initial instruction, it "enables learners to participate in strategic activity even though they may not fully understand the activity and would most certainly not be able to exercise the strategy independently" (Palincsar, 1986, p. 75). The available evidence suggests that teachers generally conduct monologues, not dialogues, and rarely use student ideas as the basis for discussion and teaching. Teachers are taught to "tell" and are rarely provided with instruction or guidance in conducting effective dialogues with students.

Level of instruction. A gradual release model of learning and instruction draws heavily on Vygotsky's (1978) view of the relationship between instruction and cognitive development. According to Vygotsky, instruction is best when it proceeds ahead of development and arouses those functions that are in the process of maturing. In other words, instruction leads development. Cognitive skills that are emerging but not yet fully mature are considered to lie within the zone of proximal or potential development. This zone is defined as:

> the distance between the actual developmental level as determined by independent problem solving and the level of potential development as determined through problem solving under adult guidance or in collaboration with more capable peers. (Vygotsky, 1978, p. 76)

This means that instruction is likely to be most effective when teachers identify the zone or levels at which students can perform with some assistance and guide them to the point of independent learning.

A familiar example offered by Au and Kawakami (1986) may be helpful in describing what instruction within the zone of proximal development might look like. They observed skilled teachers conducting reading comprehension lessons and noted that these teachers consistently posed questions they knew their students were likely to have difficulty answering. This, the authors argue, demonstrates how the children were being challenged to perform at higher levels than they were able to achieve independently. They also observed that the teachers responded to incorrect answers by helping the students work out a better answer, rather than just giving them a correct response. Thus, students were given the opportunity to carry out rather advanced comprehension skills, if only with considerable assistance.

The appropriate level of instruction may also be influenced by other factors, such as the difficulty of the materials in which students are placed. Many poor readers are placed in materials that are so difficult that they cannot identify even 80% of the words correctly (Juel, 1988). Experts argue that an astonishing 50% (Guthrie, 1980) to 60% (Ekwall & Shanker, 1985) of all elementary grade students are working with inappropriate instructional materials for reading. This and other factors influencing the appropriateness of the level of instruction are discussed in greater detail in Chapter 9.

Strategies and Tools for Assessing Instruction

Although the tools of instructional assessment are somewhat limited, it is possible to gather information about the instruction received by specific students. Some information may be collected by interviewing the teacher and/or the student. Additional information can be gathered by examining materials and assignments (see Chapter 9). However, reliable conclusions about the instructional context require some amount of classroom observation. In this chapter, we are suggesting that it is important to observe the context for learning, not just the student in that context. This can be a tricky business. It can also be extremely important.

Because teachers may be fearful about being observed (Stallings, Needels, & Sparks, 1987), the purpose of the observation should be made quite clear. It is important to keep in mind that the purpose is not to pass judgment, but rather to try to determine what, if any, contextual factors might be altered to improve the match between what the student needs and what the classroom instructional setting provides. In the following sections, we describe several ways to assess the instructional context, focusing on the focus of instruction, the degree of motivation, and the method or approach being used.

Focus of Instruction

Descriptions of the focus of instruction involve a number of interrelated issues. The curricular goals and lesson objectives generally provide the most relevant information about the instructional focus. However, because teachers frequently rely on commercially prepared materials to specify their instructional program, it will sometimes be necessary to infer an instructional focus from the content and materials being used (see Chapter 9). In this section, we focus on ways to assess the *outcomes* and *balance* of the reading program for particular students.

Recall that the overarching goal of reading instruction should be the development of strategic, motivated readers. To do this, teachers must provide instruction aimed at three large categories of outcomes: attitude outcomes, content outcomes, and process outcomes. One of the ways that assessment information about the instructional focus can be gathered is to ask teachers to complete "focus sheets" that suggest the degree to which their instruction is focused on one or another of these major outcomes. An example of a brief checklist that can be used to assess the instructional focus is provided in Figure 8.9. As always, instructional practice needs to be assessed *in relation* to important outcomes.

Another indicator of the focus of instruction is the amount of time spent on various activities. One way to organize observational data is to summarize activities in terms of the amount of time allocated to them (Good & Brophy, 1987). This technique has been used, for example, to examine the amount of direct and indirect reading activity that occurs in a given context (Leinhardt & Seewald, 1980). *Direct reading activities* are those that involve either oral or silent reading of words, sentences, or connected text. *Indirect reading activities* are those that involve manipulating materials, writing, listening, or discussing without reading silently or orally. This type of observational system can provide useful information, especially if distinctions are made in terms of the amounts of actual text reading that is done. It is apparent from Figure 8.10 that students in the remedial classes studied spent only 10 to 20% of their time actually reading connected text (even when a single paragraph is considered connected text).

Observation can be used for other purposes also. The orientation of a classroom can be determined using procedures adapted from Good and Brophy (1987) to compute the amount of time spent in various types of activity (see Figure 8.11). In this way, the various types of reading and literacy events can be examined and classroom instruction can be described more fully. Generic categories or general teaching behaviors can obscure clear differences between classrooms in how time is used. By using reading-specific time samples, it may be easier to determine possible areas for intervention.

FIGURE 8.9
Instructional Focus Sheet

Checklist for Providing a Balanced Focus in Reading/Writing Instruction

Are students being given opportunities to develop *positive attitudes* toward reading?
- Are you providing for daily SSR?
- In reading, are you encouraging students to immerse themselves in reading and responding?
- Do you provide ample opportunity to discuss interesting ideas from books and writing?
- Are students encouraged to share what they have read? What they have written?
- Do you provide guidance in selecting good books and support in reading them?
- What other practices promote a positive view of reading and writing?

Are students directed toward important *content* in their reading and writing?
- Are you providing support for students to identify the important information in text?
- Are questions focused on important information in text?
- Are students expected to integrate information from a variety of sources?

Do students have ample opportunity to acquire important *process skills*?
- Do you provide direct instruction in reading strategies and processes?
- Do you model effective reading strategies for students?
- Do you help students to acquire important information about reading?
- Are students encouraged to recognize patterns in their reading so that they can use the knowledge and skill they possess?

These types of assessment techniques are especially useful because they can also suggest the degree to which the reading program is *balanced*. In some classes, significant attention is devoted to isolated word-level work but little attention is devoted to the reading of whole texts. In others, students are rewarded for completion of specific reading products (e.g. reports or worksheets) but are not really expected to read silently during sustained reading periods. In still others, children are expected to spend time with books, but praise and rewards are delivered for quantity of books read without attention to the significance or merit of these books. Each of these can create different student outcomes, different student attitudes, and/or different student knowledge. Thus, a significant issue should be to describe as fully as possible the range of time and activity spent on various outcomes to assess the balance of the program.

Instruction and Motivation

As we have seen, instructional techniques and student motivation for learning are strongly related. Student interviews can be exceptionally useful in assessing the relationship between instruction and motivation. Some of the interviews we have already suggested may provide information about the quality and appropriateness of the instructional program (see Chapters 3 and 7) although these should clearly be designed or adapted to gather information about specific aspects of the setting or instruction that may be influencing the student.

FIGURE 8.10

*How Time Is
Spent in
Remedial
Reading
Classes*

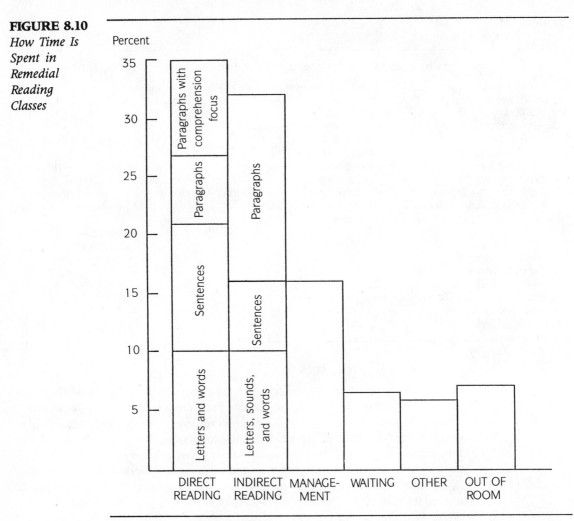

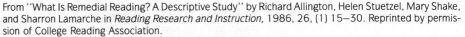

From ''What Is Remedial Reading? A Descriptive Study'' by Richard Allington, Helen Stuetzel, Mary Shake, and Sharron Lamarche in *Reading Research and Instruction*, 1986, 26, (1) 15–30. Reprinted by permission of College Reading Association.

For example, interviews can be structured to collect information about the motivational impact of units of instruction. Rogers and Stevenson (1988) asked students questions such as: What went well for you? What did you enjoy most? Should the study of _____ be a part of everyone's education? Interestingly, the last of these questions often provoked the most honest assessment of interest *and* learning. Perhaps asking a question that is more distant and less personal encourages richer thinking.

The interview information will, of course, be supplemented with data gener-

FIGURE 8.11

Teacher's Use of Time in Key Literacy Activities

Behavior Categories	Coding Instructional Activities			Summary	
	Starting time	Behavior code	Elapsed time	Behavior code	Total minutes
1. Use of basal (teacher-directed instruction)				1.	
2. Use of literature (with students)				2.	
3. Teacher read aloud				3.	
4. Teacher initiated talk (lecture)				4.	
5. Teacher-student dialogues about reading/writing				5.	
6. Student initiated talk				6.	
7. Student-student talk				7.	
8. Children reading connected text				8.	
9. Children writing connected text				9.	
10. Management, transitions, etc.				10.	
11. Other (specify)				11.	

Directions: Use the behavioral categories to code instructional activities. Note the starting time and duration of each behavior.

ated through observation. The instructional context should be examined for evidence of the motivational practices we described earlier (see Figure 8.12). Although these strategies cannot be quantified easily, this is not necessary. A strongly negative profile of instructional factors linked to motivation can provide important information about the achievement and progress of specific students.

Instruction and Strategic Learning

The issues that we have been discussing up to now have tended to be quite global, cutting across the curriculum and often touching on aspects of instruction that are important for all learning. In this section, we describe some focus questions for assessing the salient features of the reading method. Many of these issues are taken up again in Chapter 9 because the method of instruction is so closely linked—especially in elementary schools—to the instructional materials employed. Questions like the following should be used to evaluate classroom methods and approaches.

- Is the general approach to reading basal-based? literature-based? based on subskills mastery learning curriculum? some combination of these?
- Does the teacher attempt to meet individual needs by grouping? altering

FIGURE 8.12

Assessment of Motivational Strategies

Motivational Analysis of Tasks and Activities

Use: Whenever particular classroom tasks or activities are observed

Purpose: To identify the motivational elements built into the task or activity

Check each of the motivational elements that was included in the observed task or activity.

A. Extrinsic motivation strategies

_____ 1. Offers rewards as incentives for good performance

_____ 2. Calls attention to the instrumental value of the knowledge or skills developed in the activity (applications to present or future life outside of school)

_____ 3. Structures individual or group competition for prizes or recognition

B. Intrinsic motivational features of the task or activity

_____ 1. Opportunities for active response (beyond just watching and listening)

_____ 2. Opportunities to answer divergent questions or work on higher level objectives

_____ 3. Immediate feedback to students' responses (built into the task itself, rather than provided by the teacher as in C.8 below)

_____ 4. Gamelike features (the task is a game or contains gamelike features that make it more like a recreational activity than a typical academic activity)

_____ 5. Task completion involves creating a finished product for display or use

_____ 6. The task involves fantasy or simulation elements that engage students' emotions or allow them to experience events vicariously

_____ 7. The task provides opportunities for students to interact with their peers

C. Teacher's attempts to stimulate students' motivation to learn

_____ 1. Projects intensity (communicating that the material is important and deserves close attention)

_____ 2. Induces task interest or appreciation

_____ 3. Induces curiosity or suspense

_____ 4. Makes abstract content more personal, concrete, or familiar

_____ 5. Induces dissonance or cognitive conflict

_____ 6. Induces students to generate their own motivation to learn

_____ 7. States learning objectives or provides advance organizers

_____ 8. Provides opportunities for students to respond and get feedback (asks questions during group lessons, circulates to monitor performance during seatwork)

_____ 9. Models task-related thinking and problem solving ("thinks out loud" when working through examples)

_____ 10. Includes instruction or modeling designed to increase students' metacognitive awareness of their learning efforts in response to the task (includes information about mental preparation for learning, about the organization or structure built into the content, about how students can impose their own organizational structures on the content to help them remember it, or about how to monitor one's own comprehension and respond to confusion or mistakes)

Notes:

FIGURE 8.13
Observing
Instructional
Support and
Dialogue

Focus Questions:	**Yes**	**No**	**Sometimes**

1. Does the teacher encourage students' acquisition of new or difficult material?
2. Does the teacher support this process by modeling? providing guidance? Providing other supports (specify)?
3. Does the teacher engage in dialogue (versus lecture)?
4. Does the teacher support students' contributions to the dialogue?
5. Does the teacher use student ideas and link those ideas to new information?
6. Does the dialogue have a focus and direction?
7. Does the teacher make use of explicit instruction?
8. Does the teacher use feedback constructively to help students improve their responses?

content? changing the tasks? providing different levels of support? Does not appear to differentiate instruction in any way?

- How are students placed in materials?
- Is reading/language arts instruction defined (by the teacher) in terms of a specific published program (e.g., "Ginn")? Does the teacher/school draw from a variety of sources and define the reading/writing curriculum in terms of clearly established outcomes?
- What is the relationship between the method used in this classroom and that used by other teachers in the building?

Asking yourself or the teacher these questions results in useful descriptions of the instructional method employed by the teacher. In some schools these components of instructional methodology may be dictated by the administration of the school. In others these are informally decreed between and among teachers so that deviation from these practices may result in ostracism from the mainstream of professional contact. However, in most schools, teachers have a great deal of discretion about how they deliver instruction, especially if they have proved themselves to be reasonable, responsible professionals.

Other aspects of instructional method are so individual that it will be difficult to evaluate the extent to which they are used without close observation in the classroom. These two important aspects of method are the amount of scaffolding and the quantity and quality of dialogue. In addition, there are simply no good tools to evaluate these critical features of effective instruction. However, we can look for some specific teaching behaviors as we observe in the classroom (see Figure 8.13). Few teachers have been well trained in these methods, but some have developed these skills to a high degree. The presence or absence of these methods will most likely influence the achievement or involvement of some less-skilled students.

FIGURE 8.14
TIES
Components

Instructional Rating Profile

How characteristic of the student's
instructional environment are
indicators of effective instruction in
each of the following areas:

(Circle one in each row)

	Not at all	Not much	Somewhat	Very much
1. Instructional Presentation	1	2	3	4
2. Classroom Environment	1	2	3	4
3. Teacher Expectations	1	2	3	4
4. Cognitive Emphasis	1	2	3	4
5. Motivational Strategies	1	2	3	4
6. Relevant Practice	1	2	3	4
7. Academic Engaged Time	1	2	3	4
8. Informed Feedback	1	2	3	4
9. Adaptive Instruction	1	2	3	4
10. Progress Evaluation	1	2	3	4
11. Instructional Planning	1	2	3	4
12. Student Understanding	1	2	3	4

From *The Instructional Environment Scale* by James E. Ysseldyke and Sandra L. Christenson. Copyright ©
1987 by James E. Ysseldyke and Sandra L. Christenson. Reprinted by permission of PRO-ED.

The Instructional Environment Scale (TIES)

The publication of *The Instructional Environment Scale* (TIES) by Ysseldyke and
Christenson (1987) represents the first serious effort at systematically assessing
the impact of instruction on student performance. TIES is based on this premise:

> Learning and behavior are not independent of their surroundings . . . student per-
> formance in school is a function of an interaction between the student and the
> instructional environment. The relationship among student characteristics, academic
> outcomes, and the nature (or quality) of the instructional environment is reciprocal.
> (p. 1)

Thus, the focus is on evaluating individual students in their instructional environment. The authors describe two major purposes for using TIES: "(a) to systematically *describe* the extent to which a student's academic or behavior problems
are a function of factors in the instructional environment, and (b) to identify
starting points in *designing appropriate instructional interventions* for individual students" (p. 3).

Three sources of information are tapped when using TIES to judge the quality
of the instructional environment: a teacher interview, a classroom observation,
and a student interview. At the heart of TIES is the *Instructional Rating Form*. Using
research on teacher effectiveness as the basis for development, the authors created
this scale of items for 12 component areas (see Figure 8.14). The scale used on the
rating form ranges from, "very much like the student's instruction" to "not at all
like the student's instruction." Each of the 12 components is assessed using this
scale. An extensive set of "descriptors" is provided to guide the judgments in each
component.

The authors clearly state that this is not a norm-referenced test, but rather a qualitative scaling instrument. The technical adequacy of TIES appears to be acceptable for an instrument of this type. The authors rely heavily on inter-rater agreement in rating the instructional environment. Most reported that reliability coefficients are above .90 (with lower reliabilities reported for the two components of Cognitive Emphasis and Motivational Strategies). Although these suggest excellent reliability, it is very likely that untrained users of this test would generate much lower coefficients because of the large number of descriptors and categories that must be considered. The extensive research base for the component categories supports the content validity of the instrument.

Despite some difficulties with TIES, it represents a welcome addition to the repertoire of tools available for assessment. First, it broadens the database upon which decisions about children will be made. Indeed, some states now expect that this instrument will be used to gather information when a special education eligibility determination is being made. A second benefit of TIES is less obvious. So exhaustive are the indicators included in the booklet that it may provide an educative function for some teachers and supervisors. As such, it may prove helpful as teachers and support personnel strive to improve the instructional environment for all students.

FROM CLASSROOM TO CLINIC

It should be apparent that differences between classroom and clinical settings may result in dramatic differences in both teaching and learning. Students' behavior in one setting may not be at all representative of their behavior in others. Similarly, teachers may be led to provide different instructional opportunities to students depending on the context and on their assumptions about students and goals.

Teachers in both settings must reconfirm their commitment to teaching children who are having reading problems. Intransigent belief in one particular approach for all children or hubris about instructional methodology apparently prevent professionals in some settings from communicating about what is necessary for individual students. When teachers in classrooms and clinics share students, there is a professional responsibility to work toward effective instruction. This will necessitate discussions on a wide range of issues. For example, teachers must ask whether to use materials that are the same or different; whether supplemental programs should offer instruction not provided by the classroom teacher or instruction that supports the classroom teaching; and whether these programs are compensating for poor instruction in one or another setting. There are no clear-cut answers, but focused, appropriate educational programs require careful planning and thoughtful teaching.

In addition, both classroom and clinic teachers must systematically assess context, adding this information to portfolios of student work. The focus should be on gathering continuous information and exploring the effects of different setting and task conditions on the learning of particular students. It is essential to note whether and when students' performance is improved by variations in setting and method. Teachers can accomplish this using self-assessments, or they can enlist the help of other professionals to conduct interactive evaluations of students and teachers together.

It is unfortunately true that at least some students are placed in a classroom or other instructional context that is inappropriate, or worse. There are no easy answers here. Reading professionals, school administrators, and peer coaches must all take responsibility for our educational settings. Examination of instruction context is a first step toward improved teaching and learning for all children.

CHAPTER SUMMARY

The content and discussion in this chapter are relatively unusual. Reading assessment has traditionally looked to the student as the source of all academic difficulties. However, a growing body of research demonstrates that many contextual factors contribute to literacy and can enhance learning or lead to difficulty. In this chapter, we acknowledge this fact and examine ways to include contextual information in a comprehensive assessment of individual reading/writing difficulties.

First, we briefly discuss the difficulty of defining literacy, noting that standards of competent performance are determined by culture. Following this brief discussion, we devote a large segment to one specific context: the instructional setting or school environment. Several key issues are addressed to promote understanding of complex and interrelated features of school life. For example, differing *beliefs* lead different teachers to create diverse learning *environments* and to make a variety of *curricular decisions*. These can result in problems for students whose own expectations and beliefs may be at odds with the teachers. However, even when there are no significant mismatches, the level and type of *classroom activity* influences learning. Similarly, *grouping patterns* and membership affect student achievement and perceptions, often negatively. These are discussed as well as the differential treatment teachers frequently offer to members of different ability groups. More subtle differences like those related to *patterns of verbal interaction* are also described, since they influence learning. Finally, we note the importance of *congruence* between regular and remedial programs.

In the third major section of this chapter, instructional methods and practices are examined directly. The assessment of curricular goals is central to these examinations. Three types of outcomes were described: attitude, content, and process. These, in turn, were used to discuss appropriate objectives for instruction and were used to discuss effective instructional methods. We noted that effective instructional techniques share several common characteristics. For example, students are more successful when they are provided with information about how to do the task but are also given some information about the *value and usefulness* of the skill or strategy. This is often accomplished most successfully if the teacher or a competent peer *models* the task for the child. Teachers, then, ensure learning and comprehension by providing *guided practice* and planning for a *gradual release of responsibility*. Finally, teachers must provide extensive *opportunities for students to read and write for genuine purposes in meaningful settings*. Finally, effective instruction enhances motivation. Instructional practices that promote motivation are those that help students to generate *expectations for success* and also help them to focus on learning versus tasks completion as a *valued* endeavor.

Techniques for gathering information about each of these aspects of instructional setting and methods involve interviews and observations. Some of these are very informal and others are more highly structured. For example, gathering information about grouping practices will generally be done using an informal observation and summary sheet. Verbal interaction patterns, on the other hand, generally require systematic data collection and analysis. Finally, a relatively new standardized tool, TIES (The *Instructional Environment Scale*) was described and evaluated, with the conclusion that it adds an important tool to the repertoire of evaluation strategies for assessing context.

CHAPTER 9

Evaluating Instructional Materials and Tasks

INTRODUCTION

We hope it is obvious by now that instructional materials and tasks are intimately linked to the factors discussed under setting and methods in Chapter 8. This close relationship is acknowledged in the introduction of all contextual factors in Chapter 8 (see Figure 8.1, p. 331) and by the fact that we conclude this chapter with a discussion of all dimensions of the reading context as we reexamine Step 3 in the assessment-instruction process. Although the division may be somewhat arbitrary, we hope that it facilitates a closer examination of the contextual factors that can influence reading performance.

Chapter Overview

In this chapter we continue the evaluation of the instructional context by focusing on the role of instructional materials and tasks in reading performance. We describe ways to evaluate texts, teacher's manuals and instructional plans, and instructional tasks and practice activities. Finally, we examine ways to use and evaluate microcomputer software in reading instruction.

UNDERSTANDING THE ROLE OF MATERIALS AND TASKS IN READING

An increasing body of research suggests that the nature of the texts and tasks readers encounter in instructional settings has a significant effect on their learning and performance. This realization has forced both educators and publishers to examine their assumptions about the sources of reading difficulty, and has encouraged special education practitioners to promote "curriculum-based evaluations" (see Howell & Morehead, 1987). A reading assessment for any individual is incomplete until we have identified the characteristics of the texts and the tasks that are regularly used for instruction.

Text Factors

Researchers have identified a number of text factors that influence readers' comprehension, fluency, memory, and enjoyment of selections. This discussion focuses on two aspects of textual materials that are particularly relevant to our concern for evaluating instructional texts. These are the type and structure of text and the features of text that contribute to its overall "considerateness" or comprehensibility.

Text Type and Structure
A major factor in determining students' reading performance is the type of text being read. Research in this area suggests that major differences exist between

narrative (story) and expository (informational) text. Narrative text is often characterized by specific elements of information such as problem, conflict, and resolution. Expository text, by contrast, is usually described in terms of organizational structures such as cause-effect, compare-contrast, or descriptive. Generally speaking, the evidence suggests that narratives of all sorts (even unfamiliar ones) are easier to understand than expository texts (Graesser & Riha, 1984). Differences in text structure and organization, as well as purpose, probably contribute to the differences readers experience in reading narrative and expository texts. In the following section, we describe separately what is known about the structure of stories and informational texts and its influence on reading performance.

Narrative. A narrative tells a story about human events and actions. As we have noted elsewhere (see Chapters 4 and 7), researchers have concluded that narratives have an identifiable structure. Although different types of narrative such as fables, mysteries and adventures vary in specific ways, they also have some features in common. Common features of narrative include: characters; setting or time placement; complications and major goals of main characters; plots and resolutions of complications; emotional patterns; and points, morals, and themes (Graesser, Golding, & Long, 1991).

The principal purpose for stories is often assumed to be entertainment, but "the range of purposes for telling a story is as varied as the motives that underlie human behavior. Thus, stories can be used to cause pain as well as pleasure (e.g., to embarrass, to humiliate, to parody, to flatter, to console, to teach, to arouse guilt, etc.)" (Stein & Policastro, 1984, p. 116). The close connection of text type, text structure, and text purpose is worth noting, since readers and listeners anticipate organizational patterns that match the purposes of the discourse. For example, listeners do not expect the same features of discourse from a conversation or an amusing cocktail story as they do from newspaper editorials.

There is strong evidence that individuals build internal story structures and that they use them to aid comprehension during reading. Text organization helps readers predict, focus attention, and retain or recall content (McConaughy, 1982). Both children and adults comprehend better when story content is organized so that it conforms to expectations (Mandler & Johnson, 1977; Mandler, 1978; Stein & Glenn, 1979; Stein & Nezworski, 1978). When stories contain missing segments (e.g., initiating events) or altered sequence, readers comprehend and remember less (Thorndyke, 1977).

Because the internalized sense of story seems so central to comprehending narratives, it is important to understand something about its development. Even very young children appear to have a rather well-developed sense of story. Recent evidence also suggests that poor readers, at least by sixth grade, have as well-developed a sense of story as do good readers, and that they use it to enhance comprehension (McConaughy, 1985). It should also be noted that these internal story structures appear to develop as children listen to and read well-formed stories. Thus it is extremely important that disabled readers are offered well-crafted stories containing strong story structures, so that they can develop this sense of story early and make the most efficient use of this knowledge.

FIGURE 9.1
"The Shoemaker and the Elves"

Tap, Tap Story

Tap, tap, tap. See me work. I make good things.
See the red ones. See the blue ones. See the yellow ones.
No, no, no. I do not want red ones. I do not want blue ones.
I want green ones.
No, no, no. I do not want big ones. I want little ones.
No, no, no. I do not want little ones. I want big ones.
Oh, my. Oh, my. No one wants my things. I will go to bed.
I will work in the morning.

Tap, Tap Story from *Learning to Read in American Schools* by R. C. Anderson, J. Osborn, and R. J. Tierney. Copyright © 1984 by Lawrence Erlbaum Associates, Inc., Publishers. Reprinted by permission.

Unfortunately, many of the reading selections used to teach children to read and to help remedial readers are poorly written. Beck, McKeown, and McCaslin (1981) concluded as they analyzed basal stories that these types of selections can pose serious impediments to comprehension, since "the printed texts in the earliest school reading materials are not in themselves complete stories or even complete messages" (p. 780).

The "story" in Figure 9.1 is typical of a certain class of selections encountered in schools. The most obvious problem with this text is that it simply does not conform to our expectations for either the content or organization of stories. In terms of content, for example, we expect that stories will revolve around some type of conflict—environmental conflict, interpersonal conflict, or internal conflict (Bruce, 1984). The segment in Figure 9.1 contains no such elements, and it is difficult to imagine what would drive a reader through the text. The structure and organization of this selection do not conform to traditional story grammar descriptions. This type of reliance on artificial texts actually may make reading *more* difficult. Children find them uninteresting and difficult to comprehend, since they do not invite reader involvement (Bruce, 1984).

Informational texts. Whereas even young children seem able to recognize and use story structure, it appears that even middle-grade students are either unaware of or unable to use expository text structure to aid comprehension (Elliott, 1980; Taylor & Samuels, 1983). Several factors probably account for this. First, there are many ways to organize information in expository texts, and the patterns aren't so clearly defined. Five common structures are used repeatedly in textbook writing, at least in the Western hemisphere (Armbruster, 1984):

1. *Simple-listing:* Information is presented in an unordered list.
2. *Comparison/contrast:* Ideas are described in terms of their similarities and differences.
3. *Temporal sequence:* Time order of ideas or events is used to organize the text.
4. *Cause/effect:* The presentation of ideas or events focuses on the causal relationships between and among them.
5. *Problem/solution:* Relationship between and among ideas or events are linked

so that one represents a problem and the other(s) represents a solution to that problem.

The research in this area suggests that not all of these text patterns are equally easy for young readers. For example, under some conditions simple listing is more difficult than compare/contrast because it requires readers to impose an organization, often by inferring the relationships between and among listed items (Meyer & Freedle, 1984). Although the ability to use text organization to increase learning and promote comprehension improves with age, reading ability differences are also noted by the middle grades. Good readers at the junior high level are better than poor readers at recognizing and using text structure in informational texts (McGee, 1981, 1982).

A second reason why children may have less skill in reading expository text is that they typically have much more limited experience in reading this type of material. In the past, basal readers have provided very few informational selections, and what they have had typically does not represent the types of material found in textbooks. In addition, many schools do not use textbooks at the early levels for content area instruction. As is true for all aspects of reading, children must have many opportunities to hear or read informational text if they are to become proficient at reading them. Finally, differences between good and poor readers' ability to read exposition may be related to opportunity, since it appears that poor readers have even fewer opportunities to read informational text than good readers (Allington, 1984).

Even when elementary students do have the opportunity to read, they are often offered poor examples of exposition. The quality of textual materials influences performance *for all readers* (see Shimmerlik, 1978). Studies designed to compare readers' comprehension of organized versus disorganized texts have consistently demonstrated that comprehension and recall are strongly affected by the organization of ideas in text. Well-organized text that highlights the overall structure and supports the relationships between ideas contributes to comprehension and enhances recall. Poor readers appear to be affected by these factors more seriously than good readers (Meyer, Brandt, & Bluth, 1980).

Well-structured text promotes the integration of knowledge so that more cognitive resources are available to process new, more complex information. In turn, these more organized knowledge structures promote complex comprehension activities, such as generating inferences, summarizing, and evaluating (Anderson & Armbruster, 1984a). Poorly written text is difficult even for proficient readers to comprehend and remember. Students, especially those with reading problems, need to read *good* informational texts. In the next section, we turn our attention to the features of texts that contribute to comprehensibility, or considerateness, of text.

Text Features That Influence Comprehensibility

The term *considerate texts* was coined by Armbruster and T. Anderson to describe texts that enable readers to gather appropriate information with minimal effort, as opposed to inconsiderate texts that require readers to put forth extra effort in order to compensate for the inadequacies of the text (Armbruster, 1984; Anderson & Armbruster, 1984a). Although the principles for analyzing considerate text were designed for subject area textbooks, we believe that they apply equally well to narrative materials. The features of text that contribute to its considerateness are discussed briefly in the sections that follow. They are coherence, unity, audience appropriateness, and adjunct instructional aids.

Coherence. Coherence means "a sticking together" (Anderson & Armbruster, 1984a, p. 204). The ideas and concepts in texts are tied together by an underlying cohesive structure. In coherent writing, the author has moved smoothly from one idea to the next, making it easier for readers to understand the big ideas.

Coherence influences reading performance. Indeed, according to Armbruster (1984), coherence is the text factor that exerts the strongest influence on comprehension and learning. When reading coherent (versus less coherent) text, readers take less time to read, they recall more, and the integration of ideas is improved (Goetz & Armbruster, 1980). Readers are better able to build a model of the meaning of text when it has a strong cohesive structure, which functions like a "roadmap to understanding" (Binkley, 1988, p. 104).

Although hardly a routine part of reading assessment, it is absolutely essential to evaluate the texts and materials used for assessment and instruction. In coherent text, the author clarifies facts and helps the reader to understand the significance of these ideas or events. There are many ways that authors tighten relationships and increase the flow of ideas (Grimes, 1975; Halliday & Hasan, 1976). Authors can make effective use of *reference* by using pronouns to link previous or forthcoming events, people, and things. Similarly, authors use *lexical repetition and synonyms* to tie ideas together—for example, by repeating key words several times or using other words with the same meaning (e.g., *elephant* and *lumbering animal*). Both reading time and recall are improved when authors repeatedly refer to key ideas (Goetz & Armbruster, 1980). Coherent text also makes effective use of *intersentential connectives* such as *therefore* and *obviously* to tie ideas together. Finally, coherence is affected by the overall organization of the information in the text.

Inconsiderate text that does not take good advantage of cohesive devices is a particular problem for young and poor readers. Stories for young or less-able readers frequently suffer because of attempts to control difficulty by using roundabout language or by omitting information completely. This can result in highly contrived and incomplete selections such as the example provided in Figure 9.1. According to Green (1984), this excerpt is from a version of "The Shoemaker and the Elves." Key words such as *shoemaker, elves,* and *shoes* are never used (see Figure 9.1).

Both able and less-able readers appear to take a very long time to recognize fully and use most cohesive ties in text (Bridge & Winograd, 1982). However, some aspects of cohesion seem to pose special problems for less-able readers. For example, simple conjunctions such as "and" appear more difficult for less-able readers than other types of connectives (Bridge & Winograd, 1982). Since conjunction does little to illuminate the key relationships between and among ideas, readers need to make additional inferences, something that seems to be hard work for poor readers. Similarly, although the absence of explicitly stated connectives makes reading more difficult for all readers, the need to infer connectives poses more serious problems for less-able readers (Marshall & Glock, 1978–79).

Unity. Although unity in text is closely related to coherence, they are not exactly the same thing.

> Unity refers to the degree to which the text addresses a single purpose. The author of a unified text has not strayed from the purpose by including irrelevant and distracting information. (Anderson & Armbruster, 1984a, p. 209)

The importance of unity can be seen quite clearly in the sample fifth-grade social studies text presented in Figure 9.2. Although this selection suffers from several problems, one of the greatest is its lack of unity. The reader is hard-pressed to know just what is important. Readers with little knowledge of the Civil War (most fifth-grade students) will have a difficult time forming an integrated picture of the information in this section of text, since the selection moves from topic to topic so quickly. Similarly, poor readers will have trouble because there is little opportunity to use prior knowledge (either preexisting or garnered from text) as an aid to comprehension.

Text unity is likely to have an especially strong effect on both less-knowledgeable and less-able readers. In order for comprehension to occur, readers need to integrate text information with prior knowledge and also integrate the information from one part of the text with information from earlier parts. If this does not happen, readers' memory for the text will be limited because they will be forced to recall isolated facts rather than organized sets of information (Anderson & Armbruster, 1984a).

Audience appropriateness. "Audience appropriateness refers to the extent to which the text matches the reader's knowledge base—knowledge both of the content and of discourse features such as syntactic and rhetorical structures" (Anderson & Armbruster, 1984a, p. 212). Authors of books for young people, and the publishers who distribute them, have a responsibility to consider how appropriate both the content and structure of their materials are for those who are not yet expert in terms of either skill or knowledge.

Evaluating appropriateness can be extremely tricky for teachers who have had many more experiences in the world, and are themselves often content experts.

> Teachers often fail to recognize inconsiderate text because they are familiar with its content. They need to keep in mind that their students lack most of the background knowledge needed to understand the vocabulary, concepts, difficult pronoun referents, and allusions. (Wisconsin Department of Public Instruction, 1989, p. 35)

Textbook selection committees that examine materials for audience appropriateness are likely to choose exposition that does a better job of advancing both content and process goals (see Chapter 8).

FIGURE 9.2
Social Studies Text

The North and the South at War

In 1861 Lincoln became the President of a divided United States. He took the oath of office on a high platform in front of the capitol in Washington, D.C. He was dressed in a black suit, a stiff white shirt, and a high silk hat. He carried a cane with a gold handle.

Lincoln stepped forward and placed his left hand on a Bible. Raising his right hand, he promised to "preserve, protect, and defend the Constitution of the United States." People wondered how he would do this. Seven states had already left the United States. Would Lincoln try to punish them? What would he say about slavery?

Lincoln did not answer all of these questions in his Inaugural Address. He said that no state had the right to leave the United States. He warned that he would protect the forts and buildings which belonged to the United States government.

War broke out only a few weeks after Lincoln became President. It became known as the Civil War.

The war began at Fort Sumter in South Carolina. Fort Sumter was on a small island in Charleston harbor. Find it on the map. It belonged to the United States government. Union soldiers from the North held the fort. South Carolina, now a part of the Confederacy, ordered Fort Sumter to surrender. When the commander of the fort refused, the food supply was cut off.

Lincoln had food shipped to Fort Sumter. This made Confederate leaders angry. Southern soldiers fired on the fort. Northern soldiers fired back. A fierce battle took place. At last the Northern soldiers had to give up. This was the first battle of the Civil War.

Thousands offered to serve in the Union Army. Thousands rushed to join the Confederate forces, too. Everyone hoped the war would be over soon. But it wasn't. It dragged on for four years.

During the second year of the war, both sides ran short of troops. They then drafted, or ordered, people into the armies. This was the first time in United States history that soldiers were drafted.

Both sides needed money, supplies, and troops. Money-raising events were held in the Union and in the Confederacy. Groups were formed to help the families of soldiers.

Women who had never worked outside their homes went to work in offices and factories. Some women ran the family farms and businesses for the first time. Others knitted and sewed uniforms and made bandages to use in the hospitals.

Doctors and nurses went to serve on the battlefield. Mary Walker was one of the doctors. At first, she was allowed to work only as a nurse. Later, though, she became an Army officer and worked as a doctor.

Clara Barton was called the "Angel of the Battlefield." She was born on a Massachusetts farm on Christmas Day, 1821. For a while, she taught school near her home. Later she moved to Washington, D.C. She was a clerk in one of the government offices.

When the Civil War began, Clara Barton carried medicines and food to injured soldiers. The officers ordered her away. They said the battlefield was no place for a woman. But she did not give up. In fact, she got other women to join her. After a time, she ran a large hospital for wounded soldiers.

Clara Barton served suffering people the rest of her long life. She helped to find missing Union soldiers. She took care of the victims of wars in other parts of the world. She helped people who had lost homes in fires, floods, and storms. She founded the American Red Cross.

Dorothea Dix was another nurse during the Civil War. She had spent years trying to make life better for people in prisons and poorhouses. During the Civil War, though, she took time out from her work to care for wounded soldiers. She was in charge of all the nurses for the Union Army.

Even when materials are generally appropriate for the intended audience, however, mismatches can occur. This is where the knowledgeable and thoughtful teacher will need to exercise judgment. When working with special student populations or when the overall school curriculum does not support the content, we must make sure that we are judging the contribution of these materials to reader performance. Under some circumstances, failure to comprehend has very little to do with reading skill.

Adjunct aids. Adjunct aids are the structural features of texts that are intended to supplement or complement the information in the written text. They include features such as illustrations, headings and subheadings, boldfaced type, charts and figures, introductions and summaries, and questions either within or at the end of a reading selection. These features are included specifically to focus and guide readers' understanding, and are common in materials used for instructional purposes. A less common adjunct feature of text is *metadiscourse,* in which the author addresses the reader directly: "The author might point out the purpose or goal of the text, indicate what information is essential for achieving it, advise readers on how to learn from the text, and show readers how to apply information gained from the text to other situations" (Singer, 1986, p. 115). Because students' awareness of and responsibility for their own learning can be improved with metadiscourse, textbooks should be examined for evidence that this guidance is provided.

As with other features of the text, adjunct aids have an impact on students' comprehension and learning. For example, when topic sentences are clearly present, readers comprehend and recall text content better (Bridge, Belmore, Moskow, Cohen, & Matthews, 1984). Furthermore, comprehension of main ideas is enhanced when they are stated explicitly at the beginning of paragraphs or text sections (Baumann, 1986) or are highlighted in some way (Doctorow, Wittrock, & Marks, 1978).

The mere presence of such features does not ensure enhanced comprehension, however. Students must be aware of these features and understand how they contribute to understanding. Many of the adjunct aids described above are unique to the materials used for instructional purposes, and students may need direct guidance and explanation from teachers in order to take full advantage of these text features.

The Role of Commercial Reading Programs

Commercially prepared reading programs are another type of material that can influence students' learning and performance. It is estimated that at least 90% of all classrooms in the United States use commercially prepared basal programs to teach reading (Goodman, Shannon, Freeman, & Murphy, 1988), and that between 75 and 90% of the instructional time devoted to reading in American schools is occupied with the materials provided by basal reading programs (Osborn, 1989).

Basal reading programs include a multilevel series of materials for both the student and the teacher. At each level, student materials consist of an anthology of reading selections and a workbook of practice exercises. The primary material for the teacher at each level is a detailed teacher's guide that includes extensive teaching directions and suggestions. For many teachers, the basal series is their reading program. Therefore, it is important to examine these materials to understand the nature of the instruction received by many of the students who are experiencing difficulty with reading.

The student anthologies contain a variety of different types of reading selections appropriate for students at each grade/ability level. Although basal reading anthologies contain a variety of text types, narrative texts predominate. This is particularly true at the early reading levels where there has been a prevalence of "pseudo-texts" that have been created especially for these types of instructional materials. These selections contain highly controlled vocabulary and, often, distorted syntax intended to simplify initial reading experiences. However, they do not represent any authentic text types that exist outside the instructional context, and they can be unnecessarily difficult because the language and story structure are artificial.

When informational texts are included in basal reading anthologies, they are often not representative of the full range of informational materials students encounter outside the context of reading instruction. Conspicuous by their absence are informational reading selections similar to those students encounter in their subject area textbooks and for which basal programs purport to prepare students. According to Barr and Sadow (1989), the organization of materials can have a "profound effect" on teachers' use of fiction and nonfiction material. Specifically, they report that when nonfiction material is bound in separate volumes, teachers use it far less than when it is interspersed among fiction selections.

Many students with reading problems read only what is in their basal anthology. Consequently, the nature and organization of selections that students are exposed to in these readers can have a major impact on their ability to read. If basal reader anthologies are the primary instructional material, teachers must ensure that the selections in the anthologies represent the full range of materials students of a given age/ability will read in all school and non-school settings. Students must have the opportunity to read many types of age-appropriate materials for a variety of purposes if they are to become competent readers.

The reading anthologies are only one area that requires evaluation. Workbooks that accompany each level of a basal series also require careful examination. Students in basal programs spend the largest portion of their instructional time working in these materials, and the nature of workbook activities can have a significant impact on student's understanding of the nature of reading and writing. The features of these and other types of instructional tasks and practice activities are discussed further in a subsequent section of this chapter.

Finally, the teacher's guides that accompany each level in a basal reading program influence classroom practice, and the instructional activities used by teachers reflect those described in the teacher's guide (Barr & Sadow, 1989; Durkin, 1984; Shannon, 1983). Teacher's guides provide a variety of information, including replicas of both the selections and the workbook pages that appear in the students' materials; organizational procedures to follow in implementing the program; specific directions for presenting prescribed skills; suggested questions to ask when discussing selections with students; enrichment activities for use as follow-up or culminating activities; and tests that can be used to evaluate student achievement. The centerpiece of the teacher's guide is the lesson plan that is used to teach both the reading selections and the skills that comprise each instructional unit. The next section examines in detail the traditional lesson plan used in commercially prepared reading programs.

Lesson Plans

The lesson plan, used to organize instruction, is a feature of virtually all commercial reading programs. These plans exert an extremely strong influence on both the content and the delivery of reading instruction in American schools. The lesson plan, or framework, that has traditionally been used in basal reading programs is the *directed reading activity* (DRA). The DRA was first introduced by Betts in 1946 for the purposes of giving teachers a basic format for systematic group instruction, improving students' word recognition and comprehension skills, and guiding students through a reading selection. It has remained remarkably unchanged since that time.

The general framework of the DRA prescribes activities to do before, during, and after reading each selection in the anthology. Prereading activities in a DRA often include providing relevant background, creating interest, introducing meanings and/or pronunciations for new vocabulary, and establishing purposes for reading. During-reading activities are intended to guide students' reading, and often include silent reading focused on answering purpose-setting questions, oral reading and responding to questions dealing with short sections of the text, and/or oral rereading to clarify or verify a point. Postreading activities are of two types: activities focused on the reading selection, such as group discussion or end-of-selection questions; and activities focused on skill instruction and practice that may or may not be related to the reading selection.

In the following section, we provide the basis for evaluating the traditional basal lessons in the same way we suggested evaluating any instructional methods (see Chapter 8). First, we consider what is being taught: the goals and objectives. Next, we examine how it is taught: the methods and activities suggested.

What is being taught. Although the DRA is designed to facilitate readers' comprehension of the reading selection and to provide skill instruction, these two purposes have typically not been integrated. Traditional basal lessons focus on content goals in teaching the reading selection, process or skills goals in separate skills lessons and activities, and largely ignore attitude goals. Furthermore, skills objectives have taken precedence over content and attitude objectives in traditional basal lessons; "that is, the stated purpose of each lesson is to learn a particular skill (which may or may not be relevant to understanding the reading selection). Students are often held accountable for their skill learning through practice exercises and end-of-unit or end-of-level tests. However, they are rarely held accountable for their comprehension of the reading selection, except through group questioning and discussion" (Wixson & Peters, 1989, p. 22).

Effective reading lessons focus simultaneously on content, process, and attitude objectives. The goal is not simply to teach the content of given selections, or to provide isolated skills instruction, but to promote strategic, motivated reading of a variety of materials for a variety of purposes and tasks (see Chapter 8). The content of instruction should also develop students who can and will apply their knowledge about skills and strategies to a variety of reading activities on a daily basis both in and out of school.

Conventional programs do little to advance these outcomes. For example, Morrow's (1987) analysis of 6 sets of basal readers, Grades K–3, suggests that little attention is focused on the goal of voluntary reading. She analyzed the lessons for plans that promoted voluntary reading and found that only 5 (of 14 possible) activities appeared in 5% or more of the selections. Importantly, four of these occurred only in the supplementary sections of the lesson guide. Many activities, such as discussing authors and illustrators, asking children to record books read, or encouraging children to read to each other, were suggested in the plans less than 1% of the time. Given the widespread dependence on the basal along with the relatively infrequent use of supplementary activities, it would appear that students are unlikely to receive much instruction designed to promote voluntary reading.

The focus on skills instruction in basal reading programs intensified over the last two decades, but now appears to be waning somewhat. Basals are likely to change considerably in the near future, but it is not clear how well these changes will be managed. Certainly older basal lessons need careful evaluation, but newer ones will need to be held to a standard of balanced content, process, and attitude objectives also.

How it is taught. The type of instruction typically associated with the DRA is characterized by teacher-centered activities designed to teach the reading selection, and isolated instructional procedures and independent student practice activities designed to teach skills. The traditional basal lesson plan directs the teacher to ask students to practice or perform a particular task or to ask questions with specific responses.

There is a lack of scaffolded instruction involving the progression from teacher modeling and explanation to independent student practice and application (see Chapter 8). There is little support for engaging in instructional dialogue. Durkin's (1984) analysis of the teacher's guides of five major basal series supports these conclusions. Her analyses revealed the following:

1. The guides provided few suggestions for comprehension instruction but many for review, application, and practice.

2. When instructional provisions *were* offered, they often:
    a. were nonspecific;
    b. failed to link new information to reading (e.g., discussing writer's craft without indicating how this influences reading);
    c. reflected "an eagerness to get to written exercises"; the manual "mentions" the skills or strategy and then quickly moves to brief examples available in application formats;
    d. equated definitions with instruction (e.g., first person and third person narratives are defined but no instruction is offered in terms of how this information should be used during reading);
    e. failed to keep the focus on reading; peripheral skills and knowledge are granted an importance they do not deserve.
3. All the manuals examined tended to substitute application-practice activities for direct, explicit instruction.
4. None provided for good guided instruction during the application phase.

Although many students do eventually learn through these indirect practice methods, many do not, and some are actually misled by the questions and activities provided in basal lessons (Wixson & Peters, 1989).

The traditional DRA promotes the role of the teacher as the presenter and the student as the receiver of information, and encourages teacher-centered patterns of interaction. There is little opportunity for student-initiated involvement, and students have little opportunity to monitor and regulate their own reading. Although there is little direct evidence regarding the effects of different instructional frameworks, it seems safe to assume that a steady diet of teacher-centered exchange would provide different results than a more interactive pattern that placed increased responsibility on the reader (see Palincsar & Brown, 1984).

Examining the lesson plan used to teach reading can help to determine whether there have been opportunities for a particular student to learn a given content. Not infrequently, students who have difficulty reading specific texts or with certain reading skills simply have not had the instructional or practice opportunities necessary to become competent. Such an evaluation can also provide information about what has *not* proved helpful in teaching individual children to read. When an analysis of the instruction and the instructional materials suggests ample opportunity to learn but the child has not benefitted, further assessment and/or diagnostic teaching is needed (see Chapter 10).

The Role of Instructional Tasks and Practice Materials

The opportunity to learn is central to recent research findings, and school tasks are central to this opportunity. Students learn what a task requires them to do and acquire the information and operations necessary for successful task completion. Tasks are defined by Doyle (1983) as a goal and the set of cognitive operations required to meet the goal. Academic tasks are defined by the answers students are required to produce and the routes they can take to obtain these answers. Tasks influence learners by directing their attention to particular aspects of content and promoting specific ways of processing information.

Instructional tasks differ in both their content and their form, i.e., in the procedures, social organization, and products they require. The elements of tasks vary from simple to complex and combine in various ways to shape how students think and how they work by determining how information is obtained, how it is processed, and how it is presented to the teacher for evaluation.

Task Content and Form

Task content refers to the cognitive complexity of the task and reflects the objectives students are expected to attain. Different learning objectives vary in difficulty for students, because they require different levels of cognitive processing and different prerequisite skills (Doyle, 1983). Variations in the difficulty of task content affect student learning and behavior.

Students' reactions to content are also influenced by their beliefs about its inherent appeal, its difficulty, and their familiarity with the topic (Blumenfeld et al., 1987). For example, students are more likely to be discouraged when they confront difficulties with new material because they are more uncertain about their ability. Since performance in the classroom is public and subject to evaluation, few children are likely to be strongly interested in new material, where they may be confused, make errors, or have to exert a great deal of effort unless they are fairly certain they will succeed (Brophy, 1983a).

Task forms also affect learning, irrespective of their content (Blumenfeld et al., 1987). As vehicles for the transmission of content, different forms vary in the extent to which learning objectives are evident to students. Forms differ in the obviousness of their purposes, the complexity of their procedures, the social organization in which they are carried out, and the products that result. For example, the purposes and procedures for completing worksheets are generally more straightforward than those surrounding a discussion.

Certain forms may exhibit more procedural complexity than others, but this can also vary within the same form. When tasks are procedurally complex, students may spend more time carrying out procedures than focusing on the content to be learned. In addition, forms differ in the prerequisite skills they require. The more prerequisite knowledge and skill required to accomplish the task, the more hesitant students may be to work at the task (Blumenfeld et al., 1987). Finally, task difficulty is determined by the nature of the product students must complete for evaluation and by the clarity of the evaluation criteria.

When the product can be evaluated according to numerous criteria, students—particularly younger ones—tend to focus on aspects that are more objective and easier to identify and define (e.g., neatness or length) at the expense of concentrating on content or richness of ideas, clarity of explanations, or complexity of analysis (L. Anderson, 1981; L. Anderson, Brubaker, Alleman-Brooks, &

Duffy, 1985). These tendencies are obviously strengthened when teachers' evaluative comments focus on neatness or effort. If teachers rely on assessment criteria ill-matched to the original cognitive purpose of the task, students will learn to process at the levels required by these criteria. These cumulative effects will be discussed in greater detail in the next section.

The Cumulative Effects of Task

Research suggests that students rely on prior experiences with lesson format and content as a guide to interpreting current tasks. They construct knowledge structures, learning strategies and representations of the subject itself according to their experience. Even when conditions make such approaches inappropriate, students' approach to tasks is strongly influenced by their expectations concerning the form of the product and evaluative criteria to be used in assessment. If teachers do not provide information about product form or evaluation procedures, students will expect their performance to be assessed in the same way and at the same cognitive level as it was previously. So, for example, if students receive a steady diet of literal questions, they will tend to process the text at that level, and attempt to answer more thoughtful questions in the same manner as they have learned to respond to literal questions.

Generally speaking, students have to do two things as part of academic tasks: obtain information from reading/listening, and show teachers that they understand the information by producing a product. In some cases, the form in which information is obtained is different from the form of the product required for evaluation. In some of these cases, students will find it easier to obtain information than to display their knowledge/skill appropriately because the performance task is more complex. Blumenfeld et al. (1987) note that it is possible for students to possess the cognitive skills necessary to achieve the content goal, but to be unable to negotiate successfully the form in which they are required to display their knowledge. The actual problem may be failure to understand the form, rather than an inability to comprehend the content.

The more complex the task form, the more important it is for teachers to provide clear and specific explanation and feedback during the lesson to distinguish between the content and form related aspects of the learning task. Otherwise, students may spend considerable time on aspects of the task that are irrelevant to the learning objective. In such cases, actual time on task may remain high, although much of it may be devoted to aspects of the task that are irrelevant to the successful achievement of the objective.

The manner in which students approach and think about new information depends on their previous experience with the task forms. The more frequent the experience of similar task forms across subject matter, classrooms, and grades, the greater the consistency with which students approach and think about their work. If students are consistently exposed to tasks with simple forms, they will have little practice in the form-related skills of planning, organizing, selecting among several alternative strategies, and monitoring their progress toward a goal. The result is limited opportunities to learn those self-regulation skills essential for accomplishing a variety of tasks (Corno & Mandinach, 1983).

Similarly, this repeated exposure is likely to result in preferences for easy, clearly defined task forms that require minimal time or involvement on the part of the learner. This problem is further compounded when the complexity of either task content or form differs by ability group. To the extent that low achievers are assigned tasks with simple content *and* form, opportunities to develop higher level cognitive abilities become stratified and inequitable (Bowles & Gintis, 1976).

Reading Tasks

Students are confronted with a wide variety of tasks during the course of reading instruction. In many classrooms, they are expected to answer questions, complete workbook activities, read stories and books, produce book reports, write reports, engage in educational games, and complete projects. In some classrooms, they are expected to read for lengthy periods, a task that does not entail an obvious "product." In these classrooms, students are expected to respond in some way—by discussing the book in conferences, writing about the book, describing the book to others in a book talk, or creating an art project. The following sections describe more fully the two most frequently observed tasks in reading instruction—independent workbook activities and instructional questions.

Independent seatwork. Widely published reports suggest that on the average, elementary students spend fewer than 10 minutes every school day reading connected text, and between 40 and 70% of their reading time doing seatwork (L. Anderson et al., 1985; L. Anderson, 1984; Fisher et al., 1980). Since students spend so much time interacting with workbooks or other seatwork, close examination of both the content and use of these materials is essential. As Osborn (1984) has noted, well designed seatwork activities and practices can facilitate the initial teaching of what is new and the maintenance of what has already been taught. On the other hand, poorly designed seatwork activities and practices force children to spend countless hours on boring and sometimes confusing activities that do not promote reading competence.

Reviews of the content of commercially prepared workbook and skill-sheet materials suggest that these materials are unlikely to benefit students in any significant way (R. Anderson et al., 1985). Criticisms of the content of reading workbooks (Osborn, 1984; Scheu, Tanner, & Au, 1989) indicate that most of these materials:

1. involve very limited amounts of reading;
2. focus on isolated drills of skills that are often only marginally useful in learning to read;
3. involve little writing;
4. do not engage students in activities that would promote comprehension;
5. are seldom related to the selection being read.

Basal reading programs are clearly intended to promote reading ability and prepare children to read a wide range of authentic material (novels, reference books, content area textbooks, and so on). However, it is doubtful that this can occur with the steady diet of contrived texts that appear in workbooks. For example, some research suggests the transfer of knowledge and skill from one context to another is far from automatic. Hare, Rabinowitz, and Schieble (1989) found that many students who could identify the main ideas in basal-like skills texts were unable to construct main ideas in more complex, naturally occurring paragraphs.

In addition to the content of seatwork activities, we must be concerned with how seatwork materials are used. In an in-depth study of reading seatwork, L. Anderson et al. (1985) observed eight first-grade classrooms to determine what teachers and students do during the time devoted to seatwork, and how students attempt to understand and complete assigned work. Although there were some differences in seatwork assignments from one class to another, within each class the assignments were similar across time, with the same form of assignment often used two to five times a week. Also, in six of the eight classes observed, over half of the seatwork assignments were given to the whole class, despite the fact that students were assigned to different groups.

L. Anderson et al. (1985) also found that teacher instruction related to seatwork rarely included statements about what would be learned or how the assignment related to students' past learning. When teachers did attend to students doing seatwork, they most often monitored student behavior, rather than their understanding or task performance. Teachers generally emphasized keeping busy and finishing assigned work, not understanding what was being taught.

The seatwork assignments that low achievers received were particularly inappropriate. These students did poorly on their assignments and often derived answers by using strategies that enabled them to complete the assignments without understanding them. These findings are compounded by the evidence (see Chapter 8) that students assigned to lower reading groups spend even more time on worksheet exercises and less time actually reading than students in higher reading groups (Allington, Stuetzel, Shake, & Lamarche, 1986). It is not surprising that these students are especially likely to believe that reading is "finishing the workbook pages."

L. Anderson et al. (1985) suggest that poor seatwork habits developed in first grade may contribute to a subsequent passive learning style. Low achievers, who often work on assignments they do not understand, may come to believe that school work does not have to make sense; therefore, it is not necessary to obtain additional information or assistance as an aid to understanding. In contrast, high-achieving students rarely have difficulty with seatwork, so that any problems they have are more likely to motivate them to seek help.

Good and Brophy (1987) note that, because younger and lower-achieving students may spend between 300 to 400 hours a year doing reading/language arts seatwork, it is imperative that teachers find strategies and activities that enable them to use this time well. They suggest that "successful seatwork activities have the following characteristics: (1) allow students to work successfully and independently, (2) are interesting and reflect variety both in terms of the type of the assignment and how it is completed, (3) frequently allow students to read for comprehension and pleasure, (4) occasionally relate to students' personal lives'' (Good & Brophy, 1987, p. 247).

Based on the evidence available, experts have offered a variety of suggestions about how to improve the seatwork materials and practices that are a large part of reading instruction. With regard to the content of seatwork activities, Cunningham (1984; Cunningham et al., 1989) suggests that seatwork would be of more value if it focused on helping students to (1) access background knowledge and set purposes for reading, (2) follow the structure of the reading selection, (3) become increasingly independent in the use of comprehension strategies, (4) understand why they are doing it and how it will help them be a better reader. Cunningham et al. (1989) also suggest that completed worksheets not be turned in and graded. Rather, students should bring them to the reading group where students should check their own worksheets. Answers should be given and the reasoning behind the answer should be explained. Students who have made mistakes should fix them before turning in the worksheet. Finally, they recommend that teachers let the students teach others by working together to complete their seatwork assignments.

Scheu, Tanner, and Au (1989) suggest a general model for the development of seatwork activities that calls for teachers to act as decision-makers who consider both their students' needs as developing readers and the qualities of the selection to be read. According to this model, teachers should design and assign seatwork tasks based on the kinds of independent practice students need to understand specific selections and to become more proficient readers in general. Activities need to be thoroughly integrated with the reading lessons, because they give students the chance to work independently with the concepts and skills needed for a holistic understanding of a selection. The purposes of seatwork assignments should be explained and discussed. Finally, completed seatwork assignments should often serve as the basis for starting a discussion of the selection.

The increasing consensus among experts is reflected in the recommendations of the Commission on Reading: (1) children should spend less time completing workbooks and skills sheets; (2) children should spend more time in independent reading; and (3) children should spend more time writing (R. Anderson et al., 1985). According to Cunningham et al. (1989), "real" reading and writing activities should be a part of each student's daily seatwork. Unlike the time spent on traditional worksheet activities, time spent reading and writing has been shown to contribute to growth in reading ability. In addition, reading and writing are more interesting, enjoyable, and intrinsically motivating than worksheet activities.

Questions. A variety of different types of questions are used in a variety of ways each day in virtually every classroom. Questions are an integral part of teacher presentations, discussions, seatwork, examinations, homework assignments, and remedial instruction (Dillon, 1988). A variety of question taxonomies have been used to classify various types of questions.

Traditional question taxonomies that classify questions separately from the text or information being questioned (e.g., Barrett, 1976; Bloom, 1956) are inadequate, given an interactive view of reading. Any interaction that occurs as a reader answers questions about a text will have a direct effect on comprehension and/or learning. Indeed, a large body of literature indicates that the type, content, and use of questions all influence student comprehension and learning.

A taxonomy of question-answer relations proposed by Pearson and Johnson (1978) provides one means for examining questions in a more interactive manner. Questions are classified in the context of, rather than apart from, the text or information being questioned. They identify three types of questions based on the probable source of the information the reader will use to answer the question (see Chapter 7). When the information needed is stated explicitly in the text, the question is textually explicit (TE). When the answer is implied rather than explicitly stated, the question is textually implicit (TI). Finally, there are some questions for which the appropriate answer is neither explicitly stated nor implied in the text, but relies heavily on the background information/prior knowledge the reader brings to the text. Pearson and Johnson call these types of questions scriptally implicit (SI), using script as a synonym for schema or knowledge structure.

A study by Wixson (1983a) provides an example of how different types of questions affect students' comprehension of and learning from text. In this study, fifth-grade students wrote the answers to six open-ended comprehension questions after reading an expository passage (see Figure 9.3 for sample passage and questions). Students responded to only one type of question (TE, TI, or SI). One week later the students provided a written free recall of the passage they had read the week before. The results of this study indicated that TE questions promoted verbatim reproduction of the text, TI questions resulted in the generation of text-based inferences, and SI questions led to the production of inferences based on prior knowledge. The effects of different types of questions on students' comprehension and learning can be seen by examining samples of students' delayed recalls (see Figure 9.4).

A second study demonstrates how the content of questions can affect student comprehension and learning (Wixson, 1984). This study was similar to the one just described, except that the questions the students were asked varied according to the importance of the information being questioned. Students learned and remembered best the information they were questioned about, regardless of whether it was important or trivial to the important ideas in the text. For example, 57% of the students who received the question for the "Shrimp Farms" passage about where the scientists started a new kind of farm included the information that shrimp farms were started in Japan in their recalls. In contrast, only 17% of the students who were asked different questions about this passage included this information in their recalls.

It is clear that both the type and the content of questions promote different learning outcomes (Wixson, 1983b). Indiscriminate use of questions can lead readers away from, as well as toward, a desirable learning outcome. Therefore, we must use questions in a manner consistent with the goals and purposes of our instruction. For example, in situations where less inferential processing is desir-

FIGURE 9.3
Sample TE, TI, SI Questions

| Text Sample: Shrimp Farms | Sample Questions: Shrimp Farms |

Text Sample: Shrimp Farms

Some farms are used to grow corn and wheat. Other farms raise animals such as chickens, cattle and turkeys. But in Japan, a few years ago, a scientist started a new kind of farm. It was a farm for raising shrimp.

Shrimp belong to the same family as lobsters and crabs. These long thin sea animals have five pairs of legs which they use to swim backwards.

Shrimp are a valuable seafood. Fishermen usually have to use nets to catch them. But, sometimes the fishing grounds are empty. In bad weather, fishing boats cannot go to sea.

The Japanese scientist raised shrimp in large heated tanks. It took six months for the shrimp to grow from very small eggs to adult shrimp. Most shrimp are three inches long. But, the shrimp raised in the tanks were nine inches long. Also, the tanks were never empty, and the scientist did not have to wait for good weather.

So far, there are very few shrimp farms. But someday there may be many shrimp farms around the world.

Sample Questions: Shrimp Farms

Text Explicit:
   Q: How long did it take the shrimp raised in tanks to become adult shrimp?
   Q: What other animals belong to the same family as shrimp?

Text Implicit:
   Q: How common are shrimp farms?
   Q: Why is it better to grow shrimp on farms?
   Q: What problems do shrimp fishermen have?

Scriptally Implicit:
   Q: Why aren't there more shrimp farms?
   Q: Why do you think the scientist started a shrimp farm?
   Q: Why are the shrimp fishing grounds empty sometimes?

From *Reading for Concepts* by William Liddle. Copyright © 1977, 1970, Webster/McGraw-Hill. Reprinted by permission of Glencoe/McGraw-Hill.

able—such as reading directions or conducting science experiments—explicit questions may be the most appropriate. When the integration of the ideas within a text is desirable, as is often the case in subject area reading, textually implicit questions may be most helpful.

We must also remember that if we ask questions that focus on less important information, students are likely to learn this information at the expense of other, more important content. Furthermore, repeated use of similar types of questions shapes the way students approach their reading assignments. Hansen (1981a) found that students who received a steady diet of inferential questions were able to answer those kinds of questions more easily than students who had been asked only literal level questions.

Good and Brophy (1987) present the qualities of good questions and their use described by Groisser (1964). Good questions are those that are clear, purposeful, brief, natural, adapted to the level of the class/individual, and thought-provoking. Specifically:

1. Questions should clearly cue students to respond along specific lines by communicating what specific question the student should answer.

FIGURE 9.4
Sample Recalls

Sample Student Recalls According to Type of Information Questioned

Text Explicit Information: Student Recall (fifth grade)

"There was a man that started a shrimp farm in Japan. The shrimp had five pairs of legs and some of the animals that are related to them are the lobsters and crabs. When the shrimp are in the tanks they are 6 months old. The shrimp are usually caught in nets."

Text Implicit Information: Student Recall (fifth grade)

"I remember about how they could not always find shrimp in the fishing grounds they had. Or they had bad weather and could not find any. So they put eggs in tanks with all their needs then they got bigger and old and they are perfect to eat. Someday shrimp farms may get very popular and they wil be all around the world."

Scriptally Implicit Information: Student Recall (fifth grade)

"Shrimp farms are different than any other kind of farms. Other farms sometimes have animals like chickens, cows, and/or ducks and horses. Some have food like beans, potatoes, peas, corn, and/or tomatoes and lettuce. A man, I think a scientist, started shrimp farms, he lived by some kind of water, and because shrimp sold good. The Japanese like shrimp, and it is hard to get because sometimes it is not the right kind of weather. I think they found that lights attract the shrimp and they get more shrimp that way."

From *Reading for Concepts* by William Liddle. Copyright © 1977, 1970, Webster/McGraw-Hill. Reprinted by permission of Glencoe/McGraw-Hill.

2. Questions should be purposeful and should help advance the lesson's intent. Irrelevant and confusing questions keep teachers from achieving lesson goals.
3. Questions should also force students to think about facts and to integrate and apply them.
4. Questions should be planned, logical, sequential, and addressed to the group.
5. Questions should be balanced between fact and thought.

During questioning sequences, teachers should provide feedback to students, especially low achievers, about the correctness or incorrectness of their responses. Although this may seem obvious, there is evidence that teachers do not always provide effective and focused feedback (Brophy & Good, 1974).

Students' performance is also affected by the pattern of question-answering that teachers establish in the classroom. Effective questioning requires that students be allowed sufficient time to think about and to respond to questions, yet Rowe's (1974) study of *teacher "wait-time"* provided stunning evidence that students often had little opportunity to produce thoughtful responses. Her observations indicated that after asking questions, teachers waited less than one second for a response before calling on someone. In addition, after calling on a student, they waited only about a second for the student to give the answer before supplying it themselves, calling on someone else, rephrasing the question, or giving clues. Following these observations, Rowe (1974) investigated what would happen if teachers were trained to extend their wait-times to 3 to 5 seconds. These findings indicated that increased wait-times led to more active participation in lessons by a larger percentage of students, and an increase in the quality of the participation.

Subsequent research indicates that pacing and wait-time should be adjusted to the level of questions being asked and the objectives they are intended to address. A fast pace and short wait-time are appropriate for drill or review activities covering specific facts. A slow pace and longer wait times are appropriate when students are expected to think about the material and formulate original responses, rather than simply retrieve information from memory.

Currently, there is a shift away from answering teacher-posed questions with their implied "right" answers. Instead, teachers are often advised to solicit personal responses to reading (Rosenblatt, 1978; Winograd & Johnston, 1987). The long-term effects of this shift have yet to be determined. Although it appears that students can often respond to a piece of writing even though they cannot justify their responses (Galda, 1982), a steady diet of tasks that permit only literal, "correct" responses can result in students who are unengaged in reading and writing as personally important activities (Moffett, 1985; Parsons, 1990). The tension between these two approaches permeates much of the educational field today. Interestingly, this tension is also evident in discussions of the merits and potential application of microcomputer technology, to which we turn our attention in the next section.

The Role of Microcomputer Instructional Materials

The rapid growth in the use of microcomputers for reading and writing instruction demands that separate attention be paid to these specialized materials and tasks. Wisely used, microcomputers can be powerful instructional tools, providing support for instruction in the language arts. Their potential for use with less-skilled readers and writers looms large, but the concerns are no less commanding. Research evidence regarding the effects of computer-assisted instruction (CAI) is inconclusive, and analyses of computer-managed instruction (CMI) raise questions about the validity of most of these programs.

Most educators and researchers do believe that computers can help students become better readers and writers but that teachers will need to exercise both caution and judgment in selecting and using the available materials (Balajthy, 1989b; Young & Irwin, 1988). Although educators must become knowledgeable about both the hardware (the equipment itself) and the software (the programs used on the hardware) of microcomputers, we will discuss only the use of computers and the types of software available.

Microcomputers can be used for any of the normal instructional functions: teaching, application and practice, or testing (Ekwall & Shanker, 1988). However, the vast majority of software programs currently available to teachers involve practice or testing—workbooks presented on computers. Reinking, Kling, and Harper (1985) analyzed 142 software reading programs and found that roughly 70% used a drill and practice format. Similarly, Rubin and Bruce (1985) found that most reading software provided few opportunities to read connected text, dealing with print at only the letter or word level.

The problems that are characteristic of many workbook tasks (see above) also apply to these types of materials, and we will not elaborate upon them. Indeed, to the extent that the software and/or application of microcomputers in a classroom involves a simple replication of other reading or writing tasks, the problems and effects described elsewhere in this chapter can be expected to prevail. For example, students' prior knowledge appears to influence their ability to use computer programs in content area learning (Gay, 1986). Similarly, studies of the effects of various text features in computer instruction (e.g., interspersed directives, study aids, and so on) have generally replicated those with regular print presentation (see Balajthy, 1989a, pp. 111–113).

Rather than reiterate these general issues, we will describe the several specialized functions that have the most currency in instructional settings: word processing, beginning programs and voice synthesizers, and databased systems and specialized software. In so doing, we focus on the unique instructional possibilities and problems of computers and, where possible, describe the effects of computer technology on students' performance, achievement, or motivation.

Word Processing

Word processing programs offer perhaps the most powerful application of microcomputers in classrooms. Word processors are programs that permit the user to enter, delete, and manipulate text. Because these tasks can be accomplished with ease, and because they actually change the nature of the traditional reading-writing connection, word processors offer exceptional flexibility and support for writing. Indeed, the Michigan Reading Association has explicitly stated what many believe: "Students should learn to use word processing in pre-writing, organizing, writing, editing, and proofreading papers in all subjects" (1986, p. 21).

Word processing programs provide optimal support, of course, for teachers who want to focus on the writing process (see Chapters 4 and 14). For example, there is evidence that students using microcomputers produce greater amounts of text than students who are writing conventionally, and that they are more likely to revise their work (Daiute, 1983, 1986). In addition, there is some evidence that students engage in more careful editing when they are using the microcomputer (Daiute, 1986). However, Balajthy (1989a) points out that because students may not be able to view their whole composition on a computer screen, teachers may want (or students may find it necessary) to print a hard copy of the written piece for the purposes of preparing to edit.

There are many commercial software programs whose features provide support at the prewriting, writing, and postwriting phases of the writing process. Of course word processors also allow students to save their stories on disk and make books by printing them. Existing programs can keep word lists or even record the number of times the student has used each word. These can be used for subsequent word recognition activities (Balajthy, 1989b).

The clear advantage of word processors over traditional methods is that students can edit and revise their work without the tedium involved in recopying. In addition, students can produce a reasonably polished product for publication (Balajthy, 1989b). Our experience suggests that even reluctant students are willing to work and rework pieces of writing when they use a word processor. As an added feature, of course, the materials are then available to use in other, related instructional activities (e.g., spelling and word recognition).

Beginning Reading Programs and Voice Synthesizers

One of the most interesting applications of computer technology is only just emerging. Software programs, particularly word processing programs, have added voice synthesizers, or computer speech, to their existing capabilities. Because students can receive immediate word identification help, the instructional possibilities for use with young or disabled readers are significant.

The technology must be evaluated carefully. Available voice synthesizers do not always produce precise sounds, which can render words or sentences difficult to understand (Green, Logan, & Pisoni, 1986). This is a serious problem for everyone, but a critical one for disabled readers. The research does suggest that synthesized speech, in general, is not a problem. Balajthy (1989a) concluded, "While synthesized speech is not as accurately recognized as natural speech, it nonetheless is recognized at a satisfactorily high rate" (p. 123). In addition, these potential problems may be compensated for by the fact that reading comprehension is improved when readers have access to a synthesized vocabulary (Olson, Foltz, & Wise, 1986).

Teachers can expect to see continued improvement in the area of phonemic voice synthesis that will provide for even greater flexibility in use. Currently, many voice synthesizer programs function at only the word level, typically presenting isolated drill and practice activities. There are exceptions, and some commercially available programs already permit students to read full-length children's stories, with the voice synthesizer being used only as a sort of oral word bank.

We have found adaptations of voice synthesizer technology to be powerful tools for use with disabled readers. For example, when linked to word processing programs, students, teachers, or others can type in any piece of text. The voice synthesizer can be set to "read" the text word-by-word as it is being typed, or read the entire text when it is completed. Because the computer reads exactly what has been written, students are encouraged to use their available knowledge and skill to write. If the student produces correct approximations of the phonemes in a word, the result is a recognizable voice rendering of the target word. Of course, it also promotes self-corrections and editing, since gross inaccuracies can be monitored.

Databases and Other Software

There are many potentially useful software programs that "were not written to teach reading but require its use" (Dudley-Marling, 1985, p. 388). Database programs, used for the storage and retrieval of information, enable students to gain proficiency in locating, selecting, categorizing, and organizing information and in using data for drawing conclusions, making generalizations and preparing reports. These capabilities are important for teachers to understand. As Balajthy (1989a) points out:

> No longer are computers seen primarily as instructional delivery systems—as tutors and drillers. Instead, students and teachers are beginning to realize that today's immediately relevant application of the computer is as a tool. It is a tool for many of the same functions for which businesses use computers—the handling of information. (p. 147)

Because of these possibilities, computers provide ample opportunities to integrate the language arts and computer literacy into other areas of the curriculum—to use the technology to accomplish other things more easily. Software programs that involve solving mysteries, participating in simulated adventures, and following directions to solve problems in stories can also be used effectively in the reading/language arts curriculum. These offer exceptionally good practice in reading *continuous text*, something many reading programs do not provide.

There are other innovative software applications that are still not widely available, but are likely to be useful to reading teachers. A software innovation called *hypertext* offers exceptionally intriguing possibilities for teachers who work with less-skilled readers.

> Hypertext is a program that allows information to be connected to other information in any way in which the author wishes. For example, a hypertext passage about the Civil War might contain a mention of Appomattox. Students who did not know what Appomattox was could select an option that presented them with basic information about Appomattox. . . . Unfamiliar words or concepts in the hypertext explanation could also be elaborated in the same way. This system provides a way to account for the variety of student ability and interest levels with great efficiency. (Kamil, 1989, p. 396)

There are now several commercially available products that allow users to develop their own hypertext applications. Teachers could decide, for example, how to display graphics, or could connect certain information that would be helpful for students. Clearly, these types of options may make it possible for teachers to continuously adapt instructional materials and promote individual decision making and monitoring as well.

Although there is not an extensive research base for making judgments about the impact of microcomputer materials on learning, there are several conclusions emerging. First, the types of factors that influence reading of text in regular presentation modes probably affect reading from the monitor as well. In addition, the same types of features that facilitate regular instruction are also likely to benefit students as they attempt to learn from computer programs. Importantly, using the computer to deliver isolated skill and drill instruction is not likely to yield significant benefits. Finally, innovative applications of the technology hold promise for working with less-skilled readers.

Summarizing the Role of Materials and Tasks in Reading

In the preceding sections, we highlighted the role of text, commercially prepared plans, and practice tasks and materials in reading achievement. Teachers need to examine these issues quite closely, since their potential impact on students' reading performance is great. Examining the materials and plans used to teach reading can help to determine whether there have been opportunities for a particular student to learn specific content. Not infrequently, students who have difficulty reading specific texts, or with certain reading skills, simply have not had the instructional or practice opportunities necessary to become competent.

An evaluation of materials and tasks can also provide information about what has *not* proved helpful in teaching individual children to read. When an analysis of the instruction and the instructional materials suggests ample opportunity to learn, but the child has not benefitted, further assessment and/or diagnostic teaching (see Chapter 10) are needed. In order to determine the relative contributions of these factors to a student's reading difficulty, specific tools and techniques can be employed. We turn to these in the next section.

ASSESSMENT STRATEGIES AND TOOLS: MATERIALS AND TASKS

The idea that texts and tasks might exert an independent influence on readers' ability to perform is not a new one. Efforts to assess this influence, especially the relative difficulty of texts, have been fairly continuous for the past 60 years. In this section, we review some older tools and techniques and present some newer alternatives for assessing these factors. In both cases, the purpose for evaluating materials and tasks in the assessment-instruction process is actually twofold: (1) to predict the likely impact of instructional factors on reader performance—to assess the contributions of these factors to reading ability; and (2) to gain insight regarding appropriate instructional materials—to match the failing reader with texts and tasks that result in effective teaching and efficient learning.

Evaluating Text

Teachers have always been concerned about the materials their students read. They have generally recognized that "to teach reading effectively or to help students gain information from text requires a match between the difficulty of the reading material and the reading ability of the child" (Zakaluk & Samuels, 1988, p. 122). Unfortunately, achieving this match is not as easy as had been previously imagined.

We have already described the many factors that can influence how difficult a particular text is for a particular individual—the complexity of which was recognized at least 50 years ago:

> In its broadest sense, readability is the sum total—including interactions—of all those elements within a given piece of printed material that affect the success a group of readers have with it. (Dale & Chall, 1948, p. 15)

The earliest discussions of "readability" assumed that factors such as the physical appearance and format of the print, the style of written expression, language usage, and the content of the text affected the difficulty of the text (Gray & Leary, 1935). In the intervening years, researchers have demonstrated what teachers have long known: that interest, motivation, and prior knowledge also determine how readable a text will be.

Despite the early recognition that determining text difficulty was extremely complex, the tools used to measure readability have generally captured only limited aspects of text difficulty. Importantly, any serious analysis of the forms and functions of narrative and expository text did not occur until quite recently. Prompted by the desire to generate fast and efficient estimates of text difficulty, there has been a proliferation of "readability formulas." We are going to digress somewhat and present a fairly detailed discussion of them, because these formulas still dominate the area of text assessment. We will then turn our attention to a variety of contemporary alternatives.

Readability Formulas

Readability formulas are procedures that have been developed to assess difficulty objectively, generally by counting some text feature that can be easily identified. According to Klare (1988), the first readability formula was developed by Lively and Pressey in 1923. Since that time, over 50 readability formulas have been developed (Schuyler, 1982). To understand the appropriate use and potential misuse of readability formulas, it is important to understand something about their development and notable features.

Developing a readability formula. General procedures used in development are quite similar for all readability formulas (see Conard, 1984, for a complete discussion). Readability formulas are derived from detailed analyses of a small set of passages, called criterion passages. The selection and validation of the original criterion passages is a critical first step, since the difficulty of all other passages will be determined by comparison with these criterion passages and tasks. If the texts and tasks are not similar to those used by teachers, or required of students, then the predictive power of the formula will be weak. Most of the existing readability formulas were validated using extremely short criterion passages.

The criterion passages are then examined and text elements are specified as factors that are likely to contribute to passage difficulty. Once the possible text elements have been identified and quantified, analyses are conducted to determine which are the best predictors of passage difficulty. Finally, a mathematical formula is generated that provides the best description of the relationship between text elements and text difficulty.

Even the earliest readability researchers assumed that critical elements would include text features such as conceptual density and quality of writing. However, these abstract factors proved difficult to measure and were often either not selected for study or were dropped because they could not be counted reliably. The two elements that have proved to be the best predictors of text difficulty (at least using short criterion passages) are semantic difficulty and syntactic complexity of the sentences (Klare, 1984). Semantic difficulty is most often estimated using vocabulary, as measured by either frequency/familiarity or length of words; syntactic complexity is most often measured by sentence length.

Because different formulas have been developed using different criterion passages and different tasks, caution is needed in using any of the existing formulas (see Figure 9.5). For example, the Spache Formula was developed so that it is only appropriate for primary grade passages, while the Dale-Chall is only applicable to materials above the fourth-grade level.

In addition, only some formulas examine elements that have theoretical or empirical support from our newer views of the reading process, and no formula provides a totally satisfactory assessment. For example, the Dale-Chall formula, like the Spache, does not rely on word length to measure semantic difficulty. Instead, passage vocabulary is compared to an established list of familiar words. However, the Dale-Chall has been criticized because of its inadequate criterion validity (Stevens, 1980). Like many other early formulas, the Dale-Chall was developed using short passages with very suspect reliability that were never intended to be used as testing tools.

Using readability formulas. Readability formulas, like the standardized tests described in Chapter 6, have some utility. The greatest strength of readability formulas lies in their ease of use. But they must be used cautiously. One of the easiest and most frequently used formulas today is the Fry Formula (Fry, 1968). It assesses syntactic and semantic difficulty using only counts of syllables and sentence length (see Figure 9.6). Although this obviously provides a limited view of readability, the formula was developed using trade books and other real reading material. The use of rich criterion is a particularly strong feature of the Fry Formula, because the evidence suggests that readability formulas are quite reliable when applied to nonmanipulated texts to rank materials that must be read by a general population (Klare, 1984). If materials are grossly unsuitable for use in a targeted grade, readability formulas can reveal this fact in a time-saving manner so that decisions about text appropriateness may be made more rapidly. However, as the Commission on Reading (R. Anderson et al., 1985) notes, "readability formulas are useful only as a rough check on the difficulty and appropriateness of books" (p. 81).

Precise results are not likely, since you can expect variability in the scores that are generated by different readability formulas. Studies do suggest that the inter-

FIGURE 9.5

Comparison of Readability Formulas

Name of Formula Authors (Publication Date)	Criterion Passages Used for Development		
	Name or type of passages	Number of passages	Range of difficulty
Dale-Chall Formula for Predicting Readability (E. Dale-J. Chall, 1948)	McCall-Crabbs Standard Test Lessons in Reading;	376	Grades 3 to 12
	Health Education, Public Affairs Passages	133	Grades 3 to 16
Reading Ease Formula (R. Flesch, 1948)	McCall-Crabbs Standard Test Lessons in Reading	363	Grades 3 to 12
Readability Formula for Primary Grades (George Spache, 1953, 1974)	Basal and Supplementary readers; Primary science and social studies texts	100 Samples used for revision	Pre-primer to Grade 3
Readability Graph (Edward Fry, 1968, 1969, 1977)	Oxford English Reading Series Elementary Trade Books		
Harris-Jacobson Readability Formulas (A. Harris-M. Jacobson, 1974)	Six Series of Basal Readers	661	Pre-primer to Grade 6

Criterion Passages Used for Development

Criterion difficulty scores	Formulas: elements, weights and constants	Correlation with Criterion	Probable Error of Use
50%–75% Tested Comprehension	.1579 (% unfam. words) + .0496 (av. sen. len.) + 3.6365 (constant)	.70	1.65
50%–75% Comprehension Test Norms	206.835 (constant) − .846 (nbr. of syll.) − 1.105 (av. sen. len.)	.70	1.38
Publishers Grade Level PP = 1.2, P = 1.5 GR1 = 1.8 and 1.9 GR2 = 2.1 and 2.7 GR3 = 3.3 and 3.7	.121 (av. sen. len.) + .082 (% unfam. words) + .659 (constant)	.95	.2 years
Estimated to be 50%–75% comprehension	Grade levels read directly from graph	Graph scores correlate .94 with Dale-Chall scores	Approximately one grade level
Publishers Grade Level PP = 1.2, P = 1.5 GR1 = 1.8 GR2 = 2.3 and 2.7 GR3 = 3.3 and 3.7 GR4 = 4.45 GR5 = 5.45 GR6 = 6.45	Formula I .094 (% unf. words) + .168 (av. sen. len.) + .502 (constant) Formula II .140 (% unf. words) + .153 (av. sen. len.) + .560 (constant)	.90 .90	.38 years .71 years

FIGURE 9.6

*Fry
Readability
Formula*

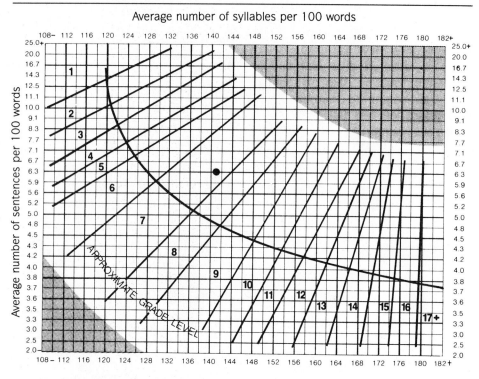

Fry Readability Formula

(Description):

1. Select three 100-word selections from the beginning, middle, and end of the text. Don't count proper nouns.
2. Count the number of sentences in each selection. Estimate to the nearest tenth of a sentence.
3. Average sentence count.
4. Count the number of syllables in each selection.
5. Average the syllable count.
6. Plot the two scores on the graph to get the grade level.

From "A Readability Formula That Saves Time" by Edward Fry (1968). *Journal of Reading, 11*, pp. 513–516, 578. International Reading Association. Reprinted by permission.

formula reliability is a cause for concern (McConnell, 1982), although this appears to be a more serious issue in the upper ranges of the readability estimates (high school and college level texts). Quite substantial variability can result when several formulas are applied to the same piece of text. Differences of two or more grade levels in the estimates generated are not unusual.

For placement purposes, the use of readability estimates alone clearly poses serious problems. When gross comparisons are needed, however, readability estimates can be helpful. If you are going to use these formulas, the tedium of analyzing text can be avoided by using one of the available microcomputer software programs available (Schuyler, 1982).

Criticisms and misuses of readability formulas. Although formulas have proved quick and efficient, there are many concerns associated with them. Some of these have to do with the formulas themselves and others have to do with their use. As Cullinan and Fitzgerald (1984) noted in the joint IRA/NCTE statement on readability (see Figure 9.7), it is not what is measured by formulas that causes concern; rather, it is what is not measured. Among the many factors that have been shown to influence text difficulty but that are not accounted for by typical formulas are text structure, interest and motivation, and prior knowledge (Entin & Klare, 1985; Fass & Schumacher, 1978). In combination, these factors may critically influence the relative difficulty of a selection. A text that may be difficult for one reader may be relatively easy for another of the same reading skill.

One of the most serious concerns about readability formulas involves their misuse in rewriting existing materials, a practice promoted by early formula developers (Dale & Chall, 1948; Flesch, 1948). There has been an understandable temptation to revise text to make it easier and more accessible to readers. However, the indiscriminate use of readability indicators, such as sentence length, to rewrite text has often had the unexpected result of making text more, rather than less, difficult (Davison, 1984; Davison & Kantor, 1982; Pearson, 1974–75). For example:

> *Version 1:* Because the law forbade blacks from sitting in the front of the bus, Rosa Parks was arrested and many black people decided to start a boycott.
> *Version 2:* The law forbade blacks from sitting in the front of the bus. Rosa Parks was arrested and many blacks decided to start a boycott.

Because version 2 requires readers to infer the relationship between two separate ideas, it is likely to be more difficult to comprehend. Most readers have more trouble understanding and remembering inferred material, but poor readers seem to find this especially difficult (Marshall & Glock, 1978–79).

Adapted versions of text also frequently focus readers' attention on information that is only peripheral, suggesting a purpose for a selection that can confuse students (see Figure 9.2). The "simplifications" resulting from use of readability formulas can and do lead to incoherence and increased text difficulty (see Figure 9.1). In addition, of course, such materials place a heavy burden on readers' prior knowledge because the text provides fewer clues for constructing meaning. Indeed, it may actually be necessary to lengthen text through elaboration, paraphrase, and example in order to enhance readability when topics are complex or difficult to understand.

These problems are pervasive in the content area textbooks used in many elementary schools. However, the use and misuse of readability formulas is not limited to these types of text. As we have already noted, many of the instructional materials used to teach beginning readers have been written with readability formulas in mind.

The benefits accrued from using readability formulas need to be assessed carefully against the potential dangers of their use. When these formulas are employed, teachers should keep specific criteria in mind (see Klare, 1984 for

FIGURE 9.7
The IRA/NCTE Readability Statement

Background Information Bulletin on the Use of Readability Formulae

Textbook adoption committees and other educators face important decisions when deciding whether instructional materials are of appropriate difficulty for the students who will use them. Many factors enter into determining the readability of materials, including the syntactic complexity of sentences, density of concepts, abstractness of ideas, text organization, coherence and sequence of ideas, page format, length of type line, length of paragraphs, intricacy of punctuation, and the use of illustrations and color. In addition, research has shown that student interest in the subject-matter plays a significant role in determining the readability of materials.

Matching students with textbooks at appropriate levels of difficulty, therefore, is a complex and difficult task. Various pressures have forced publishers to use readability formulae to assure purchasers that their textbooks are properly "at grade level." Unfortunately, these formulae measure only average sentence and word length to determine the difficulty of passages. Although long words and sentences sometimes create problems of comprehension, they do not always do so. For example, the sentence "To be or not to be" is short, but it includes difficult concepts. This sentence, "The boy has a big, red apple for lunch and some cookies for a snack," is long but simple. Readability formulae would allow the first sentence but not the second.

Serious problems occur when publishers use readability formulae. Authors of materials who are required to write to "fit the formula" often produce choppy sentences full of short words. The language doesn't sound natural to the student, who is a sophisticated speaker and whose own language may be full of complex sentences and multisyllabic words. A second problem is that complex ideas, which depend on complex sentences,cannot be adequately written in the prose style dictated by readability formulae; consequently, learning of the content may be impaired.

Third, there is a real danger that makers of instructional materials will avoid using interesting and important works of literature because those works, which often contain long words and long sentences, don't "fit the formula." Not only the student's interest but also the beginnings of the student's literary education are lost by such omissions.

Educators and publishers should use alternative approaches for measuring text difficulty. Procedures should include:

1. Teacher evaluation of proposed texts, based on the teacher's knowledge of their students' prior information and experiences, and their reading ability and interests.
2. Teacher observations of students using proposed texts in instructional settings, in order to evaluate the effectiveness of the material.
3. Checklists for evaluating the readability of the proposed materials, involving attention to such variables as student interests, text graphics, the number and difficulty of ideas and concepts in the material, the length of lines in the text, and the many other factors which contribute to relative difficulty of text material.

If readability formulae are used at all, they MUST be used in conjunction with procedures that look at all the parts of a text which affect comprehension. Readabilty formulae are simply insufficient as a guide to matching students with books and other instructional material. It is not what readability formulae measures that concerns us; it is what they do NOT measure.

Informed educational consumers must demand the authors and publishers select and develop well-written, literate text materials for students, and all who are involved in preparing and selecting text materials for the schools should cease the practice of depending on readability formulae alone to determine what is readable.

The IRA/NCTE Readability Statement (Bernice Cullinan and Sheila Fitzgerald, 1984), *The Reading Teacher.* Reprinted by permission of the International Reading Association.

further discussion). The joint IRA/NCTE statement (see Figure 9.7) provides guidance in the appropriate use of readability formulas. Importantly, these formulas should not be used to rewrite or write reading materials, and teachers should be cautious of texts that have done so. In addition, users need to be particularly alert to possible mismatches between the reader and the text; readers from nontraditional backgrounds may be influenced by factors not measured in the formula.

Finally, it is a good idea to remember that the purpose of these formulas is to *predict* the difficulty of materials. Formulas do not actually evaluate the relative difficulty that any individual reader experiences during reading of a particular text. As "tests" of reading materials (Chall, 1984), they fall short of providing comprehensive answers to our questions about text quality and appropriateness. We need other ways to evaluate these issues, and we consider alternatives in the next section.

Interactive Readability Measures

As we have noted, the problem with most approaches to text readability estimates is that they do not evaluate how specific text features might actually influence reading performance for a given reader. As Zakaluk and Samuels (1988) note:

> Readability is not an inherent property of text, but the result of an interaction between a set of particular text characteristics and the information processing characteristics of individual readers (Kintsch & Vipond, 1979). Text factors alone cannot determine readability; readers' prior knowledge and understanding influence comprehensibility and recall." (p. 128)

Efforts to develop interactive readability measures that take the reader into account are not new, but are still in need of refinement. Two interactive measures described here are the traditional cloze procedure and a more recent interactive readability formula developed by Zakaluk (Zakaluk & Samuels, 1988).

The cloze procedure. Since its development by Taylor in 1953, the cloze procedure has endured as a method for evaluating text to determine whether students can "understand" it. Although there is substantial disagreement in the reading community about the utility of the cloze procedure as a measure of comprehension, it does provide a quick estimate of the relative difficulty of a particular text for a given student.

Cloze passages are created by deleting every *n*th (usually fifth) word from a piece of text, leaving both the first and the last sentences intact (see Figure 9.8). Students are then asked to read the selection, supplying the deleted words. The rationale for this approach is that students must understand the text in order to supply the deleted words. Concerns about the task itself are more serious when cloze is used to make judgments about reading ability than when it is used to estimate the "fit" between text and reader.

To avoid any difference in judgment between scorers, students' responses are counted correct only when they have provided the exact replacements for deleted words. Verbatim scoring is required in order to use the criteria established by

FIGURE 9.8
Sample Cloze
Passage

New Guinea

New Guinea is a large island in the Pacific Ocean. New Guinea people live _____ tribes. Each tribe is _____ different but all of _____ decorate their bodies. It _____ important to the people _____ do this. In some _____ there are people called "_____ men." They cover themselves _____ river mud and put _____ masks made of mud. _____ other tribes there are "_____ men" who wear big _____ made of human hair.

_____ people in New Guinea _____ live as people did _____ thousand years ago. They _____ use sticks to plant _____ corn and other crops. _____ grow most of their _____ food and make the _____ they need.

Once a _____ tribes from all over _____ island come together for _____ big fair. This fair _____ called a sing-sing. People _____ their best animals and _____ crops to show to _____. The judges decide which _____ the winners. Then there _____ dancing and singing. The _____ and singers paint their _____. They wear fur on _____ ears and headdresses with _____ feathers.

Source: Lipson, M. Y. (1981). Third Grade Readers' Use of Prior Knowledge in Inferential Comprehension. Unpublished doctoral dissertation, The University of Michigan.

earlier studies (see below). Importantly, verbatim scoring produces relatively the same results as the more time-consuming scoring of synonyms (McKenna, 1980).

The cloze score is expressed as a percentage when the number of correct responses is divided by the total number of possible items. The following criteria, developed after substantial testing by Bormuth (1968), are generally accepted, although other criteria have been offered as well (see Pikulski & Tobin, 1982):

Above 57%   Independent Reading Level
44–57%   Instructional Reading Level
Below 44%   Frustrational Reading Level

It is evident that the cloze procedure provides information about text difficulty in terms of the *individual student*. "Formulas predict readability; cloze procedure and other similar comprehension methods measure readability" (Klare, 1984, p. 707). For clinicians this can be extremely useful. However, classroom teachers will need to make judgments about text appropriateness in different ways. In the next sections, we describe some tools for assessing the likely influence of text at a more general level.

An interactive readability formula. Zakaluk (Zakaluk & Samuels, 1988) has devised and validated a readability system for "matching readers with appropriate materials." The *Nomograph for Predicting Text Comprehensibility* is built on an interactive model of text processing and assesses the contributions of both "inside the head" reader factors and "outside the head" text/task factors (see Figure 9.9).

Procedural Guidelines:
1. Assess Inside the Head Factors
   a. Word Recognition—See IRI criteria for independent, instructional, and frustrational (Chapter 5). Points are awarded as follows: 0 = frustrational; 1 = instructional; 2 = independent.

FIGURE 9.9

Application of the Nomograph for Primary Level Text

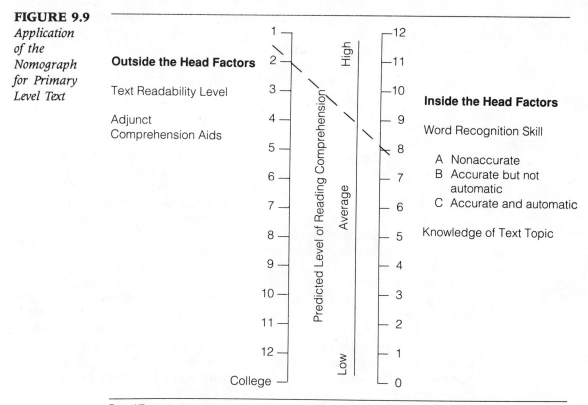

From "Toward a New Approach to Predicting Text Comprehensibility" by B. L. Zakaluk and S. J. Samuels (Eds.), *Readability: Its Past, Present, and Future* (1988). International Reading Association. Reprinted by permission.

   b. Prior Knowledge—See Word Association assessment of prior knowledge (Chapter 7). Readers receive 1 point for each "reasonable idea unit" up to a maximum of 10 points. Ideas are considered "reasonable" to the extent that they represent a focused response to the topic (the content need not be present in the actual text).

2. Assess Outside the Head Factors
   a. Readability level—Use of the existing readability formulas.
   b. Adjunct comprehension aids—Determine existence of aids such as interspersed study questions and statements of objectives. Subtract ½ point from readability score if objectives are provided and another ½ point if the text provides study questions.

3. Assess the Match
   Draw a line between the two scores to determine the ease of reading score for this reader using this text (see Figure 9.9).

Clearly, this nomographic procedure does not consider all textual and non-textual factors. However, it is an improvement over the existing formulas, and it predicts text difficulty for an individual reader. In addition, there is evidence of the validity of this technique ($r = .93$) when used to predict the actual performance of a large number of fifth-grade students (Zakaluk, 1985). Finally, given that much of this information will already have been collected as part of the assessment-instruction process, its application is relatively easy.

Evaluating Text Type and Comprehensibility

It should be quite clear by now that readability estimates alone are unlikely to provide all the information teachers need regarding the difficulty and appropriateness of textual materials for their students. First, not all text types pose the same difficulties, nor are all equally easy to read, even if the readability formula suggests otherwise. Second, the factors not accounted for by readability formulas require attention. In this section we suggest some strategies for evaluating narratives, expository texts, and basal anthologies to determine whether they are "comprehensible" or "understandable" versus "readable."

Narrative text. Two major issues must be addressed in evaluating narratives for comprehensibility. First, the text must be examined to determine if it is well-structured, conforming to conventional expectations for story structure and language use. Next, the narratives should be evaluated to see if they are interesting and enjoyable. The large class of "narratives" includes a wide range of genres, including stories, folktales, fables, fairy tales, tall tales, myths, science fiction (Flood & Lapp, 1987). However, all narratives have something in common and that must be captured in an evaluation of them; they are meant to be interesting and enjoyable.

When the characters and their relationships are well developed and their goals easily identifiable, children read with greater interest and understanding (Sundbye, 1987). Because well-formed narratives are easier to read than more ambiguous ones, they should be evaluated for the common components of narrative texts (see also Chapter 7). Using a summary form such as the one provided in Figure 9.10 might help highlight these important, but more difficult to analyze, aspects of text. In particular, the evaluation should identify the degree to which narratives have strong plots with well-defined characters whose motives and goals are clear. When these aspects of a narrative are obscure, poor readers have much more difficulty comprehending them.

Expository text. As it has become clear how strongly text features can influence text difficulty, a number of guidelines for evaluating informational texts have been generated. One of the most comprehensive of these was offered by J. Irwin & Davis (1980) and is reproduced in Figure 9.11. An especially helpful feature of their checklist is that several dimensions of text difficulty are distinguished and evaluated separately. For example, learnability and understandability are evaluated separately. Consequently, teachers can evaluate the strengths and weaknesses of texts based on the ways they wish to use them.

Expository text can be evaluated for understandability alone. However, when students are to be held accountable for learning and remembering information

FIGURE 9.10

Narrative
Evaluation
Form

Focus Questions

1. How does the story begin (setting, time)? Is the "lead," or beginning of story, powerful? weak? dull?
2. Who are the main characters? Who is telling the story (point of view)? How much do we learn about the characters?
3. What is/are the main problems or conflicts to be solved or resolved? Is the conflict interpersonal? with the environment? internal (between the character and herself)?
4. The Plot: (List episodes using abbreviations to label information: p = problem / r = response / a = action / o = outcome).

   a.

   b.

   c.

5. Does the content of the story/plot teach a lesson (ethos)? help students learn about people, reasoning, problem solving, etc. (functional)?
6. How does the story end (resolution)? Is the ending a satisfying one? interesting? powerful?
7. Other comments (e.g., use of description, language, humor).
8. If this is an anthology of stories (i.e., basal), what is the quality of the stories, in general?
9. Is there diversity?
10. How would you rate the "interestingness"?

Adapted from "The Design of Comprehensible Text" by R. C. Calfee (1987). In J. R. Squire (Ed.), *The Dynamics of Language Learning*. Urbana, IL.: ERIC Clearinghouse on Reading and Communication Skills and the National Conference on Research in English (NCRE). Reprinted by permission of Robert Calfee.

from textbooks, teachers need to evaluate texts somewhat differently. In the event that students have trouble learning information from text, an assessment of the textbook features may provide useful information about how to help them learn and remember more. Alternatively, an assessment may reveal the fact that the text obscures important or new information, making learning difficult. A helpful procedure is described by Armbruster (1984) who suggests selecting a topic from the text and generating several questions that you would expect students to be able to answer after reading about such a topic. Then, read the text and make sure that it is possible to answer these questions using *only* the textual information. When the text does not provide the information or makes it difficult to understand, teachers must be prepared to compensate for the text's inadequacies or elect not to use the text at all.

Careful examination of the text is absolutely essential. Checklists like that in Figure 9.11 can provide important guidance for the exercise of professional judgment. Teachers' estimates often compare favorably with both cloze and formula estimates of difficulty (Harrison, 1979), although the judgments of untrained teachers can vary substantially (Jorgenson, 1975). The reliability of expert estimates can increase when they are provided with criteria. Thus this checklist, like other informal instruments, will be more useful if the criteria are clearly understood and applied in an even-handed fashion.

FIGURE 9.11

Readability Checklist

This checklist is designed to help you evaluate the readability of your classroom texts. It can best be used if you rate your text while you are thinking of a specific class. Be sure to compare the textbook to a fictional idea rather than to another text. Your goal is to find out what aspects of the text are less than ideal. Finally, consider supplementary workbooks as part of the textbook and rate them together. Have fun!

Rate the questions below using the following rating system:

5 = Excellent
4 = Good
3 = Adequate
2 = Poor
1 = Unacceptable
NA = Not applicable

Further comments may be written in the space provided.

Textbook title:
Publisher:
Copyright date:

Understandability

A. _____ Are the assumptions about students' vocabulary knowledge appropriate?

B. _____ Are the assumptions about students' prior knowledge of this content area appropriate?

C. _____ Are the assumptions about students' general experiential backgrounds appropriate?

D. _____ Does the teacher's manual provide the teacher with ways to develop and review the students' conceptual and experiential background?

E. _____ Are new concepts explicitly linked to the students' prior knowledge or to their experiential backgrounds?

F. _____ Does the text introduce abstract concepts by accompanyng them with many concrete examples?

G. _____ Does the text introduce new concepts one at a time with a sufficient number of examples for each one?

H. _____ Are definitions understandable and at a lower level of abstraction than the concept being defined?

I. _____ Is the level of sentence complexity appropriate for the students?

J. _____ Are the main ideas of paragraphs, chapters, and subsections clearly stated?

K. _____ Does the text avoid irrelevant details?

L. _____ Does the text explicitly state important complex relationships (e.g. causality, conditionality, etc.) rather than always expecting the reader to infer them from the context?

M. _____ Does the teacher's manual provide lists of accessible resources containing alternative readings for the very poor or very advanced readers?

N. _____ Is the readability level appropriate (according to a readability formula)?

Learnability

Organization

A. _____ Is an introduction provided for each chapter?

B. _____ Is there a clear and simple organizational pattern relating the chapters to each other?

C. _____ Does each chapter have a clear, explicit, and simple organizational structure?

D. _____ Does the text include resources such as an index, glossary, and table of contents?

E. _____ Do questions and activities draw attention to the organizational pattern of the material (e.g. chronological, cause and effect, spatial, topical, etc.)?

F. _____ Do consumable materials interrelate well with the textbook?

FIGURE 9.11
(Continued)

Reinforcement

A. _____ Does the text provide opportunities for students to practice using new concepts?

B. _____ Are there summaries at appropriate intervals in the text?

C. _____ Does the text provide adequate iconic aids such as maps, graphs, illustrations, etc. to reinforce concepts?

D. _____ Are there adequate suggestions for usable supplementary activities?

E. _____ Do these activities provide for a broad range of ability levels?

F. _____ Are there literal questions provided for the students' self-review?

G. _____ Do some of the questions encourage the students to draw inferences?

H. _____ Are there discussion questions which encourage creative thinking?

I. _____ Are questions clearly worded?

Motivation

A. _____ Does the teacher's manual provide introductory activities that will capture students' interests?

B. _____ Are chapter titles and subheadings concrete, meaningful, or interesting?

C. _____ Is the writing style of the text appealing to the students?

D. _____ Are the activities motivating? Will they make the student want to pursue the topic further?

E. _____ Does the book clearly show how the knowledge being learned might be used by the learner in the future?

F. _____ Does the text provide positive and motivating models for both sexes as well as for various racial, ethnic, and socioeconomic groups?

Readability Analysis

Weaknesses

1. On which items was the book rated lowest?
2. Did these items tend to fall in certain categories?
3. Summarize the weaknesses of this text.
4. What can you do in class to compensate for the weaknesses of this text?

Assets

1. On which items was the book rated the highest?
2. Did these items fall in certain categories?
3. Summarize the assets of this text.
4. What can you do in class to take advantage of the assets of this text?

From "Assessing Readability: The Checklist Approach" by J. W. Irwin and C. A. Davis. *Journal of Reading*, November 1980, pp. 124–130. International Reading Association. Reprinted by permission.

The informality of this type of checklist permits teachers to evaluate texts with specific student populations in mind. A text that is appropriate for some students may not be for others. Some texts will be used as supplements, while others will be used by all students as the primary source of information about a discipline. The readability checklist permits a consideration of different responses given different purposes and different students.

Reading anthologies. Collections of stories, informational selections, poetry, and drama often provide students with the core of the material they will use in reading instruction. These anthologies are generally embedded in sets of related instructional material which will be considered in the upcoming sections. For some students, these anthologies provide the only reading material they encounter, and the quality of their reading experience is determined by the content of the anthology. They require careful evaluation.

Osborn (1989) suggests examining the student reader for both the content and the appearance of the material. Others suggest examining the content for the types of thematic organization (Searfoss & Readence, 1989). Still others suggest evaluating the quality of the message, or the "ethos" content (Schmidt, Caul, Byers, & Buchman, 1984). Of course, we also need to be sure that the content is a reasonable fit with the goals and expectations of the school and its programs. In evaluating student anthologies, the following should be considered:

Balance of Content
What proportion of the reading selections is narrative?
What proportion of the reading selections is exposition?
What other genre or type of reading is included?
If page count rather than number of selections were used to estimate proportion, would this balance change?
Does there appear to be a wide range of genre represented?
Are different narrative types represented?
Are different types of exposition represented?
Is it apparent that reading purpose might vary with the content?

Characteristics of the Selections
Are the selections representative of real reading materials or have they been written for inclusion in the anthology?
Are high-quality children's books and stories included?
Have the materials been included in unabridged versions?
Are intact (versus excerpted) materials the rule?
Are the selections representative of all racial and ethnic groups?
Are selections free of bias and "socially inappropriate allusions?"
    (Osborn, 1989, p. 291)

Physical Qualities of the Materials
Are the reading materials attractively presented?
Is comprehension enhanced (rather than diverted) by the illustrations?
Is the print clear, appropriate, and uncluttered?

Anthologies are, of course, only as good as the books and excerpts included. Thus, within these guidelines, we need to consider the qualities and characteristics of the narrative and expository selections themselves (see above). If students read *only* from an anthology, the impact of exposure and practice must be carefully considered. For example, some children may have difficulty learning to read exposition, because they have limited experience with this type of text.

Evaluating Basal Lesson Plans

In most basal readers, the content, method, and tasks are dictated by the instructional framework used to teach each selection. As we have noted, this framework is divided roughly into prereading, reading, and postreading activities. It is espe-

FIGURE 9.12

Evaluating Basal Lesson Plans

Prereading (Getting the Students Ready to Learn)

Generally, describe the prereading instruction provided by the basal lesson plan.

_____ 1. Is there evidence of content, process, and attitude goals for each lesson? Is the purpose of the lesson explicit in terms of what students will learn and why?

_____ 2. Does instruction inform students about the type of text they are asked to read, its properties, the purposes for which it might be read, and the strategies for reading it?

_____ 3. Are prerequisite skills stated and reviewed?

_____ 4. Does the text tap students' experiences, interests, and background knowledge?

_____ 5. Are key vocabulary and concepts introduced?

Guided Reading (Engaging Students During and After the Reading)

Generally, describe the guided reading instruction provided by the basal lesson plan.

_____ 1. Do activities and questions help students attain content, process and attitude goals?

_____ 2. Do instructional activities help students comprehend by extracting important information and integrating it with prior knowledge?

_____ 3. Do instructional activities challenge students to become actively engaged in reading—to take responsibility for their reading?

_____ 4. Do instructional activities challenge students to monitor and regulate their reading; to attend to its sensibleness?

_____ 5. Do teaching suggestions provide guidance for teachers to follow when students have difficulty; is guidance provided to help children understand the thinking pattern needed to complete an activity or answer a question?

_____ 6. Is the focus of instruction on teaching students how to comprehend, or merely on checking whether a student has comprehended?

cially important for teachers to evaluate the lesson frameworks and the content of commercially prepared lessons because these materials have been shown to have a powerful influence on classroom reading instruction.

Previously in this chapter (see also Chapter 8), we described the issues surrounding basal reading materials. Guidelines for evaluating basal lesson plans developed from a variety of critical reviews are provided in Figure 9.12. It is not expected that all activities will meet all the guidelines, but a program that infrequently meets these criteria is suspect, and its utility in promoting independent, motivated reading is doubtful.

The use of these procedures can be time-consuming. As Wixson and Peters (1989) point out, however, "over time, these procedures are likely to become more a 'mind set' than a series of discrete steps" (p. 60). In any event, the degree to

FIGURE 9.13
*Seatwork
Analysis Form*

Kinds of Seatwork (Check the types of seatwork that occur in this classroom)

Workbooks, Etc.
   Basal-linked workbook _____
   Supplemental workbook (specify) _____

   Commercial worksheets _____
   Teacher-generated worksheets _____
Reading of Connected Text
   Teacher assigned reading _____
   Independently selected reading
     material _____
   Reading related to other assignments
     (e.g., social studies) _____
Writing Connected Text
   Journal _____
   Process writing projects _____
   Interdisciplinary projects _____

Personal Response
   Journal _____
   Process writing projects _____
   Other _____

Proportion of Time Spent on Seatwork

1. Estimate the total percentage of the day that is spent on seatwork _____.
2. Estimate what percentage of the total reading period is spent on seatwork tasks _____.
3. Use the space next to each item above and estimate what portion of the total seatwork time is spent on that activity.

---

which detailed evaluations suggest the need for extensive modification provides one estimate of the quality of the commercial plans.

Evaluating Instructional Tasks and Practice Materials

As we have seen, children spend the majority of their school day working alone on assigned tasks. Although these are generally intended to extend instructional encounters or provide practice in newly acquired skills, the quality of these tasks is quite uneven. The dramatic yet subtle influence exerted by these tasks and practice materials cannot be over emphasized. To understand school life and the experience of a particular student requires a clear description of the kinds of tasks that are assigned and an examination of the proportion of time that is spent on different types of tasks.

A focus sheet (see Figure 9.13) used to evaluate seatwork practices will quickly reveal what types of instruction or practice tasks are used regularly. This can provide the basis for additional exploration with clients as well. For example, some teachers actually evaluate students' reading competence not on their ability to read connected text but on their ability to complete workbooks or other worksheets. On the other hand, there are classrooms in which students are regularly engaged in fruitful reading and writing activity for extended periods of time. The relationships between student performance and classroom task expectations is extremely important to ascertain. In the next sections, we examine more closely two of the most common classroom tasks: workbooks and questions.

Workbooks

Although the teachers' manuals generally dictate how instruction proceeds, the activities and reading materials used by students dictate what activities they will

FIGURE 9.14
Evaluating Workbook and Seatwork Activities

Content and Format: Generally describe the content and format of seatwork activities. Consider the following:

1. Do activities access background knowledge and set purposes for reading?
2. Are activities related to the text and do they help students develop an integrated understanding of the selection and its structure?
3. Do activities foster independence in the use of reading strategies?
4. Do some activities provide for a systematic and cumulative review of what has already been taught?
5. Do activities reflect the most important aspects of what is being taught in the reading program?
6. Are the vocabulary and concept levels of the activities consistent with the rest of the instruction and appropriate for the students?
7. Are the instructions clear, unambiguous, and easy to follow?
8. Are the student response modes the closest possible to authentic reading and writing activities?
9. Is attention given to the interrelation of reading skills?
10. Is specific instruction provided for each skill practiced independently?
11. Are the passages used representative of those for which the skill is intended?
12. Do materials avoid fragmented, isolated skill activities?

Use: Generally describe how seatwork activities are used.

1. Are activities designed and assigned on the basis of the types of independent seatwork the student needs to understand specific selections and to become a more proficient reader in general?
2. Are activities used as an integral part of classroom reading program and thoroughly integrated with reading lessons?
3. Do teachers make clear what students are to do, how to do it, why they are doing it, and how it will help them become better readers?
4. Are completed activities discussed in reading groups?
5. Do teachers use extended reading and writing activities in place of worksheet activities at least half the time?
6. Are students able to complete activities with a high success rate?
7. Do students work together on occasion to complete their seatwork?
8. Is immediate application provided for skills after they have been taught?
9. Does seatwork include both teacher-assigned activities and student-choice activities?
10. Do the activities assigned vary from low to high levels of cognitive complexity; from practicing newly acquired skills to application activities?
11. Do teachers provide constructive feedback within a reasonable time following activity completion?

experience in the name of reading. Since students spend so much time interacting with workbooks or other seatwork, it is essential to examine these materials and tasks (see Figure 9.14). Seatwork might not be a problem since "well-designed workbooks containing useful activities can be partners with teachers in the initial teaching of what is new and in the maintenance of what has already been taught" (Osborn, 1984, p. 49). On the other hand, poorly designed workbooks require students to spend countless hours on tedious and sometimes confusing activities that do not promote reading competence.

When evaluating workbooks or other tasks, it is important to try out the student activities to see if they are "do-able," if they make sense, or if they are likely to be misconstrued by students from different cultural backgrounds. Analysis should include questions related to how much reading, writing, and/or thinking is required to complete the tasks, how much time each takes to complete, and how much instructional space is likely to be devoted to such activities. As Scheu, Tanner, and Au (1989) note, "well-designed seatwork requires students to engage in extended reading and writing and focuses on skills of real value in learning to read" (p. 105).

Questions

As we have seen, the quantity and quality of question types posed by teachers and answered by students has a profound effect on what and how much is understood about specific texts. After the general assessment of instructional materials has been conducted (see above), it will be important to analyze the basal questions to determine their function, to describe more fully the demands they place on the reader, and to establish the amount of support they might provide (see also Chapter 7). The guidelines suggested here are also appropriate for use in evaluating the questions teachers may pose in class or group discussions about reading material.

Given our earlier discussions, an evaluation of questions should obviously include a check of their type and content as follows:

1. How many questions are asked?
2. What proportion focus on important, nontrivial parts of a selection?
3. Do the questions help students develop an understanding of the entire selection?
4. Do the questions require a range of cognitive functions (e.g., retrieving details, inferring connections, and so on)?

In addition, an evaluation should consider what function is served by the questions; how they are used:

5. What proportion help students integrate the content of the selection?
6. How many ask students to make predictions?
7. Are students asked to justify their responses by using information in the selection?
8. Do questions encourage students to monitor the sensibleness of the selection?
9. Are students encouraged to respond to the text in a thoughtful or emotive way?

Questions should always be evaluated in terms of the teacher's purposes (Raphael & Gavelek, 1984). Most frequently, they are meant to focus students' attention on important concepts and details. In this case, it would be vital to determine the proportion of questions that actually do focus on important aspects of the story versus unimportant details. Alternatively, questions can be used to integrate information from throughout the text to enhance comprehension and provide a review. In this event, an assessment of questions should include an examination of the degree to which they help students follow the meaning and/or identify inconsistencies in the text.

The important point to remember is that not all questions place the same requirements on the reader. In analyzing the types and forms of questions, you will need to be aware of the extent to which students' responses are shaped by the question and the degree to which it elicits a particular answer. Finally, it is worth noting that some disabled readers have a difficult time responding to some types of questions. For example, open-ended and/or ambiguous questions may confuse some students. Students who do have answers should obviously not be penalized by poorly crafted or ill-defined questions. Both the focus and the form of questions should be considered carefully before concluding that students cannot respond.

Evaluating Microcomputer Software

There are specific criteria that should be used in evaluating microcomputer software. The first question to be asked in evaluating these materials should always be: How closely does this material match the instructional and philosophical frameworks of our reading program? In the evaluation section that follows, we provide guidelines for assessing the instructional merit of the computer materials by focusing on pedagogical, theoretical, and technical considerations.

Pedagogical and Theoretical Concerns

Because computers and microcomputers are still relatively new to the educational scene, and because many teachers are uncomfortable with the technology, existing evaluation schemes often focus on features of computers that are unique to the technology. Although this type of evaluation is important, a far more basic concern may get lost. As Miller and Burnett (1986) point out, the first question to be asked in assessing computer software is: "How do you think reading (or, writing) should be taught?" (p. 164). Software that is not consistent with the prevailing theoretical or pedagogical perspective should be rejected as inappropriate rather than ineffective.

The guidelines offered by the Michigan Reading Association (1986) should prove helpful in deciding whether software can be successfully integrated into the existing reading and language arts program. Software that is pedagogically useful should:

- be consistent with local reading and language arts objectives
- provide for content modification by students or teachers
- include provisions for transfer from computer to off-screen reading situations
- feature the unique capabilities of the medium rather than duplicate features of print media

Teachers will also need to examine the content of the program carefully in order to determine the degree of theoretical and/or pedagogical appropriateness.

Although many existing guidelines assume a subskill approach to reading instruction, professional organizations have generated criteria that are more consistent with current research. For example, Michigan's guide suggests that programs should have the following features:

- include complete pieces of narrative or expository text
- present meaningful and useful information
- provide well-organized and logically developed material
- engage readers in active participation
- allow time for reflection and responses
- emphasize thinking rather than repetitive practice
- provide skills practice in real content with real purpose
- allow rereading
- take advantage of relationships between reading and writing
- be free of bias regarding race, sex, age, handicaps, and ethics

Using these assessment guidelines, it is possible to distinguish among programs for the purposes of teacher decision-making. For example, it is possible to identify computer programs that are packaged attractively and technically sound, but that promote an inappropriate view of reading/writing. If teachers are going to integrate computer technology successfully with their instructional programs "in ways that are based upon sound educational principles and are meaningful to the children being served" (Irwin, 1987, p. 37), they will need to use their scarce resources to purchase materials that accomplish important and worthwhile instructional goals. Although the educational issues should be paramount in evaluating computer materials, the technical aspects are also important.

Evaluating the Technical Aspects of Computer Programs

Because computer software *is* unique, and because it is generally meant to be used by individual students without the direct supervision of a teacher, these materials must be examined carefully. It will generally be necessary to actually use the program, since it is difficult to assess important aspects of the software through program descriptions alone.

Needless to say, computer software, like all educational material, should be accurate and free of errors. However, there are other factors to consider that are specific to computer programs. One of the most comprehensive sets of guidelines available in this area is that offered by the Michigan Reading Association (MRA) (1986). The sections having to do with general technical evaluation are reproduced in Figure 9.15.

Some software is designed for more specialized purposes and requires careful inspection using other guidelines. For example, MRA (1986) has provided guidelines for assessing word processing and simulation programs (see Figure 9.16). Similarly, Balajthy (1989a) has proposed guidelines for evaluating software with voice synthesizer features. When evaluating the voice synthesis program, he advises considering the following:

FIGURE 9.15

Guidelines for Evaluating Reading Software

Documentation and Support Features	Poor			Good	
1. Clearly written user's manual for program operation	1	2	3	4	5
2. Teacher's supplement with appropriate classroom uses and teaching activities	1	2	3	4	5
3. Pre-requisite abilities indicated	1	2	3	4	5
4. Objectives stated	1	2	3	4	5
5. Sample screens illustrated	1	2	3	4	5
6. Textual material printed for reference	1	2	3	4	5
7. Cue card for commands unique to program	1	2	3	4	5
8. Useful and efficient record-keeping capabilities, if appropriate	1	2	3	4	5
9. Records easily printed on screen or on paper	1	2	3	4	5
10. Teacher can monitor and modify individual assignments or records	1	2	3	4	5
Overall assessment of documentation and support features	1	2	3	4	5

Comments:

Technical Qualities					
1. Approach unique to computer capabilities	1	2	3	4	5
2. Varied program to maintain interest over subsequent uses	1	2	3	4	5
3. Positive feedback	1	2	3	4	5
4. Student can operate independently	1	2	3	4	5
5. Two or more students can interact cooperatively, if desired	1	2	3	4	5
6. Clear directions	1	2	3	4	5
7. Help screens available, if needed	1	2	3	4	5
8. Option to quit and to save progress at any time	1	2	3	4	5
9. Appropriate type size and attractive screen formatting	1	2	3	4	5
10. Option to bypass sound and graphics	1	2	3	4	5
Overall assessment of technical qualities	1	2	3	4	5

Comments:

Summary and Recommendations

Reviewer:

Program strengths:

Program weaknesses:

Recommendations:

"Guidelines for Evaluating Reading Software" reprinted by permission from *The Michigan Reading Journal*, *18* (4), 1985.

1. Evaluate the overall quality of the sound that is produced.
2. Is there a playback feature so that students can listen a second time to words or sentences that have not been understood?
3. Do informal tryouts with your students suggest that voice recognition is adequate for your purposes?
4. Is the voice synthesis feature an integral and important part of the program?
5. How many words are available in the system?
6. Is it possible to create new programs? How difficult is this?

FIGURE 9.16

Evaluation of Related Software for Reading

Word Processing and Database Management Programs	Poor			Good	
1. Size and spacing of characters appropriate for audience	1	2	3	4	5
2. Options to vary print formats, (e.g., page width, page length, spacing, type fonts)	1	2	3	4	5
3. Words not split at ends of lines	1	2	3	4	5
4. Actual format can be shown on screen before printing	1	2	3	4	5
5. Command keys with logical names and minimal moves	1	2	3	4	5
6. Easy editing features for erasing, inserting, centering, tabbing and underlining	1	2	3	4	5
7. Ability to reorganize large blocks of text by moving, saving on disk, inserting in other places	1	2	3	4	5
8. Provisions to restore previous action (e.g., return paragraph to original position)	1	2	3	4	5
9. Warnings at critical points (e.g., You have not saved this text)	1	2	3	4	5
10. Printer commands and capabilities available and easy for students to use	1	2	3	4	5
11. Sturdy command cards for off-screen reference	1	2	3	4	5
12. Adequate file functions including renaming, protecting, merging, and copying	1	2	3	4	5
13. Related capabilities (e.g., idea processors, spelling checkers, grammar checkers, graphics)	1	2	3	4	5
14. Ability to integrate text and illustrations	1	2	3	4	5
15. Back-up disks provided	1	2	3	4	5
16. Support materials with useful teaching ideas	1	2	3	4	5

Authoring Systems and Other Utilities					
1. Clear directions for using program to create materials	1	2	3	4	5
2. Easy to enter items	1	2	3	4	5
3. Editing possible at any point	1	2	3	4	5
4. Varied formats for developing materials (i.e., not limited to multiple choice, true/false, or simple testing types)	1	2	3	4	5
5. Can vary amount of text to be presented	1	2	3	4	5
6. Clear directions for student use of the completed program	1	2	3	4	5
7. Options for record-keeping	1	2	3	4	5
8. Options for incorporating graphics	1	2	3	4	5
9. Options for incorporating sound	1	2	3	4	5
10. Support materials with useful teaching ideas	1	2	3	4	5

Simulations and Problem-Solving Programs					
1. Content consistent with local curriculum	1	2	3	4	5
2. Realistic situations	1	2	3	4	5
3. Motivating design	1	2	3	4	5
4. Helpful feedback about user's decisions	1	2	3	4	5
5. Supplementary bibliography available, indicating sources of content and related research possibilities for students	1	2	3	4	5
6. Sample sheets provided for off-computer record-keeping, analysis and research	1	2	3	4	5
7. Teaching suggestions for integrating content within curriculum	1	2	3	4	5
8. Classroom management suggestions for using program within classroom with limited computer accessibility	1	2	3	4	5

"Evaluation of Related Software for Reading" reprinted by permission from *The Michigan Reading Journal, 18* (4), 1985.

Such evaluations take time and energy. However, the potential benefits in the areas of motivation and interactive reading/writing activities make the effort worthwhile. For some struggling readers, the computer may provide the support and interest that encourages the persistence and effort needed to become more proficient. This is not likely to happen, however, with repetitive, routinized activities. These programs offer little after the initial novelty has worn off. On the other hand, some programs provide a supportive and interactive setting within which to read and write. These are worth finding and using.

FROM CLASSROOM TO CLINIC

There are few clear distinctions to make regarding the role of materials and tasks in classroom and clinic. The instructional programs of both teachers and clinicians rely heavily on the books and activities used to teach reading/writing. The cumulative effect of exposure to materials and tasks in school settings is so powerful that classroom teachers must examine these carefully to avoid potential mismatches. We want to avoid as well the possibility that some children may become disabled by the very tasks and texts that were intended to help advance literacy. Because materials will generally be used for many years by many students, they should be purchased with care, using the guidelines suggested in this chapter. Tasks can be adapted and changed, but this cannot happen unless classroom teachers are sensitive to the need to evaluate their assignments and expectations periodically to ensure that the activities and tasks are still accomplishing their desired intent.

In clinical settings, teachers may see many students with divergent needs. Consequently, it can be more difficult to assess the impact of materials and tasks on young or disabled readers. However, we cannot afford not to evaluate these carefully. For at least some students, the problem is task- or text-related and not the result of students' limited knowledge and skill. In these cases, of course, no amount of student remediation will make the difficulties go away.

Finally, the reading professional has a responsibility to make sure that teachers and administrators make informed choices about the materials and tasks they select to teach reading and writing. In many schools, these people expect the reading professional to play an active role in educating committees and working aggressively to make good decisions. Few jobs should be taken more seriously than these, because the materials/tasks, not the formal curriculum, will typically define the instructional program for most students.

Once information about the reading context has been gathered, it is important that it be summarized. The summary information should be as specific as possible about the attributes of settings, methods, and materials/tasks the reader is encountering. It may not be necessary to include every piece of information that has been gathered. The focus should be on identifying and describing those factors that are, or might be, affecting learning for a particular student.

Using the information that has been gathered and summarized about the reader (Steps 1 and 2) and the reading context (Step 3), we are now ready to move onto the interactive decision required in Steps 4, 5, and 6, described in the next section of this text (Chapter 10).

CHAPTER SUMMARY

In this chapter, we continued to focus on evaluating the reading context, Step 3 of the assessment-instruction process. The discussion addressed the role of materials and tasks in reading and reading instruction. In the Understanding section of this chapter, we described four major aspects of materials/tasks, paying particular attention to the manner in which they influenced reading and reading achievement. First, we considered *text factors*. Here we described how text type and structure differ and how the nature of text can influence reading and learning. We also examined the features of text that influence comprehensibility—the aspects of text that can make reading easier or more difficult, and learning productive or more tedious.

Next, we examined the role of the commercial *reading programs* as a particular example of reading texts. After a brief description of the specialized nature of basal anthologies, considerable attention was devoted to helping teachers understand the role of commercially prescribed lesson plans.

In the third section, the role of instructional tasks and practice materials was examined. These aspects of the school context exert such profound influence on reading instruction that we considered these in some detail. The nature and influence of tasks were described and the cumulative effects of tasks was noted. Next, tasks specific to learning to read were discussed, with independent seatwork and questions considered separately.

Finally, the specialized materials evolving from the microcomputer technology were discussed. Three types of microcomputer materials were briefly described: word processing software programs, beginning reading programs, and specialized software programs such as databases and hypertext.

In the second major section of this chapter, strategies and tools for assessing each of these aspects of materials and tasks were described. These ranged from the highly mechanistic *readability formulas* discussed first, to the much more informal checklists provided near the end of the chapter. We provided guidelines for evaluating both texts (narrative, expository, and anthologies) and tasks (seatwork and questions). In addition, tools were provided for evaluating commercially available programs, both instructional plans and computer software.

SECTION IV

Interactions

THIS SECTION IS CENTRAL to understanding the relationship between assessment and instruction. As noted previously, the interactive nature of the assessment-instruction process requires careful observation of the ways in which the various factors may be influencing reading and reading acquisition in individual students. The single chapter in this section stands alone because it focuses exclusively on the relationship between assessment and instruction—on that moment in the assessment process when informed decision making is required of the teacher, and when the expertise and knowledge of that teacher will determine how the instructional planning to follow will proceed. Since reading ability is not viewed as a static construct, clinicians and teachers must be prepared to describe the variability observed within the individual student under different reading conditions, and to engage in continued explorations of this variability through diagnostic teaching.

The steps of the assessment-instruction process addressed in this section are shaded in the figure on the following page. They are: Step 4—Evaluating the Match Between Reader and Reading Context; Step 5—Reflection, Decision Making, and Planning; and Step 6—Identifying a Better Match: Diagnostic Teaching.

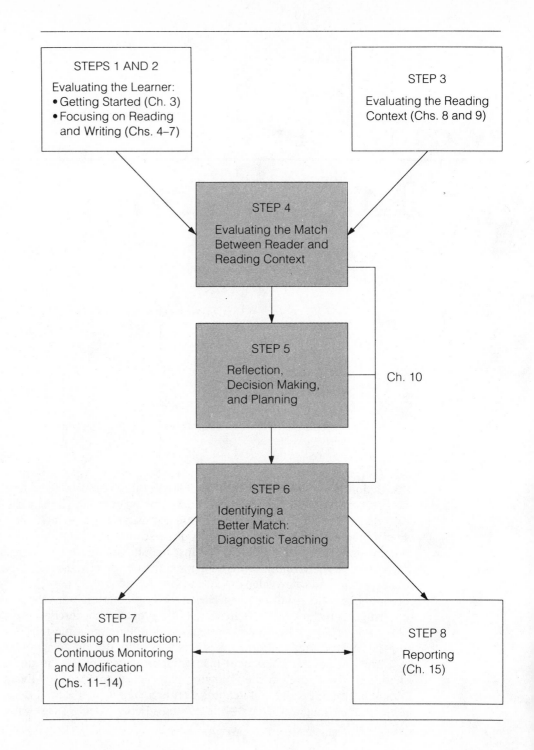

CHAPTER 10

Interactive Decision Making

INTRODUCTION

Assessment is not simply the gathering of information. The success of the assessment-instruction process depends on the teacher's ability to make informed, effective decisions. Although we can provide guidance in decision making, we cannot prescribe it. Ultimately, the quality of decision making relies on the professional knowledge, experience, and judgment of the decision maker. Therefore, it is incumbent upon the decision maker to learn as much as possible about all aspects of development, learning, and teaching in order to make informed decisions.

Informed decision making also requires a clear sense of the desired outcomes of the assessment-instruction process. We agree with Johnston (1987) when he writes, "the most fundamental goal of all educational evaluation is optimal instruction for all children and evaluation practices are only legitimate to the extent that they serve this goal" (p. 744). Similarly, Duffy and Roehler (1989) note that the first characteristic of teachers who are instructional decision makers is that they "think in terms of what students should learn, not in terms of assignments for students to complete" (p. 16).

We would also like to emphasize the value of experience in implementing the assessment-instruction process for becoming an expert evaluator and decision maker. As noted in Chapter 7, Johnston (1987) indicates that one of the most important characteristics of expert evaluators is their ability to recognize patterns. They not only know what patterns to look for, but also the conditions under which the patterns are most likely to occur.

Chapter Overview

This chapter addresses the understanding and implementation of three steps in the assessment-instruction process: Step 4—evaluating the existing match between the reader and the reading context; Step 5—reflection and generating hypotheses about what the reader needs, making decisions, and implementing a plan; Step 6—determining how to (re)establish learning through diagnostic teaching. The first half of the chapter addresses the understanding of the procedures involved in these three steps. The second half of the chapter illustrates the implementation of these three steps through the use of two case studies.

UNDERSTANDING STEP 4: EVALUATING THE MATCH BETWEEN READER AND READING CONTEXT

Using the information gathered in Steps 1–3, we are now ready to evaluate the match between the knowledge, skills, and motivation of the reader and the settings, methods, and materials/tasks within the reading context. This step provides the answer to the question: What is the current status of the interaction between the reader and the reading context? Our job in this stage of the assess-ment-instruction process is to pull together all that we know as the result of our professional efforts and experience, and to evaluate how well existing demands, expectations, and supports of the context match the reader's abilities, interests, knowledge, and level of independence.

The match between the reader and the reading context includes information about areas in which the fit is both good and poor. The information in this section comes both from an evaluation of interactions between these two sets of factors and from an evaluation of the interactions observed within the assessment itself; i.e., how the student performed differently under different reading conditions during assessment.

By the time we get to this step in the process, many of the successful and unsuccessful interactions will be obvious. If we are still uncertain about how the reader and the context interact in ways that either facilitate or inhibit learning and performance, we can examine the information in each of the categories of reader factors (i.e., background; knowledge about reading; skills application; and at-titudes and motivation) and ask ourselves how it fits with what we know about the contextual factors (i.e., settings; methods; and materials and tasks) and vice versa.

For example, the information about skills application might suggest that the reader relies too heavily on graphophonic cues for word analysis and not enough on contextual analysis, while the information about methods indicates that in-struction is focused on contextual analysis using a modified cloze procedure. This is a good match, because this instruction is likely to meet the reader's need to develop a better balance between the use of graphophonic and contextual cues in word identification. Conversely, the information about materials may suggest that instruction relies almost exclusively on drill sheets with short reading selections and that the reader performs better with the aid of additional context provided by longer reading selections. This is not a good match, because the reader needs different materials to facilitate learning. Other examples of poor matches that might be observed include:

- A third-grade student with a history of ear infections who has failed to acquire any functional sight vocabulary or word analysis strategies who is placed in a 2-2 reader and is receiving remedial instruction in isolated phonic skills.
- An eighth-grade student who does not read independently in or out of school and whose sight vocabulary and word analysis skills are below grade level on tests of isolated skills, but closer to grade level when reading coherent, full-length selections, who is receiving isolated word analysis skill-drill and is not permitted to advance beyond these isolated practices because of his weak performance on criterion tests of those skills.
- A highly verbal first-grade student who does not have the concept of a word, nor can he voice-point, whose instruction consists of dictating language experience stories without any explicit explanation about the conventions of print, and the purposes of learning to identify words.

Although it will often be quite clear how effectively the instruction and the students' needs are matched, there are times when conclusions remain ambiguous. In these cases, we need to carry our questions and concerns into the next step (see below). In other cases, we will have concluded that aspects of the match are clearly inappropriate, and in these cases, our questions and concerns will involve generating hypotheses about ways to remedy the mismatch. In either case, it is time to step back and really think about what we know or suspect and what can be done about it.

UNDERSTANDING STEP 5: REFLECTION, DECISION MAKING, AND PLANNING

After the match between the reader and the reading context has been evaluated, we need to reflect on this information and generate hypotheses about the second question guiding the assessment-instruction process: What does the reader need? At this point in the process, not everything will be guesswork. We already know some things about what the reader needs as a result of our previous analyses. Other things will still be unclear, however, and we need to begin to make some decisions about the relative importance of the various problems/needs we have identified.

Remember that we can always find a problem if we are looking for one, but that every problem is not of equal importance to the progress of the student. In evaluating the importance of the problem(s) we have identified, we should ask ourselves, "If I changed (the source of interference), is this student likely to become a better reader?" If the answer is "no," or we suspect that this intervention is unlikely to go very far in solving the problem, the problem we have identified is probably not a primary source of difficulty.

Another guide to determining what the reader needs is to reexamine the information gathered about the reader and the reading context to determine if any of the materials, methods, or settings were more effective than others. It is important to remember that we cannot decide what the reader needs without knowing the context in which the problem exists. Otherwise, we look only to the reader for the source of the problem, when in fact it is more often the interaction between reader and context.

For example, a reader with sufficient skill and major anxiety or attitude problems may display skill deficiencies, but does not need more skill instruction. What is needed instead is instruction that takes the pressure off and/or motivates the practice and application of skills. Additional examples of different types of reader needs include instruction that capitalizes on strengths while attending to weaknesses, changes perceptions of the purposes and goals of reading, or explains the how, when, and why of strategy usage rather than simply providing practice.

Generating hypotheses about students' needs is always a matter of informed decision making. It requires the use of all our knowledge and experience. Examples of specific student-needs hypotheses we have generated are listed below.

- A third-grade student with adequate word recognition skill who believes that the purpose of reading is saying all the words right needs instruction that promotes understanding of the goals of reading and practice with outside reading.
- A highly verbal first-grade student who does not understand print concepts needs exposure to written language in a variety of contexts.
- A fifth-grade student with adequate reading skills who is uninterested and unmotivated to complete assigned reading activities and to read in or out of school needs instruction that interests and motivates him.
- A fourth-grade student who functions normally at a second-grade level but is placed in a fourth-grade reader needs different materials.
- A second-grade student who functions best in holistic, contextualized instruction, who is placed in beginning material because she lacks mastery of parts, needs to be placed in higher materials and taught more whole-to-part than vice versa.

It is also important to recognize that many of these needs would never be identified if students were not examined within the instructional contexts in which their problems exist. Once hypotheses about reader needs have been generated and prioritized, we can begin planning the diagnostic teaching activities that will be used to evaluate the hypotheses.

UNDERSTANDING STEP 6: DIAGNOSTIC TEACHING

Following Steps 4 and 5, in which we reflected on the existing match and generated some preliminary hypotheses about what the reader needs, we need to address the third question guiding the assessment-instruction process: What is most likely to (re)establish learning? At this point in the process we are concerned with identifying a better or optimal match between the reader and the reading context. To accomplish this goal, we rely primarily on the technique of diagnostic teaching. The following sections describe the purposes and procedures of diagnostic teaching.

Definition and Purposes

According to Harris and Sipay (1985), the idea of using sample lessons as a diagnostic procedure for reading was developed first by Harris and Roswell in 1953. Although this type of procedure is not new, current interest in interactive views of reading and learning has resulted in significant advances in the development and implementation of these techniques. These types of procedures are referred to variously as "trial teaching" (Harris & Sipay, 1985), "dynamic assessment" (Cioffi & Carney, 1983; Feuerstein, Rand, & Hoffman, 1979), "intervention assessment" (Paratore & Indrisano, 1987), "clinical diagnosis" (Chall & Curtis, 1987), and "diagnostic teaching" (Harris, 1977; Wixson & Lipson, 1986). Although there are differences among these related procedures, they do share a critical feature: they are interactive assessments that provide for systematic modification of the instructional situation in order to observe what a student does under specified conditions.

We prefer the term *diagnostic teaching* because it reflects the dual purposes for which we use this procedure. First, the procedure is *diagnostic* because it allows the collection of additional information in order to clarify and test the hypotheses generated during the initial steps of the assessment-instruction process. Second, the procedure is *instructional* because it provides opportunities to try out methods that may be successful alternatives for working with a student. This last is a critical feature of diagnostic teaching, because it allows us to explore a student's performance under circumstances more like those encountered in the classroom on a regular basis.

Throughout this book, we have introduced numerous cautions, caveats, and concerns about traditional assessment practices. Diagnostic teaching procedures are flourishing, in part, as a response to these difficulties. The problems of traditional assessment procedures have been discussed elsewhere in the book and will not be repeated here, except for a reminder that traditional assessments, even many informal techniques, are often static measures that do not consider the possible variability within a reader's performance. The failure to test students under a range of conditions that represent authentic reading events can result in both inaccurate diagnoses and erroneous conclusions about the focus for intervention.

Problems with the static, product-oriented results of traditional assessments have also raised serious questions about *equity* issues in assessment, particularly with the use of standardized tests of achievement and intelligence. For example, Campione and Brown (1987) note that although the scores individuals attain on static tests represent only estimates of competence, all too often, the unwarranted inference is made that they are measures of ability level that are relatively permanent and resistant to change. In many cases, particularly for children from culturally different backgrounds, these scores may provide a dramatic underestimate of the potential level of performance under different circumstances. Procedures such as diagnostic teaching provide better measures of learning potential by evaluating how a student can and will perform under different conditions.

The assessment procedures described in the preceding chapters are predicated on the assumption that we need to collect information about a range of reader and contextual factors. Until now, we have not really suggested gathering information specifically to confirm predictions about the nature of the problem and how to address it. However, diagnostic teaching is hypothesis-driven. It assumes that teachers are intentionally setting out to examine more closely something that has come to their attention.

As indicated in Chapter 2, we believe that most instruction can be viewed as diagnostic teaching, particularly when it is carefully planned using our best predictions about what may work for a given student, and when we are prepared to monitor our work continually to see how adjustments have affected learning and performance. Diagnostic teaching permits the teacher to manipulate in a planned way any of the factors that are suspected to be contributing to or inhibiting reading achievement. In addition, diagnostic teaching allows us to explore the "conditions that call forth learning" (Hunt, 1961).

Skilled teachers consistently engage in "diagnostic teaching." However, because this technique is so fluid and nonstandardized, most teachers undervalue the assessment information that is generated and fail to document it. At the same time, they recognize the significant value of the instructional information it yields. Without diagnostic teaching, we have few alternatives but to believe that all students with similar presenting problems will benefit from the same instructional program. Diagnostic teaching provides an opportunity for truly integrating instruction and assessment.

Diagnostic Teaching Procedures

The procedures used for "diagnostic teaching" vary considerably from situation to situation. Because each situation is unique, it is impossible to provide step-by-step procedures for conducting diagnostic teaching sessions. However, we can describe the process of diagnostic teaching including its characteristics and tasks. The process we describe below involves three related tasks: planning, executing, and evaluating the diagnostic teaching effort.

Planning

When we reach the diagnostic teaching stage of the assessment-instruction process, we are ready to focus our efforts, rather than to continue gathering more general information. We have noted elsewhere in this text that assessment should be continuous and that diagnostic information is available any time we work with a reader. However, we are using "diagnostic teaching" here to describe specific, intentional activity, rather than a general mind-set for observing instructional interactions.

It is important to keep in mind that we are attempting to verify hunches about both the source of the problem and the instructional manipulations that are most likely to call forth learning. Because of this dual focus, diagnostic teaching requires modification and manipulation of readers and reading contexts. In order to identify the student's potential for learning under different instructional conditions or the factors and conditions that facilitate or inhibit learning, we need to view diagnostic teaching as "an interaction between an examiner-as-intervener and a learner-as-active participant, which seeks to estimate the degree of modifiability of the learner and the means by which positive changes in cognitive functioning can be induced and maintained" (Lidz, 1987, p. 4).

During planning, we need to determine how we will focus the diagnostic teaching to address the hypotheses generated in Step 5. As we have stated many times, the problems readers experience often lie in the interaction between reader knowledge, skills, and motivation and the settings, methods, and materials of the reading context. In a sense, the reader and contextual factors that enter into this interaction complement each other. For example, a reader's lack of prior knowledge is the complement of the audience appropriateness of the materials he or she is asked to read. Similarly, an instructional method that relies exclusively on independent student practice is the complement of the extent to which a reader has mastered essential skills and strategies.

Although the problem usually lies in the interaction between reader and contextual factors, when it comes to diagnostic teaching, it is easier to think about the contextual factors that can/should be altered than about manipulating reader factors. This is why Step 5 focuses on "what the *reader* needs"; it helps place the emphasis in diagnostic teaching (Step 6) on the *settings, methods, and materials* that are amenable to modification and manipulation (Campione & Brown, 1987; Paratore & Indrisano, 1987; Walker, 1988).

Changing the setting.   Using the elements of the reading context described in Chapters 8 and 9, the first area we might consider manipulating is the instructional setting. For example, we might consider attempting to alter the goals for literacy learning that a student has acquired from the instructional context. We might also consider altering the organization of instructional activities and groups (e.g., from lecture to discussion; from a teacher-led group to a cooperative work-group or individual instruction). Finally, we might consider altering the interaction patterns or "participation structures" used during instruction (e.g., from asking "known-answer" questions to more informal student-centered discussion).

Changing the methods.   The methods of instruction comprise a second element of the reading context we might consider manipulating. Within this area, we might consider altering what is being taught (focus) and/or how it is being taught (approach). For example, we might consider changing the focus of reading lessons from a heavy emphasis on individual skill instruction to the practice and application of skills in the service of constructing meaning from authentic reading materials. We may also wish to consider altering the methods of instruction being used to create motivated and/or strategic learning. For example, we may wish to change from extrinsic motivational techniques to those that are designed to enhance a student's desire to understand rather than simply comply with directions.

We may also consider moving from methods that rely heavily on independent student practice to those that provide increased teacher support during the initial stages of learning. Some authors have suggested systematically varying the level of teacher support in the administration of traditional assessment procedures as a means of obtaining better instructional information. For example, Cioffi and

Carney (1983) suggest a variety of modifications for administering an IRI, including eliminating time constraints, providing appropriate prereading instruction, observing miscues under prepared and unprepared conditions, and introducing instructional aids as needed.

Changing the materials and tasks. The third area of the reading context we might consider manipulating in diagnostic teaching consists of materials and tasks. The characteristics of the texts a student is reading can have a profound effect on learning and performance, and are therefore serious candidates for manipulation. Those that are easily modified include text type (e.g., various types of stories and/or informational materials); length, readability, familiarity, organization (e.g., temporal sequence, cause-effect), coherence/unity, and structural characteristics (e.g., headings/subheadings, illustrations, charts, italics, etc.). It is also important to consider how the task demands that are being placed on the reader might be manipulated. Specifically, we might consider altering the content (i.e., cognitive complexity) and/or the form (e.g., purpose and procedural complexity) of the tasks in which a student is asked to engage. This might include alterations such as changing from recognition tasks to open-ended or discussion tasks, or from low- to high-level tasks, or altering factors such as the quantity, mode of presentation and response (e.g., oral, written), and/or the clarity of task directions.

Generally, we should anticipate using multiple setting, method, materials and task options as we engage in diagnostic teaching. We are really attempting to set up the diagnostic teaching to represent or test certain interactions. However, not all interactions will be tested. It is important to recall that diagnostic teaching is hypothesis-driven. Only those factors and influences that appear to be likely candidates for improving learning and performance need be attempted.

Executing

It is clear that there are many ways to proceed with diagnostic teaching sessions. However, it is important to keep in mind that designing the diagnostic teaching to provide information about how a reader performs under several different or contrasting conditions can help us clarify our hypotheses about what the student needs. The many options provided above suggest at least two ways that this might be accomplished. The first is to conduct diagnostic teaching sessions that try out several distinct alternatives to solving a particular problem. For future reference, we are calling this the *alternative methods* approach.

In contrast to the alternative methods approach, we can conduct diagnostic teaching sessions in which a particular procedure is modified by providing different levels of support to the reader. This approach uses the instructional technique of scaffolding described in Chapter 8 as an assessment device and will be referred to subsequently as the *scaffolding* approach. Whichever approach is selected, the procedures need to be viable instructional techniques that are appropriate for the setting in which they will be used on a regular basis.

Alternative methods approach. The alternative methods approach involves a comparison of two or more different instructional procedures for teaching the same content or skill. An example of the alternative methods approach can be seen by rereading the case of Seth in Chapter 2, in which we described how we explored possible teaching interventions. Recall that Seth was experiencing serious word recognition problems, and in addition, he seemed to have difficulty learning either new words or the skills needed to learn new words. Therefore, our diagnostic teaching efforts involved trying out three distinct instructional approaches: phonics instruction that taught him to break the whole into component parts, phonics instruction that taught him to blend parts into wholes, and sight word instruction.

As noted in Chapter 2, Seth recalled the words he was taught using each approach equally well. However, he learned the new words in the part-to-whole phonics approach and the sight word approach in a fraction of the time it took him to learn the words using the whole-to-part phonics approach. These results, combined with Seth's perception that he had learned most easily in the part-to-whole method, led to the recommendation that he be taught to recognize words using a part-to-whole phonics approach.

Although the alternative methods approach has been used for many years (e.g., Mills, 1956), current innovations in pedagogy have led to broader applications. For example, this approach was used in one of the author's clinics with a bright, articulate first-grade student who needed to use context more as an aid to word recognition in her reading. The alternative approaches tried during diagnostic teaching included repeated readings, reading text presented in a modified cloze format, and reading text altered to include self-monitoring "checkpoints" throughout.

Scaffolding approach.   The scaffolding approach is a fairly recent innovation, making it less familiar and worthy of slightly more discussion than the alternative methods approach. This approach involves the teacher or examiner presenting the student with a reading activity, observing the response, and then introducing modifications of the task. These modifications are really hypotheses about "the minimal instructional adjustments necessary for the child to succeed in materials at or near his or her grade placement" (Cioffi & Carney, 1983, p. 768). The predominant form of these modifications is the layering of prompts. Not only must we identify candidates for manipulation in diagnostic teaching, we need to order possible interventions from least to most support. The level of support provided in diagnostic teaching can always be increased, but if we start with high levels of support it may not be clear whether the reader could perform just as well with less assistance.

Consider the case of a reader who is not able to answer questions about a grade level passage, even though word recognition is acceptable. We could plan an intervention that provided for activating background knowledge, preteaching vocabulary, focusing purpose setting, and guided reading questions (a sound example of the directed reading activity described in Chapter 8). This type of instruction represents a heavy dependence on the teacher, however. As an alternative, we could teach a lesson providing only the one component of this instructional plan that we believe is crucial to improving the match so that the reader can perform effectively. For a very young or inexperienced child, this may involve just the preteaching of vocabulary. For another child who has limited stamina for long texts, it might be providing only the guided reading questions.

The point is that we would start with one type of minimal support and increase it only as we see that the child requires it. We would prioritize, or layer, the prompts or supports so that we can clearly identify the intervention of least assistance. It is sometimes even possible to generate a highly specified set of "ordered hints" (Brown & Campione, 1986; Campione & Brown, 1987). These hints go from least support to most support and can be documented for assessment passages as we begin to use diagnostic teaching. Imagine, for example, that a reader cannot answer a question or series of questions about a selection. We can add a sequence of ordered hints such as the ones listed below and record the point at which the student *can* answer the question(s).

1. What could you do to answer that question?
2. Do you know the answer to the question?
3. Can you figure it out?
4. Is the information you need in the text?
5. Where could you find that information?

If the student still cannot respond appropriately, Paratore and Indrisano (1987) suggest the following procedures be used:

1. Ask the student to reread to find the answer.
2. If the student provides a new answer that is inadequate, ask him or her to reread a specific piece of the text to generate the answer.
3. Narrow the search to a sentence or two if necessary.
4. Finally, provide guidance at the key word level if that is required.

The next steps would involve actually engaging in instruction designed to help students locate information, infer connections, or link ideas (whatever is required by the text and task). In this manner, it will be possible to specify how much support is likely to be necessary for this student to perform under the various conditions that have been explored.

We have described these two approaches to diagnostic teaching simply to help the understanding of this procedure. We do not mean to suggest that these approaches are mutually exclusive. In fact they can be, and often are, apparent in combination within a diagnostic teaching session. An example of this comes from a diagnostic teaching session for a fourth-grade student with poor vocabulary knowledge in one of the author's clinics. The diagnostic teaching session employed vocabulary development activities both within and outside the context of reading connected text. In addition, the procedures that accompanied the text reading included the use of layered prompts to determine the level of support necessary to enable the student to identify, learn, and apply unknown words in the context of her reading.

Thus far, we have emphasized the intentional, well-planned nature of diagnostic teaching. Before leaving this section, however, it is important to understand that diagnostic teaching is also *opportunistic and flexible*. This means that a knowledgeable teacher who is able to set aside his or her own preconceived ideas about what will happen, and who can listen, is likely to gather a wealth of information from which to confirm hypotheses and plan instruction. The following exchange occurred during a diagnostic teaching session in which the tutor was using a think-aloud procedure (see Chapter 7) to explore more carefully her hunch that "Andrew" did not have many comprehension strategies available for use during reading.

> *Teacher:* Tell me what you were doing and thinking as you read that part.
> *Andrew:* Not much.
> *Teacher:* Did that part make sense to you?
> *Andrew:* Not really.
> *Teacher:* Well, do you think it would be helpful to go back and reread that part to see if you can understand it?
> *Andrew:* I don't know. You tell me. You're the teacher!

This rather extraordinary, and unexpected, exchange amply demonstrates how much readers can tell us about their reading if we will listen. It is true that Andrew uses few comprehension strategies during reading, but this exchange demonstrated the more serious fact that he is willing to be compliant but not responsible for his behaviors during reading. It appears that he approaches reading and reading instruction passively rather than as an active participant (see Johnston & Winograd, 1985).

Good diagnostic teaching requires flexibility in order to take advantage of opportunities as they arise. Over time, we develop a repertoire of both assessment and instruction procedures which can be used to respond to unexpected results or remarks. They will only be useful, however, to the extent that we recognize what is happening when it occurs and are prepared to revise our plans on the spot. This is opportunistic assessment-instruction. In the case we just described, the teacher decided to follow-up this exchange by asking Andrew what he thought it meant to be a good reader. She confirmed her new hypothesis; he believed good reading was flawless word-calling and he relied heavily on the teacher to set purposes and to monitor both word recognition and comprehension. Consequently, he paid no attention whatsoever to meaning and could not set purposes for reading. In subsequent sessions, she pursued a line of diagnostic teaching aimed at discovering how he might learn to be a more active participant in generating meaning from text.

Evaluating

The examples provided above suggest that diagnostic teaching is not usually a one-time event. Diagnostic teaching is cyclical and continuous. Generally, the results of diagnostic teaching will be used either to establish a new focus for diagnostic teaching or to plan an instructional program or sequence.

> Optimal methods of instruction and levels of difficulty suggested by trial teaching thus provide the initial approaches that teachers use in remediation. However, as students

progress and their needs in reading change, additional tryouts of methods and materials occur. (Chall & Curtis, 1987, p. 786)

The thrust of the evaluation of the diagnostic teaching is to determine the impact of the manipulations on the student's learning, performance, attitude, motivation, and/or knowledge. When alternative methods have been used, this involves noting similarities and differences in a student's performance, motivation and/or knowledge during and after the administration of the different interventions. In the case of Seth, described above, this might mean several different types of evaluation. First, we would probably want to post-test his learning of new words under the different instructional methods to compare the relative effectiveness of the different interventions. Second, we would want to observe the extent to which he participated actively in each of the interventions. Other things being equal, the extent to which he was willing to engage in the instructional activities—i.e., the extent to which the techniques "made sense" to him—is perhaps the most important criterion for future success. No matter how good the instructional technique, it is unlikely to be successful if the reader resists, rather than participates actively.

When the scaffolding approach has been used, the evaluation would focus on a comparison of the student's learning, performance, knowledge and/or motivation at various levels of support from unaided to the greatest amount of support provided. The purpose of this comparison is to find an optimal level of support; that is, the level at which the reader is challenged enough to learn, but not so much that he or she gives up in frustration, or so little that he or she does not have to become actively involved. Regardless of the nature of the diagnostic teaching, comparisons can/should be made with information about a student's performance, skill, and motivation obtained through the observations, interviews, and formal and informal measures used in Steps 1–3.

We should also not overlook the invaluable information that can be gained by interviewing the student during and/or after the intervention (see Chapter 6). We have found the following types of questions to be extremely useful indicators of student learning and knowledge.

1. What do you think we are trying to learn and why? Why am I asking you to do _____?
2. Tell me how you figured out _____?
3. What would you have done differently if you were (I asked you to) _____?
4. Which procedure/activity did you like best and why? Which did you think helped you the most and why?
5. What did you learn, how do you do it, and when would you use it/how would it help you read better?

These simple but powerful questions can reveal a great deal about the student's understanding of how to use a new skill or strategy, as well as their attitudes and motivation for engaging in particular activities. These questions also serve an instructional purpose in that they convey to the student the need to consider when and why a skill would be used during other reading acts (Paris, Lipson, & Wixson, 1983).

The need to accomplish both the implementation and evaluation of diagnostic teaching as efficiently as possible is obvious. The purpose of good assessment is to help us make efficient and significant instructional progress with our student(s). The tremendous advantage to diagnostic teaching, as we have already noted, is that it melds assessment and instruction so that we need not take a great deal of time away from teaching. At the same time, it can save months that might be wasted implementing an instructional program that has little or no impact on the reader.

IMPLEMENTING STEPS 4, 5, AND 6 OF THE ASSESSMENT-INSTRUCTION PROCESS

Thumbnail Sketch

We have found it helpful to use a summary chart we call the thumbnail sketch to facilitate and monitor our decision making as we work through the first six steps of the assessment-instruction process (see Figure 10.1). This chart, or any form of written summary for that matter, forces us to think carefully about the important factors operating in individual cases. It can also reveal missing information.

The first column of the thumbnail sketch summarizes the information gathered about the reader as part of Steps 1 and 2 (Chapters 3–7). The second column summarizes the information gathered about the reading context in Step 3 (Chapters 8 and 9). Whenever possible, the information summarized in this part of the chart should describe the actual statements, behavior, or performance of the student rather than making interpretations about these events. When generalizations or interpretations are necessary, it is helpful to indicate the sources of the information upon which they are based. It should also be noted that it is not necessary to include every piece of evidence that has been gathered. It may already be clear that certain pieces of information are irrelevant and should be disregarded. However, if there is uncertainty as to the importance of the information, it is probably best to include it.

The procedures necessary for completing the third and fourth columns of this chart are described in this chapter. The third column summarizes the decisions made about the nature of the existing match (Step 4), and hypotheses about what the reader needs (Step 5). The fourth and last column summarizes information about the nature and results of the diagnostic teaching used with the student (Step 6).

The types of information provided in the last two columns of the chart are, of necessity, more interpretive than descriptive. However, whenever possible, it is still desirable to note the evidence leading to a particular conclusion. The remainder of this chapter is devoted to illustrating the implementation of Steps 4, 5, and 6 and the thumbnail sketch through the description of two case studies.

FIGURE 10.1

Thumbnail Sketch

Reader (Steps 1 and 2)	Reading Context (Step 3)	Decision Making (Steps 4 and 5)	Diagnostic Teaching (Step 6)
Background Name: Age: Grade: Key Correlates:	*Materials*	*Evaluating the Match (Step 4)* What is the match? (Existing match)	*Planning and Implementing* What is most likely to (re)establish learning?
Knowledge About Reading	*Methods*		
Application of Reading Skill	*Settings*	*Reflection and Generating Hypotheses (Step 5)* What does the reader need?	*Evaluating the Diagnostic Sessions*
Motivation			

A Case Study of Marvin

Figure 10.2 presents a summary of the information gathered on the reader and contextual factors involved in Marvin's case. The background information on Marvin revealed that he was 11, and in the beginning of fifth grade, and that his reading level was at approximately the third-grade level. In addition, there was no indication that any physical, linguistic, or cognitive correlates were implicated in his reading problem.

Under Knowledge About Reading, Marvin's interviews and IRI performance indicated that he understood the purposes for reading, that he did not understand his own reading problems, and that he knew about phonics but not structural analysis as methods for recognizing unfamiliar words. Under Application of Reading Skill, the information from several IRIs indicated that his word recognition skills were weaker than his comprehension skills and that he did not always seem to use the phonic knowledge he possessed during reading. Although generally strong, his comprehension was variable under different reading conditions. Finally, under Motivation, his behavior in the classroom and in the clinic revealed a pleasant, cooperative individual whose behavior did not change dramatically under different contextual conditions.

The information gathered about the reading context in Marvin's case revealed several key points. First, the history of frequent family moves and school back-

FIGURE 10.2

Thumbnail Sketch: Marvin, Steps 1–3

Reader (Steps 1 and 2)	Reading Context (Step 3)	Decision Making (Steps 4 and 5)	Diagnostic Teaching (Step 6)
Background Name: Marvin Age: 11 Grade: 5 Key Correlates: • Above average IQ. • Normal vision, hearing, and overall health. • Interests: science, sports, "taking things apart." *Knowledge About Reading* • Reports that people read to learn and for recreation: reports rate adjustment for text difficulty. • Reports misperception of own problem (believes it is comprehension). • Names "breaking words down" and "asking" as the only strategies for reading unfamiliar words. • Good phonics knowledge but poor structural analysis. *Application of Reading Skill* • Achievement Test results (end of Grade 4): PR-33; Stanine-4 • Word recognition scores consistently lower than comprehension. Comprehension strong but variable (IRIs). • Question responses and recall are grade appropriate on short, expository texts and well-formed stories. • Comprehension poor for complex, ambiguous, or symbolic texts. • Has difficulty inferring main ideas, problem solutions, and linking events to self-generated theme. *Motivation* • Pleasant, cooperative demeanor during classroom and clinical sessions. • Talks freely about affective responses to text and persists without prompting on difficult tasks. • When reading in the "instruction comfort range," laughs and comments on text.	*Materials* Dated basal reader/3^2 placement (phonics-based) heavy reliance on basal worksheets and teacher-made skill sheets. *Methods* Content: • Isolated phonics • Approach-practice without explanation/modeling • Whole group basal; limited prereading component. No cooperative work, book sharing. Limited reading outside of basal. *Settings* • Multiple moves and family disruptions during K-1. English spoken in home. Few reading materials, limited interest in reading at home. • Attended several schools during K-1. Placed in private parochial school from 2–4. Large student-teacher ratio, no support services. Policy of placing *all* students in *grade* appropriate materials.	*Evaluating the Match (Step 4)* What is the match? *Reflection and Generating Hypotheses (Step 5)* What does the reader need?	*Planning and Implementing* What is most likely to (re)establish learning? *Evaluating the Diagnostic Sessions*

ground suggested that he may not have had exposure to the full range of the reading curriculum. Second, the nature of the materials and instructional methods being used with Marvin suggested that he had little opportunity to practice applying his reading skills in the context of full-length reading selections. Finally, it is important to note that his instruction was focused on isolated phonics practice, with little or no modeling or explanation.

With this information in hand, we were ready to proceed with making some decisions regarding the appropriateness of the existing match, the nature of Marvin's needs, and how to change the match in ways that would lead to improvement in Marvin's learning and performance. The first step in this process was evaluating the existing match between Marvin's strengths and weaknesses as a reader and the characteristics of the settings, methods, and materials in which he was placed.

Evaluating the Existing Match and Generating Hypotheses (Steps 4 and 5)

A summary of our evaluation of the existing match (Step 4) and of the hypotheses we generated about what Marvin needed (Step 5) is provided in the third column of the thumbnail sketch presented in Figure 10.3. Recall that we said one way to evaluate the existing match between a reader and the characteristics of the reading context in which he must operate is to examine the information in each of the categories in the reader column and ask ourselves how it fits with what we know about the context and vice versa. Using this technique, we found more weaknesses than strengths in the existing match.

First, we noted that his approximate reading level (3-2) was considerably below his grade placement level (5). Second, his knowledge about and ability to use phonics skills, combined with his lack of familiarity and ability with other word attack strategies did not match well with his current instructional emphasis on phonics. Third, his problems comprehending complex texts and dealing with "high-level" comprehension tasks were not well matched to an instructional method that contained no teacher modeling and explanation of comprehension. Finally, the lack of cooperative work assignments and authentic reading and writing tasks in his instructional environment did not capitalize on his knowledge about the purposes of reading, or his positive attitude toward reading. In short, there were a number of areas in which the match between reader and reading context might be improved in an effort to promote Marvin's learning and performance in reading.

Step 5 provided the opportunity to reflect on the existing match and generate hypotheses about what Marvin needed if he was to become a better reader. This meant setting some priorities among the various needs that had been identified. As a result of this reflection, the following priorities were established for Marvin. First, he needed to acquire much more fluency in applying the word recognition and word analysis skills he already possessed. Marvin also needed additional knowledge and skill in word analysis; particularly in the area of structural and morphemic analysis.

Second, Marvin needed to learn more about how complex stories and expositions are organized and needed many instructional opportunities to read such materials with guidance and support. These two problems converged in the need for Marvin to acquire skill in reading the type of lengthy reading assignments often expected of middle-grade students. With our priorities established, we were now ready to move on to more focused assessment using diagnostic teaching.

Diagnostic Teaching (Step 6)

Once we had generated and prioritized our hypotheses, we were then ready to plan, implement, and evaluate the diagnostic teaching to be used to confirm or deny our hypotheses and identify a match that would promote Marvin's learning and performance (see Figure 10.4).

Planning. Marvin's strength was comprehension. However, his performance in comprehension was not universally strong. Marvin's consistently poor performance was limited to selections with unstated main ideas or problems, ambiguous themes, or complex text structures (the Burns and Roe IRI). These types of selections seem to embody what caused Marvin difficulty. We suspected that he could perform better if he were provided with more information prior to reading since he seemed to make such good use of all available information in constructing meaning. Indeed, he even appeared to make use of information available *after* reading (better performance on questioning tasks than retelling ones).

Thus, one focus for diagnostic teaching involved looking at the interaction between text, prereading support, and Marvin's ability to comprehend. Because Marvin also clearly needed additional decoding skills and a great deal of attention directed toward increasing his automaticity, a second focus for diagnostic teaching involved testing out an approach to this problem. As we reflected on Marvin's needs and on what we could manipulate to "call forth learning," the following seemed to invite consideration:

What Can/Should Be Changed to Improve the Match?
*1. Amount of prereading support
*2. Type of prereading instruction/support
*3. Length of text
 4. Knowledge about structural analysis
*5. Ability to infer main ideas
 6. Reading fluency (automaticity in word recognition)
   * = focus for diagnostic teaching

Not all of our conclusions about ways to improve Marvin's performance needed to be pursued through diagnostic teaching. Although diagnostic teaching is an invaluable addition to our assessment-instruction repertoire, it is not required in all situations. For example, there was no real reason to use diagnostic teaching to confirm that Marvin lacked knowledge about how to analyze multisyllabic words. We had very good evidence about this from previous assessment efforts.

FIGURE 10.3

Thumbnail Sketch: Marvin, Steps 4 and 5

Reader (Steps 1 and 2)	Reading Context (Step 3)	Decision Making (Steps 4 and 5)	Diagnostic Teaching (Step 6)
Background Name: Marvin Age: 11 Grade: 5 Key Correlates: • Above average IQ. • Normal vision, hearing, and overall health. • Interests: science, sports, "taking things apart." *Knowledge About Reading* • Reports that people read to learn and for recreation: reports rate adjustment for text difficulty. • Reports misperception of own problem (believes it is comprehension). • Names "breaking words down" and "asking" as the only strategies for reading unfamiliar words. • Good phonics knowledge but poor structural analysis. *Application of Reading Skill* • Achievement Test results (end of Grade 4): PR-33; Stanine-4 • Word recognition scores consistently lower than comprehension. Comprehension strong but variable (IRIs). • Question responses and recall are grade appropriate on short, expository texts and well-formed stories. • Comprehension poor for complex, ambiguous, or symbolic texts. • Has difficulty inferring main ideas, problem solutions, and linking events to self-generated theme. *Motivation* • Pleasant, cooperative demeanor during classroom and clinical sessions. • Talks freely about affective responses to text and persists without prompting on difficult tasks. • When reading in the "instruction comfort range," laughs and comments on text.	*Materials* Dated basal reader/3² placement (phonics-based) heavy reliance on basal worksheets and teacher-made skill sheets. *Methods* Content: • Isolated phonics • Approach-practice without explanation/ modeling • Whole group basal; limited prereading component. No co-operative work, book sharing. Limited reading outside of basal. *Settings* • Multiple moves and family disruptions during K-1. English spoken in home. Few reading materials, limited interest in reading at home. • Attended several schools during K-1. Placed in private parochial school from 2–4. Large student-teacher ratio, no support services. Policy of placing *all* students in *grade* appropriate materials.	*Evaluating the Match (Step 4)* What is the match? a. Reading level placement below potential performance; below grade placement. b. Better reading in text is poor match to isolated phonics approach. c. Has trouble reading long/ complex selections but receives no instruction in this area. d. Is expected to read long texts in science and social studies without preparation. *Reflection and Generating Hypotheses (Step 5)* What does the reader need? a. increased practice in reading connected text b. better pre-reading preparation for reading complex or lengthy selections. c. additional skill and practice in WR to improve fluency.	*Planning and Implementing* What is most likely to (re)establish learning? *Evaluating the Diagnostic Sessions*

FIGURE 10.4

Thumbnail Sketch: Marvin, Step 6

Reader (Steps 1 and 2)	Reading Context (Step 3)	Decision Making (Steps 4 and 5)	Diagnostic Teaching (Step 6)
Background Name: Marvin Age: 11 Grade: 5 Key Correlates: • Above average IQ. • Normal vision, hearing, and overall health. • Interests: science, sports, "taking things apart." *Knowledge About Reading* • Reports that people read to learn and for recreation: reports rate adjustment for text difficulty. • Reports misperception of own problem (believes it is comprehension). • Names "breaking words down" and "asking" as the only strategies for reading unfamiliar words. • Good phonics knowledge but poor structural analysis. *Application of Reading Skill* • Achievement Test results (end of Grade 4): PR-33; Stanine-4 • Word recognition scores consistently lower than comprehension. Comprehension strong but variable (IRIs). • Question responses and recall are grade appropriate on short, expository texts and well-formed stories. • Comprehension poor for complex, ambiguous, or symbolic texts. • Has difficulty inferring main ideas, problem solutions, and linking events to self-generated theme. *Motivation* • Pleasant, cooperative demeanor during classroom and clinical sessions. • Talks freely about affective responses to text and persists without prompting on difficult tasks. • When reading in the "instruction comfort range," laughs and comments on text.	*Materials* Dated basal reader/3^2 placement (phonics-based) heavy reliance on basal worksheets and teacher-made skill sheets. *Methods* Content: • Isolated phonics • Approach-practice without explanation/modeling • Whole group basal; limited prereading component. No cooperative work, book sharing. Limited reading outside of basal. *Settings* • Multiple moves and family disruptions during K-1. English spoken in home. Few reading materials, limited interest in reading at home. • Attended several schools during K-1. Placed in private parochial school from 2–4. Large student-teacher ratio, no support services. Policy of placing *all* students in *grade* appropriate materials.	*Evaluating the Match (Step 4)* What is the match? a. Reading level placement below potential performance; below grade placement. b. Better reading in text is poor match to isolated phonics approach. c. Has trouble reading long/complex selections but receives no instruction in this area. d. Is expected to read long texts in science and social studies without preparation. *Reflection and Generating Hypotheses (Step 5)* What does the reader need? a. increased practice in reading connected text b. better prereading preparation for reading complex or lengthy selections. c. additional skill and practice in WR to improve fluency.	*Planning and Implementing* What is most likely to (re)establish learning? a. Use difficult texts with appropriate prereading preparation. b. Practice in reading connected text to build fluency. c. Additional skill in word recognition. Question: Direct instruction *or* • Try layered prompts w/IRI • Try talking dictionary *Evaluating the Diagnostic Sessions* Increased work in reading should improve fluency Performs better with preparation Can read grade appropriate text with support

Executing: Comprehension focus. Because the Burns and Roe IRI selections caused Marvin difficulty, our first diagnostic teaching efforts were focused on these selections. Of course, we could have selected passages that were similar in text structure and theme. However, our major concern during this diagnostic session was to confirm our hypothesis that Marvin's comprehension was influenced by ambiguity or complexity of theme and main idea and that it could be improved by instructional support.

Marvin had reached frustrational level on a selection without a title that dealt with a young boy's concern about a test (see Figure 10.5). Marvin missed the subtle main idea and construed the selection to be about imminent war. Having construed the selection that way, Marvin missed several related questions, resulting in a frustration level comprehension performance. Since it appeared that Marvin might be able to understand material (even at this level of difficulty) if he had some organizational support, he was asked to reread the selection, this time imagining that the story was entitled, ''Peter Worries About a Test.'' Given that much support, Marvin answered all the questions posed correctly and was able to provide a coherent and accurate summary of the selection. The exercise was repeated with two other selections, and each time Marvin was totally successful in his comprehension efforts.

Given a general idea of the topic, Marvin had no difficulty linking ideas, locating information, or supporting inferential conclusions. Our evaluation of this diagnostic teaching effort led us to conclude that Marvin could benefit from rather minimal supports in comprehending text. Next, of course, we would need to teach him to generate and use structural supports independently. This required recycling to establish a new focus, one designed to try out instructionally powerful interventions for accomplishing this. In the meantime, we wanted to attempt a trial teaching lesson directed at his rather significant word recognition/automaticity problems.

Executing: Word recognition focus. In this diagnostic teaching session, we tried a variation on a repeated reading strategy, Talking Dictionary (see Chapter 11). This technique was used for two reasons: first, we believed that Marvin's poor word recognition efforts during reading might result from limited reading practice; and second, we hoped to arrive at an approach that would permit him to use his good comprehension abilities to read grade appropriate text. The supported oral reading activity we tried permits students to ask how a word is pronounced during a first reading and evaluates the extent to which they remember these words and build fluency during a second reading of the same material.

Using grade level material (Grade 5), Marvin read 76 words correctly in a 2-minute period during the first read-through (asked for 8 words, misread 5). During the second 2-minute read of the same material, Marvin read 115 words correctly, miscalling only 3 words and correctly reading all 8 words that he had requested during the first read.

Evaluating. As we evaluated our diagnostic teaching efforts for Marvin, we examined the impact of our manipulations on his performance. In the first

FIGURE 10.5
Sample IRI Selection

About the story: *Read this story to find out about a boy named Pete and a problem that he has.*

"I see in the papers that the world is coming to an end," said Mr. Peters, reading the newspaper at the breakfast table. He chuckled.

Pete swallowed his bit of toast. "When?" he said.

His mother looked at his father and frowned, warningly.

"Not this afternoon," she said hastily to Pete.

Mr. Peters shrugged. "It doesn't say this afternoon," he agreed.

Peter munched his crisp cereal thoughtfully. If it wasn't this afternoon it wouldn't do him much good, he thought. For the test would be this afternoon—the test the substitute teacher had prepared for them.

Thinking about the test, Pete plopped into his seat at school with an unnecessary plunk. Miss Dingley frowned at him.

Burns, Paul C., and Betty D. Roe, *Informal Reading Inventory*, Second Edition. Copyright © 1985 by Houghton Mifflin Company. Used with permission.

instance, it was apparent that our instructional manipulation during the prereading phase had produced better performance than we had observed in the unaided condition. Similarly, our hypothesis that Marvin could benefit from greater exposure to print in a supported context seemed worth continuing. The word recognition/fluency manipulation was repeated in a second session during which Marvin read 64 words correctly in the first 2-minute read and 127 words correctly in the second 2-minute period. Given the effectiveness of this approach, we then integrated it into his instructional program.

The diagnostic teaching sessions generated several instructional options. In the second case, the diagnostic teaching resulted in a decision to include a specific instructional method into his ongoing program. We incorporated the repeated readings activity into every session to encourage Marvin to use his word recognition knowledge more automatically and to build fluency. In the first case, our diagnostic teaching resulted in a recycling to establish a new focus. We determined that Marvin could work, with support, in grade level material, and used it whenever possible.

Because he obviously needed more understanding of complex stories, we also initiated a new series of diagnostic teaching lessons designed to help Marvin recognize and impose story structure on lengthy narratives. Story maps (see Chapters 7 and 13) were used to guide him through text. They both supported him during reading and forced him to reconstruct meaning (generating connections) during a postreading retelling. After each of these sessions, Marvin's response to the three evaluative questions was recorded. After the first of these sessions, Marvin responded:

What did you learn?	I learned about story maps.
How do you use it?	You think about the people in the story and what they do and put it down on the chart.
When would you use it?	During reading, you look for this information. Then you don't panic.

Clearly, continuous assessment will be necessary. The results of just two small diagnostic interventions, however, yielded exceptionally good information about what types of instruction would benefit Marvin.

A Case Study of Tom

A summary of the information gathered on the reader and contextual factors involved in Tom's case is presented in the thumbnail sketch chart in Figure 10.6. The background information on Tom indicated that he was 7 years old, a beginning second-grade student who had just started reading in the first preprimer. Of the possible physical, linguistic, or cognitive correlates, the only likely factor in his reading problem was his language background as a dialect speaker.

Tom's interviews and performance suggested that he had prerequisite knowledge for learning to read and some awareness of his own reading difficulties. His performance on the TERA confirmed his readiness for reading and, more importantly, indicated that he performed better on story-based tasks such as retelling than on isolated letter and word tasks. Evidence from the word lists and the IRI confirmed good comprehension of what he could decode accompanied by poor word recognition skills. Finally, his performance in the initial assessment revealed positive attitudes and motivation when dealing with tasks related to story reading contrasted with negative attitudes and motivation for isolated letter/word tasks.

There were several notable features of the reading context in Tom's case. First, his home setting was characterized by storybook reading experience with his mother, and his school placement was a small second-grade class reserved for remedial students. Second, the exclusive focus of his reading instruction was on readiness activities such as sight word recognition and sound-symbol correspondence. In addition, the method of instruction was practice of isolated skills with no modeling or explanation and little opportunity to apply skills in any type of authentic reading or writing activities (including reading in the basal).

Given this summary of the information gathered in Steps 1–3, we were then ready to proceed to Step 4, and an evaluation of the existing match between Tom's strengths and weaknesses and key features of the reading context.

Evaluating the Existing Match and Generating Hypotheses (Steps 4 and 5)

A summary of our evaluation of the existing match (Step 4) and of the hypotheses we generated about what Tom needed (Step 5) is provided in the third column of the thumbnail sketch presented in Figure 10.7. As in Marvin's case, the match between Tom's knowledge, skills, and attitudes and the settings, methods, and materials that confront him within the reading context was not a good one. Generally, the organization, methods, and materials of his instruction maximized his weaknesses in the knowledge and application of decontextualized skills, and minimized his ability to use his understanding of reading to comprehend and

FIGURE 10.6

Thumbnail Sketch: Tom, Steps 1–3

Reader (Steps 1 and 2)	Reading Context (Step 3)	Decision Making (Steps 4 and 5)	Diagnostic Teaching (Step 6)
Background Name: Tom Age: 7 Grade: 2 Reading Level: PP1 Key Correlates: • Dialect speaker • Normal vision, hearing, and development *Knowledge About Reading* • Understands purpose of reading (interview). • Demonstrates knowledge of story structure (retelling). • Knows he has trouble with accurate oral reading. *Application of Reading Skills* • Missed 42 of 1st 100 words on Fry list; • IRI:PP level word recognition 1st+level composition; • TERA: Reading age = 6.8 performed better in retelling than isolated letter/word tasks *Motivation* • Withdrawn when asked to do traditional letter/word tasks; • Animated when discussing books his mother reads to him and when retelling stories.	*Materials* Reading placement level PP1 • Basal work-sheets and skill sheets; • Some oral reading from reader *Methods* • Focused on isolated word rec. skills; • Practice without modeling or explanation; • Little time spent with reader or other books. *Settings* • Mom reads to him at home; • Placed in special class with 18 low-achieving second graders.	*Evaluating the Match (Step 4)* What is the match? *Reflection and Generating Hypotheses (Step 5)* What does the reader need?	*Planning and Implementing* What is most likely to (re)establish learning? *Evaluating the Diagnostic Sessions*

attack unfamiliar words. A number of specific interactions between reader and context supported this conclusion.

First, Tom's excellent knowledge about reading did not fit well with an instructional context that focused almost exclusively on isolated prereading skills; he did not understand what his instruction had to do with what he knew about reading. Second, his instruction did not capitalize on his strength in comprehension as a means of aiding his word recognition. Third, his instruction did not take advantage of his increased motivation when dealing with meaningful, connected text rather than isolated skill drill. Finally, the remedial setting in which he had been placed minimized the types of interactions that were likely to be most successful with Tom.

Our evaluation of the existing match provided us with the information needed to generate hypotheses about what Tom needed to progress as a beginning reader. Our assessment was that Tom needed two things. First, he needed instruction that capitalized on his strong knowledge about reading while attending to his weaknesses in word recognition. In other words he needed "contextualized" word recognition instruction that would enable him to learn new word attack skills and apply those he had already acquired and learned. The second thing that Tom needed was to become more actively involved in his own learning and instruction.

Diagnostic Teaching (Step 6)

At this point in the process, we were ready to engage in diagnostic teaching as a means of confirming our hypotheses and identifying possible instructional interventions. A summary of Tom's diagnostic teaching and its results is presented in the thumbnail sketch in Figure 10.8.

Planning. In the planning phase of diagnostic teaching, we needed to determine the specific nature of the interventions that would address the needs identified in Step 5. To do this, as we have noted previously, it is easiest to think in terms of the features of the settings, methods, and materials that can and should be modified and manipulated. In Tom's case, there were several aspects of the classroom setting (e.g., grouping and interaction patterns) that needed to be modified to improve his involvement in his own learning and instruction. However, since we were not in a position to modify this setting, these factors were not good candidates for manipulation in diagnostic teaching. Despite this fact, there were still a variety of options that could be implemented in the tutorial program.

The characteristics of the methods, materials, and tasks of Tom's instructional context offered several alternatives for diagnostic teaching. Specifically, the instructional method could be modified to include methods and tasks that provided Tom with more support and elicited his active involvement in his own learning. In addition, his reading materials could be altered to provide him with more and better examples of interesting, connected text for use in learning and applying a variety of word recognition skills.

After considering the various alternatives, we decided to try out two alternative approaches for providing contextualized word recognition instruction. These approaches could roughly be characterized as a dictated stories approach and a cloze approach.

Executing. The dictated stories approach was a modification of the traditional language experience approach. This procedure was designed to promote Tom's active involvement in learning sight words in the context of reading his own stories. The steps used were as follows:

1. Tom dictated and the examiner transcribed a short "story" on a topic of interest (e.g., the upcoming holidays).

FIGURE 10.7

Thumbnail Sketch: Tom, Steps 4 and 5

Reader (Steps 1 and 2)	Reading Context (Step 3)	Decision Making (Steps 4 and 5)	Diagnostic Teaching (Step 6)
Background Name: Tom Age: 7 Grade: 2 Reading Level: PP1 Key Correlates: • Dialect speaker • Normal vision, hearing, and development *Knowledge About Reading* • Understands purpose of reading (interview). • Demonstrates knowledge of story structure (retelling). • Knows he has trouble with accurate oral reading. *Application of Reading Skills* • Missed 42 of 1st 100 words on Fry list; • IRI:PP level word recognition 1st + level composition; • TERA: Reading age = 6.8 performed better in retelling than isolated letter/word tasks *Motivation* • Withdrawn when asked to do traditional letter/word tasks; • Animated when discussing books his mother reads to him and when retelling stories.	*Materials* Reading placement level PP1 • Basal worksheets and skill sheets; • Some oral reading from reader *Methods* • Focused on isolated word rec. skills; • Practice without modeling or explanation; • Little time spent with reader or other books. *Settings* • Mom reads to him at home; • Placed in special class with 18 low-achieving second graders.	*Evaluating the Match (Step 4)* What is the match? Existing Match There is a poor fit between: • Good knowledge about reading and instruction focused on isolated readiness skills. • Good comprehension and decontextualized word resource instruction. • Motivation to read and lack of opportunity to read. • Active learning style and passive instruction. *Reflection and Generating Hypotheses (Step 5)* What does the reader need? • Better word resource skills. • "Contextualized" instruction. • Active involvement in his own learning.	*Planning and Implementing* What is most likely to (re)establish learning? *Evaluating the Diagnostic Sessions*

2. Tom read the story orally in its entirety.
3. The story was cut into sentence strips, the sentence strips were scrambled, and Tom was asked to put them in the correct order and reread the story.
4. The sentence strips were cut into word cards which were then scrambled, and Tom was asked to reorder the words into sentences and read aloud each sentence.
5. Tom targeted words to be entered into his word card file for future study and review.

The dictated story procedure required Tom to become actively involved in multiple readings of new words in the context of reading material he had generated for himself. In contrast, the cloze approach employed traditional early reading selections that had been altered to elicit Tom's active engagement in the application and integration of graphophonic and contextual word analysis strategies. Specifically, Tom was asked to read and supply the missing words for text in which all but the first letter of the targeted decodable words had been omitted. The targeted words were then added to his word bank for future study and review.

Both the dictated story and the cloze procedure were administered in a manner that included explaining to Tom the reason for each of the activities. In addition, he was asked frequently to reflect on what he was doing and why. This was done to help Tom understand the connections between reading instruction and independent reading activities.

Evaluating.   Several methods were used to evaluate the relative effectiveness of these two approaches. First, Tom was post-tested on his retention of the targeted words at the end of the session and after an intervening activity in which he listened to the examiner read. The results of this method of evaluation indicated that Tom recalled 100% of the words learned in the dictated story intervention and 75% of the words learned in the cloze approach.

The second method of evaluation involved asking Tom to describe the purposes of the two procedures and his feelings about completing the different activities. Tom described the purposes for both activities as learning to read words, but indicated that he liked cutting up the sentences the best.

The last, and possibly the most important, method of evaluation focused on the observation of Tom's interest and involvement in the various activities. Tom's behavior during the dictated story activities was animated and attentive. He was so interested in these activities that we had a hard time disengaging him when we needed to move on. In contrast, he was quite passive as he engaged in the cloze activities. Perhaps this procedure was too reminiscent of the activities he found so uninteresting in school. Whatever the reason, he showed a clear preference for the dictated story approach.

As a result of this diagnostic teaching experience, we devised a tutoring program based on the dictated story approach to which we added think-aloud and cloze activities that used his own stories. Tom never lost interest in this approach to learning, and proved to have a phenomenal memory for new words. We were able

FIGURE 10.8

Thumbnail Sketch: Tom, Step 6

Reader (Steps 1 and 2)	Reading Context (Step 3)	Decision Making (Steps 4 and 5)	Diagnostic Teaching (Step 6)
Background Name: Tom Age: 7 Grade: 2 Reading Level: PP1 Key Correlates: • Dialect speaker • Normal vision, hearing, and development *Knowledge About Reading* • Understands purpose of reading (interview). • Demonstrates knowledge of story structure (retelling). • Knows he has trouble with accurate oral reading. *Application of Reading Skills* • Missed 42 of 1st 100 words on Fry list; • IRI:PP level word recognition 1st + level composition; • TERA: Reading age = 6.8 performed better in retelling than isolated letter/word tasks *Motivation* • Withdrawn when asked to do traditional letter/word tasks; • Animated when discussing books his mother reads to him and when retelling stories.	*Materials* Reading placement level PP1 • Basal work-sheets and skill sheets; • Some oral reading from reader *Methods* • Focused on isolated word rec. skills; • Practice without modeling or explanation; • Little time spent with reader or other books. *Settings* • Mom reads to him at home; • Placed in special class with 18 low-achieving second graders.	*Evaluating the Match (Step 4)* What is the match? Existing Match There is a poor fit between: • Good knowledge about reading and instruction focused on isolated readiness skills. • Good comprehension and decontextualized word resource instruction. • Motivation to read and lack of opportunity to read. • Active learning style and passive instruction. *Reflection and Generating Hypotheses (Step 5)* What does the reader need? • Better word resource skills. • "Contextualized" instruction. • Active involvement in his own learning.	*Planning and Implementing* What is most likely to (re)establish learning? Compare two "contextualized" approaches to word recognition instruction • Teaching sight words taken from his dictated stories. • Teaching him to use graphic and contextual cues together to identify missing words in modified cloze passages. *Evaluating the Diagnostic Sessions* Dictated stories better than cloze because: • 100% of words learned vs 75%. • He reported preferring the "cutting" activity to all others. • More attentive, animated behavior.

to introduce as many as 10 new words in each session, and our frequent reviews indicated he rarely needed reteaching. At the end of 20 tutoring sessions, Tom's word recognition level on a repeated administration of the IRI had improved from a preprimer to a first reader level on the word lists, and from a primer to a second-grade level for passage reading. The diagnostic teaching cycle was continuing, however, with interventions that would teach Tom to expand his repertoire of word recognition strategies from memorization and contextual analysis to the use of graphophonic information he will need as he begins to encounter more complex texts.

For both Marvin and Tom, the benefits of diagnostic teaching were both immediate and long-term. Each was quickly engaged in an instructional program that held promise of addressing their needs. In addition, the tutors were able to shape these sessions to obtain good information for planning and extending the reading programs of each. It does not always happen that our first diagnostic teaching sessions yield so rich a reward. One thing is abundantly clear, however. The quality of these sessions was directly related to two factors: the quality of the assessment information that was gathered before diagnostic teaching, and the thoughtfulness of the planning that went into the diagnostic teaching segment.

FROM CLASSROOM TO CLINIC

Diagnostic teaching requires a solid knowledge base, a willingness to explore variation in student performance, and a repertoire of activities and materials for creating instructional adaptations. In the chapters to follow, we provide many suggestions for planning, adapting, and delivering good reading instruction. Many of these ideas can be incorporated into diagnostic teaching. Although the types of decision making and diagnostic teaching that can be employed by classroom teachers and clinicians may differ, the underlying principles do not. Both classroom teachers and clinicians can and should make their hunches (hypotheses) explicit, set priorities, and use them to plan and execute instructional adaptations. Good teaching, whether in the classroom or the clinic, requires that teachers establish and maintain their focus to accomplish assessment or instructional purposes. However, good teaching is also opportunistic and flexible. Interactive decision making during instruction is a hallmark of effective instruction (Duffy & Roehler, 1986). This requires careful listening and refocusing.

In order to capitalize on the diagnostic teaching procedures we have described in this chapter, classroom teachers and clinicians will need to acknowledge the strengths and limitations of their own settings. Few classroom teachers will find the time to engage in continuous full-blown diagnostic sessions such as the ones we have described, and clinicians may even find it difficult to make this a part of their regular routine. Therefore, we suggest two specific practices that may prove helpful, depending on the setting.

Target Selections for Diagnostic Teaching

Classroom teachers who are using a basal reading system can designate specific selections in each level for use as diagnostic teaching selections. In this way, conditions can be set up that reflect the focus of classroom instruction. For example, predetermined selections can be used to:

1. conduct an individual assessment that examines students' progress outside their usual group setting;
2. set up conditions that are analogous to classroom instruction and compare those to students' unaided reading of the selection;
3. manipulate aspects of the lesson that are critical for student(s) in a particular classroom;
4. select texts that make different demands as a means of exploring student flexibility.

If selections are targeted periodically, it is possible to do more elaborated assessment from time to time, rather than attempting it on a daily or even weekly basis.

Classroom teachers who are using a trade book/literature-based program can accomplish the same thing by establishing "assessment books." One of the authors has worked with a school system that so values this approach that they have established a database for over 150 books so that teachers (and students) at Grades 1 through 3 can select from a wide array of regular library books to accomplish these assessments. Teachers who may be concerned about compromising the entertainment value of these books must remember that students need practice reading for a variety of different purposes. Furthermore, if the student's personal affective response to reading is an important goal of classroom instruction, then it should be included as part of the assessment.

A Collection of Diagnostic Teaching Selections

For both classroom teachers and clinicians, the time and attention demands are so great that diagnostic teaching is more likely to be employed if the materials and tasks are readily available. Paratore and Indrisano (1987) have developed a set of materials they use for diagnostic teaching that include graded (or progressively more difficult) passages and a set of tasks and prompts to accompany these passages. These materials permit them to explore a range of student responses "on the spot."

To be effective, a collection of diagnostic teaching selections must be organized and grouped for easy use, and clearly labeled so that adjustments can be made during the assessment session. In addition, we recommend using a set of clearly tabbed task cards to facilitate administration. The following types of materials should be considered for inclusion in a diagnostic teaching collection:

- selections ranked by difficulty or a list of books to be used for assessment purposes;
- a listing of the types of tasks that can/should be used and the order in which these will be presented;
- a series of statements for each selection/book that could be expected in an adequate retelling of the text, and a place to note these;
- a summary sheet that includes key words to be used for assessment of vocabulary and/or word recognition;
- a place to make notes about student comments.

These ideas are, of course, only suggestions. Once started, a well-organized collection can and will grow. Furthermore, teachers who are committed to a portfolio approach to assessment find this type of organization absolutely essential to the effective implementation of ongoing assessment activities.

CHAPTER SUMMARY

This chapter focused on the point in assessment when informed decision making is required to determine how instructional planning will proceed. Specifically, this chapter dealt with understanding and implementing the steps in the assessment-instruction process that involve evaluating the match between reader and reading context (Step 4), reflection and generating hypotheses (Step 5), and diagnostic teaching (Step 6).

Evaluating the match between the reader and the reading context (Step 4) involves using the information gathered in Steps 1–3 to determine the fit or match between the knowledge, skills, and motivation of the reader and the settings, methods, and materials/tasks within the reading context. After the match between the reader and the reading context has been evaluated, we need to reflect on this information and generate hypotheses (Step 5) about what the reader needs. This step is designed to help us make decisions about the relative importance of the various problems/needs we have identified.

Following Steps 4 and 5, in which we reflected on the existing match and generated some preliminary hypotheses about what the reader needs, we need to identify a better or optimal match between the reader and the reading context in order to (re)establish learning. To accomplish this goal, we rely primarily on the technique of *diagnostic teaching*. This procedure is both diagnostic, because it allows the collection of additional information in order to clarify and test hypotheses, and instructional, because it provides opportunities to try out methods that may be successful alternatives for working with a student.

The process of diagnostic teaching involves three related tasks: planning, executing, and evaluating. During planning, we need to determine how we will focus the diagnostic teaching to verify our hunches about both the source of the problem and the instructional interventions that are most likely to call forth learning. Executing involves administering diagnostic teaching sessions using either the alternative methods or scaffolding approach to gain information about how a reader performs under several different or contrasting conditions. Successful execution also requires the flexibility necessary to be able to take advantage of opportunities as they arise.

The primary thrust of the evaluation of the diagnostic teaching is to determine the impact of the manipulations on the student's learning, performance, attitude, motivation, and/or knowledge. Diagnostic teaching activities can be facilitated in both the classroom and the clinic through procedures such as using targeted selections in basal reading programs or preselecting a collection of diagnostic teaching materials.

S E C T I O N   V

Instruction

THE PRECEDING CHAPTERS have focused on assessment and diagnostic teaching as a means of gathering information and gaining insight into individual learners. Decisions about how and what to teach are based on the resulting knowledge and understanding. Good decision making also requires an awareness of available instructional strategies and tools. Fortunately, there has been an upsurge of interest in recent years in advancing and promoting "best practices" in reading and writing instruction. Thoughtful teachers now have a wide array of effective instructional interventions from which to select their own preferred methods.

This section deals directly with Step 7—Focusing on Instruction: Continuous Monitoring and Modification—of the assessment-instruction process, the shaded area in the figure on the following page. Effective teaching demands a broad knowledge of the individual child and recognition that different students may need different types of instruction. Consequently, teachers must be able to select instructional strategies that are most likely to address the needs of individual children. Chapter 11 provides guidelines for creating effective literacy environments and planning good initial instruction. In the remaining chapters, we describe instructional interventions that address specific components of literacy. Chapter 12 is devoted to adapting instruction to focus on word recognition, Chapter 13 to adapting instruction to focus vocabulary, and Chapter 14 to comprehension and studying. Consistent with the focus throughout this text, these specific instructional techniques have been selected for discussion because they are a close match to the theoretical perspective of this text or because they have demonstrated their utility.

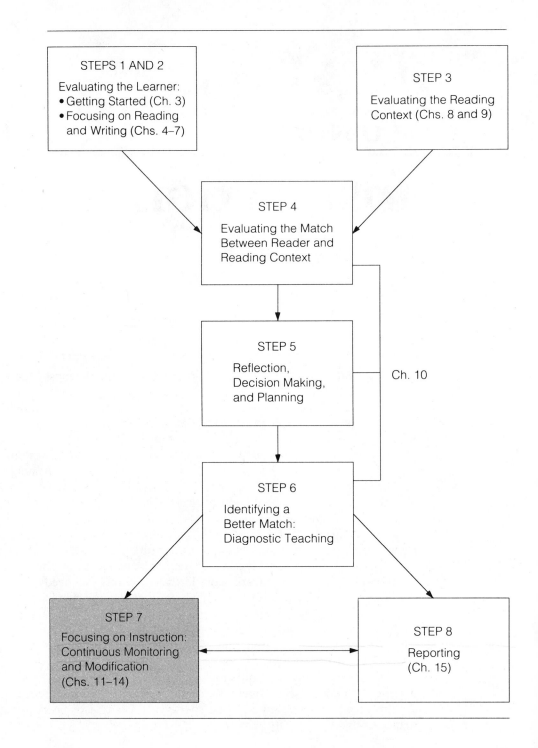

CHAPTER 11

Getting Started in Instruction

INTRODUCTION

Effective reading instruction relies heavily on the decision making powers of individual teachers. To make good decisions, teachers must orchestrate knowledge and skill in endlessly changing ways. In earlier chapters, we provided information about how to begin making good decisions using high-quality assessment information. In this chapter, we point out the types of instructional decisions that must be made and describe some effective instructional strategies for getting started.

Like assessment, instruction must begin somewhere. Of course, the multiple types of information that have been gathered, summarized, and examined quite closely in earlier steps of the assessment-instruction process (see Chapter 10) could now be used to plan an instructional program. However, it is often necessary to launch an instructional program before the assessment picture is completely clear. As we have already noted, the assessment-instruction process is continuous and requires adaptive teaching. Consequently, the issues addressed in this chapter are on the *beginnings* of instruction. This chapter lays the foundation for several chapters that follow, where more specific ideas about instructional intervention are offered.

Chapter Overview

In the next three sections of this chapter, we address three key aspects of instruction. First we discuss long-term curricular planning, describing the types of decisions that must be made to establish a program focused on important curricular goals. Next, we describe some specific instructional activities that have such high general applicability that it makes sense to use them with nearly all students. Using the techniques, it is possible to get started with a student or students even when there is still some doubt about the details of the instructional program. In the final section of this chapter, we address the issue of lesson planning for individual students, providing guidance in specifying objectives and selecting activities. The more detailed planning described in that section leads from the "getting started," "high-utility" strategies described in this chapter to the narrower instructional focus of the remaining chapters of the book (see Chapters 12–14).

MAKING DECISIONS: LONG-TERM PLANNING

Studies of school effectiveness suggest that instruction has the most impact when goals are clear and student progress is frequently monitored (Edmonds, 1980; Rupley, 1976). Given what is known about reading and reading instruction (see Chapter 8), it is clear that teachers and the programs they implement are central to student learning. The basis for effective instruction is, of course, careful planning and preparation. Teachers make both long-term and short-term plans. In this

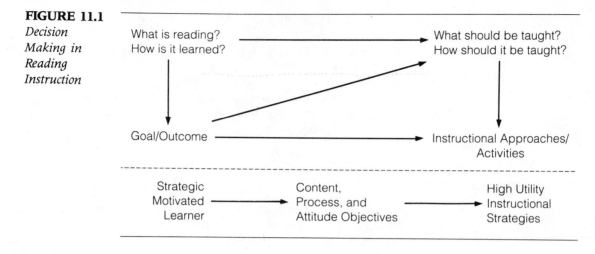

FIGURE 11.1
Decision Making in Reading Instruction

section of the chapter, we describe some of the long-term, overarching decisions and plans that must be made by teachers: deciding on goals and outcomes, selecting an organizational pattern, and selecting materials.

Goals and Outcomes

There are always a variety of ways to help students learn information and acquire competence. Effective teachers control a wide range of instructional tools that they can use flexibly. However, specific instructional activities that might be used to teach students are of far less importance than knowing what is to be accomplished. As we noted in Chapter 8, objectives are devised by teachers as they consider their knowledge of the reading process and their understanding of skilled reading, and what is known about the student. We turn to the first of these now, and to the second near the end of the chapter.

Even without exceptionally focused information about individual students, it is possible to make some judgments about appropriate practice. The framework displayed in Figure 11.1 maps the knowledge base developed in this text and upon which teacher decision making rests. It describes the flow of activity involved in planning what or how instruction should be delivered and in selecting instructional activities. Starting in the upper left-hand corner, the figure acknowledges that decisions about instruction flow from an understanding of reading and the reading process.

The curricular goals described in Chapter 8 are derived from this set of relationships and can provide important guidance in initial planning. As we stated there, the goal of reading instruction should be to create, encourage, or develop strategic, motivated readers. In refining these ideas, we noted that specific lesson objectives needed to address three major types of outcomes. We will return to the issue of lesson planning in the final section of this text. For now, it is important to remember that effective reading programs must include provisions for the development of *attitude, process,* and *content* outcomes.

In adopting these curricular goals, teachers must recognize how both the delivery system and the content of instruction influence learning. The first step toward accomplishing these ambitious long-term curricular goals to is create a context for success—an environment in which learning important outcomes is possible.

Establishing a Literate Environment

The instructional context can and does influence learning and comprehension (see Chapters 8 and 9). Attempts to separate a particular reader's problems from setting, methods, and materials are fruitless, since this separation ignores the interactive nature of reading. Similarly, instruction is most effective when the texts and tasks mimic real reading and the teaching occurs in integrated contexts. For example, there is evidence to suggest that students' reading achievement is enhanced by reading connected text with the support and guidance of a teacher, whereas there is little relationship between reading achievement and students' engagement in games or workbook activities (Leinhardt, Zigmond, & Cooley, 1981; Zigmond, Vallecorsa, & Leinhardt, 1980). Therefore, the first step in effective reading instruction, especially for less-able readers, is the creation of a literate environment. Borrowing from the work of Duffy and Roehler (1989), we described in Chapter 8 three aspects of the classroom that comprise a literate environment. Below we provide guidelines for establishing a literate environment using related descriptors: the print environment (the physical environment), meaningful enterprise (the intellectual environment), and social exchange and interaction (the social-emotional environment).

The Print Environment

The first step in establishing a literate environment is establishing accessible, inviting, and well-trafficked reading and writing centers. The reading center, or library corner, should invite students to read. The rug(s), cushions, or soft chair(s) establish this as an area of comfortable interaction with print. Characters from books can be prominently displayed in the form of stuffed animals, drawings, illustrations, or book covers, depending on the age of the group.

The available print matter should offer students a wide range of reading options. Stocking a classroom library requires some knowledge and commitment on the part of teachers. Many teachers are well-informed about books, but there is evidence that others have not developed knowledge and expertise in this area. Mangieri and Corboy (1981) report that 71% of the 571 elementary school teachers they surveyed could not name a single children's book published in the five preceding years. Only 9% of the total could name three or more such books.

The print materials should include all manner of real texts and reading materials used by literate individuals both in and out of school. The classroom reading collection might contain several books by the same author, books and stories created by children in the class, information about authors, and reference materials (maps, atlases, schedules, and so on). Some materials will be intended for recreational, self-selected reading, while others will be used more selectively by students as they complete projects or require information.

The materials in this center or library should be consulted whenever possible. When a map is needed, students should be aware that they can consult the atlas in the reading center. When they need a good book for silent reading time, they should expect to find one there as well, along with written critiques of books by children who have already read them. In addition, this area would ideally contain newspapers, magazines, and other everyday print materials.

A literate environment also contains a well-stocked and accessible *writing/ publishing center.* Students' writing folders may be kept in this area, but it should also contain writing materials, dictionaries, and, for older students, a thesaurus. Writing conference guidelines should be posted here. Many teachers and students like to have a *word wall* in this area. The word wall is simply a large, blank paper, on which the students or teacher can write words that are frequently needed but difficult to spell, words that someone has found interesting and wants to share, or theme-related words that will be useful only for a particular period. If there is room, this area should also contain at least one computer with word processing software and materials for illustrating and "publishing" books (paper, book bindings, markers, and so on). Samples of writing can also be posted, for inspiration or sharing.

Meaningful Enterprise

Setting the stage for literacy development is critical, but not easy, given the traditional focus on teacher-controlled school activity. A key feature of any setting that promotes literacy is the provision for *meaningful enterprise.* In describing the attributes of a literate environment, Raphael and Englert (1989) note that children need to read and write for "real purposes and audiences," and they need many experiences that invite sharing and extending self-generated work. The point is that students must have opportunities to use their literacy skills for their own purposes, as well as others'. Classrooms where students read and write only for the teacher (using teacher-generated topics and guidelines) are unlikely to produce people who read or write for their own purposes. The more important reason to strive for activities and materials that promote a meaningful approach to literacy is that students are more likely to see the purpose behind the activity if it strikes them as genuine. As a result, they are more likely to transfer the knowledge and skill to new settings.

Much of the instructional and practice material designed for remedial work has been excessively contrived. The temptation is great to get started in instruction by using one of the packaged remedial programs involving extensive isolated skills work. However, remedial students are generally those who have the least appreciation for reading and writing as meaningful activities. Therefore, the first approach should focus squarely on the communicative nature of reading and writing, and students should be encouraged to use their skills in authentic ways. Students may find it rewarding to:

- read to younger students
- share humorous or moving portions of stories with others
- read to find out specific information or answer a question
- read/write in order to report to others
- read/write to compile information
- read to learn how to do something or to follow directions
- read to find out how others feel or react
- read for emotional support and guidance
- read to prepare for a specific activity
- read for entertainment

Wherever possible, the materials and tasks students use to learn to read and write should permit them to advance in their appreciation of the purposes for which they are acquiring these skills. Learning to perform a skill so that you can use it at the next level in a program is not a good enough reason for learning. Students (and teachers) should understand how the new skill or knowledge can be used in real-world tasks.

Social Exchange and Interaction

Another critical feature of literate school environments is the degree of *social exchange and interaction*. In order to become literate—to acquire the language and thinking skills needed to read and understand text and write effectively—students need many opportunities to discuss, collaborate, assist, and present information and ideas. Although we will be focusing our attention on techniques that are especially useful for working with individual students, the general environment in the school/classroom is critically important. We assume that all of the specific techniques to be discussed in this and future chapters are backed by an environment that involves large amounts of writing, speaking, and listening.

In order to achieve this goal, there will need to be much more dialogue (as opposed to lecture and formal presentation) than is generally present in classroom settings (see Chapter 8, and Reciprocal Teaching, p. 487). Students need more opportunities to speak to each other, again as opposed to the formal oral presentations that are most common in schools. The smaller, less formal environments that are often characteristic of remedial instructional settings provide the perfect opportunity to promote a very dialogic, interactive mode of instruction. Unfortunately, many remedial teachers feel that they must deliver a specific skills-based program of instruction, and they often miss opportunities to promote literacy acquisition in a socially meaningful context. Teachers who are interested in establishing a social context for learning can prompt literary responses, versus answers to questions, and can encourage children to challenge and comment on their reading.

Cooperative and collaborative arrangements can support this intention. Acting on decisions to alter the classroom context or the way that instruction is delivered requires careful consideration. In the next section we will pursue these issues in some detail.

Other Long-Term Planning Considerations

Effective teachers make many decisions that require thoughtful reflection. Recent research and innovation in teaching suggest that even experienced teachers may want to examine such basic instructional decisions as how to group students and organize instruction. Similarly, new and exciting materials are available, and teachers may need to thin older texts and order or locate new, replacement books and materials.

Selecting an Organizational Pattern

There are many ways to organize students for instruction. The range of acceptable practice is quite extensive, including classrooms with individualized arrangements; learning centers and open space; and team teaching with cross-class groupings, multiaged groupings, and whole class instruction in self-contained settings. In remedial settings, one-to-one tutoring is occasionally employed. However, the most common way to meet individual differences is to organize students into ability groups (Shake, 1989) or to form homogenous ability groups in remedial settings. This type of arrangement has prevailed since the 1920s (Otto, Wolf, & Eldridge, 1984) and there is extensive, but conflicting, evidence of the benefits. Teachers certainly find it easier to plan for several small groups in which students have some similar strengths and weaknesses, and this permits students to learn together with others who may share some common needs and aptitudes as well.

Critics have recently raised serious questions about the usefulness of grouping students by ability (see Chapter 8). One major concern relates to the emotional costs of grouping students and the extent to which groups play out the expectations of teachers (Weinstein, 1986). It has also been noted that students may vary in a number of ways, and grouping by ability does not ensure that other important factors, such as prior knowledge, or interest and motivation, have been accounted for (Lipson, 1989; Otto, Wolf, & Eldridge, 1984). Although the research suggests that students *do* benefit from placement in groups (Rosenshine & Stevens, 1984), there is less evidence that these groups need to be formed on the basis of ability. Indeed, an increasingly strong body of research suggests that students of all abilities benefit from organizational patterns that involve *cooperative groups* (Dansereau, 1985; Johnson & Johnson, 1986; Slavin, 1983; Slavin, Stevens, & Madden, 1988).

One of the most widely recognized approaches to cooperative grouping for reading is Cooperative Integrated Reading and Composition (CIRC). Based on the cooperative learning principles developed by Slavin (1983; Stevens, Madden, Slavin, & Farnish, 1987), CIRC couples traditional basal reading instruction with nontraditional grouping patterns. The result has been fairly dramatic reading achievement gains for students of all abilities. As an alternative to traditional patterns, it is worth a close look, either to be used in concert with other planned arrangements or as a substitute.

Students in the CIRC program belong to two groups: their own reading group (a traditional basal program) and a mixed ability team that is composed of members from two reading groups. Students work cooperatively to help each other master the material that has been assigned to them. The reading assignments are one component of the CIRC work; various writing activities associated with a process approach to composition are another. Students work together in a variety of supportive ways: reading to one another, summarizing stories, responding to stories, and practicing a variety of reading-related tasks. Group certificates are awarded to teams based on the average performance of all team members on all reading and writing activities.

In addition to cooperative grouping arrangements, special and support teachers are confronted with a wide array of choices about how to deliver reading instruction. In some contexts it is undoubtedly better to provide in-class ("push-in") instruction; especially if students join a mixed ability cooperative group after leaving their reading support group. In other cases, students will receive more focused and effective instruction in "pull-out" programs involving small groups of like-ability students. However, reading teachers need to be sure that their grouping arrangements are not promoting negative attitudes and/or dependency behaviors in poor readers. Executing any alternative grouping patterns requires careful consideration and planning. Long term-planning is required to alter the delivery of instruction in any significant way. However, given the rapidly changing knowledge-base regarding grouping practices, teachers should remain open to the development and evolution of different approaches as the evidence of successful interventions or arrangements grows.

Materials Selection

Selecting materials is always something of a challenge for teachers of less-skilled readers. The challenge becomes even greater when we demand that the texts and tasks students encounter be high-quality, authentic ones. In reading, students need whole texts that offer authentic reading models. Stories should offer strong narrative structures that entertain and speak to students' personal experience or interests. Expository texts should be accurate and considerate, providing students with opportunities to learn and remember important information.

Careful examination of the materials to be used for direct instruction is absolutely essential. We strongly recommend that available materials be evaluated using the guidelines suggested in Chapter 9. In addition, it will be helpful to refer to a variety of resources to build a collection and a repertoire. We have included a listing of award-winning fiction books (see Appendix B) as well as some sources of information about high-interest, easy-reading books (see Appendix C). Materials especially designed for less-able readers should be examined carefully to make sure that the text resulting from application of readability formulas or vocabulary control is not terribly stilted. The literary quality of these books is very uneven, but poor readers can often find a satisfying story between the covers.

In Appendix D, we have provided a listing of *predictable and pattern books* that will be useful for teachers of young or very disabled readers. Teachers who work with disabled readers need a variety of these texts so that students can either acquire or practice their reading skills in a supported print context. Some of these books are highly predictable at the level of word or syntax level (e.g., *Brown Bear, Brown Bear,* by B. Martin), while others can be predicted only by attending to sound and symbol (e.g., *Marvin K. Mooney,* by Dr. Seuss). Other books are predictable because there is an overall pattern and students can anticipate upcoming words and events using highly familiar or meaningful context (e.g., *Little Red Hen*).

Not all students are excited by reading stories or poetry. Some would prefer nonfiction. Although it can be challenging to find good informational texts, the selection is expanding each year. Two exceptionally fine resources for selecting nonfiction and content-related books are: *Coming to Know: Writing to Learn in the Intermediate Grades* (Atwell, 1990); and *Eyeopeners* (Kobrin, 1988). Magazines and periodicals written by and for young people should also be available in classroom and clinic (see Figure 11.2). For more extensive descriptions and summaries, readers are referred to *Magazines for Children* (Stoll, 1990).

Summarizing Long-Term Planning

Establishing an environment that promotes and encourages literacy is of the utmost importance. The materials and tasks provided for in the environment and the organizational patterns used will influence students' attitude and motivation for learning, and most likely influence what is learned about reading and writing as well. However, the instructional activities that take place in that environment also affect what students learn. In the following section, we provide descriptions of several instructional techniques that we have chosen to call *high-utility strategies*.

GETTING STARTED USING HIGH-UTILITY STRATEGIES

As we noted at the beginning of this chapter, instruction must begin somewhere. As a practical matter, teachers often want or need to begin some types of instruction even without a complete diagnostic picture. In some rare cases, students arrive in the instructional setting with all the assessment information necessary. In

FIGURE 11.2
Magazines for Young People

Chart Your Course. P.O. Box 6448, Mobile, AL 36660. Targeted for gifted and talented. Ages 6–18.*

Child Life. The Children's Better Health Institute, 1100 Waterway Blvd. Indianapolis, IN 46202. Ages 8–10.*

City Kids. 1545 Wilcox, Los Angeles, CA 90028. Ages 11–14.*

Cobblestone: The History Magazine for Young People. 20 Grove Street, Peterborough, NH 03458. Ages 8–14.*

Cricket. Box 100, LaSalle, IL 61301. (See issue for rules and guidelines.) Ages 5–13.*

Ebony Jr. 820 S. Michigan Ave., Chicago, IL 60605. Ages 6–12.*

Electric Company. Children's Television Workshop, 1 Lincoln Plaza, New York, NY 10023. Ages 5–10.

Jack and Jill. The Children's Better Health Institute, 1100 Waterway Blvd. Indianapolis, IN 46202.

National Geographic World. National Geographic Society, 17th and M Sts., NW, Washington, DC 20036.

Humpty Dumpty. The Children's Better Health Institute, 1100 Waterway Blvd. Indianapolis, IN 46202.

Paw Prints. National Zoo, Washington, DC 20008. Focused on wild animal and conservation issues. Ages 6–14.*

Ranger Rick. National Wildlife Federation, 1412 16th St., NW, Washington, DC 20036. Ages 6–12.

Sesame Street Magazine. Children's Television Workshop, 1 Lincoln Plaza, New York, NY 10023. Ages 3–7.

Sprint. Scholastic, Inc., 730 Broadway, New York, NY 10003. Writing assignments in each issue. Ages 9–11.*

Stone Soup. P.O. Box 83, Santa Cruz, CA 95063. Ages 6–12.

Turtle Magazine. The Children's Better Health Institute, 1100 Waterway Blvd. Indianapolis, IN 46202.

Wee Wisdom. Unity Village, MO 64065. Ages 6–13.*

Your Big Backyard. National Wildlife Federation, 1412 16th St., NW, Washington, DC 20036. Ages 3–6.

* Magazines that publish the works of young authors.

For more extensive descriptions and summaries see: Stoll, D. R. (1990), *Magazines for children.* Newark, DE: International Reading Association.

other cases, students have been referred to the remedial setting on the basis of very little specific information (the student is "below grade level"). In other cases, there is excellent, but incomplete, information. And in the case of classroom teachers and their student(s), it is likely that the teacher has already begun instruction before realizing that a particular student is cause for concern.

It is not possible for us to anticipate all the ways that readers will use the information presented in this text. Teachers can and do need to implement the steps and use the techniques of the assessment-instruction process in a variety of ways. The need to be flexible and to exercise professional judgment is an ever-present mandate when working with students and schools. The strategies we offer in this section are admittedly selective; we might have chosen others. However, we consider these to be high-utility on the basis of four critical considerations, which we describe below.

Rationale

In deciding how to begin, teachers must rely once again on their existing knowledge base. There is an almost endless number of instructional ideas available to teachers; they must determine what criteria will be used to decide between and among them. The instructional strategies described in this section were chosen because they are theory-driven strategies, each has at least some empirical base to support its efficacy, they have broad-based applicability, and they address significant reading outcomes.

We have intentionally chosen instructional activities that we believe are theory-driven; that is, those that are consistent with what is known about the reading process. The strategies generally share the following key features:

1. They provide for reading in meaningful contexts for meaningful purposes and encourage social exchange or interaction focused on reading and writing activities.
2. Skills and strategies are integrated in whole text reading.
3. They offer flexibility in terms of what can be done with the activities and the types of materials that can be employed.

Although many activities are designed to promote reading improvement, few instructional interventions have actually demonstrated their effectiveness. Most teachers are shocked to find that long-established practices often have no empirical base. For those strategies that we expect to use with all or most students (e.g., high-utility strategies), we should demand demonstrated worth. Thus, each of the techniques described below has at least some empirical basis for its use. Finally, we have used each of these in our own clinical work. The techniques are manageable for teachers who have not used them before and effective for students.

In the Getting Started phase of instruction, the flexibility of instructional activities is especially important, and the techniques described below offer almost unlimited adaptability. Together these activities encompass the full range of reading/writing abilities, thus offering a rich beginning context for any other instruction that might be required. For example, all students can benefit from instruction activities that promote positive attitudes or increase reading power, and some provision for this should be made in the program of every student. Similarly, writing activities generally support literacy acquisition for all students, and reading programs should acknowledge that.

The fact that each technique is designed to promote skilled, independent, and self-controlled reading is particularly important. Instructional strategies must be planned to embody good practice, but also to address the important outcomes denoted in long-term planning. We have provided examples of instructional strategies designed to address each of the three major outcome categories: attitudes, process, and content. Even in the Getting Started phase, some decisions must be made and some priorities established.

Sustained Silent Reading

Sustained silent reading (SSR) practice promotes reading power and fluency, helps students develop positive attitudes toward reading, and is easy to implement in any school setting and at any grade level. Hunt (1970) provided the first descriptions of this practice, dubbing it Uninterrupted Sustained Silent Reading (USSR). In recent years, variations of the practice have been offered: SQUIRT (Sustained Quiet Reading Time), DEAR (Drop Everything and Read), and SSR (Sustained Silent Reading). Across all adaptations, however, the heart of the technique remains the same: children read silently from self-selected materials for extended periods of time for their own purposes.

When students are permitted to read from materials that they choose, *and* when teachers model silent reading themselves, insisting that no student interfere with that experience, everyone benefits. For example, Levine (1984) reported on a group of high-school students who became immersed in reading during SSR. These special education students, reading six to eight grades below grade placement, read enthusiastically during SSR.

The benefits of SSR are most clearly evident at the level of increased interest in, and motivation for, reading (Allington, 1975; Cline & Kretke, 1980; Sadowski, 1980). However, "it is also likely that researchers have not yet developed appropriate means of measuring the results of SSR" (Berglund & Johns, 1983, p. 538). If measures of students' abilities included assessments of their ability to read long, complex texts for their own purposes, it is likely that the effects of SSR would be apparent, since as Hunt (1970) has noted, SSR addresses the "essence of reading power; the ability to keep going with ideas in print" (p. 150).

Despite the ease of implementation of SSR and the demonstrable positive benefits, some teachers abandon the practice after some initial attempt, and still others are reluctant to try it. Two reasons are most often offered. First, many teachers say that there is so little time in the day that they feel guilty if they are not "teaching." This is especially true for reading support teachers, such as special educators and Chapter I teachers, and for high-school teachers, since they see students for so little time. This concern is obviously rooted in the idea that teaching only occurs during direct instruction. Although direct instruction *is* important, it is not the only way to teach. Indeed, some important literacy outcomes simply cannot be achieved via direct instruction. Such is the case with reading stamina and motivation.

With indirect instruction such as SSR, however, teachers must understand the importance of *modeling* (McCracken & McCracken, 1978). Although it is tempting to use this period for other things (grading papers, conferencing, etc.), it is critical that students see teachers and other adults reading. This communicates that teachers think reading is important—so important that other things are put aside for the serious, albeit pleasurable, business of reading real books.

A second reason that accounts for abandoning or not using SSR is that some children simply won't read, and they distract others (McCracken & McCracken,

1978). This problem requires careful thought, both in terms of initiating the program and in adapting it to fit particular students. We will address these issues below.

Launching SSR

Starting and monitoring SSR time is like implementing any other important aspect of the curriculum. There is no substitute for careful planning and good preparation. Teachers need to take time to create interest among students, on the one hand (Gambrell, 1978), and to clearly specify rules on the other (McCracken & McCracken, 1971). Unfortunately, some students will never have been expected to read for sustained periods of time and will not know how to do it. Thus, teachers must carefully prepare students and then be aware that some will need time to become proficient silent readers. The following steps should be considered before starting, and during the initial stages:

1. *Talk to your students.* Clearly describe to them what will happen and what types of behavior you expect of them. The rules for SSR should include provisions that everyone read a book that they have chosen, that everyone is quiet, and that there is no moving around during SSR.
2. *Help your students select books.* Do not assume that all of your students know how to choose a book that is good for them. Some (younger or very disabled) students may need to have several books with them during silent reading period so that they do not need to move around to get a different book when they have chosen badly, or finish a short picture book.
3. *Start with success.* Initially, choose a short block of time (as little as 5 minutes for young or disabled readers) during a period of the day that is generally quiet and productive. One of the goals of SSR is that students begin to realize that they *can* stick with books, and that they can read and enjoy longer selections. Thus, the first periods should be successful ones. The period should be so short that children should have no difficulty meeting the challenge (Mork, 1972). Do not launch SSR during a period of transition. Using SSR to "quiet" students after recess or lunch period, for example, only works after both teachers and students are experienced at reading silently for sustained periods. The silent reading period should gradually be extended so that primary grade students are reading for 15 to 20 minutes daily. Intermediate grade students should read for 30 to 45 minutes. Aim for this length of time, even if this means that SSR cannot occur every day at the upper grades.
4. *Remember that you must read during this period also.* Select a book that you are presently reading or are genuinely interested in.
5. *Plan for it, include it in the schedule, and treat it seriously.* Recently, a first grade child told one of the authors that she did not do silent reading because her "work" was not done. Sustained silent reading is "work" and students will value its importance only if teachers do.

Adapting SSR

At first, some students will not use the period wisely—a fact that should tell the teacher how much this period is needed. Teachers must be patient with students, while insisting that no individual will disrupt the period. However, some students, including very young or very disabled readers, may experience such difficulty that adaptations are needed. The most obvious adaptation is in the time provided. Some may be unable to sustain even the 5 minutes of initial time. Teachers should not hesitate to start with as little time as one minute! Some teachers find that it is helpful to set a goal together with the children and then use a kitchen timer in the beginning.

Guiding students in book selection can take care of many difficulties. Indeed, Hong (1981) has suggested that the key to success during SSR is the quality of the books. Other ways to adapt SSR that still retain the emphasis on book reading include the following:

1. *Institute a "recreational reading time"* (Morrow, 1989) or *"booktime"* (Hong, 1981) instead of SSR. This is a time when students are permitted some interaction and movement. For example, buddy reading might be permitted, students might be allowed to select new books, or the teacher might be available to provide some reading help. Morrow also suggests that any book-related activity might be permitted during this period.
2. *Introduce books to children* so that they can choose a book based on some knowledge. All teachers have experienced the rush of enthusiasm for a book that has just been read aloud. Reading aloud is one of the best ways to introduce books to children. Other ideas for introducing books include doing book talks; preparing puppet shows using the characters and events from a book; and making book-tape combinations available for students.

We do not find that these adaptations are necessary in a clinical setting, since there are generally fewer students. Occasionally we have had to remind students about how to read silently and how to attend to print during silent reading, and we have sometimes had to constrain students' choices so that they select appropriately. These adaptations are removed as soon as students have some experience successfully sustaining themselves with print. Students with any significant experience reading connected text do not generally need these supports. Students who cannot sustain themselves in print may have had too much experience with isolated skills. There *are* students who have no experience reading ordinary books, and as a result, have little idea that reading is a sense-making process. The benefits of SSR for these students include recognizing the purposes of reading, providing practice and transfer opportunities, and providing experiences with meaningful reading material.

Finally, SSR must be maintained in the curriculum, with its usefulness and purpose reviewed periodically. Although students should not be interrogated about the materials they read during SSR, they can be encouraged to keep a record of their reading. Teachers can then use this to shape the rest of the reading program. Hunt (1970) suggests that student self-evaluation is an important feature of SSR, allowing students (and their teachers) to monitor progress (see Figure 11.3). Other methods also provide this type of continuous assessment information. Graphing the number of words or pages read or keeping reading logs of all selections read can provide excellent documentation of the instructional program and rewarding feedback to students who need visible proof of their growing competence.

Dialogue Journals

Both attitude and process outcomes can be addressed with well-crafted writing strategies. We expect that all the tutors and students in our clinical settings will be doing some writing. For the youngest and least able, this often starts as dictated writing (see below). However, almost all students can do journal writing of some sort. This might involve drawing and labeling at first, then more extensive use of inventive spelling as students begin to acquire competence (see Chapter 4). Many classroom teachers have students write regularly in a personal journal. This very personal writing is often viewed as private; students are asked to share entries only when they feel comfortable doing so. Although these have obvious value, there is much to be said for more focused journal entries.

Dialogue journals, widely used in other settings, are especially well-suited to remedial settings. As the name suggests, dialogue journals involve written exchanges between a teacher and her students, or less often, between students in a group (Atwell, 1987; Fulwiler, 1980). Unlike personal journals, these are written to be shared. A dialogue journal contains a genuine conversation, written rather than spoken. It is a means by which individual students at any age can carry on a private discussion with their teacher. The interactive format of equal turns on the same topics is quite different from the traditional student personal journals, in which a teacher may sometimes make some kind of marginal comment on a student's entry, but only days or weeks after the student wrote it. The distinguishing characteristics of dialogue journals are their interactive, functional nature and the creation of mutually interesting topics (Staton, 1987, p. 49).

These journals are frequently used to encourage students to reflect on specific content to be learned, books that have been read, or ideas that are triggered by recent reading/writing activities. Like SSR, dialogue journals are aimed at addressing broad reading/writing goals and are, therefore, useful for most students. In addition, they are easy to initiate, and with commitment, easy to sustain.

Fulwiler (1987b) suggests that students use a small looseleaf notebook for all journal entries so that any writing too personal to share can be extracted before it is turned in to the teacher. The remaining portions become a "dialogue journal"— an ongoing written communication between student and teacher. Atwell (1987) has provided extensive documentation regarding the benefits of journal activity with middle-school students, concluding:

> Through our dialogue journals my students learned, too, about the world of written texts—what good writers do, what good readers do, how readers talk, what books are for and how kids can get in on it. (p. 170)

FIGURE 11.3
Questions for
Readers

How Well Did I Read Today: A Self-Check

Today's Date _____ Number of Pages Read Today _____ My Name _____

Titles of Books Read: Authors:

This sheet presents a Model Questionnaire containing sample questions to be used with children in evaluating progress in individualized reading programs. The questions are designed to produce two major goals:

1. To have the student be more reflective about his own reading process.
2. To provide a check for the teacher on student attitudes toward his own performance.

Any or all questions can be used to fit a particular program regardless of level of student and teacher needs. Each teacher is free to select those items of greatest worth for him.

PART ONE

1. Did you have a good reading period today? Did you read well?

2. Did you read better today than yesterday?

3. Were you able to concentrate today on your silent reading?

4. Did the ideas in the book hold your attention?

5. Did you have the feeling of wanting to go ahead faster to find out what happened? Were you constantly moving ahead with the ideas?

6. Was it hard for you to keep your mind on what you were reading today?

7. Were you bothered by others or by outside noises?

8. Could you keep the ideas in your book straight in your mind?

9. Were there words you did not know? _____ How did you figure them out?

10. What did you do when you got to the good parts? Did you read faster? or slower?

PART TWO

1. Why did you read this particular book?

2. Was this a good choice? Or was this a good book for you to read?

3. Could you tell what was happening all the time?

4. Was this book hard or was it easy for you to read?

5. What made it hard or easy?

6. Would you choose the same kind or a different kind of book next?

7. Did you want to keep on reading? Or did you have to force yourself to finish the book?

Adapted from "A Self-Check" from "The Effect of Self-Selection, Interest, and Motivation upon Independent, Instructional, and Frustrational Levels" by L. C. Hunt, *The Reading Teacher,* November 1970, pp. 148–149.

Atwell and her students have catalogued the topics addressed in hundreds of journal entries. These included sophisticated exchanges involving plot and action, authors and authors' craft, genre, applications to students' own writing, reading strategies and readers' affective responses, judgments regarding book recommendations, and editorial topics and mechanical advice. Finally, there is a wealth of personal anecdote and mutual support that permeates the samples Atwell provides (see Figure 11.4).

Launching Dialogue Journals

The success of dialogue journals will probably rely on the teacher's commitment to read and respond honestly to students' entries. Because many students (and many teachers too) have had little experience with writing, it is important to think about how to get students started. Although a dialogue journal can be as simple as several sheets of notebook paper stapled together, we have found that something more substantial invites students to take the activity seriously. On a practical note, a more substantial journal also tends not to get lost. Inexperienced students will need more than an attractive journal to overcome their reluctance to write, however. The following ideas should help the teacher launch the dialogue journal.

1. *Provide students with material or questions that invite response.* Reading a provocative book aloud or sharing something interesting or compelling about an author will be enough for some students. Others will need a specific question that prompts thoughtful response, like this one offered by Staton (1987, p. 49):

   Kelly: I like to read. Ev'ry time I woth a skery movy I have a drem.
   Teacher: Scary movies give me bad dreams, too, Kelly. Maybe we shouldn't watch them. What good books have you read?
   Kelly: The little red hen and Dick and Jane. I have problims some times well I hav this problim it is I am not very god on my writeing.

2. *Provide students with some model or idea of what is expected.* Gambrell (1985) suggests that students think about a format similar to letter writing and that they ask the teacher a question. Alternatively, teachers can start by asking the *students* a question that requires them to respond. Then, in the teacher response, appropriate dialogue exchange is modeled over several entries.

3. *Respond in ways that encourage individual students.* This encouragement will be based on knowledge of specific students and is likely to vary. According to Atwell (1987):

   My responses grow from what I've learned about a reader and how I hope to move the readers' thinking. In general my comments do three things, to *affirm, challenge,* or *extend* the reader's thinking. These comments take various forms: gossip, questions, recommendations, jokes, restatements, arguments, suggestions, anecdotes, instruction, and "nudges." (p. 275)

Probably the most important key to maintaining the success of dialogue journals is the teacher's commitment to respond to students' entries. Thus, it is important to give some consideration to the management of journals. Many

FIGURE 11.4
Atwell Dialogue Journal Samples

At the start of the school year Libby's letters to me stayed on the outside of written texts. She gave daily blow-by-blow accounts of plot, of what characters were up to, as in this letter about June Foley's *Love by Any Other Name.*

9/11

Dear Ms. Atwell,

Billie is getting restricted because of Bubba and his friends mostly, and partly herself. First she got restricted for being late. And then she got restricted for sitting with Bubba's friends (and a day before they got a lecture on food fights) and a girl (a friend of hers) brought in a table cloth, wine glasses, china plate ware, napkins, champagne, for them and the table! And so they all got detention for a week! But why would they get a detention, because of the champagne? Probably.

Your friend,
Libby

P.S. Have a nice day!

Every time I wrote back to Libby I wrote back about the author, using the author's name and speculating about why he or she had decided to have characters behave as they did. My response to the letter above is typical:

9/11

Dear Libby,

Well, I do think champagne is a little bit much for a cafeteria lunch, but it's a good example for what Foley is trying to do here. Can you see how she's trying to show how far and foolishly Billie is willing to go to be in with the in crowd? (And can you guess what's going to happen to Billie by the novel's end, how Foley is going to have Billie end up? I can see it coming.)

Ms. A

I nudged right through the first two months of school, modeling author talk like crazy, and by the end of October Libby had begun to come inside.

10/24

Dr. Ms. Atwell,

I have started reading *That Was Then This Is Now* by S. E. Hinton. It is a pretty good book! I didn't know that she had Ponyboy Curtis in the book as a character. That surprised me! I like the way she writes. It's like you are there in the book. You can picture what it is like and stuff.

Sincerely,
Libby

P.S. Have a nice day!

10/24

Dear Lib,

I know just what you mean. Hinton puts us inside the characters. She tells so much about what they're thinking and feeling that we see things through their eyes and feel with their hearts. In *The Outsiders,* with Ponyboy as her narrator, she really puts us there, in the book.

I loved it that Pony showed up in *That Was Then . . .* It was like an in-joke. You had to know *The Outsiders* to pick up on the reference: sort of like, be a member of the Hinton Club.

Ms. A

P.S. I'll be really anxious to know what you think of how Hinton decided to conclude this one. She shook me up but I think she was right.

teachers, for example, find that they cannot read everyone's journal every night. Gambrell (1985) suggests starting dialogue journals with only a small group of students so that it is not necessary to juggle an entire class initially. After students have some experience with this activity, some teachers require that everyone write each day but they respond to only one-third each day. If a student really wants or needs a response on a particular day, however, the system should allow for this.

Maintaining and Extending Dialogue Journals

Once teachers have made the commitment to read and react to students' writing, dialogue journals can add immeasurably to the instructional program. They can "provide a 'window' into the students' cognitive activities during writing and reading . . . giving teachers opportunities to highlight students' idea generation, planning, predicting, and monitoring" (Raphael & Englert, 1989, p. 238). Teachers' skills in this area are typically not well developed, so they should not expect to feel comfortable making responses initially. However, Atwell (1987) offers some "lessons" that are worth sharing (p. 276):

1. *"One good, thoughtful question is more than enough."* Atwell's experience suggests that students' least interesting or insightful responses came when she asked didactic questions that sounded as though she were testing the students.
2. Respond *"as a curious human being."* Dialogue journals seem to work best when they are genuine dialogues between two people who are really expressing their own ideas and sharing their own experiences.
3. *"Make no corrections on students' letters."* Dialogue entries are not final writing samples. Atwell suggests responding to mechanics only when journals cannot be read.
4. *"The journals contribute to class grades."* The grades are based on a minimum quantity (one entry per week), thoughtfulness of the responses, "use of classroom independent reading time, and progress made toward a few, individual goals set at the beginning of each quarter."

Dialogue journals can be adapted for use across the curriculum (see Fulwiler, 1987b). Classroom teachers should look for opportunities to use journal entries during non-language arts periods. It is becoming increasingly clear that when writing is used in content area disciplines, everyone benefits. "Journal writing in class stimulates student discussion, starts small group activity, clarifies hazy issues, reinforces learning experience, and stimulates imaginations" (Fulwiler, 1982, p. 15). Resource teachers should consider asking students to write about topics that are being studied in their regular classrooms.

Dictated Stories

As an instructional technique, the dictated story has its roots in the Language Experience Approach (LEA) to reading (Stauffer, 1969; 1980; Allen, 1976). As a beginning reading method, LEA promotes student awareness of the relationship between oral and written language by having students produce a "language experience story." This story then becomes the reading material that is used for the delivery of instruction. Because this eliminates any problems of a mismatch between the child's language and the reading materials, the technique has been widely used for very beginning readers, for bilingual students (Wilson & Cleland, 1989), with middle-school remedial reading students (Sharp, 1990), and with adult illiterates (Mulligan, 1974; Newton, 1977). Clearly, LEA addresses process outcomes while attending closely to both attitude and motivation.

LEA stories have traditionally been created by individuals or collaboratively by groups. For example, one of the authors was assigned to work with 17 fifth- and sixth-grade boys whose reading level was below first grade. Collaborative LEA stories revealed the group's consuming interest in football, specifically the local professional team. Using this topic and the weekly game results, students wrote, revised, and worked with football stories all fall. Newspapers, sports magazines, and special edition sports periodicals were brought into the classroom and the students began to realize that they could read the specialized accounts of football activity. In the process, they learned to analyze the patterns of print; to recognize letter combinations, compound words, base words, and to master some high-frequency sight vocabulary. The average reading gain for this group was over two grade levels in nine month's time. Most were still not exceptionally strong readers, but they had made good progress, had control over some essential skills, and more importantly, believed they could read and saw at least a few reasons for doing so.

The practice of creating group stories has recently been criticized (Heald-Taylor, 1989). However, we see no problem with the practice unless there is significant variation in the group or unless the group is so large as to severely limit the amount of literacy practice students experience. As a practical matter, classroom teachers are likely to generate group stories when they have shared an experience (e.g., a field trip) or are planning an activity (e.g., a class party). Indeed, the first step in a Language Experience Story is always considered to be the provision of an *experience* (e.g., the unexpected appearance of a skunk on the playground, a fire in a nearby building, and so on). Rich group stories can result from such experiences.

For the purposes of working with very disabled readers, individual stories may be preferred. Dictated stories, unlike LEA stories, need not be prefaced by some formal experience. As the name suggests, these stories are created as a student dictates to a recorder (teacher, parent, older student). Students may dictate any type of content they like.

Launching the Dictated Story

Always start by talking with students about what they would like to say. Some children will be ready to dictate, and a brief discussion will quickly reveal this. Other children will be floundering or have little idea about what they wish to say. The youngest and most disabled readers may want only to label. Like the other activities already suggested, dictated stories permit a range of responses and all students should be able to participate, although the responses may vary profoundly. Bridge (1989) offers the following guidelines for the dictation process:

1. Students should be able to read back the story, so it shouldn't be too long.
2. If possible, wait until the child's thought is complete, then record exactly what the student says.
3. Say each word as you write it, asking the student to watch.
4. As you record, provide some reading instruction appropriate for this student (e.g., note that there are spaces between words, that certain words begin the same way, that the story has an excellent beginning, and so on).
5. Read the story aloud for the student, encouraging students to join as they are able.
6. Have the child read the selection independently when he or she is able (this may require several readings).

Students will become more and more adept at producing dictated stories and, like the silent reading and the dialogue journals described above, this can form the core of a set of regular instructional activities. Simply producing a dictated story will be beneficial for the less-able students.

> The goal is to allow children to role play themselves as successful readers, even in the early stages of becoming readers. Through repeated readings of the words in the familiar context of the dictated language experience stories, children will add the words to their sight vocabularies and develop oral reading fluency and confidence in themselves as readers. (Bridge, 1989, p. 195)

If the stories are not used, however, the potency of the activity will hardly have been realized.

Maintaining and Using Dictated Stories

Once the dictated story has been created, it can become the focus of all kinds of effective instruction. As noted above, it can be the reading material used to deliver reading instruction. The stories can be retyped or copied for instructional purposes. Students can then underline, highlight portions, or cut the stories apart. Dictated stories around the same or similar themes can provide opportunities to develop rich vocabulary and repeated exposure to some words.

Ideally, the use of dictated stories will be reduced and a more student-controlled version of writing initiated as soon as students are able to take over the mechanics of writing (see Graves, 1983; Temple, Nathan, Burris, & Temple, 1988). Student-produced writing should not replace dictated stories until students are able to produce with some ease as much as they can dictate in a comparable period of time. Until then, students should create personal journals and drawings as well as dictated stories. The dictated stories can provide the basis for remedial or basic instructional work of the following sort.

1. Create cloze passages using these stories to provide practice in using context and writing frequently-used or favorite words.

2. Select words to focus on—sight words that appear in repeated frames, words that have the same initial sound, base words used in interesting ways—whatever is appropriate for the student.
3. Look for themes that are worth pursuing with this student. Some may require the teacher to read aloud, but others may offer reading options for the student.
4. Look for opportunities to link the dictated story to something that has been read. One way to introduce new vocabulary and linguistic patterns is to encourage children to explore, using book models.

If the stories are placed on a classroom computer, these types of multiple revisitings for various instructional purposes are obviously made much easier. Students may also be able to manage the transition from dictated stories to some independent writing if a program with voice synthesis is available (see Chapter 9).

Repeated Readings

Although very young children often hear the same story many times, once they enter school they are generally expected to read a story just once, with good fluency and comprehension, and then move on to another. The value of repeated experiences with books and stories has too often been missed by educators. One of the most potent reasons for revisiting reading materials is to build fluency. We agree with Allington (1983b) who notes: "Limitations (of the research) aside, a preponderance of empirical and clinical evidence supports the relationship of fluent oral reading and good overall reading ability" (p. 560). Although there are a variety of procedures for developing oral reading fluency (see Smith, 1979), the most widely tested technique involves *repeated readings* (Allington, 1977; Chomsky, 1978; Samuels, 1979).

There are many ways to involve students in the repeated reading of a specific piece of text. Like the other procedures already discussed, however, it offers both ease and flexibility in implementation, the point being simply to persuade and induce children to read a particular text several times so that they can improve fluency through increased familiarity and additional practice. As such, it has proven to be an extremely useful tool for teachers working with less-skilled readers. "It is important to point out that repeated reading is not a method for teaching all beginning reading skills. Rather, it is intended as a supplement in a developmental reading program" (Samuels, 1979, p. 403).

One of the most powerful characteristics of a repeated reading technique is the increased opportunity for practice that is involved—practice reading continuous and connected text. Many teachers expect resistance from students when they are asked to reread material because on the surface, this seems to be such a mechanistic and repetitive task. However, young children often choose to reread material themselves as they try to read real texts (Rasinksi, 1986). They will return to the same piece until it is familiar and can be read with understanding. Less-skilled readers generally do not get the opportunity to read much at all, much less reread material for control and fluency (Allington, 1977). Repeated readings offer them this opportunity.

Finally, repeated readings permit students to experience reading something that is (or has become) relatively easy for them to read. Allington (1983b) has suggested that this experience of reading relatively easy material may be essential in the development of fluency. Whatever the reason, we have not only found limited resistance to a repeated reading strategy in our clinical settings, we have generally found that this is a favored activity. Repeated readings focus specifically on one aspect of the reading *process,* but the strong success experiences that are evoked often produce positive attitude outcomes as well.

Launching Repeated Readings

The easiest way to initiate repeated reading is to mark off a segment of print in a text that the student is already reading and to ask the student to read and reread that section until he or she has reached some predetermined level of fluency. For example, Samuels (1979) suggested that students read repeatedly until they could read the section at a rate of 85 wpm. Others have suggested that speed is not a sufficient criterion. For example, Allington (1983b) suggests lightly marking segments of text in phrase units using Aulls' fluency scale as a guide (see Chapter 5). Students' repeated readings are then judged in terms of the degree of improvement on this scale. Still another possibility is simply to dictate how many rereadings of a text will be required (Ballard, 1978). In any event, it is necessary to decide what students will be told about how the technique will be used and when they can move on to new material.

Some sensible (although not empirically tested) guidelines for the beginning stages of repeated readings might include the following:

1. *Select materials that lend themselves to fluent oral reading.* Material that is too choppy or artificial (as commercial beginning materials tend to be) probably will not result in rewarding renderings of the text, nor in increased fluency.
2. Be sure to *talk to students about why they are doing this activity.* They should be helped to see that they are practicing a *part* of reading, much the way an athlete or musician might practice a small part in order to improve the overall performance. Emphasize that increased expression, knowledge of words, use of context, and so on will help them to comprehend text more easily. Students must see that the goal isn't exceptionally fine oral reading.
3. Since the student will be rereading the material several times, *don't hesitate to select material that will be somewhat challenging.* Clearly, it is also necessary to use good judgment about task difficulty as it affects individual students.
4. *Students should be encouraged to practice (reread) silently as much as possible.* The only real danger of repeated readings is that they may supplant productive silent reading experiences.

Maintaining and Adapting Repeated Readings

Samuels (1979) suggests several ways to maintain interest in repeated reading. One of the easiest is to keep track of the experience by graphing or logging the results (see Figure 11.5). Students, especially discouraged students, find this simple practice extremely gratifying and are often anxious to share their progress

FIGURE 11.5

Repeated
Reading Chart

If you repeatedly read the same passage, you will soon read it smoothly and easily. This sheet will help to record your progress in reading.

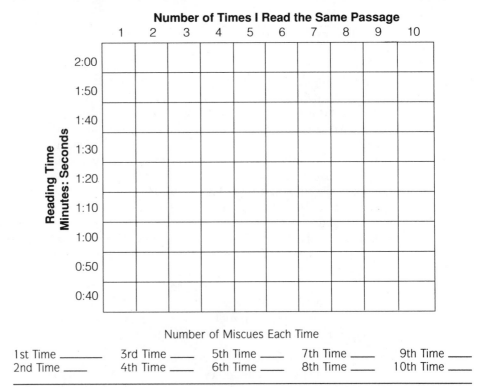

Number of Times I Read the Same Passage

Number of Miscues Each Time

1st Time _____   3rd Time _____   5th Time _____   7th Time _____   9th Time _____
2nd Time _____   4th Time _____   6th Time _____   8th Time _____   10th Time _____

with family and friends. Indeed, graphing or visually displaying progress is an excellent practice for young or less-skilled students, one that can be used with many activities and goals.

A caveat is in order, however. Feedback in the form of graphs and other displays should always be individual and private. The purpose is to compare the student's performance with his or her earlier performance; any competitive comparison or public display is probably unhelpful. Public competition is only rewarding for those who are highly successful. However, individual progress forms can help students to see their growth even when it has been slow.

Other adaptations can be initiated as practical considerations and student needs dictate (Samuels, 1979; 1988). For example, students can be encouraged to practice rereading by reading along with an audiotape. This is especially helpful for students who require a fluent model to guide them. Alternatively, students can work in peer groups to practice with a "buddy" (see Chapter 12).

As we have already noted, there are many variations on the practice. One of these, Talking Dictionary (Ballard, 1978), has been especially successful for students who require high levels of support in repeated readings. Talking Dictionary involves reading, and then rereading, a specific piece of text with the help of a "talking dictionary," or tutor. Talking Dictionary is implemented as follows (see Figure 11.6):

First Read:
1. The procedure is explained to the student.
2. The tutor selects, or helps the student to select, material that is too long to be read in one 3-minute sitting.
3. The student is asked to begin reading the selected portion of text aloud and continues reading for 3 minutes.
4. Whenever the reader encounters an unknown word, he or she asks for the pronunciation ("word please") and the tutor provides it *without comment*. The reading continues.
5. The tutor's job is to keep track of time (either 2 or 3 minutes is a reasonable amount), to provide unknown pronunciations, and to count the number of words read correctly.

Second Read:
1. The student returns to the starting point and repeats the process, again asking for any unknown words.
2. Once again, the tutor provides all requested words without comment, keeps track of time, and tallies correctly read words.

Third Read:
1. The process is repeated.
2. When the 3 minutes are completed, the results of the 3 reading attempts are graphed.

The procedure can be used quite easily by parents, who are often searching for an activity that will support their child's reading growth. One advantage of Talking Dictionary is that it permits only positive and helpful responses. In every way, the technique communicates to the student that the adult is there to provide support and will also celebrate the increased fluency that invariably results. Thus, students not only have an opportunity to practice reading connected text but also do so in a supportive environment.

Generally speaking, teachers should expect that during the second and third renderings, students will recognize at least *some* of the words that were requested and read further into the text. The first of these should be expected in any form of repeated reading. If, after several attempts (graphed along the model presented in Figure 11.6), there is still *no* improvement, some adaptation should then occur. The most common adaptations involve the need to choose an easier (or more difficult) text, remind the student that it is desirable to request help when print does not make sense, or examine the role of anxiety in the student's oral reading fluency.

FIGURE 11.6
*Talking
Dictionary*

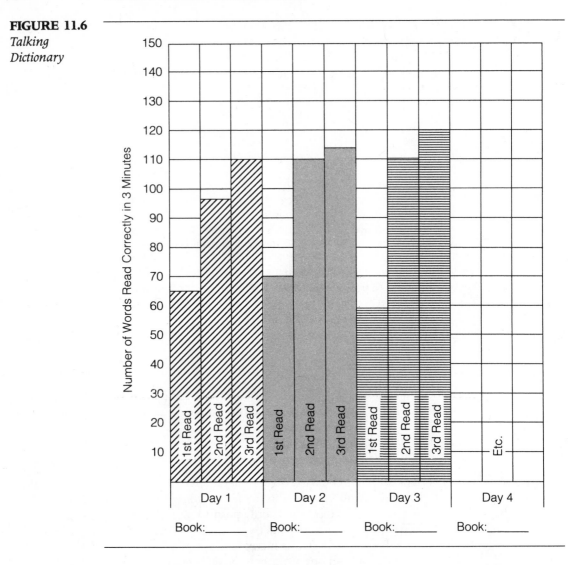

Not all students will benefit directly from repeated reading techniques. It is important to remember:

> Developing oral reading fluency should never become the only goal in beginning or remedial reading instruction, but it is at least as important as many others, e.g., identifying words in isolation or knowing letter-sound correspondences. Developing oral reading fluency is a small step in developing effective and efficient readers, but it is a step in the right direction. (Allington, 1983b, p. 561)

Although increased fluency is the most straightforward benefit to be enjoyed from repeated reading activities, it is not the only one. For example, there is evidence that young students' recognition of sight vocabulary improves when they are encouraged to reread texts (Bridge & Burton, 1982; Bridge, Winograd, & Haley, 1983; Chomsky, 1978).

There is also evidence from teacher read-aloud research that when students have repeated opportunities to hear the same stories again, their comprehension improves. Martinez and Roser (1985) report four changes that occur as children become increasingly familiar with a story:

1. Children produced more verbal responses.
2. The nature of these responses changed such that self-initiated comments and judgments became more frequent.
3. The focus on discussion changed so that children "tended to talk more about story language, events, settings, and titles as the stories became familiar" (p. 785).
4. Children appeared to gain greater insights into some segments of stories.

Because of these other benefits, teachers should find the practice of "revisiting" texts potentially powerful even if they do not use one of the more contrived repeated reading procedures. We will describe some other ways to repeatedly use text later in the chapter.

Reciprocal Teaching

Reciprocal Teaching, like several techniques that have been validated in recent years, is focused on process outcomes. The strategy was devised to promote the effective use of complex comprehension knowledge and skill (Palincsar, 1984; Palincsar & Brown, 1984). Although there is not universal agreement about the nature of comprehension ability, it is clear that it requires the orchestration of a number of complex skills and abilities.

Palincsar and Brown (1984) identified several major activities that are generally accepted as underlying comprehension ability. Skilled comprehenders understand a variety of explicit and implicit purposes for reading, activate prior knowledge, focus on important versus trivial content, and maintain this focus throughout the selection. In addition, they make critical judgments about the relationships between and among ideas in text, judge the content against prior knowledge, monitor reading for comprehension, and make inferences for the purposes of predicting, interpreting, and drawing conclusions about reading material. Reciprocal Teaching is intended to teach students to accomplish these activities as they read connected text.

Launching Reciprocal Teaching

This strategy requires that teachers have selected several expository passages and that they are prepared to work collaboratively with their students. The following steps describe the basic pattern of interaction in Reciprocal Teaching.

Step 1. The teacher meets with a small group (5–15 students) and models four comprehension-fostering strategies (predicting, self-questioning, clarifying, and summarizing). Then the teacher applies these strategies while reading a paragraph or segment from content area materials. After the procedure has been modeled by the adult teacher with several segments of text, the students take over the role of teacher.

Step 2. If the passage is new to the group, the adult teacher asks students to predict what the text will be about based on the title. If the passage is familiar, students are asked to recall and state the topic of the passage as well as the important points already covered.

Step 3. The adult teacher assigns a segment of the passage to be read (usually a paragraph) and either tells the students that she will be the teacher (especially for the initial days of instruction) or assigns one of the students as teacher for the first segment.

Step 4. When the group finishes reading the segment silently, the teacher for that segment proceeds to *ask a good question or two, clarify* the hard parts, *summarize* the paragraph or segment in a sentence, and then (starting the cycle all over again) to *predict* what the next paragraph or segment will discuss.

Step 5. Whoever is in the role of teacher for each segment must help answer the questions or suggest alternative questions, clarify the unclear parts of the text, revise the summary, and agree or disagree with the prediction.

Step 6. The adult teacher provides the guidance necessary for the student teachers to complete the preceding activities through a variety of techniques:

PROMPTING: "What question did you think a teacher might ask?"

INSTRUCTION: "Remember, a summary is a shortened version, it doesn't include a lot of detail."

MODIFYING the activity: "If you're having a hard time thinking of a question, why don't you summarize first?"

REQUESTING the help of other students: "Who can help us out with this one?"

Step 7. The adult teacher provides praise and feedback specific to the student teachers' participation: "That was an excellent summary. You provided the most important information," or "You worded that question well, but it was about a minor detail. Can you ask us about some more important information?" After this feedback, the adult teacher models any activity that continues to need improvement: "A question I would have asked is . . . " or "I would summarize by saying. . . . " The procedure continues in this manner with the teacher supporting and modeling as needed.

Maintaining and Adapting Reciprocal Teaching

The dialogic and interactive nature of Reciprocal Teaching demands a commitment on the part of teachers to engage in discussion and to respond to students' knowledge and skill. Over time, we would hope that students would not need teachers to help them craft good questions or clarify text. However, many students

FIGURE 11.7
K-W-L
Worksheet

K-W-L Strategy Sheet

K—What we know	W—What we want to find out	L—What we learned and still need to learn
1. Brainstorming		
2. Categories of information we expect to use		
A. _____		
B. _____		
C. _____		
D. _____		

Adapted from ''K-W-L: A Teaching Model That Develops Active Reading of Expository Text'' by Donna M. Ogle (1986), *The Reading Teacher*, February 1986, p. 564.

will need this support during difficult text reading, even after they have mastered the general approach. It is important to remember that Reciprocal Teaching is a *simulation* of the process of reading and comprehending. The specific strategies are not as important as the process itself. These should not be viewed as discrete activities to be trained and mastered. Instead, students (and teachers) should approach the task as a cognitive activity that is being launched interactively.

The original activity was designed for students who had adequate word identification skills but poor comprehension. It has been demonstrated to be effective with this group. However, Palincsar has subsequently adapted the technique to be used with very young or very disabled students. In the adapted form, the text is read to students, and they are encouraged to think it through during a listening task. This approach has reaped benefits for these students as well.

K-W-L

Many students who require additional help in reading have particular difficulties reading and studying expository text. Reading for informational and/or study purposes may be unfamiliar for many less-skilled readers, and too often they approach reading passively, as a word-recognition task. Carr and Ogle (1987) provide a vivid description of the problem:

> When they (middle school and secondary readers), begin to read, they do not perceive that they should learn, rather than simply "look at text." They are unaware of basic techniques, such as identifying key ideas and summarizing. When we asked one sophomore what she did when she read, she responded, "I try to take in the words and hope the teacher won't call on me." (p. 626)

Ogle (1986; 1989) has developed a simple teaching strategy that has high utility for many students across disciplines. It would be an appropriate choice for students who need support in accomplishing specific content outcomes. K-W-L is a three-step procedure to promote thinking and active reading (see Figure 11.7).

In the first step (K), the teacher helps students to activate prior knowledge and organize it into useful categories. In the second step (W), the teacher helps students to ask themselves questions and set purposes for reading. As students read, however, they are permitted to add questions to their list. Finally (in step L), students record answers to questions they have asked and the group discusses the questions and answers. Of course, students may be jotting down answers to questions as they read.

Launching K-W-L

It should be apparent that K-W-L requires no special training. It does require that a teacher be willing to help students identify what they know and permit them to pursue questions of their own determination. When introducing K-W-L, teachers should prepare a large sample worksheet so that all members of the group can see how the procedure is done. During subsequent experiences with K-W-L, children can complete their own strategy sheets with diminishing amounts of teacher guidance.

K-W-L can easily be used to adapt the traditional Directed Reading Activity (see Chapter 9) since the technique parallels the Before, During, and After phases of the DRA. However, teachers who are accustomed to high levels of teacher control and direction will need to guard against too much interference. With too much teacher direction, students will quickly come to see that they are really just reading for the teacher's purpose, and there is little point in using the K-W-L strategy. Remember that the point of K-W-L is to help students become more actively involved in reading and to enhance their memory for information identified as personally important.

On the other hand, teachers can help to shape students' question-asking behavior through skillful modeling and discussion. For example, teachers are expected to model the categorization process during the K step. Similarly, in the final discussion, students should be encouraged to see that some questions were not answered in the piece just read, or alternatively, to see that they now have new questions as a result of reading:

> The teacher helps students keep the control of their own inquiry, extending the pursuit of knowledge beyond just the one article. The teacher is making clear that learning shouldn't be framed around just what an author chooses to include, but that it involves the identification of the learner's questions and the search for authors or articles dealing with those questions. (Ogle, 1986, p. 569)

Because of these features of K-W-L, an excellent time to introduce the strategy is at the beginning of a new content area unit in which students are expected to pursue some topic for a report or presentation.

Maintaining and Adapting K-W-L

Maintaining K-W-L requires some investment in time. As Ogle (1986) notes, however, the increase in acquired knowledge makes the technique worthwhile. In addition, Ogle reports some evidence to suggest that repeated use of K-W-L encourages students to use the technique spontaneously during the reading of informational text. In order to increase the likelihood that students will transfer the strategy to other settings, the K-W-L technique has recently been adapted (Carr & Ogle, 1987). The revised technique, K-W-L Plus, adds mapping and summarization components to the original strategy and generally enhances its power and utility, especially for secondary students.

Concept mapping and summarizing are both helpful techniques for studying (see Chapter 13). Both are also quite difficult for less able readers, and they are rarely used as aids to comprehension and memory. Both are natural outgrowths of K-W-L, however. For example, concept mapping requires students to categorize information—something that has already been done as part of the basic K-W-L activity. Carr and Ogle suggest that students use text title as the central portion of a concept map and the category labels developed during K-W-L as the major concepts in the map (see Figure 11.8). In this way, students can visually display the information, helping them to understand and organize it for subsequent study.

The final step in K-W-L Plus involves using the concept map as an outline for a text summary. Carr and Ogle ask students to number the portions of the concept map in the order they wish to present information in their summary. Since the information is already quite concisely displayed, writing a summary is a relatively straightforward matter.

The important thing about K-W-L Plus is how clearly it demonstrates the value of linking *any* instructional strategy to important learning tasks. Furthermore, the adaptation combines several separate learning tools into one generally useful and powerful technique that can be used flexibly by teachers. Teachers can focus on the aspects of K-W-L Plus that will be most helpful to their students. For example, students who approach text passively, without engaging their own pre-existing knowledge base, can be encouraged to spend considerable time on step K. Other students will require significant help in answering their questions and identifying additional ones.

Summarizing Instructional Strategies

We have described some of the long-term, overarching decisions and plans that must be made by teachers, such as deciding on organizational patterns and selecting materials. In addition, teachers need to have a repertoire of instructional strategies that can be used in the initial stages of work with students. Therefore, this section also included detailed descriptions of selected instructional techniques. We have designated these *high-utility strategies*, because they have been shown to be effective, they are consistent with a known view of skilled reading, they can be shaped to meet individual needs, and they can be used with many different textual materials. There are other instructional strategies that have similar features, but this array can serve the purpose of getting started.

FIGURE 11.8

K-W-L Plus Worksheet on Killer Whales

K (Know)	**W** (Want to Know)	**L** (Learned)
They live in oceans. They are vicious. They eat each other. They are mammals.	Why do they attack people? How fast can they swim? What kind of fish do they eat? What is their description? How long do they live? How do they breathe?	D—They are the biggest member of the dolphin family. D—They weigh 10,000 pounds and get 30 feet long. F—They eat squids, seals, and other dolphins. A—They have good vision underwater. F—They are carnivorous (meat eaters). A—They are the second smartest animal on earth. D—They breathe through blow holes. A—They do not attack unless they are hungry. D—Warm blooded. A—They have echo-location (sonar). L—They are found in the oceans.

Final category designations developed for column L, information learned about killer whales: A, abilities; D, description; F, food; L, location.

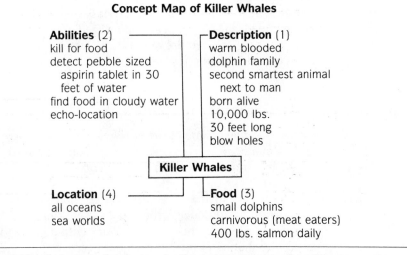

Concept Map of Killer Whales

Abilities (2)
kill for food
detect pebble sized
   aspirin tablet in 30
   feet of water
find food in cloudy water
echo-location

Description (1)
warm blooded
dolphin family
second smartest animal
   next to man
born alive
10,000 lbs.
30 feet long
blow holes

Killer Whales

Location (4)
all oceans
sea worlds

Food (3)
small dolphins
carnivorous (meat eaters)
400 lbs. salmon daily

(1) through (4) indicate the order of categories the student chose later for writing a summary.

From "K-W-L Plus: A Strategy for Comprehension and Summarization" by E. Carr and D. Ogle (1987), *Journal of Reading, 30,* pp. 626–631. International Reading Association. Reprinted by permission.

MAKING DECISIONS: PLANNING FOR INDIVIDUAL STUDENTS

Setting the stage for literacy instruction and setting in motion some effective activities are important first steps. It is possible to make these initial decisions using the knowledge base established throughout this text. However, a repertoire of techniques, no matter how good, is not sufficient. Skilled teachers and clinicians need to be simultaneously considering programs and planning in a more systematic fashion. In this section we consider instructional planning in greater detail.

Lesson Planning

Students, especially reading-disabled students, cannot afford to waste instructional time engaged in activities that they do not need or that will not help them to become more proficient. Therefore, the goals and objectives that are designed for specific students must be clearly related to the assessment that has gone before.

The most important thing to keep in mind is that there should be a clear relationship between the information that has been gathered through assessment and diagnostic teaching, the tentative conclusions about areas of need and action, and the instructional activities devised. Indeed, this is the heart of good planning—the matching of information about individual students with appropriate objectives that are, in turn, used to decide upon appropriate activities and materials.

Most teachers have been taught to use some type of generic lesson plan format. A typical lesson plan format has the following major components: (1) Topic or Focus, (2) Objectives, (3) Materials, (4) Activities/Procedures, and (5) Evaluation Plan. Clearly, writing the lesson plan following this or some other format is not what leads to success in teaching. Successful lesson planning rests on careful reflection.

Using the information that has been gathered about the particular student(s) we are working with, we decide on some specific objectives. These objectives are in turn used to adapt and refine the instructional program, making changes in either the delivery or content of instruction as appropriate for individual students.

Objectives

The available evidence suggests that effective teachers establish goals, objectives, and specific outcomes for students (Rupley, 1976). In addition, informing students of lesson objectives prior to reading improves students' performance (Duell, 1974; Maier, 1980). Despite both empirical and practical evidence that students benefit from carefully considered objectives, there is some misunderstanding about the role and function of objectives.

The objectives that are developed for a student should be clearly related to the diagnostic assessment that has gone before. It should also be evident how the objectives promote the larger important outcomes of skilled reading (see above).

Importantly, an objective should be focused on what *students* will learn or be able to do as the result of instruction. It is *not* a statement of instructional activities. Thus, an example might be:

> OBJECTIVE: Jerry will increase his interest in, and his ability to sustain himself during, silent reading.

This objective provides guidance about what to focus attention on and how to accomplish the instructional jobs that are required. Because it is not a statement of the activities to be used, it is possible to imagine a variety of activities that might address Jerry's needs. Jerry's increased knowledge and skill, not the particular program or tasks, are what is important.

The use of objectives sometimes generates concern among educators. Indeed, some believe that objectives constrain teaching and limit teachers' ability to be creative or child-centered. It is true that more mechanistic models of teaching have sometimes reduced teaching and learning to easily measured, relatively trivial behaviors. However, good objectives make it more, not less, likely that students' needs will be noticed and that important outcomes will receive attention. The format of the objective is less important than the extent to which it focuses instructional attention. There are just two principles to keep in mind when writing objectives:

1. Objectives should define what the child/student will do and learn—not what you will do as teacher.
2. Objectives must be clearly related to some demonstrated need as determined by sound assessment.

Thus, the types of objectives that are generated for a particular student are heavily dependent on what we have learned about that student and our assessment of the match (see Chapter 10).

The objectives established for some students may be largely attitude objectives. For others, the objectives generated will be more clearly process objectives, while a third group of students may need content information; their objectives will be weighted toward content objectives. Despite these variations, however, all students require some balance among the three types of objectives, and their programs should reflect this.

Activities

After the objectives have been determined, teachers can turn their attention to planning the specifics of the program they believe will best address these outcomes. This will involve selecting specific materials and tasks, and/or designing activities that will promote learning in identified areas. Some teachers select activities simply because they enjoy using them or think that their students will like them. Similarly, many novice teachers base their judgments of lesson success on the smoothness of execution or the degree to which students exhibit enthusiasm. These are not trivial issues because they may influence student learning. However, the central criteria for judging instructional success is the degree to which students make some progress toward becoming more skilled and/or motivated readers.

We start with an array of instructional strategies that are useful to many students (see the section on high-utility strategies, above). Variations of these, as well as additional techniques, are then considered (see Chapters 12 and 13). There are several major considerations in planning and selecting activities:

1. Is this activity closely linked to the student's needs?
2. How will this activity address the objectives that have been established?
3. Do the activities, in combination, form a comfortable flow of activity?
4. What level of support is required for the student to participate and how does that fit with the total instructional setting?
5. How close is the fit between this activity and what is expected of the student during normal reading/content area instruction?

It will be particularly important to think about what level of support will need to be provided to ensure that students can learn what is being taught. Expect that efficient use of learned skill and knowledge will take considerable time, and that the level of teacher support should diminish as students become more adept. This often entails adapting activities or existing programs to meet the individual needs of students.

Although some activities have high utility and are very flexible, planning must also involve selecting specific approaches or techniques to use with the particular student(s). It is important to recall that we are not describing a developmental reading program for all students. Although a balanced program is always desirable, the instruction for some individuals may reflect a more constrained focus. Some students, for example, simply have greater needs in the area of word analysis and word recognition than in comprehension.

It is also important to realize that activities are not important in themselves. Teachers must guard against viewing their instruction as merely the management of activity (see Chapter 8). The instructional program should always be designed to provide the best possible fit for specific students. In the chapters that follow, we describe specific techniques that permit teachers to make adaptations in a basically effective program in order to focus more closely on one or another aspect of reading.

Putting It All Together: Planning Lesson Frameworks

As we noted in Chapters 8 and 9 (see also Chapter 14), there are a number of basic lesson frameworks that have been employed in reading. Most of these are organized around a Before Reading, During Reading, and After Reading pattern. In general, we favor starting with a consideration of these frameworks because they assume that teachers are working with actual reading material.

Select reading materials that advance important outcomes. We have already discussed the issue of materials selection in considerable detail. In this section, we wish to emphasize selecting materials for more specific purposes. Reading materials should always be evaluated along general lines, and judgments made about the quality and merit of them. It is especially important to select materials that encourage and invite strong reader response, whenever possible (see Chapter 14). However, teachers also need to consider texts in relation to their more focused goals and objectives.

Because of the rich variety of available literature, teachers need to think about print materials as they might be used in teaching. Different books, authors, and genres invite and permit varying instructional efforts. For example, young children often enjoy the *Curious George* books by H. A. Rey, a series of books that invites discussions of cause-effect. Effective comprehension work might be done with causal relations, since the stories generally revolve around a series of events that are related only by George's curiosity and the trouble that results. On the other hand, these books would not be a good choice for teaching students about story structure, since the traditional structure of stories is not obvious in them.

When teachers think about reading instruction this way, lessons can become more text-driven than skills-driven. As Wixson and Peters (1989) point out:

> Consideration of the importance of the reading selection and its role in instruction refocuses our attention on teaching students how to read a particular type of text for particular purposes, rather than on the traditional instruction of isolated subskills. (p. 24)

Effective comprehension requires careful consideration of the relationships among the text, the objectives, and the activities. Wixson and Peters (1989) recommend that teachers engage in a three-step process; analyze the text, establish goals, and plan or modify instruction.

Analyze the text.   Map the text so that the key concepts and relationships are revealed (see Chapters 7 and 9). For stories, it is important to examine the characteristics of text that may cause problems for students or which suggest powerful response opportunities for students. These might include recognizing various plot patterns (see Figure 11.9) or looking for challenging character, setting, or theme characteristics. The text should also be scrutinized for interesting or potentially troubling uses of words and illustrations.

In analyzing expository text, teachers will need to consider different issues. Central purposes, major ideas, and supporting ideas must be identified so that teachers can see what content is present and how difficult it will be for students to read and learn from this material (Hayes & Peters, 1989; Wixson & Peters, 1989).

Establish goals.   Select content and process goals appropriate for the text and student (see Chapters 8 and 10). In establishing goals, teachers should be clear about how the goals contribute to the development of major reading outcomes. They should also be sure that the text advances and invites instructional work on these goals. Some samples of the relationship between comprehension instruction and selected materials are displayed in Figure 11.10.

Plan or modify instruction to be offered before, during, and after reading.
For commercial materials, examine the suggested instructional activities carefully to see that they provide acceptable levels of direct instruction or that they focus on

FIGURE 11.9

Structure of Reading Materials

Kind of Pattern	Description	Graphic to Clarify the Design
Step-by-step	Events flow logically one into the next. Ending can almost be anticipated. Example: James Herriot, *Bonny's Big Day* (New York: St. Martin's Press, 1987).	
Turn-about	Events flow logically one into the next, but ending takes an unexpected twist. Examples: Chris Van Allsburg, *The Garden of Abdul Gasazi* (Boston: Houghton Mifflin, 1979), and Jane Yolen, *Picnic with Piggins* (San Diego: Harcourt Brace Jovanovich, 1988).	
Circular	Events flow logically one into the next, but the action carries the main character back to where he/she began. Example: Maurice Sendak, *Where the Wild Things Are* (New York: Harper & Row, 1963, 1988).	
Just Imagine	Events repeat; each repetition varies slightly but action can be anticipated. Example: Joseph Low, *Mice Twice* (New York: Atheneum, 1981).	

Note: Encourage children to use their hands to demonstrate patterns in stories they read.

Hennings, Dorothy Grant, *Communication in Action: Teaching the Language Arts*, Fourth Edition. Copyright © 1990 by Houghton Mifflin Company. Used with permission.

important aspects of the text. If trade books are used, appropriate levels of support need to be established and focused activities planned. The important thing is that these activities be closely related to the goals established using text analysis and student assessment.

The basic DRA (see Chapter 8) can be adapted according to the needs and objectives that are established for individuals or groups. For example, the Directed-Reading and Thinking Activity (DRTA, Stauffer, 1969) is a variation that focuses on student involvement and the generation and monitoring of predictions. It is, obviously, well suited to providing strong teacher support while teaching students to assume more responsibility for learning.

Although these procedures require work, it is important for teachers of less-able readers to remember that "the point of all this, of course, is that teachers—not materials—should be the instructional decision makers for classroom reading instruction" (Wixson & Peters, 1989, p. 60). This perspective should guide all teaching, but it is absolutely essential for specialized personnel to remember, since their students are likely to be less flexible and less able to transfer or make connections from diffuse and poorly organized experiences.

FIGURE 11.10

Texts and Possible Outcomes

Text	Notable Features	Content	Process	Attitude
Amos and Boris, by W. Steig	Language usage, descriptive metaphors, characters are vivid, settings strong, plot structure parallels story grammar.	Theme of mutual aid; characteristic work of author. Story events.	Recognizing story structure; author's use of language; cause-effect; inference (theme).	Love of language, appreciation of author's craft, enjoyment of characters.
Ira Sleeps Over by B. Waber	Strong problem-solution format, first person narrator, identifiable characters with clear sequence of events.	Theme of friendship; attend to events and character feelings (response to problem).	Use problem-solution story structure to aid comprehension; identify events (details) that contribute to theme.	Enjoy reading about someone like them; identify with character; seek to read other similar stories.
My Father's Dragon by R. S. Gannett	Fantasy. Series of vignettes that rely on cause and effect surrounding animals' outrageous problems. Setting is intriguing; thin character, fairly weak plot.	Dream-like quality of the adventure; storyteller's feel to the text recognizing the problems.	Prediction of events; fantasy is a genre. Cause-effect.	Enjoy genre and humor. Appreciate a story that can be told.

An Example: Getting Started with Marvin

As we noted earlier, there are many ways that students might come to work with teachers, and many contexts in which this occurs. In this section, we describe the Getting Started phase of working with one student, Marvin (see Chapters 5–10). This instructional program was started in the university clinic setting of one of the authors. Unlike many of our students, Marvin came to this setting with a great deal of assessment information already complete.

Background and Setting

At the time of the original referral, Marvin was placed in a regular classroom, receiving no special reading support or services of any kind. His parents referred him for assessment because of their concerns about his academic problems. The assessment-instruction process was initiated by a trained reading professional (one of the authors who was working with the school). Thus, Steps 1–6 of the assessment process were executed outside of the regular classroom setting by someone other than the teacher. His instructional program, the context for literacy, and to some extent, the materials he would use in that setting were already determined.

In the university setting, the decision was made to match Marvin with another student. It was felt that there were benefits to an arrangement that was *not* one-to-one tutoring. Specifically, we felt Marvin needed opportunities to discuss reading and writing in a socially supportive environment. He was himself a gregarious young man, and many of his interests revolved around people and social interaction. In addition, his reading difficulties and the subsequent instruction he received had tended to isolate him from his peers.

Selecting High-Utility Strategies

As a result of this assessment work, Marvin was referred to our clinic. The information derived from the assessment and the diagnostic teaching sessions (see Chapter 10) suggested that there was merit in selecting at least two high-utility strategies to begin Marvin's program: USSR and Talking Dictionary. Indeed, except for those students who require teacher read-aloud as the only way to interact with books, USSR is a standard part of all our students' programs.

Although there was fairly extensive and focused individual information available about Marvin, these two high-utility strategies have merit for a wide range of students in many programs, and Marvin's case was no exception. Marvin needed to increase his ability to handle longer segments of text; reading fluency was a significant problem as well. Hence the selection of these two high-utility strategies. Although it seemed likely that Marvin could benefit from K-W-L (and we might have used this had we had less information initially), the decision to use this technique was deferred until later.

Planning for Marvin

The substantial information about Marvin could be used almost immediately to establish objectives, decide on materials, and begin to select activities. The specific objectives established for Marvin's initial sessions were:

1. *Goal/Objective:* To develop reading fluency and motivate recreational reading, Marvin will read without interruption for 5 minutes.
   Activity: USSR using *Bones on Black Spruce Mountain* (Budbill, 1978).
2. *Goal/Objective:* To increase word recognition and reading fluency, Marvin will read connected text with fluency support.
   Activity: 15-minute taped read-along using "Something Queer Is Going On" from *Electric Butterfly, Quest* (Aulls & Graves, 1985).
3. *Goal/Objective:* To increase comprehension, Marvin will be able to identify characters and the goal structure (including problem-solution) of a complex story.
   Activity: Taped read-along using "Something Queer Is Going On" from *Electric Butterfly, Quest* coupled with a story map.

It should be apparent that these objectives grow directly out of the diagnostic teaching sessions described in Chapter 10. The specific activities are essentially adaptations of the high-utility activities we have already described.

The selection of materials to use with these activities deserves some discussion. It is our experience that the appropriateness of text and task materials can have a significant effect on the success of the instruction. In Marvin's case, all of the materials were chosen with two major criteria in mind. Only full-length stories or books were to be used, since this constituted an area of need for Marvin, and these would involve fully developed complex stories with a strong goal structure. *Bones on Black Spruce Mountain* is a strongly evocative narrative involving two male characters and a strong adventure/suspense series of episodes. It was among several choices offered to Marvin during the first instructional setting, and one that sustained his interest over several weeks. In later sessions it provided a rich source of multisyllabic words from which to teach and practice structural and morphemic analysis.

The selections in the *Quest* materials are all fully-developed short stories or expository narratives (2–6 pages) of high interest. Marvin found these challenging, but he retained an interest in them. Only stories were selected initially, and we chose those with a sophisticated story structure. These short stories were used for direct instruction to develop both fluency and comprehension. In later sessions, these selections provided excellent material for use with both story mapping activities and a think-aloud strategy (see Chapter 13).

Marvin's case also illustrates what happens over time. As planning and instruction proceed, the high-utility strategies used initially are sometimes retained (e.g., SSR). More frequently, as students develop increased competence, some aspects of the initial plans are changed and adapted. The combination of initial instructional intervention and strong assessment information permits careful planning for an individual student like Marvin.

The interweaving of assessment and instruction and a commitment to continuous assessment result in subtle, yet sometimes major, adjustments in the instructional program. Most often, the program becomes more and more focused as the teacher/tutor adapts to growing competence or finds that a more and more refined focus is appropriate. These more refined techniques for building an instructional repertoire are described fully in the following chapters.

FROM CLASSROOM TO CLINIC

Classroom teachers often respond to individual differences by making placement adjustments, grouping students selectively for instruction, and changing the pace of instruction. However, because reading is a dynamic process, individualized efforts will be necessary even after groups have been formed and pacing adapted. While individualizing may be accomplished for some children by adjusting the pace of instruction, not all individual differences will be accommodated in this manner, and there are many other ways in which reading instruction may be varied to meet varying needs. Many of the high-utility strategies described in this chapter are useful to classroom teachers because they permit a wide range of responses to the same basic activity. Every student can do dialogue journals or silent reading or K-W-L. These major classes of activity promote the kinds of outcomes that we have for all students, and all students can participate.

Clinic teachers can and should look more closely at individual students. Carefully crafted objectives and individually determined activities are more likely in clinical settings. In addition, the types of sessions that are possible for individual students are different than those that are possible for whole classes of students. Many of the activities we suggest in the chapters to follow are more appropriate for remedial, individual sessions than for whole classes. Small remedial settings provide the appropriate environment for certain types of interventions, especially those that require close supervision or guidance from the teacher. Indeed, one rationale for having a different setting at all is that it permits different, not more of the same, types of instruction.

However, clinical teachers should never forget that the ultimate goal of instruction is to help students function in real classrooms under less-supported conditions. Every effort should be made to keep these long-term goals in mind. With support, classroom teachers can adapt the instructional context for individuals. Wherever possible, classroom teachers should be aided and supported so that they can respond to individual variation in students.

CHAPTER SUMMARY

In this chapter, we discussed the types of stage-setting decisions that help promote learning. Guidelines for establishing a literate environment were provided. In addition, two long-term planning issues were discussed in some detail: grouping decisions and selecting materials.

Six high-utility strategies were also described: Sustained Silented Reading, dialogue journals, dictated stories, repeated readings, reciprocal teaching, K-W-L. These specific instructional techniques were provided in this chapter, "to get started in instruction," because they have been proven effective and because they address some aspect of the attitudes, process, and content outcomes of a reading program. In discussing each of these, we provided a description of the technique, guidelines for launching the technique in the classroom, and then discussed ways to adapt the technique for special purposes of groups.

In the final sections of the chapter, we provided information about how to plan for individual students using the specific, focused assessment information that has been gathered in earlier steps of the assessment-instruction process. Finally, we returned to Marvin to provide an example of how the instructional program was initiated with him.

CHAPTER 12

Adapting Instruction to Focus on Word Recognition

INTRODUCTION

Using the assessment information gathered in the previous steps and the guidelines for sound instruction and planning as described in Chapter 11, a teacher might conclude that a student (or students) needs to concentrate more closely on acquiring or enhancing word recognition and/or vocabulary competence. In this chapter and the next chapter, we will describe the instructional approaches and materials that may be used to adapt instruction so that it provides increased instruction and support in the areas of word identification and/or vocabulary strategies.

Word recognition and vocabulary are both *word level aspects* of reading. Of course, knowledge and skill in word recognition and vocabulary affect comprehension and studying. The various components of reading are intertwined in complex ways, and it is generally not sound practice to assume that any student is experiencing difficulty in an isolated area. However, it is often necessary to focus attention more closely on a particular component of skilled reading—in this case word, recognition and/or vocabulary.

Problems at the word level, in either pronunciation or meaning association, generally pose major obstacles to wide reading. These difficulties may influence students' rate, fluency, comprehension, or enjoyment of reading. Word analysis and vocabulary ability are distinct aspects of reading, and it is quite common for students to have needs in one area but not the other. However, it is also important to understand that in skilled reading, the boundaries can be blurred. As Wilson and Hall (1990) note:

> Meaning must be the focus of all reading and word analysis must be viewed in conjunction with helping readers derive meaning from printed language. Sometimes word analysis is erroneously interpreted as being merely the use of sound-letter correspondences for deciphering unknown words. However, sentence structure (syntactic information) and the stock of word meanings and concepts (semantic information) are key elements in deriving meaning from printed language and in figuring out unfamiliar written words. (p. iii)

Chapter Overview

The information about word recognition in this chapter is presented in three large chapter sections. First, we will discuss critical issues in word recognition and word analysis instruction. These include a description of the components of word recognition ability, the debates surrounding the appropriate way to help children become competent, and the distinctions about students' word recognition based on a developmental continuum. Next, we will provide instructional guidelines that focus on word recognition and analysis. Finally, we will describe promising instructional techniques for focusing on word recognition and analysis.

ISSUES IN WORD RECOGNITION AND WORD ANALYSIS INSTRUCTION

A sizeable number of disabled readers have difficulty with some aspect of word identification. Despite the prevalence of print skill difficulties among disabled readers, there is no unified vision of the type of instruction that should be delivered to these students. This is partly because of confusion about word identification itself and partly because of a failure to distinguish between various developmental stages and student abilities. Lack of knowledge or skill in any one of the component areas of word identification (e.g., limited sight vocabulary, inability to apply phonics knowledge during reading, and so on) can cause problems. In addition, overreliance on one or another of the available word identification strategies can be debilitating for readers. In this section of the chapter, we address key issues in word recognition instruction.

Components of Word Identification

Rapid and efficient word recognition requires that readers know a number of words instantly at sight and also that they have acquired a repertoire of word identification techniques for analyzing words that are unfamiliar to them in print. In Chapter 2, we described the various components of word identification. Competent readers possess knowledge and skill in using sight word recognition, meaning-based analysis, graphophonic analysis, and structural analysis. Good readers possess a repertoire of skills and strategies that are used in concert to pronounce words and retrieve their meanings, resulting in fluent reading.

Although word pronunciation often involves meaning associations or "lexical access" (Gough, 1984), it is clearly possible for readers to be able to pronounce or decode words without having any meaning associations for them. Skilled readers of English are capable of "reading" (pronouncing) large numbers of words without assigning meaning. Indeed, they can read "pseudo-words" with equal ease (Ryder & Graves, 1980), demonstrating the degree to which good readers have internalized the sound-symbol system and structural aspects of our language. *Word identification*, *word analysis*, and *decoding* are all terms that have been used to describe a reader's ability to pronounce words. This ability requires "translating written words into spoken or subvocal words" (May, 1990, p. 34).

The tools of word identification can be placed in three large categories, with supporting skills employed as necessary:

Sight Word Recognition
  High Frequency
  High Potency
Meaning Based Word Analysis
  Contextual Analysis (Using Syntax and Semantics)
  Morphemic Analysis (Structural Analysis)

Graphophonic Analysis
Phonics
Structural Analysis—Syllabication

In a balanced reading program, provisions are made for ensuring development of each of these components of word identification. Some commercial programs attempt to teach only sound-symbol information and introduce phonics (and later structural analysis) by using nonsense words, without teaching students to make simultaneous use of other cueing systems. Other programs teach only contextual cueing (e.g. cloze formats) without providing sufficient information about the graphophonic cueing system. Teachers and others concerned about literacy need to be clear about the relationships between and among the various word identification abilities. It is especially important to recognize that word identification and phonics are not exactly the same thing.

Phonic analysis, or the use of letter-sound correspondences, is one tool among several available to the skilled reader. Knowledge and skill in using the graphophonic cueing system is essential but not in itself sufficient for good reading. Anderson et al. (1985) conclude that "all that phonics can be expected to do is help children get approximate pronunciations of written words" (p. 41). Similarly, Groff (1986) notes that phonics is not an exact science. Instead, application of phonics knowledge results in "rough estimates of the sounds that letters represent" (p. 921). Because phonics results in inexact renderings, and because reading requires more than word calling, students must attend to several aspects of print at once, *syntax cues, semantic cues,* and *graphophonic cues,* using these to help make inferences about what the exact print word is.

Clearly, knowledge of the ways in which the sound-symbol system works is critical to becoming a skilled reader. Similarly, it is clear that students must be able to use their knowledge of the graphophonic cueing system with ease and efficiency during reading. As Adams (1990) points out, the fact that students need to acquire this knowledge and skill is really not an area of dispute. How they should acquire this knowledge and skill and what knowledge is essential to becoming a skilled reader are areas of uncertainty.

Atomistic vs. Integrated Instruction

Much traditional word identification instruction employs an atomistic approach to teaching. Reading is separated into constituent parts and instruction is delivered in small pieces. The temptation to do this is great because it is relatively easy to break word identification into associated, subordinate tasks. Atomistic instruction also generally involves the introduction of these separate components in isolation and does not usually involve any presentation of words in text. Providing even sentence-length context has been relatively rare, and embedding instruction in longer patterned text is a very recent practice.

Whether students learn best when proceeding from parts to whole or from whole to parts is a debate that strikes at the heart of word identification instruction, and the answers often appear contradictory. For example, the overwhelming evidence from American researchers indicates that students learn basic sound-symbol correspondence more efficiently when they receive systematic and intensive instruction in synthetic (parts-to-whole) phonics (Johnson & Baumann, 1984). In addition, the research suggests that students who receive direct instruction in segmenting sounds and in blending are generally more adept at word recognition than students who do not receive this training (see Adams, 1990).

At the same time, it appears that such training does not result in enhanced comprehension (Resnick, 1977). Newer models of reading suggest that sound-symbol information is not the only source of information available for word identification. It is clear, for example, that meaningful context aids word identification (Goodman, 1965; Weber, 1970; West & Stanovich, 1978). As we have seen, pronouncing words during normal reading entails the use of a number of cueing systems in a coordinated fashion. However, good readers and skilled adults rely on context less heavily than do younger and poorer readers (Stanovich, 1980, 1986), presumably because they have reached high levels of word recognition proficiency.

Into these apparently conflicting results we must also insert a discussion of fluency. Some reading professionals argue that reading fluency depends on automaticity in word recognition (LaBerge & Samuels, 1974). In this view, students must learn to rapidly identify words using the sound-symbol information without depending on other cueing systems. Others argue that readers can only perform fluently when they attend more to constructing meaning from several sources and rely less on print (Clay, 1979; Goodman, 1976).

A more unified view is proposed by Barr, Sadow, and Blachowicz (1990):

> The capability to read fluently depends on two conditions: (1) instantaneous recognition of an extensive set of printed words and (2) considerable practice reading contextual selections. Many students require several years of reading experience before they acquire sufficient word knowledge and contextual practice to read unfamiliar material fluently. (p. 65)

It seems apparent that rapid and automatic word identification is desirable. However, in the early stages of reading acquisition, it is helpful for students to encounter words in the supported context of meaningful print. This does not mean that these words cannot be removed for examination. Indeed, there are good reasons for doing so, and later in the chapter, we will describe ways to focus on individual words in a less fragmented program.

Unless students are showing no growth in word recognition using a more integrated approach to reading instruction, we would argue for instruction that provides students with opportunities to see words in connected text first. Poor readers too often do not transfer the information they received during isolated skill instruction to more realistic reading materials and settings; many never receive sufficient practice in using the various component skills together. Consequently, they never achieve the high levels of automatic word identification that are the hallmark of skilled adult readers (West & Stanovich, 1978).

Children need to be *taught* to use the cue systems interactively. They need to be shown how these systems are interwoven, and then they need to be given a great deal of practice in anticipating words through using the semantic and syntactic systems and in confirming these anticipations through using the graphophonic system. They need to be *taught* strategies for changing their decisions when subsequent information proves them wrong. (Spiegel, 1984, p. 5)

As with phonics instruction, one of the persistent issues surrounding sight word instruction is the debate regarding the appropriate presentation of new words. Although the evidence is not conclusive, there is reason to believe that students benefit from the presentation of new words in meaningful contexts (Ehri & Wilce, 1980). In addition, it appears that poor readers recognize more high-frequency sight words during connected text reading than they do in isolation (Krieger, 1981), and they should have opportunities to practice in these relatively more successful settings.

In an extensive review of the literature on sight word instruction, Ceprano (1981) concluded that some students benefit from isolating the words for examination. However, more recent studies suggest that this can and should be done within a program that employs meaningful, even predictable, contexts for the reading (Bridge, Winograd, & Haley, 1983; Leu, DeGroff, & Simons, 1986). In addition, the research in writing and inventive spelling suggests that opportunities to write provide students with natural contexts for analyzing sound-symbol correspondence. Writing focuses students' attention on segmenting and isolating speech sounds. This ability seems to be a prerequisite to effective acquisition of other word identification strategies (Clay, 1979) and practices that help children to isolate and blend sounds have repeatedly proven successful (Groff, 1986).

In summary, the issues surrounding atomistic versus integrated approaches to word recognition and word analysis are complex ones. Isolated, fragmented instruction with limited opportunity to read and write real material seems doomed to failure, especially for children who are experiencing reading difficulty. On the other hand, teachers should not hesitate to provide students with information about sounds, symbols, and patterns and to pull individual words and sounds out of meaningful text experiences in order to help students notice key features (Adams, 1990). Timely, focused information about how to decode should be available to all students.

Identifying Areas of Instructional Need

Using the information gathered in previous stages of the assessment-instruction process, teachers can determine which aspects of word identification are posing the most serious difficulties for students. It is not uncommon, however, for students to demonstrate difficulties in more than one arena. For example, a student with extremely limited print skills may have weak phonics skills and limited graphophonic knowledge, but that same student may also have a weak repertoire of sight vocabulary. This should not be too surprising, since a student with few print skills tends not to try reading. Over time, students who don't read fail to acquire other abilities that result from repeated exposure to texts (Snider & Tarver, 1987; Stanovich, 1986).

Of course, students' prior experience as well as the practices and materials they encounter when they get to school will need to be considered in planning instruction (see Chapters 8 and 9). It is particularly important to recognize when direct instruction in sound-symbol associations is unlikely to be beneficial. Cohn and D'Alessandro (1978) studied the word recognition errors of 100 students referred to their clinic and concluded that "only in a small percentage of cases is it true that poor word analysis performance in decoding a list of words is attributable to a lack of knowledge of the sound-symbol relationship involved" (p. 343). In this study, students received some on-the-spot diagnostic teaching probes, such as "Please look at that word carefully and try it again." Given just this much prompting, students corrected roughly 50% of all initial miscues. If this prompt did not elicit a correct response, students were asked, for example, to examine the first letter(s) and produce the sound. This type of prompt resulted in the correction of another 29% of the miscues. Thus, at least 79% of all miscues resulted from something other than lack of sound-symbol knowledge.

Of the errors that remained uncorrected, there appeared to be three sources of difficulty: words with irregular phonic patterns (e.g., *tongue, guard*), lack of control over sound-symbol information which resulted in students sometimes pronouncing the phonic element correctly and other times not, and appearance on a word list versus in context. Like Allington and McGill-Franzen (1980), these authors found that less-skilled readers made errors on lists that they did not make in context. Cohn and D'Alessandro (1978) sensibly conclude that it is dangerous and foolish to reteach sound-symbol relationships, since it would be an attempt to "correct a situation that does not exist" (p. 343). However, these students might benefit from instruction that was designed to promote fluency, control, or flexibility.

Finally, teachers must recognize that differences exist among readers at different developmental stages. Young readers who have not advanced to formal reading and who have no print skills have different needs than students who have some, however limited, print skills. Both of these groups of students are different from older students who have acquired basic word identification skills but seem unable to use more sophisticated skills or to employ a balanced repertoire of strategies. The interactions among these various cueing systems work in different ways, depending on the knowledge and skill of the reader. In the following section, we briefly describe the special instructional issues facing teachers of various age and ability groups.

Developmental Differences in Word Identification

The issues surrounding instruction in word identification are often confounded by age and developmental stage. There is increasing evidence to support the conclusion that the very beginning stages of reading involve somewhat different tasks and behaviors than later stages of reading. For example, a developmental study by Shanahan (1984) suggests that the overall reading abilities of beginning readers are influenced most strongly by the word-level skills of word identification and spelling, whereas range of vocabulary affected older readers to a great extent.

One of the biggest problems facing teachers of disabled readers is that much of what we know about word identification instruction is based on studies of young, normal readers. Students who are experiencing reading difficulty do not generally parallel the general population in their reading achievement or progress. Therefore, describing word recognition techniques in terms of the normal stages of reading development can be problematic.

As a practical matter, students with word identification problems who appear in clinical or remedial settings generally fall into three categories: students with no or almost no print skills, students who have some print skills, and more advanced students whose print skills are not fully developed for reading multisyllabic words or specialized texts. In the following sections we will highlight the major word identification tasks of these groups.

Word Recognition for Students with No Conventional Print Skills

Reading professionals often are called upon to work with students who have acquired no functional print skills. The special education eligibility guidelines in most states require a discrepancy between ability and achievement, a standard difficult to attain in very young children who are at the beginning stages of reading acquisition. Consequently, many youngsters who are struggling are served by developmental reading or compensatory education teachers in the earliest years of schooling.

Although far less common, there are also some individuals who are not young but who have acquired virtually no functional print skills. Bilingual or LEP (Limited English Proficiency) students and illiterate adults have special needs. The issues surrounding adult literacy programs are too extensive to consider here, but some consideration of bilingual and LEP students is necessary.

Perhaps the most critical instructional issue for this group of students involves the careful consideration of emergent literacy and the degree to which the foundations of school literacy have been well-established. Careful consideration of the literacy, linguistic, and cultural environments is essential for planning effective instructional programs (see Chapters 4, 8, and 11). As a general rule, these students need to acquire some pool of sight vocabulary. They will generally require systematic introduction of sound-symbol knowledge as well as careful support for a developing view of the functional value of reading and ample opportunities to read, write, speak, and listen. If the students are young, it probably makes sense to provide many of the components of a sound developmental program. In particular, it appears to be important to increase the amount of exposure these students have to print (see Reading Recovery, p. 517).

Like other struggling young readers, bilingual and LEP students must learn to decode English print. Unlike other students, however, they do not have control over the language used to read. There is little consensus about how to approach the dual needs of such students: the need to learn to speak English and the need to become literate in English are not precisely the same problem. In addition, the challenge may not be the same for all students. For example, different solutions may be needed depending on students' literacy in their native language.

Some programs, like ESL (English as Second Language), have assumed that students must acquire proficiency in Standard English prior to literacy instruction. However, May (1990) concluded there is no evidence that learning to speak Standard English fluently is required to learn to read. "It is likely that they need abundant *exposure* to Standard English before they are expected to read it well, but fluent *speech* in Standard English is probably not necessary" (p. 479). There is relatively strong evidence to suggest that students possess an underlying language competence that can be used when learning a new language (Pflaum, 1986). Proficient speakers of one language use their knowledge of how languages work to learn a second one. Similarly, the skills used to become literate in a native language are available when learning to read and write a second language. Of course, students who are illiterate in their native language do not have these resources to draw upon.

There are differences of opinion about how to proceed with the instruction of bilingual and LEP students. "There is not, however, any disagreement that children learning a second language should be learning in a language-rich environment" (Pflaum, 1986, p. 100). Indeed, common sense would suggest that the educational programs of bilingual and LEP students should incorporate the attributes of effective instruction. May's (1990, p. 479) suggestions for instruction are consistent with the kinds of practices suggested for all students acquiring initial print skills:

1. Teachers should read aloud every day. Additional read-aloud experiences with peers and Big Books are also advised.
2. Provide ample practice for students to practice using English. Cooperative work groups and paired groupings work best.
3. Have students read predictable, patterned books and use these structures for writing as well.
4. Permit students to make limited verbal responses initially and provide guided support for increased proficiency.
5. Make use of drama and role playing.

Students whose language proficiency or literacy knowledge is not well developed will have a difficult time taking advantage of formal literacy instruction. These must be addressed as students work to acquire an awareness of language as an object of learning, as they learn to analyze spoken language into constituent sounds, and as they begin to assign symbols to sounds in their reading and writing activities. These important tasks must be accomplished or students will not prosper (Juel, Griffith, & Gough, 1986; Williams, 1980).

Word Recognition Instruction for Students with Some Conventional Print Skills

Most students who receive specialized reading instructional support have some print skills. Indeed, it is generally the case that a referral is made only after some significant attempts have been made to teach the student to read and it has become apparent that the pace or efficiency of learning is problematic.

Although the majority of remedial students have some, but not all, of the requisite print skills required for skilled reading, this is definitely not a homogenous group. It will typically be impossible to predict which print skills have been learned, which are underused, what cueing system is used most often, or whether students have generated any systematic approaches to dealing with print. Again, the careful review of assessment information is required. Although some teachers use the same commercial program for all students regardless of their specific knowledge and skill, this is clearly very undesirable.

The major differences between these students and those who have no print skills are that these students have demonstrated their ability to learn some aspects of the reading process and their skills can be used as the basis for additional learning. This information can often prove useful in planning the program. For example, students who have mastered the graphophonic elements of English orthography but who have limited sight vocabulary may require help in retaining the visual appearance of words. Many need to be informed that some words are not decodable using phonic knowledge, and may benefit from work in writing/ spelling and seeing words in familiar settings. Since such students frequently underuse context, it may be necessary to teach them these skills as well.

Sometimes students do not exhibit a specific area of difficulty. Rather, they may have what appears to be a general weakness in all aspects of word identification. An examination of the students' miscues, for example, would suggest that there is no single major area of difficulty. Miscues appear in many component areas (high-frequency sight words and several different phonic patterns), and effectiveness in using meaning-based strategies for self-correction is erratic. Such a profile suggests that the student has not achieved control over the knowledge and skill that has been taught. Lack of experience with print, not limited direct instruction, is the likely source of difficulty.

For young, poor readers it makes a great deal of sense to intensify the reading experience, but to mimic developmental reading programs wherever possible. These students have time in their future school lives to become proficient, and, with support, to practice sufficiently to regain some of the ground that was lost in the early years. Indeed, effective congruent programming may have the greatest payoff for these students (see Chapter 8).

Limited or inadequate word identification abilities are not the exclusive domain of young students. Many older, disabled readers have partial knowledge or mastery of word identification. This partial knowledge can be troublesome, since these students generally know that they are supposed to use sound-symbol information to ''sound out'' unknown words. They often attempt to do so, relying on inadequate or underdeveloped information. We frequently encounter young people who have a jumble of half-known rules and homilies stored away but little ability to identify the regularities of print or to recognize the familiar words they have seen many times.

For somewhat older students, it is important to analyze performance and knowledge in terms of opportunities to learn. If the student has already received substantial experience with one type of instruction but failed to thrive, it may be especially important to consider alternatives. This might include intensive, non-traditional training in some aspect of word recognition (e.g., the ABD program developed by Williams, 1980; described in the next section). It might also include supported reading of connected text (e.g. the Heckelman Impress, discussed on p. 528).

Although it is clear that the most desirable situation involves early acquisition of decoding skill, the appropriate intervention is not always apparent for students who have not become skilled readers. Some of these students may not have received good initial instruction, while others may not have been positioned to take advantage of traditionally successful programs (e.g., LEP children and students with poor phonemic segmentation abilities). What is clear is that many older students who have some print skills also have a history of school failure (Torgesen, 1977; Stanovich, 1986). This fact cannot be ignored in planning the instructional program for an individual student. In these cases, it is necessary to work with the existing complex of interactions.

"Jenny" is an example worth noting. Jenny was a 9-year-old second-grader when she came to our clinic. She had repeated both kindergarten and first grade and had been receiving specialized remedial help for several years. She had extremely limited mastery of phonics and an uncertain ability to associate sounds and symbols (the likely result of a long history of ear infections that had reached the critical stage between the ages of 4 and 6). In addition, she was exceptionally unreliable in her recognition of high-frequency sight words.

She had been receiving intensive phonics instruction as well as isolated practice on sight vocabulary for over a year. She had also been placed in a controlled vocabulary reader for application and practice. During our first session, Jenny was asked to read one of these simple stories aloud. She had read, haltingly, only a few words when she came to the word *there.* She stopped abruptly, held her head, and said, "That's one of *those* words—the ones I can't remember." Her intensive isolated instructional program had certainly sensitized her. She was exceptionally skilled at locating, if not pronouncing, high-frequency sight words; she had also become convinced that the task was an impossible one. Her two most frequent responses to an encounter with these words were to give up in exasperation and remark on "those" words, or to begin a fairly random run through a short list of high-frequency words, hoping to hit on the correct one. Although it is obviously desirable for Jenny to learn these words, any direct assault on them seemed doomed to failure in the immediate future.

Students like Jenny have some print skills, but they are not controlled and accessible for use. Other students have a much larger repertoire, but have not practiced them sufficiently in coordinated settings involving connected text reading. Still others have print skills that are suitable for some reading settings, but they have not acquired sufficient fluency, speed, and automaticity to direct their attention to the demands of more complex text.

It is especially important to recognize that many of these students may also appear to be unmotivated. Effective teachers and clinicians will be alert to the possibility that limited print skills have diminished the student's pleasure in reading. If this is the case, motivation will only be increased when reading is supported or skill improved. For this large group of students with some, but inadequate, word recognition and word analysis skills, differentiated instruction delivered by a thoughtful teacher is absolutely essential.

Word Recognition Instruction for Students Who Need More Advanced Print Skills

There is a third distinctive group of students who present themselves as reading problems somewhat later in school life. These students may have experienced reading difficulties earlier, but often, they were considered adequate or even good readers in the early years. These students generally have reasonably good phonic skills and are able to use phonic principles to decode unfamiliar words. Ryder and Graves (1980) found that even less-skilled seventh-grade students have more sound-symbol knowledge than was previously assumed. Indeed, there was relatively little difference between less-skilled and above-average secondary readers, in terms of their ability to identify letter-to-sound relationships.

The problem for these secondary students does not appear to be lack of knowledge. Memory (1986) argues that many of these students do have the requisite knowledge and skill but do not use (apply) it during assigned content area reading tasks.

> Possibly one reason that less-able readers in the secondary grades often do not apply their existing decoding knowledge is that the way they were taught to use that knowledge is not the way skilled readers decode words. Rather than use individual grapheme-phoneme relationships and phonic generalizations to sound out words, good readers pronounce words by putting together the sounds of familiar clusters of letters (Glass & Burton, 1973; Baron, 1977). (p. 195)

Skilled and less-skilled readers in the more advanced stages of reading development differ in other ways. Poor readers frequently do not read for meaning, and they are notably weak in their ability to read multisyllabic words. Less-skilled secondary readers often do not have a solid repertoire of skills that can be used flexibly. These problems may be related to poor meaning vocabulary (see Chapter 13) or weak comprehension abilities (see Chapter 14). In terms of word recognition, students' inability to read "long words" often stands in the way of attempts at wider reading that would, in turn, promote better vocabulary and comprehension.

Many students lack strategies for pronouncing longer, more complex words. Unfortunately, the evidence regarding the most productive approach to instruction in multisyllabic words is mixed, at best. There remains, for example, considerable controversy over the efficacy of teaching children to syllabicate words as an aid to word identification. Johnson and Baumann (1984) describe assumptions underlying syllabication instruction:

> The rationale for teaching syllabication is based on the belief that if children can segment unknown words into more manageable parts, decoding will be facilitated; that is phonics, phonogram identification, or structural skills can then be effectively applied. This position has been bolstered by the popular opinion that the syllable, not the phoneme, is the basic unit of language. . . . In addition, there is evidence that children are reasonably facile at identifying the number of syllables in words and that better readers intuitively divide unfamiliar words into syllables (cf. Schell, 1967; Sherwin, 1970). (pp. 596–597)

Researchers and educators are divided about the utility of teaching dictionary rules for syllabication. Although there is no evidence that traditional syllabication instruction improves vocabulary or comprehension, most of these studies have not demonstrated that students had difficulty in this area. The evidence does suggest improved ability to pronounce words, precisely the area of need for many less-skilled readers (see Johnson & Baumann, 1984).

What does seem unequivocal is the effectiveness of teaching students some technique for identifying elements within words. Less traditional approaches to helping students recognize word parts and apply sound-symbol information to them have proven effective in improving a wide range of reading behaviors. This type of approach is described later in the chapter.

GUIDELINES FOR INSTRUCTION FOCUSED ON WORD RECOGNITION AND WORD ANALYSIS

Word identification, like all aspects of reading performance, is influenced by the reader's knowledge and skill, the features of text, and contextual factors such as the amount of prereading support and the types of tasks. In the sections that follow, we describe instructional techniques designed primarily to influence readers' knowledge and skill. Other factors should be considered as decisions are made about what and how to teach.

In particular, it is assumed that many of the basic conditions for effective teaching described in Chapter 11 have already been established and that careful assessment has suggested that the student will benefit from instruction focused on word recognition and/or analysis. Before considering specific techniques, we offer guidelines that provide general frameworks for thinking about the content and delivery of word identification instruction.

Do Not Oversimplify the Reading Process

The close approximation of skilled reading should be the goal of all reading activities. This does not mean that students will never receive instruction focused on discrete aspects of reading; and not all students with problems in word identification can be treated the same way with success. However, wherever possible, teachers should develop instructional approaches that permit students to use several word identification skills/strategies at the same time, using relative strength to support relative weakness. Speed and accuracy in word recognition and word meaning retrieval clearly contribute to reading fluency, but so do familiarity, ability to think with print, and various text attributes.

For example, young beginning readers might use their knowledge of rhyming and text rhythms to aid word analysis in the context of a highly predictable text. Similarly, students who are more mature readers may use their extensive sight vocabulary and good decoding skills to aid in the analysis of unfamiliar words in dense informational contexts.

The dangers inherent in reducing reading to the acquisition of isolated bits and pieces are abundantly clear. The first danger is that students will come to believe that what they are experiencing is, in fact, reading. A steady diet of isolated, fragmented instruction distorts the reading process so that some students (and some teachers) find it impossible to remember that the goal is purposeful, self-directed learning and enjoyment.

A second danger in oversimplifying is that we may make reading more difficult. Highly controlled vocabulary does not make reading easier, because students are forced to apply their skills without the benefit of good information for self-checking. In Figure 12.1, an exchange between a preprimer text and Rose, a beginning first grader, demonstrates the frustration that can result. Note that Rose's confusion and difficulty do not arise because she cannot read the words. Rather, she has limited experience with commas to set off a form of address and quotation marks. Her well-developed sense of syntax tells her that Ken come is unacceptable and her desire for reading to make sense tells her that there is a semantic problem (either in the sentence or in the match between sentence and picture).

Remember That the Goal of Word Identification Instruction Is Increased Ability and Fluency During Reading

Demonstrated facility in sounding out isolated words is uninteresting and unimportant. On the other hand, students must be able to decode and recognize almost all of the words they encounter in text if they are to read with comprehension and enjoyment. Teachers should be certain that they provide systematic instruction in phonics early in reading development, but they must also remember to teach only high-utility decoding skills (Searfoss & Readence, 1989).

In addition to providing ample practice in connected text, teachers need to signal the importance of reading (versus worksheets) in every possible way. This

FIGURE 12.1
Rose's Oral Reading

From *Little Dog Laughed*, pp. 6–7, Ginn Reading Program. Ginn and Company, 1984; 1982.

must also involve evaluating students as they apply their knowledge and skill during reading and writing. In particular, teachers need to understand that students do not need to know the labels for phonic elements (blends, diphthongs, etc.), nor do they need to be able to provide an explicit rationale (rule) in order to decode effectively. Indeed, the available evidence suggests that students' ability to decode far outstrips their ability to explain what they are doing.

Tovay (1980) designed a study to examine how well children in Grades 2 through 4 understood common phonic terms like *consonant, syllable, diphthong,* and so on. In addition, she examined the relationship between explicit knowledge of terms and students' ability to apply phonics in decoding words. "The results showed that elementary grade children have a poor grasp of the meaning of phonics terms yet a far better grasp of applied phonics" (p. 431). Some of the results were especially startling. For example, only 24% of the students in Grades 2 through 4 could define or give an example of a "consonant." Similarly, there were no children who could define "consonant blend," but an average performance score in this area was 86% accuracy. These results parallel those reported by Rosso and Emans (1981). Tovay concludes that "it seems reasonable to deemphasize the use of phonics terms in deference to the functions they represent" (p. 437) and recommends a procedure that involves making comparisons with known words.

Students Should Be Taught to Examine Words for Familiar Patterns and to Make Analogies

Extremely disabled and beginning readers seem to benefit from direct instruction in analyzing, blending, and decoding unknown words (Williams, 1980). However, after a very brief initial stage of acquisition, good readers appear to move to more coordinated strategies: identifying familiar patterns in words, assigning sound relationships to those patterns, and blending elements when necessary. The rapid decay of the need for explicit information about sound-symbol relationships caused Anderson et al. (1985) to conclude:

> The right maxims for phonics are: Do it early. Keep it simple. Except in cases of diagnosed individual need, phonics instruction should have been completed by the end of second grade. (*Becoming a Nation of Readers*, p. 43)

More proficient readers rely quite heavily on spelling patterns and other familiar chunks of letters to rapidly identify words. For example, Glass and Burton (1973) reported that fully 85% of the decoding done by second- and fifth-grade students in their study involved analysis of letter *groups*. In addition, as good readers become even more skilled, they decode words by attending to larger and larger groupings of letters (Marsh, Desberg, & Cooper, 1977).

Memory (1986) argues that "if poor readers are to become even average readers, they too, must learn to see the phonetically important groupings of letters in words and take advantage of their existing knowledge of those groupings" (p. 195). The recognition of reliable letter clusters or known phonograms that remind readers of familiar words or sound-symbol patterns has proven to be effective in instruction for many years (Wylie & Durrell, 1970) and recent revisions of decoding through analogy with known words has proven equally effective (Gaskins et al., 1987).

Provide Ample Opportunities for Practice: Reading Recovery

The importance of providing students with supported opportunities to practice reading and writing cannot be overemphasized. Before launching into a discussion of specific instructional techniques, however, we describe a program that is based on the assumption that providing extensive reading and writing experiences is the appropriate response to the needs of early "at risk" students.

Reading Recovery is a program that has as its goal, "to accelerate the child's learning at a rate faster than the learning in the classroom" (Boehnlein, 1987, p. 36). Reading Recovery is based on research and instructional procedures developed by Clay (1979; 1985). The results from this ongoing research effort (see Boehnlein, 1987; Pinnel, 1985a; 1988) suggest a remarkable success rate:

> After an average of 15 to 20 weeks, or 30 to 40 hours of instruction, 90 percent of the children whose pretest scores were in the lowest 20 percent of their class catch up to

the average of their class or above and *never need remediation again.* (Boehnlein, 1987, p. 33)

Although there are no reports of efforts to single out specific features of the program that account for student progress, there are several critical attributes of Reading Recovery that probably work together.

The first is the extensive amount of reading and writing that students do. This is accomplished, in part, because of the intensive one to one instruction that occurs for 30 minutes every day for each student in the program. In addition, the program is premised on early intervention. Although every lesson conforms to a specific sequence, within that framework, students' individual needs are addressed very specifically. Students not only read widely but do so in high-quality materials (many predictable, patterned books) and receive strong oral language support as well. Finally, the program also involves extensive teacher training. Teachers are trained in the techniques that require careful observation of students, recording of information, and adapting of instruction. Teachers are observed repeatedly and both give and receive feedback on their instructional interactions.

The first 10 lessons, called "Roaming in the Known," require teachers to support students in reading easy books and writing their own stories. Teachers also read aloud, build students' confidence, and establish a pleasant relationship. Thereafter, lessons conform to the following sequence:

1. Students reread familiar material to build fluency and practice new skills.
2. Students reread the new book that was introduced the day before and the teacher does a running record (see Chapter 6).
3. Plastic letters are manipulated and identified.
4. Students write a sentence or story of their own, focusing on analyzing and writing the sounds in words.
5. The teacher copies the sentence or story that has just been composed, cuts it apart, and the student rearranges it.
6. Students experience a new book; they attend to meaning and text while teacher provides appropriate support and encouragement to use specific skills and strategies.
7. Students try to read the new book independently (Boehnlein, 1987, paraphrased).

Although the framework is the same for all students, the interactions are planned using detailed assessment information for each child. Teachers must have highly developed observational skills, because they are expected to collect observational data of each child during reading and writing. In addition, teachers are expected to shape the sessions, "actively interacting moment-by-moment with the child as he or she actually reads" (Pinnel, 1985a, p. 71).

It is not difficult to imagine how students receiving this intensive instruction from highly competent teachers would flourish. For teachers and schools not trained in the techniques, there are also lessons to be learned. Schools must find ways to provide significant blocks of time to teachers and students for literacy instruction. They must also invest in their teaching staff. We say again that there is no substitute for a knowledgeable, skilled teacher. Finally, students need to read and write daily.

INSTRUCTIONAL TECHNIQUES FOCUSED ON WORD RECOGNITION AND ANALYSIS

In this section, we provide detailed descriptions of instructional techniques designed to focus attention on word recognition and word analysis. The instructional strategies have been categorized according to their utility for use with students in the three developmental phases described above. First, we provide suggestions for working with students who have no print skills. Next, we turn our attention to students who have acquired some knowledge and skill in word recognition and, finally, we suggest some instructional approaches for working with older, more skilled readers.

Tools: Students with No Print Skills

Some students have virtually no conventional print skills. Because these students may be very diverse (very young, very disabled, bilingual, and so on), the range of techniques that might be employed with this group is also great. Some techniques involve merely tightening the focus on traditional good practice. Other strategies involve much more systematic intervention.

Establishing the Prerequisites

Age alone does not determine whether students have acquired the prerequisite knowledge and skill to become a mature reader. Although older readers are hardly ever permitted the time it would take to acquire some of the underpinnings of literacy (see Chapter 4), this is precisely what some need. In addition, most young, poor readers need at least some work on the foundations of literacy.

Developing phonemic awareness. It has become increasingly clear that students must learn to segment speech into constituent parts. Some students have mastered this skill before they enter school; most others develop the ability to isolate individual sounds rapidly as they encounter typical beginning reading instruction. There are some students, however, who do not seem to learn this early and easily. For them, the likelihood of reading failure is quite high (Juel, Griffith, & Gough, 1986). The notion that sound analysis and writing may actually precede reading is a difficult idea for most educators to grasp. Traditionally, schools have stressed learning letter names first, moving from letters to sounds. However, recent research suggests:

> A strategy of analyzing spoken words into sounds, and then going from sounds to letters may be a critical precursor to the ability to utilize the heuristic tricks of phonics. (Clay, 1979, p. 66)

As in other areas of word identification, there is disagreement about the appropriate way to deliver this instruction. For example, Clay (1979) argues that the experientially-based strategies employed in the Reading Recovery program can accomplish this. An important feature of this program is the extensive writing that occurs, with an emphasis on inventive spelling (see Chapter 4). As Clay notes, this "forces children to carry out a splendid sound analysis of the words they want to write—a first to last segmenting of the sounds in the word. They pay attention to the sounds of words and search for a visual way of representing these" (p. 66). The strong encouragement students receive for analyzing words for the constituent sounds is buttressed by activities that help students to identify orally rhyming words, to separate words that rhyme from those that don't, and finally, by activities that provide information about sound-symbol patterns.

Clay contrasts this type of visual and auditory program with the phonemic training programs used for years in Russia (see Elkonin, 1963; 1973). In Elkonin's program, children do not interact with print at all until they have mastered certain aspects of phonological segmentation. Markers are used to designate individual phonemes. Students are shown pictures with spaces beneath the picture that represent the total number of phonemes in that word. Students say the word and then they separate the word into discrete phonemes, placing a marker in each space as they say it. Over time, students are expected to do this orally, without markers or pictures.

The ABDs of Reading is a word identification program for learning disabled students designed and evaluated by Williams (1980). It focuses on teaching students to analyze, blend, and decode, using both oral training and contextual support. Williams has demonstrated that this type of program has a significant impact on the decoding abilities of learning-disabled students. Its success is probably rooted in the combination of direct instruction and supported practice. The ABDs of Reading involves the following steps:

1. Direct instruction is provided regarding the concept of word segmentation. Students are taught to identify the syllable as an element.
2. Students receive direct instruction in phoneme analysis. Nine phonemes (7 consonants and 2 vowels) are used for *auditory* analysis and practice.
3. Students receive instruction in blending phonemes into 2- and 3-phoneme units.
4. Students are taught letter-sound relationships for the 9 phonemes.
5. Students manipulate letters to learn to decode phonograms made from the 9 phonemes.
6. Six additional letter-sound relationships (5 consonants and 1 vowel) are introduced and practiced.
7. More complex patterns are introduced involving consonant combinations (e.g., CCVC).

Williams is careful to note that "this was a decoding program, not a complete reading program" (p. 4), and emphasizes the need to provide experience with words in context and the need to provide instruction in comprehension as well.

This may involve using some aspects of the program launched in Chapter 11 and providing time to focus directly on this aspect during some portion of the day. However, it seems safe to say that the instructional program of students who cannot reliably isolate sounds and blend them together should contain some focus on segmentation and blending.

Using sense and syntax. In order to take full advantage of any word identification instruction, students must understand the goals of reading, but must also be able to use sense and syntax to test out their graphophonic approximations. Students who have limited language proficiency or have had few experiences with book print should be read to extensively. Teachers, peers, older students, and parent volunteers should all be enlisted to aid in this effort.

In addition, daily oral language experiences (shared books, chants, chart stories, etc.) and opportunities to speak should also be provided. From time to time, students should also be encouraged to make their own dictated stories conform to book language. Using the frameworks or language of some read-aloud books to shape the language experience stories of less-experienced readers and writers is good practice.

There are many exceptional resources for the interested reader (see, e.g., Bridge, 1989; Pflaum, 1986; Salinger, 1988). Remember that in general, the focus of these instructional efforts should be to promote oral comprehension and the ability to predict upcoming words and ideas using the semantic and syntactic cueing systems of books.

Developing Sight Word Recognition

One of the major accomplishments of skilled reading involves recognizing instantly *at sight* large numbers of words. Some of these words have become old friends—sight words—because they occur so frequently in print that the well-read student has encountered them many times. Others have been acquired as instantly recognizable words because they have very high value (high-potency words) for the reader.

In the very early stages of formal, or conventional, reading development, there are two ways that teachers can help students recognize words at sight: embed the new word(s) in a highly familiar/strongly supported print context, or provide direct instruction of the new word(s). Both methods are described below, because effective instruction typically involves each at different times. Since the embedding method will require the least adaptation from the types of instruction started in Chapter 11, we address those procedures first.

Embedded exposure: Shared book experiences. Traditional sight word instruction has generally involved hefty amounts of skill and drill practice, often in isolation. More recently, educators and researchers have come to believe that games and isolated drill may not account for significant sight word recognition development in most children. Rather:

> Automatic recognition of a word from its graphic form is a consequence of extensive experience seeing that word in context and building up a complete linguistic identity around it. (Ehri, 1987, p. 15)

Using as a model the types of heavily supported print encounters provided by parents in literate environments, Holdaway (1979) described a cycle of activity that has been dubbed the "shared book experience." Shared reading in the classroom often involves enlarged print books, called Big Books. Big Books allow teachers and students in a group environment to read a piece of text together in a manner that mimics the intimacy and give and take of home lap reading.

> Reading to a group of children in school has little instructional value simply because the print cannot be seen, shared, and discussed. The parent is able to 'display the skill in purposeful use' and at the same time keep before the child's attention the fact that the process is print-stimulated. Teachers can do the same by using enlarged print for the experience of listening to stories and participating in all aspects of reading. (Holdaway, 1979, pp. 64–65)

Skilled teachers can develop all of the concepts of print using Big Books. They model directionality by moving their hand across the pages; they demonstrate speech-print match and concept of word by pointing; and they begin to introduce the relationship of sound-symbol by careful voice pointing across words of different length (McCracken & McCracken, 1986; Slaughter, 1983). Typical shared book experiences include the following procedures:

1. After children have settled in a group around the teacher, he or she focuses children's attention on the cover, helps children to examine other aspects of the book (e.g., author, illustrator, and so on) and asks children to predict what might happen in the book.
2. The teacher reads the book aloud for pleasure.
3. Students and teacher discuss what happened in the story, focusing on response and comprehension.
4. In later encounters, the teacher rereads the book, pointing to the words and encouraging students to read along.
5. Students do repeated readings of the text, including taped reading-alongs using small copies of the big book.

Some teachers are concerned that students, especially less-able readers, will not receive appropriate instruction if controlled vocabulary texts are not used. Although it is clearly possible, and potentially beneficial, for remedial students to receive instruction using good literature, most schools and teachers need some assurance that students are acquiring basic sight vocabulary. To this end, Eeds (1985) has analyzed 400 books appropriate for Grades K–3 and identified the high-frequency words in those books (see Figure 12.2). The 227 words listed account for 73% of all words in her sample of books. Reading teachers interested in coordinating their remedial program with a literature-based classroom program (or classroom teachers interested in supporting their less-skilled readers within the regular literature program) should find this list helpful. In particular, some direct instruction in these words, coupled with repeated exposure in good books, should prove helpful to less-skilled readers. A sampling of the books included in Eeds' analysis is provided in Figure 12.3.

FIGURE 12.2
Bookwords

Final Core 227 Word List Based on 400 Storybooks for Beginning Readers

the	1354	good	90	think	47	next	28
and	985	this	90	new	46	only	28
a	831	don't	89	know	46	am	27
I	757	little	89	help	46	began	27
to	746	if	87	grand	46	head	27
said	688	just	87	boy	46	keep	27
you	638	baby	86	take	45	teacher	27
he	488	way	85	eat	44	sure	27
it	345	there	83	body	43	says	27
in	311	every	83	school	43	ride	27
was	294	went	82	house	42	pet	27
she	250	father	80	morning	42	hurry	26
for	235	had	79	yes	41	hand	26
that	232	see	79	after	41	hard	26
is	230	dog	78	never	41	push	26
his	226	home	77	or	40	our	26
but	224	down	76	self	40	their	26
they	218	got	73	try	40	watch	26
my	214	would	73	has	38	because	25
of	204	time	71	always	38	door	25
on	192	love	70	over	38	us	25
me	187	walk	70	again	37	should	25
all	179	came	69	side	37	room	25
be	176	were	68	thank	37	pull	25
go	171	ask	67	why	37	great	24
can	162	back	67	who	36	gave	24
with	158	now	66	saw	36	does	24
one	157	friend	65	mom	35	car	24
her	156	cry	64	kid	35	ball	24
what	152	oh	64	give	35	sat	24
we	151	Mr.	63	around	34	stay	24
him	144	bed	63	by	34	each	23
no	143	an	62	Mrs.	34	ever	23
so	141	very	62	off	33	until	23
out	140	where	60	sister	33	shout	23
up	137	play	59	find	32	mama	22
are	133	let	59	fun	32	use	22
will	127	long	58	more	32	turn	22
look	126	here	58	while	32	thought	22
some	123	how	57	tell	32	papa	22
day	123	make	57	sleep	32	lot	21
at	122	big	56	made	31	blue	21
have	121	from	55	first	31	bath	21
your	121	put	55	say	31	mean	21
mother	119	read	55	took	31	sit	21
come	118	them	55	dad	30	together	21
not	115	as	54	found	30	best	20
like	112	Miss	53	lady	30	brother	20
then	108	any	52	soon	30	feel	20
get	103	right	52	ran	30	floor	20
when	101	nice	50	dear	29	wait	20
thing	100	other	50	man	29	tomorrow	20
do	99	well	48	better	29	surprise	20
too	91	old	48	through	29	shop	20
want	91	night	48	stop	29	run	20
did	91	may	48	still	29	own	20
could	90	about	47	fast	28		

From ''Bookwords: Using A Beginning Word List of High Frequency Words from Children's Literature K–3'' by M. Eeds, *The Reading Teacher,* January 1985, p. 420. International Reading Association. Reprinted by permission.

FIGURE 12.3

Book List

Author and Title	Total Words	Total Number of Different Words	Percent of Running Words Relative to Bookwords	Percent of Different Words Relative to Bookwords
50 Books for a Good Beginning				
Bancheck, Linda. *Snake In, Snake Out*	38	8	100	100
Barton, Byron. *Where's Al?*	34	18	82	89
Ginsburg, Mirra. *The Chick and the Duckling*	112	30	75	67
Burningham, John. *The Blanket*	66	33	86	85
Burningham, John. *The Friend*	51	34	86	88
Asch, Frank. *Yellow, Yellow*	97	47	70	62
Burningham, John. *The Dog*	69	48	77	69
Browne, Anthony. *Bear Hunt*	83	52	62	75
Kraus, Robert. *Whose Mouse Are You?*	108	54	77	76
Ets, Marie Hall. *Elephant in a Well*	286	56	71	64
Alexander, Martha. *Blackboard Bear*	128	62	78	70
de Paola, Tomie. *The Knight and the Dragon*	129	65	70	66
Kraus, Robert. *Leo the Late Bloomer*	166	70	68	67
Breinburg, Petronella. *Shawn Goes to School*	132	75	83	77
Mayer, Mercer. *There's a Nightmare in My Closet*	142	76	76	68
Buckley, Helen. *Grandfather and I*	291	79	90	70
Bornstein, Ruth. *Little Gorilla*	173	80	72	63
Brown, Margaret Wise. *The Runaway Bunny*	441	83	81	57
Burningham, John. *Come Away from the Water, Shirley*	129	86	74	65
Asch, Frank. *Rebecka*	203	88	87	80
Asch, Frank. *Elvira Everything*	183	92	81	73
Burningham, John. *Mr. Gumpy's Outing*	289	95	73	62
Wells, Rosemary. *Noisy Nora*	206	101	68	55
Hutchins, Pat. *The Surprise Party*	336	101	76	68
Udry, Janice. *Let's Be Enemies*	229	102	73	68
Clifton, Lucille. *Everett Anderson's Goodbye*	200	104	76	64
Brandenburg, Fritz. *I Wish I Was Sick Too*	327	107	68	63
de Paola, Tomie. *Watch Out for Chicken Feet in Your Soup*	254	107	68	63
Alexander, Martha. *Move Over, Twerp*	245	111	78	72
LaFontaine (Wildsmith). *The North Wind and the Sun*	210	113	70	59
Kellogg, Steven. *Pinkerton Behave*	233	116	65	56
Barton, Byron. *Jack and Fred*	263	118	80	72
Flack, Marjorie. *Ask Mr. Bear*	632	119	77	66
Asch, Frank. *MacGoose's Grocery*	322	123	76	70
Lionni, Leo. *Little Blue and Little Yellow*	284	123	81	71
Griffith, Helen. *Mine Will Said John*	506	124	70	69
Boynton, Sandra. *Hester in the Wild*	263	124	75	61
Sendak, Maurice. *Where the Wild Things Are*	350	129	70	57
Allard, Harry. *The Stupids Die*	296	140	55	61
Keats, Ezra Jack. *Goggles*	336	139	66	62
Hoban, Russell. *The Stone Doll of Sister Brute.*	494	143	73	65
Sharmat, Marjorie. *I Don't Care*	451	147	74	65
Keats, Ezra Jack. *Whistle for Willie*	391	149	78	69
Asch, Frank. *Sand Cake*	443	153	71	63
Delton, Judy. *New Girl in School*	379	158	80	60
Burningham, John. *Avocado Baby*	373	160	73	60
Allard, Harry. *The Stupids Step Out*	413	176	68	59
Cohen, Miriam. *Will I Have a Friend?*	464	177	74	63
Dauer, Rosamond. *Bullfrog Grows Up*	627	204	75	61
Marshall, James. *George and Martha*	645	210	75	68

From ''Bookwords: Using A Beginning Word List of High Frequency Words from Children's Literature K–3'' by M. Eeds, *The Reading Teacher,* January 1985, p. 422–423. International Reading Association. Reprinted by permission.

Predictable books technique. Using predictable books and language experience stories, Bridge, Winograd, and Haley (1983) have expanded on the "shared books" approach. They designed a program for teaching the basic sight words to beginning readers and examined its effect on students' recognition of high-frequency sight words. Their results indicate that students reading at a beginning primer level learned more basic sight words through this approach than students using a regular basal with controlled vocabulary.

The instructional strategy designed by Bridge, Winograd, and Haley involves selecting predictable books (see Appendix D) that contain the high-frequency sight words you wish students to learn. Using these materials, the teacher employs the following strategy:

Step 1: Teacher reads the book aloud. Then the teacher rereads the book, encouraging students to join in when they can predict what will come next.

Step 2: The story is transferred to a chart, without pictures to aid the reading. Students reread the story from the chart. Then students match sentence strips from the story to sentences on the chart. Finally, students match individual words to the words in the story.

Step 3: Students engage in choral rereading of the story from the chart. Word cards are presented randomly and the children match them to words in the story.

In addition to these activities, students regularly contributed to group language experience stories (see Chapter 11) that focused on sight word recognition and matching also.

Like the repeated reading techniques described in Chapter 11, strategies that involve predictable books rely on repeated exposure to high-frequency words to build sight word recognition. Big Books and charts have the additional advantage of providing opportunities to focus on individual words in the context of a whole text. Flaps or *masks* (Holdaway, 1979; Salinger, 1988) can be used to cover all or part of words so that teachers and students can work instructionally on features of interest (see Figure 12.4). If instruction began using the dictated stories technique described in Chapter 11, it might be adapted in this way to focus on word identification.

Direct instruction. Some students seem to need more explicit instruction focused clearly on the orthographic features of words (Ehri & Wilce, 1980). One of the most comprehensive of such approaches is described by McNinch (1981). He devised a framework for providing direct instruction in sight word recognition that includes some key characteristics of effective teaching. Words are introduced in sentences first and are then isolated so that students may examine them more closely. The steps in the *McNinch procedure* are:

1. The teacher chooses an unknown sight word and uses it orally in the context of discussion, introducing it to or reinforcing it in the students' oral vocabulary.

2. The teacher presents the word in written context, making sure that the new

FIGURE 12.4

Masking Techniques for Word Identification

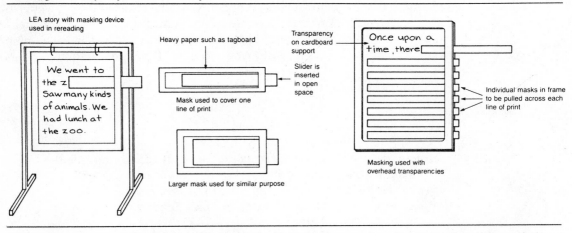

word appears in a sentence with words that are already in the students' sight vocabulary. The teacher reads the sentence and highlights the unknown sight word by underlining, circling, outlining in color, and so on.

3. The new word is isolated from the sentence and read by the teacher, who then asks a series of questions designed to focus students on critical features of the word. For example, students are asked to compare the word to the one in the sentence, to recall how many letters appear in the word, to tell what letter appears in the initial position, and so on.

4. Students read the new words in novel sentences that contain no other unknown words. McNinch applies a very strict criteria at this stage of the process. Teacher guidance and feedback is offered until students can read their sentences with 100% accuracy.

5. Students apply and practice by reading other materials containing the word(s) for meaningful purposes.

6. Students are then provided practice on the word in the form of games designed to achieve mastery of the word.

There are students who have such a difficult time learning new words that they require such intensive instructional efforts. The McNinch procedure acknowledges that some students may need extraordinary help and focuses on critical aspects of print (see Step 2). Indeed, some students require even more elaborated exposure to words, including the multisensory learning support provided by such techniques as the Fernald method.

The *Fernald method* was developed as a teaching technique to be used with students who were not learning through any normal approaches to reading instruction (Fernald & Keller, 1921; Fernald, 1943). At the heart of this approach is *tracing*, the use of visual, auditory, kinesthetic, and tactile elements (VAKT) simultaneously to teach word recognition. It was to be reserved for only the most disabled readers. Although the research support for this approach is limited to anecdotal reports, the underlying principles have proven helpful in clinical settings. The general procedure involves:

1. Self-selection of words to be learned.
2. After the child has selected a word, the teacher writes it and says it.
3. Using a finger to trace the word, the child pronounces it. The pronunciation and the tracing are to be executed in concert.
4. This tracing and then writing (with oral accompaniment) is continued until the word can be written flawlessly.
5. Using this word (and others in the sight repertoire) the child writes sentences and stories which are typed by the teacher and reread by the student.
6. The word is written on a card and filed in a wordbox.

It should be noted that very few students need such a high degree of support to learn words. The underlying principles of a multisensory approach can be used and varied, however. For example, we have occasionally had a child trace the word with markers, using a different colored marker for each trial. Some children benefit from instruction using this tactile-kinesthetic approach as a vehicle for building better visual memory for sight words. The child is stopped after each tracing and the word is removed. The child is then asked to describe any distinctive features of the word (e.g., initial or final consonants, how many letters, any tall letters, any letters that go below the line, etc.) and to use these features in recognizing and/or writing the word.

It does seem likely that a few students will find such procedures helpful, since at the very least, it often removes the emotional overlays of encountering materials and techniques that have caused failure in the past (see Myers, 1978, for a good review of the issues). However, the technique is extremely time-consuming and the rate of learning that can be accomplished is painfully slow. Once students have even a small number of words that can be recognized at sight, the instructional program should include large doses of supported practice in ways like those described in the next section.

Instructional Strategies and Tools: Students with Some Print Skills

As we have already noted, the vast majority of students who are referred with reading difficulties in the area of word recognition fall into this category. The array of teaching strategies is quite varied, since the needs of this group can be diverse.

Building on the Known: Providing Supported Practice

Students with some print skills, no matter how limited, should be supported in using those skills during authentic reading and writing events. This will frequently mean providing extensive scaffolding (see previous chapters). Although some of this can be provided by careful materials selection (see predictable books method above), for the least-skilled readers in the early stages, teachers will need to plan and execute heavily supported reading opportunities. Throughout the assessment-instruction process, we emphasize the need to determine the range of students' abilities—identifying what they can do as well as what is problematic. The instructional program should take this into account.

Heckelman Impress. The most heavily supported form of reading is the Neurological Impress Method (NIM) method described by Heckelman (1966, 1969). The teacher sits slightly behind the students and reads aloud with the student reading along for 10–15 minutes. Specific guidelines should be followed carefully:

1. The teacher should maintain a reasonably fluent pace of reading. The point is for the student to match the fluency of the teacher, not vice versa.
2. The teacher runs a finger smoothly along the print as it is being read.
3. The teacher does not launch a discussion of comprehension and does not use this experience to teach word recognition or word analysis strategies.

Although there is somewhat equivocal evidence about the effectiveness of NIM (Kann, 1983), it does appear successful in increasing both word recognition and comprehension for some students (Bos, 1982). Like Bos, we have found the procedure is most helpful for students who are experiencing extreme reading difficulty. Kemp (1987, p. 122) details a series of problems that can arise that serve as a helpful troubleshooting list. Problems occur when:

- the amount of print to be read is too great
- the complexity of the story and/or language is too difficult
- the pace set by the teacher is too fast, too slow, or without intonation
- the activity takes too long
- the child stops using the print and attends only to the teacher's voice
- the session becomes a lesson on word recognition

Henk's (1983) suggestion that NIM might reasonably replace the guided silent reading phase of a directed reading activity may prove helpful to classroom teachers who cannot otherwise accommodate such a high degree of support, and Echo Reading (B. Anderson, 1981) might also be accomplished in this fashion. Echo Reading is a variation on the impress method. The teacher reads segments of the material followed by student reading (echo) of the material.

Paired reading techniques. Paired Reading is a procedure described and evaluated by Topping (1987; 1989) that involves parents. Paired Reading is essentially a systematic variation on the NIM. The child and parent read together at the same time from a book that the child has selected. When the child feels ready, he or she reads alone. Topping reports significant gains made by students who have participated in a paired reading program, reporting progress three to five times the average on both word recognition and comprehension (Topping, 1987). The activity is meant to be done for approximately 15 minutes every day.

1. Child selects a book to be read.
2. Child and adult read together until the child, using a prearranged signal (e.g., a nudge), indicates that he or she is ready to read alone.
3. The child reads independently until an error is made or a word is encountered that is not read correctly in 5 seconds.
4. The adult immediately rejoins the child in reading together.
5. Reading together continues until the child gives the signal again and the procedure is repeated or the session ends.

Parents are encouraged to praise children for appropriate signalling, self-correcting, fluent reading, decoding difficult words independently, and for thinking about the story while reading.

The advantages to Topping's Paired Reading procedure are several. First, the student receives substantial practice with an important person in a low-risk context. Second, the student self-selects the reading material, so interest should remain reasonably high. Finally, the procedure can accommodate both extensive support and independent practice.

A different type of assistance is generally provided in repeated reading experiences, since students encounter the same words several times and have increased opportunities to add them to their sight vocabulary. The basic procedures described in Chapter 11 can be used, since the evidence suggests that poor readers with decoding problems benefit the most from repeated readings programs (Carver & Hoffman, 1981). However, adaptations can also be introduced to add additional practice in word identification or to focus and support students' development in this area. For example, the method proposed by Chomsky (1978) involves the student listening to a tape-recorded version of the text while reading along. Then the student practices until he or she can read it fluently.

An adaptation of repeated reading with the confusingly similar name of *paired repeated reading* (Koskinen & Blum, 1986) has proven helpful to students in both classroom and clinic. As the authors of this technique note, this adaptation is helpful because it "enables classroom teachers to use repeated reading with a minimum of management difficulties" (p. 71). Like traditional repeated reading, it provides practice in reading the same text several times, but it is designed especially for use with beginning readers or older students with reading difficulties. After the teacher has prepared the record form (see Figure 12.5), students work together in pairs using the following procedures:

1. Each member of the pair selects his/her own passage for reading (approximately 50 words). Each student will be reading different material; if students are reading the same book/story, they should choose different passages.
2. Passages are read silently.
3. First reader begins reading aloud. This reader will repeat the reading three

FIGURE 12.5
*Paired
Reading
Feedback Form*

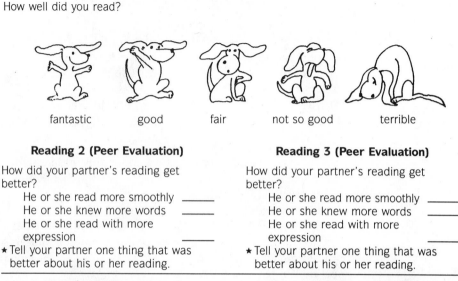

Reading 1, Reading 2, and Reading 3 (Self-Evaluation)

How well did you read?

fantastic   good   fair   not so good   terrible

Reading 2 (Peer Evaluation)	**Reading 3 (Peer Evaluation)**
How did your partner's reading get better?	How did your partner's reading get better?
He or she read more smoothly _____	He or she read more smoothly _____
He or she knew more words _____	He or she knew more words _____
He or she read with more expression _____	He or she read with more expression _____
★ Tell your partner one thing that was better about his or her reading.	★ Tell your partner one thing that was better about his or her reading.

Figure 1: Dog drawings selected from *Reading Attitude Inventory*, P. Campbell, Livonia Public Schools, Livonia, Michigan, 1966. Reprinted by permission of Livonia Public Schools. Figure 2: From "Paired Repeated Reading: A Classroom Strategy for Developing Fluent Reading" by Patricia S. Koskinen and Irene H. Blum, *The Reading Teacher*, October 1986. International Reading Association. Reprinted by permission.

times, pausing after each reading to answer the self-evaluation question (see Figure 12.5). After the second and third reading, the listener notes how the reading has improved and conveys this to reader.

4. The members of the pair switch roles and repeat the procedures.

Because this technique involves cooperative efforts between students, it is important to spend time introducing and monitoring the technique in the early stages. In addition, teachers are cautioned to help students choose independent level material.

Teaching and Extending Word Analysis

As teachers make decisions in the area of word recognition, careful consideration should be given to both what and how to teach. If the prerequisite skills are in place and students can segment the speech flow, can blend sounds, and can rhyme they will be in an excellent position to rapidly acquire the necessary word identification skills.

Systematic and carefully planned instruction is important in word analysis. Some students need explicit instruction in substituting initial consonants and consonant clusters as they create rhyming patterns and work with phonograms

FIGURE 12.6
Sample Word Analysis Lessons

A Demonstration Lesson on Initial Consonant Clusters

Instructional Steps	Lesson for *cl-/cl/*
1. Review the initial sound.	1. Ask the children to identify the initial sound in "can" and "cup."
2. Review the other phoneme.	2. Ask the children to identify the initial sound in "loud" and "lap."
3. Provide auditory experiences having combined consonant phonemes.	3. Ask the children to listen to the combined sound in "cloud," "clam," "close," etc.
4. Provide visual identification.	4. Present the children with the written words "cloud," "clam," "close," etc., and have the youngsters identify graphic similarities.
5. Ask the children to find *cl* words in their work banks.	5. Have the children supply new examples.
6. Present new *cl* words in sentence context.	6. Apply new concepts to new words.

A Demonstration Lesson for Phonograms

Instructional Steps	Lesson for *cl-an*
1. Present known words in a pattern.	1. Remind children that they know the words "pan" and "Dan."
2. Recognize rhyme and graphic similarity.	2. Encourage children to identify two common elements of -an: rhyme and letters.
3. Make a new word.	3. Write "fan"; have the children identify graphic similarity; have them use rhyming and pronounce the word.
4. Supply new and additional words.	4. Let the children suggest another word like "man," and then have them search for more examples from their word banks.
5. Make application to new words.	5. Have each child pronounce new words: for example, "ran" and "tan."

Reprinted by permission of Merrill, an imprint of Macmillan Publishing Company, from *The Development of Language and Literacy in Young Children*, 3/e by Susanna W. Pflaum. Copyright © 1986.

(see Figure 12.6). However, there is generally no magic in the exact sequence or program. In fact, students who are made to do every lesson in synthetic phonics programs are often kept from a more rapid pace of learning.

Although commercial programs and lesson frameworks can prove helpful in listing and ordering instruction, these should be used thoughtfully, as needed. The type of instruction revealed in Figure 12.6 should, of course, be followed closely (or accompanied) by ample opportunities to read and write these words. Since students generally enjoy the rhyme and rhythm afforded by poetry and nonsense books, these may be good choices.

Instructional Strategies and Tools: Print Skills for More Advanced Readers

Students who are generally skilled in word identification but who have specialized difficulties are often among the most difficult to instruct. Both students and teachers are frequently confused about where to focus attention. Indeed, there are several possible reasons for such difficulties in this area. Students may not have acquired a balanced repertoire of word recognition/word analysis skills, or they may have difficulty using both word analysis and meaning-based strategies together. Alternatively, students may not have gained control over reading, especially reading that involves complex materials with a significant number of multisyllabic words. Of course, students may not have adequate meaning vocabulary, an issue we will take up in the next chapter (see Chapter 13).

Multisyllabic and Content Words

Cunningham (1975–76; 1979) designed a compare/contrast strategy that appears to be helpful in promoting word identification of multisyllabic words. By teaching children to make analogies with known words, elementary school children (Grades 2–5) improved their ability to read unfamiliar words, and in addition, to transfer this knowledge to reading two-syllable words. The compare/contrast technique proceeds as follows:

1. Familiar sight words are placed on cards for students to manipulate.
2. Using these word cards, students are taught to compare and contrast known two-syllable words to known one-syllable words that rhyme with individual syllables of the two-syllable words (e.g., banter—can, her).
3. Students practice pronouncing the polysyllabic word and the two separate words.
4. Students practice the technique, adding other known sight words to cards for manipulation and matching them to additional two-syllable words.
5. Students receive extensive practice in executing this matching in their heads, without cards.
6. The technique is expanded to three-syllable words.

The great advantage to this technique is that it depends on flexible application of the analogy strategy. Students do not need to learn rules, but rather learn to approximate words, using sound and sense together. Finally, students can learn to identify morphemic units without memorizing long lists of prefixes and suffixes. Although the common practice of "looking for small words" is not warranted, students certainly should be taught to examine words for recurring elements and base words.

Teaching Strategies for Independence

Some students need to be taught how to approach and analyze multisyllabic words, but others need help in pulling together the skills and strategies they already know. They need to be encouraged to become independent.

Guide for attacking unknown words. Students, even very young ones, should be encouraged to attain some degree of independence and control in using their existing knowledge and skill. Most authors recommend teaching students a general strategy for word recognition and helping them to use it regularly during reading of connected text. The following steps seem reasonable:

1. Ask yourself what would make sense.
   Read ahead.
   Reread.
2. Try to sound it out.
   For one-syllable words: Compare the word to other known words: CVC, CVCe, CVVC.
   For two-syllable words: Identify the parts and compare each syllable to a known word: CVC + CVC.
   For words with more than one morpheme: Identify the root and then add the affixes.
3. Use the sound plus sense. (Get an approximation by sound-symbol and then correct or adapt using the context of the sentence.)
4. Skip it and see if it seems important.
5. If important, ask someone.

As is the case with any aspect of reading competence, independence in word identification takes substantial time and effort to accomplish on the part of both readers and teachers. Sometimes students need a copy of this guide to refer to until the steps become automatic. Teachers should teach this type of independent strategy just as carefully as they teach students the component skills.

Student monitoring and highlighting. Many less-skilled readers have difficulty transferring and coordinating their word analysis skills. In addition (perhaps consequently), they often have trouble attending to the meaningfulness of text. Pflaum and Pascarella (1980) developed a program designed to help students monitor their reading miscues, paying particular attention to those that distort meaning. In addition, these authors taught students to correct these miscues in order to retain meaning.

Reinforcing the developmental nature of some reading abilities, the program improved the reading level of learning disabled students (ages 8–13), but only if they had previously attained a reading level of second grade or higher. Thus, it appears that explicit training in monitoring and repair strategies may depend for its success on a certain level of word identification ability. Importantly, students were informed about what they were learning. In addition, the teacher discussed when to use the strategy in their own reading. The activities were modeled by the teacher, students received guided practice at each step, and then they received help in applying the strategy to their own reading. Students received instruction in two phases; half of the lessons focused on helping students to identify miscues that affect meaning and half focused on teaching students to self-correct miscues.

During the first set of lessons, students listen to an audiotape of a child who is making miscues. Students are repeatedly advised to think about whether a miscue (substitution) is "serious" (meaning-changing) or not. Specifically:

1. Students listen to 10 sentences, underlining the miscue made in each.
2. Students read five short paragraphs, underlining the two miscues in each. They discuss the seriousness of each miscue, using meaning change as the criterion.
3. Students read an instructional selection and record their own performance.
4. Students listen to their tape, underlining their own miscues. They then practice reading and recording additional passages until they reach 70% accuracy in noting miscues.
5. Students again listen to five short recorded paragraphs, underlining "serious" miscues twice. Students underline miscues once that do not distort meaning.
6. Students repeat Step 5 using their own recorded reading (underline serious miscues twice and less serious miscues once).

In the second set of lessons, students focus on learning to self-correct miscues that do not make sense. They are taught to use both context and graphophonic cues to self-correct.

1. Students listen to an audiotaped child, marking that child's self-corrections on a worksheet copy of the text.
2. Students discuss the self-corrections noting especially the technique used to self-correct and the reason underlying the self-correction (e.g., "that doesn't make sense").
3. Students practice and discuss replacements for blanks in 15 sentences (use context).
4. Students practice choosing replacement words using initial letter cues, then final letter cues.
5. Students continue practice, first listing possible words for a cloze replacement (using only context), then narrowing the choices using first initial, then finally letter information.
6. Students read their own material, record it and analyze their own miscues and self-corrections. Students are taught to correct uncorrected miscues as they listen by stopping the tape.

FROM CLASSROOM TO CLINIC

There is not a way to ensure that a particular approach to word identification instruction will be successful with a given reader. Some students need only a nudge in the right direction and an encouraging guide along the way. Others need to be lead down the path with every step guided or directed. Diagnostic teaching (see Chapter 10) can prove very helpful in narrowing the options that are likely to work with a particular child and we suggest that teachers regularly experiment before establishing a permanent approach.

Classroom teachers and clinical teachers must be especially careful to provide coherent word recognition and word analysis instruction to children who are struggling to master print skills in reading. These students are most likely to receive fragmented instruction with a heavy emphasis on isolated word identification. Indeed, many of the specialized commercial programs on the market are designed to provide instruction in the components of sound-symbol correspondence to the exclusion of meaningful practice (see Adams, 1990, for a review of the issues and concerns). Although some of these programs and materials may be useful tools in the hands of a knowledgeable teacher, they certainly should not be mistaken for a total reading/literacy program.

Classroom teachers need to guard against the temptation to believe that all children can/should learn using the same materials and methods, while specialized reading personnel need to guard against the notion that all students who are poor readers need strange and unusual instructional approaches. What is most often needed is a coherent approach that increases students' opportunities to learn (see Reading Recovery discussion in this chapter). In order to accomplish this, classroom teachers will need to find many ways to focus on print during the normal course of the school day. Clinical or special teachers should attempt to use their instructional time to enhance the program that is already being offered. Importantly, specialized instruction should not *supplant* reading and writing practice in the regular classroom, nor should it take the place of important literacy experiences such as teacher read-aloud or silent reading. These are precisely the kinds of experiences most poor readers need more of if they are to improve their literacy skills.

When special programs are advanced as appropriate for students, all concerned should be very clear about how the special program will be an improvement over methods and materials that have already been tried and how the new interventions are going to support the struggling reader in his or her work with meaningful texts. School personnel probably need to think about thinning out their materials periodically, just as librarians thin out their collections. Texts and practice tasks that were once deemed useful may no longer look so appealing in light of new information and newer resources. Similarly, classroom teachers may want to enlist the aid of knowledgeable reading professionals to review the available commercial materials while thinking about wider use of nontraditional reading texts and tasks. Early practice with print in reading and writing should take place in material that have real meaning to young students.

CHAPTER SUMMARY

In this chapter, we re-examined the components of word recognition ability and discussed several issues related to teaching word identification strategies. In particular, we described the debate surrounding the appropriate way to help students acquire effective word analysis strategies, noting that views have tended to be polarized. Some educators argue that word identification strategies will not be acquired without direct instruction, while others argue that they cannot be taught at all unless students are helped to learn them as they engage in extensive reading and writing in meaningful settings. Recent advances in knowledge and expertise permit a balanced perspective that acknowledges the importance of both positions. Importantly, there are at least three stages in the acquisition of word identification competence, and instructional approaches will be most beneficial if teachers differentiate among students who have no conventional print skills, students who have some ability to recognize words, and students with more advanced knowledge and skill in this area.

In the next major section of the chapter, we provided guidelines for teaching word identification skills to students. We emphasized the importance of providing instruction in service to meaningful activity, reminding teachers that the goal of instruction should be improved fluency during reading, not better knowledge and skill of phonics. In addition, we pointed out that instruction should help students to recognize familiar patterns in words, since it appears that this is a particularly effective approach to the teaching of word analysis. Finally, we emphasized once again the importance of providing many practice opportunities.

In the final portion of the chapter, we provided instructional techniques and strategies. These we divided into three categories, paralleling the three developmental stages of word recognition described earlier. We described techniques for embedding word analysis instruction in meaningful book experiences and we also described two direct instruction models for teaching word identification. For students with some print skills, we again described ways to support students as they interact with print and, as well, we described instructional frames for teaching students to focus on familiar and reliable patterns. For students with more advanced skills, we described some ways to help them become more facile in attacking multisyllabic words and also described ways to teach students to be somewhat more independent in their word reading abilities.

CHAPTER 13

Adapting Instruction to Focus on Vocabulary

INTRODUCTION

Words help us organize life experiences, because they represent ideas or concepts in the environment and the interrelationships among those concepts (Searfoss & Readence, 1989). As such, words facilitate our thinking processes. Reading is a thinking process; therefore, it is not surprising that vocabulary is a prime contributor to reading comprehension. Text cannot be understood unless the meanings of most of the words are known.

A wealth of research has demonstrated the strong relationship between vocabulary and comprehension. For example, Davis (1968) found that word knowledge was the single most important factor that accounted for variability in reading comprehension. Similarly, the proportion of difficult words in a text has been found to be the single most powerful predictor of text difficulty, and a reader's general vocabulary knowledge is one of the best predictors of how well that reader can understand text (Anderson & Freebody, 1981; Nagy, 1988).

As Nagy (1988) points out, the lack of adequate vocabulary knowledge is already a serious obstacle to literacy for many students, and the numbers can be expected to rise as an increasing proportion of students fall into categories considered educationally at risk. At the same time, advances in knowledge are creating an ever-larger pool of concepts and words that a person must master to be literate and employable. Thus, considerable attention to vocabulary and teaching students to derive word meanings and attach personal associations to them is vital to instruction at all levels and to success in reading and learning.

Chapter Overview

The first half of this chapter discusses the issues surrounding the controversy about when, how, and if vocabulary should be taught. In addition, goals and guidelines for vocabulary instruction are presented. The second half of the chapter describes instructional techniques that correspond to these established goals and guidelines. First, we present basic strategies for independent vocabulary learning during reading, and methods for teaching the techniques needed to support these strategies. Second, we describe techniques for providing direct instruction of key terms related to students' assigned reading. Finally, we discuss methods for promoting general vocabulary development and building interest in vocabulary learning.

UNDERSTANDING VOCABULARY INSTRUCTION

Issues

Although there is widespread consensus that vocabulary knowledge is fundamental to reading comprehension, there is a good deal of controversy about when, how, and if vocabulary should be taught. The issues surrounding this controversy are summarized in the following discussion.

Direct Instruction vs. Incidental Learning

The debate about the best way to develop students' vocabulary focuses on the question of the degree to which readers develop vocabulary through incidental learning as they are exposed to unfamiliar words in context, as opposed to direct instruction. Nagy, Herman, and Anderson (1985) have argued that direct instruction in specific words is a slow and inefficient method of vocabulary development. They have shown that readers do use context to learn the meanings of unfamiliar words. In fact, they have argued that this is the primary means of vocabulary development and that wide reading experience is probably the best means of developing students' reading vocabulary.

In contrast, others have argued that direct instruction in vocabulary is essential for good vocabulary growth. For example, a recent review by Stahl and Fairbanks (1986) concluded that, over the long term, students taught word meanings significantly outperformed students not given instruction, indicating that sustained attention to vocabulary may produce better comprehension. According to this view, the process of learning new words incidentally through repeated exposures in context is a slow and difficult means of vocabulary development.

The research cited in support of direct instruction indicates that skilled readers frequently skip over unfamiliar words as they read (Freebody & Anderson, 1983) and that intermediate grade students are not very skilled at using context to determine the meanings of unfamiliar words (Carnine, Kameenui, & Coyle, 1984). In addition, it has been found that certain unfamiliar words are learned better through direct instruction than through incidental exposures in reading material (Beck, McKeown, & McCaslin, 1983; Omanson, Beck, McKeown, & Perfetti, 1984).

The case for incidental learning. Nagy (1988) makes the case for incidental learning as follows. Very few people have received the type of intensive and prolonged vocabulary instruction that would guarantee gains in reading comprehension. However, many people have acquired extensive vocabularies. Few vocabulary programs, no matter how ambitious, cover more than several hundred words a year. Yet current research indicates that the vocabularies of school-aged students grow at the rate of 3,000 new words each year (Nagy & Herman, 1987). Furthermore, Fielding, Wilson, and Anderson (1986) found that the amount of free reading was the best predictor of vocabulary growth for students between Grades 2 and 5.

Nagy, Anderson, and Herman (1987) reported recently that students in the third, fifth, and seventh grades who read grade-level texts under fairly natural conditions had about a 1 in 20 chance of learning the meaning of any particular word from context. Thus, in the short term, it appears that learning from context is not particularly effective. However, as Nagy (1988) points out, the short term is not the whole picture.

The average fifth-grade student spends about 25 minutes a day reading in and out of school, according to Nagy (1988). Given this amount of reading, he estimates that a student encounters about 20,000 unfamiliar words a year. If 1 in

20 of these is learned from context, this would amount to a gain of about 1,000 words per year. Thus, he argues that if teachers added another 25 minutes per day to a student's reading time, an additional 1,000 words could be learned each year.

With regard to the quality of word knowledge gained from context, Nagy (1988) indicates that a single encounter with a word obviously does not provide in-depth knowledge, which is why context is not an especially effective method of instruction. However, he also maintains that extensive reading can supply all of the characteristics of intensive vocabulary instruction.

> Given that many people do develop in-depth knowledge of large numbers of words apart from much vocabulary instruction, wide reading must be able to produce the kind of word knowledge necessary for reading comprehension. Furthermore, given the number of words to be learned and the number of encounters it takes to learn them thoroughly, reading is necessarily the major avenue of large-scale vocabulary growth. (Nagy, 1988, p. 31)

Contradictory conclusions. Nagy (1988) presents the apparent contradiction regarding the degree of in-depth vocabulary knowledge necessary for comprehension as follows. On the one hand, it appears that comprehension of text depends on more in-depth knowledge than simply knowing the definitions of words. This implies that, in at least some cases, vocabulary instruction must be rich enough to teach students new concepts in-depth. An extreme response to this point of view might be to devote large portions of the school day to intensive vocabulary instruction. On the other hand, it appears that comprehension of text does not require in-depth knowledge of every word in the text. Indeed, reading itself is the major avenue of acquiring in-depth knowledge of words. An extreme response to this point of view would be to abandon vocabulary instruction in favor of increased reading time.

According to Nagy (1988), this contradiction is more apparent than real. If students are to achieve both the depth and the breadth of vocabulary knowledge that they need to become proficient adult readers, a balance between direct instruction and incidental learning is clearly necessary. Most growth in vocabulary knowledge must necessarily come through reading, because there is no way that vocabulary instruction alone can provide enough experiences with enough words to produce the necessary depth and breadth of vocabulary knowledge. Increasing the amount of students' reading is the single most important thing a teacher can do to promote large-scale vocabulary growth. However, vocabulary instruction is also necessary in cases where context does not provide essential information and knowledge of specific words is crucial to comprehension.

Teachers should also guide students in the development of strategies that promote independent word learning. There is no doubt that skilled word learners use context and their knowledge of word parts to deal effectively with new words. Independent word learning is enhanced when these techniques are taught as strategies by modeling how the knowledge of context and word parts can be used to determine the meanings of unfamiliar words encountered while reading, and by providing ample opportunity for guided practice in the use of these strategies.

Which Types of Direct Instruction?

Reviews of the literature indicate that not all types of vocabulary instruction result in improved reading comprehension (Mezynski, 1983; Stahl & Fairbanks, 1986). Nagy (1988) suggests that one reason vocabulary instruction often fails to increase comprehension is that it does not produce in-depth word knowledge. Research suggests that reading comprehension requires a high level of word knowledge, and that only those methods that produce in-depth knowledge reliably increase readers' comprehension of texts containing those words.

At a minimum, in-depth vocabulary knowledge involves at least two types of information about words—definitional and contextual knowledge (Stahl, 1986). Definitional information refers to the knowledge of the logical relations between a word and other known words as provided in dictionary definitions. Contextual information refers to knowledge of the core concept the word represents and how that core concept changes in different contexts (Stahl, 1986).

A large proportion of vocabulary instruction involves the use of definitions: some combination of looking them up, writing them down, and memorizing them. Stahl and Fairbanks (1986) report that when these approaches are used alone, they have no significant effect on comprehension. Nagy (1988) suggests that definitional approaches fail because ''reading comprehension depends on a wealth of encyclopedic knowledge and not merely on definitional knowledge of the words in the text'' (p. 7).

Another commonly used method involves teaching students to infer the meaning of a new word from the context. Again, Stahl and Fairbanks (1986) report that when a word is used only in context without the definition, there are no significant effects on comprehension. The biggest problem with contextual approaches appears to be that although a context may appear to be quite helpful to those who already know what the word means, it rarely supplies adequate information for those who have no other knowledge about the meaning of a word (Nagy, 1988).

Thus, it appears that neither definitional nor contextual methods, taken by themselves, are especially effective ways to improve reading comprehension (Nagy, 1988). Stahl and Fairbanks (1986) report that the strongest effects are found when there is a combined emphasis on definitional and contextual information, or when the balance is tipped toward contextual information. However, Nagy (1988) maintains that supplying both definitions and contexts does not necessarily guarantee gains in reading comprehension.

> It is safe to say that good definitions and contexts are minimal requirements for good instruction, but by no means do they exhaust what can be put into a good vocabulary lesson. Methods of vocabulary instruction that most effectively improve comprehension of text containing the instructed words go far beyond providing definitions and context. Such methods can be referred to as ''intensive vocabulary instruction.'' (p. 9)

Thus, the debate continues as to the most effective means of improving reading comprehension through vocabulary instruction.

When Direct Instruction Is Appropriate

Direct vocabulary instruction is needed to produce in-depth word knowledge. However, since only a fraction of the potentially unfamiliar words in a text can be taught directly, we need to determine when this type of instruction is most appropriate.

Direct vocabulary instruction is most appropriate for conceptually complex words that are not likely to be part of the students' everyday experience (Nagy, 1988). In addition, direct instruction is most worthwhile when the words to be taught are important to the understanding of the central ideas in the reading selection and to language development in general. Finally, it is beneficial to teach words in groups that have related meanings.

In further discussions of these issues, Nagy (1988) argues that students' familiarity with the words should be considered, but that it should not be a primary criterion for deciding which words to teach. The words in a selection that are least familiar may not be well suited for instruction because, for example, they may be unimportant to the central ideas of the text. Conversely, it may be important to teach certain complex concepts that may be superficially familiar to the students if a deeper knowledge of them is necessary for understanding the text.

Finally, Nagy (1988) suggests that the single most important question for the teacher who is trying to determine when direct instruction is most appropriate, is which words are likely to be conceptually difficult for the reader. Furthermore, the conceptual difficulty of the entire text, and not just the individual words, must be taken into account in determining when direct instruction is necessary. Finally, the greater the proportion of unfamiliar words in a text, the more intensive the instruction that is required to improve comprehension.

Goals

Given the evidence regarding what, when, and why vocabulary instruction is desirable, it appears that we need multiple goals for engaging students in activities designed to increase their vocabulary knowledge. The following are three primary goals for vocabulary instruction:

1. *Teach independent vocabulary learning.* Our first goal is to teach students the strategies they need to learn vocabulary independently as they read. We cannot possibly teach students all the unfamiliar words they will encounter in the course of their reading; however, we can provide them with a repertoire of strategies that will enable them to identify and learn the meanings of unfamiliar words as they read.
2. *Teach concepts important for comprehension.* Our second goal is to teach directly those concepts that are essential for comprehending specific written materials. It is important to provide intensive vocabulary instruction when in-

depth knowledge of complex concepts is critical to the understanding of reading assignments, because it is unlikely that this level of knowledge can be obtained by the student independently from context.

3. *Create an environment that promotes general vocabulary development.* Our third goal is to promote general vocabulary development by providing a vocabulary-rich environment with frequent opportunities to learn through reading. Since a major factor distinguishing between more- and less-skilled readers is their level of vocabulary knowledge, a primary goal of instruction must be the continual development and expansion of students' vocabulary knowledge.

In short, we need vocabulary instruction that teaches students strategies for acquiring new vocabulary as they read and increases their knowledge of both general vocabulary and vocabulary specific to their reading materials.

Guidelines

To accomplish the goals set forward in the previous section, research suggests that vocabulary instruction must embody the characteristics outlined in the following guidelines.

Guideline 1: Relate the New to the Known
The first property of powerful vocabulary instruction is that it integrates knowledge of instructed words with other, previously acquired, knowledge. This emphasis in instruction is an outgrowth of schema theory which has shown us that knowledge is structured into sets of relationships, and we understand new information by relating it to what we already know (Nagy, 1988).

Vocabulary instruction is effective when it helps students relate new vocabulary to their previous experience. In this way, new vocabulary becomes personally meaningful and students' understanding of new vocabulary is enhanced in ways that lead to increased reading comprehension. This practice also leads to improved learning and retention of the meanings of new words.

Guideline 2: Promote Active, In-depth Processing
Effective vocabulary instruction involves students in constructing the meanings of new words. This principle can be related to the "depth of processing" framework used in memory research (cf. Craik & Lockhart, 1972). This framework suggests that the harder one "works" to process information to be learned, the better one's retention. For example, retention will be better if one works to construct a relationship rather than simply memorizing a stated relationship.

Stahl (1986) identifies three levels of processing for vocabulary instruction. The first level is *association processing*. At this level a student simply learns an association for a word, such as a synonym or a particular context. At the second level, *comprehension processing,* the student applies a learned association to demonstrate understanding of the word. This involves doing something with the association, such as finding an antonym, fitting the word into a sentence, or classifying the word that requires the student to go beyond just giving back the association or something similar. The third level, *generation processing,* involves taking the comprehended association and generating a novel product using it. This product could be a restatement of the definition in one's own words, comparing the definition to one's own experiences, making up a novel sentence that demonstrates the word's meaning clearly, and so on.

These three increasingly deep levels of processing produce increasingly strong effects on comprehension. When students are actively processing information about each word's meaning, their comprehension of texts using those words improves. Generation could involve having students make their own sentence or definitions, developing semantic maps, breaking words down into semantic features, and so forth. What appears to be most important is that learners not only comprehend a word's meaning, but that they take that comprehension one step farther and make the word their own by interacting with it (Stahl, 1986).

Guideline 3: Provide Multiple Exposures

Another important factor for vocabulary instruction to affect comprehension is the number of times the student is exposed to a word and what types of information are given each time. According to Stahl (1986), providing the student with multiple repetitions of the same information about each word's meaning, and providing the student with multiple exposures to the word in different contexts or settings, both significantly improve comprehension. Providing only one or two exposures to a word does not have a positive effect on comprehension.

It is also important to recognize that limited or superficial knowledge of word meanings can have a detrimental effect on comprehension (Nagy, 1988). Being able to identify or produce a correct definition for a word does not guarantee that one will be able to access its meaning quickly and effortlessly during reading. Vocabulary instruction must therefore ensure not only that readers know what the word means, but also that they have had sufficient practice using it to make its meaning quickly and easily accessible during reading. In short, it appears that both the amount of time and the way time is spent in vocabulary instruction have a measurable effect on reading comprehension.

Guideline 4: Teach Students to Be Strategic

Effective vocabulary instruction teaches students to be strategic in their acquisition of new vocabulary. Students need to understand how to learn the meanings of new words they encounter in oral and written communication. This guideline can be related to the concept of a strategic reader as described by Paris, Lipson, and Wixson (1983). Strategic readers are those who are responsible for their knowledge, cognizant of that responsibility, and motivated to learn. In the context of vocabulary instruction, being strategic includes awareness of a variety of methods to acquire word meanings, ability to monitor one's understanding of new vocabulary and the capacity to change or modify strategies for understanding new words if comprehension is not forthcoming.

Teachers can help students become more strategic by teaching different methods of vocabulary learning as strategies rather than as isolated activities. This type of instruction involves modeling and explanation of how particular techniques can help students deal with unfamiliar words encountered while reading, and providing ample opportunity for guided practice, using these strategies with authentic materials.

Summarizing Vocabulary Instruction

In this first section of the chapter, we described several key issues in understanding vocabulary instruction. We conclude that vocabulary instruction requires careful reflection, since neither direct instruction nor incidental learning account for the complex interplay of learning, vocabulary, and comprehension issues. However, it is possible to conclude that wide reading contributes to vocabulary learning in important ways, and that direct instruction in vocabulary can improve students' word knowledge under some circumstances. To be effective, vocabulary instruction must foster independence and focus on conceptually difficult words that are central to understanding the reading selection. These words should ideally be taught in clusters, to enhance meaning connections. Accordingly, we list three goals for vocabulary instruction:

1. Teach independent vocabulary learning.
2. Teach concepts important for comprehension.
3. Create an environment that promotes general vocabulary development.

Because vocabulary instruction requires careful consideration of the particular students and texts, we also described four guidelines for teacher decision making. First, teachers need to relate new words to those that are already familiar. They must also promote deep processing of the vocabulary through active involvement. In addition, vocabulary acquisition requires multiple exposures, and teachers must provide these opportunities. Finally, students should be taught to approach vocabulary learning strategically. In the following sections, we describe instructional approaches that follow from these goals and guidelines.

STRATEGIES FOR VOCABULARY INSTRUCTION

This section of the chapter describes instructional techniques that correspond to the three goals of vocabulary instruction presented previously. First, we present basic strategies students can learn to use during reading, and methods for teaching the techniques needed to support these strategies. Second, we describe techniques for providing direct instruction in specific target words related to students' assigned reading. Finally, we discuss methods for promoting general vocabulary development and building interest in vocabulary learning. The various strategies and techniques adhere to the guidelines presented previously. They focus on relating the new to the known, promoting active, in-depth processing, providing repeated exposures, and promoting the acquisition of independent learning strategies.

A General Framework for Independent Vocabulary Learning

Consistent with our first goal for vocabulary instruction, we are concerned here with the ways in which we can provide the student(s) with a general framework or strategy that can be used independently to identify and learn unknown words during reading. This means that we need to teach them how to employ this type of strategy or framework. To this end, we describe here a general framework for independent vocabulary learning, a specific strategy for implementing this framework, and several techniques that can be used to support the development of the students' ability to use this framework.

The framework requires intentional effort and is designed to address vocabulary learning explicitly. Not for use with recreational reading, the framework is nevertheless critical so that vocabulary acquisition in new areas of study can become habituated. The general framework we are proposing has four phases that involve different types of reading/thinking activities.

Phase 1: Reading and identifying unknown vocabulary; activating prior knowledge regarding the words in relation to the reading.

Phase 2: Applying a repertoire of techniques to identify and learn the meanings of the unfamiliar words including the use of context, word parts, and the dictionary.

Phase 3: Relating the meanings of new words to previous knowledge as an aid to learning and memory.

Phase 4: Repeatedly studying and reviewing the meanings of new words in a variety of contexts.

This framework serves as a guide for students in independently identifying and learning unfamiliar words as they read. There are a number of ways that this framework might be implemented, including the Vocabulary Overview Guide described in the next section.

Vocabulary Overview Guide

One strategy that embodies many of the features of the general framework is the Vocabulary Overview Guide developed by Carr (1985) to teach students a series of steps for self-selecting and defining vocabulary terms from natural text. This teaches students to learn unknown words in their reading materials by establishing a network of relationships among words and relating these words to personal experiences. The students gain greater control over their reading and increase motivation to learn. It also can be used with a variety of reading materials.

The Vocabulary Overview Guide is completed by the students as they read a text. It helps them organize terms and indicate the relations among the terms, passage concepts, and their personal experience. The steps in the strategy are designed to encourage the students to self-monitor as a means of becoming independent learners. Initially, however, teacher modeling is essential to ensure mastery of the strategy. The three basic parts of this strategy are: defining the vocabulary through the use of context, completing the guide, and studying the vocabulary.

The steps involved in defining the vocabulary require the students to do the following:

1. Survey the text (titles, headings) to determine the nature of the material, and to consider what they already know about the topic.
2. Skim the materials to identify unknown or confusing vocabulary words, and underline them.
3. Read the selection and try to figure out the meaning of the word from the context of the sentences around it combined with personal experience. Check the accuracy of these definitions by asking someone or using a dictionary.
4. Write the definition in the text or on paper so that it will be available during reading.
5. Reread the passage with the defined vocabulary to ensure understanding.

After the students have reread the selection, have them fill in the guide for use in studying the selected terms. Demonstrate this procedure by presenting a sample guide, such as the one in Figure 13.1. Instruct the students to:

1. Write the title of the passage on the top line.
2. Select categories of words from the text and place them on the second row of lines. Categories should be selected by studying the vocabulary words and the text to determine what the unknown words describe or discuss. The number of categories will vary according to the vocabulary to be learned and what the words describe.
3. Fill in the vocabulary under the appropriate category on the next line.
4. Write a definition and/or synonym underneath each vocabulary word, leaving space to add more synonyms as new words are learned.
5. Add a personal clue in the box below the vocabulary word that relates the word to a personal experience or a quality or trait of someone or something that is familiar. The meaning of the word is thus related to the student's background knowledge, and more clearly understood.

After the guide has been filled in, the students are ready to study the vocabulary using the following procedures:

1. Read the title to activate background knowledge and recall words associated with the text.
2. Try to recall the meanings of the words in each category with the personal clue and definition of the word covered by a sheet of paper. If the meaning is

FIGURE 13.1
Sample of
Vocabulary
Overview
Guide

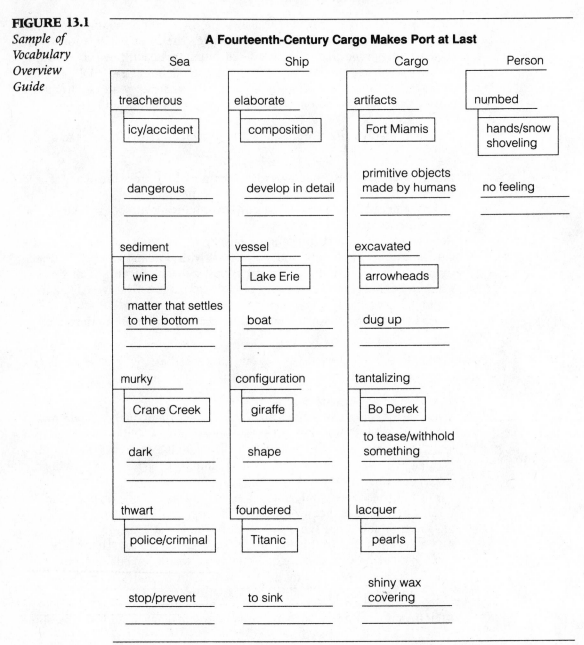

A Fourteenth-Century Cargo Makes Port at Last

Sea	Ship	Cargo	Person
treacherous	elaborate	artifacts	numbed
icy/accident	composition	Fort Miamis	hands/snow shoveling
dangerous	develop in detail	primitive objects made by humans	no feeling
sediment	vessel	excavated	
wine	Lake Erie	arrowheads	
matter that settles to the bottom	boat	dug up	
murky	configuration	tantalizing	
Crane Creek	giraffe	Bo Derek	
dark	shape	to tease/withhold something	
thwart	foundered	lacquer	
police/criminal	Titanic	pearls	
stop/prevent	to sink	shiny wax covering	

From "The Vocabulary Overview Guide: A Metacognitive Strategy to Improve Vocabulary and Retention" by E. Carr, *Journal of Reading*, May 1985, pp. 684–689. International Reading Association. Reprinted by permission.

not recalled, uncover the personal clue to jog the memory. If the meaning still cannot be recalled, uncover the definition for further study.

3. Use the guide to review the words every day until they are well known; then review them once a week as new words are learned.
4. Add synonyms to old vocabulary words as new words are learned, as a way to connect the old and the new and to refine and extend meanings.

The steps in this procedure can be summarized in a chart and given to the students as an aid until the strategy has become automatic. To ensure that the students are able to construct vocabulary overviews independently, it is important to provide frequent opportunities for practicing this strategy with a variety of reading materials. After demonstrating the strategy, complete several additional guides together, providing direction and feedback to the students. After the students understand how to create the guide, they should create several of them independently to ensure that they can monitor the correct use of the strategy.

The Vocabulary Overview Guide is one strategy for implementing the framework for independent vocabulary learning introduced previously. There are a number of other techniques that can be helpful in teaching students how to apply the framework successfully. Several of these supporting techniques are described in the next section.

Supporting Techniques

This section describes several techniques that can be used to help students learn to apply various parts of the general framework independently. These techniques are not intended to be used in isolation from the larger context of the general framework, nor are they intended to be used for extended periods of time. They are intended to be used as initial supports in teaching students how to apply the general framework.

Teaching Students to Use Context

We agree with Searfoss and Readence (1989) that the best way to teach students to use context clues is by talking through how to use these clues to gain meaning of an unknown word. Toward this end, we describe briefly the Preview in Context and Contextual Redefinition approaches developed by Readence, Bean, and Baldwin (1985), and the GLURK technique developed by Kendall and Mason (1980).

Preview in Context. This technique uses the students' experiences and teacher questioning to discover the meaning of unknown vocabulary in context. It is a very informal technique that requires little teacher preparation and lends itself to normal classroom interaction. The four steps in this procedure are as follows:

1. Select words from the material to be read that are both important to central ideas in the text and that may present difficulties for the students as they read.
2. Direct the students to the words in context. Read the material aloud as the students follow along in their own texts. Then ask the students to read the material silently.

3. Use questioning and discussion to "talk" the students toward a probable meaning for each word in its immediate context.
4. When the students have an understanding of a word's meaning in its immediate context, extend their understanding through discussion of alternative contexts, synonyms and antonyms, and the like. Encourage the students to use a dictionary or thesaurus to expand their understanding of each word. Word cards or a personal dictionary can be used as a permanent place to put words for later study and review.

Instruction of this type will have a significant cumulative effect. If students are shown how to use contextual analysis for only two words per week over the course of the school year, they will have 80 experiences with the process. This leads the student(s) to develop a habit of trying to discover the meanings of words through their own experiences and knowledge gained from the context.

Contextual redefinition. This technique was developed by Readence, Bean, and Baldwin (1985) to assist students in learning how to use context as an aid to understanding unfamiliar words. This procedure involves the following steps:

1. Select words from the assigned reading that are necessary to understand the important ideas in the text and that are likely to be unfamiliar to the students.
2. Provide a written context for each word that includes appropriate clues to the word's meaning. Sentences from the text can be used if they provide such a context.
3. Present the words in isolation and ask the students to provide a meaning for each word. The students defend their guesses and come to consensus on the best definition.
4. Present the words in context, using the sentences developed previously. Once again, the students should be asked to offer their best guesses as to the meaning of each word and to defend their definitions. Borrowing from a technique developed by Gipe (1978–79), we would suggest adding to this step the posing of a question that requires the student to relate the word to their own experience. For example, if the word is *surplus*, the question might be, "What do you or your family have a surplus of in your house?"
5. Verify the meaning of the words using a dictionary.

GLURK. Many words have multiple meanings, so we need to help students have a flexible attitude toward word meanings in order to enable them to recognize the appropriate meanings of words in context. Kendall and Mason (1980) developed a technique called GLURK to help students attend to context, so that they will select the proper meaning of polysemous words. As a first step, the teacher constructs sentences that use the less common meanings of polysemous words. After the sentences have been constructed, the polysemous word is replaced by the word GLURK (e.g., John's knees GLURKED from carrying the heavy weight. The music had a clear GLURK.).

After writing the GLURK sentences on paper or a chalkboard, the students are asked what GLURK might mean in each sentence, as well as what it could not mean. For example, they might say that John's knees "hurt," or that the music had a clear "sound." The teacher then replaces GLURK with the target word and the students discuss the intended meaning of the polysemous word (*buckled* and *beat* in our examples). This should lead to a discussion of how words can have more than one meaning and how context can be used to identify and learn new and appropriate meanings.

After the students have worked through a number of GLURK exercises, they should be shown how to apply this technique in actual reading. Using sentences from their reading that contain less common meanings of polysemous words, ask the students to identify the polysemous word and its appropriate meaning from context without first substituting the word GLURK. As a follow-up, the teacher can provide a practice activity consisting of a pair of sentences representing both a primary and a secondary meaning of a polysemous word. The students must then use the sentence context to identify the appropriate meaning for each underlined word. Responses can also be verified using a dictionary.

Teaching Students to Use Word Parts

A word itself provides information about its meaning. Analyzing a word's structure is another tool that students can use to predict meaning. When readers use word parts in combination with context, they have a powerful meaning-getting strategy at their command.

Mason and Au (1990) describe a technique that teaches students to apply their knowledge of familiar roots and affixes to word learning. This technique has the students determine whether a new word is related in meaning to any words they already know. From a knowledge of affixes, root words, and how compound words are formed, the students can have some idea of a word's meaning. They can check their initial hypotheses about it by considering the context provided by the surrounding sentence or passage.

The first step of this technique is to familiarize the students with the concept of the *word family.* Word families consist of words that are so similar that they are closely related in meaning, as in the following lists:

theory, theorist, theoretical, theorem
sense, senseless, sensitive, sensation

For instructional purposes, teachers can think of a word family as all those words derived from the same root and related in meaning. The goal, then, is to enable the students to make the connection between root words already known and the obvious variations formed from inflections and affixes.

Common prefixes and suffixes can also be introduced as part of this technique using the following steps:

1. Write a short list of familiar words in a column on paper or a chalkboard (e.g., *preview, predetermine, predate, premature*).
2. Have the students explain how the words are similar and then add some examples of their own.

3. Have the students think about how the meaning of each word is affected by the prefix and generate a rule that explains how the prefix changes the meaning.
4. Post the list and encourage the students to add to it from their reading.

At some point, the students are likely to come up with words that appear to fit the pattern, but do not (e.g., *prefer, preen, present*). These are opportunities to provide the students more information about the kinds of words that do and do not have affixes, and to show that certain affixes have more than one meaning.

After the students have become familiar with a number of prefixes and suffixes, it is important to help them develop a more general understanding of affixes. This can be done by asking the students to review several lists of words with either prefixes or suffixes, and how affixes change the meanings of words. Add one or two new examples for each affix and see if the students can figure out the meanings of these new words. Discuss how knowledge of prefixes and suffixes can be used to determine word meanings. When the students are ready to move on, introduce new words with both prefixes and suffixes. Ask the students to find the root words and identify the affixes, and see if they can figure out the meanings from reading the words in sentences.

A related technique is recommended by Readence, Bean, and Baldwin (1985), in which known parts of familiar words are transferred to parts of unfamiliar words. They recommend the following procedures:

1. Select unfamiliar words that may be troublesome for conceptual understanding of a text, and that lend themselves to an analysis of word parts.
2. Identify other words with identical word parts so that the students can associate the new words with known words.
3. Present the unknown words along with the similarly constructed known words in a manner that encourages comparison and provides the basis for predictions about the meaning of the roots or affixes in question.
4. Look up the word in the dictionary to verify predictions about the meanings of the unknown words.

Teaching Students to Use a Dictionary

The use of context and word parts are techniques that usually yield approximate meanings, rather than precise definitions, of unknown words. There are times, however, when context and word parts reveal very little about a word's meaning. At these times, or when a precise definition is needed, a dictionary is a reasonable alternative and a valuable resource for the students.

Knowing when to use a dictionary is just as important as knowing how to use one. One way to make the dictionary a functional resource is to use it to confirm predictions about word meaning arrived at through the use of context and/or word parts. In order to use a dictionary effectively, the students may require some direction. Dictionary skills that may require some assistance include the following:

1. Alphabetizing words
2. Locating words

3. Using the pronunciation key
4. Identifying the correct entry for different word forms
5. Determining which of several definitions is appropriate for a particular context

Teaching Students to Put It Together

After the students have become familiar with the various techniques that can be used to determine the meanings of unfamiliar words in context, it may be helpful to conduct a series of strategy lessons to assist them in deciding when these techniques are most appropriately applied. The procedure described here is an adaptation of the Context-Strategy Lessons presented by Searfoss and Readence (1989), and involves analyzing the text to determine how much help it provides in determining the meanings of unknown words in context.

Strategy lessons teach the students to select an appropriate technique for identifying the meanings of unknown words in a text by analyzing the material to determine the amount of help it provides in understanding the unfamiliar words. The students are taught to look first for direct help in the form of context clues that provide definitions, synonyms, and/or comparisons, as in the following examples.

1. *Context clues of definition.* The *ecologist*, a scientist who studies the environment, is usually quick to attack new sources of air pollution.
2. *Context clues of comparison.* Unlike Lyn, who was flattering in his actions with people, John was stubbornly *flippant.*

When no direct help is provided, the students are taught to look for indirect help from familiar root words and/or affixes. Searfoss and Readence (1989) provide an example of such a situation from a text with the sentence "John's mother has *hydrophobia.*" The teacher helps the students recognize that since there is no direct help from the context, they need to look for indirect help from familiar root words and affixes. The teacher then guides the students in breaking down the word and identifying the meanings of its component parts by comparing the parts to other known words and their parts (e.g., *phobia, hydroplane, hydroelectric*).

Finally, when the text provides neither direct nor indirect help, the students are taught to consult a dictionary to identify a meaning that is appropriate to the context. Thus, these lessons focus on analyzing the amount of help provided by the text as a means of deciding which techniques should be applied to determine the meanings of unknown words. Naturally, the number and variety of techniques (and therefore the strategy lessons) may be varied according to the needs of the individual student.

Consistent with the gradual release model of instruction described in Chapters 8 and 11, the amount of support provided by the teacher in the use of the techniques described in this section should depend on the students' level of development. Students in the initial stages of acquisition require a great deal of teacher support in the form of modeling and explanation. Students who have acquired some knowledge and skill in vocabulary learning may only require a brief period of guided instruction before they are ready to work independently. Finally, students who have mastered the integrated use of vocabulary learning strategies should be provided opportunities for independent application.

Strategies for Teaching Specific Vocabulary for a Text

Consistent with our second goal for vocabulary instruction, it is important to provide direct vocabulary instruction when in-depth knowledge of complex concepts is critical to the understanding of reading assignments. The following techniques can be used for this purpose.

List-Group-Label

The list-group-label lesson was originally developed by Hilda Taba (1967) to assist students in dealing with the technical vocabulary in subject area reading. Although the foundation of these procedures is in subject content area reading, the concept can be broadened to all areas and levels of vocabulary learning.

To implement the procedure, a one- or two-word topic is selected by the teacher as a stimulus word and written at the top of a chalkboard or large sheet of paper. Topics may be drawn from either literary themes (e.g., fear, trust) or subject area content (e.g., social studies unit on independence). Although general topics such as events of the school year (e.g., Martin Luther King Day, President's Day) or places (e.g., school, home) could be used, we are recommending this procedure primarily for development of specific vocabulary in preparation for reading a particular text.

After the topic is presented, the students are asked to think of related words or expressions. For example, the teacher might ask, "What comes to mind when you think about this topic?" All responses are recorded until a reasonable list has been compiled (i.e., between 15 and 25 words). Then the teacher rereads the list orally, or asks the students to do so. The students are then asked to break the larger list into smaller lists of three words or more that have something in common. The students are also asked to give each group of words a label indicating the common characteristics they share. The students must then explain why the words have been grouped in a certain manner. All groupings should be accepted and recorded, although the teacher should point out that meaningful associations are preferable to groupings based on surface-level features such as spelling.

A number of variations of this procedure are possible for students who may need more assistance. For example, the teacher may provide the initial list of words and ask the students to group and label them. Alternatively, the teacher could provide the groups of words and ask the students to label them, or the teacher can supply the list and the label and have the students group the words.

Semantic Mapping

Johnson and Pearson (1984) describe another well-practiced version of the list-group-label strategy, called *semantic mapping*. Semantic maps are a graphic representation of text concepts that typically consist of three levels of information about

FIGURE 13.2
*Prereading
Semantic Map*

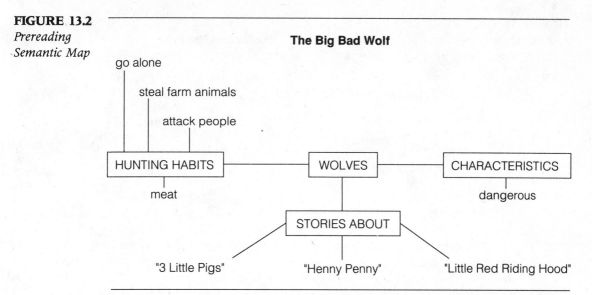

The Big Bad Wolf

the main topic in a central hub, "spokes" labeled to indicate major ideas or categories, and branches containing specific supporting details. Maps can be used either to organize the students' brainstorming before reading a text or as the basis for summarizing ideas after reading.

To implement this procedure, begin by placing the topic in a central hub and eliciting major category labels related to the topic. Then ask the students either to brainstorm or search the selection for supporting information within each of the categories. After the supporting information has been categorized, the teacher can bring up any important ideas not suggested by the students and ask them to try to place them in an appropriate category. With students who require more structure, a prestructured map with empty slots can be supplied and the students asked to fill these in as the material is discussed. Figure 13.2 presents a semantic map constructed prior to reading an expository selection on wolves.

List-group-label and semantic mapping procedures can also be used as a measure of how well the students have learned the vocabulary from a particular lesson. They can be used at different points in a lesson or unit to determine if the students are beginning to use and categorize the key vocabulary. Each time a list-group-label lesson or semantic map has been completed, the categories can be compared to the previous ones as a means of evaluating progress. Figure 13.3 presents a semantic map for wolves created after the students read, embellished, and made corrections as necessary. A comparison between this postreading map and the prereading map reveals increased knowledge about the general attributes and specific characteristics of wolves.

FIGURE 13.3
*Postreading
Semantic Map*

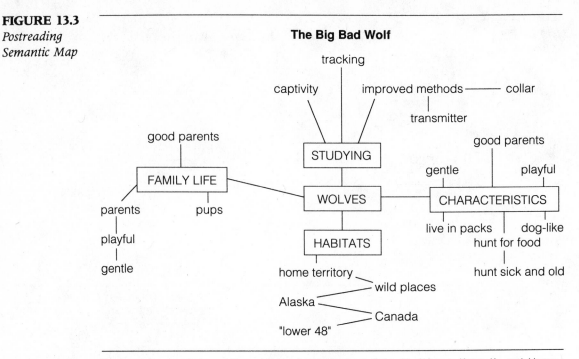

Structured Overview or Graphic Organizer

Structured overviews or graphic organizers are visual representations of the relationships among important vocabulary terms and concepts in a text. They are generally more structured than semantic maps and more tied to the hierarchical structure of the information presented in a text. For this reason, they are particularly well suited for subject areas texts.

According to Nelson-Herber (1986), these overviews or organizers have three purposes: to help students expand their knowledge of vocabulary by building from the known to the new, to help students refine their understanding of word meanings and the ways that words interrelate, and to support students in the use of their word knowledge in reading, writing, and speaking. They are also used to introduce vocabulary in a way that helps students relate new material to what they already know, and to provide an advance organizer for the reading assignment.

The overview or organizer itself is a tree diagram with the most inclusive concepts subsuming subordinate ones. Relationships among the concepts are indicated by the connecting lines between terms (see Figure 13.4). These diagrams can be designed by the teacher prior to instruction or can be developed jointly by the teacher and the students during instruction. As the students work with the

FIGURE 13.4
Structured
Overview

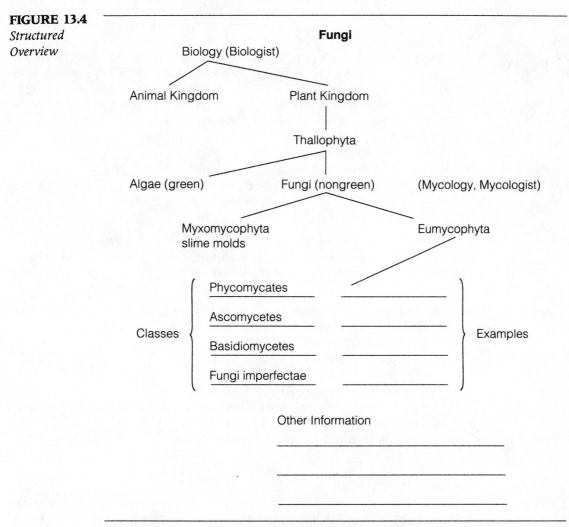

Fungi

Biology (Biologist)

Animal Kingdom   Plant Kingdom

Thallophyta

Algae (green)   Fungi (nongreen)   (Mycology, Mycologist)

Myxomycophyta   Eumycophyta
slime molds

Classes {
Phycomycates _____   _____
Ascomycetes _____   _____
Basidiomycetes _____   _____
Fungi imperfectae _____   _____
} Examples

Other Information

_____

_____

_____

Adapted from ''A Structured Overview: Fungi'' from ''Expanding and Refining Vocabulary in Content Areas'' by Joan Nelson-Herber, *Journal of Reading*, April 1986, p. 630.

text, they refer to the diagram and use it to organize and learn key concepts as presented in their reading.

The following steps are suggested for developing the diagram and introducing it to students (cf. Barron, 1969; Herber, 1978; Nelson-Herber, 1986):

1. Analyze the text and list the major concepts and key terms that are to be stressed in instruction and therefore are important for students to understand.
2. Arrange the list of words into a diagram that shows the interrelationships among the concepts in a manner that relates to and expands on what is already known by the students. The arrangement depends on the teacher, the

number of concepts to be learned, and the students' prior knowledge of the concepts.

3. Evaluate the overview. Are the major relationships shown clearly? Can the diagram be simplified and still effectively communicate the key ideas? Add to the diagram any vocabulary necessary for students to understand the relationships between the text information and the discipline as a whole.

5. Introduce and talk the students through the diagram. Encourage them to apply previously learned knowledge by adding to the diagram. Engage students in the construction of word meanings from context, experiences, and reasoning in small group interactive discussions of words and meanings.

6. After discussing the concepts and their interrelationships, leave the diagram in full view of the students as a reference point during reading and/or discussion following reading.

Nelson-Herber (1986) also recommends the use of follow-up activities to provide contexts for students to construct, refine, and reinforce word meanings. Using the concepts from the diagram shown in Figure 13.4, she provides the following sample activities:

1. Directions: Work together to choose the word that best completes the analogy.
   a. Green: chlorophyllous as nongreen:
      1. phyla   2. achlorophyllous   3. mycology
   b. Green: nongreen as algae:
      1. protist   2. mycologist   3. fungi

2. Directions: Circle the word in each set that does not belong and be ready to explain why the other three go together.
   a. fungi, heterotrophic, vascular, achlorophyllous
   b. algae, chlorophyllous, nongreen, autotrophic

Semantic Feature Analysis

Semantic feature analysis (SFA) is a procedure for helping students see how words within a category are alike and different, and to relate the meanings of new words to previous knowledge and experience. The guidelines presented here are recommended by Anders and Bos (1986) as an adaptation of the SFA teaching strategies proposed by Johnson and Pearson (1984). These guidelines were designed and tested for use with subject area reading material.

The first step in the SFA procedure is to read the text thoroughly and make a list of the major ideas that students will encounter. Next, examine the list and determine which ideas represent the superordinate concepts. Then identify words that represent the supporting or subordinate ideas related to the superordinate concepts. This information should then be organized into a relationship chart with the superordinate concepts as column headings across the top and the related vocabulary as row headings down the side (see Figure 13.5).

Each student should receive a copy of the relationship chart before reading the assignment. Then, using a copy of the chart, either on the board or on an

FIGURE 13.5

Sample Semantic Feature Analysis Relationship Chart

The Fourth Amendment

Important Ideas

Important Vocabulary	Citizen's right to privacy versus	Society needs to keep law and order	Police search with a search warrant	Police search without a search warrant	Evidence allowed in court
Search and seizure					
Unreasonable search and seizure					
Probable cause to search					
Your property and possessions					
Absolute privacy					
You give consent					
Hot pursuit					
Moving vehicle					
Stop-and-frisk					
Plain view					
During an arrest					
Evidence					
Exclusionary rule					

From "Semantic Feature Analysis: An Interactive Strategy for Vocabulary Development and Text Comprehension" by P. L. Anders and C. S. Bos, *Journal of Reading*, April 1986, p. 613. International Reading Association. Reprinted by permission.

overhead projector, the students should be introduced to the topic of the assignment and the meaning of each superordinate word or phrase. Following the discussion of the superordinate concepts, introduce each subordinate concept, giving a simple definition. Students should be encouraged to add their personal experiences or understandings of the terms during these discussions. One key to a successful discussion is to ask students how and why they arrived at a certain relationship rating.

Next, lead a discussion with the students to determine the relationship between each superordinate term or phrase and each subordinate concept. Fill in the relationship chart using the following symbols to signify the nature of the relationship: a plus sign (+) for a positive relationship, a minus sign (−) for a negative relationship, a zero (0) for no relationship, and a question mark (?) when no consensus can be reached without further information.

After completing the relationship chart, the students read to confirm their predictions and to determine the relationship between the terms for which no agreement could be reached. Following the reading, review with the students the relationship chart, changing any of the relationships if necessary, and reach consensus on the previously unidentified relationships.

A more general, less text-specific, application of semantic features analysis uses a group of words that are closely related. These words serve as the headings for the rows, whereas the headings for the columns are the semantic features or phrases describing components of meaning shared by some of the words or that distinguish a word from other meanings. Thus, SFA can be used to promote general vocabulary development in addition to specific vocabulary learning for a particular text.

Summarizing Procedures for Teaching Vocabulary

As Nagy (1988) has noted, the procedures described above for teaching vocabulary for specific texts serve several purposes. First, they activate appropriate background knowledge, encouraging students to think about experiences in their own lives that relate to the central concepts of the reading. Second, they help students understand the semantic relations and organization of the concepts in their text. Third, they allow the teacher to identify and assess the specific background knowledge of their students. The teacher can then clear up misconceptions and make sure that new concepts and words are related to experiences that are meaningful to those particular students. Finally, these techniques provide a rich basis for further reading, writing, and discussion.

General Vocabulary Development

Consistent with our third goal, it is important to promote general vocabulary development in a variety of ways. One that has been mentioned frequently throughout this chapter is extensive reading, both in and out of school (Nagy, 1988). In addition to wide reading, this section presents a well-documented method for teaching general vocabulary, and several suggestions for building interest in and enthusiasm for vocabulary learning as a lifelong process.

Teaching General Vocabulary

Beck and McKeown (1983) describe a vocabulary learning program based on introducing words by semantic categories. This program emphasizes the development of "word consciousness," with the aim of making students more aware of words in general. Grouping the words into meaningful sets helps students learn and remember subtle differences in word meanings.

The program is designed to give students an in-depth knowledge of word meanings through a carefully planned sequence of activities using groups of 8 to 10 words at a time. For example, a category of words about *moods* would include words such as *cautious, jovial, glum, placid, enthusiastic, envious,* and *impatient.* Words are grouped in this manner to allow the students to build relationships among them.

The students receive a 5-day cycle of instruction on each set of words. Each day's lesson lasts about 30 minutes. The first few lessons are designed to be fairly easy, while the later lessons are more demanding. Each cycle covers a range of tasks, including defining, sentence generation, oral production, and games calling for rapid responding. The point of presenting students with a variety of tasks is to help them develop a rich understanding of the words and the ability to use them flexibly.

Beck and McKeown (1983) use a variety of activities for teaching semantically related words. For example, students are asked to compare the features of two new words and consider if the two are mutually exclusive. They are asked questions such as "Could a *virtuoso* be a *rival*?" or "Could a *philanthropist* be a *miser*?" In another activity, a clue word is used to elicit a newly defined word (e.g., *crook* is used to elicit *accomplice*). Then the students are required to explain why these two terms should be associated with each other.

In a word-association activity, the teacher says a familiar word, and the students are supposed to respond with a closely related word selected from among those being taught. If the day's words are *virtuoso, accomplice, philanthropist,* and *novice,* the teacher might say *crook.* The students are expected to respond with the word *accomplice* and to be able to defend their choice.

A final activity is completion of sentences containing the target words, for example: "The *accomplice* was worried because . . . " The use of sentence completion, as opposed to the more open-ended task of "using the word in a sentence," helps steer students in the direction of sentences that really use the meaning of the word, instead of producing stereotyped answers, such as "I saw X yesterday."

As Nagy (1988) suggests, the exact activity is not the issue, and any of these or similar activities can be adapted for particular classrooms, words, and/or students. What is important is that students be given practice at tasks that require them to *use,* rather than state, the meanings of words they are learning in natural sentence contexts.

Building Interest and Enthusiasm for Vocabulary Learning

In the final analysis, the students who are interested in words are likely to be the most motivated to attend to vocabulary learning. It is important to try and instill in the students a sense of excitement in word learning that will compel them to make vocabulary learning a part of their daily life. A good way for teachers to build students' enthusiasm for words and word learning is to engage them in vocabulary games and other interesting activities.

Creating an environment for word learning. Students often enjoy sharing with others new words they have learned outside of school (Taylor, Harris, & Pearson, 1988). The teacher simply sets aside a few minutes once or twice a week for the students to present and define new words. The students share how they came across the word and the context in which it was used. Students' attention to unfamiliar words often increases if they know they have the opportunity to share them.

As an additional incentive, the students can be responsible for making a bulletin board display to present new words they have encountered outside of school. Bulletin board displays can also be used by the teacher to stimulate interest in key concepts from the students' reading materials through items such as pictures, cartoons, advertisements, magazine or newspaper articles.

Student committees can also be formed to preview reading assignments for new or unusual words and to explain them. An example from Vacca and Vacca (1989) illustrates this type of activity nicely.

> An English class committee called the Word Searchers found this passage from *Flowers for Algernon:* "Sculpture with a living element. Charlie, it's the greatest thing since junkmobiles and tincannia." The Word Searchers introduced the terms *junkmobiles* and *tincannia* to the class. They explained that the two words would not be found in the dictionary. Then the committee challenged the class to come up with definitions that would make sense. To top off the presentation the committee prepared Exhibit A and Exhibit B to demonstrate the words—a mobile made of various assortments of junk and an *objet d'art* made from tin cans, jar lids, and the like. (p. 331)

Playing with words. There are a variety of ways students can be encouraged to play with words that are likely to enhance their interest and understanding of new vocabulary. For example, crossword puzzles are useful for developing vocabulary and increasing interest in words. In addition to the crossword puzzles that are already available for students to use, many students enjoy constructing their own crossword puzzles for others to complete.

Adapted versions of vocabulary games such as "Spill-and-Spell," "Scrabble," "Bingo," and "Concentration" also can be valuable for increasing students' interest in and learning of new vocabulary. To adapt these games for this purpose, simply include new rules about giving definitions and/or examples of the words that are constructed, identified, or matched as part of each game.

Goldstein (1986) has suggested that cartoons and comics can be used as an inexpensive source for developing interest in and knowledge of vocabulary. Both the teachers and the students locate cartoons and comics that illustrate the use of new vocabulary, or old vocabulary used in new ways. The teacher and the students discuss the meanings of the words and expressions both in and out of the humorous context provided by the cartoon or comic. Then the students keep a record of the vocabulary or expressions in notebooks, journals, or on cards according to categories such as figurative language, colloquial expressions, puns, and palindromes. The students can also use their notes to make humorous constructions of their own.

Word histories. Brief discussions of word derivations or histories often increase students' interest in words and make the words more memorable. Teachers can collect word origins that have a clear connection to the current meaning of a word and use them as mnemonic devices. Examples provided by Vacca and Vacca (1989) from *Picturesque Word Origins* (1933) include:

> *Muscle.* Metaphorically, the scurrying of a mouse. A Latin word *musculus* means "mouse." The French adapted it because they associated the rippling of a muscle with the movement of a mouse.

Calculate. Originally, the counting stones of the Romans. The Latin word *calx* means "limestone." The ancient Romans used little stones called *calculus* to add and subtract. From this derived the English word *calculate* and its many derivatives.

Vacca and Vacca (1989) suggest that interest and enthusiasm also can be created by discussions of *eponyms* and *acronyms.* Eponyms are words originating from persons or places such as *pasteurize, maverick,* or *chauvinistic.* Acronyms are words formed from the beginning letters or groups of letters that make up phrases. For example, *scuba* is the acronym for *s*elf-*c*ontained *u*nderwater *b*reathing *a*pparatus, and *snafu* stands for *s*ituation *n*ormal *a*ll *f*ouled *u*p. As Vacca and Vacca (1989) note, "interesting words abound. If they appear in a text assignment, don't miss the opportunity to teach them to students" (p. 333).

FROM CLASSROOM TO CLINIC

Strategies for three different types of vocabulary instruction have been described in this chapter: (1) strategies for teaching independent vocabulary learning during reading; (2) strategies for teaching key vocabulary in preparation for reading specific texts; and (3) strategies for creating an environment that promotes general vocabulary development. Given the differences in the type of contact classroom teachers and clinic personnel have with individual students, it is likely that the priority given to these three types of instruction will differ between these two settings.

Because of the limited amount of time clinic or resource personnel spend with individual students, it probably makes the most sense for the focus in these settings to be on teaching students the strategies they need for independent vocabulary learning. Students learn strategies that can be applied any time they read, in or out of the clinical setting, both at home or at school. In this way, specialists are most likely to promote long-term vocabulary growth in their students.

Secondarily, resource specialists might focus on preteaching the vocabulary prior to reading specific selections, either in the clinical setting or in the classroom. The third type of vocabulary instruction, teaching general vocabulary, is realistically not likely to be accomplished satisfactorily in clinical settings.

In contrast to clinical settings, the daily contact that classroom teachers have with individual students makes the classroom an ideal setting for focusing on the development of general vocabulary. Using meaningful categories of words to teach general vocabulary and creating an atmosphere of enthusiasm for and interest in word learning are the ways that classroom teachers are likely to have the greatest impact on students' long-term vocabulary development.

Secondarily, classroom teachers should employ strategies for teaching independent vocabulary learning and for teaching key terms related to reading assignments at different times, depending on the purpose of instruction and the needs of individual students. Specific strategy lessons in independent vocabulary learning may be warranted for students who have no such strategies. As students begin to acquire independent vocabulary strategies, they should be practiced through application to a variety of reading activities both in and out of school.

Techniques for preteaching key vocabulary prior to reading specific texts may be used to provide students with an initial awareness of a concept as an aid to understanding specific content. These techniques may be used either when a student's independent learning strategies are weak or when it is particularly important to highlight certain concepts prior to reading.

CHAPTER SUMMARY

This chapter discussed the role of vocabulary and vocabulary instruction in reading comprehension and presented a variety of strategies for teaching vocabulary. Vocabulary knowledge has long been recognized as a significant factor in reading comprehension; however, how this relationship works and what it implies for instruction are still open to debate.

The first half of the chapter discussed the issues surrounding the controversy about when, how, and if vocabulary should be taught, and presented goals and guidelines for vocabulary instruction. The major issues addressed were the debate about whether students learn vocabulary best through direct instruction or incidental learning; the debate regarding which types of direct vocabulary instruction (e.g., definitional, contextual, "intensive") are most effective; and the debate regarding when direct vocabulary instruction is most appropriate. These issues were then translated into the following goals and guidelines for vocabulary instruction.

Goals
Teach independent vocabulary learning.
Teach concepts important for comprehension.
Create an environment that promotes general vocabulary development.
Guidelines
Guideline 1: Relate the new to the known.
Guideline 2: Promote active, in-depth processing.
Guideline 3: Provide multiple exposures.
Guideline 4: Teach students to be strategic.

The second half of the chapter described instructional techniques that corresponded to the established goals and guidelines. First, a general framework for independent vocabulary learning during reading was presented that consisted of four phases: reading and identifying unknown vocabulary, applying a repertoire of techniques to identify and learn the meanings of the words, relating the meanings of the new words to previous knowledge to aid learning and memory, and reviewing and studying the meanings of the new words in a variety of contexts. This was followed by a description of the Vocabulary Overview Guide, a strategy that embodies the features of the general framework, and of methods for teaching the techniques (e.g., using context or word parts) needed to support independent vocabulary learning.

Strategies for teaching vocabulary for specific texts and for general vocabulary development were also presented. The four strategies described for direct instruction of vocabulary related to specific reading assignments were: list-group-label, semantic mapping, structured overviews or graphic organizers, and semantic feature analysis. Finally, methods for using semantic categories to teach general vocabulary and for building interest and enthusiasm for vocabulary learning (e.g., word play, word histories) were described.

CHAPTER 14

Adapting Instruction to Focus on Comprehension and Studying

INTRODUCTION

The ability to read with comprehension for age-appropriate purposes is the hallmark of skilled reading. In the past, however, prevailing views of reading provided little reason to devote attention to comprehension instruction, since comprehension was assumed to rely exclusively on the ability to pronounce words, coupled with adequate meaning vocabulary. The view of reading presented throughout this text differs considerably from those earlier, skills-based models.

Readers unquestionably need skills and strategies to attain high levels of ease and efficiency in reading, but these abilities are the means, not the end itself. Effective readers *use* skills and strategies to comprehend, but it is the reader's response and comprehension that are important, not the acquisition of skills and strategies themselves. The challenge is to find instructional approaches and techniques that promote the active use of knowledge and skill to accomplish self-generated and imposed purposes.

Chapter Overview

Previous chapters in this section suggested instructional responses for students who require a reading program focused on word identification or vocabulary. The focus of this chapter is on providing instruction that improves students' ability to understand (learn, enjoy, and/or remember) information from different types of texts read under a variety of different conditions. First, we describe the nature of comprehension instruction, discussing issues and providing guidelines. Then, we turn to a wide array of instructional techniques designed to focus on comprehension and studying. These are divided into techniques for supporting students' comprehension and studying, and techniques for helping students learn to comprehend and study. Finally, we describe advances in the teaching of writing that have implications for teaching reading.

UNDERSTANDING INSTRUCTION FOCUSED ON COMPREHENSION AND STUDYING

We have described skilled reading and comprehension in some detail in earlier chapters. We noted, for example, that the success of the reading act is dependent on purpose, and we described how perception, memory and prior knowledge interact with other aspects of the reading process. Reading is a functional skill. This means that people engage in reading for a variety of purposes that include reading for enjoyment and reading to complete work tasks, both academic and non-academic. In school settings, students read for at least two additional purposes; to improve their reading and to learn about the world and about themselves (DuBois

& Stice, 1981). Of course, these purposes are not mutually exclusive, but they do often require different reading behaviors.

Some students have difficulty comprehending texts for any purpose. More commonly, students can read and understand some materials, but not all, and can read for some purposes, but not many. These students have not acquired the knowledge and skill to read flexibly for a wide range of purposes. The consequences of this problem become more and more serious as students move through each subsequent grade in school. To succeed in school and work settings, "students must learn to think in such a way that they can tackle, unravel, and understand any author's communication" (Sardy, 1985, p. 216). In the following sections, we discuss some issues surrounding comprehension and comprehension instruction and provide some guidelines for comprehension instruction.

Issues

In earlier chapters, we described the nature of comprehension (Chapters 1 and 2) and also addressed many of the issues surrounding comprehension instruction (Chapters 8, 9, and 11). Several additional issues will be discussed below. These include an expanded discussion of comprehension and comprehension ability, additional definitional notes on the nature of instruction, and new discussions of the purposes and nature of reading.

The Nature of Comprehension Instruction

Among the most hotly debated issues is whether students can or should be taught to comprehend at all. Until recently, comprehension instruction was limited to helping students learn to comprehend by helping them to understand the particular text being read. Students were expected to generate knowledge and skill through repeated exposure to texts and questions (Durkin, 1978–79). In the decade since Durkin reported these findings, educators have often taken one of two views (see Kameenui & Shannon, 1988) in a debate that is similar to the one presented in Chapter 13. Some argue for structured programs involving direct instruction in various comprehension skills (Carnine, Silbert, & Kameenui, 1990), while others suggest that students will learn to comprehend without any direct instruction at all (Goodman, 1989). Regarding this issue, we argue for balance.

Although many students seem to comprehend without apparent effort, the weight of recent research and practice suggests that some students require more thoughtful instruction than has generally been offered in the past (see Pearson & Gallagher, 1983; Tierney & Cunningham, 1984 for summaries). That some students need only the opportunity to read does not relieve us of the responsibility to provide instruction to others who need it.

On the other hand, the available evidence suggests that comprehension instruction focused on discrete components of reading is fruitless. For example, recent research suggests that good decoding skills are no assurance of good comprehension or study strategies (Adams, Carnine, & Gersten, 1982). While underlying skills and strategies may account for many students' inability to comprehend, other etiologies are possible as well.

Students need ample opportunities to practice reading comprehension, but many also require accurate, accessible information about how to comprehend text. Some young or disabled readers simply do not understand when or why they should use the skills and knowledge they do possess (Paris, Lipson, & Wixson, 1983). Without sufficient understanding of the functional value (usefulness) of these skills, students are unlikely to use them during reading. Others do not realize that reading demands attention to meaning. Recently, Susan, a seventh-grade student, was asked to talk about what she had been thinking as she read a portion of text. Her response captures the problem: "Oh, I don't usually think while I read."

Unfortunately, it appears that even when students have acquired some comprehension abilities, they may not make good use of them. There is increasing reason to believe that limited awareness of cognitive activity and limited ability to control it may account for at least some of the problems disabled readers encounter in their attempts to understand text (Torgesen & Licht, 1983). Recent research points to the conclusion that the types of instruction typically offered to disabled readers contribute to the problem (Duffy & McIntyre, 1982). In focusing on understanding specific texts, teachers may have inadvertently denied students the instruction they need to learn how to learn. We discuss this issue next.

Text Comprehension vs. Comprehension Ability

The traditional emphasis for comprehension instruction has been on *text-specific* comprehension. In all likelihood, this has prevented educators from generating techniques for developing comprehension *ability* (Johnston, 1985a).

> The more obvious or painful the student's lack of comprehension, the more likely that the teacher will explain the content rather than the text . . . From experience, teachers learn which kinds of written materials, when not understood, will produce the most obvious classroom problems, and they often give up assigning such materials altogether. The result is that many students have very little experience reading important types of material. (MacGinitie, 1984, pp. 145–146)

Although this picture of traditional practice is distressing, there is increasing reason to celebrate, as more and more teachers and researchers find that students' comprehension abilities *can* be improved. It should be pointed out that teachers have traditionally emphasized content versus process, because the processes involved in comprehending text were not well understood. Some aspects of the mental activity involved in comprehending have become clearer over the past two decades. There is still much to be learned about how readers cope with text, but some reading behaviors that distinguish skilled and less-skilled readers can be articulated. These reading behaviors deserve closer attention, since they can provide a focus for some promising instructional activities. We will briefly describe some of these later in this chapter.

Effective readers activate existing knowledge prior to reading and make predictions about text content based on the title and other available clues. Most poor readers are capable of making predictions, but they often fail to do so in appropriate settings.

Skilled readers also monitor their reading to check the sensibleness of the text. They ask themselves if there is any portion of just-read text that is not understood. Poor readers, on the other hand, rarely reflect on the meaning of the text, more often believing that the goal is simply to "say the words" (Paris & Myers, 1981). Similarly, effective readers check to see if their initial (and interim) predictions were accurate. Finally, they attempt to accommodate new information by checking to see if it is necessary to change the meaning they have constructed. This requires the reader to take a great deal of responsibility for comprehension. However, poor readers often fail to monitor their reading efforts, and therefore are typically insensitive to their comprehension failures (Kennedy & Miller, 1976).

Successful comprehension requires readers to fit new (text) information with prior knowledge, and also to integrate information from several parts of text to form a coherent whole. Readers must use available prior knowledge and be alert to the need to change their minds if the text contradicts their preexisting notions. Younger and less-skilled readers often fail to use textual information to acquire new information or change their minds (see Lipson, 1983).

Finally, effective readers ask themselves questions about the text and reread portions of text, as necessary, to clarify ideas and relationships. In the process, proficient readers use available skills and strategies to decode unknown words, to understand new concepts, or to check text meanings. Poor readers have often acquired a passive approach to reading in which they expect the teacher to clarify any important misconceptions they may have about the text, rarely attempting to do so themselves.

The balance between focusing on text comprehension and teaching students to comprehend is a delicate one. Although students often do not receive the instruction they need to acquire comprehending ability, a note of caution is in order. We should not assume that a student cannot comprehend *anything* because we have seen that she cannot understand *something*. Too often, a student who cannot answer the teacher's questions about a specific textbook assignment is assumed to have generalized reading and studying problems. This may be the case, but it is also possible that this student is capable of reading and understanding other materials for other purposes.

When students do not respond to specific texts or tasks, it is important to remember that this represents only a small sample of reading behavior. Sometimes students only need information about how to use and adapt existing skills and knowledge to the special demands of a new discipline or a new kind of task. In this case, extensive global comprehension instruction would be unnecessary and unwise.

Aesthetic vs. Efferent Reading

Effective comprehension instruction also seems to require careful consideration of the various purposes for reading. Rosenblatt (1982) has argued that readers adopt one of two possible approaches during any "reading event"; the *efferent stance* or the *aesthetic stance*. Her descriptions of reading for aesthetic purposes focus on personal attitudes, responses, and feelings.

> In aesthetic reading, we respond to the very story or poem that we are evoking during the transaction with the text. In order to shape the work, we draw on our reservoir of past experience with people and the world, out past inner linkage of words and things, our past encounters with spoken or written texts. . . . We participate in the story, we identify with the characters, we share their conflicts and their feelings. (Rosenblatt, 1982, p. 270)

Readers' prior knowledge affects the types of response they experience in reading literature. It is clearly true, as Purves (1985) suggests, that certain pieces of literature have special or personal meaning for individual readers. However, it is also possible for this work to have a meaning that is shared by many readers. "A large number of readers may share a response to a work of literature, and at the same time no two responses will be exactly alike" (Mason & Au, 1990, p. 75).

Individual reader response is patterned by certain recurrent factors. For example, reader response appears to vary as a function of development. Younger readers have different kinds of involvement with stories than older readers, often fusing fiction and nonfiction (Applebee, 1978). Similarly, children will only gradually acquire the abstract thinking skills needed to analyze the literacy qualities of stories. On the other hand, there are special reading demands in efferent or informational reading:

> When a reader approaches a reading event with an *efferent stance*, attention is focused on accumulating what is to be carried away from the reading. Readers using this stance may be seeking information, such as in a textbook; they may want directions for action, as in a driver's manual; or they may be seeking a logical conclusion, as in a political article. (Vacca, Vacca, & Gove, 1987, p. 258)

In school settings, reader response is influenced by teachers and peers, as well as by students' prior knowledge and personal experience.

Teachers who promote and support a diversity of responses are in a position to recognize when students are comprehending in an unanticipated way. Bleich (1975, 1980) has developed a useful categorization scheme for thinking about readers' interactions with text. He argues that there are three approaches to text and that these can be employed in classrooms to promote rich responses to literature:

> *Reconstructing the text.* Readers try to summarize the text as the author wrote it, "telling the story in your words."
> *Text association.* Readers make connections between the text (events, characters, etc.) and their own personal experiences.

Value judgments. Readers make judgments about the merit of the selection, at both the emotional and literary level.

In working with students in classrooms, Bleich suggests that students learn to retell, make associations, and render judgments. The range of these responses, of course, must be encouraged and developed by teachers. Consistent with the interactive view of reading, an individual's response to literature is influenced by the social context (Purves, 1985). It is fair to say that teachers have generally not encouraged such personal responses, and in fact may undermine the personal response to literature by asking closed questions with discrete answers.

Students receive little direct information about how to read stories and little encouragement to respond aesthetically to them, and it is even less common for them to acquire knowledge about how to study from, learn about, or manage informational materials. Students are often asked questions, frequently take tests, and are commonly responsible for learning information defined by the teacher for school-based tasks, but they are not helped to acquire expertise in these tasks.

Teachers who do not provide instruction for students in how to accomplish school-imposed tasks are obviously shortchanging their students and are failing to prepare them for their future school lives. Perhaps even more serious is the failure of schools to provide quality instruction in the types of activities students will need once they leave school.

Students rarely have opportunities to determine purposes and match materials and strategies to self-imposed needs. Yet the world outside of schools places a high premium on the ability to determine a goal, marshal the resources needed to meet that goal, and communicate with others about it. As Vacca, Vacca, and Gove (1987) point out:

> In most reading situations, there is both an efferent and aesthetic response to the text. . . . Although one stance usually predominates over the other in most reading events, the text itself does not dictate a reader's stance. A text is chosen because it satisfies a reader's intended purpose. (p. 258)

In order to encourage strategic reading for a wide range of purposes, teachers will need to move beyond routine tasks such as completing workbook pages. They will also need to pose questions and encourage responses that are richer and more complex than past practice has dictated. Discussions can often be prompted by the right question (see Figure 14.1). Personal response allows for a range of responses, and there is no one correct answer (see Parsons, 1990). Students should be challenged to defend their responses, however, and both teachers and students will need to develop discussion skills that promote exploration of divergent responses. Finally, both teachers and students should be able to make clear distinctions between these stances and shift their approach appropriately for reading and writing different tasks and texts.

The Relationship Between Reading and Writing

Earlier views of literate activity characterized reading as a receptive activity and writing as an expressive one. Construed as more or less opposite processes, they

FIGURE 14.1
Sample
Questions

Prompting Personal Response

- As you think ahead to your next day's reading, what possible directions might the story take? How do you hope the story will unfold?
- What surprised you about the section you read today? How does this change affect what might happen next in the story?
- As you read today, what feelings did you experience in response to events or characters (e.g., irritation, wonder, disbelief, recognition, dislike), and why do you think you responded this way?
- What questions do you hope to have answered next day as you read more of this story?
- What startling/unusual/effective words, phrases, expressions, or images did you come across in your reading today that you would like to have explained or clarified? Which ones would you like to use in your own writing?
- If the setting and characters were changed to reflect your own neighborhood and friends and acquaintances, how would the events of the story also have to change and why would that be so?
- Have you ever had a dream or daydream that seemed similar to an event or theme in this book? Try to describe the dream or daydream and trace the parallels.

- After reading this far, what more do you hope to learn about what these characters plan to do, what they think, feel, believe, or what happens to them?
- Do you ever wish that your own life or the people you know were more like the ones in the story you're reading? In what ways would you like the real world to be more like the world of your book?
- With what characters do you identify most closely or feel the most sympathy? What is it about these characters that makes you feel this way?
- How much do you personally agree or disagree with the way various characters think and act and the kinds of beliefs and values they hold? Where do you differ and why?
- What issues in this story are similar to real-life issues that you've thought about or had some kind of experience with? How has the story clarified or confused or changed your views on any of these issues?
- What characters and situations in the story remind you of people and situations in your own life? How are they similar and how do they differ?
- How did the characters or events in this book remind you of characters or events in other books you've read or movies or television shows you've seen? Do you prefer one of these treatments over the others? If so, why?

From *Response Journals* by Les Parsons. Copyright © 1990 Pembroke Publishers Limited. Reprinted by permission.

were also assumed to develop differently. Educators generally assumed that reading ability preceded writing ability, and little writing activity was undertaken until students had acquired at least some reading ability.

Current thinking suggests that reading and writing are actually two facets of the same process, and that they emerge simultaneously in terms of literacy development (Kucer, 1985; Squire, 1983; Tierney & Pearson, 1983). "Students learn to write as they begin to read; they learn to read as they begin to write" (Hennings, 1990, p. 16). In fact, it is possible that writing activity precedes reading development when students are allowed to explore in meaning-centered environments (Clay, 1975; see Chapters 4 and 11).

The relationships between reading and writing are apparent beyond the initial stages of literacy acquisition as well.

> Without exception, researchers cite the reciprocal benefits between reading and writing. The two should be developed concurrently from an early age. Children borrow ideas from reading stories and incorporate them into their own stories. Through reading, they build a richer store of meanings from which to write. Reading their own writing provides practice in reading. Writing helps children to see how written and oral language are related and expands their understanding of the parts of print: phonics, spelling, syntax, and semantics. As they write, children begin to think of themselves as writers just as they think of themselves as readers when they read. (Jewell & Zintz, 1990, p. 102)

Despite these realizations, it is still much more common for reading and writing to be taught in separate blocks of time and as completely separate and unrelated activities. Additionally, many schools and teachers have continued the traditional practice of teaching the mechanics and study of language to young children without providing students with adequate understanding of the reasons for doing so. Just as readers need to acquire word recognition abilities, writers need to acquire the mechanics of writing. But, like word recognition, the mechanics (spelling, grammar, punctuation) are tools for effective communication; they do not have much importance by themselves. Unless students have ample opportunities to write for a wide range of purposes, the mechanics will remain unintegrated and students will fail to apply these skills spontaneously.

Guidelines for Instruction Focused on Comprehension

There is increasingly solid evidence that suitable instruction can improve students' comprehension and comprehension ability. Effective comprehension instruction does not happen spontaneously, however. It requires thoughtful preparation, careful execution, and continuous monitoring and adjustment. For example, instruction must focus on important versus trivial reading and writing experiences and tasks.

Just as isolated practice in word identification and vocabulary seem inadequate, isolated comprehension exercises completed with small, fragmented texts do not seem to result in improved ability to read real books, poems, newspapers, or brochures for authentic purposes. Thus, before turning our attention to specific instructional practices, in this section we will review and expand upon some guiding principles for comprehension instruction.

Provide Information (Explicit Instruction)

As we have already noted, the issue of direct or explicit instruction is presently the source of substantial debate. Our position is that many students need information about reading and the reading process that can and should be delivered by thoughtful teachers. In Chapter 8, we provided a lengthy discussion of direct, explicit instruction and planned release of responsibility, and a review of that chapter may be helpful.

Direct instruction need not be trivial. The approach should provide poor readers with information about skills and strategies in terms of how these would be helpful during real reading tasks. Indeed, there is growing evidence from a number of research studies that we can increase children's use of learned skills and strategies by providing, during instruction, some explicit information about the when and why of strategy use (Paris, Lipson, & Wixson, 1983; Paris, Newman, & McVey, 1982; Roehler, Duffy, & Meloth, 1986).

Such studies are most encouraging, not only because they demonstrate that readers' comprehension *and* comprehension ability can be improved, but also because they provide teachers with strategies for structuring their formal classroom lessons in very specific ways. The key aspects of direct instruction appear to be clear, specific teacher explanation; conveying information about when and why to use the skills; feedback on the utility of the action; and scaffolded instruction with dialogue. Teacher provision of this type of information and structure appears to aid comprehension.

Students need help in understanding specific reading material, but they also need to acquire skills and strategies that will provide them with the confidence that their comprehension accomplishments can be duplicated in the future. This generally will require teachers to be very specific about how to employ the skill or strategy and when and why to use it (see Paris, Lipson, & Wixson, 1983). Then, this knowledge and skill must be reinforced during application. Teachers need to be sure that students receive reinforcement for the right kind of reading behaviors as well as the right answers.

Develop Independence and Self-Control

Recent research paints a picture of the reading disabled child as an inactive learner (Torgesen & Licht, 1983). Students in remedial settings often seem willing to be compliant, but not responsible, readers of text. They often appear willing to do what we ask, but they do not demonstrate any independent ability to apply skills in transfer settings. Often these children seem to use skills and strategies only when they are explicitly directed to do so (Keeney, Canizzo, & Flavell, 1967). Lipson and Wickizer (1989, p. 29) provide the following example of this type of disabled reader:

> *Tutor:* So, you didn't really understand that part (of the text)?
> *Student:* No.
> *Tutor:* Well, do you think it would be helpful to go back and reread that part to see if you can understand it?
> *Student:* I don't know. You tell me. You're the teacher!

Some possible reasons for this failure to perform mastered skill in context are suggested by recent research (cf. Brown, 1980). Attention has recently focused on the metacognitive aspects of skilled reading—those components of skilled reading that focus on evaluating tasks before reading, monitoring (paying attention to meaning) during reading, and regulating (or "fixing problems") throughout (Brown, 1980; Flavell, 1977). The lack of metacognitive awareness seems to limit adaptive (flexible) reading behaviors among young and disabled children.

Some students need explicit instruction that promotes flexibility and strategic reading, and all students need ample opportunities to develop these abilities. Students should develop the ability to adapt for the demands of varying texts. Similarly, they should be flexible in varying reading to suit the purpose, studying, gaining personally meaningful information, reading recreationally, and reading to "do" (assemble, cook, etc.).

Two related factors appear to contribute to students' inability to efficiently use available resources when they are needed: lack of knowledge about how to control existing skills and strategies and limited understanding of the usefulness of these skills and strategies. Research suggests that effective comprehension instruction must address both factors. In the techniques sections, we describe some recent instructional strategies that demonstrate how these might be addressed.

Provide Support (Make Reading as Easy as Possible)

Although students should receive clear, direct information designed to help them read, this will be most effective when teachers view the information (both content and delivery) as a means of supporting *students'* reading. When teachers provide information that is not needed or for which students are not ready, no learning occurs (Duckworth, 1979). The hallmark of effective teaching is thus for teachers to listen and observe carefully so that they identify what information and guidance students might use to become more proficient and strategic.

It is attractive to imagine an area that prescribes the content, difficulty, and pace of instruction appropriate for a given student. The Russian psychologist Vygotsky advanced the idea that students' readiness might be described as "the zone of proximal development" (Vygotsky, 1978; Campione, Brown, Ferrara, & Bryant, 1984). This zone is viewed to be the distance between a student's unaided performance and his or her performance when supported and guided by someone with greater knowledge and expertise. When there is little difference between these two, the child is not likely to take advantage of the proffered support and guidance. On the other hand, the distance is sometimes much greater. "Here, the implication is that with proper input, she could be expected to perform much more capably than her current level would indicate" (Campione et al., 1984, p. 265).

The notions of scaffolded instruction, dialogue, and release of responsibility were described in earlier chapters. It is important for teachers to acquire a strong sense of the importance of supportive teaching, both in the environment and in the interactions with students. Vygotsky strongly believed that learning occurs as a collaborative effort between adults and children, with competence acquired gradually. In classrooms, this means that students are not left at a level of lesser performance. Instead, as they become able to read and write some things for some purposes, they are asked to perform increasingly challenging tasks and are supported in doing so. The teacher's job is not to move students through some set curriculum or to teach and assess, in isolation, some set of comprehension skills. Rather, teachers must introduce texts and tasks that will challenge their students, and then provide the support to help them respond to the text and/or acquire needed information from it.

This type of instruction cannot be scripted, and it relies heavily on the judgments of knowledgeable teachers. However, the past two decades have produced several specific instructional techniques that conform in important ways to this type of teaching. The Reciprocal Teaching technique introduced in Chapter 11 is one such approach. We will describe others later in this chapter.

Create Extensive Opportunities for Practice and Personal Response

In Chapter 8, we described the characteristics of classrooms that promote reading. From Morrow's extensive research (e.g., Morrow, 1989), we know that a print-rich environment, active student involvement with reading, and adult-child interactions focused on literature contribute to students' comprehension of text. These ideas were discussed expansively in Chapter 11, as were the benefits of Sustained Silent Reading.

These instructional principles should serve as guidelines for all instruction, but particularly instruction focused on comprehension. No matter how skillful the instruction, students probably cannot become mature, competent comprehenders, skillful at studying, unless they have extensive opportunities for practice in connected text. Teachers must expand students' reading/writing repertoire, and teaching should always include instructional activities that approximate real literacy events and invite a rich array of responses. Students should have opportunities to retell and judge a wide range of materials. Discussions and projects that promote a personal relationship with characters and/or books is essential.

Teachers also need to take responsibility for directing students to texts and setting tasks that will ensure experiences with a wide range of reading materials, read for a variety of purposes. The promotion of voluntary, self-selected reading is unquestionably a neglected but desirable goal. It is not the only objective of reading instruction, however. Students who cannot read for work, for purposes assigned by others, or to complete real-world tasks will be just as handicapped as the students who cannot read stories for pleasure. Furthermore, practice and skill in one type of reading does not ensure success and expertise in other types.

Integrate Reading and Writing

The research results of the past two decades leave little room to question the desirability of providing more unified experiences in reading and writing. Whereas reading and writing had been defined as opposite processes, current thinking suggests that competence in reading and writing are acquired in an interrelated fashion.

Teachers must help struggling readers to integrate their abilities with continuous instructional support. When the reading material warrants substantial consideration, students should be encouraged to respond in writing to it, from either an aesthetic or efferent stance. Similarly, students should also be encouraged to do free-writing as a pre-reading activity to stimulate prior knowledge and interest (see Fulwiler, 1989).

These activities vary from traditional ones only in their focus on student knowledge and response. Other aspects of an integrated approach to reading and writing are more subtle and require more pervasive changes in the environment. The suggestions in Chapter 11 regarding the creation of a literate environment and recommendations for using dialogue journals should be reviewed. The adoption of a process approach to writing instruction enhances the likelihood that a reading-writing connection will be made (see Graves, 1983; Hansen, 1987). When they write extensively:

> Students see that writing occurs because an author has a purpose and an audience with whom she or he wishes to communicate. They learn through discussion that writing is a decision-making process and that writers consider the needs and expectations of their audience when creating their stories and articles and that they monitor how well their ideas are communicated, revising when needed. Through writing and talking about writing, they learn to view published written materials through the eyes of the author as well as from the perspective of the reader. (Raphael & Englert, 1989, pp. 237–238)

In addition to this general promotion of the relationships between reading and writing, various researchers and educators have developed specific suggestions for improving students' abilities in these areas. We discuss some of these in the following section.

INSTRUCTIONAL TECHNIQUES TO FOCUS ATTENTION ON COMPREHENSION AND STUDYING

Students who are having difficulty understanding what they read generally need support in two areas. They need help comprehending and/or learning the content of the specific texts they read for school and recreational purposes, and they need to learn to comprehend these and other materials. Reading professionals need to know how to adapt the instructional context, and they need skill in teaching students strategies for reading and learning. Consequently, they are almost always engaged in a balancing act, trying to respond to the sometimes competing demands of these two needs.

Supporting Students' Comprehension and Studying

There is certainly nothing new in the idea that good teachers help students comprehend and learn from their reading materials. For over 40 years, teachers have been trained to use standard lesson frames that provide extensive support for understanding texts. Over the years, the basic pattern of the the Directed Reading Activity (DRA) described in Chapter 9 has been altered and changed to meet new challenges or to provide different kinds of teacher guidance (Spiegel, 1981). We describe several of these below, and we also provide some suggestions for other ways to help students understand specific reading materials. Finally, we describe some specific aids to learning and studying that teachers can use to help students with specific texts and tasks.

Directed-Reading-Thinking Activity

The Directed-Reading-Thinking Activity (DRTA) was one of the very first variations on the basic DRA. Developed by Stauffer (1969; 1980), the DRTA is based on a view of reading as thinking, requiring reconstruction of the authors ideas and an ability to critically examine them. The DRTA provides much less teacher guidance in reading than the DRA. It is designed to promote students' ability to set purposes for reading and to monitor their comprehension.

One of the major contributions of the DRTA is its focus on actively involving students in their reading. The following steps are generally followed when using the DRTA:

1. *Elicit student predictions* about the outcomes (for fiction) or topic (for nonfiction) of the selection. If students have not done this sort of activity before, they may need help in surveying the title, pictures, and other print clues that can help in making focused predictions.
2. *Students read silently* to confirm, alter, or reject predictions. This may involve reading the whole, or any part of the selection, depending on student skill and text difficulty.
3. *The cycle of predict-read-monitor predictions* continues, with the teacher helping as little as possible.
4. *After-reading activities* include student summarization, student-teacher discussion, evaluation of the DRTA process, and involvement in any vocabulary or skills work that the teacher deems important.

According to Stauffer (1969), the teacher's role in Steps 1–3 above should be to direct students' reading and thinking. In Step 4, other skills instruction more commonly associated with the DRA is conducted.

Although the DRTA was originally designed as a lesson framework to be used with group instruction, it is possible to adapt the DRTA so that students are working even more independently. The Reading Forecaster Guide displayed in Figure 14.2 is one that we have used successfully in our clinics for many years. Most suitable for younger students and for fiction, it can even be used as a listening activity, as long as the teacher is willing to record the predictions and the prediction checks. We have also used more focused prediction guides with success. The guide in Figure 14.3, for example, supplements a basal lesson and was designed to focus specifically on story structure elements.

Similarly, Nichols (1983) devised a prediction guide that works well with expository material. The teacher prepares a prediction guide ahead of time by listing statements about the selection to be read. Some of the statements accurately state information conveyed in the selection; some are misleading, wrong, or simply not supported by the text. These statements are positioned next to two

FIGURE 14.2
Prediction Monitoring Guide

Be a Reading Forecaster
A weather forecaster tries to tell what the weather will be like BEFORE it happens. Forecasters use clues to help them make PREDICTIONS about what is going to happen in the future. A reading forecaster does the same thing. Reading forecasters try to PREDICT what will happen in a story by using clues.

	Page	Happened	Will not happen	Still might happen
1. My prediction is _____	_____	_____	_____	_____
2. My prediction is _____	_____	_____	_____	_____
3. My prediction is _____	_____	_____	_____	_____
4. My prediction is _____	_____	_____	_____	_____
5. My prediction is _____	_____	_____	_____	_____

From *Instructor's Resource Book to Accompany Reading Instruction for Today* by Jana M. Mason and Kathryn H. Au. Copyright © 1986 Scott, Foresman and Company.

columns. Before reading, students predict (check off in column A) the topics/content that they think will appear in their reading. After reading, students turn to column B. They place a check next to those statements that were supported in the text, a zero next to those statements that were refuted by the text, and a question mark next to those statements not addressed or answered in the text.

The DRTA and prediction guides help students to realize that they already have some ideas about the topic to be considered. Both also provide help and support during reading, so that students are encouraged to monitor and check their comprehension. Prediction guides especially can be useful for students who require even more structured support than, for example, the K-W-L provides. They work best when students' ideas about the text are reasonably congruent with the text information and when students have sufficient prior knowledge to facilitate reading (Spiegel, 1981).

Some students will require even more help in the area of prior knowledge. Some may benefit from additional instruction in the area of vocabulary (see Chapter 13). Others may benefit from instructional support that focuses on combining the areas just described. The VLP and ETR are two other variations on the directed reading activity that warrant a closer look.

Vocabulary-Language-Prediction (VLP)
The VLP provides support for students in several ways (Wood & Robinson, 1983). There is extensive prereading support, and the activity combines vocabulary and oral language development with prediction and monitoring. The VLP is especially attractive because it can so easily be embedded in the normal DRA procedures for

FIGURE 14.3

Basal Lesson Prediction Guide

NAME: _____ STORY: *Amelia and the Bear*
Day 1
My predictions are:
1. Prediction Question #1:
   What do you think life was like for Amelia's family?

   _____

                YES   NO

   _____
   _____

2. Prediction Question #2:
   What do you think the bear has to do with the story?

   _____

                YES   NO

   _____
   _____

3. Prediction Question #3:
   How do you think Amelia feels about bears?

   _____

                YES   NO

   _____
   _____

NAME: _____ STORY: *Amelia and the Bear*
Day 2
My predictions are:
1. Prediction Question #1:
   What do you think Amelia will do?

   _____

                YES   NO

   _____

2. Prediction Question #2:
   How do you think Amelia's actions will affect the bear?

   _____

                YES   NO

   _____

3. Prediction Question #3:
   How do you think the story will end for Amelia and her family?

   _____

                YES   NO

   _____
   _____

---

teaching basal selections. It requires some preparation by the teacher; indeed, Steps 1–3 have to do with selecting and preparing the vocabulary:

> *Vocabulary*
>> *Steps 1–3:* Select vocabulary, determining which words are important and will cause students difficulty (see Chapter 13). Decide what skill(s) will be addressed in this lesson and how vocabulary is related to the skill(s). The words are then written on individual cards with the page number from the story on them.
>> *Step 4:* The words are displayed for the students; students are told they will see these words in the selection and that they will do some activities with the words.

Students can point to or pick up the cards that contain the correct word during the following steps.

> *Oral language*
>> *Step 5:* The teacher asks questions about the structural and conceptual features of the words. Relevant activities could include discussions of categories, context, synonyms, and so on.

Prediction

    Step 6: The teacher directs children to use these words to predict what the story will be about and predictions are written on the board. Wood and Robinson suggest the following as possible prediction questions (p. 394):

        Characterization: "Which words probably tell you about the main character?"

        Setting: "Which words tell where she/he lives?"

        Events/Outcomes: "Which words give clues about events in the story?"

    Step 7: Children are asked to confirm, reject, or modify their predictions during reading.

Because of the focus on vocabulary and prereading preparation, the VLP can be used with Limited English Proficiency (LEP) students as well as students reading highly unfamiliar material. In addition, the link between story vocabulary and prediction helps students to see other ways to generate hypotheses about the text besides using the title and pictures. Finally, the focus on monitoring in Step 7 helps students to connect the prereading instruction and the postreading discussion—an important feature of the next framework.

Experience-Text-Relationship (ETR)

When students' prior knowledge is a significant factor, other adaptions may be needed, and the experience-text-relationship (ETR) variation was developed for these circumstances (Au, 1979). ETR is designed so that teachers take an active role in discussing the text and text-related ideas with students. In addition, the teacher models skilled reading for students, helping them to build a concept of reading as a meaningful activity. Thus, before reading, the teacher must preview the reading material and identify concepts or themes that might be especially interesting or relevant for students. Before reading, as well, teachers should identify places where silent reading can be stopped for students who need to read in smaller segments. ETR itself consists of the following steps:

1. The *Experience or E phase* occurs before reading. The teacher evaluates students' prior knowledge of the themes, concepts, or ideas central to reading the selection. The teacher guides the discussion in two ways, always leading toward the selection by showing pictures or using ideas, and helping students to see the relationships between their knowledge and the text. Then, students make predictions about the selection.

2. The *Text or T phase* is like a combination of guided reading (DRA) and the reading-thinking step of the DRTA. Students read, pause, discuss their predictions, receive help from the teacher, and generate new predictions as they work their way through segments of text. This phase may take more than one day, depending on the text and the students.

3. The *Relationship or R phase* begins once the text has been completed. The teacher asks questions and leads discussions intended to help students make

connections between the selection and their knowledge and experience. Teachers can ask students whether they have had a similar problem, or they can help students to see that though the events might be somewhat different, the underlying motivations are similar to their own.

This focus on connecting past experience and knowledge with text information needs to be done quite explicitly for some students. Teachers should be aware of these connections as well and should actively seek ways to focus students on the important ideas in text. For example, urban children can all understand the motivation of the Little Red Hen as she relished the warm bread at the end of her story, even though most will not have ever seen wheat, a miller, or bread baking in an oven. The *underlying* relationships describing how people feel when they do not get the help or cooperation they desire do not require such specific prior knowledge.

Techniques for Using Text Structure and/or Identifying Patterns

Although the use of lesson frameworks is the most common way to support students' understanding of specific texts, it is not the only way. In recent years, there has been a proliferation of ideas designed to guide and support students in reading specific texts (or types of texts). These generally involve helping students to comprehend by revealing the structure and/or relationship patterns of texts.

Text mapping. We have already discussed in some detail the elements of narrative and exposition and the issue of mapping to reveal important ideas and themes in text (see Chapters 7 and 9). A good map will help children to see the relationships between the events in a story or informational piece. Students are guided to understand the selection because the map directs their attention. In addition, students generally find it easier to recall information when it has been organized coherently, and maps help here as well. The techniques for mapping stories described earlier in the text should be used to create frameworks that can be used by students who need help perceiving the organization of ideas in stories.

Maps that reveal the structure of expository paragraphs have also been used successfully with students in Grades 4 through 6 (Schmidt, 1986; see Figure 14.4). A close relative to story maps are *pattern guides,* designed to help students identify important ideas and see how concepts are related in informational text. McNeil (1987) described steps for generating expository guides which we believe are useful in generating all types of maps:

1. Decide what central idea or concept students should derive from the text.
2. Characterize the major text pattern used in the selection (e.g., cause-effect).
3. Visually display the pattern and model for students how it was identified.
4. Inform students about the tasks (it should relate to working with the major pattern of relationships).
5. Students work with the pattern guide, using it to complete the task as defined by the teacher.

FIGURE 14.4

Sample Text Map

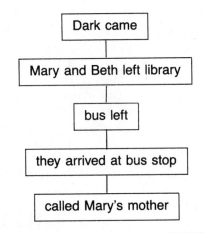

Time Ladder Map

It was already dark by the time Beth and Mary left the library. They immediately started walking as quickly as possible to the bus stop. Unfortunately, the bus had already left when they got there. They had to telephone Mary's mother for a ride home.

Dark came

Mary and Beth left library

bus left

they arrived at bus stop

called Mary's mother

Illustration 2, "The Time Ladder Map" Practical Ideas by Marion B. Schmidt, *The Reading Teacher*, October 1986, pp. 113–117.

Maps can be used to accommodate a wide range of student abilities by altering the degree of prereading and during-reading support that is provided. For example, students can be provided with a blank but fully structured story map so that their task is to read for the purpose of completing the network. For some children, this will provide the right degree of support. For others, who have comprehension abilities that are even less well developed, or who are reading especially difficult material, portions of the map can be filled in, leaving only a few blanks to be completed.

As useful as maps can be, it is important to remember that they are intended to help students comprehend specific materials. As soon as students have control over the various structures and can use them to help them understand difficult or unfamiliar text, then the maps should be abandoned in favor of more usual school- or work-response modes.

Text frames. Creating text-specific maps is a great deal of work, and many classroom teachers will not be able to find the time to do this. Fowler (1982) suggests a somewhat more generic technique for supporting students in text. He developed the idea of story frames, featuring the common characteristics of stories that could be used with elementary students (see Figure 14.5). "Once a frame is constructed it can be used with new passages so long as the passage can support the line of thought or argument implied with the frame" (p. 176).

Fowler suggests using story frames after reading in place of questions, as a part

FIGURE 14.5
Sample Story
Frame

Story Summary with One Character Included

Our story is about _____

_____.   _____ is an

important character in our story.   _____

tried to _____.

The story ends when _____.

Figure 1, "Developing Comprehension Skills in Primary Students Through the Use of Story Frames" by Gerald Fowler, *The Reading Teacher*, November 1982, p. 177

of the traditional DRA. Students can be guided to complete the frames, and the frames themselves can be shaped to focus on particular elements. Fowler provides copies of frames for focusing on plot, setting, character, and character comparison. He also suggests that students work together to clarify and complete their early frames. We have found that some students with very weak comprehension abilities benefit from being introduced to the frames *before* reading so that they can use the frames to guide them through text.

As Fowler notes, the same story frames can be used with students of widely varying abilities, since they permit open-ended responses. In addition, they are generic enough so that they provide routine structure and students can do new stories without new instructions. This is especially helpful in working with young or less-skilled readers. The idea of frames evolved, however, from earlier work by Nichols (1980), who examined recurrent types of paragraph structures and used a similar technique with high-school students reading narrative texts.

There are also well-tested frames for helping students to read exposition. Armbruster, Anderson, and Ostertag (1989) have demonstrated that students' comprehension (and writing) improved when they were instructed in the use of text structure. They have developed quite sophisticated frames to be used with middle-grade students (see Figure 14.6). Using these frames, students are taught the general frame (e.g., compare/contrast pattern), are taught to recognize examples of this structure, and are taught to use this pattern to summarize text.

Supported Studying

We have already described one of the most useful teacher-supported activities for use with expository texts. K-W-L (see Chapter 11) is an instructional technique that provides appropriate teacher support in two ways. First, it helps students to focus on the purpose for reading informational text: to add to one's knowledge base or to learn new ideas. Second, it guides students through a series of steps so that they can more easily accomplish this goal. The K-W-L strategy, however, is not always an appropriate technique.

Students must learn to set their own purposes and decide what they want or need to know from specific materials. However, educators must acknowledge that studying places very specific demands on students, demands that are not always consistent with the student's own goals. Studying requires students to identify or

FIGURE 14.6
Frame for Expository Text

Compare/Contrast Frame

Example [contrast]:

Marsupials are either meat eaters or plant eaters. Generally speaking, one can tell what type of food a marsupial eats by looking at its teeth. Meat-eating marsupials have a great many small sharp teeth designed to tear flesh. In contrast, the front teeth of the plant eating marsupials are large and designed for nipping and cutting. The feet of meat-eating marsupials also differ from those of plant-eating marsupials. The meat eaters have feet that look rather like a dog's or cat's foot. The plant eater's feet are quite different. The second and third toes on the hind feet are joined together and the big toe is opposed to the other toes, just as a person's thumb is to their fingers.

General frame:

	Concept A	Concept B
Feature 1		
Feature 2		
.	.	.
.	.	.
.	.	.
Feature *n*		

Frame for example:

	Meat-eating marsupials	Plant-eating marsupials
Teeth	Many small sharp teeth	Large front teeth, designed for nipping and cutting
Feet	Look like dog's or cat's foot	Second and third toes joined; big toe opposed

Summary pattern:

A. Comparison

_____ and _____ are similar in several ways. Both _____ and _____ _____. _____ and _____ have similar _____. Finally, both _____ and _____ _____.

B. Contrast

_____ and _____ are different in several ways. First of all, _____, while _____. Secondly, _____ but _____. In addition, while _____, _____. Finally, _____ _____, while _____.

recognize an (usually) external purpose. Learning in school texts often demands that students know not only what to read but what the associated tasks are or will be.

Teachers set purposes for students in many school settings, and decide what tasks must be accomplished with the information acquired. Teachers can help students to learn the information they have identified as important. Often the use of these practices would help most students, not just the ones who are struggling in the area of reading.

Lesson frameworks in content text. Using a Before, During, and After approach to reading specific texts will often help students learn the content of informational texts. Before reading, teachers should take care to introduce any content-specific words or note cases where vocabulary usage varies from everyday meanings. Structured overviews (see Chapter 13) and other prereading activities can also help students focus and prepare. In addition, teachers can either set a purpose for reading themselves, thereby informing students what they deem important, or they can elicit purpose-setting ideas from the group, thereby assessing students' ability to identify appropriate purposes.

During reading, students can be provided with guided reading questions (either orally or in writing) that many find helpful as an aid to comprehension. These can, of course, be used later as a study guide. After reading, students can be helped to revisit the text to organize information or gather ideas that were missed on an initial read through the text.

When working with students who need additional guidance and conceptual support, teachers may wish to employ the modifications suggested by the *concept-text-application* (CTA) approach developed by Wong and Au (1985). The CTA, like the ETR, is a variation on the traditional DRA that places particular emphasis on students' prior knowledge. During the concept (C) phase, teachers assess students' knowledge of the major concepts to be encountered in text. Where appropriate and necessary, unfamiliar vocabulary or concepts are pretaught. Students read predetermined segments silently during the text (T) phase and teachers lead discussions that help students build background knowledge and/or fit new information to older concepts.

It may seem obvious that this teacher-guided lesson framework would be useful in reading the types of dense, unfamiliar texts often encountered for study. Unfortunately, many teachers, even those who use a DRA during reading instruction, do not apply the principles of this plan during the reading of other texts (see Alvermann, 1989). As a result, reading teachers and other support personnel may need to help students acquire important content. Creating study aids such as study guides is one option, but so is helping regular teachers to adapt their reading expectations. Both techniques are described next.

Study guides. Studying from content area textbooks is challenging for even the most able school-aged students. It requires students to recognize important information and to locate it in dense, often poorly written text (see Chapter 9). Even when studying from considerate text, students must be able to make use of complex text structures, using these to help identify major ideas and supporting details.

One of the most well-documented techniques for helping students maintain their focus in text is the study, or reading, guide (Earle, 1969; Herber, 1970; 1978).

> It is the purpose of a study guide to facilitate readers' understanding of text content while improving their ability to deal with patterns of ideas (cause and effect; comparison and contrast; sequence or time order; and simple listing) as well as levels of text presentation. (Tierney & Cunningham, 1984, p. 626)

These guides generally involve segmenting text into smaller pieces and interspersing checkpoints throughout that are designed to help students check their comprehension or monitor their progress. This level of support has generally proved helpful for readers of all abilities (Armstrong, Patberg, & Dewitz, 1988).

There are presently a wide array of study guide models available to teachers. Herber's (1970) *three-level guide* focuses students' attention on different levels of meaning. A *pattern guide* is a variation on the three-level guide that helps students understand the major text relationships in the reading material. Since these two types of guides are so similar, it is possible to discuss both at once.

Herber (1970) contended that there are three levels of comprehension required of students in content area reading: literal, interpretive, and applied. Therefore, he designed the three-level guide to help students interact with the text in three fairly distinct stages. The three questions students are guided to answer in a three-level guide are: What does the author say? What does the author mean? and How does this relate to your own life/How can you use this information? (see Figure 14.7). The pattern guide retains this three-level view of text processing, but makes explicit provision for using text structure (patterns) as an aid to studying.

Preparation is obviously very important. It proceeds in the following way for both three-level and pattern guides (Herber, 1978; Vacca & Vacca, 1989):

1. Analyze the text. Identify the major text organization pattern.
2. Make decisions. Decide what knowledge and abilities your students have and what your objectives are.
3. Decide what quantity and quality of comprehension you require for this reading assignment.

Once these steps have been completed, teachers need to think about how much support will be provided by the study guide. Then they will probably need to reanalyze the text as they create a guide.

The major distinction between a three-level guide and a pattern guide occurs at the literal level where the reader receives additional help recognizing the text pattern used to answer the question, What does the author say? (see Figure 14.7). For some students this additional support will be helpful; for others, unnecessary. In either case, it should be apparent that these guides require significant amounts of teacher time and effort, and although they are intended to help students acquire independence in studying, they are heavily teacher-directed. In addition, these

FIGURE 14.7
Sample Three-Level Guide

I. *Directions:* Check the items you believe say what the author says. Sometimes the exact words will be used; other times other words may be used.

—— 1. Letters of reprimand were to be written for two teachers and their department head.
—— 2. The school committee decided the teachers made an error in judgment.
—— 3. The teachers were finally suspended for three days.
—— 4. Students and parents generally felt the "lecture" was a mistake.
—— 5. School officials approved the prostitute's visit beforehand.
—— 6. Control over the program will be tightened in the future.

II. *Directions:* Put a check on the line beside any of the statements below which you think are reasonable interpretations of the author's meaning.

—— 1. Emotion rather than reason prevailed among some members of the community.
—— 2. Parents and students seemed to view the controversy differently.
—— 3. A few vocal parents led the attack against the teachers.
—— 4. The prostitute's lecture is another example of teachers and students trying to take over the schools.
—— 5. The teachers involved in the controversy were glad to be reprimanded and not suspended.

III. *Directions:* To apply what you read means to take information and ideas from what you have read and connect them to what you know. Place a check in the blank beside any statements below which are supported by statements in level II and by previous experience or study. Be sure you can defend your answers.

—— 1. A prostitute can contribute to one's formal education.
—— 2. Schools should be run more *for* students than *by* them.
—— 3. Ends justify means.
—— 4. Ideas and actions alien to the status quo usually precipitate aggressive reaction and restrictive requirements.

Guest Lecturer

The tension in the air could be sliced with a knife. The hearing had lasted nearly five hours. More than two hundred people, many of them students, were in the meeting room where the session was held. Bob Herring and Ray Weatherman, the two American history teachers, sat attentively. They didn't blink an eyelash at the verdict: letters of reprimand were to be written for the two teachers and their department head.

The Hard Rock School Committee had concluded that the teachers made an error in judgment but didn't deserve to be suspended. Little did Bob and Ray realize the community turmoil that would be . . . .

guides reflect a hierarchical view of text comprehension that is somewhat outdated (see Chapters 1 and 7).

A recent variation on the study guide technique addresses several of these concerns. The Textbook Activity Guide (TAG) developed by Davey (1986) avoids focusing on discrete levels of comprehension and does not require that the ideas in the text be organized in a specific pattern. The sample in Figure 14.8 also demonstrates another feature of TAG: that it "emphasize(s) active student involvement through cooperative learning and a self monitoring component" (p. 490).

FIGURE 14.8

Sample TAG

Geography Affected Indian Ways

Names: _____ _____ Date initiated: _____

Strategy Codes:

DP = Read and discuss with your partner

PP = Predict with your partner

WR = Each partner writes response on separate paper

Map = Complete the semantic map

Skim = Read quickly for the purpose stated; discuss with your partner

Self-Monitoring Codes:

__+__ I understand this information.

__√__ I'm not sure if I fully understand this information.

__?__ I do not understand this information. I need to restudy.

1. PP   pp. 21–25   title and headings
   What do you think you will learn about from this section? List at least eight things.
2. DP   p. 21   heading and first three paragraphs
____ Explain the second sentence in this section, beginning "The type of shelter . . . ."
   What are some examples from the passage? What are some examples from today?
3. WR   p. 21   right column, first and second paragraphs
____ a. Why did the Haidas and the Iroquois need different kinds of boats?
____ b. Using other resource books in the classroom, draw an Iroquois canoe and a Haida
        boat. Add them to your booklet on Indians.
4. Skim   p.. 21, last two paragraphs, p. 22, first paragraph
____ Purpose: Find out about the shelter and food of the Plains Indians.
5. DP   p. 22   second to sixth paragraphs
   How did the climate of the Southwest affect:
____ the materials the Pueblo Indians used for their shelters?
____ the way they built their shelters?
____ the way they grew their food?
6. Skim   p. 22   second to last paragraph of section
____ Purpose: Find out about the features of homes of the Mayan Indians.
7. WR   p. 22   last paragraph of section
   Give an example from the section to prove each of the following:
____ Geography influenced Indian homes.
____ Geography influenced Indian clothing.
____ Geography influenced Indian food.
8. DP, Map   pp. 24, 25
____ Compare and contrast two types of Indian homes.

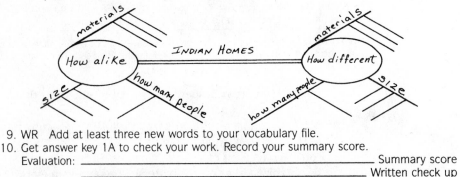

9. WR   Add at least three new words to your vocabulary file.
10. Get answer key 1A to check your work. Record your summary score.
    Evaluation: _____ Summary score
    _____ Written check up
    _____ Teacher conference

From "Using Textbook Activity Guides to Help Students Learn from Textbooks" by B. Davey, *Journal of Reading, 29,* March 1986, p. 491. International Reading Association. Reprinted by permission.

Task slicing. There are, of course, times when even the most skillful teacher management of lessons and study guides will not provide sufficient support for students as they interact with assigned reading. Assigning fewer papers, less reading, and so on, are unsatisfactory responses in most cases, because students will only slip further and further behind in terms of the conceptual demands of the content. In such cases, teachers may try "task slicing" (Readence & Moore, 1980), in which minor changes in task assignment allow students to work with the same texts as others in the class. "Slicing refers to reexamining the tasks required of students in text assignments and then recasting them to ease their demands" (p. 112).

The authors describe several ways that tasks can be adapted, depending on a reader's skill and knowledge. For example, teachers might limit the scope of the information search. Readers can often cope with difficult text as long as they are not held accountable for all the ideas, concepts, or events. To limit the scope of the information search:

> The number of concepts for which students are responsible can be varied by adding or deleting the number of assigned tasks on their study guides or end-of-chapter questions. Some students may be responsible for 15 concepts while others may deal with only five. These concepts may or may not be exclusive of each other. Whatever the case, whole-class discussion should follow the directed reading so that all students are exposed to the desired information. (p. 113)

When you adapt the scope of the information search, you do not alter the amount of material to be read, only the degree to which students are expected to understand the material.

The power of this type of slicing is that it helps to focus students' attention on important information and, for those who need it, limits their focus so that they do not have to make as many judgments about what is important and what should be learned. Another way to accomplish this is to create an information index. This method of supported studying helps students to locate information by providing interspersed questions throughout the selection and then keying questions to the place in text (page, paragraph, sentence) where the information to answer the question can be found. According to Readence and Moore (1980), "the degree of question interspersing and information indexing may be varied according to the importance of the concept reflected in the questions, the level of thinking required, and students' reading ability" (p. 114).

A note about note-taking, outlining, and summarizing. Although both notetaking and outlining are generally perceived to be helpful for studying, few students in Grades 1–8 are skilled enough in these areas to use the techniques effectively. Of particular concern is the fact that though students are often told to use these strategies, they seldom receive instruction in them (Irvin, 1990).

For example, a well-executed outline is a helpful study tool (Anderson & Armbruster, 1984b), but only if the content of the outline is reasonable. Outlining is often taught structurally. That is, students are taught the mechanics of outlining; where to put Roman numerals, letters, and so on. Students rarely receive help in the difficult tasks of identifying important ideas, recognizing supporting details, and generating large themes or main ideas. These same problems and criticisms apply to summarization and note-taking activities in most schools. Because these activities *are* useful in studying, they should be taught as tools for independence. Thus, we will return to these activities in the next section.

Teaching Students to Comprehend Text

It is extremely important for teachers to help students comprehend the specific texts they must read. This is an especially critical issue during studying, when some students require extensive and focused support in order to learn the informational content of their textbooks and related materials. However important these supporting tasks, permanent maintenance is not desirable. Students need to learn how to read and how to learn so that they can do so across many settings over a lifetime. To accomplish this often requires different types of instructional activity.

One of the most promising approaches to this problem involves teaching students strategies for comprehending texts. There is increasing interest in learning strategies instruction among educators who work with disabled readers and learning disabled students. Indeed, the University of Kansas Institute for Research in Learning Disabilities has designed a complete set of "task-specific learning strategies" (Deshler & Schumaker, 1986) that is a significant departure from the earlier attempts to teach specific content. In this section we describe techniques that can be used to help students "learn to learn" (Brown, Campione, & Day, 1981).

A General Plan to Teach for Independence

A recurrent finding among researchers and educators over the past two decades is that students need explicit instruction to acquire reading competence (Paris, Cross, & Lipson, 1984; Pearson, 1984). In addition, teachers need to be sure that they provide for a release of responsibility if they hope that students will transfer and apply newly acquired skills and strategies (Pearson & Gallagher, 1983). Using research evidence from several research efforts, Palincsar (1986) concluded that effective comprehension instruction should include *metascripts*, or action plans, that involve general suggestions for instruction but also allow teachers to be responsive to the students' behaviors during teaching.

The metascripts suggested by Palincsar involve several stages in instruction and it seems reasonable to suggest that teachers' long-term planning should include three instructional phases: Heavy Coaching, Supported Reading (Working Together), and Independent Application (On Your Own).

Heavy Coaching. When students are learning brand new skills and strategies or transferring newly acquired skills to difficult material, they need teachers to guide their reading and provide significant coaching. During this phase of instruction, teachers have responsibility for much of the reading/learning event (see Palincsar, 1986, for examples). Teachers should:

FIGURE 14.9
Reading
Monitoring
Guide

Constructing Meaning Think Sheet

Comprehension	*Decoding*	*Word Meanings*
• Did that make sense?	• Can I read these words?	• Do I know what the important words mean?
• Do the ideas fit together?	• How did I figure them out? (What strategies/skills did I use?)	• How did I know the meanings?
• If there's a problem, what is it?	• If there is a problem, what is it?	• If there is a problem, what is it?
• What can I (we) do?	• What can I (we) do?	• What can I (we) do?
• What strategies did I use?		
• What do I think about this story (selection)?		

- make explicit statements of lesson focus and content
- model the skill or strategy (Teacher Talk Thru)
- support students' contributions
- use students' ideas and link them to new knowledge
- maintain focus and direction

Supported Reading (Working Together). As students become increasingly competent, they should begin to gain more control over the knowledge and skill they are acquiring. During this phase, teachers should encourage students to take responsibility, but would provide guidance and maintenance functions to support successful reading and learning. Teachers should take primary responsibility for maintaining the focus and direction of the reading/studying event. In other respects, however, there is a shared responsibility:

- students (with teacher support) state the lesson focus
- students (with teacher support) model the skill or strategy (Student Talk Thru)
- students and teacher support students' contribution
- students and teachers use each others ideas and link them to new knowledge

Independent Application (On Your Own). Student independence is the goal of the reading instructional program. Success in this area results from careful and supportive instruction that includes an explicit self-control component (Brown, Campione, & Day, 1981; Paris, Newman, & McVey, 1982; Dewitz, Carr, & Patberg, 1987). In this phase, students are encouraged to generalize their learning to unstructured settings. In addition, students and teachers "troubleshoot" so that the various components work in concert for the desired purposes. Teachers and students often find a monitoring sheet of some sort useful in this phase. In Figure 14.9, a checksheet is offered that brings together a variety of skills and strategies. These generic suggestions can be used in any reading situation to help students learn any of a variety of reading strategies. There are also some specific ideas for teaching students to comprehend; we will describe several of these next.

Providing Support Across the Curriculum

Instruction should not be limited to those periods when reading is being taught directly. The first step in empowering students and helping them gain control over their reading is to help them use and control their skills as they read in a variety of contexts. Supported Think Aloud during Reading (STAR) is an instructional strategy designed to focus students on the *processes* of effective comprehension whenever they are reading (Lipson & Wickizer, 1989; Lipson et al., 1987). Because poor readers often do not understand when and why to use their skills and strategies, teachers need to teach students about the functional value of these behaviors during all reading events.

STAR is a technique that involves student-teacher dialogues about a reading selection. The purpose of these dialogues is to encourage students to actively use the skills and strategies they have available, but often do not use. The key to STAR is the teacher's ability to elicit student talk about reading and then to respond with supportive remarks about the value of the student's approach. To do this, students are stopped periodically as they read and they are encouraged to talk about what they had been doing and thinking as they read each portion of text.

These interruptions open dialogues that provide teachers with instructional opportunities. As students talk, teachers can offer feedback—not just about the products of students' cognitive activity, but about the quality of the cognitive activity itself. In addition, teachers ask questions that focus on the process versus the products of reading in order to lead students toward self-control and encourage them to take increased responsibility for their own learning. The specific guidelines below should be considered.

1. *Keep instruction focused.* Many students must first become aware of the reading behaviors that are likely to improve comprehension. The teacher can help to focus students' attention on their own strategies for understanding using a checklist of behaviors used by skilled readers (see Figure 14.10). When students do not use a range of appropriate reading strategies, teachers can prompt them to become more active in one of the component areas: pause and reflect, hypothesize, monitor, integrate, and clarify.

2. *Provide appropriate feedback.* Because many teachers are not accustomed to teaching with extensive dialogue, Lipson and Wickizer (1989) found that most needed some guidance about how to conduct these teacher-student exchanges. They describe some steps to be used when using STAR in the early stages of instruction:

   Listen carefully to what the child is saying.
   Attend to what the child is *doing* as well as to the accuracy of the response.
   Acknowledge (by naming) the strategy used to understand the text.
   Affirm its use with praise or feedback (p. 30).

Often students' statements suggest, but do not explicitly name, a strategy, and it appears that they are relatively unaware that they have employed a useful approach to the task. Under these circumstances, it is even more important that

FIGURE 14.10

Supported Think-Aloud Checklist

Prompts	Stop 1	Stop 2	Stop 3	Stop 4	Stop 5
PAUSE & REFLECT					
1. Does this part make sense?	✓	✓	✓	✓	✓
2. Do the words and sentences in this section make sense together?			✓	✓	✓	✓
HYPOTHESIZE					
3. What do you think will be presented next? (or what will the next part talk about?)				✓	✓	
4. What do you think this story is going to be about?	✓				
MONITOR					
5. Is there any part you didn't understand?			✓		✓
6. Did this part talk about what you predicted (expected)?		✓		✓	✓
7. Did you change your mind about anything?		✓		✓	
INTEGRATE					
8. Does the information in this part fit with what you knew before reading?		✓			
9. Does the information in this part fit with the information presented earlier in the text?			✓	✓	
10. What's the most important thing(s) in this part? (or what is the main idea of this part?)				✓	✓
11. Did you get any pictures in your head about this part?			✓		✓
CLARIFY					
12. Did you ask yourself questions about this part?		✓		✓	
13. Do you need to go back in the text to clarify anything? (or do you need to reread anything?)			✓	✓	✓
14. What did you do when you didn't understand a word, a sentence, or a part of a sentence?			✓		✓

the teacher use acknowledgement and affirmation. For example, in the exchange below, the student does not name the strategy himself and must be informed of its use:

> *Student:* I didn't get that. I couldn't understand it because of that word there.
>
> *Teacher:* Okay. It's really helpful to try to make sense out of what you're reading. It's important to ask yourself if it makes sense or not and I'm glad you're doing that. Okay, Mitchell, when that happened, what did you do?

This teacher is helping Mitchell to become aware of his reading strategies and to see which ones are productive. These patterns of interaction are essential for many older and disabled readers. It appears that middle-school students, even very disabled ones, can benefit from these procedures, improving their comprehension during teacher-supported reading activities but also during silent unsupported reading (see Lipson et al., 1987).

Teaching Students to Monitor and Manage Their Own Comprehension

One of the major problems confronting some students is their failure to attend to meaning as they read. Clearly, these students probably should not have been permitted to entertain such a peculiar view of reading over the years, but unfortunately, many disabled readers do not know how to manage their own reading.

Some students have become discouraged because they have run into difficulties and do not know how to overcome them. For these students, the plan for repairing comprehension failures suggested by Collins and Smith (1980) should be helpful.

1. *Ignore the problem and read on.* This is useful when the problem area involves unimportant information.
2. *Wait and see.* This helps when readers think that the problem will be cleared up by subsequent text.
3. *Generate a hypothesis.* This is useful when readers believe they can make an educated guess about the meaning; they continue reading to test their tentative hypotheses.
4. *Reread.* Readers can reread the sentence or use bigger chunks of prior context to help clarify or identify the problem.
5. *Seek help from an expert source.* Readers may need to do this when the first steps have failed to resolve the comprehension problem and they still do not understand the text. This may involve referring to a dictionary, for example, or seeking aid from a teacher or other competent person.

If students do not have sufficient knowledge or skill, then these techniques will not be helpful, of course. In that case, teachers will need to engage in direct instruction regarding the purposes for reading, the strategies to be used during reading, and the ways to repair reading problems. Paris, Cross, and Lipson (1984) developed a program for teaching students about reading and reading strategies. Informed Strategies for Learning (ISL) is a series of lessons that use metaphors and

FIGURE 14.11
Comprehension Skill Training Modules

I. Awareness of reading goals, plans, and strategies
  1. Goals and purposes of reading
     "hunting for reading treasure"
  2. Evaluating the reading task
     "be a reading detective"
  3. Comprehension strategies
     "a bag full of tricks for reading"
  4. Forming plans
     "planning to build meaning"
  5. Review

II. Components of meaning in text
  6. Kinds of meaning and text content
     "turn on the meaning"
  7. Ambiguity and multiple meanings
     "hidden meaning"
  8. Temporal and causal sequences
     "links in the chain of events"
  9. Clues to meaning
     "tracking down the main idea"
  10. Review

III. Constructive comprehension skills
  11. Making inferences
      "weaving ideas"
  12. Preview and review of goals and tasks
      "surveying the land of reading"
  13. Integrating ideas and using context
      "bridges to meaning"
  14. Critical reading
      "judge your reading"
  15. Review

IV. Strategies for monitoring and improving comprehension
  16. Comprehension monitoring
      "signs for reading"
  17. Detecting comprehension failures
      "road to reading disaster"
  18. Self-correction
      "road repair"
  19. Text schemas and summaries
      "round up your ideas"
  20. Review
      "plan your reading trip"

Comprehension Skill Training Modules, Fig. 7.1, p. 126, *Contexts of School-Based Literacy* by Taffy E. Raphael, 1986 Random House. Reproduced with permission of McGraw-Hill, Inc.

direct explanation to help elementary-aged students acquire important information about reading. The materials and methods of ISL were created using many of the principles we have already noted as important for effective instruction. Teaching activity involved informing, discussing, and coaching (Paris, 1986).

In addition, the content of these lessons provided students with an opportunity to receive needed information about the nature of reading (see Figure 14.11). This figure also shows the nature of the metaphors used in the ISL lessons, an element that appeared helpful in sharing strategic information with elementary-aged students. Teachers may welcome the specific lessons and activities in programs like ISL, but they should remember that "the magic is in the strategies and awareness; their ordered presentation to children; and teachers' communication that these strategies are important and beneficial" (Paris, 1986, p. 128). Teachers can and should find ways to adapt these ideas into their own daily curriculum.

Teaching Students to Ask and Answer Questions
As we have already noted (Chapters 7 and 9), asking and answering questions is perhaps the most persuasive activity in formal school settings. We have also seen that the quantity, quality, and placement of questions all influence students'

performance and learning. Although teachers often receive vast amounts of advice about how to become better at asking questions (see Chapter 9), relatively little attention has traditionally been directed at ways to help students become better at answering them.

Students need to gain control over answering the types of questions often asked in schools, and teachers need to help them learn this skill. In addition, if students are to grow into competent adults, they must become highly skilled at asking their own questions and knowing how to answer them, using one or more sources of printed material.

Question-Answer Relationships (QARs). Using Pearson and Johnson's (1978) taxonomy, Raphael (1982; 1986) developed a training program that has proven effective in improving students' abilities to answer comprehension questions (see Chapters 7 and 9). As with other effective teaching strategies, Raphael suggests using effective instructional features such as feedback, gradual release of responsibility and increasing independence, and movement toward longer and more complex texts. In addition, the QAR training program suggests structuring lessons in the following way.

Lesson 1. Introduce QARs using a chart or transparency to help students focus attention (see Figure 14.12). Particular attention should be paid to helping students understand how QAR knowledge will help them answer questions more effectively. Following this lesson, in which each type of question is clearly described, students engage in practice activities that increase in complexity. First students receive two- or three-sentence passages that are accompanied by questions, answers, and QARs. Teacher and students discuss and provide a rationale for each of the QARs. The next practice session involves using the same short passages plus questions and answers, but the students must identify the QAR. Finally, students practice with short passages and questions, answering the questions and identifying the QAR.

Lesson 2. Students receive passages of 75–150 words with questions representing each of the types of relationships. The students read the passage(s), answer the questions and assign a QAR to it. Students must be able to defend their choices, although responses may vary. In this part of the training, teachers should be prepared to help students correct wrong decisions about question-answer-relationships. However, they must also respond to incorrect answers.

Lesson 3. Students work with a basal-length passage that has been divided into at least four segments, with six questions for each segment (two of each type). The first segments should be done as a group, while later sections can be done independently if students seem able.

Lesson 4. The QAR training is applied to normal reading material as used in the classroom. Students identify the QARs and then answer the questions.

Maintenance. For young children (Grades 4 and below), Raphael suggests periodic sessions with shorter passages.

Teachers should use QAR training cautiously. Although many students will benefit from the types of discussion that can occur in this program, the training is not explicitly designed to assure correct question-answering results. Of course,

**FIGURE
14.12**

*Illustrations to
Explain QARs
to Students*

In the Book QARs	In My Head QARs
Right There	**Author and You**

Right There
The answer is in the text, usually easy to find. The words used to make up the question and words used to answer the question are Right There in the same sentence.

Author and You
The answer is *not* in the story. You need to think about what you already know, what the author tells you in the text, and how it fits together.

Think and Search
(Putting It Together)
The answer is in the story, but you need to put together different story parts to find it. Words for the question and words for the answer are not found in the same sentence. They come from different parts of the text.

On My Own
The anwer is not in the story. You can even answer the question without reading the story. You need to use yur own experience.

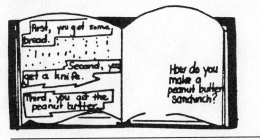

From "Teaching Question-Answer Relationships, Revisited" by T. E. Raphael, *The Reading Teacher, 39,* February 1986, pp. 516–522. International Reading Association. Reprinted by permission.

students who know where to look for an answer are at least part of the way toward success. Vacca and Vacca (1989) have demonstrated the use of QAR training for content area teaching-learning, and it is easy to see how this type of activity could enhance work with a three-level study guide as well.

   Reciprocal Questioning (ReQuest). Developed by Manzo (1969), ReQuest addresses a different aspect of skilled reading: the ability to formulate and pursue reasonable questions and purposes for reading. ReQuest is often used in regular classrooms as an adaptation to the DRA, but it was originally designed for use in clinical, remedial settings and it is ideally suited for work with inactive readers who comprehend poorly. It can be used with any instructional materials being read by the students, but teachers should be sure that the text is appropriate for the students. As with any new activity, careful introduction is essential. Manzo (1969) suggests that students are told:

> The purpose of this lesson is to improve your understanding of what you read. We will each read silently the first sentence. The we will take turns asking questions about the sentence and what it means. You will ask questions first, then I will ask questions. Try to ask the kind of questions a teacher might ask, in the way a teacher might ask them. You may ask me as many questions as you wish. When you are asking me questions, I will close my book. When I ask questions, you close your book. (p. 124)

Both students and the teacher read the material silently; then the students begin questioning the teacher. The teacher responds to *all* questions to the best of his/her ability. Teachers should not pretend a level of ignorance or fail to answer a question because they wish a student to answer it.

Similarly, when the roles are reversed and the students are questioned, they are not permitted to respond with, "I don't know." Instead, they can provide an explanation for their inability to answer or ask for additional information to respond. Question clarification and/or reworking are permissible if either the teacher or the student does not understand the question itself. Finally, when answering questions, individuals should refer to their source of information (the text or their own experience) as a way to justify answers. Clearly, many students will initially have a difficult time with this, but teachers are participating, providing models and responding to questions (see also Reciprocal Teaching, Chapter 11, if students have many comprehension problems).

Teaching Students to Study

Teachers generally believe that students who understand will perform well on their tests, problems, and projects. Although this is often true, there is a sizeable group of students who do not know how to respond to the demands of teachers or tasks and therefore do not demonstrate the knowledge and skill they possess. A much larger group of students do not understand the content, but could if they were provided with tools for learning and remembering important information.

There are some troubling trends in this regard. Although many content area teachers recognize their students' inability to read and comprehend their textbooks, they often respond by circumventing the books altogether.

> Limited as it is, the research on the use of textbooks in helping students learn from text has several implications. First, it suggests that students will not read their content-area textbooks if teachers fail to expect them to learn from text. Second, the research suggests that teachers rarely spend time teaching students how to use their content-area texts. (Alvermann, 1989, p. 257)

In this section, we address only the types of techniques designed to help students study and learn from texts. Since teachers are unlikely to employ text reading if they do not believe students can comprehend and remember the material, the situation is not likely to improve until they and their students move in the direction of effective study skills instruction.

SQ3R. The grandfather of study strategies, SQ3R (Survey, Question, Read, Recite, Review) was developed by Robinson in 1946. SQ3R is meant to be taught to students as an organized method for dealing with study and learning tasks in assigned textbook reading. Students are taught to approach their textbook reading/studying using the following procedures.

Survey. Students are told to preview the material to get a general overview of the chapter. This step will be most helpful if students are provided with information about how to preview a text effectively. For example, they should be taught to ask themselves questions such as: What appears to be the main topic of this chapter? How has the author organized the information? In addition, students should be taught to survey any maps, figures, captions, and so on for useful information about the topics.

Question. The information students have gained by surveying the text is used to generate questions to guide their reading. Students are specifically directed to restate boldface headings as questions. For example, when using this step of the technique to study the present chapter, a reader might pose the question, "What is SQ3R?"

Read. Using the questions and purposes established in the first steps to guide them, students read the assigned material.

Recite. Students are expected to pause periodically and "recite," or think about their reading (see STAR, p. 594). Students are encouraged to try to provide answers to their questions given the reading they have done.

Review. When students have completed the assigned reading, they are expected to stop, review the material, and summarize or take notes on the important information.

There are many variations of SQ3R that have been proposed, some designed for study in specific content areas. SQ3R is still widely taught and appears to be an effective technique for students who use it. The biggest concern expressed by critics involves the relatively low incidence of student use (Adams, Carnine, & Gersten, 1982). This is probably related to the failure of teachers to provide explicitly for careful instruction in how or why to employ the technique. The next strategy addresses this concern.

SMART. A Self-Monitoring Approach to Reading (SMART) is comprised of a series of steps that students are taught to use. Developed by Vaughan and Estes (1986), the strategy is especially helpful for students who need help attending to meaning in reading.

Step 1: Students are taught to keep track of their comprehension by putting a √ or a ? in the margins as they read. The √ indicates understanding, the ? confusion.

Step 2: Students self-check, explaining in their own words the concepts or ideas they have understood.

Step 3: Students are taught to deal with comprehension failures: reread, identify the problem (e.g., word? relationships? etc.), generate possible solutions, review the text, and so on.

Step 4: Students continue using Steps 1–3 as a cycle of activity to read long passages. Then they self-check and review.

It should be apparent that none of these specific activities is new. All are often suggested to students. What *is* different is that the students would be taught these steps as a systematic approach to the problem of reading and understanding. In addition, students are encouraged to think about solutions to their problems and to use the skills and strategies they possess. According to Irvin (1990):

> Successful study skills training programs have three main components: (1) training and practice in the use of task-specific strategies (knowing *what* to apply); (2) instruction in the monitoring of these skills (knowing when and how to apply strategies); and (3) information concerning the significance and outcomes of these activities and their range of utility (knowing why we apply strategies) (Paris, Newman, & McVey, 1982). (p. 140)

Underlining and notetaking. Although easy and widely used, underlining is unevenly effective as a study strategy (Anderson & Armbruster, 1984b). After an extensive review of the research on notetaking, these authors also concluded that it can be an effective strategy but that it is most useful when it involves focusing students' attention in specific ways. Students are most likely to enjoy benefits from notetaking when they attend to and note information in ways that closely approximate the way the information will subsequently be used. Thus, if students are going to need to write compare/contrast essay questions, their notes should reflect this organization as well. Thus, taking good notes clearly requires that students be able to recognize these text patterns.

If students merely copy information verbatim from the text, as many research results suggest they typically do (Bretzing & Kulhavy, 1981), then the benefits of notetaking may be less startling. Indeed, it is possible that students who simply reread or effectively underline will do at least as well under those circumstances. They could spend more time thinking about the material since a read-rereading strategy takes less time than recording information that they may recall anyway:

> Research has shown that people tend to remember the "most important" information anyway. . . . Therefore, note takers may be learning "main ideas" very well, but at the expense of learning other information. On the other hand, subjects who use less time-consuming studying techniques (e.g., read-reread and underline) are able to distribute their attention and effort more evenly over the passage. (Anderson & Armbruster, 1984b, p. 668)

Effective notetaking and underlining both require that students be able to distinguish important from unimportant information. Most students, of course, will require some instruction and discussion in these areas before they will be able to manage successfully. Yet one researcher reports that only 17% of college students ever received any instruction in how to take notes!

It is possible to teach one of the available systems of notetaking such as the Cornell Notetaking Method (Pauk, 1974) or the Notetaking System for Learning (Palmatier, 1973). The format of the notetaking system and the specifics are less important than the guidance students receive in learning to note important information and use notes to study. Irvin (1990) suggests the following guidelines be applied when teaching notetaking:

1. Students should be asked to preview the chapter before beginning, attending especially to the structure of the material.
2. Textbooks with clear headings and subheadings should be used during initial instruction.
3. Practice with shorter texts should precede work with longer assignments.
4. Students should be provided with examples and feedback, and their initial attempts at notetaking should be reviewed.
5. Students should receive instruction and practice in using notes to accomplish others tasks; e.g., to write a summary, make outlines, etc.
6. Finally, students' notes should be used to study for a test.

In reviewing students' notes with them and helping them to use them for study, teachers should be asking the following questions (Tierney, Readence, & Dishner, 1985, p. 203):

- Has this student noted the essential concepts and supporting detail emphasized in the unit?
- Is the material organized in a way that will lead to successful study of the material for testing purposes?

When students are having difficulty with either of these aspects of notetaking, additional instruction will be needed. It is also possible that students will benefit from instruction designed to focus them more clearly on the central information in texts (see previous sections) or in summarizing (see below).

Summarization. To summarize means to eliminate extraneous information so that only the main points remain. As a study strategy, summarizing is useful only under some circumstances. First, students must be well-equipped to engage in summarization. This often (always with poor readers) involves specific instruction in how to write a summary. A second condition is that the subsequent tasks students are required to do demand the kind of information and thinking that is represented in a summary. Clearly, writing a good summary is not likely to enhance performance on a short-answer/multiple-choice objective test.

In order to summarize effectively, students need to learn how to identify the prevailing text structure, how to recognize or generate important ideas and connections, and how to produce an overarching statement of topic. Fortunately, several effective instructional programs have been designed to teach students how to summarize information in texts. For example, Brown, Campione, and Day (1981) taught students five rules for generating summaries:

1. Delete irrelevant or trivial information.
2. Delete redundant information.
3. Select topic sentences.
4. Substitute a superordinate term or event for a list of terms or actions.
5. Invent topic sentences when none are provided by the author.

FIGURE 14.13

Hierarchical Summary for Text Selection Containing One Heading and Six Subheadings

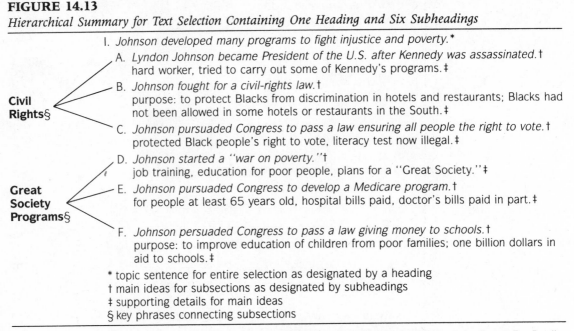

I. *Johnson developed many programs to fight injustice and poverty.* *

A. *Lyndon Johnson became President of the U.S. after Kennedy was assassinated.* †
hard worker, tried to carry out some of Kennedy's programs. ‡

B. *Johnson fought for a civil-rights law.* †
purpose: to protect Blacks from discrimination in hotels and restaurants; Blacks had not been allowed in some hotels or restaurants in the South. ‡

C. *Johnson pursuaded Congress to pass a law ensuring all people the right to vote.* †
protected Black people's right to vote, literacy test now illegal. ‡

D. *Johnson started a "war on poverty."* †
job training, education for poor people, plans for a "Great Society." ‡

E. *Johnson pursuaded Congress to develop a Medicare program.* †
for people at least 65 years old, hospital bills paid, doctor's bills paid in part. ‡

F. *Johnson persuaded Congress to pass a law giving money to schools.* †
purpose: to improve education of children from poor families; one billion dollars in aid to schools. ‡

Civil Rights§

Great Society Programs§

* topic sentence for entire selection as designated by a heading
† main ideas for subsections as designated by subheadings
‡ supporting details for main ideas
§ key phrases connecting subsections

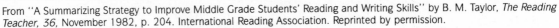

From "A Summarizing Strategy to Improve Middle Grade Students' Reading and Writing Skills" by B. M. Taylor, *The Reading Teacher, 36,* November 1982, p. 204. International Reading Association. Reprinted by permission.

Using rules very much like these, and feedback and practice with modeling, Hare and Borchardt (1984) successfully taught high-school students to summarize texts. Similarly, sixth-grade students who were taught rules for summarizing and learned to use them effectively showed improvement in comprehension (Bean & Steenwyk, 1984).

Taylor (1982, 1986) has developed a somewhat more sophisticated strategy that has been found effective with middle-school students: the Hierarchical Summary Procedure. It is intended to improve students' ability to summarize using the structure and organization of text. The steps in this procedure are somewhat involved, and it is helpful to see a completed example before you begin (see Figure 14.13).

> *Step 1: Preview.* Students survey a segment of text (3–5 pages) and examine the headings, subheadings, and so on. Teacher and students generate an outline framework that reflects each of the major sections. Thus, a Roman numeral is recorded for each major section (but not filled in) and a capital letter is used to designate every major subsection. Spaces are left to enter details at a later point.
>
> *Step 2: Read.* Students read each segment of the text, noting the important information as they read.

Step 3: Outline. Students summarize using the outline. This can be done as students read or may be conducted in a revisiting of the text. They write a topic sentence next to each of the Roman numerals and details under each of the capitals.

Step 4: Study. Students then connect related ideas by using some superordinate term.

The value of Hierarchical Summaries is that students receive substantial amounts of practice in identifying important ideas and additional experience displaying ideas in relation to each other (major and supporting details, for example). With explicit instruction, Taylor reports that middle-grade students can complete hierarchical summaries independently after five or six sessions.

Needed: A Functional, Integrated Approach to Study Skills Instruction

Teachers have always bemoaned the apparent absence of study skills on the part of their students. Until recently, however, only a meager array of tools and strategies were passed along, and students were more often admonished to engage in them than they were taught to employ them (Palmatier & Bennett, 1974). The situation has begin to change quite rapidly in recent years, as educators have demonstrated that study strategies and studying approaches could be taught and, more importantly, transferred to other settings.

The wide array of available techniques does not, however, assure that students will use them appropriately or voluntarily. The increasing interest in this area has revealed what earlier examinations of comprehension in general did: that studying is a complex cognitive activity that involves knowledge, skills, and motivation in at least equal parts (see Weinstein, Goetz, & Alexander, 1988). If students are going to become effective studiers, they will need an integrated and well-conceived repertoire of knowledge and skills.

The only comprehensive approach to this problem at the moment appears to be the Learning Strategies Curriculum (Schumaker, Deshler, Alley, & Warner, 1983). Three large strands comprise the set of instructional materials. Almost all important strategies for studying are included in this set of materials. Unfortunately, the view of studying as a highly specialized reading activity is somewhat diluted by the organization of the strands and by the mixture of strategies. Strategies like Multi-Pass (a strategy for working with textbook chapters in a study condition), coupled with strategies like Self-Questioning might be organized to provide students with a coherent studying plan.

However, students and teachers also need to learn and use strategies at the point of need. Students will probably never acquire good, independent studying strategies if they do not receive at least some encouragement and direction from content teachers.

Paris (1988) has summarized the characteristics of successful strategy instruction. Not surprisingly, many of these parallel the characteristics of effective comprehension instruction, including the need for explicit instruction and transfer of responsibility from teachers to students. He notes several other characteristics that seem especially important in the promotion of independent study behaviors:

1. Students must believe in the utility and necessity of using the strategies.
2. Teachers must provide a demonstration of how the strategies can be used and when and why they are valuable.
3. The strategies must be appropriate for the student in terms of his/her abilities and willingness to expend effort.
4. Strategy instruction should result in improved student confidence and belief in their own competence.

The ability to study effectively is merely a specialized type of comprehension ability. As with all aspects of comprehension ability, studying ability emerges over time and in response to need and instruction. It is clear that teachers must provide much more intentional, focused, and continuous instruction in studying if students are going to become independent in this area.

Reading and Writing

A somewhat different, but no less promising, approach to improved reading comprehension ability involves providing much more extensive experience with writing. Programs that promote a process (versus product) view of writing have great potential for enhancing students' reading as well as writing abilities. Ours is an admittedly slim review of the issues and techniques. Although it is well beyond the scope of this text to explore the writing process at length, or to describe the teaching of writing as a legitimate enterprise, we do believe reading teachers need to be much better informed about the connections and the issues. Interested readers are referred to one of the many fine books on this topic for more information (e.g., Calkins, 1986; Graves, 1983; Hansen, 1987; McVitty, 1986; Newkirk & Atwell, 1988).

Generically called "process writing programs," the newer approaches to teaching writing have grown out of a clearer understanding of writing and writers. We describe the phases of the writing cycle briefly below. Then, we suggest some ways to help support students as writers and ways to manage writing and reading activities in the classroom so that writing will be sustained as an important, *daily* activity.

The Writing Process

The writing process is generally conceived of as having five stages, some of which can be collapsed under certain writing conditions by some individuals: prewriting or rehearsing, drafting, revising, editing, and sharing or publishing (see Murray, 1982).

Prewriting or rehearsing. During this phase, authors may be thinking about ideas, jotting down information, or generating topics. Classroom teachers can facilitate this phase of writing by providing ample time for brainstorming, noting ideas, and free-writing (see Chapter 11). In older product-oriented approaches to writing, students were rarely given adequate time to reflect and *plan* their writing. Many students will need extensive help and guidance in topic selection.

Drafting. This is stage one in which authors actually begin to shape their piece, "the stage in which drafts, or unfinished attempts, are created" (Temple & Gillet, 1989, p. 219). At this stage, students will be writing and reading and, often, rethinking their piece.

Revising. Revising will sometimes happen as a distinct phase and will sometimes occur almost simultaneously with the drafting stage. There are times when authors have a full draft and then work at revising it, but just as often authors revise as they draft, changing, deleting, and adding as they go.

Editing. In this stage, authors create a final copy of their work. This generally involves addressing both physical appearance and mechanical errors (in spelling, grammar, etc.). In this regard, it is important to remember the developmental abilities of the student.

> The teacher always considers what will help the writer grow. There is always a margin of editing that the child can work with prior to publication. The teacher needs to think through the individual dosage that will still make the child take responsibility for his work. (Graves, 1983, p. 58)

Sharing or publishing. Authors write to communicate. People do, occasionally, write for themselves (lists, notes, and journals). But generally speaking, students need opportunities to share their writing with others because that is the function and nature of writing. Sharing can be quite formal, as in the publication of classroom or individual books, or it can be quite intimate, as in the one-on-one sharing of a piece during a conference.

The writing process is played out in classrooms through a variation of whole class (e.g., brainstorming) and individual (drafting) activities. Individuals in these classrooms regularly confer about the writing that they are doing. Students confer with each other to provide guidance and seek help. The classroom teacher also has conferences with students, but these should generally follow a conference between peers.

Students who have had opportunities to write continuously and to confer with others about their work bring the knowledge they acquire about writing, structure, and communication to their reading (Hansen, 1987). Word usage, the effectiveness of titles, and the relationships between ideas will all be discussed as a piece progresses. Having struggled with various ways to convey meaning themselves, they are likely to recognize and use this knowledge to aid comprehension. Students' writing also often begins to reflect some aspects from their reading: ideas, language use, and genre, for example (Paley, 1981).

Instructional Suggestions

The writing activity of process classrooms is significantly different from traditional writing programs. Gone are the days of assigning one topic for all students, having all students write together for some predetermined period, and then handing in the work to be corrected by the teacher. So are the days when that piece would be returned full of markings, to be recopied as the final product for display on the board.

There is no question that process writing programs can produce quite different products. The product is the student as author, a person who writes and who is willing to work with a piece of writing and a set of ideas for more than a brief period. It takes a knowledgeable teacher to advance these outcomes. There are several suggestions for supporting students as they write and read.

Write with the students. Just as it is important for teachers to model reading, it is important for them to model writing. During uninterrupted sustained writing periods, teachers should work on their own writing pieces if at all possible.

Maintain writing folders. Students (and teachers) should understand that not all pieces of writing will proceed smoothly from prewriting to publication. Many good ideas will go dry after writing has begun; others will be derailed by a more pressing topic. Still others require more time to develop. Thus, students should keep a folder, not only for their current writing, but as a place to keep other story ideas, notes on topics to be pursued, and early drafts of some project that has not been completed. Teachers and students together should cull this folder periodically for ideas and decide on pieces that should really be brought to completion.

Help students select topics. Encourage them to write about things that interest them. Try to ensure that students have more than one topic idea so that they can turn to a different one if the first doesn't seem to be working. Atwell (1987) suggests the following ways to help students in topic selection. Students should interview each other and keep a list of "My Ideas for Writing." Be sure that students know that they can ask for a conference to discuss ideas for generating and selecting topics, and be ready to provide stimulus questions such as: What is special about you? or Who's your best friend? What's special about him/her? Teachers who are unhappy with the topics of students' writing need to take responsibility for helping students choose more wisely.

Develop and teach conference skills. In order to conduct effective and fruitful writing conferences, both individuals need to know what is expected and how to behave. The author should have a clear goal in mind: seeking advice about the title, requesting help on a difficult section, or soliciting overall reaction to the ideas in a piece. Meaning discussions should *always* precede mechanics discussion, although mechanical difficulties may account for difficulties in conveying meaning.

Classroom teachers will obviously conduct conferences regularly, but they should not feel that they must do it all. Even primary aged children can and should be taught to have productive conferences with their peers. First, the author reads his or her draft aloud to the conference partner. The author may volunteer a reason for the conference, or the conference partner can provide feedback. Students need clear guidelines for responding, and many teachers find it helpful to provide a conference guide that is either placed in the students' folder or posted on the wall of the writing center. Peer conferees should be given a set of prompts like the following:

- Listen carefully to the author.
- Tell the author:
    What your response to the piece was. (How did it make you feel?)
    What you liked best about the piece.
    What you found difficult to understand.
- Help the author:
    Answer the author's questions.
    Tell where you think there should be more detail.
    Tell where you think sentences could be combined or information deleted.

Some teachers have found it helpful to make a videotape that demonstrates effective conferencing so that students can see others working through the process. Not only will teachers find it easier to maintain process writing programs if they invest in conference training with their students, these students will benefit from the opportunity to think about other students' writing, and provide feedback to them.

Provide opportunities for sharing. Students should not be expected to share all pieces of writing. However, there is no clearer motivation for taking writing and revising seriously than to make sure that authors have opportunities to share their work. This may involve bookmaking activities or word processing and desk-top publishing (see Chapter 8). Some children's magazines regularly publish written work of young people and these may be interesting for some teachers and students (see Chapter 11).

Teachers should find ways to celebrate students' writing outside of the classroom. However, these activities can become quite elaborate projects. Teachers can find other ways to share student writing that are less involved and, in some cases, equally gratifying. For example, many teachers have long known the power of having older students read to younger ones. This can be extended to having students read their own stories and descriptions to younger students. Many teachers and students have been attracted to the idea of an "author's chair" (Graves & Hansen, 1983). This special chair provides a place for authors to sit as they read their work to the class. Teachers may also sit there to read trade books for the purpose of author discussion. These less formal forums for sharing can be powerful social forces for literacy acquisition. They also provide additional models for students who need topic ideas or suggestions for new ways to express themselves.

As we learn more about the reading-writing connection, it is possible that we will find what appeared earlier to be unlikely results. For example, in a university reading clinic, we recently worked with a 10-year-old boy who was an extremely reluctant and unskilled reader, but who nevertheless discovered that he loved to write. His own explanation for this is interesting: "I like to make my own ideas for what will happen . . . I don't like reading because you have to get the ideas *they* wrote." The dialogue journal that had been started early took shape as a prewriting idea log. In addition, he avidly listened as his tutor read *Dear Mr. Henshaw* (Cleary, 1983) about a young boy who wanted to be an author. Over time, he found that there were things he liked to read as well, and although still struggling, he is no longer stalled.

Writing and Learning

In recent years, educators and effective teachers in a variety of disciplines have been exploring the use of writing as a tool to learn. Whereas most process writing programs originate with English professionals and remain the responsibility of language arts teachers, writing as a learning tool is an altogether different thing:

> Writing is basic to thinking about, and learning, knowledge in all fields as well as to communicating that knowledge. (Fulwiler, 1987a, p. 1)

Writing in these cases is viewed as a tool; students are required to write in order to advance content learning goals. This extremely powerful means of supporting students' learning is only just coming clear (see Atwell, 1990; Fulwiler, 1987b; Young & Fulwiler, 1986).

Others have taken the tack that students can be taught to write certain expository forms as a way to improve reading and studying ability. For example, Armbruster, Anderson, and Ostertag (1989) taught middle-school students to identify the text structure in social sciences texts and to write summaries that conformed to that pattern (see Figure 14.10). "A write-to-learn program recognizes that content ideas can be expressed through a variety of writing forms. These discourse forms can be easily incorporated into the context of writing assignments" (Vacca & Vacca, 1989, p. 274; see Figure 14.14).

This thinking is very similar to that underlying the Cognitive Strategy Instruction in Writing (CSIW) program developed by Raphael and Englert (1989; 1990; Raphael, Kirschner, & Englert, 1988). As they explain it, "the CSIW program combines principles of process writing with principles underlying the teaching of cognitive strategies such as those used during reading writing" (Raphael & Englert, 1989, p. 242).

CSIW relies heavily on helping students to cope with text organization. Students use a variety of "think sheets" to help them plan, draft, monitor and revise their texts. For example, students use one think sheet to get started on the first phases of prewriting and planning. They are directed to ask themselves questions such as Why am I writing this? What do I already know about my topic? Then, students are introduced to another think sheet that helps them to plan how they will organize their ideas. The think sheets in this second stage reflect the various types of text structure and are similar to the pattern guides discussed earlier.

CSIW also calls for teachers to model the writing process, and think sheets are provided to guide writing and editing (see Figure 14.15). It should be apparent that though the process is similar to the process writing procedures described above, the focus for this writing is content and structure. Thus, students' attention is drawn to the specialized features of expository writing. Such explicit instruction in writing exposition apparently provides substantial benefits for reading it as well (Raphael, Kirschner, & Englert, 1988).

FIGURE 14.14

Discourse Forms for Content Area Writing

Journals and diaries (real or imaginary)	Editorials	Utopian proposals
Biographical sketches	Commentaries	Practical proposals
Anecdotes and stories:	Responses and rebuttals	Interviews:
from experience	Newspaper "fillers"	actual
as told by others	Fact books or fact sheets	imaginary
Thumbnail sketches:	School newspaper stories	Directions:
of famous people	Stories or essays for local papers	how-to
of places	Proposals	school or neighborhood guide
of content ideas	Case studies:	survival manual
of historical events	school problems	Dictionaries and lexicons
Guess who/what descriptions	local issues	Technical reports
Letters:	national concerns	Future options, notes on:
personal reactions	historical problems	careers, employment
observations	scientific issues	school and training
public/informational	Songs and ballads	military/public service
persuasive:	Demonstrations	Written debates
to the editor	Poster displays	Taking a stand:
to public officials	Reviews:	school issues
to imaginary people	books (including textbooks)	family problems
from imaginary places	films	state or national issues
Requests	outside reading	moral questions
Applications	television programs	Books and booklets
Memos	documentaries	Informational monographs
Resumés and summaries	Historical "you are there" scenes	Radio scripts
Poems	Science notes:	TV scenarios and scripts
Plays	observations	Dramatic scripts
Stories	science notebook	Notes for improvised drama
Fantasy	reading reports	Cartoons and cartoon strips
Adventure	lab reports	Slide show scripts
Science fiction	Math:	Puzzles and word searches
Historical stories	story problems	Prophecy and predictions
Dialogues and conversations	solutions to problems	Photos and captions
Children's books	record books	Collage, montage, mobile,
Telegrams	notes and observations	sculpture
	Responses to literature	

From *Teaching Writing in the Content Areas: Elementary School* by Stephen N. Tchudi and Susan J. Tchudi. Copyright © 1983 National Education Association of the United States. Reprinted by permission.

In summary, writing can provide additional techniques for improving reading in both narrative and expository situations. A review of the characteristics of effective writing programs (Tiedt, 1989) suggests that students:

- Write frequently.
- Learn to write by writing and by reading.
- Write for varied purposes and audiences.
- Discuss the writing process.
- Edit and revise their own work

Writing Conference Guides

Author's Name _____   Editor's Name _____

Read to check information

What is the paper mainly about?

What do you like best? Put a * next to the part you liked best and tell here why you like it:

What parts are not clear? Put a ? next to the unclear parts, and tell what made the part unclear to you:

Is the paper interesting? Tell why or why not:

Question yourself to check organization

Did the author:

Tell what two things are compared and contrasted?	YES	SORT OF	NO
Tell the things that they are being compared to and contrasted with?	YES	SORT OF	NO
Tell how they are alike?	YES	SORT OF	NO
Tell how they are different?	YES	SORT OF	NO
Use key words clearly?	YES	SORT OF	NO

Plan revision

What two parts do you think should be changed or revised? (For anything marked "sort of" or "no," tell whether the author should add to, take out, or reorder.)

1. _____
   _____

2. _____
   _____

What could help make the paper more interesting?

Talk

Talk to the author of the paper. Talk about your comments on this think sheet. Share ideas for revising the paper.

Reprinted by permission of the publisher from Raphael, T. E., and Englert, C. S., "Integrating Writing and Reading Instruction" in Winograd, Peter N., Wixson, Karen K., & Lipson, Marjorie Y., eds., *Improving Basal Reading Instruction* (New York: Teachers College Press, © 1989 by Teachers College, Columbia University. All rights reserved), p. 248.

- Help others to edit and revise
- Share their writing with others in a public forum
- Confer often with the teacher

When students have opportunities to write with the guidance of others, they appear to learn to write but they often learn a great deal about reading. General comprehension abilities and specialized study skills can be improved when students write on a regular basis and receive focused information about writing from skilled teachers.

FROM CLASSROOM TO CLINIC

There is little in this chapter that is not applicable to both classroom and clinic, nor is there even one instructional guideline or technique that cannot be done in either classroom or clinic. Indeed, teachers working in more isolated clinical settings may have a harder time implementing some of the suggestions in this chapter, since our suggestions rely so heavily on relevant practice in authentic environments. Every developmental or remedial reading teacher and special educator knows that transfer from one setting to another is painfully difficult unless there is a close approximation of the classroom texts and tasks.

Generally speaking, classroom teachers should be particularly concerned about providing appropriate support for students so that they can read and/or study the materials they are using in their classrooms. Consequently, teachers may find it especially helpful to review the general guidelines for comprehension instruction and then to become quite comfortable with a range of the strategies provided in the Supporting Students' Comprehension and Studying section of this chapter. The lesson frames, in particular, are easily adapted to most classrooms.

On the other hand, clinical teachers must be absolutely concerned that they are providing students with instruction aimed at improving their ability to comprehend and study. The array of techniques provided in this chapter should be helpful here. However, specialized reading personnel should also consider carefully the implications of the "general plan to teach for independence." The intentional planning for self-controlled learning is of the utmost importance and will be difficult to achieve in an isolated clinical setting. Reading teachers and classroom teachers must find ways to collaborate to advance this primary goal.

CHAPTER SUMMARY

After a brief introduction, we reviewed several issues related to comprehension instruction. Specifically, we noted that contemporary debates regarding the nature of comprehension instruction have resulted in considerable knowledge about effective teaching and productive learning. We argued that teachers should strike a balance, providing rich literacy contexts as well as good explicit instruction regarding the reading process. Next, two aspects of comprehension instruction were discussed and a distinction was made between comprehending specific texts and promoting comprehension ability. We noted that the latter results in generalized knowledge and skill necessary to comprehend many texts. Third, we devoted a section to discussing the varying purposes for which people read. Here, we described recent distinctions between "aesthetic" and "efferent" purposes, noting that readers' responses differ depending on their approach to the text/task. Finally, five key guidelines were provided to shape teachers' thinking about comprehension instruction, including a strong suggestion that reading and writing instruction need to be more closely aligned.

In the next major section of this chapter, we provided detailed descriptions of instructional techniques for focusing on comprehension and studying. These were divided into two classes of technique: those designed to support students as they comprehend and study particular texts, and those designed to teach students to become better able to comprehend a wide range of texts. Strategies such as DRTA, text mapping, and study guides were described in the first group. In the second group, we described a general plan for teaching students to become independent, and then described several specific techniques such as QAR training, ReQuest, and SQ3R. Finally, specific guidelines for developing a more integrated approach to reading and writing in the curriculum were provided, as well as a brief description of process approaches to the teaching of writing.

SECTION VI

The Reading Professional

TEACHERS WHO CONDUCT EFFECTIVE assessment and thoughtful, well-designed instruction may feel that they have completed their responsibilities. However, work in assessment and instruction always requires accountability to a wide array of groups and individuals (such as administrators, other teaching professionals, parents, and community personnel). Consequently, the final step in the assessment-instruction process emphasizes the need to effectively communicate with others about their students and the curriculum (see the figure on the following page).

The single chapter in this section contains a focus on the responsibilities of reading professionals that extend beyond working with an individual student or client. We discuss the importance of skillful communication with parents and the need for accurate reporting procedures. Teachers will be guided through the process of writing formal reports and also will be provided with samples of exemplary written reports. Finally, we discuss the ethics and responsibilities of reading professionals.

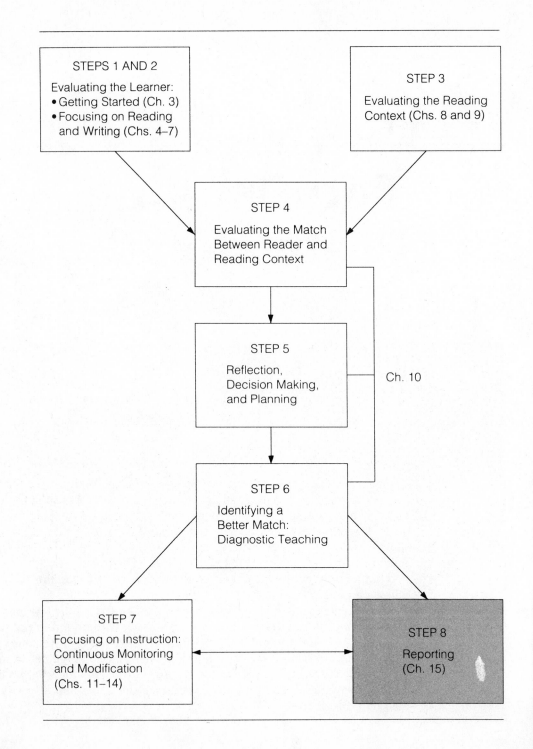

CHAPTER 15

The Reading Professional

INTRODUCTION

In this text we have focused on some specific roles important to the reading professional, roles involving assessment and instruction. However, most reading professionals are actually expected to fulfill many roles. Certainly they are expected to be preeminently knowledgeable in reading instruction (Wylie, 1969), but there are many other expectations of reading professionals as well, including consulting, supervising, and providing in-service functions.

Skillful communication with parents and community is absolutely essential to the assessment-instruction process. Sophisticated assessment and well-designed instruction must be accompanied by clear and accurate reporting procedures. Otherwise, it is possible for lay people, and even other professionals, to be confused or to misunderstand the implications of the work done with students or clients.

Throughout the early portions of the text, we advocated an approach to assessment that valued multiple sources of information collected fairly continuously. Converting the instructionally useful information that is gathered in a portfolio into information suitable for communicating with others is one issue facing teachers, especially classroom teachers. Similarly, it can be challenging to communicate the results of diagnostic teaching and other innovative approaches to assessment and instruction. Finally, teachers must also be able to convey the results of standardized tests in a clear and concise manner.

Chapter Overview

In this chapter, we describe the range of functions and responsibilities that may be associated with various reading professional roles. A listing of competencies helpful for reading professionals is provided. Among the most important of these is the ability to communicate effectively. Consequently, we provide a major section on reporting to others that includes some general guidelines and some suggestions for organizing and reporting on the contents of portfolios. In addition, teachers are guided through the process of writing formal reports and are also provided with samples of exemplary written reports. We describe how different types of reports may be appropriate for different purposes and discuss conferences as well as written reporting. In the final section of this chapter, we describe the professional and ethical responsibilities associated with providing reading services to students and clients.

THE ROLE(S) OF THE READING PROFESSIONAL

There is actually a great deal of disagreement about the appropriate roles and functions of reading teachers. For example, Bean (1979) reports that classroom teachers valued in-service and conferring activities considerably more highly than they did either group or individual diagnosis. However, Pikulski and Ross (1979) report that whereas teachers do expect reading specialists to be well-informed about reading and to provide some consultative service, they clearly preferred that reading personnel spend most of their time delivering reading instruction to individual students. Frequently, the perception of appropriate roles appears to vary with the audience (Mangieri & Heimberger, 1980).

Confusion over the appropriate functions led the International Reading Association (1986) to identify roles and responsibilities of various reading professionals. The list includes the following three categories: Category I, Classroom teachers; Category II, Reading Specialists; and Category III, Allied Profession. Category II is the largest category, encompassing all roles involving consulting, coordinating reading programs, and delivering diagnostic-remedial services. The Allied Profession category includes special educators, administrators, and others such as counselors and psychologists.

Within each of the broad categories, specific roles are identified and defined. For example, Role 3 (within Category II) is Diagnostic-Remedial Specialist. This role includes such functions as assessing reading and planning instructional programs. In addition, it designates coordinating services for individual students. Role 5, Reading Consultant/Reading Resource Teacher, lists somewhat different functions, including organizing and administering school reading programs, providing staff development, and coordinating reading specialist/other specialist activity.

In many school situations, however, the reading professional is expected to perform a variety of functions spanning several roles. Indeed, the situation is made even more complex by the existence of various mandated special education programs, as well as the wide variety in reading programs and functions. Sometimes special education programs employ individuals who are expected to assess reading and deliver reading instruction but who are not well-versed in reading themselves. Other situations exist where both the special education and the compensatory reading programs are run by the same persons.

Whatever the formally designated role, there is a need for school-level leadership surrounding reading and reading disabilities. No matter what the title, professionals who are well-versed in reading and reading instruction will have a responsibility to function as an educational leader in the school or school district. Although somewhat dated, the competencies described by Garry as most highly valued by reading professionals in 1974 are generally desirable today as well (see Figure 15.1). What many of these have in common is an emphasis on effective communication.

REPORTING TO OTHERS

Reading professionals are often expected to report to a wide range of people regarding the reading abilities and progress of students. There are a number of ways reading professionals communicate with others. Reporting may be as infor-

FIGURE 15.1

Desirable Competencies of Reading Personnel

Ability and Skill in:

1. Working with teachers to plan appropriate instruction for readers who need special support, in the classroom, and in special programs.
2. Working with small instructional groups of disabled readers.
3. Helping teachers to interpret test results.
4. Helping classroom teachers to assess the strengths and weaknesses of students in their classroom.
5. Providing expertise in diagnosing students with extreme reading difficulties and in suggesting instructional programs for them.
6. Referring students to appropriate specialized service personnel.
7. Determining the degree of reading difficulty.
8. Identifying students for special reading services and programs.
9. Helping teachers to document progress in reading.
10. Recommending and modeling the use of instructional techniques and materials.
11. Using and generating tools and techniques for improving students' "higher level" reading skills.
12. Supporting teachers as they develop additional strategies for teaching reading.

Adapted from "Desirable Competencies of Reading Personnel" from "Competencies That Count Among Reading Specialists" by V. V. Garry, *Journal of Reading*, May 1974, pp. 608–613.

mal as a chat in the teachers' lounge, as routine as a parent-teacher conference, or as formal as a complete case report. Its purpose should always be to communicate or solicit information about an individual student.

In this section we provide some guidelines for effective reporting, describe some ways to use the portfolio in reporting to others, and discuss several types of written reports. Finally, specific procedures for writing formal reports are detailed.

General Guidelines

No matter what form the reporting takes, there are some guidelines that should be considered:

1. *Provide a clear summary* of what has been done in both assessment and instruction. The tools, strategies, and techniques should be clear, and the results should be understandable, apparent, and reasonable. Effective reports provide detailed descriptions so that others can understand the reader and the reading context with little chance of confusion.
2. *Include only relevant information.* No matter how interesting, information should not be included unless there appears to be a close link to reading/academic performance. When sensitive personal information is discussed, this should be treated as discreetly as possible.
3. *Highlight the most important information* about the reader and the reading context. Always make sure that the reader's most salient strengths and obvious difficulties are described as priorities. Similarly, critical positive supports in the instructional context should be noted along with suggestions for

instruction that are likely to be effective for the student. Less central information should be discussed later in the reporting session or at the end of any written report. It is not necessary or desirable to report the same information about all individuals; the report should reflect the particular needs and abilities of the reader.

4. *Use language and format appropriate for the audience.* When reporting to parents it is important to keep discussions free of jargon and as straightforward as possible. When specialized terms seem necessary to use, be sure to define them. If there is any reason at all to suspect the literacy skills of parents or guardians, all information should be communicated orally. On the other hand, when reporting to teachers, schools, or other agencies, the form and language should be professional and technical terms should be used to ensure precision.

In deciding on the form of reporting, it is important to consider the needs of the audience as well as the purposes for communicating. Too often, reading professionals believe that reporting must always involve transmitting and interpreting formal test data. Yet, parents often would prefer periodic meetings that inform them about their children's general progress. This is where assessment portfolios are particularly powerful tools in reporting.

Reporting via Portfolio Summaries

Throughout this text we have made periodic references to assessment portfolios. In our view, a portfolio should contain *all* types of available information about an individual student. It should include *at least* three types of information:

1. formal, standardized test information, where available (see Chapter 6);
2. the results of intentionally planned assessments of reading/writing ability such as retellings (see Chapter 7);
3. work samples collected as representative of the activities and abilities of that student/classroom.

These pieces of evidence are themselves relatively uninformative, however. They are essentially raw data unless a knowledgeable teacher organizes the information and interprets its significance.

When preparing to report the contents of portfolios to others, it is helpful to organize the information in some way so that it takes on meaning for others who are less well-informed. Even a simple cover sheet stapled to a folder can systematize the information (see Figure 15.2). Listing the pieces of information in the portfolio and the dates collected can help the teacher and any others to see the range of information available. If, in addition, the teacher writes a narrative periodically (for example, at conference time), then the information can be even more accessible to others.

For the purposes of reporting to others, it may be important to organize the information and the patterns of reading behavior to an even greater extent. In such

FIGURE 15.2
*Portfolio Cover
Sheet*

Name _____   Teacher(s) _____
Grade _____   Birthdate _____

CONTENTS   DATE

1. _____
2. _____
3. _____
4. _____
5. _____
6. _____
7. _____
8. _____

COMMENTS   DATE

_____
_____
_____
_____
_____
_____

cases, teachers can use a Portfolio Analysis Sheet (see Figure 15.3). The example provided is only suggestive, since teachers should use an analysis system that parallels the types of assessment and instruction that are most central to their program.

It is important that the portfolio analysis offer systematic evaluation of the contents of the portfolio—analysis that could be replicated by others who are interested in this student's performance. While the contents may be helpful to classroom teachers as they work with students, they are unlikely to be informative to others (or considered valid and reliable) unless some additional effort is made to interpret and formalize the results. If this effort is made, however, both parents and administrators are likely to be pleased with the specificity of information and the depth of knowledge available.

There are times, of course, when the information about students must be interpreted and summarized for other purposes or in other ways. Written reports vary in both type and purpose, and are discussed in the next section.

Report Writing: Different Types for Different Purposes

Writing reports is an essential part of the job of most reading professionals. However, these may vary from very brief reports to extensive formal case reports. Parents generally want to know what is happening in the clinical or classroom setting, especially when the student is receiving specialized help for an identified problem. Brief reports about the student's program and progress can and should be sent periodically to parents and other involved professionals. This kind of report can alert parents and teachers to special accomplishments that have occurred or to problems that have been identified. At other times, this report may be used to enlist the help of parents and classroom teachers (see Figure 15.4).

It is also important for classroom teachers and specialized personnel to communicate with each other. Issues of congruence discussed earlier (see Chapters 8 and 9) have obvious implications for reporting. As Shake (1989) has noted:

> It seems safe to say that remedial teachers cannot provide instruction that either introduces or reinforces the classroom reading curriculum if they do not know what that curriculum contains. Both classroom and remedial teachers report concern regarding the lack of time for communication about programs and target students. (Allington & Shake, 1986; Johnston, Allington, & Afflerbach, 1985). (p. 74)

Clearly, the type of reporting called for in this situation is somewhat different, though no less important. Shake suggests that teachers and specialists keep a record form (see Chapter 8) that travels with the student. This type of documentation can diminish the need for extensive formal reporting at a later date and also increases the likelihood that instruction will have some coherence across settings. Of course, if a portfolio system is being employed, then the student as well as all teachers can and should contribute samples, observations, and evaluations.

Just as the audience and format for reporting may vary, so may the content. For example, all of the specially funded programs for reading and related difficulties require some sort of reporting procedures. These programs often require the teacher only to report program data; extensive individual reporting is not

FIGURE 15.3
Portfolio Analysis Sheet

Observations of Reading and Writing

Date	Student Interview
	Summarize results of
	Observations
	Record observations of student's development in reading/writing

FIGURE 15.3
(Continued)

Reading Materials/Tasks

Date	
	Books/selections read (assigned)
	Books/selections read (self-selected)
	Book/reading-related written work completed
	Group activities

Reading Performance (Note materials, task, level of support)

Date	
	Word recognition ability
	Oral reading fluency
	Comprehension: Question answering
	Comprehension: Retelling
	Strategy use
	Studying strategies

FIGURE 15.3
(Continued)

Writing Development

Date	
	Describe writing samples (include all drafts)
	Note types of writing represented
	Summarize writer's development of written mechanics (spelling and writing conventions)
	Student-selected "best piece" (describe)
	Evaluate writing development (progress over time and in terms of age-appropriateness)

Summary

Date	
	Student's reading development
	Student's writing development

FIGURE 15.4
Parents/
Teacher
Report Form

Student _____   Date _____
Teacher _____

Summary of the following instructional periods (dates/times of sessions):

_____

Summary of reading/writing abilities: _____

_____

_____

Summary of instructional program (materials, activities): _____

_____

_____

Summary of progress: _____

_____

_____

Comments: _____

_____

_____

_____

necessary. Even when formal individual case reports are expected, they may vary depending on the audience and the program.

Sometimes it is important to write much more comprehensive case reports that include summaries of all available standardized test information and interpretations of the results for specific uses. A written report of a student's reading ability generally includes all or some of the following: background information, summary of assessment information, summary of factors influencing reading performance, and implications for instruction or future placement (or summary of instructional progress).

Formal reports about individual students in public school settings are used most often when the student has been referred for special services or for a determination of eligibility for special education (as called for in PL 94–142; see Chapter 1). These often make recommendations regarding the student's eligibility for services, but are less helpful regarding the specific implications for instructional programs.

As we have seen, reading professionals may be asked or required to perform in a variety of contexts and may need to be responsive to different people and their needs. Perhaps the most frequent responsibility, however, involves the need to pull together an array of assessment information and use it to plan an instructional program. This type of reporting, something we call the *case report,* is described in much greater detail in the next section.

Procedures for Writing Diagnostic Case Reports

Fully executed case reports are very time-consuming to write, and few settings require such extensive documentation. Although it is the not the most frequent format for reporting and communicating about students, it is the format that reading professionals often use as the vehicle for learning how to report. A formal, written report requires discipline in organizing information, ability to interpret results, and well-developed writing skills. It demands careful examination of all information regarding a student, and involves learning to communicate that information to others in a much more public forum than many teachers typically experience.

Choosing and using a fairly standard format for writing case reports saves time. There are a wide array of formats used. Several factors need to be considered in selecting a format. First, it should accommodate and support reporting of the types of information that you wish to communicate. Second, it should be flexible enough so that it can be shaped to take the focus appropriate to the particular individual and purpose (see above). Third, it should offer a format that is convenient for the consumer of the report—considerate both in terms of what is expected and familiar and clearly organized for ease of reading. Finally, there is a political consideration as well. Although the situation is rapidly changing, the educational community still has a bias toward data gathered from standardized, norm-referenced tools. Since we include large amounts of non-traditional information in our reports, we are particularly sensitive to the ways in which we display these data.

The format described in this section has an overall appearance that is similar to traditional case reports and provides for formally reporting all existing assessment information. We want consumers to take the information seriously and to consider it as reliable and valid as the more familiar test scores (see Figure 15.6). The format also offers flexibility in accommodating the types of information we have advocated throughout this text. If the Thumbnail Sketch was done earlier (see Chapter 10), this information will be very useful in preparing the case report.

The case of "Marvin," discussed periodically throughout this text, is now used to illustrate the sections in a diagnostic case report (a second full case report is presented in Appendix A). Each of the procedures described below parallels a major component of the diagnostic case report (see Figure 15.5).

Display the Assessment Information

The cover sheet should contain a concise, yet complete, description of the assessment information. To the extent possible, all available information about the reader should be displayed on a cover sheet (see Figure 15.6). This includes identifying information such as name, age, school, and so on. It should also clearly indicate the date of the report, who has prepared the report, and who administered the tests (if this was different). The date and source of the report should be easy to find. Remember, these reports end up in files, and often follow students for some time. It can be both irritating and confusing to find a report in a file and to be unable to tell when the results were generated.

Previous results may be included on the cover sheet when they are recent and the data are useful in the total report (e.g., a recent psychological report, an existing IEP, etc.; see Appendix A). In such cases, both the examiner and the date of testing should be clearly labeled. School achievement test data can be provided

FIGURE 15.5
Diagnostic
Case Report
Format

Cover Sheet(s)
 Identifying information for student
 Name of reporter and date of report
 Summary of assessment results

Background Information
 Reason for referral
 Distinctive developmental history
 School history
 Results of initial student, parent,
  teacher interviews

Summary of Assessment Results
 Reader factors (areas discussed as
 appropriate for individual):
  Emergent literacy development
  Word recognition
  Vocabulary
  Comprehension
  Studying
  Writing
  Integrated discussion of results
 Instructional factors
  Results of classroom/other
   observation
  Analysis of text and task
   demands

Diagnostic Teaching
 Strategies
 Results

Diagnostic Statement
 Summarize major findings
 Summarize reader's strengths/
  weaknesses
 Note factors that influence
  performance (peaks/valleys)

Suggestions for Instruction
 Content of instruction
 Delivery of instruction
 Materials
 Level of support

Other Suggestions/Recommendations
 Home involvement
 Additional assessment
 Special placement

as well, when they demonstrate a pattern or are relevant to the referral or the summary.

The remainder of the cover sheet involves presenting both formal and informal data in brief numerical or descriptive form. This serves two purposes. First, the report reader can get an overview of what has been done and what pattern of results is emerging without reading the entire report. Second, it eliminates the need to include extensive numerical data in the body of the report, thus focusing attention on the interpretation of these results.

Describe Background Information

This section should open with a clear statement about who referred the student for special evaluation and instruction, and the reason for this referral. The content of the remainder of this section of the report will vary. For some students, it is important to describe rather extensive amounts of relevant background information. Critical aspects of health history, notable school factors, or particularly disruptive emotional incidents would all need to be included. There are other students for whom this section is brief, since there are no factors that seem related to the reading/writing difficulties. In these cases, simply noting that the student's development appears normal and the school history uneventful should be appropriate.

It is also helpful to convey in this background section both the student's and

FIGURE 15.6

Cover Sheet

Confidential Diagnostic Report

NAME Marvin B.   DATE December 27, 1988

EXAMINER Majorie Y. Lipson, Ph.D.

NAME OF PARENT/GUARDIAN Joan and Phillip B.

ADDRESS 15 East View   PHONE 923-6570

         Lakeville, VT   BIRTHDATE _____

SCHOOL Apple Elementary School   AGE 11   GRADE 5

         Lakeville, Vermont

Previous Test Information

WISC-R (Administered 4/88 by M. Hawkins, Psychologist):

     Verbal: 109   Performance: 114   Full scale: 112

Metropolitan Achievement Tests (Administered 4/88, 4th grade)

Total Reading:	37th percentile (4th stanine)
Word Identification:	23rd percentile (3rd stanine)
Comprehension:	45th percentile (5th stanine)

Summary of Assessment Results

Woodcock Reading Mastery (Form B)	Relative Mastery	Percentile Rank
Letter Identification	93%	58
Word Identification	7%	10
Word Attack	32%	9
Word Comprehension	55%	15
Passage Comprehension	29%	8

Analytic Reading Inventory	Independent Reading Level	Instructional Reading Level	Frustrational Reading Level
Word Recognition	2	3	5–6
Oral Comprehension	2 & 3	4 & 5	6
Silent Comprehension	2–4	5	6

Classroom Reading Inventory			
Word Recognition	NA	1	2–6
Oral Comprehension	1–4 & 6	5	7
Silent Comprehension	2, 3, & 5	4	6

Burns and Roe, Informal Reading Inventory			
Word Recognition	NA	2	3–5
Oral Comprehension	NA	2	3–5
Silent Comprehension	NA	2 & 3	4 & 5

Summary

Comprehension Scores:

     Highest Instructional/Independent Level: (7-Ind, Silent)

     Lowest Instructional: 1 (Oral and Silent)

     Lowest Frustrational: 2 (Oral)

Listening Comprehension: (Analytic Reading Inventory)

     Independent: Grades 2–6; Instructional: Grade 7

Relevant Instruction Information

Grades K–1:	Conrad Elementary, Lakeville Public Schools Readiness and Primer levels of Ginn 360 (1982)
Grades 2–4:	St. Mary's School, Lakeville Vermont Basal books for Grades 2–4, synthetic phonics series
Currently:	Fifth grade, recently placed in Apple School, Lakeville Public Schools. Literature-based individualized reading program.

the family's attitude toward reading/writing activities and toward the student's particular problems. Information gleaned from interviews and from observations should be summarized here and used to support any statements made about attitudes, motivation, or the influence of correlational factors (see Figure 15.7).

Summarize the Assessment Information

The section called Summary of Assessment Results is designed to convey critical aspects of reading performance as clearly as possible. There are a number of ways to do this, and the emphasis and focus should reflect the *particular* reader being described. In some cases, the reader will be the focus of the summary and analysis; in other cases, instructional factors will loom large.

Information about the reader. This section is not designed to reiterate tests scores that have already been summarized, although these can be used when needed for clarity. Rather, it is designed to interpret and pull into clear view the overall performance patterns of the reader. As the various components of reading are discussed, all pieces of evidence about that component are described (see Figure 15.8). When the test or some aspect of the assessment task contributes strongly to the results, they should be discussed and interpreted also. In Marvin's case, this type of description was offered to help interpret the results of the various IRIs (see Figure 15.8).

It is important to point out again that the reports of specific students may vary considerably from this. Effective reporting describes the reader and focuses attention on important aspects of his or her performance. In some cases, this may be done more effectively by using subheads that parallel the various components of reading that are posing problems for that student. For example, there might appear within the Summary of Results section a subsection on Emergent Literacy Development, another on Vocabulary, and another on Word Recognition, but no separate heads for Studying or Writing, if those were less critical areas for the student.

On the other hand, the reports for other students seem to be more straightforward and coherent when the various tests are discussed and the results interpreted. This format is likely to be most helpful when the tests themselves contribute to a student's performance and a discussion of the test or assessment strategy is needed. This organization can be helpful when there are important anecdotal aspects to the student's interactions. This variability is demonstrated using a brief excerpt from another young student (see Figure 15.9).

Summarize the instructional factors. This portion is the least common in traditional reports. In some cases, it would make more sense to include observations and information about the instructional factors in the Background Section (see p. 628). In others, the information is included as a part of the discussion regarding the test results. In still other cases, it is important only to state that the instructional context has included appropriate instruction and reading experiences for the student. However, there are times when the information collected in the assessment-instruction process warrants separate commentary.

FIGURE 15.7

*Case Report:
Background
Information
Section*

Reason for Referral
Marvin has just returned to a public school setting, having been enrolled in a private parochial school for three years. Concerns about Marvin's reading abilities, expressed by both school and parents, led to a referral for reading assessment.

Observation and Interview Information
Neither Marvin's mother nor the available records suggest any remarkable health or development problems. Throughout the current series of assessment activities Marvin appeared to be an engaging, friendly, and open fifth-grade boy. His manner was quite easy-going and he appeared to have excellent self-confidence. He approached each task with vigor, never tired of the activities, and always appeared ready for the next one. He smiles easily and does not appear ruffled by even the most difficult tasks. Marvin has extraordinary stamina for reading activities, especially given his slow pace and rate.

These observations are somewhat at odds with Marvin's case history (see Confidential Psychological Report in files). Marvin's mother reports that the family has experienced significant disruption for the past two years as a result of a separation and impending divorce between Marvin's parents. A psychologist's report suggests that Marvin's reading difficulties may result from his inability to attend to school tasks and from high levels of anxiety related to these family problems. At the present time, the family appears to have settled into a more regular routine and Marvin regularly visits with his father and he reports enjoying these visits.

When asked to reflect on reading in general and his own abilities in particular, Marvin offered very little. He could neither think of anything to say about how he viewed reading nor describe what a good reader was like. With regard to his own reading ability he believes he is a "medium" reader and that his biggest problem is "understanding what I read." On the other hand, Marvin believes that people read "to learn and to get away from things." He suggests that he reads because "it's fun—but, not all the time."

Marvin exhibits enthusiastic curiosity about a wide range of topics and he brings this interest to bear on his reading. He becomes actively involved with reading, stopping to comment and/or chuckle over parts of the text. He indicated an interest in reading books with a high degree of action and humor and also said he likes to read books about his hobbies and about machines and the outdoors. He is not, however, interested in reading about American heroes, biographies, or sports. Marvin builds model cars as a hobby and he says he generally likes to "take stuff apart."

School/Instructional History
Due to family moves, Marvin attended two different schools during kindergarten and first grade. During these early years, Marvin was reported to be struggling with reading. Because his parents were concerned about his limited reading abilities after first grade, they decided to send him to a private parochial school for second grade. He remained there throughout the second, third, and fourth grades. During Marvin's fourth-grade year, his teacher reported that Marvin was experiencing serious difficulties in reading; precipitating a psychological evaluation (see file). At least partly because this private school does not have any remedial services, Marvin's parents decided to return him to the public school in their neighborhood and he was referred for reading assessment at that time.

Marvin has received reading instruction within a basal reading program since kindergarten. In Grades K–1, the program was an eclectic one published in the early 1980s and he progressed as a member of the lowest reading group. From Grades 2 through 4, he was placed in the phonics-oriented basal used in his new school. No grouping or special support was employed in this school, so he progressed through the materials at the pace determined appropriate for the whole class. The reading methods of the school appear to revolve around daily oral reading of assigned basal selections

FIGURE 15.7
(Continued)

followed by independent completion of assigned workbook pages. Neither silent reading time nor process writing activities were provided on a regular basis. Starting in fourth grade, the school used textbooks for science and social studies, although it is not clear how often students received reading assignments in these materials.

Marvin has only just been placed in the fifth grade of a public school. Although the classroom program is a literature-based individualized one, with individual work folders assigned to each student, the least-able readers are often placed in a dated basal series. The teacher is anxious to receive information about Marvin's reading abilities in order to make some instructional decisions. Oral reading occurs in this classroom during one-to-one conferences with the teacher and generally involves student-selected and prepared excerpts from books of stories. Silent reading is a daily activity although writing activities are more irregular and generally involve writing book reports and research reports.

In summary, Marvin presents himself as a vigorous, active, and undaunted boy who is remarkably at ease in new settings.

In Marvin's case, there seemed to be little point in conducting a classroom observation, since he had only just transferred to the school/classroom. Critical information about instructional history was placed here in the Background Section (see Figure 15.7). It was important to note that he had received no individualized instruction in his program and that the methodologies were quite sparse. Specific information about texts and tasks that influence Marvin's performance was placed in the Summary of Assessment Results section (see Figure 15.8).

Describe and Report the Results of Diagnostic Teaching

In this section, specific manipulations of the reading event should be described. Since diagnostic teaching is not included in most traditional assessment plans, it is important to describe briefly the purpose of such activity. The reader should understand both what was done and why this was attempted. In addition, the section should conclude with a summary that interprets the results.

In Marvin's case (see Figure 15.10), the specific procedures were developed using a framework like that described earlier (see Chapter 10). The evaluation was conducted by someone other than school personnel, and for very specific purposes. The descriptions of diagnostic teaching may be a much more substantial part of some reports. This is especially true when the reports are written after significant instructional contact (see Progress Reports, p. 635).

Provide a Diagnostic Summary Statement

This section provides a brief, coherent statement of the student's strengths and weaknesses (see Figure 15.11). In a straightforward way, the report reader is reminded of the ground that has been covered and helped to see the big picture. Because no assessment data are specifically cited here, it is especially important that there be no surprises. This is not the time to introduce new information. In addition, what is concluded in this section should be clearly related to the earlier data that were described.

FIGURE 15.8
Case Report:
Summary and
Interpretation
of Results

Summary of Assessment Results

The pattern of Marvin's performance is quite stable. An examination of the pattern of results for the various informal reading inventories (IRIs) demonstrates that his word recognition scores are consistently poor and he reaches frustrational level on word recognition at Level 3 on all three IRIs (see Cover Sheet). On the other hand, his comprehension scores are consistently higher than his word recognition scores and, on two IRIs, he does not reach frustrational level in comprehension until Grade 6 or 7.

Marvin's performance on the word analysis subtest reflects his limited ability to decode non-meaningful words out-of-context. He does, however, demonstrate adequate knowledge of the basic phonic relationships. There are two possible phonic components that may also require additional instruction: [1] consonant blends and digraphs, and [2] complex vowel combinations like "ea," "ou," and "oi." Marvin's miscues on these ("tragic" for "task," "find" for "friend," etc., and a persistent problem with "ea" words) suggest that he has not yet mastered these phonic elements. It should be noted, however, that his phonics skills *overall* appear to be adequate except as he fails to apply these skills to multisyllabic words.

An analysis of Marvin's miscues (see Chapter 5) demonstrates the large number of word recognition difficulties he experiences during reading. Many of these miscues appear on high-frequency sight words ("the" for "our," "and" for "the," "the" for "her," etc.). Thus, it would appear that Marvin needs continued opportunities to practice these high-frequency words. Many of Marvin's remaining miscues involve word endings — inflectional endings and suffixes (for example: "safe" for "safer," "means" for "meant," "quick" for "quickly," etc.). Marvin consistently deletes such endings, and occasionally adds endings not present. There is also evidence that Marvin has underdeveloped syllabication skills ("engenical" for "energetic," "detoof" for "develop," etc.) and it would appear that direct instruction in structural analysis as a word recognition strategy would be helpful to Marvin.

The disparity between his word recognition and comprehension performance is substantial. Marvin demonstrated good to excellent comprehension of most materials read. He was able to answer questions following both oral and silent reading with ease and he appears capable of answering a broad range of question types. Analysis of his rate of self-correction and the proportion of meaningful miscues (see Chapter 5) provide additional evidence of Marvin's substantial comprehension abilities. His rate of self-correction is extremely high (especially at lower levels), suggesting that he actively monitors his reading progress and attempts to construct meaning from text. Indeed, when his rate of self-correction is coupled with the percentage of meaningful miscues (i.e., the "error" does not affect the meaning of the text), it becomes apparent how impressive Marvin's efforts to understand really are. He rarely produces nonsensical substitutions or "wild guesses" and, often, his substitutions could go undetected since they do not significantly affect the meaning of the selection.

Though Marvin's comprehension abilities are quite robust (note the overall pattern of performance), he also demonstrates differential ability across the texts and tasks. [Note both his "peak" — silent reading on the CRI (instructional at Grade 7) and his "valley" (frustrational comprehension at Grade 3 on the oral reading Burns and Roe)]. It is obvious that the Burns and Roe passages were more difficult for him than any others. In fact, if only the Burns and Roe IRI had been administered, it would have appeared that limited power and automaticity in decoding skills was the sole source of his comprehension problems, so that as decoding accuracy decreased, so did comprehension.

This explanation obviously cannot account for Marvin's performance at other times. His performance on the other two IRIs in fact suggests exactly the opposite — that comprehension ability drives his reading efforts and that he is likely to perform poorly

FIGURE 15.8
(Continued)

overall only when the reading process cannot be driven from a position of understanding. Marvin's weakest performance occurred while reading several rather ambiguous texts in the Burns and Roe IRI. Two are set in a foreign country and are guided almost entirely by a type of lyrical internal response structure. All three are fragments from longer texts and none have a very strong story structure. While Marvin often understood all the relevant explicit information in these texts, he did not always make the inferences necessary to answer the question. Thus, while neither the type of text (exposition versus narrative) nor the type and number of questions significantly affect Marvin's performance, other factors such as coherence and conformity to expected story structures did. The diagnostic teaching pursued with Marvin supports this conclusion and this segment of the assessment is described in the next section.

The diagnostic statement should synthesize information across the various assessment and instructional contexts. The results of the diagnostic teaching are embedded to inform the conclusions drawn. The summary statement should contain enough information to function as an overview of the entire report so that individuals who cannot read or reread the whole document can read an accurate statement that captures the reading process for that student/client.

Describe Recommendations for Instruction
In this section, the specific implications for instruction are described. Again, there should be no surprises here. Suggestions for improving word identification cannot be offered when no evidence for a problem in this area was provided earlier. There should be a clear link between the assessment portions of the report and these instructional suggestions.

There are several types of instructional advice that can be offered in this section, both of which are evident in Marvin's report (see Figure 15.12). Suggestions often include ideas for shaping reading instruction and/or offering instructional support (Recommendations 1, 3, and 4). Of course, instructional recommendations should also specify the component areas of reading to be emphasized in instruction (Recommendations 2 and 3).

Other suggestions for instruction may involve naming particular instructional strategies or techniques (Recommendation 3). In these cases, it is important to make sure that teachers reading the report are familiar with the techniques. If there is any doubt about the familiarity of the method, strategy, or text suggested, the information should be provided as a part of the report. This can be done in the body of the report for brief recommendations. For instructional techniques that require greater additional explanation, an appendix works best.

Note Any Additional Suggestions and/or Recommendations (Optional)
There are times when the reading professional completes an assessment and is aware that there is more to be done. Often, it would be desirable to collect information from other professional sources. For example, medical services may be needed to explore health, vision, or auditory contributions to the reading

FIGURE 15.9
Excerpt from Summary and Interpretation of Assessment

Jason, February, Grade 2

The scores on the Woodcock Reading Mastery Test placed Jason at or near the 2.1 grade level on all subtests. Errors on the Letter Identification section occurred, for the most part, because he had not yet been introduced to cursive writing. On the Word Identification section, Jason's errors showed high similarity to the printed form (farm/from, sheep/sleep). The Word Attack subtest provided some insight into Jason's analysis skills. He read 12 of 27 nonsense words correctly. Of the 15 errors, 13 had the same initial and final sound as the stimulus word. Jason misread all medial portions of the words. On the Word Comprehension subtest, Jason remarked that he could not read the words so he could not figure out the answers. Of the 15 errors on this section, Jason made no attempt or said, "I don't know" to 10 of the items. Even though Jason was given the direction to read each item on the Passage Comprehension section to himself, he read all items out loud. As the passages got more difficult, Jason read to himself with lip movement.

The Bader Informal Reading Inventory contributed important information concerning Jason's reading performance. His word recognition and independent oral reading level of pre-primer and his instructional level of primer to second grade place him at or below his present second-grade class placement. A high percentage of Jason's miscues were structurally similar to the story word (meal/mail; hurt/hit). He made few attempts to self-correct for meaning. For example, he read, "She saw that her leg was hard" and did not correct it to the print version: "She saw that her leg was hurt."

difficulties. Alternatively, it might be concluded that a psychologist and/or special educator should become involved to determine eligibility for special services. Referrals to other professionals should be done generally; specific recommendations should be avoided.

The reporter may also wish to recommend that the student receive additional support services. Again, the nature and/or duration of the support should be described, but the report should avoid recommending specific sources of service. The obvious exception is the case where the person reporting is also responsible for delivering the type of service recommended (as in special school programs).

Finally, it is often desirable to specify what types of activities would be appropriate in the home environment (see Figure 15.13). It is not possible to ensure home involvement and support, but parents often welcome specific suggestions for helping their children. We often attach some parent information to each report, since many parents are unaware of the importance of some simple ways they can help. Tips about reading to children, local sources of good books, guidelines for controlling TV watching, and directions for supporting students with specific techniques are generally welcomed.

Progress Reports

The procedures described above are appropriate for an initial and complete diagnostic assessment. Students often become involved in special programs or receive special instructional services as the result of such reports. In such cases, periodic reports may be very desirable, but there is no need to write such a

**FIGURE
15.10**

*Case Report:
Diagnostic
Teaching*

Diagnostic Teaching

In order to clarify Marvin's problem, diagnostic teaching was attempted with him. Diagnostic teaching involves manipulating the assessment process in any of a number of ways. The purpose of manipulating the assessment process is twofold: to collect additional information to clarify and test the hypotheses about Marvin's reading problems, and to try out potential methods of instruction.

Marvin clearly needs additional decoding skills and a great deal of attention directed toward increasing his automaticity. Marvin's strength is comprehension. However, his performance in comprehension was not universally strong and it was in this area that more information might be useful.

Because he had performed poorly on the Burns and Roe IRI, these selections were used in the diagnostic teaching. Marvin had reached frustration level on a selection without a title that dealt with a young boy's concern about a test. The main idea of this selection was subtle and Marvin constructed a different main theme for the selection. Marvin also asked several questions related to the main theme. It seemed likely that Marvin might be able to understand challenging material if some organizational support were provided. Therefore, he was asked to reread the selection, this time imagining that the story was entitled, ''Peter Worries About a Test.'' Given that much support, Marvin answered all the questions posed correctly and was able, in addition, to provide a coherent and accurate summary of the selection. The exercise was repeated with two other selections and each time Marvin was totally successful in his comprehension efforts. Given a general idea of the topic, Marvin has no difficulty linking ideas, locating information, or supporting inferential conclusions.

It is clear that Marvin's forte involves responding to questions after reading coherent or well-structured text (even when his percentage of miscues is extremely high). However, Marvin also will need to be able to comprehend text on his own. Thus, a final activity was employed. Marvin was asked to silently read a very lengthy (5-page) narrative story written at the high third/low fourth-grade readability and to do a retelling of the story. Marvin appeared very interested in the selection and launched into the retelling with enthusiasm. Despite this obvious interest, Marvin's reconstruction of the story left out vital events and concepts and his recount involved no sound sequence. In addition, his recount failed to name the important characters, to identify their problem in the story, or to accurately identify the final solution to the problem. On the other hand, when Marvin was asked specific questions about the selection, he was able to demonstrate a far clearer understanding of the text or, perhaps more accurately, he was able to use the questions asked to *re*-organize his understanding of the story.

---

comprehensive diagnostic report. The format for progress reports is somewhat different, with a focus on instruction rather than assessment (see Figure 15.14).

The first two sections of a Progress Report are almost identical to a Diagnostic Report. Only minor variations in the cover sheet and background information components are obvious. For example, the Cover Sheet may include both test and retest information. Since the Progress Report is written after some period of instructional intervention, it is important to date and note this information carefully. Similarly, the Background Information component may contain information that has been gathered over a considerable period of time. Thus, it is important to note if an observation was made early in the program or was made more recently.

In a Progress Report, one of the most important components is the Diagnostic

FIGURE
15.11
*Case Report:
Diagnostic
Summary*

Diagnostic Summary

Marvin has a great many strengths, not the least of which is his interest in reading and his obvious enjoyment of it. Marvin makes an excellent showing in silent reading comprehension, especially as measured by ability to answer questions. In addition, Marvin has good to excellent memory skills which he uses to aid his understanding. He uses all pre-reading information (introductory statements, for example) to the greatest possible extent to drive his reading efforts. In addition, Marvin actively attends to his reading. He self-corrects frequently, does not produce "wild guesses," and is able to respond effectively to what he reads. He uses context very effectively to aid his word recognition and to derive meaning from text.

Marvin has serious word recognition difficulties, including limited sight-word recognition. He also has difficulty reading multisyllabic words and has not acquired a strategy for coping with words that require structural analysis (including syllabication). He also demonstrates limited ability to apply knowledge of consonant blends and digraphs and vowel digraphs and dipthongs. He will need to improve his word recognition skills if he is not to be overwhelmed by lengthy reading assignments, since his lack of automaticity slows him down.

While comprehension is generally a strength for Marvin, his ability to impose structure and meaning on longer, denser, or less-considerate text is limited. He seems to lack experience reading different types of materials. In addition he has had limited opportunities to read for a variety of purposes or for different tasks.

Marvin is capable of handling much of the material at his grade level, although he will not sound fluent in oral reading situations. His performance is improved significantly when relevant pre-reading supports are provided. Narrative selections are easier for Marvin to read than expository ones. In addition, dense, poorly organized texts of all types are more difficult for him to read and should be avoided wherever possible.

Summary. This section should be written carefully, because it essentially provides the rationale for the instructional program that is described. This brief, accurate, and focused statement is usually not more than a page in length. It may refer to earlier assessments (by date and examiner) but should not be viewed as a complete diagnostic report.

The Summary of the Instructional Program is also a critical component of the Progress Report. It should describe exactly what was done and why. The excerpt in Figure 15.15 demonstrates how instructional goals are linked to specific activities. These activities are either described in the body of the report or descriptions can be provided in an appendix. If there were changes in the instructional program, these should be noted also. It is obviously quite common for student progress to occur that results in refocusing the program or changing the activities. The rationale for program decisions should be carefully described.

The Summary of Progress section should contain a description of the student's reading performance at the current time. Quantitative and/or qualitative evidence should be provided regarding areas of improvement. In addition, there should be clear descriptions of the types of texts, tasks, or skills that require continued attention. Finally, the report should contain recommendations about changes in instructional focus, the desirability of continued reading support services, and the need for continued support at home.

FIGURE 15.12

Case Report: Recommendations for Instruction

Recommendations

Marvin is a very able, hard-working, eager boy who should progress in reading if offered the opportunity. It is entirely possible that his history (see Confidential Psychological Report in school files) has slowed his progress in reading and that he is currently in a position to take advantage of some remedial help.

1. Marvin needs to have his reading assignments structured for him. Wherever possible, pre-reading questions will help Marvin significantly. In addition, visual story "maps," structured overviews, etc. would be very helpful to Marvin, and he should be able to learn to construct them for himself in a very short time.

2. Some direct instruction in structural analysis skills (specifically, syllabication and recognizing suffixes) is essential. This instruction should be coupled with a reminder to Marvin that he can employ his rather good phonics skills after he has analyzed the structure of the words (thus, this provides the opportunity for review in phonics as well). Since Marvin enjoys "taking things apart," he should be able to employ these skills to good effect once he understands how this will aid his reading.

3. Marvin could benefit from a holistic approach to his word recognition problems. I would recommend two strategies for Marvin (as opposed to more isolated work in phonics or word recognition): [a] Repeated Readings Approach, or its variation, the Talking Dictionary; and [b] taped read-alongs requiring Marvin to read in a book along with an oral rendition that has been taped for him. Several commercial companies produce good tape-book combinations. The Neurological Impress (NIM) might also be a good approach to use with Marvin in a tutorial or other one-on-one setting.

4. Every effort should be made to sustain Marvin's positive attitude and cooperation in any remedial program. At the moment he has an excellent approach to reading and school and he should be encouraged to develop his substantial strengths.

FIGURE 15.13

Case Report: General Recommendations

Additional Recommendations

Marvin could benefit from additional individualized or small group instruction. A tutorial or clinical setting would be beneficial to him. Additional testing does not, however, seem necessary at this time.

At home, Marvin should set aside a short period each day for silent reading. Marvin's mother reads regularly herself and might consider setting aside a "family reading time" each evening. It might be helpful if Marvin were encouraged to read aloud (after practice) to his younger brother and sister as well.

Marvin could also benefit from doing the Talking Dictionary at home several times a week. This should be a relaxed, enjoyable time for both Marvin and whomever he is reading with. Family participation in word and memory games could be helpful to Marvin. Games such as Scrabble and Memory could increase Marvin's word analysis skills. Finally, Marvin should be encouraged to write as often as possible. Letters and notes to family and friends should be actively encouraged. He might also be charged with making lists of activities and notes to remind family members of special events.

Marjorie Y. Lipson, Ph.D.   Date

**FIGURE
15.14**
*Progress
Report Format*

Cover Sheet(s)
Identifying information for student
Name of reporter and date of report
Summary of existing assessment
  information
Summary of new or retest
  information

Background Information
Summary of relevant referral
  information
Summary of continuing observation
  or interview data

Diagnostic Summary
Brief summary of relevant
  assessment information
Conclusions re: major instructional
  implications

Summary of Instructional Program
Description of instructional goals
Description of instructional activities/
  program

Summary of Progress
Description of areas of improvement
  (with evidence)
Description of areas that remain
  problematic

Recommendations
Further intervention and instructional
  programs
Parental support

Conferences

Conferences are a common format for reporting to others. They differ somewhat from other forms of reporting because they are generally less formal. The skills and strategies for conducting interviews (see Chapter 3) are helpful in conducting conferences. Whereas the purpose of an interview is to gather information, the purpose of a conference is to report or clarify information.

As in all forms of reporting, there are a variety of reasons why conferences are conducted. For example, reading professionals are frequently expected to confer with classroom teachers, administrators, and other specialized professionals about the abilities or progress of individual students. Reading professionals are also often expected to participate in formal conferences like those conducted for IEP hearings. And, of course, there are usually regularly scheduled conferences for parents.

The different types of conferences are likely to be focused on slightly different issues, and often require slightly different skills. A conference with a classroom teacher sometimes involves specific issues about which there has been ongoing communication prior to the conference. Perhaps, for example, the classroom teacher and the reading teacher have been keeping an eye on the progress of one young girl, ''Krista.'' They have set a conference time to examine all the pieces of information they have about her and to review her progress and performance in the classroom. As a result, they may decide to continue observing, or they may decide that Krista should be evaluated more fully by the reading professional.

Conferences can also focus on solving problems or sharing perceptions. The classroom teacher may report, for example, that ''Jay'' is having trouble with some task in the classroom. The conference may involve:

- evaluating the appropriateness of that task for the child
- examining the task itself
- other evidence that the child has problems in a particular area

**FIGURE
15.15**
*Excerpt from
Summary of
Instructional
Program*

Much of Jason's instruction this term has focused on two main areas: foundation skills, designed to help him see the purposes of reading, and comprehension. Comprehension activities were designed to help Jason see reading as a process of getting meaning from text and to help him acquire strategies for understanding.

The Think Aloud activity has been used several times with Jason to encourage more active comprehension. The first time he did this activity, it was clear that word recognition greatly affected his performance. He offered very little in response to the initial prompt of, "What were you doing and thinking as you read that part?" Jason's main concern centered around how well he was going to read. Since then, Jason's responses to prompts have been more focused on comprehension. He prefaces his responses with, "Well, I was thinking about . . ." or, "That makes sense." Recently, during a Think Aloud selection, when he was asked what he had been doing or thinking as he read, Jason responded: "I wasn't thinking about nothing, but I made a picture in my mind about a cave with stone pictures." When he was asked if he had to think to make a picture in his mind, Jason paused and said, "Yeah—I guess I do think!"

- developing ways to work on this problem in the reading support program,
- developing ways to address the problem in the regular classroom

Reading professionals and administrators sometimes confer about specific children. This may happen because a parent has expressed concern to the principal, because the principal has observed the child in some context, or because the reading professional is concerned. More often, though, conferences with administrators focus on issues of program administration, budget, testing policies, or requests for professional evaluations of new methods or materials.

Particular care must be taken when conferring with parents. Parents can react emotionally to information about their children, and this may prevent them from receiving the information as you intended. It is important to help parents understand the significance of what you are saying. In addition, you should always be sensitive to different cultural modes of interacting. Every effort should be made to communicate in the language most comfortable to the parents and to use interactional styles appropriate to them. If that is not possible, then it will be important to maintain contact and to follow up on any requests for parental action.

It is important to provide clear, concise information during a conference. It is also important to listen carefully and attend to the other individual(s). Be especially alert to the possibility that the parent or teacher has not clearly understood what you are saying. Also be sure to request new or additional information about the student or the situation. Finally, be sure to enlist the support of these individuals. Be as specific as possible about the ways that they can help.

FROM CLASSROOM TO CLINIC

Like all those who work with people, reading professionals must be careful to attend to their ethical responsibilities. Since reading professionals often work with young or vulnerable people, these responsibilities must be taken particularly seriously. The International Reading Association Code of Ethics (see Figure 15.16)

FIGURE 15.16
IRA Code of Ethics

The members of the International Reading Association who are concerned with the teaching of reading form a group of professional persons obligated to society and devoted to the service and welfare of individuals through teaching, clinical services, research, and publication. The members of this group are committed to values which are the foundation of a democratic society—freedom to teach, write, and study in an atmosphere conducive to the best interests of the profession. The welfare of the public, the profession, and the individuals concerned should be of primary consideration in recommending candidates for degrees, positions, advancements, the recognition of professional activity, and for certification in those areas where certification exists.

Ethical Standards in Professional Relationships

1. It is the obligation of all members of the International Reading Association to observe the Code of Ethics of the organization and to act accordingly so as to advance the status and prestige of the Association and of the profession as a whole. Members should assist in establishing the highest professional standards for reading programs and services, and should enlist support for these through dissemination of pertinent information to the public.

2. It is the obligation of all members to maintain relationships with other professional persons, striving for harmony, avoiding personal controversy, encouraging cooperative effort, and making known the obligations and services rendered by professionals in reading.

3. It is the obligation of members to report results of research and other developments in reading.

4. Members should not claim nor advertise affiliation with the International Reading Association as evidence of their competence in reading.

Ethical Standards in Reading Services

1. Professionals in reading must possess suitable qualifications for engaging in consulting, clinical, or remedial work. Unqualified persons should not engage in such activities except under the direct supervision of one who is properly qualified. Professional intent and the welfare of the person seeking services should govern all consulting or clinical activities such as counseling, administering diagnostic tests, or providing remediation. It is the duty of the professional in reading to keep relationships with clients and interested persons on a professional level.

2. Information derived from consulting and/or clinical services should be regarded as confidential. Expressed consent of persons involved should be secured before releasing information to outside agencies.

3. Professionals in reading should recognize the boundaries of their competence and should not offer services which fail to meet professional standards established by other disciplines. They should be free, however, to give assistance in other areas in which they are qualified.

4. Referral should be made to specialists in allied fields as needed. When such referral is made, pertinent information should be made available to consulting specialists.

5. Reading clinics and/or reading professionals offering services should refrain from guaranteeing easy solutions or favorable outcomes as a result of their work, and their advertising should be consistent with that of allied professions. They should not accept for remediation any persons who are unlikely to benefit from their instruction, and they should work to accomplish the greatest possible improvement in the shortest time. Fees, if charged, should be agreed on in advance and should be charged in accordance with an established set of rates commensurate with that of other professions.

Breaches of the Code of Ethics should be reported to IRA Headquarters for referral to the Committee on Professional Standards and Ethics for an impartial investigation.

IRA Code of Ethics, *The Reading Teacher,* November 1987, p. 143. Reprinted by permission of the International Reading Association.

should be given careful consideration by all reading professionals. The portion regarding ethical standards in reading services has critical implications for teachers and clinicians who work with disabled readers.

This statement conveys most of what we believe to be important professional conduct, but there are two other responsibilities that we believe reading professionals should shoulder. First, reading professionals should be advocates for students and their families. This means ensuring that parents and clients understand forms they must sign, and that those who cannot read are provided with information to make informed decisions about their programs and options.

Being an advocate involves much more, of course. It means insisting that inadequate programs are revised, that misleading test results be reconsidered, and that instructional programs respond to students' needs. It means being concerned with issues of equity, funding, and politics. Clearly, this is not easy, and an in-depth discussion is beyond the scope of this text. However, disabled readers often need strong voices, and the families of poor readers frequently need an advocate as well. Institutions are not always responsive to the needs of individuals; reading professionals must be, to the fullest extent possible.

A second responsibility that reading professionals should accept is the responsibility to remain current regarding developments and research in the field. They must make a commitment to read and communicate about the important advances and techniques available. In doing so, they should advance high standards in assessment and instruction for all students. We opened this book with a section entitled Why Theory? We close with an admonishment to continue in the areas of professional growth and development, since there is every reason to believe that the field will remain dynamic for several years to come. New information, better practice, and fresh approaches are all likely to emerge. The effective reading professional must take as an ethical responsibility the responsibility to be informed.

CHAPTER SUMMARY

In the first section of this chapter we described the various roles that reading professionals are expected to perform. These range from direct instructional contact with students to consultative roles with teachers. We noted that these critical roles all share a common requirement for effective communication. We argued that reading teachers must be able to interact with a wide array of people, sharing information and advocating effective assessment and instructional practices.

We described several modes for reporting including summaries of portfolios and the most formal type of communication, case reports. We detailed the contents of a formal case report, using the case of Marvin (see earlier chapters) to exemplify each section. These sections include descriptions of background information, summaries of assessment information, descriptions and reports of the results of diagnostic teaching, a diagnostic summary statement, and recommendations for instruction. In addition to formal case reports, we described progress reports, noting the similarities and differences between various reporting forms. Finally, we described the role of conferences in the reporting process.

In the final portion of this chapter, we presented the International Reading Association Code of Ethics. Several aspects of this code were elaborated to focus on issues of particular importance to professionals who work with reading-disabled students.

Sample Case Report: Seth

COLLEGE OF EDUCATION READING CLINIC
PROGRESS REPORT

Name: Seth C.   *Date of Report:* May 19, 1986
Address: Route 390
       Pleasantville, Vermont
Phone: 624-0111
Birthdate: 6/26/76
Age: 9 years   *Grade:* 3 (R1)   *School Name:* Pleasantville Elementary
School Address: Pleasantville, Vermont
Parent's/Guardian's Name: Mr. & Mrs. C.
Tutor: W. Jorgan

Attendance for Tutoring
   A. *Times present:* 12
   B. *Times absent:* 12
   C. *Reasons for absences:* NA
   D. *Attitude toward tutoring:* Seth appears highly motivated to work hard in
      those areas where he feels he is competent and/or where he is succeeding.
      Seth appears tired much of the time. He yawned several times during the
      classroom observation and yawns and rubs his eyes three to five times
      during each clinic session. Seth is an open and friendly child who smiles
      often, is animated in discussions, makes eye contact when working with
      the examiner, and likes to laugh.

SUMMARY OF ASSESSMENT RESULTS

Dolch Word List (2-27-86)	*Recognized 192/220*
Post Test (4-24-86)	*Recognized 196/220*
Peabody Picture Vocabulary	
Test (form M)	*Standard Score Equivalent: 95*
Date of Testing: 2-13-86	*Percentile Rank: 37*
Age: 9 years, 8 months	*Age Equivalent: 8 years, 11 months*
El Paso Phonics Survey	*Frustrational level errors: 2.9*
Date of Testing: 2-20-86	*Level 1.9 errors: 19/30*
Post Test (4-24-86)	*Retest of skills taught at grade 1.9:*
	22/30 correct
Analytical Reading Inventory	
by Mary Lynn Woods and	*Instructional: primer-1*
Alden J. Moe	*Frustrational: 2*
Date of Testing: 2-6-86	*Hearing Capacity: 2*
Durrell Analysis of Reading Difficulty:	
Visual Memory of Words Subtest	
Date of Testing: 2-20-86	*Low second grade*

Auditory Discrimination of Pairs (Bader)
    Date of Testing: 2-13-86   *29/30 items correct (competent)*
Hearing Letter Names in Sounds (Bader)
    Date of Testing: 2-13-86   *912 items correct (competent)*
Woodcock Reading Mastery Tests (Form B)

	Relative Mastery	Percentile Rank
Letter Identification	93%	58
Word Identification	7%	10
Word Attack	32%	9
Word Comprehension	55%	15
Passage Comprehension	29%	8

Specific Areas of Reading Difficulty: Despite a reading expectancy of 4.1, Seth demonstrates difficulty in skills taught as early as first grade. Specific areas needing attention are vowels, reversals, visual discrimination, blending, sight words, fluency in oral reading, the graphemes *g, ch, sch, sp, str, squ, spl, qu,* and *s,* ending consonant sounds, and comprehension strategies.

BACKGROUND INFORMATION

Reason for Referral
Seth's reading level is considerably below his grade placement. The Chapter I reading teacher in Seth's school requested that Seth be tested for further data and insight.

Family and Medical History
Seth lives at home with both parents, who are farmers. When asked to tell the examiner something about himself, the first thing Seth mentioned was that he lived on a farm. At the beginning of nearly every clinic session, when asked how he's been doing, Seth invariably tells a story about something that has happened on the farm. Seth's primary interest beyond the farm is his four-wheeler; the friend he plays with most is a 12-year-old from down the road with whom he rides his four-wheeler. Seth has mentioned special days he has spent in the fields and woods as well.

    Seth says that he doesn't like television that much; he says that he doesn't like "being cooped up" and would rather play outside. He watches television about 1/2 hour after school and 1 to 1 1/2 hours in the evenings—usually movies on his VCR.

    Seth indicated that no one in his family reads and that only occasionally does either his mother or his sister read to him. Despite this, there is obvious concern about Seth's reading difficulties on the part of the family, and the commitment that they have made to drive him the considerable distance to the clinic each week is indicative of this. In addition, the interview with Seth's mother and sister revealed that despite Seth's contention that he does not read at home, he has been reading as part of a Pizza Hut promotion, his family is aware of his favorite kind of book, he does read a farm journal occasionally, and he receives *Humpty-Dumpty* magazine.

Seth was 11½ pounds at birth and several weeks late. Forceps were used as a result of a difficult delivery, pinching nerves in his left arm. It is shorter than the right arm, and because of a lack of motility, he receives physical therapy. Beyond this, Seth's health has been normal except for a series of ear infections suffered during his first year in the first grade. Tubes were inserted to rectify his problems.

Seth goes to bed between 8:00 and 8:30 on weeknights and gets up at 7:00. He goes to sleep with the radio playing.

School History and Teacher Comments

Seth is in a third-grade classroom with Mrs. Garvey, an experienced teacher who replaced Seth's regular teacher when the latter went on maternity leave in February. Seth repeated first grade after a difficult year of health and academic problems. Mr. Williams, the Chapter I reading teacher with whom Seth works, feels that the phonetic approach used by Seth's teacher that first year was inappropriate, given Seth's ear problems. Presently, Seth receives help from Mr. Williams in reading and math.

Mrs. Garvey reports that Seth seems much younger than the other children in the class and that he sometimes asks questions or makes comments that are "babyish"; she says at times even the other children react negatively to his immaturity. She feels that Seth acts "cute" when he can't do something or wants help. Seth is required to complete all assigned tasks before going out to recess. Mrs. Garvey reports that he really likes recess and doesn't like to miss it.

SUMMARY OF ASSESSMENT RESULTS

Reader Factors

On the Metropolitan Achievement Tests (most recently administered in Seth's school in the fall of 1985), Seth scored in the first percentile in reading comprehension. No other subtest scores were available.

Seth underwent an extensive psychoeducational evaluation in November, 1985, at the request of the Special Educator at his school. The results of the Wechsler Intelligence Scale for Children—Revised (WISC) indicate a Full Scale score of 88. Results of the Bender Visual Motor Gestalt Test and the Visual Aural Digit Span Test appear to demonstrate a preference for visual processing; however, his score on the former reflects a slightly more than one-year delay, and his scores on visual processing subtests of the latter placed him in the 25th to 50th percentile.

Seth's standard score equivalent on the Peabody Picture Vocabulary Test (PPVT) was 95, and, consistent with the WISC-R results, his score places Seth in the low-average to average range of ability.

Observations made by the examiner during the administration of the Analytic Reading Inventory indicate that Seth only sporadically attempts to construct meaning from the text. On a primer-level selection, Seth omitted the word "I" at the beginning of three different sentences, rendering them semantically and syntactically incorrect. Other miscues as early as the primer level reflect an inattention to meaning; for example, "I can run as fast as a turn (train)."

Some miscues, however, do reflect an effort on Seth's part to construct meaning from the passage. This was particularly evident on a passage about a boy's dog being hit by a car. "Hit" was misread as "hurt" twice, "pup lying" became "puppy laying," and "badly hurt" was misread as "belly hurt." On this selection, Seth's miscues (16) rendered a score of frustrational level. However, he had only two comprehension errors, both of which may be construed as logical, based on Seth's experience. When asked how the child felt seeing his pet hurt, Seth answered "sad" (the correct answer being "scared"). In answer to the question "What does the child say to make you think he loved the dog?" Seth answered, "I'll hurry right home" (to get help for the dog). The writers of the inventory consider the answer to be "Shep is my best friend."

The nature of many of Seth's miscues on this story and his level of comprehension appear to be a result of the structure and content of the story. Both primer-level selections and one of the first-grade passages appear to begin in the middle of stories; they lack a strong structure and interesting plot. The story about the dog getting hit by a car (Level 2) had no clear resolution, but elements of the story (i.e., the subject, the clear statement of a problem, Seth's ability to relate to a child with a hurt pet) may have encouraged him to construct meaning from it. Seth's other strong comprehension performance was on a Level 1 passage with a clear story line (about a child who brings home stray animals) and a conclusion (his mother puts a halt to it). Not only did Seth answer four out of six questions competently, he retold the story in detail and made a well-formulated statement of the main idea.

Despite Seth's performance on the second-grade passage about the hurt dog, the examiner weighed the large number of miscues (16) as well as his comprehension on a second-grade passage that he read silently (42%) to determine this level as frustrational. Seth's listening level was determined by weighing his answers to traditional postreading questions and the quality of his retellings. Seth was tested at the third-grade level twice. In both cases, he answered a percentage of questions correctly, which placed this level on the instructional/frustrational border for him. However, his retellings in both cases lacked organization and missed the main ideas. Based on this, the examiner determined Seth's instructional listening level to be second-grade.

Analysis of Seth's miscues reveals strong attention to initial letters, i.e., *hit-hurt* (with any pair of words or phrases listed in this case report, the first word or phrase will represent the text and the second will represent Seth's word calling). Other miscues demonstrate use of both beginning and ending sounds (*drop-drip, thud-tried, anyway-always*). Seth also appears to rearrange letters in the medial portions of words to create new words (*felt-flat, still-sitting, train-turn*). Miscues on the Word Identification subtest of the Woodcock Reading Mastery Tests (WRMT) reflect these patterns as well (*grow-grew, happen-hope, heart-hurt*).

Except for the Letter Identification subtest, all of the other subtests of the WRMT indicate that Seth is far below the norm in these tasks. Seth's Word Comprehension score reveals this as an area of some strength. Seth's only errors prior to reaching a ceiling level were with analogies in which Seth could not read one or more of the words. For diagnostic purposes, the examiner gave Seth those words. In all cases, Seth was able to complete the analogies. The results of the Passage Comprehension subtest confirm observations made by the examiner during clinic sessions. The cloze exercise requiring Seth to use context to determine the meanings of words is especially difficult for him.

Word analysis skills were tested with two different instruments. The results of both the Word Attack subtest of the WRMT and the El Paso Phonics Survey indicate difficulties in a number of decoding skills. The validity of tests requiring children to read nonsense words has been questioned, and indeed, Seth did miscall a number of the nonsense words as legitimate words. A second weakness of the testing situation—the tendency for Seth's eyes to wander to letters above and below the word which he was reading—was eliminated when the El Paso Phonics Survey was readministered with the words written on cards.

Despite the drawbacks of these kinds of tests, the skill difficulties that surfaced consistently are worth noting. Although Seth is capable of reading the phonograms *up, in,* and *am,* in 4 out of 22 cases he had difficulty blending one of these with an initial consonant. Vowels, both long and short, surfaced as an area of weakness for Seth on the Word Attack subtest of the WRMT. Other error patterns include adding an *m* before a final *p* (*shup-shump*), changing the initial sound entirely despite a correct pronunciation of it prior to word analysis (*quam-cume*), adding ending consonants (*blin-blant*), and separating the letters of blends (*plip-pilip*). It should be noted, however, that Seth performed accurately on 26/32 blends taught as late as Grade 3.5.

The Visual Memory subtest of the Durrell Analysis of Reading Difficulty (DARD) reveals a weakness in visual memory and discrimination (level attained: low second-grade). This weakness is evident in other areas of Seth's reading. The reading inventory miscues noted earlier which appear to be a rearrangement of letters (*felt-flat*), as well as several on the Dolch Word List (*could-cloud*), may be evidence of a visual memory problem, as are miscues such as *plip-pilip*. Seth says he prefers to read with his finger underlining the words; he missed entire lines on the reading inventories, thus adding additional support to the suggestion that he has difficulty with visual discrimination and tracking.

The Bader auditory tests were administered because of Seth's history of ear problems. No deficiencies in discrimination surfaced.

A second testing of the Dolch Word List demonstrated that Seth lacks automaticity on many of the words which he read correctly on the first testing. Although he had only 24 errors on the second testing, 18 of these were not repeat errors.

Instructional Factors

Seth receives instruction both in a regular classroom and in a Chapter I reading program outside the classroom. Seth is not part of a regular reading group within the classroom, although workbook tasks are assigned frequently. He is rarely expected to read full-length texts in either setting. In the Chapter I classroom, his reading instruction has focused largely on word analysis and work is assigned from a program that emphasized visual and auditory perception of letter clusters in words. The method of instruction used by this particular program emphasized the analysis of words into their constituent parts.

The classroom teacher indicated Seth was responsible for the same assigned work required of all other children in the class, and that there was no differentiation of tasks among students. The language arts, spelling, and social studies books used in Seth's classroom are standard third-grade texts with readability estimates ranging from a 2.5 to a 5.0 grade level. Seth is expected to complete all classroom assignments before going to recess. The teacher reported that Seth really likes recess and does not like to miss it, although he frequently does because his work is incomplete.

The examiner observed Seth in his classroom for approximately one hour on April 7, 1986. At the beginning of the observation period, Mrs. Garvey was phasing children into a painting project. Seth was one of the first students done with his project. While the majority of the class continued to paint, Seth washed his hands and returned to his desk.

Throughout the period during which Seth painted, as well as during the work period, no other children initiated an interaction with him. Seth appears to enjoy the other children, often responding and laughing at general comments made by others to the group as a whole.

Only occasionally did Seth look up from his work after returning to his desk. Six children were coloring on the floor near him, two children were painting at the table behind him, and except for three other children working, the rest of the class was engaging in one of these activities around the room. Despite the noise level and the proximity of two groups of children chatting, Seth seemed undistracted.

Although Seth appears to work well independently, he is very reliant on his teacher. He asks questions frequently, requiring her help on nearly every individual task on which the examiner observed him working.

DIAGNOSTIC TEACHING

Using three different approaches to instruction and three groups of five words, Seth was systematically taught to recognize the words instantly. The instructional sequence was timed to determine how long it took under each set of instructional circumstances for him to learn the five words in each set. He was retested on these words after $1\frac{1}{2}$ hours to see how many he had retained from each sequence. Thus, both effectiveness and efficiency were evaluated. Finally, Seth was asked to tell which method he thought had been most effective for him.

At delayed retesting, Seth knew all 15 new words at sight (2-second flash). Thus, all three instructional approaches were equally effective. However, using one approach he learned the five new words in 1 1/2 minutes, whereas, using a different approach, it took 10 minutes for him to learn the words! In terms of efficiency, Seth is likely to benefit from a phonics program that blends parts into wholes, as opposed to a phonics program that breaks the whole into component parts. It should be noted, however, that he learned the words with equal ease when they were presented as sight words. The approach that was least efficient for Seth was the whole-to-part phonics approach, similar to his current instructional program. Seth's perception confirmed these conclusions. He felt he had learned the words most easily in the part-to-whole phonics approach.

In order to clarify issues related to approach and content, we initiated a language experience activity designed to allow Seth to read and write about topics of interest to him. During the first diagnostic teaching segment we were chagrined to find that, while Seth was enthusiastic about discussing a personal encounter with a "coydog" (half dog, half coyote), the story he dictated was sparse and incoherent. Subsequent work with a conference partner did nothing to improve the quality of the product. Two additional trials, yielding similar results, led to the conclusion that this was not the most effective method for improving Seth's word recognition or comprehension skills at the present time.

DIAGNOSTIC STATEMENTS AND SUGGESTIONS FOR INSTRUCTION

Structuring concepts for Seth will be valuable in all remedial activities. Evidence indicates that he is not grasping the "whole" and that "parts-to-whole" instruction may be helpful in improving comprehension as well. Seth needs to acquire a *story schema,* including a knowledge of story grammar. By focusing Seth's attention on the elements of story structure with prereading and postreading questions and activities, he will begin to acquire a sense of the parts of a well-written story. Given Seth's limited independent reading, it is suggested that this be done initially with books read aloud by the teacher.

Another vehicle for structuring reading selections for Seth is concept mapping. This spatial visualization task may fit his learning style, given his preference for visual processing as indicated on the psychoeducational report. A variety of models exist. For story structure, a map can be constructed to show the flow of the problem/resolution pattern, completed initially with teacher direction. Other models can be specifically used to map expository writing. Mapping can also be used to help Seth structure his own writing. As with expository maps, he could begin with his superordinate concept and extend his map with subordinate details.

To further expand instruction in the concept of the whole as a sum of its parts, *writing* can be taught through conventional parts of a piece of writing. In the clinic

Seth has generated ideas for a piece of writing through discussion with the examiner. After Seth has written what he believes is a finished product, the examiner rewrites it with an introduction, episode, and conclusion. It is read to Seth and the parts of a strong piece of writing are discussed, as is the importance of writing for an audience. One of the examiner-written parts is then excluded and Seth composes that part. This process is continued until Seth has rewritten the entire piece within this framework. Thus far, it has been a successful technique, although repetition and reinforcement are indicated. Seth's revisions have become more detailed, but his initial drafts are still only two or three sentences about the episode.

Of extreme importance are instructional programs that would teach Seth to think about what he is reading. By attending to the meaning of what he is reading, Seth will correct miscues that are not appropriate to the text. A number of strategies can be employed to improve Seth's *thinking/reading skills*. Think-Aloud, a program which requires the reader to discuss what s/he is thinking about while reading, has been used, as have teacher-directed cloze activities. Cloze exercises that are guided and directed by the teacher will encourage Seth to look for contextual cues for a word that he doesn't know, improve his understanding of the structure of language, inform the teacher of his instructional needs, and allow the teacher to provide activities that are specifically designed to fill those needs.

In addition to monitoring his reading comprehension, Seth needs to attend to the word display. An analysis of Seth's errors on the El Paso Phonics Survey indicated that at times he retrieves letters from lines above and below where he is reading. Specific decoding exercises that require that Seth attend to the symbols and sounds will provide less opportunity for his eyes to wander. Although such procedures defy common views of reading as holistic, Seth's lack of progress and his demonstrated difficulties with the whole (both words and concepts) indicate that a parts-to-whole approach may be appropriate.

Seth's concept of reading and of himself as a reader would improve with more *fluency* in his oral reading. In addition, fluency and phrasing facilitates comprehension by redirecting the child's focus from the individual words to the flow of writing as "talk written down." Neurological impress is a method for improving fluency with which Seth has met success in the clinic. He is anxious to try reading the practice passage himself and likes to bring it home to read to his parents. Also appended is an article describing ways to improve comprehension by using this technique.

As the test results indicate, Seth has specific areas of instructional need. His *sight vocabulary* is adequate, but the results of the posttest indicate a lack of automaticity on at least 18 words (read correctly on the pretest but incorrectly on the posttest) in addition to the 28 he missed on the pretest. It is critical in this, and in all of Seth's instruction, that a variety of techniques be employed. Initial presentation of each word should be in a variety of modes; Seth should say the word, write it, hear it said and used in a sentence, and use it himself. Suggesting that he note configuration and providing opportunities for him to experience the word kinesthetically (such as tracing or building the word) would also be helpful. Of particular value in the clinic has been the use of VAKT, a technique that will capitalize on Seth's preference for visual processing and help him to focus on the display of the word.

There are other methods which can encourage Seth to attend to all parts of the word. Because of the wide range of vowel errors, it is suggested that *vowel instruction* include all vowel sounds and be concurrent with instruction in *phonograms*. Activities should require Seth to say, hear, write, read, and feel the vowels and phonograms taught.

Seth's tendency to rearrange letters in the medial portions of words and add letters near the end suggests a need for instruction in structural analysis. Initially, instruction in this area needs to focus on the parts of simple words. Instruction could build on vowel and phonogram instruction with the teacher asking Seth to identify in what part of a word he hears a sound (i.e., when teaching the long *o* have him hold up a card with the word *middle* on it to demonstrate that he heard the *o* in the middle of the word *boat*). Written exercises can be designed on this same premise.

Seth's miscues indicate that he lacks skill in *blending*. While teaching any of the skill areas, the teacher could include activities that provide practice in blending the sound taught to produce a word. Many enjoyable and productive oral and kinesthetic activities can be employed to aid Seth in learning to blend all parts of a word. The teacher can point to each part of a word, having Seth say and hold the sound represented until the teacher moves his/her finger to the next word part. Letters could be placed on the floor and Seth could "skate" from one phoneme of a word to the next while saying the word aloud. These and other activities would be especially beneficial when teaching Seth vowels and *ending consonant sounds* that testing identified as weak.

A technique that may be of benefit to Seth in seeing the whole and its parts is that of using one book in all reading exercises in a given day. There is added power in doing this. It will be easier for him to operate within a familiar and consistent context, and to be working on varying skills toward one purpose: to complete and understand the story.

SUGGESTIONS AND RECOMMENDATIONS

The above are specific skill areas in which Seth needs instruction. Other strategies can be employed both in school and at home to improve his reading.

1. The lack of self-reliance that Seth demonstrated in the classroom indicates a need to provide assignments and tasks on which he can become self-directed. Seth must fulfill this high standards set for him; however, he will benefit from a quantity of work that he can complete and a level of work at which he can succeed.
2. An accompanying shift of responsibility to Seth at home may benefit him.

Perhaps he could do more chores in the barn or around the house to help build an image of himself as a mature and helpful member of the family.

3. Goal-setting is a technique that might be employed to encourage responsibility for himself and his work at both school and home. If Seth is exhibiting difficulty in completing tasks, he can set a goal for himself (i.e., finishing a number of math problems before recess).

4. Seth should be encouraged to use a marker when reading, to limit the distraction of extraneous print.

5. As noted above, Seth will benefit tremendously from using one book in all reading exercises in a given day.

6. Seth needs help choosing books that are appropriate for his reading ability and interests. His performance on the passage about a dog who gets hit by a car indicates an interest in exciting stories that he can relate to personally. In conversations with the examiner Seth had indicated an interest in horse stories as well. These interests are one of Seth's strengths in reading, a major part of what he brings to the process, and it will be to his benefit to capitalize on them.

7. Seth needs more exposure to reading and language. At home this could be accomplished by trips to the library, a family "reading time," and a time during which Seth is to read to daily. It is recommended that Seth be read to daily at school as well. Only with repeated exposure to story structure will Seth utilize it as a comprehension strategy.

8. Seth's parents may employ the Talking Dictionary approach to oral reading. Seth enjoyed his success in this activity at the clinic and loved to graph his progress.

9. It is recommended that Seth go to bed earlier. He seemed very tired in school and at the clinic. It is also recommended that Seth receive complete physical and eye examinations. Some of his fatigue may be due to health problems.

10. It is recommended that objectives be stated for Seth. He will benefit from clear direction in instruction.

Seth brings to the reading process specific interests and a positive attitude toward most tasks asked of him. The examiner believes that with opportunities to succeed, more exposure to literature that meets his interests, and most importantly, a unified instruction plan across all of Seth's academics, his reading will improve.

_____   _____
Clinician   Date

Award-Winning Books for Children and Youth

CALDECOTT MEDAL WINNERS (1961–1991)

The Caldecott Medal has been awarded since 1938 by the American Library Association. It is awarded to the most distinguished picture book for children and honors the illustrators of these books.

1991 *Black and White.* David Macaulay. Boston: Houghton Mifflin, 1990.

1990 *Lon Po Po: A Red Riding Hood Story from China.* Ed Young. New York: Philomel, 1989.

1989 *Song and Dance Man.* Karen Ackerman. Illus. by Stephen Gammell. New York: Knopf, 1988.

1988 *Owl Moon.* Jane Yolen. Illus. by John Schoenherr. New York: Philomel, 1987.

1987 *Hey, Al.* Arthur Yorinks. Illus. by Richard Egielski. New York: Farrar, Straus and Giroux, 1986.

1986 *The Polar Express.* Chris Van Allsburg. Boston: Houghton Mifflin, 1985.

1985 *Saint George and the Dragon.* Retold by Margaret Hodges. Illus. by Tina Schart Hyman. Boston: Little, Brown, 1984.

1984 *The Glorious Flight: Across the Channel with Louis Bleriot.* Alice and Martin Provensen. New York: Viking, 1983.

1983 *Shadow.* Blaise Cendrars. Illus. by Marcia Brown. New York: Scribner's, 1982.

1982 *Jumanji.* Chris Van Allsburg. Boston: Houghton Mifflin, 1981.

1981 *Fables.* Arnold Lobel. New York: Harper & Row, 1980.

1980 *Ox-Cart Man.* Donald Hall. Illus. by Barbara Cooney. New York: Viking, 1979.

1979 *The Girl Who Loved Wild Horses.* Paul Goble. New York: Bradbury, 1978.

1978 *Noah's Ark.* Peter Spier. New York: Doubleday, 1977.

1977 *Ashanti to Zulu.* Margaret Musgrove. Illus. by Leo and Diane Dillon. New York: Dial, 1976.

1976 *Why Mosquitoes Buzz in People's Ears.* Verna Aardema. Illus. by Leo and Diane Dillon. New York: Dial, 1975.

1975 *Arrow to the Sun.* Gerald McDermott. New York: Viking, 1974.

1974 *Duffy and the Devil.* Retold by Harve Zemach. Illus. by Margot Zemach. New York: Farrar, Straus and Giroux, 1973.

1973 *The Funny Little Woman.* Retold by Arlene Mosel. Illus. by Blair Lent. New York: Dutton, 1972.

1972 *One Fine Day.* Nonny Hogrogian. New York: Macmillan, 1971.

1971 *A Story A Story.* Gail Haley. New York: Atheneum, 1970.

1970 *Sylvester and the Magic Pebble.* William Steig. New York: Windmill Books, 1969.

1969 *The Fool of the World and the Flying Ship.* Retold by Arthur Ransome. Illus. by Uri Shulevitz. New York: Farrar, Straus and Giroux, 1968.

1968 *Drummer Hoff.* Adapted by Barbara Emberley. Illus. by Ed Emberley. Englewood Cliffs, N.J.: Prentice-Hall, 1967.

1967	*Sam, Bangs, and Moonshine.* Evaline Ness. New York: Holt, Rinehart and Winston, 1966.

1966	*Always Room for One More.* Sorche Nic Leodhas. Illus. by Nonny Hogrogian. New York: Holt, Rinehart and Winston, 1965.

1965	*May I Bring a Friend?* Beatrice Schenk de Regniers. Illus. by Beni Montresor. New York: Atheneum, 1964.

1964	*Where the Wild Things Are.* Maurice Sendak. New York: Harper & Row, 1963.

1963	*The Snowy Day.* Ezra Jack Keats. New York: Viking, 1962.

1962	*Once a Mouse.* Marcia Brown. New York: Scribner's, 1961.

1961	*Baboushka and the Three Kings.* Ruth Robbins. Illus. by Nicolas Sidjakov. Orleans, Mass.: Parnassus, 1960.

NEWBERY MEDAL WINNERS (1961–1991)

The Newbery Medal is awarded each year by the American Library Association. Since 1922 this medal has been awarded to honor the author of the book that is deemed to be the most distinguished contribution to children's literature.

1991	Maniac Magee. Jerry Spinelli. Boston: Little, Brown, 1990.

1990	*Number the Stars.* Lois Lowry. Boston: Houghton Mifflin, 1989.

1989	*Joyful Noise: Poems for Two Voices.* Paul Fleischman. New York: Harper & Row, 1988.

1988	*Lincoln: A Photobiography.* Russell Freedman. Boston: Houghton Mifflin, 1987.

1987	*The Whipping Boy.* Sid Fleischman. New York: Greenwillow, 1986.

1986	*Sarah, Plain and Tall.* Patricia MacLachlan. New York: Harper & Row, 1985.

1985	*The Hero and the Crown.* Robin McKinley. New York: Greenwillow, 1984.

1984	*Dear Mr. Henshaw.* Beverly Cleary. New York: William Morrow, 1983.

1983	*Dicey's Song.* Cynthia Voigt. New York: Atheneum, 1982.

1982	*A Visit to William Blake's Inn: Poems for Innocent and Experienced Travelers.* Nancy Willard. New York: Harcourt Brace Jovanovich, 1981.

1981	*Jacob Have I Loved.* Katherine Paterson. New York: Crowell, 1980.

1980	*A Gathering of Days.* Joan Blos. New York: Scribner's, 1979.

1979	*The Westing Game.* Ellen Raskin. New York: Dutton, 1978.

1978	*Bridge to Terabithia.* Katherine Paterson. New York: Crowell, 1977.

1977	*Roll of Thunder, Hear My Cry.* Mildred D. Taylor. New York: Dial, 1976.

1976	*The Grey King.* Susan Cooper. New York: Atheneum, 1975.

1975	*M. C. Higgins, the Great.* Virginia Hamilton. New York: Macmillan, 1974.

1974	*The Slave Dancer.* Paula Fox. New York: Bradbury, 1973.

1973	*Julie of the Wolves.* Jean Craighead George. New York: Harper & Row, 1972.

1972	*Mrs. Frisby and the Rats of NIMH.* Robert O'Brien. New York: Atheneum, 1971.

1971   *Summer of the Swans.* Betsy Byars. New York: Viking, 1970.

1970   *Sounder.* William H. Armstrong. New York: Harper & Row, 1969.

1969   *The High King.* Lloyd Alexander. New York: Holt, Rinehart and Winston, 1968.

1968   *From the Mixed-up Files of Mrs. Basil E. Frankweiler.* E. L. Konigsburg. New York: Atheneum, 1967.

1967   *Up a Road Slowly.* Irene Hunt. Chicago: Follett, 1966.

1966   *I, Juan de Pareja.* Elizabeth Borton de Trevino. New York: Farrar, Straus and Giroux, 1965.

1965   *Shadow of a Bull.* Maia Wojciechowska. New York: Atheneum, 1964.

1964   *It's Like This, Cat.* Emily Neville. New York: Harper & Row, 1963.

1963   *A Wrinkle in Time.* Madeleine L'Engle. New York: Farrar, Straus and Giroux, 1962.

1962   *The Bronze Bow.* Elizabeth George Speare. Boston: Houghton Mifflin, 1961.

1961   *Island of the Blue Dolphins.* Scott O'Dell. Boston: Houghton Mifflin, 1960.

CORETTA SCOTT KING AWARD (1970–1989)

This award was established in 1969 "to commemorate the life and works of the late Dr. Martin Luther King, Jr; to honor Mrs. King for her courage to continue to fight for peace and world brotherhood; to encourage creative artists and authors to promote the cause of brotherhood through their work; and to inspire children and youth to dedicate their talents and energies to help achieve these goals." The award is presented annually. Since 1979, an additional award has been presented for illustration.

1970   *Martin Luther King, Jr.: Man of Peace.* Lillie Patterson. Illus. by Victor Mays

1971   *Black Troubadour: Langston Hughes.* Charlemane Rollins.

1972   *Seventeen Black Artists.* Elton Clay Fax. Illus. with photographs.

1973   *I Never Had It Made.* Jackie Robinson as told to Alfred Duckett.

1974   *Ray Charles.* Sharon Bell Mathis. Illus. by George Ford.

1975   *The Legend of Africania.* Dorothy Robinson. Illus. by Herbert Temple.

1976   *Duey's Tale.* Pearl Bailey. Photographs by Arnold Skolnick and Gary Azon.

1977   *The Story of Stevie Wonder.* James Haskins. Illus. with photographs.

1978   *African Dream.* Eloise Greenfield. Illus. by Carole Byard.

1979   *Escape to Freedom: A Play About Young Frederick Douglass.* Ossie Davis.

1979   Special Award for Illustration
        Something on My Mind. Nikki Grimes. Illus. by Tom Feelings.

1980   Author
        The Young Landlords. Walter Dean Myers.

1980   Illustration
        Cornrows. Camille Yarbrough. Illus. by Carole Byard.

1981   Author
        This Life. Sidney Poitier.
1981   Illustration
        Beat the Story-drum, Pum-pum. Written and illus. by Ashley Bryan.
1982   Author
        Sweet Whispers, Brother Rush. Virginia Hamilton.
1982   Author Honorable Mention
        This Strange New Feeling. Julius Lester.
1982   Illustration
        Black Child. Written and photographed by Peter Magubane.
1983   Author
        Let the Circle Be Unbroken. Mildred D. Taylor.
1983   Illustration
        Mother Crocodile—Maman-Caiman. Birango Diop. Trans. and adapted by
        Rosa Guy. Illus. by John Steptoe.
1984   Author
        Everett Anderson's Goodbye. Lucille Clifton. Illus. by Ann Grifalconi.
1984   Illustration
        My Mama Needs Me. Mildred Pitts Walter. Illus. by Pat Cummings.
1984   Honorable Mention
        Because We Are. Mildred Pitts Walter.
        Bright Shadow. Joyce Carol Thomas.
        Lena Horne. James Haskins. Illus. with photographs.
        The Magical Adventures of Pretty Pearl. Virginia Hamilton.
1984   Special Citation
        The Words of Martin Luther King, Jr. Selected by Coretta Scott King.
1985   Literature
        Motown and Didi. Walter Dean Myers.
1985   Literature Honorable Mention
        Little Love. Virginia Hamilton.
        The Circle of Gold. Candy Dawson Boyd.
1985   Illustration
        No Award.
1986   Literature
        The People Could Fly. Virginia Hamilton. Illus. by Leo and Diane Dillon.
1986   Literature Honorable Mention
        Junius Over Far. Virginia Hamilton.
        Trouble's Child. Mildred Pitts Walter.
1986   Illustration
        The Patchwork Quilt. Valerie Fluornoy. Illus. by Jerry Pinkney.
1986   Illustration Honorable Mention
        The People Could Fly. Virginia Hamilton. Illus. by Leo and Diane Dillon.
1987   Literature
        Justin and the Best Biscuits in the World. Mildred Pitts Walter. Illus. by
        Catherine Stock.

1987   Literature Honorable Mention
        Which Way Freedom? Joyce Hansen.
        The Lion and the Ostrich Chicks. Written and illus. by Ashley Bryan.
1987   Illustration
        Half a Moon and One Whole Star. Crescent Dragonwagon. Illus. by Jerry Pinkney.
1987   Illustration Honorable Mention
        C.L.O.U.D.S. Written and illus. by Pat Cummings.
1988   Literature
        The Friendship. Mildred Taylor. Illus. by Max Ginsburg.
1988   Illustration
        Mufaro's Beautiful Daughters. Written and illus. by John Steptoe.
1989   Literature
        Fallen Angels. Walter Dean Myers.
1989   Illustration
        Mirandy and Brother Wind. Patricia McKissack. Illus. by Jerry Pinkney.
1990   Literature
        A Long Hard Journey. Patricia and Frederick McKissack.
1990   Illustration
        Nathaniel Talking. Eloise Greenfield. Illus. by Jan Gilchrist.

JANE ADDAMS CHILDREN'S BOOK AWARD WINNERS (1953–1990)

This award is presented annually for the book that "best promotes peace, dignity, and equality for all people, as well as social justice." The award was created in 1953 by the U.S. section of the Women's International League for Peace and Freedom to honor Jane Addams.

1953   *People Are Important.* Eva Knox Evans. Illus. by Vana Earle.
1954   *Stick-in-the Mud: A Tale of a Village, a Custom and a Little Boy.* Jean Ketchum. Illus. by Fred Ketchum.
1955   *Rainbow Around the World: A Story of UNICEF.* Elizabeth Yates. Illus. by Betty Alden and Dirk Gringhuis.
1956   *Story of the Negro.* Arna Wendell Bontemps. Illus. by Raymond Lufkin.
1957   *Blue Mystery.* Margaret Benary Isbert. Trans. by Clara and Richard Winston. Illus. by Enrico Arno.
1958   *The Perilous Road.* William O. Steele. Illus. by Paul Galdone.
1959   No Award.
1960   *Champions of Peace: Winners of the Nobel Peace Prize.* Edith Patterson Meyer. Illus. by Eric von Schmidt.
1961   *What Then, Raman?* Shirlee Lease Arora. Illus. by Hans Guggenheim.
1962   *The Road to Agra.* Aimee Sommerfelt. Illus. by Ulf Aas.
1963   *The Monkey and the Wild, Wild Wind.* Ryerson Johnson. Illus. by Lois Lignell.

1964   *Profiles in Courage.* John F. Kennedy. Illus. by Emil Weiss.

1965   No Award.

1966   *Berries Goodman.* Emily Cheney Neville.

1967   *Queenie Peavy.* Robert Burch. Illus. by Jerry Lazare.

1968   *The Little Fishes.* Eric Christian Haugaard. Illus. by Milton Johnson.

1969   *The Endless Steppe: Growing Up in Siberia.* Esther Hautzig.

1970   No Award.

1971   *Jane Addams: Pioneer for Social Justice, a Biography.* Cornelia L. Meigs. Illus. with photographs.

1972   *The Tamarack Tree.* Mary Betty Underwood. Illus. by Bea Holmes.

1973   *The Riddle of Racism.* S. Carl Hirsch.

1973   Honor

    The Upstairs Room. Johanna Reiss.

1974   *Nilda.* Written and illus. by Nicholasa Mohr.

1974   Honor

    A Hero Ain't Nothing But a Sandwich. Alice Childress.

    Men Against War. Barbara Habenstreit.

    A Pocket Full of Seeds. Marilyn Sachs.

1975   *The Princess and the Admiral.* Charlotte Pomerantz. Illus. by Tony Chen.

1975   Honor

    My Brother Sam Is Dead. James Lincoln Collier and Christopher Collier.

    Viva La Raza! The Struggle of the Mexican-American People. Elizabeth Sunderland Martinez and Enriqueta Martinez.

    The Eye of Conscience. Milton Meltzer and Bernard Cole.

1976   *Paul Robeson.* Eloise Greenfield. Illus. by George Ford.

1976   Honor

    Song of the Trees. Mildred D. Taylor. Illus. by Jerry Pinkney.

    Dragonwings. Laurence Yep.

    Z for Zachariah. Robert C. O'Brien.

1977   *Never to Forget: The Jews of the Holocaust.* Milton Meltzer.

1977   Honor

    Roll of Thunder, Hear My Cry. Mildred D. Taylor. Illus. by Jerry Pinkney.

1978   *Child of the Owl.* Laurence Yep.

1978   Honor

    Mischling, Second Degree: My Childhood in Nazi Germany. Ilse Koehn.

    Alan and Naomi. Myron Levoy.

1978   Special Recognition

    Amifka. Lucille Clifton. Illus. by Thomas DiGrazia.

    The Wheel of King Asoka. Written and illus. by Ashok Davar.

1979   *Many Smokes, Many Moons: A Chronology of American Indian History Through Indian Art.* Jamake Highwater. Illus. with photographs.

1979   Honor

    Escape to Freedom: A Play About Young Frederick Douglass. Ossie Davis.

    The Great Gilly Hopkins. Katherine Paterson.

1980   *The Road from Home: The Story of an Armenian Girl.* David Kherdian.

1980 West Coast Honor Book
Woman from Hiroshima. Toshio Mori.

1980 Special Recognition
Natural History. Written and illus. by M.B. Goffstein.

1981 *First Woman in Congress: Jeanette Rankin.* Florence Meiman White.

1981 Honor
Chase Me, Catch Nobody! Erik C. Haugaard.
Doing Time: A Look at Crime and Prisons. Phyllis E. Clark and Robert Lehrman.
We Are Mesquakie, We Are One. Hadley Irwin. Illus. with maps.

1982 *A Spirit to Ride the Whirlwind.* Athena V. Lord.

1982 Honor
Lupita Manana. Patricia Beatty.
Let the Circle Be Unbroken. Mildred D. Taylor.

1983 *Hiroshima No Pika.* Written and illus. by Toshi Maruki.

1983 Honor
The Bomb. Sidney Lens. Illus. with photographs.
If I Had a Paka: Poems in Eleven Languages. Charlotte Pomerantz. Illus. by Nancy Tafuri.

1983 West Coast Honor Book
All the Colors of the Race: Poems. Arnold Adoff. Illus. by John Steptoe.
Children as Teachers of Peace, by our children. Ed. by Gerald G. Jampolsky. Foreword by Hugh Prather.

1984 *Rain of Fire.* Marion Dane Bauer.

1985 *The Short Life of Sophie Scholl.* Hermann Vinke. Trans. by Hedwig Pachter.

1985 Honor
The Island on Bird Street. Uri Orlev. Trans. by Hillel Halkin.
Music, Music for Everyone. Written and illus. by Vera B. Williams.

1986 *Ain't Gonna Study War No More: The Story of America's Peace Seekers.* Milton Meltzer.

1986 Honor
Journey to the Soviet Union. Samantha Smith. Illus. with photographs.

1987 *Nobody Wants a Nuclear War.* Written and illus. by Judith Vigna.

1987 Honor
All in a Day. Written and illus. by Mitsumasa Anno.
Children of the Maya: A Guatemalan Indian Odyssey. Brent Ashabranner. Photographs by Paul Conklin.

1988 *Waiting for the Rain: A Novel of South Africa.* Sheila Gordon.

1989 *Anthony Burns: The Defeat and Triumph of a Fugitive Slave.* Virginia Hamilton.

1989 Honor
Looking Out. Victoria Boutis.

1990 *Long Hard Journey: The Story of the Pullman Porter.* Patricia and Frederick McKissack.

APPENDIX C

High Interest, Easy-Reading Books

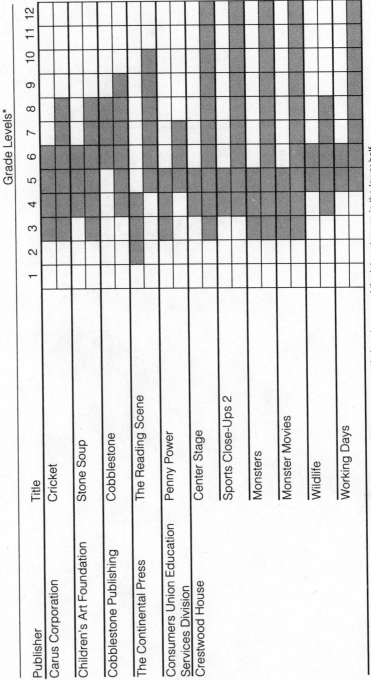

*The reading level of each series or periodical is indicated in the upper half of each row and the interest range in the lower half.

Grade Levels*

Publisher	Title		1	2	3	4	5	6	7	8	9	10	11	12
EMC Publishing	Easy-to-Read Classics	reading			▓	▓	▓	▓						
		interest						▓	▓	▓	▓	▓	▓	▓
	Encounter	reading			▓	▓	▓							
		interest							▓	▓	▓	▓	▓	▓
Fearon Education (Davis S. Lake)	Doomsday Journals	reading			▓	▓								
		interest						▓	▓	▓	▓	▓	▓	▓
	Fastbacks	reading				▓								
		interest						▓	▓	▓	▓	▓	▓	▓
	Double Fastbacks	reading				▓								
		interest							▓	▓	▓	▓	▓	▓
	Flashbacks	reading				▓	▓							
		interest							▓	▓	▓	▓	▓	▓
	Galaxy 5	reading		▓	▓									
		interest						▓	▓	▓	▓	▓	▓	▓
	Space Police	reading		▓										
		interest				▓	▓	▓	▓	▓				
	Laura Brewster Books	reading		▓										
		interest						▓	▓	▓	▓	▓	▓	▓
	Pacemaker Classics	reading		▓										
		interest					▓	▓	▓	▓	▓	▓	▓	▓
	Specter	reading		▓										
		interest						▓	▓	▓	▓	▓	▓	▓
	Super Specter	reading			▓	▓								
		interest						▓	▓	▓	▓	▓	▓	▓

*The reading level of each series or periodical is indicated in the upper half of each row and the interest range in the lower half.

Grade Levels*

Publisher	Title	1	2	3	4	5	6	7	8	9	10	11	12
Fearon Education (David S. Lake)	Sportellers												
	Talespinners												
	South City Cops												
Field Publications	Current Events												
	Current Science												
	Know Your World Extra												
	Read												
	Weekly Reader, Senior Edition												
	Weekly Reader, Editions 4, 5, and 6												
Globe Book Company	Myths and Folk Tales												
High Noon Books	Tom and Ricky Mystery Series												
	The Road Aces												

*The reading level of each series or periodical is indicated in the upper half of each row and the interest range in the lower half.

Grade Levels*

Publisher	Title	1	2	3	4	5	6	7	8	9	10	11	12
High Noon Books	Life Line Series	■		■	■	■	■						
	Meg Parker Mystery Series		■	■	■	■	■						
	Scoop Dougan and Skip Malone		■	■	■		■						
	High Adventures		■	■	■	■	■						
	9-5 Series		■	■	■	■	■						
	Main Street Books	■	■	■	■	■	■						
	Perspective Novels		■	■	■	■	■						
	You Are Series		■	■	■	■	■	■					
National Geographic Society	National Geographic World			■	■	■	■	■	■				
New Readers Press	Sundown Books			■	■							■	■
Pendulum Press	Illustrated Classics				■	■	■	■	■	■			

*The reading level of each series or periodical is indicated in the upper half of each row and the interest range in the lower half.

Grade Levels*

Publisher	Title	1	2	3	4	5	6	7	8	9	10	11	12
Raintree Publishers	Great Unsolved Mysteries			▓	▓	▓	▓	▓					
	Myth, Magic & Superstition			▓	▓	▓	▓	▓	▓	▓			
	Quest, Adventure, Survival			▓	▓	▓	▓	▓	▓	▓	▓		
	Science Fiction Shorts					▓	▓	▓	▓	▓	▓	▓	▓
Random House	Reader's Digest Top Picks		▓	▓	▓	▓	▓	▓	▓				
	Reader's Digest Reading Skill Builder				▓	▓	▓	▓	▓	▓	▓		
Scholastic	Sprint Library				▓	▓	▓	▓					
	Action Library				▓	▓	▓	▓	▓	▓			
	Double Action Library						▓	▓	▓	▓	▓	▓	▓
	Action				▓			▓	▓	▓	▓	▓	▓
	Sprint					▓	▓	▓	▓				
	Scope					▓	▓	▓	▓	▓	▓	▓	▓
	U.S. Express						▓	▓	▓	▓	▓	▓	▓

*The reading level of each series or periodical is indicated in the upper half of each row and the interest range in the lower half.

APPENDIX D

Listing of Predictable Books

PREDICTABLE BOOKS

Books with a repetitive pattern in which a certain phrase or sentence is repeated throughout the story.

Ahlberg, Janet & Allan. *Peek-a-boo*. Viking Press, 1981.

Allen, Roach Van. *I Love Ladybugs*. DLM Teaching Resources, 1985.

Balina, Lorna. *Mother's Mother's Day*. Abingdon Press, 1982.

Barrett, Judi. *Animals Should Definitely Not Act Like People*. Atheneum, 1980.

Barrett, Judi. *Animals Should Definitely Not Wear Clothes*. Atheneum, 1981.

Barrett, Judi. *A Snake Is Totally Tail*. Atheneum, 1983.

Barton, Byron. *Harry Is a Scaredy-Cat*. Macmillan, 1974.

Berenstain, Stan & Jan. *Old Hat New Hat*. Random House, 1970.

Brooke, Leslie. *Johnny Crow's Garden*. F. Warne & Co., 1941.

Brooke, Leslie. *Johnny Crow's New Garden*. F. Warne & Co., 1938.

Brown, Margaret Wise. *Goodnight Moon*. Harper & Row, 1947.

Brown, Margaret Wise. *The Friendly Book*. Western Publishing, 1954.

Brown, Margaret Wise. *The Important Book*. Harper & Row, 1949.

Brown, Margaret Wise. *Where Have You Been?* Hastings House, 1952.

Brown, Ruth. *A Dark Dark Tale*. Dial Press, 1981.

Caldwell, Mary. *Henry's Busy Day*. Viking Press, 1984.

Carle, Eric. *The Grouchy Ladybug*. Thomas Y. Crowell Co., 1977.

Crews, Donald. *Light*. Greenwillow Books, 1981.

Degen, Bruce. *Jamberry*. Harper & Row, 1983.

deRegniers, Beatrice Schenk. *Going for a Walk*. Harper & Row, 1961.

Domanska, Janina. *If All the Seas Were One Sea*. Macmillan, 1971.

Eastman, P.D. *Go, Dog, Go!* Random House, 1961.

Galdone, Paul. *The Teeny-Tiny Woman*. Clarion Books, 1984.

Ginsburg, Mirra. *The Chick and the Duckling*. Macmillan, 1972.

Hamsa, Bobbie. *Dirty Larry*. Children's Press, 1983.

Harper, Anita. *How We Work*. Harper & Row, 1977.

Harper, Anita & Roche, Christine. *How We Live*. Harper & Row, 1977.

Hutchins, Pat. *Goodnight Owl*. Macmillan, 1972.

Isadora, Rachel. *I See*. Greenwillow Books, 1985.

Krauss, Ruth. *A Hole Is to Dig*. Harper & Row, 1952.

Krauss, Ruth. *I Write It*. Harper & Row, 1970.

Kraus, Robert. *I'm a Monkey*. Windmill Books, 1975.

Krauss, Ruth. *The Happy Day*. Harper & Row, 1949.

Langstaff, John M. *Oh, A-Hunting We Will Go*. Atheneum, 1977.

Malloy, Judy. *Bad Thad*. E. P. Dutton, 1980.

Martin, Bill. *Brown Bear, Brown Bear*. Holt, Rinehart & Winston, 1970.

Martin, Bill. *King of the Mountain*. Holt, Rinehart & Winston, 1970.

Martin, Bill. *Silly Goose and the Holidays*. Holt, Rinehart & Winston, 1970.

Martin, Bill. *The Haunted House*. Holt, Rinehart & Winston, 1970.

Martin, Bill. *Up and Down the Escalator*. Holt, Rinehart & Winston, 1970.

Mosel, Arlene. *Tikki Tikki Tembo*. Holt, Rinehart & Winston, 1968.

Muntean, Michaela. *I Like School*. Golden Press, 1980.

Paterson, Diane. *If I Were a Toad*. Dial Press, 1977.

Peek, Merle. *Mary Wore Her Red Dress*. Clarion Books, 1985.

Preston, Edna Mitchell. *Where Did My Mother Go?* Four Winds Press, 1978.

Quackenbush, Robert. *Skip to My Lou*. J. B. Lippincott, 1975.

Rockwell, Anne. *Thump Thump Thump!* E. P. Dutton, 1981.

Scheer, Julian. *Rain Makes Applesauce*. Holiday House, 1964.

Seuss, Dr. *The Foot Book*. Random House, 1968.

Shaw, Charles G. *It Looked Like Spilt Milk*. Harper & Row, 1947.

Simon, Norma. *I Know What I Like*. Whitman, 1971.

Titherington, Jeanne. *Big World, Small World*. Greenwillow Books, 1985.

Udry, Janice May. *A Tree Is Nice*. Harper & Row, 1956.

Watanabe, Shigeo. *I Can Ride It!* Philomel Books, 1981.

Watanabe, Shigeo. *Where's My Daddy?* Philomel Books, 1979.

Williams, Barbara. *Never Hit a Porcupine*. E. P. Dutton & Co., 1977.

Books with predictable plots in which the events occur in such a way as to enable the reader to predict future events.

Aliki. *At Mary Bloom's*. Greenwillow Books, 1976.

Allard, Harry. *I Will Not Go to Market Today*. Dial Press, 1979.

Aylesworth, Jim. *Hush Up!* Holt, Rinehart & Winston, 1980.

Balian, Lorna. *Where in the World is Henry?* Abingdon, 1972.

Barton, Byron. *Buzz, Buzz, Buzz*. Puffin Books, 1979.

Brown, Margaret Wise. *The Runaway Bunny*. Harper & Row, 1972.

Burningham, John. *Mr. Gumpy's Outing*. Scholastic, 1974.

Charlip, Remy. *Fortunately*. Four Winds Press, 1964.

Emberley, Ed. *Klippity Klop*. Little, Brown and Co., 1974.

Fregosi, Claudia. *Are There Spooks in the Dark?* Four Winds Press, 1977.

Galdone, Paul. *The Three Bears*. Scholastic, 1972.

Galdone, Paul. *The Three Billy Goats Gruff*. Scholastic, 1963.

Galdone, Paul. *The Three Little Pigs*. Seabury Press, 1970.

Ginsburg, Mirra. *Where Does the Sun Go at Night?* Greenwillow Books, 1981.

Joslin, Sesyle. *What Do You Do, Dear?* Young Scott Books, 1961.

Klein, Leonore. *Brave Daniel*. Scholastic, 1958.

Lobel, Arnold. *A Treeful of Pigs*. Greenwillow Books, 1979.

Mayer, Mercer. *Just for You*. Golden Press, 1975.

Nodset, Joan. *Who Took the Farmer's Hat?* Scholastic, 1963.

Silverstein, Shel. *Who Wants a Cheap Rhinoceros?* Macmillan, 1983.

Stevenson, James. *Could Be Worse!* Greenwillow Books, 1977.

Tobias, Tobi. *A Day Off*. G. P. Putnam's Sons, 1973.

Zolotow, Charlotte. *Do You Know What I'll Do?* Harper & Row, 1958.

Books with a repetitive-cumulative pattern in which a word, phrase, or sentence is repeated in each succeeding episode and with each episode adding a new word, phrase, or sentence to the sequence.

Aardema, Verna. *Bringing the Rain to Kapiti Plain.* Dial Press, 1981.

Aardema, Verna. *Why Mosquitoes Buzz in People's Ears.* Scholastic, 1975.

Berenstain, Stan & Jan. *The B Book.* Random House, 1971.

Berenstain, Stan & Jan. *C is for Clown.* Random House, 1972.

Berenstain, Stan & Jan. *Inside Outside Upside Down.* Random House, 1968.

Bonne, Rose. *I Know an Old Lady.* Scholastic, 1961.

Brenner, Barbara. *The Snow Parade.* Crown Publishers, 1984.

Dodd, Lynley. *Hairy Maclary from Donaldson's Dairy.* Gareth Stevens, Inc., 1983.

Emberley, Barbara. *Drummer Hoff.* Prentice-Hall, Inc., 1967.

Ets, Marie Hall. *Elephant in a Well.* Viking, 1972.

Galdone, Paul. *Chicken Little.* Seabury Press, 1968.

Galdone, Paul. *The Greedy Old Fat Man.* Clarion Books, 1983.

Galdone, Paul. *The Old Woman and Her Pig.* MacGraw-Hill, 1960.

Granowsky, Alvin. *Pat's Date and Plate.* D. C. Heath & Co., 1975.

Guilfoile, Elizabeth. *Nobody Listens to Andrew.* Scholastic, 1957.

Hogrogian, Nonny. *One Fine Day.* Collier Books, 1971.

Hoguet, Susan R. *I Unpacked My Grandmother's Trunk.* E. P. Dutton, 1983.

Kalan, Robert. *Jump, Frog, Jump.* Greenwillow Books, 1981.

Kent, Jack. *Jack Kent's Twelve Days of Christmas.* Scholastic, 1973.

Kent, Jack. *The Fat Cat.* Scholastic, 1971.

Lobel, Arnold. *The Rose in My Garden.* Greenwillow Books, 1984.

Parnall, Peter. *The Mountain.* Doubleday, 1971.

Patrick, Gloria. *A Bug in a Jug and Other Funny Rhymes.* Scholastic, 1970.

Peppe, Rodney. *The House That Jack Built.* Delacorte Press, 1970.

Quackenbush, Robert. *No Mouse for Me.* Franklin Watts, 1981.

Sadler, Marilyn. *It's Not Easy Being a Bunny.* Random House, 1983.

Seuss, Dr. *Green Eggs and Ham.* Random House, 1960.

Shoemaker, Kathryn. *Children, Go Where I Send Thee.* Winston Press, 1980.

Silverstein, Shel. *A Giraffe and a Half.* Harper & Row, 1964.

Tolstoy, Alexi. *The Great Big Enormous Turnip.* Franklin Watts, 1968.

Wood, Audrey. *The Napping House.* Harcourt Brace Jovanovich, 1984.

Books with a repetitive refrain in which a certain phrase or sentence is repeated at various points in the story.

Aardema, Verna. *The Vinganese and the Tree Toad.* Frederick Warne & Co., 1983.

Aardema, Verna. *Who's in Rabbit's House?* Dial Press, 1969.

Bang, Betsy. *The Old Woman and the Rice Thief.* Greenwillow Books, 1978.

Brown, Margaret Wise. *Home for a Bunny.* Golden Press, 1980.

Brown, Margaret Wise. *Wait Till the Moon Is Full.* Harper & Row, 1948.

daPaola, Tomie. *Marianna May and Nursey.* Holiday House, 1983.
Gag, Wanda. *Millions of Cats.* Coward, McCann & Geoghegan, 1977.
Littledale, Freya. *The Magic Fish.* Scholastic, 1967.
Shannon, George. *The Piney Woods Peddler.* Greenwillow Books, 1981.

Books with rhyming patterns, many of which have rhyme combined with repetition and cumulative-repetition.

Aliki. *Hush Little Baby.* Prentice-Hall, 1968.
Battaglia, Aurelius. *Old Mother Hubbard.* Golden Press, 1972.
Cameron, Polly. *"I Can't" Said the Ant.* Scholastic, 1961.
Cranstoun, Margaret. *1, 2, Buckle My Shoe.* Holt, Rinehart & Winston, 1967.
Einsel, Walter. *Did You Ever See?* Scholastic, 1962.
Hawkins, Colin & Jacqui. *Pat the Cat.* G. P. Putnam's Sons, 1983.
Kessler, Leonard. *Hey Diddle Diddle.* Garrard Publishing, 1980.
Krauss, Ruth. *Bears.* Harper & Row, 1948.
Petersham, Maud & Miska. *The Rooster Crows: A Book of American Rhymes and Jingles.* Macmillan, 1971.
Schermer, Judith. *Mouse in a House.* Houghton Mifflin, 1979.
Sendak, Maurice. *Pierre.* Harper & Row, 1962.
Seuss, Dr. *I Can Read with My Eyes Shut!* Random House, 1978.
Seuss, Dr. *The Cat in the Hat.* Random House, 1957.
Spier, Peter. *London Bridge Is Falling Down.* Doubleday & Co., 1967.
Stadler, John. *Cat at Bat.* E. P. Dutton, 1979.
Withers, Carl. *Favorite Rhymes from a Rocket in My Pocket.* Scholastic, 1967.
Zolotow, Charlotte. *Some Things Go Together.* Thomas Y. Crowell, 1969.
Zuromskis, Diane. *The Farmer in the Dell.* Little, Brown & Co., 1978.

Books with a wordplay pattern in which pictures illustrate characteristics of words.

Gwynne, Fred. *The King Who Rained.* Windmill Books, 1970.
Hanson, Joan. *Antonyms.* Lerner Publishing Co., 1972.
Hanson, Joan. *Homographic Homophones.* Lerner Publishing Co., 1973.

Sequenced Books

Books with patterns based on familiar cultural sequences (cardinal and ordinal numbers, alphabet, months of the year, days of the week, seasons and colors).

Numbers

Anno, Mitsumasa. *Anno's Counting Book.* Thomas Y. Crowell Co., 1975.
Anno, Masaichiro & Mitsumasa. *Anno's Mysterious Multiplying Jar.* Philomel Books, 1983.
Bang, Molly. *Ten, Nine, Eight.* Greenwillow Books, 1983.

Berenstain, Stan & Jan. *Bears on Wheels*. Random House, 1969.

Bruna, Dick. *I Can Count*. Methuen Children's Books, 1968.

Carle, Eric. *1, 2, 3 to the Zoo*. Philomel Books, 1968.

Cleveland, David. *The April Rabbits*. Coward, McCann & Geoghegan.

Duvoisin, Roger. *Two Lonely Ducks*. Alfred A. Knopf, 1955.

Emberley, Barbara. *One Wide River to Cross*. Scholastic, 1966.

Feelings, Muriel. *Moja Means One: Swahili Counting Book*. Dial Press, 1971.

Ginsburg, Mirra. *Kitten from One to Ten*. Crown Publishers, Inc., 1980.

Hoberman, Mary Ann. *The Looking Book*. Alfred A. Knopf, 1973.

Hopkins, Lee Bennett. *Small Circus*. Macmillan, 1975.

Hughes, Shirley. *When We Went to the Park*. Lothrop, Lee & Shepard Books, 1985.

Hutchins, Pat. *1 Hunter*. Greenwillow Books, 1982.

Keats, Ezra Jack. *Over in the Meadow*. Scholastic, 1971.

Kredenser, Gail & Mack, Stanley. *1 One Dancing Drum*. S. G. Phillips, 1971.

LeSieg, Theo. *I Can Write!* Random House, 1971.

Lewin, Betsy. *Cat Count*. Dodd, Mead & Co., 1981.

Martin, Bill. *Ten Little Squirrels*. Holt, Rinehart & Winston, 1970.

McLeod, Emilie Warren. *One Snail and Me*. Little, Brown & Co., 1961.

Nedobeck, Don. *Nedobeck's Numbers Book*. Ideal Publishing Co., 1981.

Peek, Merle. *Roll Over! A Counting Song*. Clarion Books, 1981.

Scarry, Richard. *The Best Counting Book Ever*. Random House, 1975.

Schertle, Alice. *Goodnight, Hattie, My Dearie, My Dove*. Lothrop, Lee & Shepard Books, 1985.

Smollin, Michael J. *I Can Count to 100 . . . Can You?* Random House, 1979.

Alphabet

Anno, Mitsumasa. *Anno's Alphabet*. Thomas Y. Crowell Co., 1974.

Arnosky, Jim. *Mouse Writing*. Harcourt Brace Jovanovich, 1983.

Attwell, Lucie. *Lucie Attwell's ABC 123 Pop-up Book*. Deans International Publishers, 1984.

Baskin, Leonard. *Hosie's Alphabet*. Viking Press, 1972.

Bridwell, Norman. *Clifford's ABC*. Scholastic, 1983.

Brown, Marcia. *All Butterflies—an ABC*. Charles Scribner's Sons, 1974.

Carle, Eric. *All About Arthur (An Absolutely Absurd Ape)*. Franklin Watts.

Duke, Kate. *The Guinea Pig ABC*. E. P. Dutton, 1983.

Duvoisin, Roger. *A for the Ark*. Lothrop, Lee & Shepard Co., 1952.

Eastman, P. D. *The Alphabet Book*. Random House, 1974.

Eichenberg, Fritz. *Ape in a Cape—An Alphabet of Odd Animals*. Harcourt Brace & World, 1952.

Elting, Mary & Folsom, Michael. *Q is for Duck*. Clarion Books, 1980.

Emberley, Ed. *Ed Emberley's ABC*. Little, Brown & Co., 1978.

Gretz, Susanna. *Teddy Bears ABC*. Follett, 1977.

Hoban, Tana. *A. B. See!* Greenwillow Books, 1982.

Isadora, Rachel. *City Seen from A to Z.* Greenwillow Books, 1983.

Kitchen, Bert. *Animal Alphabet.* Dial Books, 1984.

Miller, Elizabeth, & Cohen, Jane. *Cat and Dog and the ABCs.* Watts Publishing Co., 1981.

Munari, Bruno. *Bruno Munari's ABC.* Collins/World Publishing Company, Inc., 1960.

Ruben, Patricia. *Apples to Zippers.* Doubleday, 1976.

Schmiderer, Dorothy. *The Alphabeast Book.* Holt, Rinehart & Winston, 1971.

Sendak, Maurice. *Alligators All Around.* Harper & Row, 1962.

Seuss, Dr. *ABC.* Random House, 1963.

Stevenson, James. *Grandpa's Great City Tour.* Greenwillow Books, 1983.

Tallon, Robert. *Rotten Kidphabets.* Holt, Rinehart & Winston, 1975.

Warren, Cathy. *Victoria's ABC Adventure.* Lothrop, Lee & Shepard, 1984.

Wildsmith, Brian. *Brian Wildsmith's ABC.* Franklin Watts, 1962.

Yolen, Jane. *All in the Woodland Early.* Collins, 1979.

Colors

Miller, J. P., & Howard, Katherine. *Do You Know Colors?* Random House, 1978.

O'Neill, Mary. *Hailstones and Halibut Bones.* Doubleday & Co., 1961.

Rossetti, Christina G. *What Is Pink?* Macmillan, 1971.

Days

Carle, Eric. *The Very Hungry Caterpillar.* Philomel Books, 1983.

Clifton, Lucille. *Some of the Days of Everett Anderson.* Holt, Rinehart & Winston, 1970.

Domanska, Janina. *Busy Monday Morning.* Greenwillow Books, 1985.

Elliott, Alan C. *On Sunday the Wind Came.* William Morrow & Co., 1980.

Hooper, Meredith. *Seven Eggs.* Harper & Row, 1985.

Quackenbush, Robert. *Too Many Lollipops.* Scholastic, 1975.

Sharmat, Mitchell. *The Seven Sloppy Days of Phineas Pig.* Harcourt Brace Jovanovich, 1983.

Yolen, Jane. *No Bath Tonight.* Thomas Y. Crowell, 1978.

Months and Seasons

Clifton, Lucille. *Everett Anderson's Year.* Holt, Rinehart & Winston, 1974.

Lionni, Leo. *Mouse Days.* Pantheon Books, 1981.

Sendak, Maurice. *Chicken Soup with Rice.* Scholastic, 1962.

Wolff, Ashley. *A Year of Birds.* Dodd, Mead & Co., 1984.

Zolotow, Charlotte. *Summer Is . . .* Abelard-Schuman, 1967.

Bibliography

Adams, A., Carnine, D., & Gersten, R. (1982). Instructional strategies for studying content area texts in the intermediate grades. *Reading Research Quarterly, 18,* 27–55.

Adams, M. J. (1990). *Beginning to read: Thinking and learning about print.* Cambridge, MA: The MIT Press.

Adelman, H., & Taylor, L. (1977). Two steps toward improving learning for students with (and without) "learning problems." *Journal of Learning Disabilities, 10,* 455–461.

Agee, H. (Chair). (1984). *High-interest easy reading for junior and senior high school students* (4th ed.). Urbana, IL: National Council of Teachers of English.

Agnew, A. T. (1982). Using children's dictated stories to assess code consciousness. *The Reading Teacher, 35,* 450–454.

Allen, R. V. (1976). *Language experience in communication.* Boston: Houghton Mifflin.

Allington, R. L. (1975). Sustained approaches to reading and writing. *Language Arts, 52,* 813–815.

Allington, R. L. (1977). If they don't read much how they ever gonna get good? *Journal of Reading, 21,* 57–61.

Allington, R. L. (1980). Teacher interruption behaviors during primary grade oral reading. *Journal of Educational Psychology, 72,* 371–377.

Allington, R. L. (1983a). The reading instruction provided readers of differing reading abilities. *Elementary School Journal, 83,* 548–558.

Allington, R. L. (1983b). Fluency: The neglected reading goal. *The Reading Teacher, 36,* 556–561.

Allington, R. L. (1984). Content coverage and contextual reading in reading groups. *Journal of Reading Behavior, 16,* 85–96.

Allington, R. L., Chodos, L., Domaracki, J., & Truex, S. (1977). Passage dependency: Four diagnostic oral reading tests. *The Reading Teacher, 30,* 369–375.

Allington, R. L., & Johnston, P. (1989). Coordination, collaboration, and consistency: The redesign of compensatory and special education intervention. In R. Slavin, M. Madden, & N. Karweit (Eds.), *Preventing school failure: Effective programs for students at risk* (pp. 320–354). Boston: Allyn and Bacon.

Allington, R. L., & McGill-Franzen, A. (1980). Word identification errors in isolation and in context: Apples vs. oranges. *The Reading Teacher, 33,* 795–800.

Allington, R. L., & Shake, M. C. (1986). Remedial reading: Achieving curricular congruence in classroom and clinic. *The Reading Teacher, 39,* 648–654.

Allington, R. L., Stuetzel, H., Shake, M., & Lamarche, S. (1986). What is remedial reading? A descriptive study. *Reading Research and Instruction, 26,* 15–30.

Almy, M., & Genishi, C. (1979). *Ways of studying children.* New York: Teachers College Press.

Altwerger, B., Diehl-Faxon, J., & Dockstader-Anderson, K. (1985). Read-aloud events as meaning construction. *Language Arts, 62,* 476–484.

Alvermann, D. E. (1984). Second graders' strategic preferences while reading basal stories. *Journal of Educational Research, 77,* 184–189.

Alvermann, D. E. (1989). Creating the bridge to content-area reading. In P. Winograd, K. Wixson, & M. Y. Lipson (Eds.), *Improving basal reading instruction* (pp. 256–270). New York: Teachers College Press.

American Educational Research Association (AERA) (1985). *Standards for educational and psychological testing.* Washington, DC: American Psychological Association.

Anders, P. L., & Bos, C. S. (1986). Semantic feature analysis: An interactive strategy for vocabulary development and text comprehension. *Journal of Reading, 29,* 610–616.

Anderson, B. (1981). The missing ingredient: Fluent oral reading. *Elementary School Journal, 81,* 173–177.

Anderson, L. M. (1984). The environment of instruction: The function of seatwork in effective commercially developed curriculum. In G. G. Duffy, L. R. Roehler, & J. Mason (Eds.), *Comprehension instruction: Perspectives and suggestions* (pp. 93–103). New York: Longman.

Anderson, L. M. (1981). Short-term student responses to classroom instruction. *Elementary School Journal, 82,* 97–108.

Anderson, L. M., Brubaker, N. L., Alleman-Brooks, J., & Duffy, G. G. (1985). A qualitative study of seatwork in first-grade classrooms. *Elementary School Journal, 86,* 132–140.

Anderson, R. C., & Freebody, P. (1981). Vocabulary knowledge. In J. T. Guthrie (Ed.), *Comprehension and teaching: Research perspectives* (pp. 71–117). Newark, DE: International Reading Association.

Anderson, R. C., Hiebert, E. H., Scott, J. A., & Wilkinson, I. G. (1985). *Becoming a nation of readers: The report of the Commission on Reading.* Washington, DC: The National Institute of Education.

Anderson, R. C., Reynolds, R., Schallert, D., & Goetz, E. (1977). Frameworks for comprehending discourse. *American Educational Research Journal, 14,* 367–381.

Anderson, R. C., Wilson, P. T., & Fielding, L. G. (1988). Growth in reading and how children spend their time outside of school. *Reading Research Quarterly, 23,* 285–303.

Anderson, T. H., & Armbruster, B. B.

(1984a). Content area textbooks. In R. C. Anderson, J. Osborn, & R. J. Tierney (Eds.), *Learning to read in American schools: Basal readers and content texts* (pp. 193–226). Hillsdale, NJ: Lawrence Erlbaum.

Anderson, T. H., & Armbruster, B. B. (1984b). Studying. In P. D. Pearson, R. Barr, M. Kamil, & P. Mosenthal (Eds.), *Handbook of reading research* (pp. 657–679). New York: Longman.

Applebee, A. N. (1978). *A child's concept of story.* Chicago: University of Chicago Press.

Armbruster, B. B. (1984). The problem of "inconsiderate text." In G. G. Duffy, L. R. Roehler, & J. Mason (Eds.), *Comprehension instruction* (pp. 202–217). New York: Longman.

Armbruster, B. B., & Anderson, T. H. (1981). Research synthesis on study skills. *Educational Leadership, 39,* 154–156.

Armbruster, B. B., Anderson, T. H., & Ostertag, J. (1989). Teaching text structure to improve reading and writing. *The Reading Teacher, 43,* 130–137.

Armstrong, D. P., Patberg, J., & Dewitz, P. (1988). Reading guides—Helping students understand. *Journal of Reading, 31,* 532–541.

Asher, S. (1980). Topic interest and children's reading comprehension. In R. J. Spiro, B. C. Bruce, & W. F. Brewer (Eds.), *Theoretical issues in reading comprehension* (pp. 525–534). Hillsdale, NJ: Lawrence Erlbaum.

Ashton-Warner, S. (1963). *Teacher.* New York: Simon and Schuster.

Atwell, N. (1987). *In the middle.* Portsmouth, NH: Boynton/Cook.

Atwell, N. (1990). *Coming to know: Writing to learn in the intermediate grades.* Portsmouth, NH: Heinemann.

Au, K. H. (1979). Using the experience-text-relationship method with minority children. *The Reading Teacher, 32,* 677–679.

Au, K. H. (1980). Participation structures in a reading lesson with Hawaiian children: Analysis of a culturally appropriate instructional event. *Anthropology and Education Quarterly, 11,* 91–115.

Au, K. H., & Kawakami, A. J. (1986). The influence of the social organization of instruction on children's text comprehension ability: A Vygotskian perspective. In T. E. Raphael (Ed.), *The contexts of school-based literacy* (pp. 63–77). New York: Random House.

Au, K. H., & Mason, J. (1981). Social organizational factors in learning to read: The balance of rights hypothesis. *Reading Research Quarterly, 17,* 115–167.

Aulls, M. W. (1982). *Developing readers in today's elementary school.* Boston: Allyn & Bacon.

Aulls, M. W., & Graves, M. S. (Eds.). (1985). *Electric butterfly and other stories (Quest series).* New York: Scholastic Inc.

Bader, L. A. (1980). *Reading diagnosis and remediation in classroom and clinic.* New York: Macmillan.

Bader, L. A. (1983). *Bader reading and language inventory.* New York: Macmillan.

Baker, L., & Brown, A. L. (1984). Metacognitive skills and reading. In P. D. Pearson, R. Barr, M. Kamil, & P. Mosenthal (Eds.), *Handbook of reading research* (pp. 353–394). New York: Longman.

Balajthy, E. (1989a). *Computers and reading: Lessons from the past and the technologies of the future.* Englewood Cliffs, NJ: Prentice-Hall.

Balajthy, E. (1989b). The printout: Holistic approaches to reading. *The Reading Teacher, 42,* 324.

Ballard, R. (1978). *Talking dictionary.* Ann Arbor, MI: Ulrich's Books.

Baron, J. (1977). Mechanisms for pronouncing printed words: Use and acquisition. In D. LaBerge & S. J. Samuels (Eds.), *Basic process in reading: Perception and comprehension* (pp. 175–216). Hillsdale, NJ: Lawrence Erlbaum.

Barr, R. (1974–75). The effect of instruction on pupil reading strategies. *Reading Research Quarterly, 10,* 555–582.

Barr, R., & Sadow, M. W. (1989). Influence of basal programs on fourth-grade reading instruction. *Reading Research Quarterly, 24,* 44–71.

Barr, R., Sadow, M., & Blachowicz, C. (1990). *Reading diagnosis for teachers.* New York: Longman.

Barrett, T. C. (1976). Taxonomy of reading comprehension. In R. Smith & T. C. Barrett (Eds.), *Teaching reading in the middle grades* (pp. 53–58). Reading, MA: Addison-Wesley.

Barron, R. (1969). The use of vocabulary as an advance organizer. In H. L. Herber & P. L. Sanders (Eds.), *Research in reading in the content areas: First report* (pp. 29–39). Syracuse, NY: Syracuse University Reading and Language Arts Center.

Baumann, J. F. (1986). Effect of rewritten content textbook passages on middle grade students' comprehension of main ideas: Making the inconsiderate considerate. *Journal of Reading Behavior, 28,* 1–21.

Baumann, J. F. (1988). *Reading assessment: An instructional decision-making perspective.* Columbus, OH: Charles E. Merrill.

Bean, R. M. (1979). Role of the reading specialist: A multifaceted dilemma. *The Reading Teacher, 32,* 409–413.

Bean, T. W., & Steenwyk, F. L. (1984). The effect of three forms of summarization instruction on sixth graders' summary writing and comprehension. *Journal of Reading Behavior, 16,* 297–306.

Beck, I. L., & McKeown, M. G. (1981). Developing questions that promote comprehension: The story map. *Language Arts, 58,* 913–918.

Beck, I. L., & McKeown, M. G. (1983). Learning words well—A program to enhance vocabulary and comprehension. *The Reading Teacher, 36,* 622–625.

Beck, I. L., McKeown, M. G., & McCaslin, E. S. (1981). Does reading make sense? Problems of early readers. *The Reading Teacher, 34,* 780–785.

Beck, I. L., McKeown, M. G., & McCaslin, E. S. (1983). Vocabulary development: All contexts are not created equal. *Elementary School Journal, 83,* 177–181.

Beck, I. L., Omanson, R. C., & McKeown, M. G. (1982). An instructional redesign of reading lessons: Effects on comprehension. *Reading Research Quarterly, 17,* 462–481.

Beers, J., & Henderson, E. H. (1977). A study of developing orthographic concepts among first graders. *Research in the Teaching of English, 11,* 133–148.

Bender, L. (1938). *A visual-motor Gestalt test and its clinical use.* New York: American Orthopsychiatric Association.

Berglund, R., & Johns, J. (1983). A primer on uninterrupted sustained silent reading. *The Reading Teacher, 36,* 534–539.

Betts, E. A. (1936). *The prevention and correction of reading difficulties.* Evanston, IL: Row, Peterson.

Betts, E. A. (1946). *Foundations of reading instruction.* New York: American Books.

Bialystok, E., & Ryan, E. (1985). A metacognitive framework for the development of first and second language skills. In D. L. Forrest-Pressley, G. E. MacKinnon, & T. G. Waller (Eds.), *Metacognition, cognition, and human performance* (pp. 207–252). New York: Academic Press.

Binkley, M. R. (1988). New ways of assessing text difficulty. In B. L. Zakaluk & S. J. Samuels (Eds.), *Readability: Its past, present, and future* (pp. 98–120).

Newark, DE: International Reading Association.

Bleich, D. (1975). *Readings and feelings.* Urbana, IL: National Council of Teachers of English.

Bleich, D. (1980). *Subjective criticism.* Bloomington: Indiana University Press.

Bloom, B. S. (Ed.). (1956). *Taxonomy of educational objectives. Handbook I: Cognitive domain.* New York: David McKay.

Blumenfeld, P. C., Hamilton, V. L., Bossert, S. T., Wessels, K., & Meece, J. (1983). Teacher talk and student thought: Socialization into the student role. In J. Levine & M. Wang (Eds.), *Teacher and student perceptions: Implications for learning* (pp. 143–192). Hillsdale, NJ: Lawrence Erlbaum.

Blumenfeld, P. C., Mergendoller, J. R., & Swarthout, S. W. (1987). Task as a heuristic for understanding student learning and motivation. *Journal of Curriculum Studies, 19,* 135–148.

Boehm, A. E. (1986). *Boehm Test of Basic Concepts—Revised.* San Antonio, TX: The Psychological Corporation.

Boehnlein, M. (1987). Reading intervention for high-risk first graders. *Educational Leadership, 44* (6), 32–37.

Boggs, S. T. (1985). *Speaking, relating and learning: A study of Hawaiian children at home and at school.* Norwood, NJ: Ablex.

Bormuth, J. R. (1968). Cloze test readability: Criterion scores. *Journal of Educational Measurement, 5,* 189–196.

Bos, C. S. (1982). Getting past decoding: Assisted and repeated readings as remedial methods for learning disabled students. *Topics in Learning and Learning Disabilities, 1,* 51–57.

Bossert, S. T. (1979). *Tasks and social relationships in classrooms.* New York: Cambridge University Press.

Botel, M. (1982). New informal approaches to evaluating word recognition and comprehension. In J. J. Pikulski & T. Shanahan (Eds.), *Approaches to the informal evaluation of reading* (pp. 30–41). Newark, DE: International Reading Association.

Bowerman, M. (1978). The acquisition of word meaning: An investigation into some current conflicts. In N. Waterson, & C. E. Snow (Eds.), *The development of communication* (pp. 263–287). London: Wiley & Sons.

Bowles, S., & Gintis, H. (1976). *Schooling in capitalist America.* New York: Basic Books.

Bradley, J. M., & Ames, W. S. (1976). The influence of intrabook readability variation on oral reading performance. *Journal of Educational Research, 70,* 101–105.

Bradley, J. M., & Ames, W. S. (1977). Readability parameters of basal readers. *Journal of Reading Behavior, 9,* 175–183.

Bransford, J. D., & Johnson, M. K. (1972). Contextual prerequisites for understanding: Some investigations of comprehension and recall. *Journal of Verbal Learning and Verbal Behavior, 11,* 717–726.

Bransford, J. D., & McCarrell, N. S. (1974). A sketch of a cognitive approach to comprehension. In W. Weimer & D. S. Palermo (Eds.), *Cognition and the symbolic processes* (pp. 189–229). Hillsdale, NJ: Lawrence Erlbaum.

Brecht, R. D. (1977). Testing format and instructional level with the informal reading inventory. *The Reading Teacher, 31,* 57–59.

Brennan, A. D., Bridge, C. A., & Winograd, P. N. (1986). The effects of structural variation on children's recall of basal reader stories. *Reading Research Quarterly, 21,* 91–104.

Bretzing, B. B., & Kulhavy, R. W. (1981). Note-taking and passage style. *Journal of Educational Psychology, 73,* 242–250.

Bricker, D. D. (1986). *Early education of at-risk and handicapped infants, toddlers, and preschool children.* Glenview, IL: Scott, Foresman.

Bridge, C. A. (1989). Beyond the basal in beginning reading. In P. Winograd, K. Wixson, & M. Lipson (Eds.), *Improving basal reading instruction* (pp. 177–209). New York: Teachers College Press.

Bridge, C. A., Belmore, S., Moskow, S., Cohen, S., & Matthews, P. (1984). Topicalization and memory for main ideas in prose. *Journal of Reading Behavior, 16,* 27–40.

Bridge, C. A., & Burton, B. (1982). Teaching sight vocabulary through patterned language materials. In J. A. Niles & L. A. Harris (Eds.), *New inquiries in reading research and instruction* (31st Yearbook of The National Reading Conference, pp. 119–123). Washington, DC: National Reading Conference.

Bridge, C. A., & Winograd, P. N. (1982). Readers' awareness of cohesive relationships during cloze comprehension. *Journal of Reading Behavior, 14,* 299–312.

Bridge, C. A., Winograd, P. N., & Haley, D. (1983). Using predictable materials vs. preprimers to teach beginning sight words. *The Reading Teacher, 36,* 884–891.

Brigance, A. H. (1976). *BRIGANCE® Diagnostic Inventories.* North Billerica, MA: Curriculum Associates.

Brophy, J. E. (1983a). Conceptualizing student motivation. *Educational Psychologist, 18,* 200–215.

Brophy, J. E. (1983b). Research on the self-fulfilling prophecy and teacher expectations. *Journal of Educational Psychology, 75,* 631–661.

Brophy, J. E., & Good, T. L. (1974). *Teacher-student relationships: Causes and consequences.* New York: Holt, Rinehart & Winston.

Brown, A. L. (1978). Knowing when, where, and how to remember: A problem of metacognition. In R. Glaser (Ed.), *Advances in instructional psychology 1* (pp. 77–165). Hillsdale, NJ: Lawrence Erlbaum.

Brown, A. L. (1980). Metacognitive development and reading. In R. Spiro & W. Brewer (Eds.), *Theoretical issues in reading comprehension* (pp. 453–481). Hillsdale, NJ: Lawrence Erlbaum.

Brown, A. L., Armbruster, B. B., & Baker, L. (1986). The role of metacognition in reading and studying. In J. Orasanu (Ed.), *A decade of reading research: Implications for practice* (pp. 49–75). Hillsdale, NJ: Lawrence Erlbaum.

Brown, A. L., & Campione, J. C. (1986). Psychological theory and the study of learning disabilities. *American Psychologist, 14,* 1059–1068.

Brown, A. L., Campione, J. C., & Day, J. D. (1981). Learning to learn: On training students to learn from texts. *Educational Researcher, 10,* 14–21.

Brown, J. S., Collins, A., & Duguid, P. (1989). Situated cognition and the culture of learning. *Educational Researcher, 18,* 32–42.

Brown, V. L., Hammill, D. D., & Wiederholt, J. L. (1986). *Test of Reading Comprehension.* Austin, TX: Pro-Ed.

Bruce, B. (1984). A new point of view on children's stories. In R. C. Anderson, J. Osborn, & R. J. Tierney (Eds.), *Learning to read in American schools: Basal readers and content texts* (pp. 153–174). Hillsdale, NJ: Lawrence Erlbaum.

Bruner, J. S. (1964). The course of cognitive growth. *American Psychologist, 19,* 1–15.

Bruner, J. S. (1973). *Beyond the information given: Studies in the psychology of knowing.* Selected, edited, and introduced by J. M. Anglin. New York: W. W. Norton.

Budbill, D. (1978). *Bones on black spruce mountain.* NY: Bantom Skylark Books.

Burns, P. C., & Roe, B. D. (1985). *Informal reading inventory* (2nd ed.). Boston: Houghton Mifflin.

Buros, O. K. (Ed.) (1975). *Reading tests and reviews II.* Highland Park, NJ: Gryphon Press.

Butkowsky, I. S., & Willows, D. M. (1980). Cognitive-motivational characteristics of children varying in reading ability: Evidence for learned helplessness in poor readers. *Journal of Educational Psychology, 72,* 408–422.

Calfee, R. C., & Drum, P. A. (1979). *Teaching reading in compensatory classes.* Newark, DE: International Reading Association.

Calfee, R., Lindamood, P., & Lindamood, C. (1973). Acoustic-phonetic skills and reading: Kindergarten through twelfth grade. *Journal of Educational Psychology, 64,* 293–298.

Calkins, L. M. (1986). *The art of teaching writing.* Portsmouth, NH: Heinemann.

Campione, J. C., & Brown, A. L. (1987). Linking dynamic assessment with school achievement. In C. S. Lidz (Ed.), *Dynamic assessment* (pp. 82–109). New York: Guilford.

Campione, J. C., Brown, A. L., & Ferrara, R. A. (1982). Mental retardation and intelligence. In R. J. Sternberg (Ed.), *Handbook of human intelligence.* New York: Cambridge University Press.

Campione, J. C., Brown, A. L., Ferrara, R. A., & Bryant, N. R. (1984). The zone of proximal development: Implications for individual differences and learning. In B. Rogoff & J. Wertsch (Eds.), *New directions for child development: Children's learning in the "zone of proximal development"* (Vol. 23, pp. 265–294). San Francisco: Jossey-Bass.

Carlson, J. S., & Wiedl, K. H. (1979). Toward a differential testing approach: Testing-the-limits employing the Raven matrices. *Intelligence, 3,* 323–344.

Carnine, D. W., Kameenui, E. J., & Coyle, G. (1984). Utilization of contextual information in determining the meaning of unfamiliar words. *Reading Research Quarterly, 19,* 188–204.

Carnine, D., Silbert, J., & Kameenui, E. J. (1990). *Direct instruction reading* (2nd ed.). Columbus, OH: Charles E. Merrill.

Carr, E. (1985). The vocabulary overview guide: A metacognitive strategy to improve vocabulary and retention. *Journal of Reading, 28,* 684–689.

Carr, E., & Ogle, D. (1987). K-W-L Plus: A strategy for comprehension and summarization. *Journal of Reading, 30,* 626–631.

Carr, E. M., & Wixson, K. K. (1986). Guidelines for evaluating vocabulary instruction. *Journal of Reading, 29,* 588–595.

Carter, L. F. (1984). The sustaining effects study of compensatory and elementary education. *Educational Researcher, 13* (7), 4–13.

Carver, R., & Hoffman, J. (1981). The effect of practice through repeated reading on gain in reading ability using a computer-based instructional system. *Reading Research Quarterly, 16,* 374–390.

Cavanaugh, J. C., & Perlmutter, M. (1982). Metamemory: A critical examination. *Child Development, 53,* 11–28.

Cazden, C. B. (1983). Adult assistance to language development: Scaffold, model and direct instruction. In R. Parker & S. Davis (Eds.), *Developing literacy* (pp. 3–18). Newark, DE: International Reading Association.

Cazden, C. B. (1986). Classroom discourse. In M. C. Wittrock (Ed.), *Handbook of research on teaching* (3rd ed., pp. 432–463). New York: Macmillan.

Center for Language in Primary Education (CLPE). (1988). *The primary language record*. Portsmouth, NH: Heinemann.

Ceprano, M. (1981). A review of selected research on methods of teaching sight words. *The Reading Teacher, 35,* 314–322.

Chall, J. S. (1983). Literacy: Trends and explanations. *Educational Researcher, 12,* 3–8.

Chall, J. S. (1984). Readability and prose comprehension: Continuities and discontinuities. In J. Flood (Ed.), *Understanding reading comprehension* (pp. 233–246). Newark, DE: International Reading Association.

Chall, J. S., & Curtis, M. E. (1987). What clinical diagnosis tells us about children's reading. *The Reading Teacher, 40,* 784–789.

Chomsky, C. (1978). When you still can't read in third grade: After decoding, what? In S. J. Samuels (Ed.), *What research has to say about reading instruction* (pp. 13–30). Newark, DE: International Reading Association.

Chomsky, C. (1981). Write now, read later. *Childhood Education, 47,* 296–299.

Cioffi, G., & Carney, J. J. (1983). Dynamic assessment of reading disabilities. *The Reading Teacher, 36,* 764–768.

Clark, C. H. (1982). Assessing free recall. *The Reading Teacher, 35,* 434–439.

Clark, C. M. (1984). Teacher planning and reading comprehension. In G. G. Duffy, L. R. Roehler, & J. Mason (Eds.), *Comprehension instruction* (pp. 58–70). New York: Longman.

Clarke, J. H., Raths, J., & Gilbert, G. L. (1989). Inductive towers: Letting students see how they think. *Journal of Reading, 33,* 86–95.

Clay, M. M. (1966). *Emergent reading behavior.* Unpublished doctoral dissertation, University of Auckland, New Zealand.

Clay, M. M. (1975). *What did I write?* Auckland/Portsmouth, NH: Heinemann.

Clay, M. M. (1979). *Reading: The patterning of complex behavior* (2nd ed.). Auckland/Exeter, NH: Heinemann.

Clay, M. M. (1982). *Observing young readers.* Exeter, NH: Heinemann.

Clay, M. M. (1985). *The early detection of reading difficulties* (3rd ed.). Auckland, New Zealand: Heinemann.

Cleary, B. (1983). *Dear Mr. Henshaw.* New York: Bantam Doubleday Dell Publishing, Inc.

Cline, R. L., & Kretke, G. L. (1980). An evaluation of long-term SSR in the junior high school. *Journal of Reading, 23,* 503–506.

Cohn, M., & D'Alessandro, C. (1978). When is a decoding error not a decoding error? *The Reading Teacher, 32,* 341–344.

Coles, G. S. (1978). The learning-disabilities test battery: Empirical and social issues. *Harvard Educational Review, 48,* 313–340.

Coles, G. S. (1987). *The learning mystique.* New York: Pantheon.

Collins, A., & Smith, E. E. (1980). *Teaching the process of reading comprehension* (Tech. Rep. No. 182). Urbana, IL: University of Illinois, Center for the Study of Reading.

Conard, S. S. (1984). *On readability and readability formula scores* (Ginn Occasional Papers No. 17). Columbus, OH: Ginn and Co.

Cook, D. (Ed.). (1986). *A guide to curriculum planning in reading* (Bulletin No. 6305). Madison, WI: Department of Public Instruction.

Cooley, W. W., & Leinhardt, G. (1980). The instructional dimensions study. *Educational Evaluation and Policy Analysis, 2,* 7–25.

Cooper, J. L. (1952). *The effect of adjustment of basal reading materials on reading achievement.* Unpublished doctoral dissertation, Boston University, Boston.

Corno, L., & Mandinach, E. (1983). Student interpretive processes in the classrooms. *Educational Psychologist, 18,* 88–108.

Covington, M. V., & Omelich, C. L. (1979). Effort: The double-edged sword in school achievement. *Journal of Educational Psychology, 71,* 169–182.

Craik, F., & Lockhart, R. (1972). Levels of processing: A framework for memory research. *Journal of Verbal Learning and Verbal Behavior, 11,* 671–684.

Cramer, R. L. (1982). Informal approaches to evaluating children's writing. In J. J. Pikulski & T. Shanahan (Eds.), *Approaches to the informal evaluation of reading* (pp. 80–93). Newark, DE: International Reading Association.

Critchley, M. (1975). Specific developmental dyslexia. In E. H. Lenneberg & E. Lenneberg (Eds.), *Foundations of language development* (Vol. 2, pp. 361–366). New York: Academic Press.

Crowell, D. C. (1980). *Kamehameha reading objective system.* Honolulu: Kamehameha Schools.

Cullinan, B., & Fitzgerald, S. (1984). *Statement on readability.* Joint statement by the Presidents of the International Reading Association and the National Council of Teachers of English.

Cunningham, A. E. (1990). Explicit vs. implicit instruction in phonemic awareness. *Journal of Experimental Child Psychology, 50.*

Cunningham, P. M. (1975–76). Investigating a synthesized theory of mediated word identification. *Reading Research Quarterly, 11,* 127–143.

Cunningham, P. M. (1978). Decoding polysyllabic words: An alternative strategy. *Journal of Reading, 21,* 608–614.

Cunningham, P. M. (1979). A compare/contrast theory of mediated word identification. *The Reading Teacher, 32,* 774–778.

Cunningham, P. M. (1984). What would make workbooks worthwhile? In R. C. Anderson, J. Osborn, & R. T. Tierney (Eds.), *Learning to read in American schools* (pp. 113–120). Hillsdale, NJ: Lawrence Erlbaum.

Cunningham, P. M., Moore, S. A., Cunningham, J. W., & Moore, D. W. (1989). *Reading in elementary classrooms* (2nd ed.). New York: Longman.

Daiute, C. (1983). The computer as stylus and audience. *College Composition and Communication, 34,* 134–145.

Daiute, C. (1986). Physical and cognitive factors in revision: Insights from studies with computers. *Research in the Teaching of English, 20,* 141–159.

Dale, E., & Chall, J. (1948). A formula for predicting readability. *Educational Research Bulletin, 27,* 11–20, 37–54.

Dansereau, D. F. (1985). Learning strategy research. In J. Segal, S. Chipman, & R. Glaser (Eds.), *Thinking and learning skills: Relating instruction to basic research* (Vol. 1, pp. 209–240). Hillsdale, NJ: Lawrence Erlbaum.

Davey, B. (1986). Using textbook activity guides to help students learn from textbooks. *Journal of Reading, 29,* 489–494.

Davis, F. B. (1968). Research in comprehension in reading. *Reading Research Quarterly, 3,* 499–545.

Davison, A. (1984). Readability—Appraising text difficulty. In R. C. Anderson, J. Osborn, & R. T. Tierney (Eds.), *Learning to read in American schools: Basal readers and content texts* (pp. 121–140). Hillsdale, NJ: Lawrence Erlbaum.

Davison, A., & Kantor, R. N. (1982). On the failure of readability formulas to define readable texts: A case study from adaptations. *Reading Research Quarterly, 17,* 187–209.

Day, K. C., & Day, H. D. (1986). Tests of metalinguistic awareness. In D. B. Yaden & S. Templeton (Eds.), *Meta-*

linguistic awareness and beginning literacy: Conceptualizing what it means to read and write (pp. 187–198). Portsmouth, NH: Heinemann.

Dechant, E. V. (1970). *Improving and teaching of reading* (2nd ed.). Englewood Cliffs, NJ: Prentice-Hall.

DeFord, D. E. (1980). Young children and their writing. *Theory into Practice, 19,* 157–162.

DeFord, D. E. (1985). Theoretical orientation to reading profile (TORP). *Reading Research Quarterly, 20,* 351–367.

DeFord, D. E. (1986). Classroom contexts for literacy learning. In T. E. Raphael (Ed.), *The contexts of school-based literacy* (pp. 163–180). New York: Longman.

deHirsch, K., Jansky, J. J., & Langford, W. S. (1966). *Predicting reading failure.* New York: Harper & Row.

Deshler, D. D., & Schumaker, J. B. (1986). Learning strategies: An instructional alternative for low-achieving adolescents. *Exceptional Children, 52,* 583–590.

Dewitz, P., Carr, E. M., & Patberg, J. P. (1987). Effects of inference training on comprehension and comprehension monitoring. *Reading Research Quarterly, 22,* 542–546.

Dillon, J. T. (1988). *Questioning and teaching: A manual of practice.* New York: Teachers College Press.

Dixon, C. N. (1977). Language experience stories as a diagnostic tool. *Language Arts, 54,* 501–509.

Doctorow, M., Wittrock, M. C., & Marks, C. (1978). Generative processes in reading comprehension. *Journal of Educational Psychology, 70,* 109–118.

Dolch, E. W. (1942). *Basic sight word test.* Champaign, IL: Garrard.

Dombey, H. (1987). Learning the language of books. In M. Meek (Ed.), *Opening moves: Work in progress in the study of children's language development* (Bedford Way Papers 17, pp. 26–43). London: Institute of Education, University of London, Turnaround Distribution Ltd.

Downing, J. (1970). Children's concepts of language in learning to read. *Educational Research, 12,* 106–112.

Downing, J. (1978). Linguistic awareness, English orthography and reading instruction. *Journal of Reading Behavior, 10,* 103–114.

Downing, J., Ayers, D., & Schaefer, B. (1983). *Linguistic Awareness in Reading Readiness (LARR) Test.* Slough, England: NFER-Nelson.

Downing, J., & Leong, C. K. (1982). *Psychology of reading.* New York: Macmillan.

Doyle, W. (1983). Academic work. *Review of Educational Research, 53,* 159–199.

Doyle, W. (1986). Classroom organization and management. In M. C. Wittrock (Ed.), *Handbook of research on teaching* (3rd ed., pp. 392–431). New York: Macmillan.

Drahozal, E. C., & Hanna, G. S. (1978). Reading comprehension subscores: Pretty bottles for ordinary wine. *Journal of Reading, 21,* 416–420.

Dreeben, R. (1968). The contribution of schooling to the learning of norms. In *Socialization and schools* (Harvard Educational Review Reprint Series No. 1). Cambridge, MA: Harvard University Press.

DuBois, D., & Stice, C. (1981). Comprehension instruction: Let's recall it for repair. *Reading World, 20,* 173–183.

Duckworth, E. (1979). Either we're too early and they can't learn it or we're too late and they know it already: The dilemma of "applying Piaget." *Harvard Educational Review, 49,* 297–312.

Dudley-Marling, C. C. (1985). Microcomputers, reading, and writing: Alternatives to drill and practice. *The Reading Teacher, 38,* 388–391.

Duell, O. K. (1974). Effect of types of objective, level of test questions, and judged importance of texted materials upon posttest performance. *Jour-*

nal of Educational Psychology, 66, 225–232.

Duffy, G. G., & McIntyre, L. (1982). A naturalistic study of instructional assistance in primary grade reading. *Elementary School Journal, 83,* 15–23.

Duffy, G. G., & Roehler, L. R. (1989). *Improving classroom reading instruction: A decision making approach* (2nd ed.). New York: Random House.

Duffy, G. G., Roehler, L. R., Meloth, M. S., Vavrus, L. G., Book, C., Putnam, J., & Wesselman, R. (1986). The relationship between explicit verbal explanations during reading skills instruction and student awareness and achievement: A study of reading teacher effects. *Reading Research Quarterly, 21,* 237–252.

Dunn, L. M., & Dunn, L. M. (1981). *Peabody Picture Vocabulary Test–Revised.* Circle Pines, MN: American Guidance Service.

Durkin, D. (1978). *Teaching them to read* (3rd ed.). Boston: Allyn & Bacon.

Durkin, D. (1978–79). What classroom observations reveal about reading comprehension instruction. *Reading Research Quarterly, 14,* 481–533.

Durkin, D. (1981). Reading comprehension instruction in five basal reader series. *Reading Research Quarterly, 16,* 515–544.

Durkin, D. (1983). *Teaching them to read* (4th ed.). Boston: Allyn & Bacon.

Durkin, D. (1984). Is there a match between what elementary teachers do and what basal reader manuals recommend? *The Reading Teacher, 37,* 734–749.

Durkin, D. (1987). Testing in kindergarten. *The Reading Teacher, 40,* 766–770.

Durr, W. K. (1973). Computer study of high frequency words in popular trade journals. *The Reading Teacher, 27,* 37–42.

Durrell, D. D., Nicholson, A., Olson, A. V., Gavel, S. R., & Linehan, E. B. (1958). Success in first grade reading. *Journal of Education, 140,* 2–48.

Dweck, C. S. (1975). The role of expectancies and attributions in the alleviation of learned helplessness. *Journal of Personality and Social Psychology, 31,* 674–685.

Dweck, C. S., & Bempechat, J. (1983). Children's theories of intelligence: Consequences for learning. In S. G. Paris, G. M. Olson, & H. S. Stevenson (Eds.), *Learning and motivation in the classroom* (pp. 239–258). Hillsdale, NJ: Lawrence Erlbaum.

Dykstra, R. (1968). The effectiveness of code- and meaning-emphasis beginning reading programs. *The Reading Teacher, 22,* 17–23.

Earle, R. A. (1969). Developing and using study guides. In H. L. Herber & P. L. Sanders (Eds.), *Research in reading in the content areas: First year report* (pp. 71–92). Syracuse, NY: Reading and Language Arts Center, Syracuse University.

Easley, J., & Zwoyer, R. (1975). Teaching by listening—Toward a new day in math classes. *Contemporary Education, 47,* 19–25.

Edmonds, R. (1980). *A discussion of the literature and issues related to effective schooling.* St. Louis, MO: Cemrel.

Eeds, M. (1985). Bookwords: Using a beginning word list of high frequency words from children's literature K-3. *The Reading Teacher, 38,* 418–423.

Ehri, L. (1979). Linguistic insight: Threshold of reading acquisition. In T. G. Waller & G. E. MacKinnon (Eds.), *Reading research: Advances in theory and practice* (Vol. 1, pp. 63–114). New York: Academic Press.

Ehri, L. (1985). Effects of printed language acquisition on speech. In D. R. Olson, N. Torrance, & A. Hildyard (Eds.), *Literacy, language, and learning* (pp. 333–367). Cambridge, England: Cambridge University Press.

Ehri, L. (1987). Learning to read and spell

words. *Journal of Reading Behavior, 19,* 5–32.

Ehri, L., & Wilce, L. S. (1980). Do beginners learn to read function words better in sentences or in lists? *Reading Research Quarterly, 15,* 451–476.

Eisenberg, L. (1975). Psychiatric aspects of language disability. In D. Duane & M. Rawson (Eds.), *Reading, perception, and language* (pp. 215–229). Baltimore: York Press.

Ekwall, E. E. (1979). *Ekwall reading inventory* (1st ed.). Boston: Allyn & Bacon.

Ekwall, E. E. (1986). *Ekwall reading inventory* (2nd ed.). Boston: Allyn & Bacon.

Ekwall, E. E., & Shanker, J. L. (1983). *Diagnosis and remediation of the disabled reader* (2nd ed.). Boston: Allyn & Bacon.

Ekwall, E. E., & Shanker, J. L. (1985). *Teaching reading in the elementary school.* Columbus, OH: Charles E. Merrill.

Ekwall, E. E., & Shanker, J. L. (1988). *Diagnosis of the disabled reader* (3rd ed.). Boston: Allyn & Bacon.

Elkonin, D. E. (1963). The psychology of mastering the elements of reading. In B. Simon & J. Simon (Eds.), *Educational psychology in the U.S.S.R.* (pp. 165–179). London: Routledge.

Elkonin, D. E. (1973). U.S.S.R. In J. Downing (Ed.), *Comparative reading: Cross-national studies of behavior and processes in reading and writing* (pp. 551–579). New York: Macmillan.

Elley, W. B. (1989). Vocabulary acquisition from listening to stories. *Reading Research Quarterly, 24,* 174–187.

Elliot, S. N. (1980). Children's knowledge and uses of organizational patterns of prose in recalling what they read. *Journal of Reading Behavior, 12,* 203–212.

Ellis, A. (1984). *Reading, writing and dyslexia: A cognitive view.* Hillsdale, NJ: Lawrence Erlbaum.

Entin, E. B., & Klare, G. R. (1985). Relationships of measures of interest, prior knowledge, and readability to comprehension of expository passages. In B. Hutson (Ed.), *Advances in reading/language research* (Vol. 3, pp. 9–38). Greenwich, CT: JAI Press.

Ericsson, K. A., & Simon, H. A. (1980). Verbal reports as data. *Psychological Review, 87,* 215–251.

Estes, T. H., & Vaughan, J. L. (1973). Reading interest and comprehension: Implications. *The Reading Teacher, 27,* 149–153.

Estes, T. H., & Vaughan, J. L. (1978). *Reading and learning in the content classroom.* Boston: Allyn & Bacon.

Evans, M., Taylor, N., & Blum, I. (1979). Children's written language awareness and its relation to reading acquisition. *Journal of Reading Behavior, 11,* 7–19.

Fass, W., & Schumacher, G. M. (1978). Effects of motivation, subject activity, and readability on the retention of prose materials. *Journal of Educational Psychology, 70,* 803–808.

Federal Register (29 December 1977). Washington, DC: 65082–65085.

Fernald, G. M. (1943). *Remedial techniques in basic school subjects.* New York: McGraw-Hill.

Fernald, G. M., & Keller, H. B. (1921). Effects of kinesthetic factors in development of word recognition. *Journal of Educational Research, 4,* 355–377.

Ferreiro, E. (1978). What is written in a written sentence? A developmental answer. *Journal of Education, 160,* 25–39.

Ferreiro, E. (1980, May). *The relationship between oral and written language: The children's viewpoints.* Paper presented at the 25th Annual Conference of the International Reading Association, St. Louis, MO.

Ferreiro, E., & Teberosky, A. (1979/1982). *Literacy before schooling.* Exeter, NH: Heinemann.

Feuerstein, R., Rand, Y., & Hoffman, M. B. (1979). *The dynamic assessment of re-*

tarded performance. Baltimore, MD: University Park Press.

Fielding, L. G., Wilson, P. T., & Anderson, R. C. (1986). A new focus on free reading: The role of trade books in reading instruction. In T. E. Raphael (Ed.), *The contexts of school-based literacy* (pp. 149–160). New York: Random House.

Filby, N., & Barnett, B. (1982). Student perceptions of better readers in elementary classrooms. *The Elementary School Journal, 82*, 435–450.

Fillion, B., & Brause, R. S. (1987). Research into classroom practices: What have we learned and where are we going? In J. R. Squire (Ed.), *The dynamics of language learning* (pp. 201–225). Urbana, IL: ERIC Clearinghouse on Reading and Communications Skills and the National Conference on Research in English.

Fisher, C. W., Berliner, D. C., Filby, N., Marliave, R., Cohen, L., Dishaw, M., & Moore, J. (1980). Teaching behaviors, academic learning time, and student achievement: An overview. In C. Denham & A. Lieberman (Eds.), *Time to learn* (pp. 7–32). Washington, DC: National Institute of Education.

Flanders, N. (1971). Teacher influence, pupil attitudes, and achievement. In J. Raths, J. R. Pancella, & J. S. Van Ness (Eds.), *Studying teaching* (2nd ed., pp. 43–69). Englewood Cliffs, NJ: Prentice-Hall.

Flanders, N. (1975). The use of interaction analysis to study pupil attitudes toward learning. In R. A. Weinberg & F. H. Wood (Eds.), *Observation of pupils and teachers in mainstream and special education settings: Alternative strategies* (pp. 41–74). Minneapolis: The Leadership Training Institute/Special Education, The University of Minnesota.

Flavell, J. H. (1977). *Cognitive development*. Englewood Cliffs, NJ: Prentice-Hall.

Flavell, J. H. (1978). Metacognitive aspects of problem-solving. In L. B. Resnick (Ed.), *The nature of intelligence* (pp. 231–235). Hillsdale, NJ: Lawrence Erlbaum.

Flavell, J. H., & Wellman, H. M. (1977). Metamemory. In R. Kail, Jr., & J. W. Hagen (Eds.), *Perspectives on the development of memory and cognition* (pp. 3–33). Hillsdale, NJ: Lawrence Erlbaum.

Flesch, R. (1948). A new readability yardstick. *Journal of Applied Psychology, 32*, 221–233.

Flood, J., & Lapp, D. (1987). Forms of discourse in basal readers. *The Elementary School Journal, 87*, 299–306.

Forester, A. D. (1980). Learning to spell by spelling. *Theory into Practice, 19*, 186–193.

Fowler, G. L. (1982). Developing comprehension skills in primary students through the use of story frames. *The Reading Teacher, 36*, 176–184.

Fowler, J. W., & Peterson, P. L. (1981). Increasing reading persistence and altering attributional style of learned helpless children. *Journal of Educational Psychology, 73*, 251–260.

Fox, B., & Routh, D. K. (1976). Phonemic analysis and severe reading disability in children. *Journal of Psycholinguistic Research, 9*, 115–119.

Fox, C. (1987). Talking like a book: Young children's oral monologues. In M. Meek (Ed.), *Opening moves: Work in progress in the study of children's language development* (Bedford Way Papers 17, pp. 12–25). London, UK: Institute of Education, University of London, Turnaround Distribution Ltd.

Fraatz, J. M. (1987). *The politics of reading: Power, opportunity, and prospects for change in America's public schools*. New York: Teachers College Press.

Francis, H. (1973). Children's experience of reading and notions of units of language. *British Journal of Educational Psychology, 43*, 17–23.

Freebody, P., & Anderson, R. C. (1983). Effects on text comprehension of differing proportions and locations of difficult vocabulary. *Journal of Reading Behavior, 15,* 19–40.

Fry, E. (1968). A readability formula that saves time. *Journal of Reading, 11,* 513–516, 578.

Fry, E. (1980). The new instant word list. *The Reading Teacher, 34,* 284–289.

Fulwiler, T. (1980). Journals across the disciplines. *English Journal, 69,* 14–19.

Fulwiler, T. (1982). The personal connection: Journal writing across the curriculum. In T. Fulwiler & A. Young (Eds.), *Language connections: Writing and reading across the curriculum* (pp. 15–32). Urbana, IL: National Council of Teachers of English.

Fulwiler, T. (Ed.). (1987a). *The journal book.* Portsmouth, NH: Boynton/Cook.

Fulwiler, T. (1987b). *Teaching with writing.* Portsmouth, NH: Boynton/Cook.

Galda, L. (1982). Assessment: Responses to literature. In A. Berger & H.A. Robinson (Eds.), *Secondary school reading: What research reveals for classroom practice* (pp. 111–125). Urbana, IL: National Council of Teachers of English and ERIC Clearinghouse on Reading and Communication Skills.

Gallagher, J. (1984). Policy analysis and program implementation/PL 94–142. *Topics in Early Childhood Special Education, 4* (1), 43–53.

Gambrell, L.B. (1978). Getting started with sustained silent reading and keeping it going. *The Reading Teacher, 32,* 328–331.

Gambrell, L.B. (1985). Dialogue journals: Reading-writing interaction. *The Reading Teacher, 38,* 512–515.

Gardner, E.F. (1978). Bias. *Measurement in Education, 9,* 1–4.

Garner, R. (1981–82). Good and poor comprehender's differences in knowing and regulating reading behaviors. *Educational Research Quarterly, 6,* 5–12.

Garner, R. (1982). Verbal report data on reading strategies. *Journal of Reading Behavior, 14,* 159–167.

Garner, R. (1987). *Metacognition and reading comprehension.* Norwood, NJ: Ablex.

Garner, R., & Reis, R. (1981). Monitoring and resolving comprehension obstacles: An investigation of spontaneous text lookbacks among upper-grade good and poor comprehenders. *Reading Research Quarterly, 16,* 569–582.

Garry, V.V. (1974). Competencies that count among reading specialists. *Journal of Reading, 17,* 608–613.

Gaskins, I. (1988). Helping teachers adapt to the needs of students with learning problems. In S.J. Samuels & P.D. Pearson (Eds.), *Changing school reading programs* (pp. 143–160). Newark, DE: International Reading Association.

Gaskins, I., Downer, M., Anderson, R., Cunningham, P., Gaskins, R., & Schommer, M. (1987). A metacognitive approach to phonics: Using what you know to decode what you don't know. *RASE, 9,* 36–41.

Gates, A.I., McKillop, A.S., & Horowitz, E.C. (1981). *Gates-McKillop-Horowitz reading diagnostic tests* (2nd ed.). New York: Teachers College Press.

Gavelek, J.R., & Palincsar, A.S. (1988). Contextualism as an alternative worldview of learning disabilities: A response to Swanson's "Toward a metatheory of learning disabilities." *Journal of Learning Disabilities, 21,* 278–281.

Gay, G. (1986). Interaction of learner control and prior understanding in computer-assisted video instruction. *Journal of Educational Psychology, 78,* 225–227.

Genishi, C., & Dyson, A.H. (1984). *Language assessment in the early years.* Norwood, NJ: Ablex.

Gentry, J.R. (1982). An analysis of developmental spelling in GNYS at WRK. *The Reading Teacher, 36,* 192–200.

Gerke, R. (1980). Critique of informal reading inventories: Can a valid instructional level be obtained? *Journal of Reading Behavior, 12,* 155–158.

Gesell Institute of Child Development (1978). *Gesell School Readiness and Kindergarten Screening Tests.* Rosemont, NJ: Programs for Education.

Gillet, J., & Temple, C. (1982). *Understanding reading problems* (1st ed.). Boston: Little, Brown.

Gillet, J., & Temple, C. (1990). *Understanding reading problems* (3rd ed.). Glenview, IL: Scott, Foresman.

Gipe, J. (1978–79). Investigating techniques for teaching word meanings. *Reading Research Quarterly, 14,* 624–644.

Glass, G. G., & Burton, E. H. (1973). How do they decode? Verbalizations and observed behaviors of successful decoders. *Education, 94,* 58–64.

Glazer, S. M., & Searfoss, L. (1988). *Reading diagnosis and instruction: A C-A-L-M approach.* Englewood Cliffs, NJ: Prentice Hall.

Goetz, E., & Armbruster, B. (1980). Psychological correlates of text structure. In R. J. Spiro, B. C. Bruce, & W. F. Brewer (Eds.), *Theoretical issues in reading comprehension* (pp. 201–220). Hillsdale, NJ: Lawrence Erlbaum.

Golden, J. M. (1984). Children's concept of story in reading and writing. *The Reading Teacher, 37,* 578–584.

Goldstein, B. S. (1986). Looking at cartoons and comics in a new way. *Journal of Reading, 29,* 657–661.

Good, T. L., & Brophy, J. E. (1987). *Looking in classrooms* (4th ed.). New York: Harper & Row.

Good, T. L., & Marshall, S. (1984). Do students learn more in heterogeneous or homogeneous achievement groups? In P. Peterson, L. Cherry-Wilkinson, & M. Hallinan (Eds.), *The social context for instruction* (pp. 15–38). New York: Academic Press.

Goodman, K. S. (1965). A linguistic study of cues and miscues in reading. *Elementary English, 42,* 639–643.

Goodman, K. S. (1969). Analysis of oral reading miscues: Applied psycholinguistics. *Reading Research Quarterly, 5,* 9–30.

Goodman, K. S. (1973). Miscues: Windows on the reading process. In K. S. Goodman (Ed.), *Miscue analysis: Applications to reading instruction* (pp. 3–14). Urbana, IL: ERIC Clearinghouse on Reading and Communication Skills and the National Council of Teachers of English.

Goodman, K. S. (1976). Behind the eye: What happens in reading. In H. Singer & R. B. Ruddell (Eds.), *Theoretical models and processes in reading* (2nd ed., pp. 470–496). Newark, DE: International Reading Association.

Goodman, K. S. (1989). Whole language is whole: A response to Heymsfeld. *Educational Leadership, 46*(6), 69–70.

Goodman, K. S., & Goodman, Y. M. (1977). Learning about psycholinguistic processes by analyzing oral reading. *Harvard Educational Review, 47,* 317–333.

Goodman, K. S., Shannon, P., Freeman, Y. S., & Murphy, S. (1988). *Report card on basal readers.* New York: Richard C. Owen.

Goodman, Y. M. (1980). The roots of literacy. In M. Douglass (Ed.), *Claremont Reading Conference Forty-Fourth Yearbook* (pp. 1–32). Claremont, CA: The Claremont Reading Conference.

Goodman, Y. M. (1981). Test review: Concepts About Print test. *The Reading Teacher, 34,* 445–448.

Goodman, Y. M. (1986). Children coming to know literacy. In W. H. Teale & E. Sulzby (Eds.), *Emergent literacy: Writing and reading* (pp. 1–14). Norwood, NJ: Ablex.

Goodman, Y. M., & Burke, C. L. (1972).

Reading miscue inventory. New York: Richard C. Owen.

Goodman, Y. M., Watson, D. J., & Burke, C. L. (1987). *Reading miscue inventory: Alternative procedures.* New York: Richard C. Owen.

Gordon, C., & Braun, C. (1983). Using story schema as an aid to reading and writing. *The Reading Teacher, 37,* 116–121.

Gordon, C., & Pearson, P. D. (1983). *The effects of instruction in metacomprehension and inferencing on children's comprehension abilities* (Tech. Rep. 269). Urbana, IL: University of Illinois, Center for the Study of Reading.

Gough, P. B. (1984). Word recognition. In P. D. Pearson, R. Barr, M. Kamil, & P. Mosenthal (Eds.), *Handbook of reading research* (pp. 225–253). New York: Longman.

Gove, M. K. (1983). Clarifying teachers' beliefs about reading. *The Reading Teacher, 37,* 261–268.

Graesser, A. C., Golding, J. M., & Long, D. L. (1991). Narrative representation and comprehension. In R. Barr, M. L. Kamil, P. Mosenthal, & P. D. Pearson (Eds.), *Handbook of reading research* (Vol. II, pp. 171–205). New York: Longman.

Graesser, A. C., & Riha, J. R. (1984). An application of multiple regression techniques to sentence reading times. In D. Kieras & M. Just (Eds.), *New methods in comprehension research* (pp. 183–218). Hillsdale, NJ: Lawrence Erlbaum.

Graves, D. H. (1983). *Writing: Teachers and children at work.* Portsmouth, NH: Heinemann.

Graves, D. H., & Hansen, J. (1983). The author's chair. *Language Arts, 60,* 176–183.

Graves, M. F., Cooke, C. L., & LaBerge, M. J. (1983). Effects of previewing short stories. *Reading Research Quarterly, 18,* 262–276.

Gray, W. S. (1920). The value of informal tests of reading achievement. *Journal of Educational Research, 1,* 103–111.

Gray, W. S. (1941/1984). Reading. In J. T. Guthrie (Ed.), *A research retrospective, 1881/1941.* Newark, DE: International Reading Association.

Gray, W. S., & Leary, B. E. (1935). *What makes a book readable?* Chicago: University of Chicago Press.

Greaney, V. (1980). Factors related to amount and type of leisure reading. *Reading Research Quarterly, 15,* 337–357.

Green, B., Logan, J. S., & Pisoni, D. B. (1986). Perception of synthetic speech produced automatically by rule: Intelligibility of eight text-to-speech systems. *Behavior Research Methods, Instruments, and Computers, 18,* 100–107.

Green, G. (1984). On the appropriateness of adaptations in primary-level basal readers. In R. C. Anderson, J. Osborn, & R. J. Tierney (Eds.), *Learning to read in American schools: Basal readers and content texts* (pp. 175–191). Hillsdale, NJ: Lawrence Erlbaum.

Green, J., & Bloome, D. (1983). Ethnography and reading: Issues, approaches, criteria, and findings. *Searches for meaning in reading/language processing and instruction* (32nd Yearbook of The National Reading Conference, pp. 6–30). New York: National Reading Conference.

Grimes, J. E. (1975). *The thread of discourse.* The Hague, Netherlands: Mouton.

Groff, P. (1986). The maturing of phonics instruction. *The Reading Teacher, 39,* 919–923.

Groisser, P. (1964). *How to use the fine art of questioning.* New York: Teachers' Practical Press.

Gronlund, N. E. (1981). *Measurement and evaluation in teaching* (4th ed.). New York: Macmillan.

Gronlund, N. E. (1985). *Measurement and evaluation in teaching* (5th ed.). New York: Macmillan.

Gump, P. V. (1969). Intra-setting analysis: The third grade classroom as a special but instructive case. In E. Willems & H. Rausch (Eds.), *Naturalistic viewpoints in psychological research* (pp. 200–220). New York: Holt, Rinehart & Winston.

Guthrie, J. T. (1980). Research reviews: Time in reading programs. *The Reading Teacher, 33,* 500–502.

Guthrie, J. T., & Seifert, M. (1978). Education for children with reading disabilities. In H. R. Myklebust (Ed.), *Progress in learning disabilities* (Vol. 4, pp. 223–255). New York: Grune & Stratton.

Hall, N. A. (1976). Children's awareness of segmentation in speech and print. *Reading, 10,* 11–19.

Halliday, M. A. K. (1975). *Learning how to mean: Explorations in the development of language.* New York: Elsevier North-Holland Inc.

Halliday, M. A. K., & Hasan, R. (1976). *Cohesion in English.* London: Longman.

Hammill, D. D., & Larsen, S. C. (1988). *Test of Written Language—2.* Austin, TX: Pro-Ed.

Hansen, J. (1981a). The effects of inference training and practice on young children's reading comprehension. *Reading Research Quarterly, 16,* 391–417.

Hansen, J. (1981b). An inferential comprehension strategy for use with primary grade children. *The Reading Teacher, 34,* 665–669.

Hansen, J. (1987). *When writers read.* Portsmouth, NH: Heinemann.

Hare, V. C. (1984). What's in a word? A review of young children's difficulties with the construct of "word." *The Reading Teacher, 37,* 360–364.

Hare, V. C., & Borchardt, K. (1984). Direct instruction of summarization skills. *Reading Research Quarterly, 20,* 62–78.

Hare, V. C., Rabinowitz, M., & Schieble, K. M. (1989). Text effects on main idea comprehension. *Reading Research Quarterly, 24,* 72–88.

Hare, V. C., & Smith, D. C. (1982). Reading to remember: Studies of metacognitive reading skill in elementary school-aged children. *Journal of Educational Research, 75,* 157–164.

Harp, W. (1987). What are your kids writing during reading time? *The Reading Teacher, 41,* 88–89.

Harris, A. J. (1977). Ten years of progress in remedial reading. *The Reading Teacher, 31,* 29–35.

Harris, A. J., & Roswell, F. G. (1953). Clinical diagnosis of reading disability. *Journal of Psychology, 63,* 323–340.

Harris, A. J., & Sipay, E. R. (1985). *How to increase reading ability* (8th ed.). New York: Longman.

Harris, A. J., & Sipay, E. R. (1990). *How to increase reading ability* (9th ed.). New York: Longman.

Harrison, C. (1979). Assessing the readability of school texts. In E. Lunzer & K. Gardner (Eds.), *The effective use of reading* (pp. 72–107). London: Heinemann.

Harter, S. (1981). A model of mastery motivation in children: Individual differences and developmental change. In W. A. Colliers (Ed.), *Aspects of the development of competence: The Minnesota Symposium on Child Psychology* (Vol. 14, pp. 215–255). Hillsdale, NJ: Lawrence Erlbaum.

Hartlage, L. C., Lucas, D. G., & Main, W. H. (1972). Comparison of three approaches to teaching reading skills. *Perceptual and Motor Skills, 34,* 231–232.

Haskins, R., Walden, T., & Ramey, C. (1983). Teacher and student behavior in high- and low-ability groups.

Journal of Educational Psychology, 75, 865–876.

Hayes, B., & Peters, C. W. (1989). The role of reading instruction in the social studies. In D. Lapp, & J. Flood (Eds.), *Handbook of instructional theory and practice* (pp. 152–178). Englewood Cliffs, NJ: Prentice-Hall.

Hayes, D. A., & Tierney, R. J. (1982). Developing readers knowledge through analogy. *Reading Research Quarterly, 17,* 256–280.

Heald-Taylor, G. (1989). *Administrator's guide to whole language.* Katonah, NY: Owen Publishers.

Heath, S. B. (1981). Questioning at home and at school: A comparative study. In G. Spindler (Ed.), *Doing ethnography: Educational anthropology in action* (pp. 102–131). New York: Holt, Rinehart & Winston.

Heath, S. B. (1983). *Ways with words: Language, life, and work in communities and classrooms.* Cambridge, England: Cambridge University Press.

Heckelman, R. G. (1966). Using the neurological impress remedial technique. *Academic Therapy Quarterly, 1,* 235–239.

Heckelman, R. G. (1969). Neurological impress method of remedial reading instruction. *Academic Therapy Quarterly, 4,* 277–282.

Henderson, E. H., & Beers, J. (Eds.). (1980). *Developmental and cognitive aspects of learning to spell.* Newark, DE: International Reading Association.

Henk, W. A. (1983). Adapting the NIM to improve comprehension. *Academic Therapy Quarterly, 19,* 97–101.

Hennings, D. G. (1990). *Communication in action: Teaching the language arts.* Boston: Houghton Mifflin.

Herber, H. L. (1970). *Teaching reading in the content areas.* Englewood Cliffs, NJ: Prentice-Hall.

Herber, H. L. (1978). *Teaching reading in the content areas* (2nd ed.). Englewood Cliffs, NJ: Prentice-Hall.

Herber, H. L., & Riley, J. D. (1979). *Re-search in reading in the content areas: Fourth year report.* Syracuse, NY: Syracuse University Reading and Language Arts Center.

Herman, P. A., Anderson, R. C., Pearson, P. D., & Nagy, W. E. (1987). Incidental acquisition of word meaning from expositions with varied text features. *Reading Research Quarterly, 22,* 263–284.

Hiebert, E. H. (1981). Developmental patterns and interrelationships of preschool children's print awareness. *Reading Research Quarterly, 16,* 236–260.

Hiebert, E. H. (1983). An examination of ability grouping for reading instruction. *Reading Research Quarterly, 18,* 231–255.

Hiebert, E. H., Winograd, P. N., & Danner, F. W. (1984). Children's attributions for failure and success in different aspects of reading. *Journal of Educational Psychology, 76,* 1139–1148.

Hieronymus, A. N., Hoover, H. D., & Linquist, E. F. (1986). *Iowa Test of Basic Skills.* Chicago, IL: Riverside.

Hinshelwood, J. (1917). *Congenital word-blindness.* London: Lewis.

Holdaway, D. (1979). *Foundations of literacy.* Sydney, Australia: Ashton Scholastic.

Holdaway, D. (1986). Guiding a natural process. In D. R. Tovay & J. E. Kerber (Eds.), *Roles in literacy learning* (pp. 42–51). Newark, DE: International Reading Association.

Holmes, B. C., & Roser, N. L. (1987). Five ways to assess readers' prior knowledge. *The Reading Teacher, 40,* 646–649.

Hong, L. K. (1981). Modifying SSR for beginning readers. *The Reading Teacher, 34,* 888–891.

Hood, J. (1978). Is miscue analysis practical for teachers? *The Reading Teacher, 32,* 260–266.

Hood, J. (1985). Review of the Test of Reading Comprehension, 1978 Edition. In J. V. Mitchell (Ed.), *The ninth mental measurements yearbook* (pp. 1588–1589). Lincoln, NE: Buros Institute of Mental Measurements.

Howell, K. W., & Morehead, M. K. (1987). *Curriculum-based evaluation for special and remedial education.* Columbus, OH: Charles E. Merrill.

Huey, E. B. (1908/1968). *The psychology and pedagogy of reading.* Cambridge, MA: MIT Press. (Republished: Cambridge, MA: MIT Press, 1968)

Hughes, M. M. (1971). The model of good teaching. In J. Raths, J. R. Pancella, & J. S. Van Ness (Eds.), *Studying teaching* (2nd ed., pp. 21–24). Englewood Cliffs, NJ: Prentice-Hall.

Hunt, L. C. (n. d.). *Vocabulary development is a simple dumbbell operation.* Burlington, VT: University of Vermont.

Hunt, L. C. (1970). Effect of self-selection, interest, and motivation upon independent, instructional, and frustrational levels. *The Reading Teacher, 24,* (2), 146–151.

Hynd, C. R., & Alvermann, D. E. (1986). Prior knowledge activation in refutation and non-refutation text. In J. A. Niles & R. Lalik (Eds.), *Solving problems in literacy: Learners, teachers, and researchers.* (Thirty-fifth Yearbook of The National Reading Conference, pp. 55–60). Rochester, NY: National Reading Conference.

Hynd, G. W., & Hynd, C. R. (1984). Dyslexia: Neuroanatomical/neurolinguistic perspectives. *Reading Research Quarterly, 19,* 219–239.

Ilg, F. (1982). *Scoring notes: The developmental examination.* New Haven, CT: Gesell Institute of Human Development.

Ilg, F. L., & Ames, L. B. (1965). *Gesell Developmental Tests of School Readiness.* Lumberville, PA: Programs for Education.

Indrisano, R. (1982). An ecological approach to learning. *Topics in Learning and Learning Disabilities, 3,* 11–15.

International Reading Association. (1986). *Guidelines for the specialized preparation of reading professionals.* (Professional Standards and Ethics Committee). Newark, DE: International Reading Association.

International Reading Association. (1987). IRA Code of Ethics. *The Reading Teacher, 41,* 143.

Irvin, J. L. (1990). *Reading and the middle school student.* Boston: Allyn & Bacon.

Irwin, D. M., & Bushnell, M. M. (1980). *Observational studies for child study.* New York: Holt, Rinehart & Winston.

Irwin, J. W., & Davis, C. (1980). Assessing readability: The checklist approach. *Journal of Reading, 24,* 124–130.

Irwin, M. (1987). Connections: Young children, reading, writing, and computers. *Computers in Schools, 4,* 37–51.

Irwin, P. A., & Mitchell, J. N. (1983). A procedure for assessing the richness of retellings. *Journal of Reading, 26,* 391–396.

Jaggar, A. (1985). On observing the language learner: Introduction and overview. In A. Jaggar & M. T. Smith-Burke (Eds.), *Observing the language learner* (pp. 1–7). Newark, DE: International Reading Association.

Jewell, M. C., & Zintz, M. V. (1990). *Learning to read and write naturally* (2nd ed.). Dubuque, IA: Kendall/Hunt.

Johns, J. J. (1978). Do comprehension items really test reading? Sometimes! *Journal of Reading, 21,* 615–619.

Johns, J. J. (1988). *Basic reading inventory* (4th ed.). Dubuque, IA: Kendall/Hunt.

Johnson, D. D. (1971). A basic vocabulary for beginning reading. *The Elementary School Journal, 72,* 29–34.

Johnson, D. D., & Baumann, J. F. (1984). Word identification. In P. D. Pearson, R. Barr, M. Kamil, & P. Mosenthal (Eds.), *Handbook of reading research* (pp. 583–608). New York: Longman.

Johnson, D. D., & Pearson, P. D. (1984). *Teaching reading vocabulary* (2nd ed.). New York: Holt, Rinehart & Winston.

Johnson, D. W., & Johnson, R. T. (1986). *Learning together and alone* (2nd ed.). Englewood Cliffs, NJ: Prentice-Hall.

Johnson, M. S., & Kress, R. A. (1965). *Informal reading inventories.* Newark, DE: International Reading Association.

Johnston, P. H. (1985a). Teaching students to apply strategies that improve reading comprehension. *Elementary School Journal, 85,* 635–645.

Johnston, P. H. (1985b). Understanding reading disability: A case study approach. *Harvard Educational Review, 55,* 153–177.

Johnston, P. H. (1987). Teachers as evaluation experts. *The Reading Teacher, 40,* 744–748.

Johnston, P. H., Allington, R. L., & Afflerbach, P. (1985). The congruence of classroom and remedial reading instruction. *Elementary School Journal, 85,* 465–477.

Johnston, P. H., Allington, R., & Franzen, A. (1985, April). Obstacles to an integrated understanding of reading failure. In M. Y. Lipson (Chair.), *Research on reading disabilities: Theoretical and methodological issues.* Symposium conducted at the meeting of the American Educational Research Association, Chicago, IL.

Johnston, P. H., & Winograd, P. N. (1985). Passive failure in reading. *Journal of Reading Behavior, 17,* 279–301.

Jones, B. F. (1983, April). *Integrating learning strategies and text research to teach high order thinking skills in schools.* Paper presented at the Annual Meeting of the American Educational Research Association, Montreal, Canada.

Jongsma, E. A. (1982). Test review: Peabody Picture Vocabulary Test–Revised (PPVT–R). *Journal of Reading, 20,* 360–364.

Jongsma, K. S., & Jongsma, E. A. (1981). Test review: Commercial informal reading inventories. *The Reading Teacher, 34,* 697–705.

Jorgenson, G. W. (1975). An analysis of teacher judgments of reading levels. *American Education Research Journal, 12,* 67–75.

Judd, C. H. (1918). *Reading: Its nature and development* (Supplementary Educational Monographs, No. 10). Chicago: University of Chicago Press.

Judd, C. H., & Buswell, G. T. (1922). *Silent reading: A study of the various types* (Supplementary Educational Monographs, No. 23). Chicago: University of Chicago Press.

Juel, C. (1988). Learning to read and write: A longitudinal study of fifty-four children from first through fourth grade. *Journal of Educational Psychology, 80,* 437–447.

Juel, C., Griffith, P. L., & Gough, P. B. (1986). Acquisition of literacy: A longitudinal study of children in first and second grade. *Journal of Educational Psychology, 78,* 243–255.

Juola, J. F., Schadler, M., Chabot, R., McCaughey, M., & Wait, J. (1979). What do children learn when they learn to read? In L. B. Resnick & P. A. Weaver (Eds.), *Theory and practice of early reading* (Vol. 2, pp. 91–108). Hillsdale, NJ: Lawrence Erlbaum.

Just, M. A., & Carpenter, P. A. (1987). *The psychology of reading and language comprehension.* Boston: Allyn & Bacon.

Kagan, J., & Lang, C. (1978). *Psychology and education.* New York: Harcourt Brace Jovanovich.

Kalmbach, J. R. (1986a). Evaluating informal methods of assessment of retellings. *Journal of Reading, 30,* 119–129.

Kalmbach, J. R. (1986b). Getting at the point of retellings. *Journal of Reading, 29,* 326–333.

Kameenui, E. J., & Shannon, P. (1988). Point/counterpoint: Direct instruction reconsidered. In J. Readence, R. Baldwin, J. Konopak, & P. O'Keefe, *Dialogues in literacy research* (37th Yearbook of the National Reading Conference, pp. 35–44). Chicago: National Reading Conference.

Kamil, M. (1988). Uses of computers in reading and writing instruction. In G. G. Duffy & L. R. Roehler (Eds.), *Improving classroom reading instruction* (2nd ed., pp. 390–412). New York: Random House.

Kann, R. (1983). The method of repeated readings: Expanding the neurological impress method for use with disabled readers. *Journal of Learning Disabilities, 16,* 90–92.

Kappelman, M., Kaplan, E., & Ganter, R. (1969). A study of learning disorders among disadvantaged children. *Journal of Learning Disabilities, 2,* 262–268.

Karlsen, B., & Gardner, E. (1985/1986). *Stanford Diagnostic Reading Test* (3rd ed.). San Antonio, TX: The Psychological Corporation.

Kastler, L. A., Roser, N. L., & Hoffman, J. V. (1987). Understanding the forms and functions of written language: Insights from children and parents. In J. E. Readence & R. S. Baldwin (Eds.), *Research in literacy: Merging perspectives* (36th Yearbook of the National Reading Conference, pp. 85–92). Rochester, NY: National Reading Conference.

Kaufman, A. S., & Kaufman, N. L. (1972). Tests built from Piaget's and Gesell's tasks as predictors of first grade achievement. *Child Development, 43,* 521–535.

Kaufman, M. (1976). Comparison of achievement for DISTAR and conventional instruction with primary pupils. *Reading Improvement, 13,* 169–173.

Kaufman, N. L. (1985). Review of the Gesell Preschool Test. In J. V. Mitchell (Ed.), *The ninth mental measurements yearbook 1* (Vol. 1, pp. 607–608). Lincoln, NE: Buros Institute of Mental Measurements.

Keeney, T. J., Canizzo, S. R., & Flavell, J. H. (1967). Spontaneous and induced verbal rehearsal in a recall task. *Child Development, 38,* 953–966.

Kemp, M. (1990). *Watching children read and write: Observational records for children with special needs.* Portsmouth, NH: Heinemann.

Kendall, J., & Mason, J. (1980). *Comprehension of polysemous words.* Paper presented at the Annual Meeting of the American Educational Research Association, Boston, MA.

Kennedy, B. A., & Miller, D. J. (1976). Persistent use of verbal rehearsal as a function of information about its value. *Child Development, 47,* 566–569.

Kibby, M. W. (1979). Passage readability affects the oral reading strategies of disabled readers. *The Reading Teacher, 32,* 390–396.

Kilgallon, P. A. (1942). *A study of relationships among certain pupil adjustments in reading situations.* Unpublished doctoral dissertation, Pennsylvania State College, Pennsylvania.

King, L. H. (1983). Pupil classroom perceptions and the expectancy effect. *South Pacific Journal of Teacher Education, 11,* 54–70.

Kintsch, W., & Vipond, D. (1979). Reading comprehension and readability in educational practice and psychological theory. In L. G. Nilsson (Ed.), *Perspectives on memory research* (pp. 329–366). Hillsdale, NJ: Lawrence Erlbaum.

Klare, G. (1984). Readability. In P. D. Pearson (Ed.), *Handbook of reading research* (pp. 681–744). New York: Longman.

Klare, G. (1988). The formative years. In B. L. Zakaluk & S. J. Samuels (Eds.), *Readability: Its past, present, and future* (pp. 14–34). Newark, DE: International Reading Association.

Klesius, S. E. (1972). Perceptual motor development and reading—A closer look. In R. C. Aukerman (Ed.), *Some persistent problems in beginning reading* (pp. 151–159). Newark, DE: International Reading Association.

Kobrin, B. (1988). *Eyeopeners.* New York: Penguin Books.

Koppitz, E. M. (1963). *The Bender Gestalt Test for Young Children*. New York: Grune & Stratton.

Koppitz, E. M. (1975). *The Bender Gesalt Test for Young Children: Volume II: Research and application, 1963–1973*. New York: Grune & Stratton.

Koskinen, P. S., & Blum, I. H. (1986). Paired repeated reading: A classroom strategy for developing fluent reading. *The Reading Teacher, 40,* 70–77.

Kounin, J. S. (1970). *Discipline and group management in classrooms*. New York: Holt, Rinehart & Winston.

Krieger, V. K. (1981). Differences in poor readers' abilities to identify high-frequency words in isolation and context. *Reading World, 20,* 263–272.

Kucer, S. (1985). The making of meaning: Reading and writing as parallel processes. *Written Communication, 2,* 317–336.

LaBerge, D., & Samuels, J. (1974). Toward a theory of automatic information processing in reading. *Cognitive Psychology, 6,* 293–323.

Laffey, J., & Kelley, D. (1979). Test review: Woodcock Reading Mastery Test. *The Reading Teacher, 33,* 335–339.

Langer, J. A. (1981). From theory to practice: A prereading plan. *Journal of Reading, 25,* 152–156.

Langer, J. A. (1982). Facilitating text processing: The elaboration of prior knowledge. In J. Langer & M. T. Smith-Burke (Eds.), *Reader meets author/bridging the gap* (pp. 149–162). Newark, DE: International Reading Association.

Langer, J. A. (1984). Examining background knowledge and text comprehension. *Reading Research Quarterly, 19,* 468–481.

LaPray, M., & Ross, R. (1969). The graded word list: Quick gauge of reading ability. *Journal of Reading, 12,* 305–307.

Leinhardt, G., & Seewald, A. (1980). *Student level observation of beginning reading manuals*. Pittsburgh, PA: University of Pittsburgh, Learning Research and Development Center.

Leinhardt, G., Zigmond, N., & Cooley, W. (1981). Reading instruction and its effects. *American Educational Research Journal, 18,* 171–177.

Leong, C. K. (1976–77). Spatial-temporal information processing in children with specific reading disability. *Reading Research Quarterly, 12,* 204–215.

Leslie, L., & Caldwell, J. (1990). *Qualitative reading inventory*. Glenview, IL: Scott, Foresman.

Leu, D., DeGroff, L. C., & Simons, H. D. (1986). Predictable texts and interactive-compensatory hypothesis: Evaluating individual differences in reading ability, context use, and comprehension. *Journal of Educational Psychology, 78,* 347–352.

Levine, S. G. (1984). USSR: A necessary component in teaching reading. *Journal of Reading, 27,* 394–400.

Liberman, I. Y., & Shankweiler, D. (1979). Speech, the alphabet, and teaching to read. In L. B. Resnick & P. A. Weaver (Eds.), *Theory and practice of early reading* (Vol. 2, pp. 109–134). Hillsdale, NJ: Lawrence Erlbaum.

Lidz, C. S. (1987). Historical perspectives. In C. S. Lidz (Ed.), *Dynamic assessment* (pp. 3–34). New York: Guilford.

Lindfors, J. W. (1980). *Children's language and learning*. Englewood Cliffs, NJ: Prentice-Hall.

Lipson, M. Y. (1982). Learning new information from text: The role of prior knowledge and reading ability. *Journal of Reading Behavior, 14,* 243–262.

Lipson, M. Y. (1983). The influence of religious affiliation on children's memory for text information. *Reading Research Quarterly, 18,* 448–457.

Lipson, M. Y. (1989). Individualizing within basal instruction. In P. Winograd, K. Wixson, & M. Y. Lipson (Eds.), *Improving basal reading instruction* (pp. 140–176). New York: Teachers College Press.

Lipson, M. Y., Bigler, M., Poth, L., & Wickizer, B. (1987, December). *Instructional applications of a verbal report methodology.* Paper presented at the 37th Annual Meeting of the National Reading Conference, St. Petersburg, FL.

Lipson, M. Y., Cox, C., Iwankowski, S., & Simon, M. (1984). Explorations of the interactive nature of reading: Using commercial IRIs to gain insights. *Reading Psychology, 5,* 209–218.

Lipson, M. Y., Irwin, M., & Poth, E. (1986). The relationships between metacognitive self-reports and strategic reading behavior. In J. Niles & R. Lalik (Eds.), *Solving problems in literacy: Learners, teachers and researchers* (35th Yearbook of The National Reading Conference, pp. 460–476). Rochester, NY: National Reading Conference.

Lipson, M. Y., & Wickizer, E. (1989). Promoting reading independence through instructional dialogue. *Teaching Exceptional Children, 21* (2), 28–32.

Lipson, M. Y., & Wixson, K. K. (1986). Reading disability research: An interactionist perspective. *Review of Educational Research, 56,* 111–136.

Lipson, M. Y., & Wixson, K. K. (1989). Student evaluation and basal instruction. In P. Winograd, K. K. Wixson, & M. Y. Lipson (Eds.), *Improving basal reading instruction* (pp. 109–139). New York: Teachers College Press.

Lively, B. A., & Pressey, S. L. (1923). A method for measuring the "vocabulary burden" of textbooks. *Educational Administration and Supervision, 9,* 389–398.

Lomax, R. G., & McGee, L. M. (1987). Young children's concepts about print and reading: Toward a model of word reading acquisition. *Reading Research Quarterly, 22,* 237–256.

Lund, N. J., & Duchan, J. F. (1988). *Assessing children's language in naturalistic contexts.* Englewood Cliffs, NJ: Prentice-Hall.

Lytle, S. (1987, May). Interviewing. In M. Y. Lipson, & K. K. Wixson (Chairs), *New approaches to individual and group reading assessment: An interactionist perspective.* Institute conducted at the 32nd Annual Convention of the International Reading Association, Anaheim, CA.

MacGinitie, W. H. (1984). Readability as a solution adds to the problem. In R. C. Anderson, J. Osborn, & R. T. Tierney (Eds.), *Learning to read in American schools* (pp. 141–151). Hillsdale, NJ: Lawrence Erlbaum.

MacGinitie, W. H., Kamons, J., Kowalski, R. L., MacGinitie, R., & McKay, T. (1978). *Gates-MacGinitie Reading Test—Readiness Skills.* New York: Columbia University, Teachers College Press.

MacGinitie, W. H., & MacGinitie, R. K. (1989). *Gates-MacGinitie Reading Tests* (3rd ed.). Chicago, IL: Riverside.

Maier, A. A. (1980). The effect of focusing on the cognitive processes of learning disabled children. *Journal of Learning Disabilities, 13,* 143–147.

Mandler, J. M. (1978). A code in the node: The use of story schema in retrieval. *Discourse Processes, 1,* 14–35.

Mandler, J. M., & Johnson, N. S. (1977). Remembrance of things parsed: Story structure and recall. *Cognitive Psychology, 9,* 111–115.

Mangieri, J. N., & Corboy, M. R. (1981). Recreational reading: Do we practice what is preached? *The Reading Teacher, 34,* 923–925.

Mangieri, J. N., & Heimberger, M. J. (1980). Perceptions of the reading consultant's role. *Journal of Reading, 23,* 527–530.

Manzo, A. V. (1969). The request procedure. *Journal of Reading, 13,* 123–126.

Maria, K. (1986, December). *Refuting misconceptions: Its effect on middle grade children's comprehension.* Paper presented at the 35th Annual Meeting of the National Reading Conference, Austin, TX.

Maria, K. (1990). *Reading comprehension instruction: Issues and strategies.* Parkton, MD: York Press.

Markwardt, F. C. (1989). *Peabody Individual Achievement Battery–Revised.* Circle Pines, MN: American Guidance Service.

Marsh, G. P., Desberg, P., & Cooper, J. (1977). Developmental changes in reading strategies. *Journal of Reading Behavior, 9,* 391–394.

Marshall, H. H., & Weinstein, R. S. (1984). Classroom factors affecting students' self-evaluations: An interactional model. *Review of Educational Research, 54,* 301–325.

Marshall, N. (1983). Using story grammar to assess reading comprehension. *The Reading Teacher, 36,* 616–621.

Marshall, N., & Glock, M. (1978–79). Comprehension of connected discourse: A study into the relationship between the structure of text and information recalled. *Reading Research Quarterly, 14,* 10–56.

Martinez, M., & Roser, N. (1985). Read it again: The value of repeated readings during storytime. *The Reading Teacher, 38,* 782–786.

Mason, G. (1967). Preschooler's concepts of reading. *The Reading Teacher, 21,* 130–132.

Mason, J. (1980). When do children begin to read: An exploration of four-year-old children's letter and word reading competencies. *Reading Research Quarterly, 15,* 203–227.

Mason, J. M., & Au, K. H. (1990). *Reading instruction for today* (2nd ed.). Glenview, IL: Scott, Foresman.

Mason, J., Osborn, J., & Rosenshine, B. (1977). *A consideration of skill hierarchy approaches to the teaching of reading* (Tech. Rep. No. 42). Urbana, IL: University of Illinois, Center for the Study of Reading.

Mason, J., Roehler, L. R., & Duffy, G. G. (1984). A practitioner's model of comprehension instruction. In G. G. Duffy, L. R. Roehler, & J. Mason (Eds.), *Comprehension instruction* (pp. 299–314). New York: Longman.

May, F. B. (1990). *Reading as communication: An interactive approach.* Columbus, OH: Charles E. Merrill.

McConaughy, S. H. (1982). Developmental changes in story comprehension and levels of questioning. *Language Arts, 59,* 580–589, 600.

McConaughy, S. H. (1985). Good and poor readers' comprehension of story structure across different input and output modalities. *Reading Research Quarterly, 20,* 219–232.

McConnell, C. R. (1982). Readability formulae as applied to college economics textbooks. *Journal of Reading, 26,* 14–17.

McCormick, S. (1987). *Remedial and clinical reading instruction.* Columbus, OH: Charles E. Merrill.

McCracken, R. A., & McCracken, M. (1971). Initiating sustained silent reading. *Journal of Reading, 14,* 521–524, 582–583.

McCracken, R. A., & McCracken, M. (1978). Modeling is the key to sustained reading. *The Reading Teacher, 31,* 406–408.

McCracken, R. A., & McCracken, M. J. (1986). *Stories, songs, and poetry to teach reading and writing.* Chicago: American Library Association.

McDermott, R. P. (1977). The ethnography of speaking and reading. In R. W. Shuy (Ed.), *Linguistic theory: What can it say about reading?* (pp. 153–185). Newark, DE: International Reading Association.

McDermott, R. P. (1985). Achieving school failure: An anthropological approach to illiteracy and social stratification. In H. Singer & R. B. Ruddell (Eds.), *Theoretical models and processes of reading.* (3rd ed., pp. 558–594). Newark, DE: International Reading Association.

McGee, L. A. (1981). Good and poor readers: Ability to distinguish among and recall ideas on different levels of importance. In M. Kamil (Ed.), *Directions in reading: Research and instruction* (30th Yearbook of National Reading Conference, pp. 162–168). Washington, DC: National Reading Conference.

McGee, L. A. (1982). Awareness of text structure: Effects on children's recall of expository text. *Reading Research Quarterly, 17,* 581–590.

McGinnis, D. J., & Smith, D. E. (1982). *Analyzing and treating reading problems.* New York: Macmillan.

McKenna, M. C. (1980). *An introduction to the cloze procedure: An annotated bibliography.* Newark, DE: International Reading Association.

McKenna, M. C. (1983). Informal reading inventories: A review of the issues. *The Reading Teacher, 36,* 670–679.

McNeil, J. D. (1987). *Reading comprehension: New directions for classroom practice* (2nd ed.). Glenview, IL: Scott, Foresman.

McNinch, G. H. (1981). A method for teaching sight words to disabled readers. *The Reading Teacher, 35,* 269–272.

McVitty, W. (1986). *Getting it together: Organizing the reading-writing classroom.* Portsmouth, NH: Heinemann.

McWilliams, L., & Rakes, T. A. (1979). *Content inventories: English, social studies, science.* Dubuque, IA: Kendall/Hunt.

Medley, D. M. (1985). Systematic observation schedules as measuring instruments. In R. A. Weinberg & F. H. Wood (Eds.), *Observation of pupils and teachers in mainstream and special education settings: Alternative strategies* (pp. 97–106). Minneapolis, MN: University of Minnesota, Leadership and Training Institute/Special Education.

Meltzer, N. S., & Herse, R. (1969). The boundaries of written words as seen by first graders. *Journal of Reading Behavior, 1,* 3–14.

Memory, D. M. (1986). Guiding students to independent decoding in content area classes. In E. K. Dishner, R. W. Bean, J. E. Readence, & D. W. Moore (Eds.), *Reading in the content areas* (2nd ed., pp. 194–201). Dubuque, IA: Kendall/Hunt.

Menyuk, P. (1984). Language development and reading. In J. Flood (Ed.), *Understanding reading comprehension* (pp. 101–121). Newark, DE: International Reading Association.

Meyer, B. J., Brandt, D. M., & Bluth, G. S. (1980). Use of top-level structure in text: Key for reading comprehension of ninth-grade students. *Reading Research Quarterly, 16,* 72–103.

Meyer, B. J., & Freedle, R. O. (1984). Effects of discourse type on recall. *American Educational Research Journal, 21,* 121–143.

Mezynski, K. (1983). Issues concerning acquisition of knowledge: Effects of vocabulary training on reading comprehension. *Review of Educational Research, 53,* 253–279.

Michaels, S. (1981). "Sharing time": Children's narrative styles and differential access to literacy. *Language in Society, 10,* 423–442.

Michigan Reading Association (1986). *Computers in the reading program.* Grand Rapids, MI: Michigan Reading Association.

Miller, L., & Burnett, J. D. (1986). Theoretical considerations in selecting language arts software. *Computer Education, 10,* 159–165.

Mills, R. E. (1956). An evaluation of techniques for teaching word recognition. *Elementary School Journal, 56,* 221–225.

Mitchell, J. V. (1985). *The ninth mental measurements yearbook.* Lincoln, NE: Buros Institute of Mental Measurements.

Moffett, J. (1985). Hidden impediments to

improving English teaching. *Phi Delta Kappan, 67,* 50–56.

Monroe, M. (1932). *Children who cannot read.* Chicago: University of Chicago Press.

Morgan, A. L. (1987). The development of written language awareness in black preschool children. *Journal of Reading Behavior, 19,* 49–68.

Morgan, D. P. (1981). *A primer on individualized education programs for exceptional children.* Reston, VA: The Foundation for Exceptional Children.

Morgan, W. P. (1896). A case of congenital word blindness. *British Medical Journal, 2,* 1612–1614.

Mork, T. A. (1972). Sustained silent reading in the classroom. *The Reading Teacher, 25,* 438–441.

Morphett, M. V., & Washburne, C. (1931). When should children begin to read? *The Elementary School Journal, 31,* 496–508.

Morris, D. (1981). Concept of word: A developmental phenomenon in the beginning reading and writing processes. *Language Arts, 58,* 659–668.

Morrow, L. M. (1983). Home and school correlates of early interest in literature. *Journal of Educational Research, 76,* 221–230.

Morrow, L. M. (1986). Encouraging voluntary reading: The impact of a literature program on children's use of library centers. *Reading Research Quarterly, 21,* 330–346.

Morrow, L. M. (1987). Promoting voluntary reading: Activities represented in basal reader manuals. *Reading Research and Instruction, 26,* 189–202.

Morrow, L. M. (1988). Retelling stories as a diagnostic tool. In S. M. Glazer, L. W. Searfoss, & L. M. Gentile (Eds.), *Reexamining reading diagnosis: New trends and procedures* (pp. 128–149). Newark, DE: International Reading Association.

Morrow, L. M. (1989). Creating a bridge to children's literature. In P. Wino-

grad, K. Wixson, & M. Lipson (Eds.), *Improving basal reading instruction* (pp. 210–230). New York: Teachers College Press.

Mosenthal, P., & Na, T. (1980). Quality of children's recall under two classroom testing tasks: Towards a socio-psycholinguistic model of reading comprehension. *Reading Research Quarterly, 15,* 504–528.

Moss, M. (1979). *Test of Basic Experiences (TOBE).* Monterey, CA: CTB/McGraw-Hill.

Mulligan, J. (1974). Using language experience with potential high school dropouts. *Journal of Reading, 18,* 206–211.

Murray, D. (1982). *Learning by teaching: Selected articles on writing and reading.* Montclair, NJ: Boynton-Cook.

Myers, C. A. (1978). Reviewing the literature on Fernald's technique of remedial reading. *The Reading Teacher, 31,* 614–690.

Myers, M., & Paris, S. G. (1978). Children's metacognitive knowledge about reading. *Journal of Educational Psychology, 70,* 680–690.

Nagy, W. E. (1988). *Teaching vocabulary to improve reading comprehension.* Urbana, IL: ERIC Clearinghouse on Reading and Communication Skills and the National Council of Teachers of English.

Nagy, W. E., & Anderson, R. C. (1984). How many words are there in printed school English? *Reading Research Quarterly, 19,* 304–330.

Nagy, W. E., Anderson, R. C., & Herman, P. (1987). Learning word meanings from context during normal reading. *American Educational Research Journal, 24,* 237–270.

Nagy, W. E., & Herman, P. (1987). Breadth and depth of vocabulary knowledge: Implications for acquisition and instruction. In M. G. McKeown & M. E. Curtis (Eds.), *The nature of vocabulary acquisition* (pp.

19–36). Hillsdale, NJ: Lawrence Erlbaum.

Nagy, W. E., Herman, P. A., & Anderson, R. C. (1985). Learning words from context. *Reading Research Quarterly, 20,* 233–253.

Neill, D. M., & Median, J. (1989). Standardized tests: Harmful to educational health. *Phi Delta Kappan, 70,* 688–697.

Nelson-Herber, J. (1986). Expanding and refining vocabulary in content areas. *Journal of Reading, 29,* 626–633.

Newcomer, P., & Hammill, D. D. (1988). *Test of Oral Language Development–2 Primary.* Austin, TX: Pro-Ed.

Newkirk, T., & Atwell, N. (1988). *Understanding writing: Ways of observing, learning and teaching.* Portsmouth, NH: Heinemann.

Newton, E. S. (1977). Andragogy: Understanding the adult as learner. *Journal of Reading, 20,* 361–363.

Nichols, J. N. (1980). Using paragraph frames to help remedial high school students with written assignments. *Journal of Reading, 24,* 228–231.

Nichols, J. N. (1983). Using prediction to increase content area interest and understanding. *Journal of Reading, 27,* 225–228.

Nicholson, T., Pearson, P. D., & Dykstra, R. (1979). Effects of embedded anomalies and oral reading errors on children's understanding of stories. *Journal of Reading Behavior, 11,* 339–354.

Nisbett, R. E., & Wilson, T. D. (1977). Telling more than we can know: Verbal reports on mental processes. *Psychological Review, 84,* 231–257.

Norton, D. E. (1980). *The effective teaching of language arts.* Columbus, OH: Charles E. Merrill.

Nurss, J. R. (1979). Assessment of readiness. In T. G. Waller & G. E. MacKinnon (Eds.), *Reading research: Advances in theory and practice* (Vol. 1, pp. 31–62). New York: Academic Press.

Nurss, J. R., & McGauvran, M. E. (1976/1986). *Metropolitan Readiness Tests (MRT).* San Antonio, TX: The Psychological Corporation.

Ogle, D. M. (1986). K-W-L: A teaching model that develops active reading of expository text. *The Reading Teacher, 39,* 564–570.

Ogle, D. M. (1989). The know, want to know, learn strategy. In K. D. Muth (Ed.), *Children's comprehension of text: Research into practice* (pp. 205–223). Newark, DE: International Reading Association.

Olshavsky, J. E. (1978). Comparison profiles of good and poor readers across materials of increasing difficulty. In P. D. Pearson & J. Hansen (Eds.), *Reading: Disciplined inquiry in process and practice* (27th Yearbook of The National Reading Conference, pp. 73–76). Washington, DC: National Reading Conference.

Olson, M. W. (1985). Text type and reader ability: The effects of paraphrase and text-based inference questions. *Journal of Reading Behavior, 17,* 199–214.

Olson, R., Foltz, G., & Wise, B. (1986). Reading instruction and remediation with the aid of computer speech. *Behavior Research Methods, Instruments, and Computers, 18,* 93–99.

Omanson, R. C., Beck, I. L., McKeown, M. G., & Perfetti, C. A. (1984). Comprehension of texts with unfamiliar versus recently taught words: An assessment of alternative models. *Journal of Educational Psychology, 76,* 1253–1268.

Orton, S. T. (1925). Word-blindness in school children. *Archives of Neurology and Psychiatry, 14,* 582–615.

Osborn, J. H. (1984). The purposes, uses, and contents of workbooks and some guidelines for publishers. In R. C. Anderson, J. Osborn, & R. J. Tierney (Eds.), *Learning to read in American schools: Basal readers and content texts* (pp. 45–112). Hillsdale, NJ: Lawrence Erlbaum.

Osborn, J. H. (1989). Summary: Improving basal reading programs. In P. Winograd, K. Wixson, & M. Y. Lipson (Eds.), *Improving basal reading instruction* (pp. 203–226). New York: Teachers College Press.

Otto, W., Wolf, A., & Eldridge, R. (1984). Managing instruction. In P. D. Pearson, R. Barr, M. Kamil, & P. Mosenthal (Eds.), *Handbook of reading research* (pp. 799–828). New York: Longman.

Page, W. D., & Pinnell, G. S. (1979). *Teaching reading comprehension: Theory and practice*. Urbana, IL: ERIC Clearinghouse on Reading and Communication Skills and the National Council of Teachers of English.

Paley, V. (1981). *Wally's stories*. Chicago: University of Chicago Press.

Palincsar, A. S. (1984). The quest for meaning from expository text: A teacher-guided journey. In G. G. Duffy, L. R. Roehler, & J. Mason (Eds.), *Comprehension instruction* (pp. 251–264). New York: Longman.

Palincsar, A. S. (1986). The role of dialogue in providing scaffolded instruction. *Educational Psychologist, 21*, 73–98.

Palincsar, A. S., & Brown, A. L. (1984). Reciprocal teaching of comprehension-fostering and monitoring activities. *Cognition and Instruction, 1*, 117–175.

Palmatier, R. A. (1973). A notetaking system for learning. *Journal of Reading, 17*, 36–39.

Palmatier, R. A., & Bennett, J. M. (1974). Notetaking habits of college students. *Journal of Reading, 18*, 215–218.

Pany, D., & Jenkins, J. (1978). Learning word meanings: A comparison of instructional procedures and effects on measures of reading comprehension with learning disabled students. *Learning Disabilities Quarterly, 1*, 21–32.

Paratore, J. R., & Indrisano, R. (1987). Intervention assessment of reading comprehension. *The Reading Teacher, 40*, 778–783.

Paris, S. G. (1986). Teaching children to guide their reading and learning. In T. E. Raphael (Ed.), *Contexts of school-based literacy* (pp. 115–130). New York: Random House.

Paris, S. G. (1988). Models and metaphors of learning strategies. In C. Weinstein, E. T. Goetz, & P. A. Alexander (Eds.), *Learning and study strategies: Issues in assessment, instruction, and evaluation* (pp. 299–321). San Diego: Academic Press.

Paris, S. G., Cross, D. R., & Lipson, M. Y. (1984). Informed strategies for learning: A program to improve children's reading awareness and comprehension. *Journal of Educational Psychology, 76*, 1239–1252.

Paris, S. G., & Jacobs, J. (1984). The benefits of informed instruction for children's reading awareness and comprehension skills. *Child Development, 55*, 2083–2093.

Paris, S. G., & Lindauer, B. K. (1982). The development of cognitive skills during childhood. In B. Wolman (Ed.), *Handbook of developmental psychology* (pp. 333–349). Englewood Cliffs, NJ: Prentice-Hall.

Paris, S. G., Lipson, M. Y., & Wixson, K. K. (1983). Becoming a strategic reader. *Contemporary Educational Psychology, 8*, 293–316.

Paris, S. G., & Myers, M. (1981). Comprehension monitoring in good and poor readers. *Journal of Reading Behavior, 13*, 5–22.

Paris, S. G., Newman, R. S., & McVey, K. A. (1982). Learning the functional significance of mnemonic actions: A microgenetic study of strategy acquisition. *Journal of Experimental Child Psychology, 34*, 490–509.

Paris, S. G., Olson, G., & Stevenson, H. (Eds.). (1983). Learning and motivation in the classroom. Hillsdale, NJ: Lawrence Erlbaum.

Paris, S. G., & Wixson, K. K. (1987). The development of literacy: Access, acquisition and instruction. In D. D. Bloome (Ed.), *Literacy and schooling* (pp. 35–54). Norwood, NJ: Ablex.

Paris, S. G., Wixson, K. K., & Palincsar, A. S. (1986). Instructional approaches to reading comprehension. In E. Rothkopf (Ed.), *Review of research in education* (pp. 91–128). Washington, DC: American Educational Research Association.

Parsons, L. (1990). *Response journals.* Portsmouth, NH: Heinemann.

Pauk, W. (1974). *How to study in college.* Boston: Houghton Mifflin.

Pearson, P. D. (1974–75). The effects of grammatical complexity on children's comprehension, recall, and conception of certain semantic relations. *Reading Research Quarterly, 10,* 155–192.

Pearson, P. D. (1982). *Asking questions about stories* (Ginn Occasional Papers, No. 15). Lexington, MA: Silver Burdett & Ginn.

Pearson, P. D. (1984). Direct explicit teaching of reading comprehension. In G. G. Duffy, L. R. Roehler, & J. Mason (Eds.), *Comprehension instruction: Perspectives and suggestions* (pp. 222–233). New York: Longman.

Pearson, P. D. (1986). Twenty years of research in reading comprehension. In T. E. Raphael (Ed.), *Contexts of school-based literacy* (pp. 43–62). New York: Longman.

Pearson, P. D., & Gallagher, M. (1983). The instruction of reading comprehension. *Contemporary Educational Psychology, 8,* 317–344.

Pearson, P. D., Hansen, J., & Gordon, C. (1979). The effect of background knowledge on young children's comprehension of explicit and implicit information. *Journal of Reading Behavior, 11,* 201–209.

Pearson, P. D., & Johnson, D. (1978). *Teaching reading comprehension.* New York: Holt, Rinehart & Winston.

Perfetti, C. A. (1985). *Reading ability.* New York: Oxford Press.

Perfetti, C. A., & Hogaboam, T. (1975). The relationship between single word decoding and reading comprehension skill. *Journal of Educational Psychology, 67,* 461–469.

Peterson, J., Greenlaw, M. J., & Tierney, R. J. (1978). Assessing instructional placement with an IRI: The effectiveness of comprehension questions. *Journal of Educational Research, 17,* 247–250.

Pflaum, S. W. (1986). *The development of language and literacy in young children* (3rd ed.). Columbus, OH: Charles E. Merrill.

Pflaum, S. W., & Pascarella, E. T. (1980). Interactive effects of prior reading achievement and training in context on the reading of learning-disabled children. *Reading Research Quarterly, 16,* 138–158.

Philips, S. U. (1982). *The invisible culture: Communication in classroom and community on the Warm Springs Indian Reservation.* New York: Longman.

Piaget, J. (1960). *Language and thought of the child.* London: Routledge & Kegan Paul.

Picturesque word origins (1933). Springfield, MA: Merriam.

Pikulski, J., & Ross, E. (1979). Classroom teachers' perceptions of the role of the reading specialist. *Journal of Reading, 23,* 126–135.

Pikulski, J. J., & Shanahan, T. (1982). Informal reading inventories: A critical analysis. In J. J. Pikulski & T. Shanahan (Eds.), *Approaches to the informal evaluation of reading* (pp. 94–116). Newark, DE: International Reading Association.

Pikulski, J. J., & Tobin, A. W. (1982). The cloze procedure as an informal assessment technique. In J. J. Pikulski & T. Shanahan (Eds.), *Approaches* to the informal evaluation of reading (pp. 42–62). Newark, DE: International Reading Association.

Pinnell, G. S. (1985a). Helping teachers help children at risk: Insights from the Reading Recovery Program. *Peabody Journal of Education, 62,* 70–85.

Pinnell, G. S. (1985b). Ways to look at the functions of children's language. In A. Jaggar & M. T. Smith-Burke (Eds.), *Observing the language learner* (pp. 57–72). Newark, DE: International Reading Association.

Pinnell, G. S. (1987). Helping teachers see how readers read: Staff development through observation. *Theory into Practice, 26,* 51–58.

Pinnell, G. S. (1988). Holistic ways to help children at risk of failure. *Teachers Networking: The Whole Language Newsletter, 9,* 1, 10–13.

Polloway, E. A. (1985). Review of the Test of Written Language, 1983 Education. In J. V. Mitchell (Ed.), *The ninth mental measurements yearbook* (pp. 1600–1602). Lincoln, NE: Buros Institute of Mental Measurements.

Popham, W. J. (1978). *Criterion-referenced measurement.* Englewood Cliffs, NJ: Prentice-Hall.

Poplin, M. (1984). Summary rationalizations, apologies and farewell: What we don't know about the learning disabled. *Learning Disabilities Quarterly, 7,* 130–134.

Poplin, M. (1988). The reductionist fallacy in learning disabilities: Replicating the past by reducing the present. *Journal of Learning Disabilities, 21,* 389–400.

Potts, M., & Savino, C. (1968). The relative achievement of first graders under three different reading programs. *Journal of Educational Research, 61,* 447–450.

Powell, W. R. (N. D.). *The finger count system for monitoring reading behavior.* Unpublished paper, University of Florida, Gainesville.

Powell, W. R. (1980). Measuring reading performance informally. *Journal of Children and Youth, 1,* 23–31.

Powell, W. R., & Dunkeld, C. G. (1971). The validity of IRI reading levels. *Elementary English, 48,* 637–642.

Purves, A. C. (1985). That sunny dome: Those caves of ice. In C. R. Cooper (Ed.), *Researching response to literature and the teaching of literature: Points of departure* (pp. 54–69). Norwood, NJ: Ablex.

Rakes, T. A., & Smith, L. (1986). Assessing reading skills in the content areas. In E. K. Dishner, T. W. Bean, J. E. Readence, & D. W. Moore (Eds.), *Reading in the content areas: Improving classroom instruction* (2nd ed., pp. 145–159). Dubuque, IA: Kendall/Hunt.

Raphael, T. E. (1982). Question-answering strategies for children. *The Reading Teacher, 36,* 186–190.

Raphael, T. E. (1986). Teaching questions-answer relationships, revisited. *The Reading Teacher, 39,* 516–522.

Raphael, T. E., & Englert, C. S. (1989). Integrating writing and reading instruction. In P. Winograd, K. Wixson, & M. Lipson (Eds.), *Improving basal reading instruction* (pp. 231–255). New York: Teachers College Press.

Raphael, T. E., & Englert, C. S. (1990). Writing and reading: Partners in constructing meaning. *The Reading Teacher, 43,* 388–400.

Raphael, T. E., & Gavelek, J. R. (1984). Question-related activities and their relationship to reading comprehension: Some instructional implications. In G. G. Duffy, L. R. Roehler, & J. Mason (Eds.), *Comprehension instruction* (pp. 234–250). New York: Longman.

Raphael, T. E., Kirschner, B. W., & Englert, C. S. (1988). Expository writing program: Making connections between reading and writing. *The Reading Teacher, 41,* 790–795.

Raphael, T. E., Winograd, P., & Pearson, P. D. (1980). Strategies children use in answering questions. In M. L. Kamil & A. J. Moe (Eds.), *Perspectives in reading research and instruction* (29th Yearbook of The National Reading Conference, pp. 56–63). Washington, DC: National Reading Conference.

Rasinski, T. V. (1986). Repeated readings—naturally. *The Reading Teacher, 39,* 244.

Ravitch, M. M. (1985). Review of Metropolitan Readiness Tests, 1976 Edition. In J. V. Mitchell (Ed.), *The ninth mental measurements yearbook* (Vol. 1, pp. 968–970). Lincoln, NE: Buros Institute of Mental Measurements.

Readence, J. E., Bean, T. W., & Baldwin, R. S. (1985). *Content area reading: An integrated approach* (2nd ed.). Dubuque, IA: Kendall/Hunt.

Readence, J. E., & Moore, D. (1980). Differentiating text assignments in content areas: Slicing the task. *Reading Horizons, 20,* 112–117.

Reid, D. K., Hresko, W. P., & Hammill, D. D. (1989). *The Test of Early Reading Ability (TERA–2).* Austin, TX: Pro-Ed.

Reid, J. F. (1966). Learning to think about reading. *Educational Research, 9,* 56–62.

Reimer, B. L., & Warshow, L. (1989). Questions we ask of ourselves and our students. *The Reading Teacher, 42,* 596–607.

Reinking, D. P., Kling, M., & Harper, M. K. (1985). *Characteristics of computer software in reading: An empirical investigation.* Unpublished manuscript, Rutgers Graduate School of Education, New Brunswick, NJ.

Resnick, L. B. (1977). *Theory and practice in beginning reading instruction.* Pittsburgh, PA: Pittsburgh University. (ERIC Document Reproduction Service No. ED 149 292).

Resolutions passed by the Delegates Assembly. (1981). *Reading Research Quarterly, 16.*

Reutzel, D. R. (1985). Story maps improve comprehension. *The Reading Teacher, 38,* 400–404.

Rey, H. A. (1941). *Curious George.* Boston: Houghton Mifflin.

Ringler, L. H., & Weber, C. K. (1984). *A language-thinking approach to reading.* San Diego: Harcourt Brace Jovanovich.

Robinson, F. P. (1946). *Effective study.* New York: Harper & Row.

Robinson, H. M. (1946). *Why pupils fail in reading.* Chicago: University of Chicago Press.

Robinson, H. M. (1972). Perceptual training—Does it result in reading improvement? In R. C. Aukerman (Ed.), *Some persistent questions in beginning reading* (pp. 135–150). Newark, DE: International Reading Association.

Robinson, R., & Good, T. L. (1987). *Becoming an effective reading teacher.* New York: Harper & Row.

Roehler, L. R., & Duffy, G. G. (1984). Direct explanation of comprehension processes. In G. G. Duffy, L. R. Roehler, & J. Mason (Eds.), *Comprehension instruction: Perspectives and suggestions* (pp. 265–280). New York: Longman.

Roehler, L. R., & Duffy, G. G. (1991). Teachers' instructional actions. In R. Barr, M. L. Kamil, P. Mosenthal, & P. D. Pearson (Eds.), *Handbook of reading research* (Vol. II, pp. 861–883). New York: Longman.

Roehler, L. R., Duffy, G. G., & Meloth, M. (1986). What to be direct about in direct instruction in reading: Content-only versus process-into-content. In T. E. Raphael (Ed.), *Contexts of school-based literacy* (pp. 79–96). New York: Random House.

Rogers, D. B. (1984). Assessing study skills. *Journal of Reading, 27,* 346–354.

Rogers, V. R., & Stevenson, C. (1988). How do we know what kids are learning in school? *Educational Leadership, 45* (5), 68–75.

Rosenbaum, J. E. (1980). Social implications of educational grouping. In D. C. Berliner (Ed.), *Review of Research in Education* (Vol. 8, pp. 361–401). Washington, DC: American Educational Research Association.

Rosenblatt, L. (1978). *The reader, the text, and the poem: The transactional theory of literary work.* Carbondale: Southern Illinois University.

Rosenblatt, L. (1982). The literary transaction: Evocation and response. *Theory into Practice, 21,* 268–277.

Rosenshine, B. V. (1979). Content, time, and direct instruction. In P. L. Peterson & H. J. Walberg (Eds.), *Research on teaching: Concepts, findings, and implications* (pp. 28–56). Berkeley, CA: McCutchan.

Rosenshine, B. V., & Stevens, R. (1984). Classroom instruction in reading. In P. D. Pearson (Ed.), *Handbook of reading research* (pp. 745–798). New York: Longman.

Rosenthal, R., & Jacobson, L. (1968). *Pygmalion in the classroom: Teacher expectation and pupils' intellectual development.* New York: Holt, Rinehart & Winston.

Rosso, B. R., & Emans, R. (1981). Children's use of phonetic generalizations. *The Reading Teacher, 34,* 653–658.

Rowe, M. B. (1974). Wait time and rewards as instructional variables, their influence on language, logic, and fate control: Part One—Wait time. *Journal of Research in Science Teaching, 11,* 81–94.

Rubin, A., & Bruce, B. (1985). QUILL: Reading and writing with a microcomputer. In B. Hutson (Ed.), *Advances in reading/language research* (Vol. 3, pp. 97–117). Greenwich, CT: JAI Press.

Ruddell, R. B. (1965). Effect of the similarity of oral and written language structure on reading comprehension. *Elementary English, 42,* 403–410.

Rumelhart, D. (1977). Toward an interactive model of reading. In S. Dornic (Ed.), *Attention and performance VI* (pp. 573–603). Hillsdale, NJ: Lawrence Erlbaum.

Rupley, W. H. (1976). Effective reading program. *The Reading Teacher, 29,* 616–623.

Rupley, W. H., & Blair, T. R. (1983). *Reading diagnosis and remediation: Classroom and clinic.* Boston: Houghton Mifflin.

Ryan, E. B. (1981). Identifying and remediating failures in reading comprehension: Toward an instructional approach for poor comprehenders. In T. G. Waller & G. E. MacKinnon (Eds.), *Reading research: Advances in theory and practice* (Vol. 3, pp. 224–262). New York: Academic Press.

Ryder, R. J., Graves, B. B., & Graves, M. F. (1990). *Easy reading: Book series and periodicals for less able readers.* Newark, DE: International Reading Association.

Ryder, R. J., & Graves, M. F. (1980). Secondary students' internalization of letter-sound correspondence. *Journal of Educational Research, 73,* 172–178.

Sadowski, M. (1980). Ten years of uninterrupted sustained silent reading. *Reading Improvement, 17,* 153–156.

Salinger, T. (1988). *Language arts and literacy for young children.* Columbus, OH: Charles E. Merrill.

Salvia, J., & Ysseldyke, J. E. (1988). *Assessment in special education and remedial education* (4th ed.). Boston: Houghton Mifflin.

Samuels, S. J. (1979). The method of repeated readings. *The Reading Teacher, 32,* 403–408.

Samuels, S. J. (1988). Decoding and automaticity: Helping poor readers become automatic at word recognition. *The Reading Teacher, 41,* 755–760.

Samuels, S. J., & Kamil, M. L. (1984). Models of the reading process. In P. D. Pearson, R. Barr, M. Kamil, & P. Mosenthal (Eds.), *Handbook of reading research* (pp. 185–224). New York: Longman.

Sarason, S. B., & Doris, J. (1979). *Educational handicap, public policy, and social history.* New York: Free Press.

Sardy, S. (1985). Thinking about reading.

In T. L. Harris & E. J. Cooper (Eds.), *Reading, thinking and concept development* (pp. 213–229). New York: College Entrance Examination Board.

Sawyer, D. J. (1987). *Test of Awareness of Language Segments (TALS)*. Rockville, MD: Aspen.

Sawyer, W. S., & Wilson, B. A. (1979). Role clarification for remedial reading and learning disabilities teachers. *The Reading Teacher, 33*, 162–166.

Schank, R. C. (1973). Identification of conceptualizations underlying natural language. In R. C. Schank & K. M. Colby (Eds.), *Computer models of thought and language* (pp. 187–248). San Francisco: Freeman.

Schell, L. M. (1967). Teaching structural analysis. *The Reading Teacher, 21*, 133–137.

Schell, L. M., & Hanna, G. S. (1981). Can informal reading inventories reveal strengths and weaknesses in comprehension subskills? *The Reading Teacher, 35*, 263–268.

Scheu, J. A., Tanner, D. K., & Au, K. H. (1989). Integrating seatwork with the basal lesson. In P. Winograd, K. K. Wixson, & M. Y. Lipson (Eds.), *Improving basal reading instruction* (pp. 58–73). New York: Teachers College Press.

Schmidt, M. B. (1986). The shape of content: Four semantic map structures for expository paragraphs. *The Reading Teacher, 40*, 113–117.

Schmidt, W., Caul, J., Byers, J., & Buchman, M. (1984). Content of basal reading selections: Implications for comprehension instruction. In G. Duffy, L. R. Roehler, & J. Mason (Eds.), *Comprehension instruction* (pp. 144–162). New York: Longman.

Schmuck, R. A. (1980). The school organization. In J. H. McMillan (Ed.), *The social psychology of school learning* (pp. 169–214). New York: Academic Press.

Schumaker, J. B., Deshler, D. D., Alley, G. R., & Warner, M. M. (1983). Toward the development of an intervention model for learning disabled adolescents. *Exceptional Education Quarterly, 3* (4), 45–50.

Schuyler, M. R. (1982). A readability program for use on microcomputers. *Journal of Reading, 25*, 560–591.

Scott, Foresman Publishing Co. (1981). Standards for evaluating expository writing and standards for evaluating narrative writing. In R. L. Cramer et al., *Language structure and use, Teacher's Edition 8*. Glenview, IL: Scott, Foresman.

Scribner, S., & Cole, M. (1981). *The psychology of literacy: A case study among the Vai*. Cambridge, MA: Harvard University Press.

Searfoss, L. W., & Readence, J. E. (1985). *Helping children learn to read* (1st ed.). Englewood Cliffs, NJ: Prentice-Hall.

Searfoss, L. W., & Readence, J. E. (1989). *Helping children learn to read* (2nd ed.). Englewood Cliffs, NJ: Prentice-Hall.

Sendak, M. (1963). *Where the wild things are*. New York: Harper & Row.

Shake, M. C. (1989). Grouping and pacing with basal materials. In P. Winograd, K. K. Wixson, & M. Y. Lipson (Eds.), *Improving basal reading instruction* (pp. 62–85). New York: Teachers College Press.

Shanahan, T. (1984). The reading-writing relation: An exploratory multivariate analysis. *Journal of Educational Psychology, 76*, 466–477.

Shannon, P. (1983). The use of commercial reading materials in American elementary schools. *Reading Research Quarterly, 19*, 68–85.

Sharp, S. J. (1990). Using content subject matter with LEA in middle school. *Journal of Reading, 33*, 108–112.

Shepard, L. A. (1986, April). *School readiness and kindergarten retention: A policy analysis*. Paper presented at the Annual Meeting of the American Educational Research Association, San Francisco, CA.

Shepard, L. A., & Smith, M. L. (1986). Synthesis of research on school readiness and kindergarten retention. *Educational Leadership, 20*, 78–86.

Shepard, L. A., & Smith, M. L. (1987). Effects of kindergarten retention at the end of first grade. *Psychology in the Schools, 24*, 346–357.

Sherwin, J. S. (1970). Research and teaching of English. *English Record, 21*, 2.

Shimmerlik, S. (1978). Organization theory and memory for prose: A review of the literature. *Review of Educational Research, 48*, 103–121.

Shnayer, S. W. (1969). Relationships between reading interest and reading comprehension. In J. A. Figurel (Ed.), *Reading and realism* (pp. 698–702). Newark, DE: International Reading Association.

Shuy, R. W. (1981). What the teacher knows is more important than text or test. *Language Arts, 58* (8), 919–929.

Silvaroli, N. J. (1982). *Classroom reading inventory* (4th ed.). Dubuque, IA: William C. Brown.

Silvaroli, N. J. (1986). *Classroom reading inventory* (5th ed.). Dubuque, IA: William C. Brown.

Silvaroli, N. J., Kear, D. J., & McKenna, M. C. (1982). *A classroom guide to reading assessment and instruction*. Dubuque, IA: Kendall/Hunt.

Singer, H. S. (1986). Friendly texts: Description and criteria. In E. K. Dishner, T. W. Bean, J. E. Readence, & D. Moore (Eds.), *Reading in the content areas* (pp. 112–128). Dubuque, IA: Kendall/Hunt.

Sipay, E. R. (1984). *Sipay Word Analysis Tests*. Cambridge, MA: Educators Publishing Service.

Slaughter, J. P. (1983). Big books for little kids: Another fad or a new approach for teaching beginning reading? *The Reading Teacher, 36*, 758–763.

Slavin, R. E. (1983). *Cooperative learning*. New York: Longman.

Slavin, R. E., Stevens, R. J., & Madden, N. A. (1988). Accommodating student diversity in reading and writing instruction: A cooperative learning approach. *RASE, 9*, 60–66.

Sleeter, C. E. (1985, March). *Why is there learning disabilities? A critical analysis of the birth of the field in its social context*. Paper presented at the Annual Meeting of the American Education Research Association, Chicago, IL.

Slobin, D. (1979). *Psycholinguistics*. Glenview, IL: Scott, Foresman.

Slosson, R. L. (1983). *Slosson Oral Reading Test/Slosson Intelligence Test (2nd ed.)*. East Aurora, NY: Slosson.

Smith, D. D. (1979). The improvement of children's oral reading through the use of teacher modeling. *Journal of Learning Disabilities, 12*, 39–42.

Snider, V. E., & Tarver, S. G. (1987). The effect of early reading failure on acquisition of knowledge among students with learning disabilities. *Journal of Learning Disabilities, 20*, 351–356, 373.

Spache, G. S. (1981). *Diagnostic Reading Scales*. Monterey, CA: CTB/McGraw-Hill.

Spache, G. S., & Spache, E. (1986). *Reading in the elementary school*. Boston: Allyn & Bacon.

Spiegel, D. L. (1981). Six alternatives to the Directed Reading Activity. *The Reading Teacher, 34*, 914–923.

Spiegel, D. L. (1984). Helping children to identify words by using all three cue systems of the language. In J. F. Baumann & D. D. Johnson (Eds.), *Reading instruction and the beginning teacher* (pp. 2–15). Minneapolis, MN: Burgess.

Spiro, R. J., & Myers, A. (1984). Individual differences and underlying cognitive processes. In P. D. Pearson, R. Barr, M. Kamil, & P. Mosenthal (Eds.), *Handbook of reading research* (pp. 471–504). New York: Longman.

Squire, J. (1983). Composing and comprehending: Two sides of the same basic process. *Language Arts, 60,* 581–589.

Stahl, S. A. (1986). Three principles of effective vocabulary instruction. *Journal of Reading, 29,* 662–668.

Stahl, S. A., & Fairbanks, M. (1986). The effects of vocabulary instruction: A model-based meta-analysis. *Review of Educational Research, 56,* 72–110.

Stallings, J., Needels, M., & Sparks, G. M. (1987). Observation for the improvement of classroom learning. In D. C. Berliner & B. V. Rosenshine (Eds.), *Talks to teachers* (pp. 129–158). New York: Random House.

Stanovich, K. E. (1980). Toward an interactive-compensatory model of individual difference in the development of reading fluency. *Reading Research Quarterly, 16,* 32–71.

Stanovich, K. E. (1982a). Individual differences in the cognitive processes of reading: I. Word decoding. *Journal of Learning Disabilities, 15,* 485–493.

Stanovich, K. E. (1982b). Individual differences in the cognitive processes of reading: II. Text level processes. *Journal of Learning Disabilities, 15,* 549–554.

Stanovich, K. E. (1986). Matthew effects in reading: Some consequences of individual differences in the acquisition of literacy. *Reading Research Quarterly, 21,* 360–406.

Staton, J. (1987). The power of responding in dialogue journals. In T. Fulwiler (Ed.), *The journal book* (p. 63). Portsmouth, NH: Heinemann.

Stauffer, R. (1969). *Teaching reading as a thinking process.* New York: Harper & Row.

Stauffer, R. (1980). *Directing the reading-thinking process.* New York: Harper & Row.

Stein, N. L., & Glenn, C. G. (1979). An analysis of story comprehension in elementary school children. In R. O. Freedle (Ed.), *New directions in discourse processing* (Vol. 2, pp. 53–120). Norwood, NJ: Ablex.

Stein, N. L., & Nezworski, M. T. (1978). The effects of organization and instructional set on story memory. *Discourse Processes, 1,* 177–193.

Stein, N. L., & Policastro, M. (1984). The concept of a story: A comparison between children's and teachers' viewpoints. In H. Mandl, N. L. Stein, & T. Trabasso (Eds.), *Learning and comprehension of text* (pp. 113–158). Hillsdale, NJ: Lawrence Erlbaum.

Stevens, K. C. (1980). Readability formulae and McCall-Crabbs Standard Test Lessons in Reading. *The Reading Teacher, 33,* 413–415.

Stevens, R. J., Madden, N. A., Slavin, R. E., & Farnish, A. M. (1987). Cooperative integrated reading and composition: Two field experiments. *Reading Research Quarterly, 23,* 433–454.

Stoll, D. R. (1990). *Magazines for children.* Newark, DE: International Reading Association.

Stoodt, B. D. (1988). *Teaching language arts.* New York: Harper & Row.

Stotsky, S. (1984). Research on reading/writing relationships: A synthesis and suggested directions. In J. Jensen (Ed.), *Composing and comprehending* (ED 243 139, pp. 7–22). Urbana, IL: ERIC Clearinghouse on Reading and Communication Skills and the National Conference on Research in English.

Sulzby, E. (1985). Children's emergent reading of favorite storybooks: A developmental study. *Reading Research Quarterly, 20,* 458–481.

Sulzby, E. (1986a). Children's elicitation and use of metalinguistic knowledge about "word" during literacy interactions. In D. B. Yaden & S. Templeton (Eds.), *Metalinguistic awareness and beginning literacy* (pp. 219–234). Portsmouth, NH: Heinemann.

Sulzby, E. (1986b). Writing and reading:

Signs of oral and written language organization in the young child. In W. H. Teale & E. Sulzby (Eds.), *Emergent literacy: Writing and reading* (pp. 50–89). Norwood, NJ: Ablex.

Sulzby, E., & Teale, W. H. (1985). Writing development in early childhood. *Educational Horizons, 64,* 8–12.

Sundbye, N. (1987). Text explicitness and inferential questioning: Effects on story understanding and recall. *Reading Research Quarterly, 22,* 82–98.

Swanson, H. L., & Watson, B. L. (1982). *Educational and psychological assessment of exceptional children.* St. Louis: Mosby.

Taba, H. (1967). *Teacher's handbook for elementary social studies.* Reading, MA: Addison-Wesley.

Taylor, B. M. (1982). A summarizing strategy to improve middle grade students' reading and writing skills. *The Reading Teacher, 36,* 202–205.

Taylor, B. M. (1986). Teaching middle grade students to summarize content textbook material, In J. F. Baumann (Ed.), *Teaching main idea comprehension* (pp. 195–209). Newark, DE: International Reading Association.

Taylor, B. M., Harris, L. A., & Pearson, P. D. (1988). *Reading difficulties: Instruction and assessment.* New York: Random House.

Taylor, B. M., & Samuels, S. J. (1983). Children's use of text structure in the recall of expository material. *American Educational Research Journal, 20,* 234–237.

Taylor, N. E. (1986). Developing beginning literacy concepts: Content and context. In D. B. Yaden & S. Templeton (Eds.), *Metalinguistic awareness and beginning literacy: Conceptualizing what it means to read and write* (pp. 173–184). Portsmouth, NH: Heinemann.

Taylor, N. E., & Blum, I. H. (1980). *Written Language Awareness Test (WLAT)* (Experimental Ed.). Washington, DC: Catholic University.

Taylor, N. E., Blum, I. H., & Logsdon, D. M. (1986). The development of written language awareness: Environmental aspects and program characteristics. *Reading Research Quarterly, 21,* 132–149.

Taylor, W. L. (1953). Cloze procedure: A new tool for measuring readability. *Journalism Quarterly, 30,* 415–433.

Tchudi, S., & Yates, J. (1983). *Teaching writing in content areas: High school.* Washington, DC: National Education Association.

Teale, W. H., Hiebert, E. H., & Chittenden, E. A. (1987). Assessing young children's literacy development. *The Reading Teacher, 40,* 772–777.

Teale, W. H., & Sulzby, E. (Eds.). (1986). *Emergent literacy: Writing and reading.* Norwood, NJ: Ablex.

Temple, C., & Gillet, J. W. (1989). *Language arts: Learning processes and teaching practices* (2nd ed.). Glenview, IL: Scott, Foresman.

Temple, C., Nathan, R., Burris, N., & Temple, F. (1988). *The beginnings of writing.* Boston: Allyn & Bacon.

Thorndyke, P. W. (1977). Cognitive structures in comprehension and memory of narrative discourse. *Cognitive Psychology, 9,* 77–110.

Tiedt, I. M. (1989). *Writing: From topic to evaluation.* Boston: Allyn & Bacon.

Tierney, R. J., & Cunningham, J. W. (1984). Research on teaching reading comprehension. In P. D. Pearson (Ed.), *Handbook of reading research* (pp. 609–655). New York: Longman.

Tierney, R., & Pearson, P. D. (1983). Toward a composing model of reading. *Language Arts, 60,* 568–580.

Tierney, R., Readence, J. E., & Dishner, E. (1985). *Reading strategies and practices: A compendium* (2nd ed.). Boston: Allyn & Bacon.

Tikunoff, W. J., & Ward, B. A. (1983). Collaborative research on teaching. *Elementary School Journal, 83,* 453–468.

Tinker, M. A., & McCullough, C. M. (1968). *Teaching elementary reading*

(3rd ed.). New York: Appleton-Century-Crofts.

Tonjes, M. J., & Zintz, M. (1987). *Teaching reading, thinking and study skills in content classrooms.* Dubuque, IA: William C. Brown Publishers.

Topping, K. (1987). Paired reading: A powerful technique for parent use. *The Reading Teacher, 40,* 608–614.

Topping, K. (1989). Peer tutoring and paired reading: Combining two powerful techniques. *The Reading Teacher, 42,* 488–494.

Torgesen, J. K. (1977). The role of non-specific factors in the task performance of learning disabled children: A theoretical assessment. *Journal of Learning Disabilities, 10,* 24–34.

Torgesen, J. K. (1980). Conceptual and educational implications of the use of efficient task strategies by learning-disabled children. *Journal of Learning Disabilities, 13,* 364–371.

Torgesen, J. K., & Licht, B. G. (1983). The learning disabled child as an inactive learner: Retrospect and prospects. In J. McKinney & L. Feagans (Eds.), *Topics in learning disabilities* (Vol. 1, pp. 3–31). Norwood, NJ: Ablex.

Tovay, D. R. (1980). Children's grasp of phonics terms vs. sound-symbol relationships. *The Reading Teacher, 33,* 431–437.

Trabasso, T. (1981). On the making of inferences during reading and their assessment. In J. T. Guthrie (Ed.), *Comprehension and teaching: Research reviews* (pp. 56–76). Newark, DE: International Reading Association.

Tunmer, W. E., Herriman, M. L., & Nesdale, A. R. (1988). Metalinguistic abilities and beginning reading. *Reading Research Quarterly, 23,* 134–158.

Vacca, J. L., Vacca, R. T., & Gove, M. K. (1987). *Reading and learning to read.* Boston: Little, Brown.

Vacca, R. T., & Padak, N. D. (1990). Who's at risk in reading? *Journal of Reading, 33,* 486–488.

Vacca, R. T., & Vacca, J. L. (1989). *Content area reading* (3rd ed.). Glenview, IL: Scott, Foresman.

Valencia, S. (1990a). A portfolio approach to classroom assessment: The whys, whats, and hows. *The Reading Teacher, 43,* 338–340.

Valencia, S. (1990b). Portfolio assessment: Separating the wheat from the chaff. *The Reading Teacher, 44,* 60–61.

Valencia, S., McGinley, W., & Pearson, P. D. (1990). Assessing reading and writing: Building a more complete picture. In G. Duffy & P. Anders (Eds.) *Reading in the middle schools* (pp. 124–153). Newark, DE: International Reading Association.

Valencia, S., & Pearson, P. D. (1987). Reading assessment: Time for a change. *The Reading Teacher, 40,* 726–733.

Valencia, S., Stallman, A. C., Commeyras, M., Hartman, D. K., Pearson, P. D., & Greer, E. A. (1987, December). *Three methods of assessing prior knowledge: A validation study.* Paper presented at The National Reading Conference, St. Petersburg, FL.

Valmont, W. J. (1972). Creating questions for informal reading inventories. *The Reading Teacher, 25,* 509–512.

Vaughan, J. L., & Estes, T. H. (1986). *Reading and reasoning beyond the primary grades.* Boston: Allyn & Bacon.

Vellutino, F. R. (1977). Has the perceptual deficit hypothesis led us astray? *Journal of Learning Disabilities, 10,* 375–384.

Vygotsky, L. S. (1978). *Mind in society: The development of higher psychological process.* Cambridge, MA: Harvard University Press.

Wade, S. E. (1990). Using think alouds to assess comprehension. *The Reading Teacher, 43,* 442–453.

Walker, B. J. (1988). *Diagnostic teaching of reading: Techniques for instruction and assessment.* Columbus, OH: Charles E. Merrill.

Walp, T. P., & Walmsley, S. A. (1989). Instructional and philosophical congruence: Neglected aspects of coordination. *The Reading Teacher, 42,* 364–368.

Walsh, W. B., & Betz, N. E. (1990). *Tests and assessment* (2nd ed.). Englewood Cliffs, NJ: Prentice-Hall.

Warncke, E. W., & Shipman, D. A. (1984). *Group assessment in reading: Classroom teacher's handbook.* Englewood Cliffs, NJ: Prentice-Hall.

Watson, D. (1985). Watching and listening to children read. In A. Jaggar & M. T. Burke (Eds.), *Observing the language learner* (pp. 115–128). Newark, DE: International Reading Association.

Weber, R. (1970). A linguistic analysis of first-grade reading errors. *Reading Research Quarterly, 3,* 429–451.

Weinstein, C. E., Goetz, E. T., & Alexander, P. A. (1988). *Learning and study strategies: Issues in assessment, instruction, and evaluation.* San Diego: Academic Press.

Weinstein, R. S. (1976). Reading group membership in first grade: Teacher behaviors and pupil experience over time. *Journal of Educational Psychology, 68,* 103–116.

Weinstein, R. S. (1986). Teaching reading: Children's awareness of teacher expectations: In T. E. Raphael (Ed.), *The contexts of school-based literacy* (pp. 233–252). New York: Random House.

Wells, G. (1982). Story reading and the development of symbolic skills. *Australian Journal of Reading, 5,* 142–152.

Wells, G. (1985). Preschool literacy-related activities and success in school. In D. R. Olson, N. Torrance, & A. Hildyard (Eds.), *Literacy, language, and learning* (pp. 229–255). Cambridge, England: Cambridge University Press.

Wells, G. (1986). *The meaning makers: Children learning language and using language to learn.* Portsmouth, NH: Heinemann.

West, R. F., & Stanovich, K. (1978). Au-

tomatic contextual facilitation in readers of three ages. *Child Development, 49,* 717–727.

Westby, C. (1988). Test Review: Test of Language Development–2. Primary. *The Reading Teacher, 42,* 236–237.

Wiederholt, J. L., & Bryant, B. R. (1986). *Gray Oral Reading Test–Revised.* Austin, TX: Pro-Ed.

Wigfield, A., & Asher, S. R. (1984). Social and motivational influences on reading. In P. D. Pearson, R. Barr, M. Kamil, & P. Mosenthal (Eds.), *Handbook of reading research* (pp. 423–452). New York: Longman.

Williams, J. P. (1980). Teaching decoding with an emphasis on phoneme analysis and phoneme blending. *Journal of Educational Psychology, 72,* 1–15.

Williams, J. P., Taylor, M. B., & deCani, J. S. (1984). Constructing macro structure for expository text. *Journal of Educational Psychology, 76,* 1065–1075.

Wilson, R. M., & Cleland, C. J. (1989). *Diagnostic and remedial reading for classroom and clinic.* Columbus, OH: Charles E. Merrill.

Wilson, R. M., & Hall, M. (1990). *Programmed word attack for teachers.* Columbus, OH: Charles E. Merrill.

Winograd, P. N., & Johnston, P. (1987). Some considerations for advancing the teaching of reading comprehension. *Educational Psychologist, 22,* 213–230.

Wisconsin Department of Public Instruction. (1989). *Strategic learning in the content areas.* Madison, WI.

Wittrock, M. C., Marks, C., & Doctorow, M. (1975). Reading as a generative process. *Journal of Educational Psychology, 67,* 484–489.

Wixson, K. K. (1979). Miscue analysis: A critical review. *Journal of Reading Behavior, 11,* 163–175.

Wixson, K. K. (1983a). Postreading question-answer interactions and children's learning from text. *Journal of Educational Psychology, 30,* 413–423.

Wixson, K. K. (1983b). Questions about a text: What you ask about is what children learn. *The Reading Teacher, 37,* 287–293.

Wixson, K. K. (1984). Level of importance of postquestions and children's learning from text. *American Educational Research Journal, 21,* 419–434.

Wixson, K. K. (1986). Vocabulary instruction and children's comprehension of basal stories. *Reading Research Quarterly, 21,* 317–329.

Wixson, K. K., Bosky, A. B., Yochum, M. N., & Alvermann, D. E. (1984). An interview for assessing student's perceptions of classroom reading tasks. *The Reading Teacher, 37,* 354–359.

Wixson, K. K., & Lipson, M. Y. (1986). Reading (dis)ability: An interactionist perspective. In T. E. Raphael (Ed.), *Contexts of school-based literacy* (pp. 131–148). New York: Random House.

Wixson, K. K., & Lipson, M. Y. (1991). Perspectives on reading disability research. In R. Barr, M. L. Kamil, P. Mosenthal, & P. D. Pearson (Eds.), *Handbook of reading research* (Vol. II, pp. 539–570). New York: Longman.

Wixson, K. K., & Peters, C. W. (1984). Reading redefined: A Michigan Reading Association position paper. *Michigan Reading Journal, 17,* 4–7.

Wixson, K. K., & Peters, C. W. (1989). Teaching the basal selection. In P. Winograd, K. K. Wixson, & M. Y. Lipson (Eds.), *Improving basal reading instruction* (pp. 21–61). New York: Teachers College Press.

Wixson, K. K., Peters, C. W., Weber, E. M., & Roeber, E. D. (1987). New directions in statewide reading assessment. *The Reading Teacher, 40,* 749–755.

Wixson, S. E. (1985). Test review: The Test of Early Reading Ability (TERA). *The Reading Teacher, 38,* 544-547.

Wong, B. Y. L., Wong, R., & Le Mare, L. (1982). The effects of knowledge of criterion tasks on comprehension and recall in normally achieving and learning disabled children. *Journal of Educational Research, 76* (2), 119–126.

Wong, J., & Au, K. H. (1985). The concept-text-application approach: Helping elementary students comprehend expository text. *The Reading Teacher, 38,* 612–618.

Wood, D. J., Bruner, J. S., & Ross, G. (1976). The role of tutoring in problem solving. *Journal of Child Psychology and Psychiatry, 17,* 89–100.

Wood, K. D. (1988). Techniques for assessing students' potential for learning. *The Reading Teacher, 41,* 440–447.

Wood, K. D., & Robinson, N. (1983). Vocabulary, language, and prediction: A prereading strategy. *The Reading Teacher, 36,* 392–395.

Woodcock, R. W. (1987). *Woodcock Reading Mastery Test–Revised.* Circle Pines, MN: American Guidance Service.

Woods, M. L., & Moe, A. J. (1985). *Analytical reading inventory* (3rd ed.). Columbus, OH: Charles E. Merrill.

Wylie, R. E. (1969). Diversified concepts of the role of the reading consultant. *The Reading Teacher, 22,* 519–522.

Wylie, R. E., & Durrell, D. D. (1970). Teaching vowels through phonograms. *Elementary English, 47,* 787–791.

Yopp, H. T. (1988). The validity and reliability of phonemic awareness tests. *Reading Research Quarterly, 23,* 159–177.

Young, A., & Fulwiler, T. (Eds.). (1986). *Writing across the disciplines.* Portsmouth, NH: Boynton/Cook.

Young, D., & Irwin, M. (1988). Integrating computers into adult literacy programs. *Journal of Reading, 31,* 648–652.

Ysseldyke, J. E., & Christenson, S. L. (1987). *The Instructional Environment Scale (TIES).* Austin, TX: Pro-Ed.

Zakaluk, B. (1985). *Toward a new approach*

to predicting text comprehensibility using inside- and outside-the-head information and a nomograph. Unpublished doctoral dissertation, University of Minnesota, Minneapolis.

Zakaluk, B.L., & Samuels, S.J. (1988). Toward a new approach to predicting text comprehensibility. In B.L. Zakaluk & S.J. Samuels (Eds.), *Read-*

ability: Its past, present, and future (pp. 121–144). Newark, DE: International Reading Association.

Zigmond, N., Vallecorsa, A., & Leinhardt, G. (1980). Reading instruction for students with learning disabilities. *Topics in Language Disorders, 1,* 89–98.

Zintz, M.V. (1970). *The reading process.* Dubuque, IA: William C. Brown.

Index

AUTHOR